Readings in Investments

Readings in Investments

Edited by
Stephen Lofthouse

JOHN WILEY & SONS
Chichester • New York • Brisbane • Toronto • Singapore

First published 1994 by John Wiley & Sons Ltd,
Baffins Lane, Chichester,
West Sussex PO19 IUD, England

International (+44)243 779777
National Chichester 0243 779777

Library of Congress Cataloging-in-Publication Data

Lofthouse, Stephen.
  Equity investment management: how to select stocks and
  markets / Stephen Lofthouse
      p. cm.
  Includes bibliographical references and index.
  ISBN 0-471-95208-7 (paper)
    1. Portfolio management   2. Investment analysis.   I. Title.
  HG4529.5.L63   1994
  332.6 — dc20   93-29957
                                                  CIP

British Library Cataloguing in Publication Data

A catalogue record for this book is available from the British Library

ISBN 0-471-95208-7 (paper)

Typeset in 10/12pt Times from editor's disks by Laser Words, Madras
Printed and bound in Great Britain by Redwood Books, Trowbridge, Wiltshire.

Contents

Preface

The objective of this book is to provide an interesting and informative collection of articles, which supplement the major undergraduate and MBA investment textbooks. It is not geared to one country, and is suitable for an international readership.

Faced with an enormous number of worthy articles, my guidelines for selection were:

- The articles as a whole had to reflect a variety of research methods, styles of argument and presentation. They should not simply repeat material available in the textbooks, but genuinely supplement the textbooks.

- The majority of articles had to be accessible to readers with limited mathematical and statistical skills. That did not rule out up-to-date research methods, providing the reader would be able to grasp the gist of the argument without necessarily being able to follow all the details.

- A preference for articles that would help students see how investment theory is, or is not, applied in the real world and would also be useful to practitioners. Although this book is intended to supplement the standard textbooks, I have assumed that the readership will include investment practitioners and not just university students. Many of the articles are by practitioners.

- A greater international orientation than the major textbooks. These argue the importance of international investment but then usually devote only one chapter to international issues. The largest stock market in terms of market capitalization is the U.S. market and U.S. academics and practitioners have been the most prolific producers of high quality research. Inevitably the majority of articles included here have been drawn from U.S. sources, but nearly a quarter of the articles discuss general international issues or non-U.S. markets.

- Articles were selected for their information content rather than merely having been published very recently.

- Whenever possible, articles were selected from journals or publications not readily available in most university libraries.

The articles have been divided into seven parts which correspond to broad topic areas that appear in most of the textbooks. At the start of each section I give a brief discussion of some of the factors that led me to include the topics and articles that you have before you. I hope you enjoy the selection. If I have missed one of your favourite articles and you feel it should be included in a second edition, please write and tell me.

I am grateful to the writers and publishers who have allowed me to reprint their work and to abridge some pieces. The affiliation of the authors stated in the text is that shown in the original publication except where I know the author has since moved. I have removed footnotes that give the authors' affiliations, their thanks to various readers and organizations and so forth. Other footnotes have been placed as "end notes". I have also deleted glossaries of terms from some articles. Finally, I am grateful to the Library of Congress and the Central Reference Library of the New York Public Library for use of their resources.

Stephen Lofthouse
September 1993

PART ONE
Risk, Return and Diversification

Notions of risk and return are central to investment theory. Two of the most important ideas are that investors will only bear risk for additional returns and that risk is reduced by diversification. In Part One, I have selected four articles that bear on these issues.

Investors who wanted only to maximize their returns in the stockmarket would find what seemed to them to be the best stock and hold only that one stock. But most investors do not do that. Nobody can be sure which is the best stock, indeed the stock chosen may turn out to be the worst. Faced with uncertainty about outcomes, investors are likely to take into account risk, as well as return. Holding several stocks will reduce the risk, providing all stocks do not behave in the same way. We know that when the market goes up and down, most stocks move the same way as the market. But stocks do not all move exactly the same amount, and most days when the market goes down you can find some stocks that have gone up, and vice versa. Why is that?

One can think of stocks as bearing two kinds of risk: systematic or market risk, and unsystematic or unique risk. Each stock will bear both sorts of risk. Every company is unique and its stock will be subject to company-specific risks. However all companies tend to be subject to the economic cycle so all stocks will also have some common risks. When a portfolio of stocks is constructed, the variability of the portfolio returns will decline as more and more stocks are added because the unsystematic risks will tend to wash out: sunny weather will hurt the umbrella business, but it will do wonders for the ice cream business. If you own stocks in both industries, you won't be affected as much by changing weather as you would if you held only one. But diversification will not completely remove risk, because the market, or systematic risk, cannot be diversified away. If the economy goes into recession, no matter the weather, fewer umbrellas and ice creams are likely to be sold. How quickly does diversification reduce risk? Various studies show that it doesn't take many stocks — 10 or so, at most 20 — to eliminate most of the unsystematic risk, leaving the portfolio subject mainly to unavoidable systematic risk. Consequently many textbooks argue that investors need hold only 10–20 stocks to achieve the benefits of diversification. I will return to this later.

The above analysis assumes random selection of securities. Securities whose returns tend to move together (for example, the stocks of companies in the same industry) will not have the same diversification impact as will securities whose returns are less closely related. The importance of diversification in portfolio construction and the importance of the correlation of returns between assets was first analyzed by Harry Markowitz. He showed that to construct an efficient portfolio, i.e., one with the highest return for a given risk, or the lowest risk for a given return, one needs to know every asset's expected return, standard deviation of returns and the correlation of returns between assets (strictly speaking, the covariance of returns, a statistical measure related to correlation). The statistical program that does the calculation is known as an optimizer. Optimizers are not widely used in the investment community for constructing share portfolios but are more widely used for asset allocation — they are discussed in Part Four.

As well as for portfolio theory, systematic and unsystematic risk are important concepts for asset pricing theory. The basic textbook treatment of asset pricing runs as follows. If unsystematic risk can be eliminated by diversification (and institutional investors do diversify, even if private investors often do not) it is unlikely that bearing unsystematic risk will be rewarded. Return is likely to be related to the unavoidable systematic, or market-related, risk. A relative measure of the sensitivity of a stock's (or other asset's) return to that of the market is its beta. The market has a beta of one. Stocks with a beta greater than one will tend to have returns which exaggerate market movements — they are more volatile or risky. When the market goes up, stocks with a high beta will tend to return more than the market and when the market goes down these stocks will tend to do worse. And vice-versa for low beta stocks. According to this view, beta is the relevant risk measure for pricing assets. Investors will expect to get the risk-free rate from a stock with a zero beta, i.e., a stock whose returns are unrelated to the market's, and the market return from a security with a beta of one. A bit of algebraic manipulation produces the following equation, which is the capital asset pricing model, usually abbreviated to CAPM:

expected return from security = risk free rate + (security beta)

× (expected return from market − risk free rate)

That is the gist of the CAPM, which is discussed at length in the textbooks and is outlined at the start of Chapter 2 of this book. Here I will focus on whether the theory is true, i.e., whether beta is related to return in the real world. The early empirical evidence favoured the theory. Later U.S. evidence suggested the theory was false, as did the majority of foreign studies. These studies were largely ignored until Fama and French (1992) reported that there was no relationship between betas and return in the U.S. over the period 1963–90. Had beta finally been laid to rest? In Chapter 1, Louis Chan and Josef Lakonishok, both of whom are professors at the University of Illinois at Urbana-Champaign, argue that beta is not yet dead. (Lakonishok, it might be noted, was the co-author of a study published a decade ago that found beta was not related to returns.) Using 60 years' return data, Chan and Lakonishok show that there does appear to be a relationship between returns and beta but, because of the noisy nature of the data, statistical significance is not attained. This may mean that beta is not related to returns or that we simply do not have enough observations to know. They note that beta is not related to returns in the last decade and one can view this as untypical, and a reason why statistical significance is not attained for long periods which include the last few years or, alternatively, as the likely pattern from now on. Chan and Lakonishok suggest that investment managers may be as interested in extreme situations as they are in what happens on average over very long periods. For example, in market crashes, do high beta stocks perform worse than others? It seems they do.

Well, what is one to conclude from all this? Chan and Lakonishok give three conclusions supporting beta and three against. Readers must make up their own minds which side to come down on. The uncertainty surrounding the value of beta provides an interesting case in scientific method. It raises questions as to how one tests scientific theories and what is considered to be adequate evidence to reject a theory. For example, are the authors right to argue: "If a hypothesis is based on a sound theory (some might say 'story') and is relatively free of data-snooping biases, it may not be the most productive way to proceed if we insist unthinkingly on a significance level of 5% before we can reject the null hypothesis."? (Readers especially interested in statistical testing of theories might also read Summers, 1986, on similar statistical problems encountered when testing the efficient market theory.)

Even if beta is related to returns, many investors and academics would argue that there is more to risk than beta, and this has spurred the search for a better theory. Indeed, some academics who believe the evidence on beta is weak, are nonetheless not willing to reject the CAPM until they find a better theory to take its place. The major academic rival to the CAPM is the Arbitrage Pricing Theory, or APT. The APT is covered in the textbooks but a complete discussion involves a lot of mathematics and statistics, especially if factor analysis is discussed, making the exposition difficult to follow. Some textbooks get round this problem by giving only the briefest of outlines, which leaves the reader unsure what APT is about. Here I have tried to tread the middle path. In Chapter 2, Richard Roll and Stephen Ross, professors at the University of California at Los Angeles and Yale University respectively, and co-proprietors of a financial consulting firm, set out the basic notions of APT and compare it to the CAPM. The article is useful for its presentation of APT and its empirical merits, but there is an additional reason for including this piece. Textbook writers tend to take a balanced stance, carefully noting the pluses and minuses of competing theories. One of the authors of Chapter 2, Stephen Ross, was the original proponent of APT. This chapter is more fun than the typical textbook treatment because it does not sit on the fence: APT is the better theory — according to the authors. The discussion is orientated to a specific problem — determining the cost of capital for regulated utility companies.

Like the CAPM, the APT envisages both systematic and unsystematic risk factors and argues that the unsystematic risks can be diversified away and therefore will not be priced. However, instead of the single systematic factor of the CAPM, the market, the APT is a multi-factor model. Stocks' returns are priced in relation to their exposure to unexpected returns in the systematic factors. In essence the APT says:

$$\text{expected return} = \text{risk-free return} + \beta_1(\text{factor 1}) + \beta_2(\text{factor 2}) + \cdots + \beta_n(\text{factor } \mathbf{n}) + e$$

A major problem with the theory is that it does not tell us how many factors there are or what the factors are. We are left to find the factors ourselves. There are two ways of doing this. One is by pre-specifying likely factors (for example factors that the dividend discount model implies might be relevant) and then testing to see if they are relevant. The second way is by a complex statistical technique which can determine if factors exist in sets of data, although it will not identify those factors in terms of meaningful economic or financial variables; we simply discover that statistically derived factors X, Y and Z exist. A multi-factor theory of risk and return corresponds better to most investors' view of how the world works than does the single factor CAPM. But, at the level of empirical application, it leaves itself open to charges of data-mining: factors found at one time period for one set of data may not apply at another period or for another data sample. Where theoretically pre-specified factors are involved, this charge may have less force. Nonetheless, the academic literature contains a large number of studies which find different numbers of factors, different factors for different periods and so forth. APT is interesting, but it has not yet proved to be *the* theory of risk and return.

Outside of the U.S., there has been less work on testing the CAPM and APT. In the European markets, beta has generally not been found to be a very useful tool. In the U.K. there have been a number of studies of the APT. Some studies suggest that there are indeed several risk factors. Unfortunately these factors vary from study to study and in some studies it has been found that the factors change over time. Elton and Gruber (1988) studied the risk structure of the Japanese market. They concluded that there was more than one factor, and that four factors were sufficient to describe the risk structure. It is clear from the diverse findings for the U.S. and the rest of the world that more work has to be done on the nature of risk.

To the extent the CAPM and the APT are valid, they have implications for managing investments. In both theories, it is assumed that markets are efficient (discussed in Part Two) and investors can only get extra returns by bearing extra risk. In the CAPM, if you want the chance of extra returns, you must bear more risk than the market. This can be achieved by holding high beta stocks or holding a leveraged position on the market. In the APT each source of systematic risk has its own volatility and returns. The return return/risk ratios of each source of risk can differ, and may change over time. If a portfolio is constructed that is overweight in high return/risk factors, the portfolio will outperform the market. But this poses the question as to whether this is genuine outperformance or merely reflects the obvious — if investors bear different risks than the market, they get a different return.

Although the CAPM and the APT are interesting, investors grappled with risk before the theories were invented, and many still grapple with risk along traditional lines. The bond rating services use traditional common-sense variables to assess risk and more investors will describe a risky share as one with high gearing, in a cyclical industry and so forth, than as one with a high beta. Of course, there may be a correlation between beta and gearing, etc., but why not examine the value of the traditional approaches? One problem is that they tend to be informal and non-quantitative, making testing hard, although some organizations have formulated disciplined approaches. The *Value Line Investment Survey* is an independent, weekly, investment advisory service covering U.S. stocks. It claims to be the largest advisory service in the world measured in terms of revenues and numbers of subscribers. For the 1,700 stocks *Value Line* reviews, it produces a Safety Rank which includes a measure of financial strength based on "traditional" variables. In Chapter 3, Russell Fuller and Wenchi Wong relate three measures of risk to return. One measure of risk is the CAPM beta (systematic risk), one is a stock's standard deviation of returns (total risk), and the third is *Value Line's* Safety Rank. For the period studied, the Safety Rank was the best measure of risk. The authors suggest that our understanding of risk might be improved by examining the practices of investment professionals. At the time the article was written, Fuller was a professor at Washington State University and Wong at DePaul University. Fuller is currently President of RJF Asset Management, Inc.

At the start of this Part, I noted that the textbooks tell us that since a portfolio of 10–20 stocks eliminates most unsystematic risk, the benefits of diversification can be achieved with that number of stocks. In Chapter 4, Meir Statman, a professor at Santa Clara University, challenges this conclusion. Recalling first year economics, Statman points out that activities should be carried out up to the point where marginal benefits equal marginal costs, i.e., investors should diversify until the risk reduction benefits of diversification equate with the extra transaction costs. Statman constructs a security market line using the risk-free rate and the historical return on the S&P 500. He then uses data on the standard deviation of returns for the market and for a 10 stock portfolio, 20 stock portfolio, and so on. The limited diversification portfolios are riskier than the market and we can read off from the security market line the extra return that the smaller portfolios should receive as reward for the extra risk. Of course it would be hard for most investors to hold every stock in the S&P 500, so Statman looks at the return from a retail index fund. It has returned about $\frac{1}{2}$% less than the index. Assuming the limited diversification portfolios achieve the market return, investors should diversify until the required extra return for a limited diversification portfolio's extra risk is $\frac{1}{2}$%. On this basis investors should hold portfolios of between at least 30 and 40 stocks, i.e., investors should be more diversified that the textbooks tell us. In coming to this conclusion, Statman makes a number of assumptions which readers may wish to list and consider. Do the assumptions undermine the analysis? Statman notes that surveys show that private investors are not well diversified. They seem to act contrary to the standard assumptions of finance theory. This raises the question why these investors forego the benefits of diversification, and what that implies for financial theory.

REFERENCES

Elton, E.J. and Gruber, M.J. 1988. A Multi-Index Risk Model of the Japanese Stock Market. *Japan and the World Economy*, **1**, 21–44.

Fama, E.F. and French, K.R. 1992. The Cross-Section of Expected Stock Returns. *Journal of Finance*, **47**, 427–65.

Summers, L.H. 1986. Does the Stock Market Rationally Reflect Fundamental Values? *Journal Of Finance*, **41**, 591–601.

1

Are the Reports
of Beta's Death Premature?

Louis K.C. Chan and Josef Lakonishok

Many would name the concept of beta risk as the single most important contribution of academic researchers to the financial community. At first slow to accept beta, practitioners have come to use it widely as a risk measure and for computing expected returns. In European capital markets, the concept of beta is now beginning to gain popularity. Yet, just as beta seems to be on the verge of widespread use, an article by Fama and French [1992a] has caused both academics and practitioners to re-examine the empirical support for beta's importance.

In retrospect, some earlier studies of beta (Fama and MacBeth [1973]; Black, Jensen, and Scholes [1972]) do not provide conclusive evidence in support of beta. Later studies dating from the 1980s (such as Reinganum [1982]; Lakonishok and Shapiro [1986]; and Ritter and Chopra [1989]) are not able to detect any significant relation between beta and average returns.

The negative findings of these later studies, however, have been largely ignored. The recent study of Fama and French [1992a], which echoes the results of some of these papers from the 1980s, has been interpreted as the final nail in the coffin.

Do we really have sufficient evidence to bury beta? The question assumes added urgency when we consider how dramatically the practice of portfolio management has changed in the last five years.

More money managers, for example, are beginning to use optimization techniques to find efficient portfolios. This trend is still growing, and the technology is being developed to optimize over thousands of assets to form portfolios. One outcome may be that more investors will come to emphasize systematic risk, leading thereby to a tighter relation between returns and beta.

It would be highly ironic if, after continuing to accept beta for twenty years without solid empirical support, we were to discard beta just when the move toward portfolio optimization is gaining speed, and when beta might emerge as an important risk measure.

Reprinted from: Chan, L.K.C. and Lakonishok, J. 1993: Are the Reports of Beta's Death Premature? *Journal of Portfolio Management*, 19, Summer, 51–62. This copyright material is reprinted with permission from The Journal of Portfolio Management, 488 Madison Avenue, New York, NY 10022.

We should, instead, bear in mind how very difficult it is to draw any definitive conclusions from empirical research on stock returns. Fischer Black [1986] has alerted us all to the pervasive influence of "noise," which clouds our ability to test our theories definitively.

In this article, we examine whether the very noisy and constantly changing environment generating stock returns permits strong statements about the importance of beta. Things instead may be much more complicated, and we may simply have to admit that we are not sure what drives stock returns.

We provide direct evidence on how the limitations of the available data make it difficult to draw firm inferences about the relation between betas and returns, as well as the relation between returns and other variables used in previous studies. By examining the entire history of returns, we also consider the sensitivity of the results to the choice of time period.

There are, of course, numerous reasons why returns might not be related to betas. Roll [1977] and Roll and Ross [1992] emphasize the problems with testing the relation between betas and returns when the true market portfolio is unobservable.

We do not dispute that this difficulty underlies all the existing empirical tests of the CAPM. Our approach is instead pragmatic: we focus on the CAPM as it is used in practice. The standard approach is to specify some broad-based proxy for the market index, calculate betas with respect to this proxy, and relate future returns to these betas. We ask whether high-beta stocks outperform low-beta stocks, and whether the compensation for beta risk is equal to $r_m - r_f$, the rate of return on the market less the risk-free rate, as implied by the Sharpe–Lintner version of the CAPM.

Fama and French [1992a] find no association between returns and betas, even when beta is the only explanatory variable. This is the finding we wish to focus on. In so doing, we exclude from our regressions other variables, such as size and the book-to-market ratio, that have been found to have explanatory power for returns, and focus solely on beta. While it is true that other variables may help to explain returns, there are no firm guidelines as to what variables to include in addition to beta.

Even if there were no compensation for beta risk, this does not mean that betas serve no use for investment decision-making. As long as beta is a stable measure of exposure to market movements, investors should still consider the "beta factor" of a stock.[1] A market timer, for example, would want to be long in high-beta stocks if a rise in the market is expected. A manager who wishes to track a given target portfolio would also have to consider the beta of a stock.

We examine whether betas indeed serve as reliable measures of exposure to market movements. In October 1987, for instance, when the market tumbled by 22%, did high-beta stocks do worse than low-beta stocks? Many institutional investors think of risk in precisely these terms — as sensitivity to market movements.

There is a widespread belief among financial researchers that only risk drives returns. If conventional market betas cannot explain returns, then there must be some other measures of risk that will do the job better. The search is thus on for these multidimensional measures of risk. Given the dangers of this kind of collective data-snooping exercise (Lakonishok and Smidt [1988], Lo and MacKinlay [1990]), however, the results of this search must be taken with a grain of salt.

An alternative explanation for why it is so difficult to detect the relation between risk and return is that other behavioral and institutional factors unrelated to risk may be at work. There is an extensive literature documenting both investors' tendency to over-react over longer horizons (De Bondt and Thaler [1985]), and the existence of momentum over shorter horizons (Jegadeesh and Titman [1993]).

In this article, we study one specific institutional feature: the effect of the trend toward indexed investment and performance evaluation on the prices of stocks in the S&P 500. The rising demand for stocks in the index could result in higher returns for stocks in this exclusive fraternity, unrelated to their riskiness.

Our results should in no way be construed as providing unconditional support for beta's importance for returns. Rather, our point is that, given the limitations of the data, it is still an open question whether beta is dead or alive as a determinant of expected returns.

NOISY STOCK RETURNS

Twenty years is a long time in financial markets. Needless to say, the horizon of the money management business is very much shorter than twenty years. There are only a handful of countries where it is possible to obtain comprehensive data going back twenty years. Most of the international data bases available to money managers extend back no farther then ten years. Widely used commercial data bases, for example, carry accounting information on Swiss companies from 1986 onward only. Even the data that are available are plagued with problems, as they focus only on surviving companies.

It is thus fair to say that many would feel that having a complete monthly history of twenty years of data on thousands of stocks should be more than adequate to answer the simple question whether there is a significant relation between beta and returns. Yet is twenty years really enough?

One popular procedure to test for the existence of a relation between betas and returns comes from Fama and MacBeth [1973]. Monthly cross-sectional regressions are run relating stock returns to betas. The slope coefficient from each regression is our estimate of the compensation per unit of beta in that particular month. The average of the monthly slopes is thus the estimate of the compensation per unit of beta risk received by investors on average. We can then use the standard deviation of the monthly series on the slope coefficients to examine whether the average slope is statistically significantly different from zero.

Suppose that each month for the last twenty years in the U.S. we follow the standard methodology and run monthly cross-sectional regressions relating returns to betas. Suppose, moreover, that every month we obtain a slope coefficient exactly equal to $r_m - r_f$, the return on the market minus the risk-free rate. This accords perfectly with the Sharpe–Lintner CAPM. Indeed, we cannot obtain a more favourable result than this for the model.

Yet would our regressions reveal that beta plays a significant role in explaining stock returns? From our regressions, we would obtain an annualized average slope coefficient of 5.05%, and an annualized standard deviation of the slope coefficient of 16.58%. The standard procedure is to test whether the average slope coefficient is significantly different from zero. The t-statistic for testing for the significance of the premium for beta risk is 1.36, significant at a level of about 9%. This significance level is not enough to reject the null hypothesis that the premium is zero, given our typical insistence on a 5% significance level.

Given the level of noise in the last twenty years of stock returns, we would need a risk premium of about 7.4% per year before we could reliably reject the null hypothesis. What if the compensation per unit of risk were lower, 4% per year, consistent with the Black [1972] model but still a non-negligible number? How many years then would we need before we could declare the premium statistically significant? We would have to report back to you in sixty-nine years.

Because we assume in this exercise that the premium for beta risk is indeed equal to $r_m - r_f$, what we are doing is the same as testing for the existence of an equity risk premium (i.e., whether stocks do better than T-bills). We thus infer that the annual difference of 5.05% per year does not suffice to reject reliably the null that stocks do not outperform T-bills. A dollar invested in T-bills at the beginning of the twenty-year period in question would have grown to $4.41, while an equivalent investment in stocks would have yielded $9.21. Yet this huge difference is still not statistically significant at the 5% level.

beyond testing whether high-beta stocks outperform low-beta stocks. Strategies based on B/M (the book-to-market ratio) have recently gained popularity (Chan, Hamao, and Lakonishok [1991], Fama and French [1992a]). Following this tack, for each year from 1968 to 1990, we form ten portfolios from the universe of NYSE and AMEX stocks, ranked by B/M. We compare the returns of the two extreme portfolios: the portfolio comprising those stocks with the highest B/M ratio, and the portfolio made up of those stocks with the lowest B/M portfolio.

The standard error of the difference is 3.6%, implying that unless the high B/M portfolio outperforms the low B/M portfolio by at least 7.2% a year, the difference will not be significant. Luckily for the partisans of B/M, the difference over the sample period is 8.7%, passing the test of significance.

Strategies developed in hindsight do not ensure successful future performance for a money manager, however. How confident can one be that high B/M stocks will continue to outperform low B/M stocks at such a pace?

On the one hand, the publicity that we have collectively given to B/M may make high B/M stocks less attractive in the future. On the other hand, if B/M is simply proxying for risk, then we might expect similar returns in the future for high B/M stocks. Many of us, however, have serious doubts whether the extraordinary performance of high B/M stocks can be explained by their riskiness (see Lakonishok, Shleifer, and Vishny [1992a]).

Another popular trading strategy is based on market capitalization. We compare the returns over the period 1979–1991 on the Russell 2000 index to the returns on the S&P 500. The standard error for the difference in returns is 3.63% per year. Unless the return on small stocks is at least twice this much (7.26%) over the return on the S&P 500, we cannot judge the difference to be significant.

As it turns out, the mean returns over the last thirteen years differ by 0.28% per year. This difference does not amount to much — should we conclude that the size effect is dead?

In a different context, take a money manager who outperforms a benchmark by 2% a year, representing an extraordinary feat. Assume that tracking error is 5% a year, which is below the median for active money managers (based on the SEI universe of equity managers).

We would still need to accumulate twenty-five years of data on returns earned by this manager before we can reject the null hypothesis that performance of this magnitude is no better than the benchmark. This example highlights how dangerous our assumption of stability can be. Are we getting twenty years later the same money manager as the one responsible for the extraordinary early performance?

These examples illustrate how difficult it is to make unambiguous inferences from the very noisy and ever-changing environment generating stock returns. While our research is often posed as clear-cut black-and-white statements, we often do not have the luxury of drawing such unqualified conclusions from the data at hand. If a hypothesis is based on a sound theory (some might say "story") and is relatively free of data-snooping biases, it may not be the most productive way to proceed if we insist unthinkingly on a significance level of 5% before we can reject the null hypothesis.

TESTS OF THE CAPM

We use all the available data on the monthly Center for Research on Security Prices (CRSP) tape from 1926 to 1991 to examine the relation between beta and returns, following the Fama–MacBeth procedure. The first three years of monthly observations are used in a market model regression to estimate each stock's beta relative to the CRSP value-weighted market index. Our universe is restricted to NYSE and AMEX stocks.

The stocks are then ranked on the basis of the estimated betas and assigned to one of ten portfolios. Portfolio 1 contains stocks with the lowest betas, while Portfolio 10 contains stocks with the highest betas.

The assignment of stocks to portfolios in part reflects measurement errors in the betas. Such errors would result in a "regression to the mean."

To avoid such bias, an intermediate step is necessary: the beta of each stock in a portfolio is re-estimated using the next three years of returns; a portfolio's beta is then a simple average of the betas of the individual stocks assigned to that portfolio. Thus the first three-year period is used to classify stocks to portfolios, and the next three-year period is used to estimate betas for the portfolios.

In each month of the subsequent year, we regress the returns on the ten portfolios on their estimated betas. Note that this is a predictive test in the sense that the explanatory variable (beta) is estimated over a period disjoint from the period over which returns are measured. At the end of the year, we repeat the process of forming portfolios from three years of data, estimating betas over three years, and adding twelve more cross-sectional regressions. Ultimately we obtain 720 cross-sectional regressions.

Table 1.1 provides summary statistics on the betas for the ten portfolios and their average returns. There is a positive relation between betas and average returns: a finding consistent with a recent paper by Black [1992].

Table 1.2 provides results from the monthly cross-sectional regressions. The mean estimated slope coefficient is 0.47% per month, with a marginally significant t-statistic of 1.84.[2] Given our standard errors, it is as likely that the compensation per unit of beta is 0% per year as it is 12% per year. The realized market premium $(r_m - r_f)$ over this period averages 0.76% per month. Thus our estimated premium is 62% of the market excess return, in line with the results of earlier work.

The Sharpe–Lintner CAPM implies that the risk premium is equal to the mean of $(r_m - r_f)$ — the absolute difference between the average slope and the average market excess

Table 1.1 Mean, standard deviation (in %), and beta of returns on portfolios formed on beta, January 1932–December 1991

	(Low) 1	2	3	4	5	6	7	8	9	(High) 10
Mean	1.30	1.33	1.32	1.46	1.56	1.59	1.52	1.65	1.54	1.60
Standard Deviation	5.51	6.07	6.55	7.36	7.50	7.87	8.58	9.12	9.08	10.37
Beta	0.90	1.03	1.12	1.25	1.26	1.32	1.44	1.49	1.51	1.70

Table 1.2 Monthly Fama-MacBeth cross-sectional regressions

Sample period	Intercept	Slope	R^2	T-test for slope $= r_m - r_f$
Jan. 1932–Dec. 1991	0.0059	0.0047	0.48	−1.15
($r_m - r_f = 0.0076$)	(3.50)	(1.84)		
Jan. 1932–Dec. 1961	0.0075	0.0074	0.48	−1.01
($r_m - r_f = 0.0115$)	(2.80)	(1.82)		
Jan. 1962–Dec. 1991	0.0042	0.0020	0.47	−0.57
($r_m - r_f = 0.0038$)	(2.10)	(0.64)		

return is only 29 basis points, so we cannot reject the null hypothesis that the mean slope coefficient is equal to the average market excess return (the t-statistic is −1.15).

In contrast, over the period 1963–1990, Fama and French [1992a] obtain a much lower point estimate for the slope coefficient (0.15% per month), with a t-statistic of 0.46. The case against beta is thus much stronger in Fama and French's sample period.

Upon reflection, however, their finding may not be as striking as it first seems. In order for them to obtain a t-statistic of 2, the compensation per unit of beta risk would have to be 7.83% per year — undoubtedly on the high side relative to the experience of the last thirty years, or relative to any projection of future returns. So the failure to find a statistically significant role for beta should not come as a total surprise.

Figure 1.1 plots the average cumulative monthly difference between the estimated premium for beta risk and $r_m - r_f$, the value predicted by the Sharpe–Lintner CAPM.

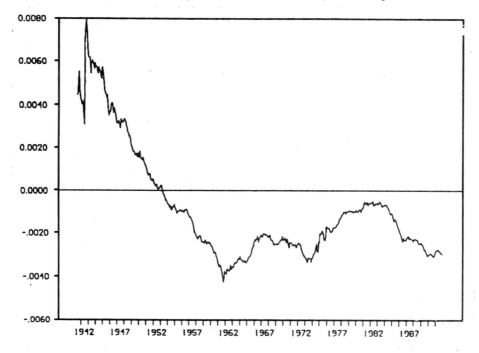

Figure 1.1 Cumulative average difference between estimated slope and excess market return, January 1942–December 1991

We start cumulating the difference from January 1932, although the exhibit focuses on the post-1942 experience.

It is clear from the figure that the relation between betas and returns varies considerably over time. If we were to stop our test in 1982, we would conclude that there is a lot of support for the CAPM. Up until 1982, the estimated compensation for beta risk is strikingly close to $r_m - r_f$: the average slope is 0.0070 (2.47 times its standard error), while the average market excess return is 0.0076, yielding a minuscule difference of 6 basis points (the t-statistic for the difference is -0.32).

On the other hand, the last nine years have not been kind to beta — the gap between the estimated compensation for beta risk and the realized market premium widens substantially. Figure 1.1 reinforces our earlier discussion of the difficulties posed by noise in the data. The conclusions based on a period of as much as fifty years of data turn out to be quite fragile, given that adding nine years to the sample can dramatically alter our results.

What one takes away from all this depends on one's prior beliefs. A die-hard believer in beta could make a good argument that the poor performance of beta over the last nine years should be viewed as an aberration. During this period small stocks, which tend to have higher betas, have performed poorly relative to larger companies with lower betas, perhaps because, as Fama and French [1992b] suggest, unanticipated economic developments in the recent period had an adverse effect on low-capitalization stocks.

One could, however, with equal ease, argue that it is the earlier period that presents problematic evidence for beta. There appears to be a very strong relation between betas and returns in the earlier years, even before Markowitz formulated the mean-variance concepts underlying the CAPM. If anything, then, the model seems to work "too well" until the

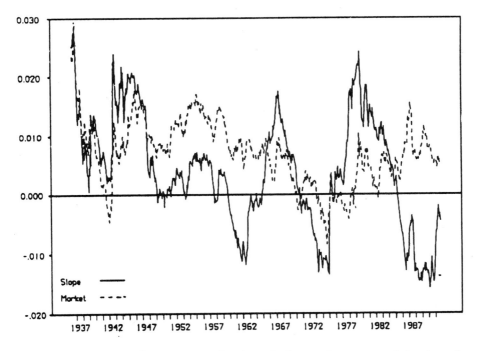

Figure 1.2 Five-year moving averages of estimated slope and excess market return, January 1937–December 1991

mid-fifties. It is possible that Markowitz's ideas were not so new after all, and the marginal investor knew how to form efficient portfolios long before Markowitz was born.

Figure 1.2 presents five-year moving averages of the estimated slope and the excess return on the market. Each point on the graph represents the average of the last sixty months of observations on the variable. There seems to be a close correlation between the two series for much of the sample period. For whatever reason, the most pronounced discrepancy appears in the more recent period, as noted above.

THE IMPORTANCE OF THE BETA FACTOR

The noisy, dynamic environment generating stock returns clouds our ability to reach firm conclusions with respect to the compensation for beta risk. It may be a less difficult task to verify whether the beta factor is important in driving stock returns. In particular, the case for beta would be more plausible if it were indeed true that stocks with high betas represent higher risk than stocks with low betas.

Extensive conversations with money managers suggest that downside risk is their major concern. Since beta represents the sensitivity of a stock's return to market rises and declines, it should be a good measure of downside risk. If, for example, stock prices were to fall in general, the prices of high-beta stocks should decline more than the prices of low-beta stocks.

There is no automatic presumption that this should be so — there may, for instance, be other factors driving stock returns, and these factors may change in such a way as to distort the association between market movements and the movement in individual stock prices. Another possibility is that the relation between past betas and future betas is unstable.

In order to address this issue, Table 1.3 presents the experience of the ten largest "down-market" months (a down-market month is a month when $r_m - r_f$ is negative). These are precisely the sort of months that cause sleepless nights for investors.

For each of these ten months, we report the excess market return, the coefficients and R^2 of the cross-sectional regression, and the returns on the ten beta-sorted portfolios. In each month, the returns on the ten portfolios are nearly monotonically related to their betas. On average, the R^2 is a remarkable 74%.

October 1987 is still fresh in the memories of many: in that month the excess market return is -22.43%, compared to the estimated slope of -22.59%. The returns on the ten beta-sorted portfolios are all negative, ranging from -17.10% for the portfolio with the lowest beta to -33.76% for the portfolio with the highest beta (a difference of 16.66 percentage points). The R^2 of the cross-sectional regression is 83%.

The results for the ten largest up-market months in Table 1.4 are qualitatively similar. In months when the market falls (rises), investors in high-beta stocks do indeed experience larger losses (gains) than investors holding low-beta stocks.

More generally, Table 1.5 provides averages of the cross-sectional slope coefficients across all down-market and all up-market months. In the down-market subsample (Panel A), the average excess return on the market is -3.81% per month. With this large a "signal," it should become easier to detect whether the beta factor is important. The average slope in this subsample is -3.55% per month, remarkably close to the average market excess return.

Panel B of Table 1.5 performs the same exercise with respect to the up-market months (where the market excess return $r_m - r_f$ is positive). Once more we see a close correspondence between the average realized premium (3.88%) and the average slope (3.21%).

Table 1.3 Ten largest down-market months: excess market return $(r_m - r_f)$, estimated cross-sectional slope, R^2, and returns on portfolios formed on beta

Month	Market	Slope	R^2	Returns on portfolios formed on beta									
				(Low) 1	2	3	4	5	6	7	8	9	(High) 10
1 3/38	−23.61	−16.06	96.50	−19.35	−21.17	−24.24	−27.06	−28.58	−32.77	−32.67	−35.36	−37.72	−37.13
2 10/87	−22.43	−22.59	83.20	−17.10	−16.88	−25.70	−26.88	−25.90	−27.46	−29.79	−30.08	−29.70	−33.76
3 5/40	−22.00	−5.38	83.74	−22.10	−24.63	−25.44	−25.68	−27.07	−28.61	−29.24	−26.73	−31.77	−30.51
4 5/32	−20.75	−8.43	27.00	−20.88	−20.02	−25.31	−21.32	−18.95	−16.45	−21.09	−21.10	−22.08	−27.74
5 4/32	−18.11	−4.84	28.90	−19.46	−16.33	−18.17	−19.07	−18.30	−22.58	−20.84	−20.59	−20.72	−20.06
6 9/37	−13.52	−9.27	96.56	−10.82	−14.44	−14.71	−16.40	−20.25	−20.96	−22.63	−22.52	−24.82	−26.36
7 2/33	−13.28	−13.08	76.44	−7.05	−8.93	−12.20	−9.75	−12.47	−12.13	−13.73	−12.18	−19.19	−17.47
8 10/32	−13.06	−14.93	60.85	−11.60	−15.83	−16.38	−19.86	−14.39	−15.22	−22.32	−20.52	−17.36	−23.45
9 3/80	−12.80	−8.40	92.33	−12.14	−13.33	−11.64	−14.79	−13.49	−14.21	−15.54	−15.96	−17.40	−19.26
10 11/73	−12.33	−12.58	94.49	−9.13	−12.05	−12.26	−16.05	−14.90	−17.92	−19.01	−19.42	−20.76	−23.54
Average	−17.19	−11.56	74.00	−14.96	−16.36	−19.00	−19.68	−19.43	−20.83	−22.69	−22.45	−24.15	−25.93

Table 1.4 Ten largest up-market months: excess market return $(r_m - r_f)$, estimated cross-sectional slope, R^2, and returns on portfolios formed on beta

| Month | Market | Slope | R^2 | Returns on portfolios formed on beta | | | | | | | | | |
				(Low) 1	2	3	4	5	6	7	8	9	(High) 10
1 4/33	38.18	45.83	72.21	37.84	44.73	36.40	47.57	47.84	74.40	54.56	58.67	60.08	72.34
2 8/32	36.45	60.30	56.05	49.06	54.76	61.02	81.73	47.75	43.92	64.07	86.44	61.58	84.96
3 7/32	33.06	19.97	28.28	38.93	46.62	47.46	52.70	50.13	40.57	62.93	44.26	49.72	57.70
4 6/38	23.54	22.96	96.93	16.98	18.57	23.34	28.09	34.32	35.17	37.81	39.18	40.98	43.33
5 5/33	21.07	14.67	21.92	43.56	50.31	49.34	50.35	69.25	59.17	57.30	57.53	46.55	59.28
6 10/74	16.02	-2.43	26.59	10.90	13.83	13.42	13.88	8.82	11.49	10.95	12.17	8.51	10.25
7 9/39	15.94	49.96	86.40	6.96	17.87	23.21	36.35	40.09	46.20	69.01	64.49	53.48	56.93
8 4/38	14.53	17.26	73.52	13.85	15.20	18.96	19.88	18.45	23.45	22.72	23.13	27.83	42.41
9 6/33	13.35	19.54	48.04	13.92	19.19	14.59	13.04	23.82	24.53	34.15	25.37	22.77	28.79
10 1/75	13.32	37.02	65.14	23.84	20.68	22.51	21.52	29.06	31.18	33.15	31.90	40.10	42.89
Average	22.55	28.51	57.51	25.58	30.18	31.02	36.48	36.95	39.01	44.66	44.31	41.16	49.89

Table 1.5 Cross-sectional regression results and excess return on market, classified by down-market months (where $(r_m - r_f) < 0$) and up-market months (where $(r_m - r_f) > 0$)

Sample period	Intercept	Slope	R^2	$r_m - r_f$
(A) Down-market months				
All down months	−0.0008	−0.0355	0.54	−0.0381
(292 months)	(−0.34)	(−13.98)		
Large down months[a]	−0.0092	−0.0524	0.63	−0.0626
(146 months)	(−2.56)	(−14.19)		
Small down months[b]	0.0076	−0.0186	0.45	−0.0136
(146 months)	(2.94)	(−6.45)		
(B) Up-market months				
All up months	0.0104	0.0321	0.44	0.0388
(428 months)	(4.46)	(9.62)		
Large up months	0.0139	0.0530	0.51	0.0625
(214 months)	(3.49)	(9.20)		
Small up months	0.0069	0.0112	0.37	0.0151
(214 months)	(2.86)	(4.14)		

[a] A large down- (up-) month is defined as a month where $(r_m - r_f)$ is larger in magnitude than the median of those observations that are negative (positive).

[b] A small down- (up-) month is defined as a month where $(r_m - r_f)$ is smaller in magnitude than the median of those observations that are negative (positive).

Note that in both the up-market and down-market subsamples, the estimated slope is close to the realized market premium in magnitude: the subsample slopes are 93% and 83% of the market excess return in down- and up-market months, respectively. Even a small relative difference between the estimated slope and the excess market return in down- or up-market months, however, translates into being off by 29 basis points when pooled over the entire sample (Figure 1.3).

The statistical researcher who is aware of the stability of covariances between portfolio returns will find little that is surprising in Tables 1.3–1.5. That the message is familiar to some, however, does not make it any less worthy of repetition — it is our experience, in particular, that the majority of professional money managers are struck by how well the beta factor fares in predicting which portfolios will take the biggest beating in down-markets. Beta can thus be useful to any investor who casts risk in terms of downside exposure. More generally, a stock's beta would be relevant to a market timer, or an investor tracking a target portfolio.

We should stress, however, that our strong results for down- and up-market months should not be taken as evidence that, on average, high-beta stocks necessarily earn higher returns than low-beta stocks. The estimated coefficients tend to move in the same direction as the market premium, so that the slope is high (low) when $r_m - r_f$ is high (low).

In a regression of the monthly observations of the cross-sectional slopes on the monthly market excess return $r_m - r_f$ over the period January 1932 to December 1991, the intercept is −0.0023, and the slope coefficient of the regression is 0.91, which is impressively close to 1.0. The R^2 of the regression is 0.52, which is remarkably high, given the variability in monthly rates of return.

The estimated monthly cross-sectional slope does not exactly match the excess market return, however, so it might be the case that when averaged across all market cycles high-beta stocks do not necessarily earn higher returns than low-beta stocks. Our results in this section

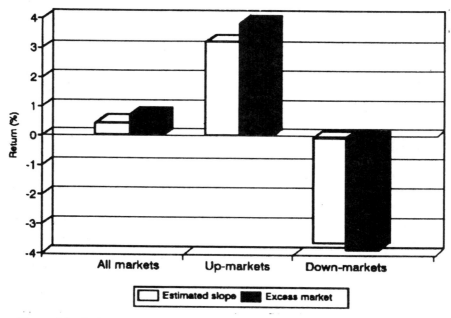

Figure 1.3 Estimated slope and excess return on market for all up- and down-markets

are thus consistent with alternative factor models of returns that feature no compensation for beta.

One example is a factor model of the form

$$r_{it} - r_{ft} = k + b_i[r_{mt} - r_{ft} - E(r_{mt} - r_{ft})] + e_{it}, \qquad (1)$$

where $E(\ )$ is the expectation operator, and e_{it} is an error term uncorrelated with the market. Here the slope of any monthly cross-sectional regression differs from the excess market return only by a constant, yet expected returns are not related to betas but are constant across stocks.

If we were handed a realization of this factor model where the average excess market return $r_m - r_f$ is high (say, 10% per year), we would find that high-beta stocks outperform low-beta stocks. We would be led to conclude — incorrectly — that beta is a highly significant variable determining expected returns.

The question remains, however, whether this realization corresponds with "normal" experience, and whether beta will still be a significant explanatory variable for expected returns in a more representative environment, where the excess market return is more likely to be 5% per year. This point is particularly relevant for tests of the CAPM applied to foreign markets, where sample periods are relatively short and hence not necessarily representative of the normal experience of these markets.

While the beta factor is important, therefore, it may not necessarily be priced. Nonetheless, if enough investors become aware of the close correspondence between beta and downside risk, they may require a higher return for holding a stock with a higher beta, so beta may ultimately play a more important role for the pricing of stocks.

Even if high-beta stocks in the future earn higher returns, however, the compensation for beta risk may still not equal $r_m - r_f$. Investors may be unable or unwilling (Black [1972,

1993]) to take on sufficient leverage to exploit divergences from the compensation predicted by an equilibrium model.

Furthermore, as long as the performance of investment managers is evaluated relative to an index such as the S&P 500, active money managers may prefer stocks with high betas, thereby bidding up their prices relative to stocks with low betas. The latter possibility illustrates the potential impact of institutional or behavioral considerations ("investor psychology" in Black's [1993] discussion) on stock returns.

THE S&P INDEX EFFECT ON STOCK RETURNS

The discussion so far indicates that it might be premature to bury beta. If we focus on the point estimates, however, all the existing evidence suggests that the estimated risk premium is smaller than predicted by the Sharpe–Lintner model.

It is of course possible that beta is a very poor measure of risk, and much better risk measures exist but have not been uncovered. When we uncover these superior measures of risk, we will fully understand the relation between return and risk.

An alternative·explanation is that behavioral and institutional factors, unrelated to risk, play a major role in generating stock returns, thereby confounding the relation between risk and return (Shleifer and Summers [1990]). A recent article by Lakonishok, Shleifer, and Vishny [1992b] discusses the complicated agency relations within the money management industry. One aspect of these many conflicts of interest is that risk might mean different things to different parties.

For example, a plan sponsor might view the risk of the portfolio in terms of the standard deviation of its return. The money manager, whose performance is being evaluated relative to the S&P 500 index, is more concerned about tracking error. This concern with tracking error is not unreasonable, given the very short horizons in the money management industry.

Robert Haugen, for example, has analyzed the properties of the minimum-variance portfolio, using various time periods and samples of stocks. The out-of-sample returns of his "efficient portfolio" are on average no lower than that of the S&P 500, but the volatility is much lower.

Imagine that we can expect in the future the same performance from Haugen's minimum-variance portfolio as in the past. Would everybody flock to this portfolio? What about tracking error? If the bench-mark is the S&P 500, quite a few money managers will understand that such a strategy is risky, as the tracking error is quite large.

We investigate one particular institutional aspect of equity markets and its effect on stock prices. There are good reasons to believe that over the past decade there is a positive effect on stock returns associated with being in the S&P 500 index. First, indexation has become a big industry. For example, in 1980 only about 2% of the equity investment of the top 200 pension funds was indexed to the S&P 500; the number now is close to 20%, even without counting the closet indexers.

Second, the emphasis on performance evaluation is now much stronger than it was ten or fifteen years ago, and the S&P 500 index is, without any doubt, the most popular benchmark for performance evaluation. These reasons have prompted an additional demand for stocks belonging to the exclusive fraternity of the S&P index. Does this extra demand translate to higher returns from belonging to the index?

Our sample period is 1977–1991, and the universe comprises all NYSE, AMEX, and NASDAQ stocks whose market capitalization exceeds $50 million (1991) dollars. Every year, we run a cross-sectional regression with the annual holding-period return on each stock as the dependent variable.

The explanatory variables are: the beta of the stock, its market capitalization, its book-to-market-ratio, a dummy variable for the stock's industry classification, and a dummy variable for whether the stock is included in the S&P 500 index. All our explanatory variables are measured at the end of the year prior to the interval over which returns are measured. We thus try to control for all the other generally accepted influences on stock returns when examining the excess return from belonging to the exclusive S&P club.

Table 1.6 presents the yearly estimates of the coefficient of the dummy variable for S&P membership. Even after controlling for all the other influences, we find a sizable average excess return of 2.19% per year. The excess return is highly significant (the t-statistic is 2.33), and is consistent with the notion that institutional factors unrelated to risk play an important role.

The premium for membership in the index is impressive, amounting to almost half the average annual market excess return $r_m - r_f$ (5.77%) over this period. The average excess return for S&P membership in the period beginning in 1980, when indexation really began to catch on, is even more striking at 3.03% (the t-statistic is 3.90).

It is interesting to speculate on how the S&P index effect may show up in future stock returns. Given the performance of active money managers, one possibility is that the shift toward indexation will continue. In this case, extra buying pressure may continue in the future to produce excess returns from belonging to the index (assuming that the expected future price pressure has not already been incorporated into current stock prices).

Another possibility is that the push for indexation has passed its peak. If so, the question arises as to whether the stocks in the index are overpriced. Insofar as membership in the index has bestowed an average excess return of 2.19% per year for the last fifteen years, one might argue that a correction in prices is due for these stocks.

Table 1.6 The "S&P index effect" on stock returns, 1977–1991

Year	Excess Return (%) on S&P 500
1977	−3.99
1978	−4.85
1979	5.33
1980	2.39
1981	3.17
1982	6.94
1983	1.58
1984	4.69
1985	−0.08
1986	2.21
1987	5.92
1988	3.45
1989	4.87
1990	−2.94
1991	4.15
Average	2.19
t-statistic	2.33

SUMMARY AND CONCLUSIONS

Although the empirical support for beta was never strong, most of us have accepted beta unquestioningly for many years as a measure of risk. The tide now seems to be turning against beta; many of us seem ready to discard beta and to begin searching for better risk measures. This collective data-snooping exercise poses grave dangers and raises doubts whether the outcome will be "true" measures of risk.

We have tried here to evaluate whether we truly have sufficient evidence to dump beta. When we began this research, the case for beta seemed to us tenuous. Upon finishing it, we have by no means become die-hard supporters of beta, but we also do not feel that the evidence for discarding beta is clear-cut and overwhelming.

The inconclusive nature of the results has to do with the very noisy and constantly changing environment generating stock returns. The noise is so pervasive that even if returns and betas are indeed related, as implied by the CAPM over the last twenty years, we would still not be able to reject the hypothesis that returns and betas are unrelated, at standard levels of statistical significance. This is the case even though the realized premium on the market over this period is 5.05%.

If we were to plead the case for beta before a jury, we would emphasize these findings of our study:

1. If we use the entire CRSP history of stock returns in the U.S., the estimated average compensation for beta risk is 0.47% per month and is close to being significant. Moreover, the estimated compensation is not significantly different from the average excess return on the market $(r_m - r_f)$ of 0.76% per month.

2. If we were to stop the study in 1982, the support for beta would be overwhelming. The last nine years, which have not been favourable for beta's explanatory role for returns, are an aberration.

3. Examination of the monthly behavior of the estimated and actual premiums indicates a close association between the two variables, in line with the Sharpe–Lintner CAPM. For example, in months when the market takes a deep dive, high-beta stocks substantially underperform low-beta stocks.

On the other hand, a prosecuting attorney could use the same results to discredit beta's importance for returns:

1. Even with sixty years of data on returns, spanning many generations of money managers, the t-statistic for the estimated average compensation for beta risk is a paltry 1.84.

2. The most recent period, which is perhaps more representative of current experience, provides much weaker support for beta. To drive the point home, the strongest support for beta comes from the earlier period, long before Markowitz's findings on forming stocks into efficient portfolios.

3. Including other variables may substantially diminish beta's role in explaining stock returns.

What is the verdict? The data simply do not lend themselves to a clear-cut conclusion either way. To complicate the situation further, it very well may be the case that returns are driven not only by risk but also by a host of other institutional and behavioral aspects of equity markets. The extremely strong effect we find from membership in the S&P 500 index is but one example of the many other possible confounding influences from institutional or behavioral factors.

ENDNOTES

1. By "beta factor," we mean more precisely the market factor underlying returns; beta is the sensitivity to this market factor. This usage appears frequently in the literature.

2. Some researchers have argued that the relation between beta and returns may be stronger at the level of an annual holding period, rather than a monthly holding period. We also checked for this possibility by replicating the results of Table 1.2 using annual as well as semiannual and quarterly holding periods. The general conclusions remain unchanged. For example, over the sample period 1932–1991, the average estimated slope coefficient is 0.0368 (with a t-statistic of 1.08) for annual returns. For semiannual and quarterly returns, the average estimated slope coefficients are 0.0262 (corresponding to 5.24% on an annualized basis, with a t-statistic of 1.46), and 0.0136 (or 5.44% per year, with a t-statistic of 1.49), respectively.

REFERENCES

Black, Fischer. "Capital Market Equilibrium With Restricted Borrowing." *Journal of Business*, **45** (1972), pp. 444–455.

— —. "Presidential Address: Noise." *Journal of Finance*, **41** (1986), pp. 529–544.

— —. "Beta and Return." *Journal of Portfolio Management*, **20**, Fall, 1993, pp. 8–18.

Black, Fischer, Michael C. Jensen and Myron Scholes. "The Capital Asset Pricing Model: Some Empirical Tests." In M. Jensen, ed., *Studies on the Theory of Capital Markets*. New York: Praeger, 1972.

Chan, Louis, K., Yasushi Hamao and Josef Lakonishok. "Fundamentals and Stock Returns in Japan." *Journal of Finance*, **46** (1991), pp. 1739–1789.

De Bondt, Werner, F.M. and Richard, H. Thaler. "Does the Stock Market Overreact?" *Journal of Finance*, **40** (1985), pp. 557–581.

Fama, Eugene, F. and Kenneth R. French. "The Cross-Section of Expected Stock Returns." *Journal of Finance*, **47** (1992a), pp. 427–465.

— —. "The Economic Fundamentals of Size and Book-to-Market Equity." Working paper, University of Chicago, 1992b.

Fama, Eugene, F. and James MacBeth. "Risk, Return and Equilibrium: Empirical Tests." *Journal of Political Economy*, **81** (1973), pp. 607–636.

Jegadeesh, Narasimhan and Sheridan Titman. "Returns to Buying Winners and Selling Losers: Implications for Market Efficiency." *Journal of Finance*, **48** (1993), pp. 65–91.

Lakonishok, Josef and Alan C. Shapiro. "Systematic Risk, Total Risk and Size as Determinants of Stock Market Returns." *Journal of Banking and Finance*, **10** (1986), pp. 115–132.

Lakonishok, Josef, Andrei Shleifer and Robert Vishny. "Contrarian Investment, Extrapolation and Stock Returns." Working paper, University of Illinois, 1992a.

— —. "The Structure and Performance of the Money Management Industry." *Brookings Papers: Microeconomics*, 1992b, pp. 339–391.

Lakonishok, Josef and Seymour Smidt. "Are Seasonal Anomalies Real? A Ninety-Year Perspective." *Review of Financial Studies*, **1** (1988), pp. 403–425.

Lo, Andrew, W. and A. Craig MacKinlay. "Data-Snooping Biases in Tests of Financial Asset Pricing Models." *Review of Financial Studies*, **3** (1990), pp. 431–468.

Reinganum, Marc, R. "A Direct Test of Roll's Conjecture on the Firm Size Effect." *Journal of Finance*, **37** (1982), pp. 27–35.

Ritter, Jay, R. and Navin Chopra. "Portfolio Rebalancing and the Turn-of-the-Year Effect." *Journal of Finance*, **44** (1989), pp. 149–166.

Roll, Richard. "A Critique of the Asset Pricing Theory's Tests; Part I: On Past and Potential Testability of Theory." *Journal of Financial Economics*, **4** (1977), pp. 129–176.

Roll, Richard and Stephen A. Ross. "On the Cross-Sectional Relation Between Expected Returns and Betas." Working paper, Anderson Graduate School of Management, UCLA, 1992.

Shleifer, Andrei and Lawrence Summers. "The Noise Trader Approach to Finance." *Journal of Economic Perspectives*, **4** (1990), pp. 19–33.

—— 2 ——

The Arbitrage Pricing Theory
versus
the Capital Asset Pricing Model
Richard W. Roll and Stephen A. Ross

The capital asset pricing model (CAPM) is rapidly becoming the preferred methodology for the computation of fair rates of return in regulatory proceedings. This is not surprising given the amount of attention the model has received in the academic literature, but what is surprising is its seemingly unqualified acceptance by some regulatory bodies. Paradoxically, as the CAPM has gained favor amongst regulators, it is losing favor among financial scholars.

The major goal of this article is to describe a new scholarly view of how assets are priced in the financial markets and its implications for computing the cost of capital. This alternative approach is known by the acronym APT which stands for the arbitrage pricing theory. We believe that this theory provides a sounder theoretical basis than the CAPM for determining the cost of capital and that it is a more sensible methodology for such computations in rate of return regulation. It has a further advantage that it can be easily understood, particularly by anyone familiar with the CAPM.

THE CAPM — THE CURRENT STATE OF AFFAIRS

The popularity of the CAPM is based much less on its theoretical underpinnings than upon the intuitive descriptions that surround it. Central to this intuition is the notion of risk. The common argument goes roughly as follows. In a well-functioning capital market, investors must be rewarded for assuming risks. An investor always has the option of investing in nearly riskless securities, such as Treasury bills. To induce him to invest in equity with its greater risks, he must be promised a higher return than the riskless rate offered by Treasury bills. By the same reasoning, the greater the risk the greater must be the promised return.

Reprinted from: Roll, R.W. and Ross, S.A. 1983: "Regulation, the Capital Asset Pricing Model, and the Arbitrage Pricing Theory". *Public Utilities Fortnightly*, 111, May 26, 22–28. Reprinted with Permission of *The Fortnightly*.

Of course, the return offered by the equity is just the cost of that capital to the equity issuer.

All of this has a very satisfying Calvinist appeal; if you want to have a higher return then you must bear more risk. The problems really begin when we go beyond this simple perspective and start to ask what is really meant by risk and exactly how it can be measured. The CAPM provides one approach to this question. According to the CAPM, each security has an associated quantity called its "beta" coefficient which is the sole measure of risk. The beta coefficient, b for short, is defined by the theory to be the sensitivity of the return of the security to the return of the "market" portfolio. In theory, the market portfolio is the portfolio composed of all securities and assets existing in the entire world, from simple stocks and bonds to Japanese electronics factories and Nigerian real estate. In practice, there is an enormous simplification to some familiar stock market index such as the Standard & Poor's 500. Given the index, the beta coefficient for an individual security is obtained by any of a variety of statistical techniques all of which essentially involve finding the best measure of b in the following equation:

$$\text{return on stock} = \text{constant} + b \times (\text{return on S\&P 500}).\qquad(1)$$
$$\text{(cost of capital)}$$

In other words, beta is the response of the returns on this stock to the returns on the market index. A beta of one would imply that when the S&P 500 went up or down by 10% the stock would tend to go up or down by the same 10%. A beta higher than one, say two, would magnify market movements. Such a stock would move twice as much as the market. Similarly, a beta of less than one would diminish the importance of market movements. For example, if beta was one-half, when the market went up by 10% this stock would on average only go up by 5%. In the extreme, a stock could actually have a negative beta (gold stocks and some lines of the insurance industry exhibit such behavior). Such stocks respond in reverse to market movements, tending to go up when the market goes down and down when it goes up.

Having computed beta, the CAPM then argues that this measure of risk is the sole determinant of return. Any additional variability which might be caused by events peculiar to the individual asset can be "diversified away." In other words, in large diversified portfolios, the type of portfolios held by the investors who determine prices, only the nondiversifiable risk, the systematic risk, is relevant.

To find the cost of capital for a given stock we need only recognize that it must offer a return premium over and above that offered by a riskless asset. By the theory this premium will be proportional to the beta of the stock. Furthermore, since we can measure the average return on the S&P 500 we can use this to figure out the constant of proportionality. If, for the sake of illustration, the S&P 500 has an average return of 9.5% while Treasury bills have averaged 5%, then we would conclude that it has had an average return premium of 9.5% − 5% = 4.5%. Since the S&P 500 clearly has a beta of one with itself it follows that the constant of proportionality is 4.5%. All of this is summarized in the following equation which is the cornerstone of the CAPM:

$$\text{return on stock} = \text{riskless return} + \text{beta} \times (\text{S\&P 500} - \text{riskless return})$$
$$\text{(cost of capital)}\qquad(2)$$
$$= \text{Treasury bill rate} + 4.5\% \times \text{beta}.$$

But is beta really all that there is to the story? More precisely, does beta really capture all that is systematic in the risk of a security, and is it a sufficient measure of this risk for an adequate determination of the cost of capital?

In recent years these questions have become central to the academic debate of capital asset pricing. The doubts that have been raised concerning the practical significance of the CAPM and its use in the determination of the fair rate of return, have their counterparts in the theoretical and academic discussions as well. There is a lengthy literature on this debate. By way of a quick summary, the major points of contention have centered on the somewhat artificial nature of the theory and on the inability to test the theory statistically. To date there is yet to be an adequate test of the CAPM. Those tests that have been conducted, if accepted at face value, have not been generally supportive. The theory says that a particular portfolio, the market portfolio of all the assets in the world, is the proper benchmark against which to measure risk. In the parlance of the theory, it is a mean-variance efficient portfolio. The theory does not say that the S&P 500 is such an efficient portfolio, and, in fact, current evidence suggests that neither this index nor any other familiar single index will suffice.

Given this unfortunate state of affairs, why then is the CAPM so popular? It is our view that this popularity stems not from the theory itself, but rather from the intuition which the theory attempts to embody. There is nothing wrong with the general idea. Somehow it all sounds plausible, but the final results just do not make much sense.

A newer alternative model has been developed in the academic literature which captures all of the fine intuitions of the CAPM, seems more sensible, and produces much more reasonable results. This model is called the arbitrage pricing theory. Like the CAPM, the APT determines the cost of capital from the systematic risk of the security, but unlike the CAPM, it allows assets to be subject to more than a single source of systematic risk.

THE ARBITRAGE PRICING THEORY, APT

The APT begins with a simple description of the way in which uncertain and unpredictable events influence asset returns. The returns on an individual stock in, say, the coming year will depend upon a variety of anticipated and unanticipated changes in the economy over that period of time. These changes in the overall economic environment affect all stocks in systematic ways, and the response of any particular stock depends upon its sensitivity to the general economic environment. Those changes that are anticipated will be incorporated by investors into their expectations of returns on individual stocks, and the market prices will reflect such expectations. Generally, though, well over half of the return actually realized will be the result of unanticipated changes. Of course, change itself is anticipated and investors know that the most unlikely occurrence of all would be for them to get exactly what they now expect to be the most probable future scenario. But, even though they know that the economy will change in some currently unforeseen ways, they do not know either the direction or magnitude of these changes. What they can know is the sensitivity of stock returns to these events.

Asset returns are also affected by factors that are not systematic to the economy as a whole. These factors are the amalgam of all of those forces which influence individual firms or particular industries, but are not directly related to overall economic conditions. We call these forces idiosyncratic to distinguish them from the systematic forces which describe the major movements in market returns.

Large portfolios will have their returns influenced by changes in the major systematic factors and, through the process of diversification, they will be nearly immune to the idiosyncratic effects on individual assets. As a consequence, the systematic factors alone determine the returns on large portfolios, and the actual return on any given portfolio depends upon the sensitivity of that portfolio to unanticipated movements in the common factors. Since the factors are the major sources of risk in large portfolios, a portfolio that is so hedged as to be insensitive to the common factors and sufficiently large and well proportioned so as to diversify away idiosyncratic risk, is essentially riskless. It follows that exposure to the unpredictable movements in the common factors is the risk that the capital market is most concerned about in the determination of the cost of capital.

The logic behind this reasoning is not simply the usual economic argument that if you want more return you must be prepared to bear more risk. While this line of reasoning certainly captures an important truth, there is a far simpler reason why the expected return on a portfolio is related to its sensitivity to factor movements. The argument is the same as that which leads to the conclusion that two three-month Treasury bills or two shares of the same stock must sell for the same price. Two assets which are very close substitutes must sell for about the same price, and nowhere in the entire economy are there any items which are closer substitutes than two financial assets which offer the same returns.

Two diversified portfolios with identical sensitivities to systematic economic forces are very close substitutes. In effect, they differ only in the limited amount of idiosyncratic, or residual risk that they might still bear. Consequently, they must offer the investor very nearly identical expected returns, just as the two Treasury bills or the two shares of the same stock offer identical expected returns.

At this point a bit of mathematics is probably desirable if not inevitable. We will use the letter b to stand for the sensitivity to factor movements. We will let a capital R denote the actual return on a portfolio or stock, and we use a capital E to stand for the expected return on the portfolio or the stock. Since E denotes the expected return to the investor, it is also simply the cost of capital. The whole thrust of this theory is to relate E to the systematic risk. A lower case f will stand for the actual unpredictable return on the systematic economic factors and a lower case e will denote the return on the unsystematic, idiosyncratic factor. Armed with this notation we can break the actual return on any asset, be it a stock, a bond, real estate, or even a portfolio, into its three constituent parts:

$$R = E + bf + e. \tag{3}$$

In words, this equation reads,

$$\text{Actual return } = \text{ Expected return}$$
$$+$$
$$\text{Factor sensitivity} \times \text{Factor movement}$$
$$+$$
$$\text{Idiosyncratic risk.}$$

As we have been stressing, though, there is not simply a single systematic factor; rather empirical research has found that there are at least three or four important ones, so

$$R = E + (b1)(f1) + (b2)(f2) + (b3)(f3) + (b4)(f4) + e, \tag{4}$$

where each systematic economic factor has been explicitly broken out. Each of the four middle terms in the above equation is the product of the unanticipated returns on a particular economic factor and the given asset's sensitivity to that factor.

What are these factors? They are the underlying economic forces which are the primary influences on the asset market. Our research has suggested that three of the most important factors are unanticipated movements in inflation, in industrial production, and in the general cost of risk bearing. For the determination of the cost of capital using the APT it is not necessary to identify which economic forces actually are the most important influences on market returns, but doing so does aid the intuition and is further confirmation that the cost of capital has been correctly measured.

Since we have already argued that the expected returns on large portfolios are influenced almost exclusively by these systematic factors and not by the idiosyncratic terms, if we carefully choose four different portfolios in just such a way that they each have different sensitivities to the systematic factors, then these portfolios can be indices for the factors. The easiest way to illustrate this argument is to assume, for the moment, that there are two completely unknown and unidentifiable factors which influence returns. Even though we have no idea what these factors are and may, in fact, disagree strongly about them, nevertheless we can still compute the cost of capital for an individual stock in an unequivocal manner. To do so we need only find two large, well-diversified portfolios whose returns regularly differ from each other; i.e., are not very well correlated. This assures us that one of the portfolios is more heavily weighted towards one of the unknown factors than is the other portfolio; if they had the same weights then they would tend to have nearly identical returns. Now we can simply compute the sensitivity of the given stock to each of these "mimicking" portfolios and use these sensitivities to determine the cost of capital for the stock. In what follows, then, we will simply interpret the four factors in equation (4) as four portfolios of assets, since identifying them more carefully will not influence the determination of the cost of capital.

Equation (4) is the basic description of how the returns on a given security are related to the overall returns on the four portfolios which mimic the economic factors. We use this model of the capital market to determine the cost of capital, E, by proving that there must be a particular relationship between the cost of capital, E, and the systematic risk measures for the stock; i.e., $(b1)$, $(b2)$, $(b3)$, and $(b4)$.

Suppose that there are two stocks, A and B, with identical factor sensitivities, but whose costs of capital, E, differ. Let us look at this situation from the point of view of an investor with a large portfolio. For such an investor contemplating purchasing or retaining shares in these two companies, the only relevant measures of the risk are the factor sensitivities, and these are the same for the two companies. The respective idiosyncratic risks of A and B do not matter since these will be diversified away in the large portfolio. But if, for example, the expected return on asset A, denoted by EA is larger than that for asset B, EB, then all such investors would want to hold the stock of company A and none of them would want company B. Since there would be no demand for company B's stock, its price must fall. If company B is to retain its stockholders, it must pay just as much as A in order to attract capital. In other words, two companies with the same systematic sensitivities must have the same costs of capital; the cost of capital is determined by the b's.

To show exactly how the b's and E are related, a simple example will be sufficient. We will refer to the factor sensitivities, the b's, as factor betas or just betas for short. For illustrative simplicity, assume that the assets being considered have identical sensitivities to

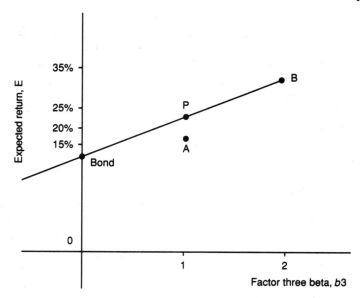

Figure 2.1 Portfolio sensitivity

Table 2.1

	Bond	Stock A	Stock B
E (Expected return, cost of capital)	15%	20%	35%
b (Factor sensitivity)	0	1	2

all but, say, the third factor portfolio, $f3$. The accompanying Figure 2.1 plots the costs of capital and the third factor betas of two stocks and a riskless bond. The characteristics of the three assets are displayed in Table 2.1.

Notice that the riskless asset, the bond, offers a yield that (we assume) is unaffected by the systematic factor that influences the other two assets. Suppose that we form a portfolio that is evenly divided between the bond and the stock B. Such a portfolio will have a return that is a simple average of the returns of the two constituent assets. Hence the expected return on such a portfolio will be given by

$$E = 1/2 \times 15\% + 1/2 \times 35\% = 25\%.$$

Similarly, the sensitivity of this portfolio, its $b3$, will also be halfway between the sensitivities of the bond and B,

$$b3 = 1/2 \times 0 + 1/2 \times 2 = 1.$$

This portfolio is plotted as point, P, in the accompanying figure. Notice that P lies directly above stock A. Consider what this means. By forming a portfolio of the bond and the higher risk stock, B, we have exposed our investment to the same systematic factor risk as we would have by investing in stock A. While stock B is twice as sensitive as stock A, only half of our investment is at risk and the remainder has gone into the bond. The combination therefore has exactly the same sensitivity to the third factor as asset A.

But, with this same sensitivity we have obtained a higher expected return! The expected return on the portfolio is 25% while that on asset A is only 20%. It does not matter whether investors like the systematic risk or not, what is essential is that the portfolio P is exactly like stock A in all relevant features except for one: It has a higher expected return, 25% versus 20%. No matter what happens with unforeseeable economic forces, the portfolio P will have a higher rate of return.

By our previous argument, though, any two assets with the same returns must have the same cost of capital. In other words, the expected return on portfolio P cannot differ from the expected return on stock A. In symbols, $EP = EA$. In well-functioning capital markets such opportunities cannot persist; they are quickly eliminated by astute traders. This arbitrage takes place, by investors reducing their holdings of stock A and purchasing portfolio P, causing the price of A to fall. Since B is in the heavily demanded portfolio, the price of B will rise. At a lower price, stock A will become more attractive and at a higher price B will be less attractive. The process stops when stock A offers the same return as portfolio P.

Such arbitrage opportunities will cease to exist only when all three of the assets in the figure lie on the same line. Otherwise, we would be able to find another portfolio that beat or was beaten by one of the two stocks. This implies, then, that there is a line relating each of the b's and the cost of capital.

More generally, it follows from the same argument that the cost of capital is given by the risk-free interest rate, r, plus a weighted average of the factor sensitivities,

$$E = r + (k1)(b1) + (k2)(b2) + (k3)(b3) + (k4)(b4). \tag{5}$$

The weights, $k1$, $k2$, $k3$, and $k4$, are the return premiums (in excess of the riskless return) earned by each of the four portfolios, $f1$, $f2$, $f3$, and $f4$. By way of illustration, suppose, for example, that $f3$ had an average return of 8%. Using the previous average of 5% for the risk-free rate would produce a return premium of

$$
\begin{aligned}
k3 &= \text{return on } f3 - \text{ risk-free interest rate} \\
&= 8\% - 5\% \\
&= 3\%.
\end{aligned}
\tag{6}
$$

COMPARING THE APT AND THE CAPM

The CAPM and the APT have quite different implications for the determination of the cost of capital for regulated utilities. Table 2.2, column 1, displays the alphas for a sample of regulated utility companies. (No attempt has been made to examine the companies in the sample individually. For example, the reported results are for the entire company and not just for the regulated subsidiaries.) The alpha reported is simply the difference between the historical average past return on equity; i.e. the past average cost of equity capital, and the cost of capital obtained by the CAPM theory described in the first section of this article, and using equation (2). The consistently positive alphas indicate that the CAPM theory has consistently underestimated the cost of capital for these firms relative to their historic capital costs.

Table 2.2

Regulated utilities	CAPM alphas (Per cent – Per year)	APT alphas (Per cent – Per year)	APT cost of capital – CAPM cost of capital
Alagasco Inc.	1.602	0.496	1.106
Allegheny Pwr. Sys. Inc.	2.457	−0.104	2.561
American Elec. Pwr. Inc.	1.160	0.479	0.681
American Nat. Res. Co.	2.471	1.240	1.231
American Teleph. & Teleg.	0.713	−0.146	0.859
Arizona Pub. Svc. Co.	−4.046	−3.288	−0.758.
Atlantic City Elec. Co.	1.509	−0.191	1.700
Baltimore Gas & Elec.	0.084	−0.647	0.731
Bay St. Gas Co.	7.685	6.378	1.307
Boston Edison Co.	0.337	−1.158	1.495
Brooklyn Un. Gas Co.	3.270	1.046	2.224
CP Natl. Corp.	2.394	3.268	0.874
Carolina Pwr. & Lt. Co.	0.756	0.214	0.542
Cascade Nat. Gas Corp.	1.546	3.424	−1.878
Central & South West.	1.820	0.147	1.673
Central Hudson Gas & Elec.	1.344	0.075	1.269
Central Ill. Lt. Co.	−0.173	−1.592	1.419
Central Ill. Pub. Svc.	1.102	−0.936	2.038
Central Me. Pwr. Co.	−1.055	−1.793	0.738
Cincinnati Bell Inc.	1.259	1.145	0.114
Cincinnati Gas & Elec.	2.166	0.638	1.528
Cleveland Elec. Illum.	1.567	0.074	1.493
Columbia Gas Sys. Inc.	4.659	2.853	1.806
Columbus & Southern Oh.	1.090	−0.507	1.597
Commonwealth Edison	−0.347	−2.382	2.035
Consolidated Edison	1.725	−0.490	2.215
Consolidated Nat. Gas	3.328	1.837	1.491
Consumers Pwr. Co.	−0.464	−1.129	−0.665
Continental Teleph. Corp.	−3.951	−4.440	0.489
Dayton Pwr. & Lt. Co.	−0.416	−1.944	1.528
Delmarva Pwr. & Lt. Co.	0.565	−0.625	1.190
Detroit Edison Co.	0.058	−1.464	1.522
Duke Pwr. Co.	−1.753	−0.419	−1.334
Duquesne Lt. Co.	−0.452	−1.716	1.264
Eastern Utils. Associates	−2.279	−1.928	−0.351
El Paso Co.	2.633	1.387	1.246
Empire Dist. Elec. Co.	2.536	0.624	1.912
Enserch Corp.	4.270	2.599	1.671
Equitable Gas Co.	3.841	1.800	2.041
Florida Pwr. & Lt. Co.	3.274	2.394	0.880
Florida Pwr. Corp.	2.879	2.119	0.760
Gas Svc. Co.	−3.156	−3.925	0.769
General Pub. Utils. Co.	−2.709	−4.096	1.387
General Teleph. & Elec.	2.226	1.611	0.615
Gulf Sts. Utils. Co.	1.911	0.058	1.853
Hawaiian Elec. Inc.	−1.718	−2.067	0.349
Houston Inds. Inc.	2.115	0.150	1.965
Idaho Pwr. Co.	1.225	−0.654	1.879
Illinois Pwr. Co.	1.684	−0.172	1.856
Indiana Gas Inc.	−0.951	−3.259	2.308
Indianapolis Pwr. & Lt.	1.685	−0.533	2.218

Table 2.2 (*continued*)

Regulated utilities	CAPM alphas (Per cent − Per year)	APT alphas (Per cent − Per year)	APT cost of Capital − CAPM cost of capital
Interstate Pwr. Co.	1.311	−0.602	1.913
Iowa Elec Lt. & Pwr. Co.	−1.204	−2.538	1.334
Iowa-Ill. Gas & Elec.	1.060	−0.663	1.723
Iowa Pub. Svc. Co.	−1.150	−1.460	0.310
Kansas City Pwr. Co.	0.500	−0.985	1.485
Kansas Gas & Elec. Co.	0.054	−2.189	2.243
Kansas Pwr. & Lt. Co.	1.865	0.688	1.177
Kentucky Utils. Co.	−2.937	−2.184	−0.753
Laclede Gas Co.	2.153	0.454	1.699
Long Island Ltg. Co.	2.291	0.687	1.604
Louisville Gas & Elec.	1.498	−0.213	1.711
Mid-Continent Teleph. Co.	−2.010	−2.350	0.340
Middle South Utils. Inc.	0.964	−0.149	1.113
Minnesota Pwr. & Lt. Co.	1.651	0.303	1.348
Missouri Pub. Svc. Co.	−0.964	−1.811	0.847
Montana-Dakota Utils.	2.720	1.058	1.662
Montana Pwr. Co.	2.357	0.443	1.914
Mountain Fuel Supply	5.986	4.175	1.811
National Fuel Gas Co.	1.821	−0.011	1.832
Nevada Pwr. Co.	−0.146	−0.318	0.172
New England Elec. Sys.	1.282	−0.275	1.557
New England Gas & Elec.	1.496	4.085	−2.589
New York St. Elec. & Gas	0.592	−0.482	1.074
Niagara Mohawk Pwr. Corp.	−0.436	−1.649	−2.521
Nicor Inc.	3.351	2.045	1.306
Northeast Utils.	−2.631	−2.866	0.235
Northern Ind. Pub. Svc.	−3.631	−3.393	−0.238
Northern Sts. Pwr. Co.	1.906	0.337	1.569
Ohio Edison Co.	0.641	−0.791	1.432
Oklahoma Gas & Elec.	1.226	−0.892	2.118
Orange & Rockland Utils.	−2.006	−1.695	−0.311
Pacific Gas & Elec. Co.	0.235	−1.450	1.685
Pacific Ltg. Corp.	1.466	0.097	1.369
Pacific Pwr. & Lt. Co.	0.695	0.246	0.449
Pacific Teleph. & Teleg.	0.104	−0.762	0.866
Panhandle Eastern Pipe	6.165	3.792	2.373
Pennsylvania Pwr. & Lt.	0.444	−1.077	1.521
Philadelphia Elec. Co.	−0.504	−1.945	1.441
Piedmont Nat. Gas Inc.	2.879	4.739	−1.860
Portland Gen. Elec. Co.	−1.999	−1.467	−0.532
Potomac Elec. Pwr. Co.	1.743	0.367	1.376
Public Svc. Co. Colo.	1.856	0.497	1.359
Public Svc. Co. Ind. Inc.	0.808	−0.443	1.251
Public Svc. Co. N. Il.	−2.645	−0.321	−2.324
Public Svc. Co. N. Mex.	−0.042	4.158	−4.200
Public Svc. Elec. & Gas	0.005	−1.455	1.460
Puget Sound Pwr. & Lt.	−0.221	−1.843	1.622
Rochester Gas & Elec.	0.918	−0.595	1.513
Rochester Teleph. Corp.	4.286	2.986	1.300

continued overleaf

Table 2.2 (*continued*)

Regulated utilities	CAPM alphas (Per cent – Per year)	APT alphas (Per cent – Per year)	APT cost of Capital – CAPM cost of capital
St. Joseph Lt. & Pwr. Co.	1.046	0.156	0.890
San Diego Gas & Elec.	1.001	−0.448	1.449
Savannah Elec. & Pwr.	−4.336	−4.148	−0.188
Sierra Pacific Pwr. Co.	−2.635	−1.641	−0.994
South Carolina Elec.	1.639	−0.165	1.804
South Jersey Inds. Inc.	2.179	1.017	1.162
Southern Calif. Edison	0.849	−0.837	1.686
Southern Co.	5.474	3.887	1.587
Southern Ind. Gas & Elec.	2.673	1.711	0.962
Southern New England	1.249	2.566	−1.317
Southwestern Pub. Svc.	1.030	−0.234	1.264
Tampa Elec. Co.	−2.262	−0.513	−1.749
Texas Eastern Corp.	7.022	3.186	3.836
Texas Gas Transmis.	4.976	3.401	1.575
Texas Utils. Co.	3.014	1.476	1.538
Toledo Edison Co.	0.516	−1.722	2.238
Tucson Elec. Pwr. Co.	0.845	4.441	−3.596
UGI Corp.	4.067	1.968	2.099
Union Elec. Co.	−0.550	−1.963	1.413
United Illum. Co.	−1.685	0.379	−2.064
United Telecom.	−1.388	−0.928	−0.460
Utah Pwr. & Lt. Co.	1.504	−2.088	1.792
Virginia Elec. & Pwr.	0.335	−1.242	1.577
Washington Gas Lt. Co.	2.696	1.023	1.673
Washington Wtr. Pwr. Co.	0.407	−0.881	1.288
Westcoast Transmission	4.122	1.915	2.207
Western Un. Corp.	−1.896	−1.463	−0.433
Wisconsin Elec. Pwr. Co.	2.458	0.285	2.173
Wisconsin Pub. Svc. Co.	1.992	0.652	1.340
Mean Alpha	0.974	0.013	0.961

This table contains the results for a sample of regulated utility companies with publicly traded equity. The sample period runs from December, 1925, to December, 1980. Thirteen companies were eliminated from the sample because they had unusually high abnormal returns which were associated with their holdings of significant natural resources. (Many of these companies were specifically engaged in oil and gas explorations.)

Table 2.2, column 2, displays the alphas for the same sample of firms using the APT. The differences between the CAPM alphas and the APT alphas are reported in Table 2.2, column 3. These differences are the additional cost of capital implied by the APT. As can be seen in Table 2.2, column 3, the estimated costs of capital are, on average, significantly greater for the APT than for the CAPM. No attempt has been made here to do anything more than compute simple long-run average estimates. We have argued that the resulting APT estimates for the cost of capital are much more realistic than those obtained from the CAPM. By including the additional forces which influence the systematic risk of equity, the APT theory can better explain the cost of capital than the CAPM. In effect, the APT can explain, significantly lessen, and remove the biases in the CAPM's alphas.

In particular, regulated utilities differ substantially in the pattern of their factor sensitivities from the pattern exhibited by a broad stock market index such as the S&P 500 (which is dominated by nonregulated manufacturing and service companies). Regulated utilities have a much greater sensitivity to the second factor portfolio, the portfolio that mimics unanticipated inflation. This is hardly surprising. Regulated utilities are interest rate sensitive and interest rates respond dramatically to inflation. This sensitivity to inflation is a risk for which investors in regulated utilities require compensation; it is a risk that increases the cost of capital.

The CAPM, unlike the APT, cannot portray this risk properly. The single CAPM beta of a regulated utility merely measures how sensitive the utility is to that particular mix of factors in the S&P 500. For example, suppose that the S&P 500 had b's, sensitivities to the underlying economic forces, of

$$b1s = 0.8, \text{ industrial production,}$$

and

$$b2s = 0.2, \text{ inflation,}$$

and suppose also, that the return premiums for the factor sensitivities were:

$$k1 = 9\%,$$

and

$$k2 = 7\%,$$

with a riskless rate of 15%

Suppose that a particular regulated utility had a different pattern of sensitivities, say,

$$b1u = 0.2,$$

and

$$b2u = 0.8.$$

In other words, the utility is more sensitive to inflation and less sensitive to industrial production than is the typical manufacturing stock in the S&P 500. The true expected returns — i.e., the costs of capital — for the S&P 500 and the utility are, as calculated from equation (5),

$$Es = 15\% + (0.8)(9\%) + (0.2)(7\%) = 23.6\%,$$

and

$$Eu = 15\% + (0.2)(9\%) + (0.8)(7\%) = 22.4\%.$$

But, the CAPM beta of the utility will be the sensitivity of the utility's return to the S&P 500 return, not to the true factors. If, for simplicity, we assume that the factors are not correlated and are equally variable, then

$$
\begin{aligned}
\text{CAPM } b &= ((0.2)(0.8) + (0.8)(0.2))/((0.8)(0.8) + (0.2)(0.2)) \\
&= 0.32/0.68 \\
&= 0.47
\end{aligned}
$$

The CAPM would therefore predict that the utility's cost of capital would be, using equation (2),

$$\text{CAPM } Eu = 15\% + (0.47)(23.6\% - 15\%) = 19\%.$$

There is a shortfall of $22.4\% - 19\% = 3.4\%$, between the true (APT) cost of capital and the CAPM cost of capital and this appears as the "alpha" in the CAPM. Note the magnitude of this shortfall; simply because the utility has a different pattern of sensitivities to underlying economic forces than that of the typical company in the S&P 500 index, the CAPM underestimates the cost of capital by nearly 20% ($3.4\%/19\% = 18\%$).

One way to view the alphas of the CAPM and the APT is to recognize that they are the result of two distinct forces. Since they capture the differences between historical costs and what the respective theories predict, they are the consequence of both errors in the theories and any actual differences between current and historical equity costs. The striking feature of the alphas in Table 2.2 from the CAPM is that they do not look at all like random statistical errors. On the contrary, they are predominantly positive, indicating that the CAPM consistently predicts lower capital costs (risk premia) for the regulated utilities than their historical costs. Aside from the incongruity of predicting lowered costs in an era of unprecedented inflation, this is prima facie evidence of a missing factor which influences returns in this industrial sector.

The APT, on the other hand, produces a much more reasonable pattern of alphas (see Table 2.2, column 2); some are negative and some are positive. This is precisely what we should expect from ordinary statistical errors rather than the theoretical errors of the CAPM with its systematic underprediction of capital costs.

SUMMARY AND CONCLUSIONS

In the foregoing article we have described the arbitrage pricing theory, APT for short, and have compared this alternative theory to the CAPM. We have argued that it provides a superior method, from both a theoretical and a pragmatic perspective, for computing the cost of equity capital. Furthermore, we have demonstrated its application to a sample of utilities and derived much more sensible estimates of the costs of equity capital than those produced by the CAPM.

BIBLIOGRAPHY

The first reference cited below provides a legal critique of the application of the capital asset pricing model in rate making, and the remaining references provide the academic papers which underly the authors' economic critique of the CAPM and the development and testing of the APT.

"The Case Against the Use of the Capital Asset Pricing Model in Public Utility Rate Making," by Joe Chartoff, George W. Mayo, Jr. and Walter A. Smith, Jr., unpublished manuscript, Hogan & Hartson, Washington, D.C.

"A Critique of the Asset Pricing Theory's Tests," by Richard Roll, *Journal of Financial Economics* **4**, May, 1977, pp. 129–176.

"Ambiguity When Performance Is Measured by the Securities Market Line," by Richard Roll, *Journal of Finance* **33**, September, 1978, pp. 1051–1069.

"Testing a Portfolio for Ex Ante Mean-Variance Efficiency," by Richard Roll, in *"TIMS Studies in the Management Sciences,"* Elton, E. and Gruber, M. Eds., Amsterdam: North-Holland, 1979.

"An Empirical Investigation of the Arbitrage Pricing Theory," by Richard Roll and Stephen Ross, *Journal of Finance* **35**, December, 1980. pp. 1073–1103.

"Return, Risk, and Arbitrage," by Stephen Ross, in *Risk and Return in Finance*, I, Irwin Friend and James Bicksler, Eds., Ballinger, Cambridge, Massachusetts, 1977, pp. 189–218.

"The Arbitrage Theory of Capital Asset Pricing," by Stephen Ross, *Journal of Economic Theory* **13**, December, 1976, pp. 341–360.

"The Current Status of the Capital Asset Pricing Model (CAPM)," by Stephen Ross, *Journal of Finance* **3**, June, 1978, pp. 885–890.

3

Traditional versus Theoretical Risk Measures

Russell J. Fuller and G. Wenchi Wong

"Great deeds are usually wrought at great risk."

Herodotus, 485–425 B.C.

The best known model of risk and return in the investment field to date is the Capital Asset Pricing Model (CAPM) developed in the mid-1960s by Sharpe, Lintner and others.[1] In addition to a theory describing the relation between risk and return, the CAPM provides an explicit measure of risk — i.e., the security's beta. Long before the advent of the CAPM, however, investors were attempting to quantify risk, even though they may not have had a well-developed theory to explain the relation between their particular risk measure and return.

Bond rating agencies, for example, have no particular theory to go by in constructing their traditional risk measures. Nor is there a theory indicating exactly what the relation between bond returns and bond ratings should be. Rather, it is *common sense* that suggests that bonds are riskier if the issuing firm has a relatively high level of debt, if the coverage ratios of the bond are low, if the earnings of the firm are erratic and so forth. Common sense also suggests that bonds with low ratings (say, BB) should be priced to provide, on average and over time, higher returns than bonds with high ratings (say, AAA).

Similarly, on the basis of common sense and experience, analysts have constructed traditional measures of risk for common stocks. This article examines the relative explanatory powers of two theoretical risk measures — beta and standard deviation — and one traditional risk measure — the Value Line Safety Rank.[2]

THE RISK MEASURES

Value Line assigns rankings from 1 (highest safety) to 5 (lowest safety) to all the common stocks it follows. Table 3.1 describes how, in general, the Value Line Safety Rank is determined.

Reprinted, with permission from: Fuller, R.J. and Wong, G.W. 1988: Traditional versus Theoretical Risk Measures. *Financial Analysts Journal*, 44, March–April, 52–57, 67. Copyright 1988, The Financial Analysts Federation, Charlottesville, Va. All rights reserved.

Table 3.1   The Value Line Safety Rank

The Value Line Safety Ranks range from 1 to 5, with a rank of 1 indicating the lowest risk and a rank of 5 indicating the greatest risk. The safety rank is computed by averaging two other Value Line indexes — the price stability index and the financial strength index.

The price stability index is a ranking based on the standard deviation of weekly stock price changes over the most recent five years. The 5% with the lowest standard deviations receive a ranking of 95 and so on down to a ranking of 5 for the highest standard deviations.

The financial strength ratings range from A++ for those firms deemed to have the best relative financial strength to a low of C. The primary variables used to determine this rating are equity coverage of intangibles, quick ratio, accounting methods, variability of return, fixed charge coverage, stock price stability and company size.

Source: A. Bernhard, *How to Use the Value Line Investment Survey, A Subscriber's Guide* (Value Line Inc., New York).

The safety rank takes into account two primary factors — the stock's price stability index, which is a ranking of the stock's standard deviation of returns compared with the standard deviation of returns for all other stocks followed by Value Line, and the stock's financial strength rating, which is based on such variables as debt coverage ratios, firm size, quick ratio and accounting methods. The safety rank is thus based on both statistical concepts and fundamental variables.

The CAPM beta, by contrast, is based solely on statistical concepts, although there is an economic interpretation of beta as a measure of relative market risk. The beta for the ith stock (β_i) is measured as the covariance of the stock's returns with the market index's returns (Cov_{im}) divided by the variance of the market's returns (σ_m^2):

$$\beta_i = \frac{\text{Cov}_{im}}{\sigma_m^2}. \tag{1}$$

Beta can also be expressed as the correlation coefficient of the ith stock's returns with the market's return (ρ_{im}) multiplied by the ratio of the standard deviation of returns for the ith stock divided by the standard deviation of returns for the market index:

$$\beta_i = \rho_{im} \left[\frac{\sigma_i}{\sigma_m} \right] \tag{2}$$

Both beta and the Value Line Safety Rank are at least partly determined by a common variable — the stock's standard deviation of returns. This suggests that the two risk measures should be correlated. But the two risk measures differ with respect to other variables. They are thus not perfect proxies for each other.

As both safety rank and beta are partly determined by the stock's standard deviation of returns (sigma), we also considered this risk measure. Sigma (frequently called total risk) can be shown theoretically to be the appropriate measure of risk for individual securities in circumstances where only limited diversification is possible.[3]

DATA AND METHOD

To examine the relation between realized stock returns and the three risk measures, we collected data for three four-year subperiods — 1974–77, 1978–81 and 1982–85. We used Value Line Safety Ranks and beta estimates for each available stock as of the beginning of 1974, 1978 and 1982.[4] Monthly returns for each stock were taken from the CRSP tapes

Table 3.2 Number of sample stocks in each rank by subperiod

Subperiod	Rank 1	Rank 2	Rank 3	Rank 4	Rank 5	Total
1974–1977	72	225	413	184	60	954
1978–1981	63	235	486	181	49	1014
1982–1985	105	182	520	127	60	994

for New York and American stock exchange stocks. The sample consisted of all stocks for which complete data sets (Value Line Safety Rank, Value Line betas and monthly returns) were available.

For each stock in a particular four-year (48-month) subperiod, we calculated the arithmetic mean monthly return.[5] Sigma was measured as the standard deviation of returns based on the 48 months prior to the start of the subperiod in question. By using the prior 48 months of returns, we based sigma on data that would have been available to investors at the start of the subperiod, just as the Value Line Safety Ranks and beta estimates would have been available.

As noted, Value Line assigns each stock to one of five safety ranks, rank 1 being the least risky and 5 being the most risky. The distribution of stocks across the five ranks is not uniform, and the distribution varies somewhat over time. Of the approximately 1,700 stocks currently followed by Value Line, approximately 140 (about 8%) are assigned a safety rank of 1; approximately 240 (about 15%) are assigned a rank of 2; 140 or so are assigned a rank of 5; about 240 are ranked 4; and the balance (approximately 900 stocks currently) are assigned what is considered an average safety rank of 3. Value Line used this same general type of distribution at the beginning of our first subperiod (i.e., 1974).

Two factors caused the number of sample stocks in each rank to vary by subperiod. First, the number of stocks followed by Value Line varied slightly over the entire time period of the study, and at any point in time Value Line might not assign a safety rank or beta estimate to every stock. Second, our criteria for inclusion in the sample required that a stock must have a complete record of return data, as well as a safety rank and beta estimate; this meant some stocks were eliminated. The number of stocks in rank 1 for subperiod 1974–77, for example, was reduced from 102 to 72. Table 3.2 lists the number of sample stocks in each safety rank for each of the three subperiods.[6]

For the purpose of comparing the three risk measures (safety rank, beta and sigma), we assigned beta ranks and sigma ranks to stocks to duplicate the distribution for the Value Line Safety Rank, shown in Table 3.2. That is, for subperiod 1974–77, we assigned the 72 stocks with the lowest betas (sigmas) a beta (sigma) rank of 1, the next 225 lowest betas (sigmas) a rank of 2, and so on.[7]

RESULTS

We would expect the three risk measures to be positively correlated, because sigma is one of the variables involved in determining both the safety rank and beta. This turned out to be the case for our sample. Table 3.3 reports correlation coefficients for the three risk measures by subperiod.

The correlation coefficients fall in the range of 0.4 to 0.8 and are all highly significant statistically. For example, the correlation between safety rank and beta rank is 0.705 for the 1974–77 subperiod. While the correlations are high, however, the risk measures are not

Table 3.3   Correlation coefficients for risk measures

Subperiod	Safety rank and beta rank	Safety rank and sigma rank	Beta rank and sigma rank
1974–1977	0.705	0.820	0.702
1978–1981	0.434	0.703	0.510
1982–1985	0.501	0.760	0.616
Averages	0.547	0.761	0.609

perfectly correlated and therefore not perfect proxies for each other. It is of interest to see which risk measure is most strongly associated with return.

Table 3.4 presents simple descriptive statistics for each of the risk measures. Over the first two subperiods (1974–77 and 1978–81), there is a very strong, positive relation between risk and return. That is, as the risk ranking increases, mean monthly return also generally increases, regardless of the risk measure being considered.

Table 3.4   Descriptive statistics

		Statistics for safety ranks				
Subperiod	Averages	Rank 1	Rank 2	Rank 3	Rank 4	Rank 5
1974–1977	Monthly return	1.104%	1.016%	1.484%	2.263%	2.573%
1978–1981	Mean return	0.759%	1.125%	1.617%	2.118%	2.700%
1982–1985	Mean return	1.966%	1.841%	1.771%	1.393%	1.438%
Averages for 1974–1985	Mean return	1.276%	1.327%	1.624%	1.925%	2.237%

		Statistics for beta ranks				
Subperiod	Averages	Rank 1	Rank 2	Rank 3	Rank 4	Rank 5
1974–1977	Monthly return	1.382%	1.329%	1.417%	1.980%	2.312%
	Beta value	0.585	0.819	1.077	1.401	1.760
1978–1981	Mean return	1.391%	1.365%	1.567%	1.959%	1.827%
	Beta value	0.586	0.733	1.028	1.318	1.599
1982–1985	Mean return	2.056%	2.054%	1.772%	1.374%	0.596%
	Beta value	0.597	0.773	1.021	1.306	1.552
Averages for 1974–1985	Mean return	1.610%	1.583%	1.585%	1.771%	1.578%
	Beta value	0.589	0.788	1.042	1.342	1.637

		Statistics for sigma ranks				
Subperiod	Averages	Rank 1	Rank 2	Rank 3	Rank 4	Rank 5
1974–1977	Monthly return	1.129%	1.001%	1.540%	2.235%	2.297%
	Sigma value	4.657%	6.990%	10.034%	13.386%	16.986%
1978–1981	Mean return	1.002%	1.143%	1.604%	2.098%	2.496%
	Sigma value	5.704%	7.703%	10.618%	15.351%	21.546%
1982–1985	Mean return	2.091%	1.984%	1.749%	1.271%	1.230%
	Sigma value	4.987%	6.663%	9.796%	14.114%	19.003%
Averages for 1974–1985	Mean return	1.407%	1.376%	1.631%	1.868%	2.008%
	Sigma value	5.116%	7.119%	10.149%	14.284%	19.178%

For the 1982–85 subperiod, however, there is a strong but negative relation between risk and return. This could be easily explained *if* the 1982–85 period had been a bear market. During bear markets, we would expect a negative relation between risk and return; it is the nature of risk that the most risky securities should provide the poorest returns in poor markets. But the 1982–85 period would have to be classified as a bull market.[8] We can offer no explanation for this peculiar result, other than the usual caveat: During relatively short periods of time, anything can happen in the securities markets.

Averaging results over all three subperiods provides an interesting picture. The bottom row for each risk measure in Table 3.4 presents simple averages, which are plotted in Figure 3.1. For each of the three risk measures, five sets of bars represent the return for each rank; that is, the first of the five bars represents the return for rank 1 stocks (lowest risk) and the fifth bar represents the return for rank 5 stocks (highest risk).

For the safety ranks there is a strongly positive relation between risk and return; for the entire 1974–85 period, the average return increases as the safety rank increases. This is also true for the sigma ranks, with the one exception that the average return for sigma rank 1 was slightly greater than the return for sigma rank 2. For the beta ranks, however, the relation between risk and return is not so clear. In fact, simple observation of Figure 3.1 suggests that there is no relation between risk, as measured by beta, and realized return.

The process of averaging over time periods and across securities by forming portfolios (as is the case for the results reported in Figure 3.1) can sometimes obscure a true underlying relationship. To provide a more formal test of the relation between return and the three risk measures, we regressed the average return for *individual* stocks against each stock's three risk rankings over each of the three subperiods. Table 3.5 reports the results.

For the first subperiod, 1974–77, the first regression (denoted #1) lists the results of regressing individual stock mean returns for the 48-month subperiod against safety rank at the beginning of the subperiod. The regression co-efficient for safety rank is a positive 0.0047 and is highly significant in the statistical sense; the t-statistic of 12.76 is significant at the 1% level. The R^2 is 0.146, which means that roughly 15% of the variation in stock returns can be explained by safety rank.[9]

The second regression (#2) lists the results of regressing individual stock mean returns against beta rank at the beginning of the sub-period. While the coefficient for beta rank is positive (0.0026) and statistically significant (t-statistic of 6.69), the relation between return and beta rank is not nearly as strong as the return-safety rank relationship. The beta rank R^2 is only 0.044–about one-third the size of the safety rank R^2.

The third regression lists the results using the sigma ranks as the risk measure. The relation between return and sigma rank is positive and statistically significant. It is stronger than the result for beta rank, but not quite as strong as that for safety rank.

In general, the results for the 1978–81 subperiod mirror those for the 1974–77 sub-period. Safety rank is the most powerful explanatory risk measure, sigma rank the second most powerful; beta rank is a distant third. For this subperiod, the R^2 for safety rank is over six times as large as the R^2 for beta rank.

This is not the case for the third subperiod, 1982–85. For this subperiod, beta rank is the best explanatory variable, even though its R^2 is only 0.047. This is also the subperiod for which there was a peculiar negative relation between beta risk and return, despite the fact that it was a period of generally rising stock prices. Furthermore, the regression coefficient for each of the risk measures is negative. We are thus inclined to view the results for this subperiod with a healthy dose of skepticism.

44

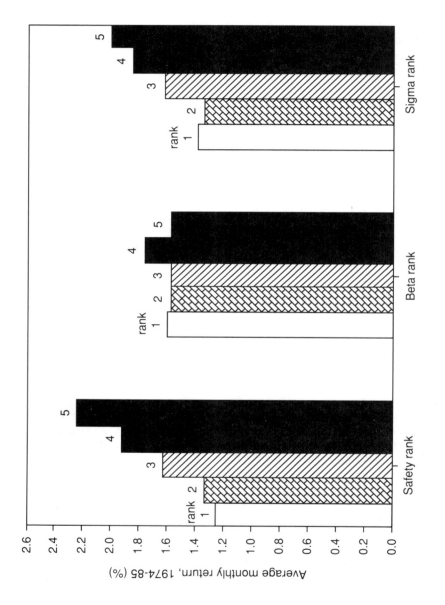

Figure 3.1 Return and three risk measures

Table 3.5 Regression analysis of risk measures (*t*-statistics in parentheses)

Subperiod	Regression	Intercept	Safety Rank	Beta Rank	Sigma Rank	R^2	F Ratio**
1974–1977	#1	0.0019 (1.70)	0.0047 (12.76)**			0.146	162.88
	#2	0.0080 (6.67)**		0.0026 (6.69)**		0.044	44.69
	#3	0.0031 (6.75)**			0.0043 (11.51)**	0.122	132.58
1978–1981	#1	0.0017 (1.41)	0.0049 (12.66)**			0.136	160.29
	#2	0.0106 (8.71)**		0.0019 (4.59)**		0.019	21.07
	#3	0.0037 (3.05)**			0.0042 (10.65)**	0.100	113.40
1982–1985	#1	0.0218 (16.27)**	−0.0016 (−3.52)**			0.011	12.42
	#2	0.0264 (19.56)**		−0.0031 (−7.06)**		0.047	49.84
	#3	0.0246 (18.51)**			−0.0025 (−5.77)**	0.032	33.23
Total Period 1974–1985	#1	0.0088 (11.90)**	0.0025 (10.11)**			0.138	102.26
	#2	0.0121 (15.39)**		0.0013 (4.95)**		0.036	24.51
	#3	0.0090 (12.13)**			0.0024 (9.76)**	0.129	95.28

*Significant at the 5% level.
**Significant at the 1% level; all F ratios are significant at the 1% level.

As a final check on the risk-return relationships, we calculated the average return for each stock over the entire 12 years of the study, 1974–85. We then regressed this 12-year average return against each stock's risk measures at the beginning of the period, 1974. These results are reported at the bottom of Table 3.5. The results are similar to those for the first two subperiods. Safety rank is the most powerful explanatory risk measure, followed by sigma rank, with beta rank a distant third.[10]

IMPLICATIONS

Our results suggest that the intuitive notions of risk utilized by investment professionals in constructing risk measures have been closer to the mark than the theoretically more rigorous risk measures developed by academics.

One interpretation of the many recent findings of market inefficiency (such as the small-firm effect, *P/E* effect and earnings "surprises") is that the theoretical model for risk and return is misspecified, and the risk measure (typically beta) is consequently inadequate or inappropriate. For example, a recent study found that, in addition to beta, measures of liquidity risk need to be accounted for in the risk-return model.[11]

Liquidity risk has long been one of the intuitive notions of risk considered by investors; in fact, by incorporating such variables as firm size and stock price stability in their safety ranks, Value Line analysts may be trying to account for this risk. The safety rank may also reflect other traditional notions of risk, such as business risk. If so, this would suggest that our theoretical understanding of the relation between risk and return might be improved by carefully observing the practices of investment professionals.[12]

ENDNOTES

1. See, for example, Sharpe, W. "Capital Asset Prices: A Theory of Market Equilibrium Under Conditions of Risk," *Journal of Finance*, September 1964 and Lintner, J. "The Valuation of Risky Assets and the Selection of Risky Investments in Stock Portfolios and Capital Budgets," *Review of Economics and Statistics*, February 1965, as well as Treynor, J.L. "Toward a Theory of the Market Value of Risky Assets" (unpublished, 1961), Mossin, J. "Equilibrium in a Capital Asset Market," *Econometrica*, October 1966, and Black, F. "Capital Market Equilibrium with Restricted Borrowing," *Journal of Business*, July 1972. Another example of the evolutionary struggle to define the risk-return relationship is the Arbitrage Pricing Theory of Ross, S. "The Arbitrage Theory of Capital Asset Pricing," *Journal of Economic Theory*, December 1976.

2. Other traditional risk measures for common stocks include Standard & Poor's earnings and dividends ranking and Fitch's quality rating. We concentrate on the Value Line Safety Rank for several reasons. First, the data are readily available to investors, as Value Line is the world's largest investment advisory organization. Second, as Standard & Poor's is careful to point out, its earnings and dividends rankings do not pretend to reflect all the factors, tangible or intangible, that bear on stock quality (*Standard & Poor's Stock Guide*, page 7.)

3. See, for example, Levy, H. "Equilibrium in an Imperfect Market: A Constraint on the Number of Securities in the Portfolio," *American Economic Review*, September 1972.

4. The choice of the starting date was dictated by the fact that 1972 was the earliest period for which we could get both Value Line Safety Ranks and Value Line beta estimates. We also estimated simple OLS betas using the CRSP data as well as OLS betas adjusted for their tendency to regress toward the mean. The procedures presented in the text using Value Line betas were repeated using simple OLS betas and adjusted OLS betas and the results were all qualitatively the same as those reported in Tables 3.3, 3.4 and 3.5.

5. We also computed the geometric mean for each stock and repeated the procedures reported in the text. All the results based on the geometric mean were qualitatively the same as those based on the arithmetic mean.

6. As might be expected, our selection criteria tended to eliminate more stocks ranked 4 or 5 for safety than those ranked 1 or 2. For example, over the three subperiods the rank 1 stocks in our sample averaged 8.1% of the total sample, whereas for all stocks followed by Value Line, those with a safety rank of 1 averaged 6.5%. It is not clear what effect, if any, this bias had on our results.

7. We also assigned beta (sigma) ranks based on equal-size quintiles. Although these quintile rankings are not directly comparable to the method used by Value Line in determining safety ranks, we nevertheless repeated all the tests reported in the text using equal-size quintiles; the results were qualitatively the same.

8. Theoretically, we would expect to see an *ex post* negative risk-return tradeoff during market periods when the return on the risk-free asset exceeds the return on the risky market portfolio. This was not the case during the period 1982–85; for example, the geometric mean return on the S&P 500 was 20.2% during the period, compared with 9.2% for Treasury bills.

9. An R^2 of 0.146 may not seem very high, but bear in mind that this is a regression of *individual* security returns against risk. The R-squares for portfolios are typically much higher.

10. Over this long a time period, individual security risk characteristics can obviously change, which reduces the power of this test. However, the stability of the stocks' risk characteristics over time are perhaps higher than one might think. For example, the correlation coefficient for individual stocks' safety ranks at the beginning of 1974 with their safety ranks at the beginning of 1982 was 0.605. Listed below are the serial correlation coefficients for the three risk measures:

	1974 vs. 1978	1978 vs. 1982	1974 vs. 1982
Safety Rank	0.762	0.710	0.605
Beta Rank	0.691	0.653	0.675
Sigma Rank	0.621	0.597	0.646

11. See Amihud, Y. and Mendelson, H. "Asset Pricing and the Bid-Ask Spread,' *Journal of Financial Economics*, December 1986.

12. Unfortunately, it does not appear that simply substituting the Value Line Safety Rank for beta will make such anomalies as the small-firm and *P/E* effects disappear. We replicated the tests of Banz and Reinganum for the small-firm effect and the low-PE effect for the period of our study (1974–85), using first beta and then safety rank as the risk measure. The size of both the small-firm effect and the low-PE effect was substantially reduced when safety rank was used as the risk measure, but both anomalies remained and were still statistically significant. See Banz, R.W. "The Relationship Between Return and Market Value of Common Stocks," *Journal of Financial Economics*, September 1981 and Reinganum, M. "Misspecification of Capital Asset Pricing: Empirical Anomalies Based on Earnings' Yields and Market Values," *Journal of Financial Economics*, March 1981.

4

How Many Stocks Make a Diversified Portfolio?

Meir Statman

I. INTRODUCTION

How many stocks make a diversified portfolio? Evans and Archer [9] concluded that approximately ten stocks will do. They stated that their results "Raise doubts concerning the economic justification of increasing portfolio sizes beyond 10 or so securities" (p. 767). Evans and Archer's conclusion has been widely adopted and cited in many current textbooks, but is it correct? No. The primary purpose of this paper is to show that no less than 30 stocks are needed for a well-diversified portfolio. A secondary purpose is to compare this finding to the levels of diversification observed in studies of individual investors' portfolios.

II. PORTFOLIOS AND RISK

The risk of a stock portfolio depends on the proportions of the individual stocks, their variances, and their covariances. A change in any of these variables will change the risk of the portfolio. Still, it is generally true that when stocks are randomly selected and combined in equal proportions into a portfolio, the risk of a portfolio declines as the number of different stocks in it increases. Evans and Archer observed that the risk reduction effect diminishes rapidly as the number of stocks increases. They concluded that the economic benefits of diversification are virtually exhausted when a portfolio contains ten or so stocks.

Evans and Archer's conclusion has been cited in many textbooks. For example, Francis ([10], p. 749) wrote:

> [P]ortfolio managers should not become overzealous and spread their assets over too many assets. If 10 or 15 different assets are selected for the portfolio, the maximum benefits from naive diversification most likely have been attained. Further spreading of the portfolio's assets is *superfluous diversification* and should be avoided. [Emphasis in the original.]

Reprinted from: Statman, M. 1987: How Many Stocks Make a Diversified Portfolio? *Journal of Financial and Quantitative Analysis*, 22, 353–363.

Stevenson and Jennings ([22], pp. 532–533) wrote:

> The results of the Evans and Archer study indicate that a portfolio of approximately eight to sixteen randomly-selected stocks will closely resemble the market portfolio in terms of fluctuations in the rate of return. Other studies have shown similar results and an unusual consistency using different time periods, different groups of stocks, and different research techniques. Consequently, while the CAP model requires the purchase of the market portfolio, essentially the same result can be achieved from a practical standpoint with a much smaller portfolio.

Gup ([11], pp. 363–364) wrote:

> Proper diversification does not require investing in a large number of different industries or securities ... [T]he diversifiable risk is reduced as the number of stocks increases from one to about eight or nine ... [W]hen the number of securities is increased to about nine, almost all of the diversifiable risk is eliminated.

Table 4.1 Expected standard deviations of annual portfolio returns

Number of stocks in portfolio	Expected standard deviation of annual portfolio returns	Ratio of portfolio standard deviation to standard deviation of a single stock
1	49.236	1.00
2	37.358	0.76
4	29.687	0.60
6	26.643	0.54
8	24.983	0.51
10	23.932	0.49
12	23.204	0.47
14	22.670	0.46
16	22.261	0.45
18	21.939	0.45
20	21.677	0.44
25	21.196	0.43
30	20.870	0.42
35	20.634	0.42
40	20.456	0.42
45	20.316	0.41
50	20.203	0.41
75	19.860	0.40
100	19.686	0.40
200	19.423	0.39
300	19.336	0.39
400	19.292	0.39
450	19.277	0.39
500	19.265	0.39
600	19.247	0.39
700	19.233	0.39
800	19.224	0.39
900	19.217	0.39
1000	19.211	0.39
Infinity	19.158	0.39

Source: Elton and Gruber [8], p. 35. Portfolios are equally weighted. Elton and Gruber reported variances of weekly returns. We have converted these to standard deviations of annual returns.

Reilly ([18], p. 101) wrote:

> In terms of overdiversification, several studies have shown that it is possible to derive most of the benefits of diversification with a portfolio consisting of from 12 to 18 stocks. To be adequately diversified does *not* require 200 stocks in a portfolio [Emphasis in the original.]

Early studies, including that by Evans and Archer, reached their conclusions by simulating the relationship between risk and the number of stocks. Elton and Gruber [7] investigated the relationship between risk and the number of stocks in a portfolio further and provided an analytical solution for the relationship between the two.[1] Elton and Gruber's results, presented in Table 4.1, imply that 51% of a portfolio standard deviation is eliminated as diversification increases from 1 to 10 securities. Adding 10 more securities eliminates an additional 5% of the standard deviation. Increasing the number of securities to 30 eliminates only an additional 2% of the standard deviation.

III. THE COSTS AND BENEFITS OF DIVERSIFICATION

The principle that marginal costs should be compared to marginal benefits in determining the optimal levels of production or consumption is fundamental to economic theory. The fact that "almost all" of the portfolio's unsystematic risk is eliminated when it contains 10 or 100 stocks is meaningless when presented by itself.

Diversification should be increased as long as the marginal benefits exceed the marginal costs. The benefits of diversification are in risk reduction. The costs are transaction costs. The usual argument for limited diversification is that marginal costs increase faster than marginal benefits as diversification increases. For example, Mayshar [17] developed a model that shows that it is optimal to limit diversification in the presence of transaction costs.

Comparison of benefits and costs requires a common measure. We use returns as our measure. The risk reduction benefits of diversification, in units of expected return, can be determined through a simple comparison of any two portfolios. The analysis is similar to that by Blume and Friend ([5], pp. 52–58).

We use a 500-stock portfolio as our benchmark portfolio and compare other, less diversified portfolios to it. We use a 500-stock portfolio as an example of an attainable, fairly diversified portfolio, but we claim neither that a 500-stock portfolio is a proxy for the market portfolio, nor that we cannot obtain better diversified portfolios.

The 500-stock portfolio can be levered, through borrowing or lending, to form portfolios $P(n)$ with combinations of expected returns and standard deviations according to the equation

$$E\left[R_{P(n)}\right] = (R_F + \alpha) + \left\{ \frac{E\left|R_{P(500)}\right| - (R_F + \alpha)}{\sigma_{P(500)}} \right\} \sigma_{P(n)}, \tag{1}$$

where $E[R_{P(n)}]$ = the expected return of portfolio $P(n)$,

$\quad R_F$ = the risk-free rate,

$\quad \alpha$ = the excess of the borrowing rate over the lending or risk-free rate for a borrowing investor, and zero for a lending investor,

$E[R_{P(500)}]$ = the expected return of the 500-stock portfolio,

$\quad \sigma_{P(n)}$ = the standard deviation of portfolio $P(n)$, and

$\quad \sigma_{P(500)}$ = the standard deviation of the 500-stock portfolio.

Equation (1) defines what we will call the 500-stock line and all portfolios $P(n)$ lie on it (see Figure 4.1). The 500-stock line is composed of two segments. The first, from R_F to $P(500)$, represents the portfolio combinations for a lending investor. The lending rate is R_F, the risk-free rate. The second, from $P(500)$ through $P(10)$, represents the portfolio combination for a borrowing investor. The borrowing rate is $R_F + \alpha$, where α is the excess of the borrowing rate over the lending rate.

Markowitz [16] developed a formula for the expected variance of a portfolio on n securities. That formula has been used by Elton and Gruber. We assume, as in Elton and Gruber, that an investor draws randomly from all stocks to form portfolios that differ in the number of stocks but have identical expected returns. We use the findings of Ibbotson Associates [12] about the risk premium on a particular 500-stock portfolio, the Standard and Poor's (S&P) 500 Index. Note that the S&P 500 Index is one attainable 500-stock portfolio. While Elton and Gruber use equally weighted portfolios, the S&P 500 Index is value weighted. We assume, for now, that the cost of maintaining an equally weighted 500-stock portfolio is identical to the cost of maintaining a value weighted 500-stock portfolio.

We use an Ibbotson Associates ([12], p. 42) estimate of the risk premium on the 500-stock portfolio, $E[R_{P(500)}] - R_F$. The arithmetic mean of the risk premium over the period 1926–1984 is 8.2% per year. We use 2.0% per year as an estimate of α, the excess of the borrowing rate over the risk-free or lending rate. The estimate is based on a comparison between the Treasury Bill rate, a proxy for the lending rate, and the Call Money rate. The Call Money rate is the rate charged on loans to brokers on stock exchange collateral (i.e, margin loans), and it provides a starting point for the estimate of the borrowing rate. The Call Money rate is less than 2% higher than the Treasury Bill rate (see Table 4.2). However, brokers typically charge their borrowing customers somewhat more than the Call Money rate. An estimate of 2% for α seems reasonable.

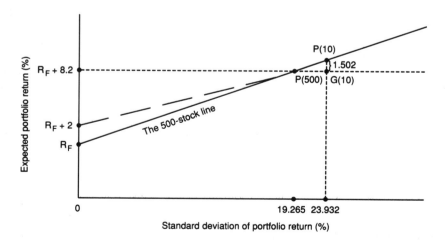

Figure 4.1 An expected return 1.502 percent higher than that of a 500-stock portfolio, $P(500)$, is necessary to offset the higher risk, due to limited diversification, of teh 10-stock portrfolio $G(10)$. A portfolio $P(10)$ can be constructed by leveraging $P(500)$ where the expected return of $P(10)$ is 1.502 percent higher than that of $G(10)$, while the two have identical risks. Data on standard deviations of portfolio returns are from Table 1. An estimate of 2 percent was used for α, the excess of the borrowing rate over the lending rate. An estimate of 8.2 percent was used for the risk premium.

Table 4.2 Difference between the Call Money rate and the Treasury Bill rate

Date	(1) Call Money rate (%)	(2) Treasury Bill rate (%)	(1)–(2) Difference
Jan. 15, 1985	9.25	7.74	1.50
Feb. 15, 1985	9.38	8.20	1.18
March 15, 1985	9.75	8.48	1.27
April 15, 1985	9.50	8.14	1.36
May 15, 1985	9.00	7.69	1.31
June 14, 1985	8.63	7.21	1.42
July 15, 1985	8.63	6.92	1.71
Aug. 15, 1985	9.25	7.14	2.11
Sept. 15, 1985	8.75	7.22	1.53
Oct. 17, 1985	8.88	7.20	1.68
Nov. 15, 1985	9.13	7.21	1.92
Dec. 16, 1985	9.00	7.05	1.95
			1.58

Source: Data are from the Money Rate tables of the *Wall Street Journal* on the specified dates. We used data from the *Wall Street Journal* for the 15th of each month during 1985, or a date close to the 15th if data for the 15th were not available. The Call Money rate is the mean of the range of rates provided. The Treasury Bill rate is the rate for the most recent auction of 13-week bills.

To calculate the risk reduction benefits of diversification, compare, for example, a portfolio of ten randomly selected stocks, $G(10)$, to a portfolio $P(10)$, that lies on the 500-stock line and has a standard deviation identical to that of portfolio $G(10)$. We know from Elton and Gruber (Table 4.1) that portfolio $G(10)$ has an expected standard deviation, $\sigma_{G(10)}$ of 23.932%, and that the expected standard deviation of the 500-stock portfolio, $\sigma_{P(500)}$, is 19.265%. The standard deviation, $\sigma_{G(10)}$, exceeds $\sigma_{P(500)}$ as portfolio $G(10)$ contains more diversifiable risk than portfolio $P(500)$.

If stocks are chosen randomly, every stock and every portfolio has an expected return of $R_F + 8.2\%$, composed of the risk-free rate and an 8.2% risk premium. Thus, the expected returns of both the 10-stock portfolio, $G(10)$, and the 500-stock portfolio, $P(500)$, are equal to $R_F + 8.2\%$.

How much would a portfolio $P(10)$, that levers the 500-stock portfolio, $P(500)$, be expected to yield if $P(500)$ were levered so that the standard deviation of the returns on portfolio $P(10)$ is 23.932%? Using Equation (1) we find that

$$E\left[R_{P(10)}\right] = (R_F + 2) + \left\{ \frac{(R_F + 8.2) - (R_F + 2)}{19.265} \right\} 23.932 = R_F + 9.702.$$

An investor obtains the $R_F + 9.702\%$ expected return on portfolio P(10) by borrowing 0.242 of his or her wealth and investing 1.242 of his or her wealth in the 500-stock portfolio (see Figure 4.1).

The return differential between the levered 500-stock portfolio, $P(10)$, and the 10-stock portfolio, $G(10)$, is $E[R_{P(10)}] - E[R_{G(10)}] = [R_F + 9.702] - [R_F + 8.2] = 1.502$.

The 1.502% differential in the expected return between the levered 500-stock portfolio $P(10)$ and the 10-stock portfolio $G(10)$ can be interpreted as the benefit that an investor derives from increasing the number of stocks in the portfolio from 10 to 500. In general, the benefit from increasing the number of stocks in a portfolio from n to 500 is

$$E\left[R_{P(n)}\right] - E\left[R_{G(n)}\right] = \left\{\frac{\sigma_{P(n)}}{\sigma_{P(500)}} - 1\right\}\left\{E\left[R_{G(n)}\right] - (R_F + \alpha)\right\}. \quad (2)$$

For the 10-stock portfolio, discussed earlier, we have

$$E\left[R_{P(10)}\right] - E\left[R_{G(10)}\right] = \left\{\frac{23.932}{19.265} - 1\right\}\{(R_F + 8.2) - (R_F + 2)\} = 1.502.$$

Benefits, in terms of expected returns, of increasing the number of stocks in various portfolios to 500 are presented in Table 4.3.

We turn now from the measurement of the benefits of diversification to the measurement of its costs. Assume, for now, that no costs are incurred in buying, selling, and holding of portfolios $G(n)$ composed of less than 500 stocks. A leveraged 500-stock portfolio, $P(n)$, is preferable to a portfolio $G(n)$ if the costs of $P(n)$ are lower than the benefits that come with increased diversification.

A 500-stock portfolio is available to all investors in the form of the Vanguard Index Trust, a no-load index fund that mimics the S&P 500 Index. The fund provides a return that is lower than that of the S&P 500 Index because investors pay transaction costs and administrative expenses. The mean annual return differential for the years 1979–1984 is 0.49% (see Table 4.4). Of course, 0.49 is less than 1.502, so the Vanguard portfolio dominates a ten-stock portfolio even when the cost of buying, selling, and holding these ten securities is zero.

Note that the Vanguard Index Trust serves only as an example of an attainable well-diversified and unmanaged mutual fund. Similar funds with various combinations of securities would be offered, if investors demand them.

A comparison of the 0.49% figure to the figures in Table 4.3 makes clear that the Vanguard Index Trust dominates a 30-stock portfolio, $G(30)$, for a borrowing investor, and

Table 4.3 Difference between expected annual return of a portfolio of n stocks, $G(n)$, and expected annual return of a portfolio $P(n)$ that levers a 500-stock portfolio such that standard deviations of returns of portfolios $G(n)$ and $P(n)$ are equal[a]

Number of stocks in portfolio (n)	Return differences for borrowing and lending investors	
	Borrowing investor	Lending investor
10	1.502	1.986
20	0.776	1.027
30	0.517	0.683
40	0.383	0.507
50	0.302	0.399
100	0.135	0.179

[a]The figures in this table were calculated using Equation 2 with data from Table 4.1. The risk premium is estimated as 8.2%, the arithmetic mean risk premium. Risk premium data are from Ibbotson Associates [12], p. 42. The value of α, the excess of the borrowing rate over the lending rate, was estimated as 2%.

Table 4.4 Comparison of returns to investors in the Standard and Poor's (S&P) 500 Index and Vanguard Index Trust, 1979–1984

Year	(1) Rate of return on S&P 500 Index (%)	(2) Rate of return on Vanguard Index Trust (%)	Difference (1)–(2)
1979	18.44	18.04	0.40
1980	32.42	31.92	0.50
1981	−4.91	−5.21	0.30
1982	21.41	20.98	0.43
1983	22.51	21.29	1.22
1984	6.27	6.21	0.06
		Mean	0.49

Source: Vanguard Index Trust returns data are from Wiesenberger Financial Services [23]. S&P 500 Index returns data are from Ibbotson Associates [12].

a 40-stock portfolio, $G(40)$, for a lending investor, even if we assume that no costs exist for buying, selling, and holding stocks in portfolios $G(30)$ and $G(40)$ while the Vanguard Index Trust costs are paid.

The figures quoted above were obtained under a set of particular assumptions, and they may increase or decrease as the assumptions change. We will consider here some prominent cases.

First is the issue of transaction costs. So far we have assumed that investors pay the costs of the Vanguard Index Trust, but they pay nothing for buying and selling and holding stocks of less diversified portfolios, $G(n)$. This assumption leads to an underestimation of the advantage of the Vanguard Index Trust over portfolios $G(n)$. For example, consider the case where costs associated with portfolios $G(n)$ amount 0.1% per year of the value of the portfolio. The effect of these costs on the relative positions of portfolios $G(n)$ and the Vanguard Index Trust is equal to the effect of reducing the Vanguard Index Trust annual costs by 0.1%, from 0.49 to 0.39. Such a change makes the Vanguard Index Trust superior to a portfolio of 35 stocks, rather than 30 stocks, for the case of a borrowing investor, and 50 stocks, rather than 40 stocks, for the case of a lending investor.

The estimation of annual costs associated with portfolios $G(n)$ is difficult because they depend on the interval between stock trades; costs are higher for those who trade frequently. However, the earlier example probably underestimates the advantages of the Vanguard Index Trust. The cost of a round trip stock trade is probably not lower than 1%, and the mean holding period of a stock is probably not much higher than one year. (See [20], p. 306.)

Second, the reliability of the standard deviation estimate for returns of portfolios consisting of few stocks is low relative to that of portfolios of many stocks. Elton and Gruber ([17], Table 8) reported that the standard deviation of the estimate of the standard deviation of the portfolio return is 1.8% for a portfolio of 10 stocks, and 0.3% for a portfolio of 50 stocks, but it drops to virtually zero for a portfolio of 500 stocks. We do not know how to measure the loss that is due to the inherent unreliability of the estimate of the standard deviation of portfolio returns in portfolios of few stocks. However, it is another disadvantage of low levels of diversification.

The case for the Vanguard Index Trust may have been overstated because of two reasons. First, investors may be able to choose superior stocks and use the returns on these stocks to compensate for the additional risk due to lack of diversification. Indeed, there is some evidence that investors are able to choose stocks that offer return advantages sufficient to eliminate some of the negative effects of transaction costs. For example, Schlarbaum, Lewellen, and Lease ([20], Table 14) found that individual investors had mean returns, after transaction costs, that were identical to the mean returns of mutual funds. However, Schlarbaum *et al.* adjusted only for the systematic risk of stocks in both individuals' portfolios and mutual funds. The lack of diversification in individuals' portfolios relative to that of mutual funds implies that individuals may do worse than mutual funds when proper consideration is given to both systematic and unsystematic risk.

Second, stocks in the Vanguard Index Trust are value weighted while the analysis here is based on equally weighted portfolios. It is possible that the cost of the Vanguard Index Trust underestimates the costs of an equally weighted 500-stock portfolio, since transaction costs per dollar investment are generally higher for small company stocks than for large company stocks.

IV. DO INDIVIDUALS FOLLOW MARKOWITZ'S PRESCRIPTION ON DIVERSIFICATION?

The framework in which individuals construct portfolios by choosing combinations of expected return and risk, measured as the standard deviation of the return, is a crucial building block for much work in finance. Markowitz developed the prescriptive (normative) framework.

An important prediction of the CAPM, a descriptive (positive) model based on Markowitz's idea, is that every investor would hold a portfolio of all securities available in the market (given efficient markets, perfectly divisible securities, and no transaction costs).

Evidence, however, suggests that the typical investor's stock portfolio contains only a small fraction of the available securities. Blume, Crockett, and Friend [3] found that in 1971, 34.1% of investors in their sample held only one dividend-paying stock, 50% held no more than 2 stocks, and only 10.7% held more than 10 stocks. A 1967 Federal Reserve Board Survey of Financial Characteristics of Consumers showed that the average number of stocks in the portfolio was 3.41 (see [4]). A survey of investors who held accounts with a major brokerage company revealed that the average number of stocks in a portfolio ranged from 9.4 to 12.1, depending on the demographic group [15].

Of course, the number of securities in the portfolio is not the sole determinant of the degree of diversification. Studies by Jacob [13] and others have shown that an investor can reduce unsystematic risk significantly with few securities if he or she chooses securities judiciously. However, there is no evidence that investors follow the suggested rules on optimal diversification with few securities. Blume and Friend ([5], p. 49) reported that the actual degree of diversification in 70% of the investors in their study *was lower* than suggested by the number of securities in the portfolios. Blume and Friend concluded that

> The empirical results show, however, that many investors, particularly those of limited means, do not hold well-diversified portfolios. The analysis of the returns realized by them confirms that these investors have exposed themselves to far greater risks than necessary (p. 58).

Observing individuals' stock portfolios provides only limited information about the level of diversification in their overall portfolios. While we know that there are only few stocks in the typical portfolio, it is possible that diversification is accomplished through bonds, real estate, and other assets. However, recent evidence by King and Leape [14] strongly suggests that limited diversification is observed even where assets other than stocks are included. Their study was based on a detailed survey of 6,010 U.S. households conducted in 1978. The survey oversampled high-income families and therefore provides a rich source of information on the composition of portfolios. One conclusion of King and Leape was that

> the differences in portfolio composition across households cannot be fully explained within the framework of the conventional portfolio choice model. The households in our sample, though wealthy, own a surprisingly small number of assets and liabilities, and this lack of diversification was found to be important when estimating asset demand equations. Given that the mean net worth of the sample was almost a quarter of a million dollars in 1978, it is hard to imagine that transactions costs, as traditionally defined, played a decisive role in producing incomplete portfolios (pp. 33–34).

It seems that a descriptive theory of portfolio construction, based on Markowitz, does not hold. People forego available opportunities for diversification, and transaction costs are not likely to provide a complete explanation for it.

V. CONCLUSION

We have shown that a well-diversified stock portfolio must include, at the very least, 30 stocks for a borrowing investor, and 40 stocks for a lending investor. This conclusion contradicts earlier results, quoted in many current textbooks, that the benefits of diversification for stock portfolios are exhausted when the number of stocks reaches 10 or 15. Moreover, observation of individuals' portfolios suggests that people do not hold portfolios that are well diversified.

Why do people forego the benefits of diversification? Maybe investors are simply ignorant about the benefits of diversification. If ignorance is the problem, education may be the solution. However, existing evidence does not warrant a claim that investors should indeed be educated to increase diversification.

Alternative approaches to portfolio construction exist. One is the framework in which investors are concerned about the skewness of the return distribution as well as with the mean and variance. (See, for example, [6].) The other is the "safety first" framework (see [19]). However, we are not sanguine about the ability of either of these two theories to provide an adequate description of the way portfolios are built because neither is consistent with the following two common observations.

First, people do not seem to treat their assets as parts in an integrated portfolio. For example, some people borrow at 15% interest to finance a car rather than "borrow" from the college education fund they have set for their young children that pays only 10% interest. As Black [2] wrote, people "keep their money in separate pockets." Second, people display risk seeking and risk aversion that varies with the various "pockets." Many people seek risk by buying lottery tickets, while they are extremely risk averse with assets in retirement accounts. (For a discussion of these issues in the context of portfolio construction, see [21].)

We have to know much more about investors' goals and preferences to develop a framework that describes how they form portfolios. Meanwhile, we should not rush to conclude that investors should be educated to hold fully diversified portfolios.

ENDNOTES

1. Bird and Tippett [1] have shown that studies using the simulation methodology are deficient. In particular, simulation studies tend to exaggerate the rate of decline in portfolio risk as the number of stocks in the portfolio increases.

REFERENCES

[1] Bird, R. and Tippett, M. "Naive Diversification and Portfolio Risk: A Note." *Management Science*, **32** (Feb. 1986), 244–251.

[2] Black, F. "The Future for Financial Services." Working Paper, M.I.T. (Oct. 1982).

[3] Blume, M.E., Crockett, J. and Friend, I. "Stock Ownership in the United States: Characteristics and Trends." *Survey of Current Business*, **54** (Nov. 1974), 16–40.

[4] Blume, M.E. and Friend, I. "The Asset Structure of Individual Portfolios and Some Implications for Utility Functions." *Journal of Finance*, **30** (May 1975), 585–603.

[5] ── ──*The Changing Role of the Individual Investor: A Twentieth Century Fund Report*. New York: John Wiley & Sons (1978).

[6] Conine, T.E. and Tamarkin, M.J. "On Diversification Given Asymmetry in Returns." *Journal of Finance*, **36** (Dec. 1981), 1143–1155.

[7] Elton, E.J. and Gruber, M.J. "Risk Reduction and Portfolio Size: An Analytical Solution." *Journal of Business*, **50** (Oct. 1977), 415–437.

[8] ── ──*Modern Portfolio Theory and Investment Analysis*, 2nd ed. New York: John Wiley & Sons (1984).

[9] Evans, J.L. and Archer, S.H. "Diversification and the Reduction of Dispersion: An Empirical Analysis." *Journal of Finance*, **23** (Dec. 1968), 761–767.

[10] Francis, J.C. *Investments: Analysis and Management*, 4th ed. New York: McGraw-Hill (1986).

[11] Gup, B.E. *The Basics of Investing*, 2nd ed. New York: John Wiley & Sons (1983).

[12] Ibbotson Associates. *Stocks, Bonds, Bills, and Inflation: 1985 Yearbook*. Chicago: Ibbotson Associates, Inc. (1985).

[13] Jacob, N.L. "A Limited-Diversification Portfolio Selection Model for the Small Investor." *Journal of Finance*, **29** (June 1974), 837–857.

[14] King, M.A. and Leape, J.I. "Wealth and Portfolio Composition: Theory and Evidence." #1468, NBER Working Paper Series, Cambridge, MA: National Bureau of Economic Research (Sept. 1984).

[15] Lease, R.C., Lewellen, W. and Schlarbaum, G. "Market Segmentation: Evidence on the Individual Investor." *Financial Analysts Journal*, **32** (Sept. 1976), 53–60.

[16] Markowitz, H. *Portfolio Selection: Efficient Diversification of Investments*. New York: John Wiley & Sons (1959).

[17] Mayshar, J. "Transaction Cost in a Model of Capital Market Equilibrium." *Journal of Political Economy*, **87** (Aug. 1979), 673–700.

[18] Reilly, F.K. *Investment Analysis and Portfolio Management*, 2nd ed. San Francisco: Dryden Press (1985).

[19] Roy, A.D. "Safety-first and the Holding of Assets." *Econometrica*, **20** (July 1952), 431–449.

[20] Schlarbaum, G.G., Lewellen, W.G. and Lease, R.C. "Realized Returns on Common Stock Investments: The Experience of Individual Investors." *Journal of Business*, **51** (April 1978), 299–325.

[21] Shefrin, H.M. and Statman, M. "A Mental Accounting-Based Portfolio Theory." Working Paper, Santa Clara Univ. (Nov. 1985).

[22] Stevenson, R.A. and Jennings, E.H. *Fundamentals of Investments*, 3rd ed. San Francisco: West Publ. Co. (1984).

[23] *Wiesenberger Investment Companies Service: Investment Companies* 1985. New York: Wiesenberger Financial Services. (1985).

PART TWO
The Efficient Market and Stock Selection

Risk is one of the central notions of investment theory—although not well understood. Another important idea is that of the efficient market. At its simplest, the efficient market theory says that security prices reflect all available information. This is no more than what we would expect if investors are keen to make money. If there is information that has some financial value, profit-orientated investors will quickly act on it and prices will then fully discount that information. Of course, if there are costs involved in acquiring information, prices will only reflect that information to the point at which the costs of acquiring it equate with the benefits from doing so. Nonetheless, we would expect a constant pressure for prices quickly to discount new information. This has some important implications for investors, specifically:

- investors can't use public information to earn abnormal returns;
- new information that implies a change in intrinsic value will be acted upon quickly.

How much faith investors have in the efficient market theory should determine their approach to managing investments. Funds may be managed passively or actively. A passive manager simply aims to match the return on some appropriate index whereas an active manager aims to purchase mispriced securities and assets and thereby earn a positive abnormal rate of return. Passive managers assume that:

- the market does not misprice securities or assets; *or*
- the market does misprice securities and assets but managers are not able to take advantage of the mispricing.

Passive managers would adopt a strategy of determining the appropriate strategic asset class allocation and then diversifying within each asset class. This might be achieved via index funds.

Active managers assume that:

- the market misprices securities and/or assets; *and*
- managers are able to recognize the mispricing.

Active managers may attempt to outperform by either or both of:

- security selection;
- asset class selection.

Clearly it is important to know if the efficient market theory is true. Unfortunately it is hard to test the theory. To know if a stock price fully reflects all available information, we need to know what the proper price for the stock is. To be able to tell that, we need to have a theory of asset pricing, for example the CAPM or APT. Thus, when we test the efficient market theory, we are also testing an asset pricing theory. This is known as the joint hypothesis problem — we always test two hypotheses together and it is hard to know which theory is refuted if a stock is not "properly" priced. Numerous studies have been made to test the efficient market theory and the studies encounter the joint hypothesis problem to varying degrees. Four broad conclusions appear to emerge (for a full discussion see Fama, 1991).

(a) Studies of specific events, especially related to corporate announcements, suggest that the market is broadly efficient and quickly reflects certain types of information. However some information, for example earnings surprises, appears to take months to be fully reflected in prices. The joint hypothesis problem is not much of an issue for these studies.

(b) Private information seems to give investors an edge. Corporate officers, dealing in the shares of their own companies, seem to earn abnormal returns although it is less clear how much investors who follow the officers will benefit; brokerage recommendations, if properly processed, may be worth following; press recommendations may also be useful. Still, all of these yield small returns.

(c) If the CAPM is correct, only beta matters — variables such as the size of the firm and its price–earnings ratio should not also be related to returns. The evidence is that they are. This means that the CAPM (or APT, which also struggles to account for these effects) is wrong, or the market is inefficient, or both. Most researchers believe that it is the capital asset pricing model that is mis-specified. For example, small stocks may be more risky, albeit not in a way that beta measures, and so the extra return small stocks earn is not a result of market inefficiency but a reward for risk. Alternatively, we know that small stocks are, for example, less liquid than large stocks, and perhaps investors dislike both illiquidity and risk, and expect to be rewarded for bearing either. Whatever the reason, these empirical findings of variables related to returns will be of interest to investors. If, for example, we believe illiquidity to be the cause of excess returns for small stocks, investors who are not concerned by poor liquidity should tilt their portfolios in that direction to earn higher returns. And it may be that the market is inefficient.

(d) There is some evidence of return predictability — especially at the market level. If equity market returns have been poor for a period of years, they are likely to reverse. Equity market returns are also related to the market dividend yield, the price–earnings ratio and, in the U.S., to the spread of low- over high-grade bond yields. These findings are not statistically very powerful, and there is some dispute as to whether they contradict the efficient market theory. All they might show is that when things look bad, investors demand a higher risk premium to hold stocks. Prices have to fall enough to make the market sufficiently attractive to offset the poorer prospects. A higher risk premium will mean, amongst other things, higher dividend yields and this will be associated with higher returns. In short, dividend yields should predict returns. Whatever one concludes on the theoretical arguments, the empirical findings are of some interest to investors.

In Part Four, I discuss some of the return predictability issues in the context of tactical asset allocation. In this Part, I focus on some of the other aspects of an efficient market and on stock selection.

A major source of information about companies is their published accounts. If the market is efficient, this information should be reflected in share prices. But what if companies engage in creative accounting, i.e., they stay the right side of the law but try to present their accounts so as to give an especially favourable view of earnings or the balance sheet? There have been a number of studies on this topic, some looking at the effect of differences in depreciation policy which affect stated earnings but not cash flow or real earnings power. The textbooks typically state that the market is not fooled by creative accounting. Actually, only some studies find this, whereas others do not. Most investment professionals probably believe that creative accounting fools some investors. A common view would be that the market discounts a lot, but not everything, and that careful analysis of accounts can yield substantial benefits in some cases.

In Chapter 5, George Foster, a professor at Stanford University, makes a relatively straightforward test of the effect of creative accounting. Abraham Briloff was a well-known critic of U.S. accounting standards. He published a number of articles critical of the accounts of particular companies. If the market is efficient, it might be thought that it should have seen through the creative accounting and should not react to his articles. Foster shows that for the Briloff articles he examined, the prices of the stocks discussed fell on average by 8% after the articles appeared. Foster offers a number of suggestions as to why this might be, with market inefficiency a serious candidate.

Chapter 6 is by Donald Keim, a professor at the University of Pennsylvania. Keim discusses some of the empirical regularities that relate to returns. His article was published in 1988, and there has been a flood of research in this area since then. Nonetheless, while not the last word, Keim gives careful discussion of a number of regularities and he ties his discussion into the joint hypothesis problem. Keim discusses abnormal returns in relation to high yields, small capitalization, low price–earnings ratios, *Value Line* recommendations and calendar effects. Other factors and strategies that have been related to abnormal returns include reacting to earnings and dividend surprises and following earnings and dividend forecast revisions, as well as buying stocks which have low price-to-sales ratios, low price, high book-to-market value or are neglected or new issues.

Many of the attributes that are related to abnormal returns are those that might be associated with good value — for example, high yields, low price–earnings ratios and high book-to-market. These attributes have been the basis of value investing for many decades. Why might these strategies work? One argument is that profits are much more random than most investors believe. Investors are inclined to extrapolate past profits and growth trends. Firms with good records sell on high ratings and those with poor histories sell on low ratings. But future prospects don't justify the ratings.

This general line of argument has recently received empirical support in an article by Josef Lakonishok, Andrei Shleifer and Robert Vishy (1993). I would like to have included the paper in this book but it was only in Working Paper format at the time this book was put together and was still being reviewed by one of the academic journals. The gist of the article is, however, worth reporting here. The authors looked at various value-based versus glamour-based strategies, including for example, low (i.e., value) versus high (i.e., glamour) price–earnings ratio stocks, high versus low book-to-market and high versus low cash flow to price. They found that value stocks outperformed.

They then looked at the five-year average growth of earnings, cash flow, sales and operating income for each decile of the attribute being studied, i.e., earnings-price, book-to-market, etc., *prior* to portfolio formation. For most value-based strategies there was a strong relationship between past growth and the attribute studied — for example high market-to-book stocks (value) had low past growth and low book-to-market stocks (glamour) had high past growth.

Based on these findings we might argue that past performance leads to stocks being seen as glamour or value stocks and that the value stocks have the better stock market performance. Why do value strategies work and glamour strategies fail? For just the reasons we suggested above — the market prices glamour stocks on the basis of extrapolating past growth but, sometimes in the short run, certainly in the long run, the growth rates of glamour and value stocks converge or overshoot.

Lakonishok, Shleifer and Vishny looked at the riskiness of the value-based strategies in a number of ways. They looked at how the strategies performed in poor economic conditions, poor stock markets and also at risk as measured by the standard deviation of returns and beta. The value strategies turned out to be *less* risky. These strategies appear to offer a sure way of making money. Why are they not discounted? First, the strategies don't work every year. Second, there may be consistent psychological biases in the way that investors process information. (This is discussed in Chapter 8.) Third, institutional investors and trustees may be willing to buy glamour stocks because they appear to be more prudent purchases. Because investment managers and trustees are not the owners of the assets they control, they may try to avoid doing things that might lay them open to criticism. Being wrong with the crowd may be acceptable, buying controversial, and cheap, stocks may not be if you get blamed for the losers and thought to be just lucky with the winners. In short, the market may not be fully efficient.

Before we move on to other topics, it is worth noting that the sort of variables both Keim and Lakonishok, Shleifer and Vishny discuss for the U.S. have been examined in other markets. For example, Mario Levis (1989) found that high dividend yield, low share price, small market capitalization and low price–earnings ratios were associated with excess returns in the U.K. For Japan, Louis Chan, Yasushi Hamao and Josef Lakonishok (1991), found that stocks with high earnings yield, high book-to-market ratio, small size and high cash flow yield all earned excess returns. These findings relate to each variable taken on its own. When the variables were considered together, the picture changed to some extent. Keim mentions some of the research on seasonal or calendar effects. Many of the world's markets have now been studied. William Ziemba (1994) reviews some of the international evidence. Often the findings have been broadly similar to the U.S. findings. For example, Ziemba, (1991, p. 144) found that "the seasonality regularities in Japan during the 1949–88 period were quite similar to the corresponding effects in U.S. security markets. Differences occur because of alternative institutional and cultural patterns in Japan."

In Chapter 7, one of the empirical regularities is looked at in some depth. It has been known for many years that around the world, initial public offerings (IPOs) have generated abnormal positive returns. Many reasons have been put forward to explain the apparent mis-pricing of IPOs. Recently, there have been studies looking at the long-term record which has lead to some re-assessment of the explanations. The evidence for the U.K. and the U.S. is that after the initial good performance, IPOs underperform over at least the next three years. In Chapter 7, Mario Levis, a Reader at the City University (London) details both the initial outperformance and the subsequent underperformance. He argues that while there may be some deliberate underpricing of new issues, the evidence is consistent with some kind of investor overreaction: investors are overoptimistic about the earnings prospects of some companies. Thus the stocks with the best initial performance tend to do worst over the next three years, and those with the worst aftermarket performance tend to marginally outperform subsequently.

Many students and investment practitioners think finance theory is too dominated by economic theorizing and think psychological analysis is underutilized. There have been some signs that there is a modest shift taking place to make greater use of psychological reasoning. While some writers have looked at topics such as the psychology of successful traders and others at crowd and mob behaviour, it is cognitive psychology that has had the greatest impact. The researchers who have had most impact on investment thinking are Professors Tversky and Kahneman (see, for example, Tversky and Kahneman, 1981, for a general discussion of some of their work). Chapter 8 consists of an informal introduction to some cognitive psychology by Harvey Pines, a psychology professor at Canisius College. He discusses some of the cognitive psychology research and its possible investment applications: it is this sort of psychological theory that might explain, in part, the findings of Lakonishok *et al.*, the overreaction reported by Levis or many of the anomalies reported by Keim.

I turn now to selecting shares. Investors who believe that the market is inefficient will want to construct a portfolio of shares that are cheap, i.e., underpriced. The classic textbook way of selecting shares is not by focusing on the empirical regularities or anomalies that have been discussed, but by a valuation technique, the dividend discount model. The dividend discount model states that the value of a share is the value of all the dividends it will ever pay, discounted at some appropriate rate. The textbooks explain the difficulties of forecasting dividends to eternity and explain some simplifying assumptions that can be made. The textbooks do this clearly enough, but they are usually slightly misleading on dividend discount models. They imply that they are in general use, which is not true. Relatively few investment firms rely mainly on dividend discount models for portfolio construction, and those that do are mainly in the U.S. Second, the texts do not give a very good idea of the practical problems involved in developing and maintaining such a model in an organizational context. Third, the dividend discount model, like most stock selection techniques has good and bad periods. In the long run the value that a dividend discount model hunts for may pay off, but during some periods the market may neglect value. For example, in a recession, when many firms produce unpleasant profit surprises, investors may scurry into stocks which appear to be recession-proof, even if they appear to be overvalued in terms of discounted dividends.

Probably the best known adherent of the dividend discount model is the investment management firm Sanford C. Bernstein. For many years it used just the dividend discount model for assessing shares. However, a number of studies have shown that a stock selection strategy can be built on the basis of earnings revisions and surprises. When a stock's earnings forecasts are revised, they tend to continue to be revised in the same direction. The decision rule is then simple: buy positive revisions and sell negative revisions. This is a strategy where results are likely to be seen in the short-term. In 1991 Bernstein added an earnings revision strategy to its dividend discount approach, i.e., it developed a two factor stock selection model, using a short-term and a long-term factor. In Chapter 9, Michael Goldstein, Michael Sommer and Robert Pari, all working at Bernstein, describe that firm's model. This chapter provides information on three topics — a real world dividend discount model, earnings revisions and share selection model construction.

As an aside, it is worth noting that earnings revisions appear to be important in non-U.S. markets as well as in the U.S. For example, Elton and Gruber examined the effect of changes in analysts' forecasts of earnings and sales per share on the subsequent price performance of Japanese stocks. Their findings were very similar to what is found in the West: "earnings, not sales, drive stock prices in Japan. Analysts' estimates are incorporated in stock prices but changes in analysts' estimates are incorporated with a lag. Because of this lag, extra returns can be earned by buying stocks immediately after an upward revision in analysts earning estimates." (1989, p. 401).

Most investors do not use a dividend discount model for share selection. Many use some combination of factors such as accounting ratios and accounting analysis, the economic prospects of the firm whose shares are being appraised, and some of the anomalies we have discussed (low price–earnings ratio, low book-to-market, small market capitalization, etc.). These factors may be combined in an informal manner, or a formal manner such as optimization, some form of weighted scoring method, or by screening. These approaches should be carried out in a manner that allows for adequate diversification in terms of, say, market sectors.

Of the formal approaches, screening is much the simplest. This can produce a portfolio that has a large overlap with one constructed by more complex weighted scoring methods such as multiple regression. Yet, while the textbooks mention screening, few pay it much attention, and many managers who sometimes screen stocks as a supplement to their decision-making process do it in a quite unsystematic manner.

Chapter 10 is an extract on screening from a book by Avner Arbel, a professor at Cornell University, which will help readers be more systematic in their screening. Arbel has published a number of papers on neglected, or what he calls generic, stocks, i.e., stocks neglected by investment analysts and the investing institutions. He shows that they outperform. Arbel's discussion of screening assumes that screening by degree of neglect is the important starting point. You don't have to agree with that, or the value of any of the other screens he uses, to find the discussion useful. Some sentences referring to other parts of the book from which the extract is taken have been omitted. The location of omitted sentences is indicated by ellipses.

After reading Arbel, students might like to put together a portfolio of 30 stocks by screening and see how it performs over the course of the academic year. Less than a year isn't much of a test, but if you outperform you will surely claim to be talented, and if you don't, you need only consider yourself as having flunked if you aren't able to provide a reason for your poor performance. This is surprisingly good training for real investment management! In putting together a set of screens don't use too many — every screen reduces the universe of investable stocks and if you use too many you will end up with no stocks. What one wants to do is use a few screens that measure different aspects of a stock. Four will probably suffice.

Investors who decide that the market is efficient, or that even if it is not, but that it is still unlikely that they will be able to outperform, should consider indexing their portfolio. Although indexation is mentioned in the textbooks, few explain the practical mechanics. In Chapter 11, I offer a short, non-technical, discussion of the mechanics of indexation.

REFERENCES

Chan, L.K.C., Hamao, Y. and Lakonishok, J. 1991. Fundamentals and Stock Returns in Japan. *Journal of Finance*, **46**, 1739–64.

Elton, E.J. and Gruber, M.J. 1989. Expectational Data and Japanese Stock Prices. *Japan and the World Economy*, **1**, 391–401.

Fama, E.F. 1991. Efficient Capital Markets: II. *Journal of Finance*, **46**, 1575–1617.

Lakonishok, J., Shleifer, A. and Vishny, R.W. 1993. *Contrarian Investment, Extrapolation, and Risk.* Faculty Working Paper No. 93–0128, College of Commerce and Business Administration, University of Illinois at Urbana-Champaign.

Levis, M. 1989. Stock Market Anomalies: A Re-Assessment Based on the U.K. Evidence. *Journal of Banking and Finance*, **13**, 675–96.

Tversky, A. and Kahneman, D. 1981. The Framing of Decisions and the Psychology of Choice. *Science*, **211**, 30 January, 453–58.

Ziemba, W.T. 1991. Japanese Security Market Regularities: Monthly, Turn-of-the-Month and Year, Holiday and Golden Week Effects. *Japan and the World Economy*, **3**, 119–46.

Ziemba, W.T. 1994. World Wide Security Market Regularities. *European Journal of Operational Research*, **74**, 198–229.

5
Briloff and the Capital Markets
George Foster

Abraham Briloff is a noted critic of contemporary financial reporting standards.[1] A distinctive feature of his approach is detailed analysis of the financial reports of individual companies. Several observers (e.g., Bernstein [1975]) have cited the "sharp declines" in the prices of companies criticized by Briloff at the time several of his articles were published (notably articles on land developers and computer leasors) as evidence consistent with capital market inefficiency. This note examines the security market reaction to companies criticized by Briloff in his published articles. One concern is whether the cited reactions of the land developers and computer leasors are ex post chosen because of their price drop or whether they are representative of the market reaction to companies cited in Briloff's articles. The evidence presented in Section 2 indicates that companies whose accounting practices are criticized by Briloff, suffer (on average) a price drop of approximately 8% on the day the article is published. In Section 3, a variety of explanations for this result are discussed.

1. ARTICLES EXAMINED

Two criteria were used to select the articles to examine: (a) the day the article became "publicly available" must be readily ascertainable,[2] and (b) the accounting practices of specific companies must be criticized. Fifteen articles met these two criteria. A resumé provided by Briloff as well as an independent check of several financial journals were used in selecting the articles. Table 5.1 (columns 1 and 2) details these fifteen articles and their date and place of publication. The specific companies criticized in each article were noted and security returns on as many as possible collected. In all, security returns on twenty-eight companies cited in the articles were collected.[3] Table 5.1 (column 3) details these companies.

2. METHODOLOGY AND RESULTS

Past research has reported that the announcement of such items as annual and interim earnings, dividends, and secondary issues appears to have an observable effect on the capital

Reprinted from: Foster, G. 1979: Briloff and the Capital Markets. *Journal of Accounting Research*, 17, 262–74. © Institute of Professional Accounting, 1979. Reprinted with permission.

Table 5.1 Articles of Briloff examined

Article	Journal/publication date	Companies cited that are examined in this note
1. "Dirty Pooling"	*Barron's* (July 15, 1968)	Gulf and Western; Ling-Temco-Vought (LTV)
2. "All a Fandangle?"	*Barron's* (December 2, 1968)	Leasco Data Processing; Levin-Townsend
3. "Much-Abused Good-will"	*Barron's* (April 28, 1969)	Levin-Townsend; ¹National General Corp.
4. "Out of Focus"	*Barron's* (July 28, 1969)	Perfect Film & Chemical Corp.
5. "Castles of Sand?"	*Barron's* (February 2, 1970)	Amrep Corp.; Canaveral International; Deltona Corp.; General Development Corp.; Great Southwest Corp.; Great Western United, Major Realty; Penn Central
6. "Tomorrow's Profits?"	*Barron's* (May 11, 1970)	Telex
7. "Six Flags at Half-Mast?"	*Barron's* (January 11, 1971)	Great Southwest Corp.; Penn Central
8. "Gimme Shelter"	*Barron's* (October 25, 1971)	Kaufman & Broad Inc.; U.S. Home Corp.; U.S. Financial Inc.
9. "SEC Questions Accounting"	*Commercial and Financial Chronicle* (November 2, 1972)	Penn Central
10. "$200 Million Question"	*Barron's* (December 18, 1972)	Leasco Corp.
11. "Sunrise, Sunset"	*Barron's* (May 14, 1973)	Kaufman & Broad
12. "Kaufman & Broad — More Questions"	*Commercial and Financial Chronicle* (July 12, 1973)	Kaufman & Broad
13. "You Deserve a Break. . . ."	*Barron's* (July 8, 1974)	McDonald's
14. "The Bottom Line: What's Going on at I.T.T." (Interview with Briloff)	*New York Magazine* (August 12, 1974)	I.T.T.
15. "Whose Deep Pocket?"	*Barron's* (July 19, 1976)	Reliance Group Inc.

market; moreover, much of this effect appears to be concentrated in a two-day period surrounding the announcement.[4] Given these results, I decided to use daily security returns in the analysis. The period covering thirty trading days before to thirty trading days after the publication of each article was chosen for examination. Given past research, any security price effect associated with the publication of Briloff's articles should be observable over this sixty-one-trading-day period.

The following model of capital market equilibrium is assumed to describe the pricing of capital assets (see Black [1972]):

$$E(\tilde{R}_{it}) = (\tilde{R}_{zt}) + \beta_i[E(\tilde{R}_{mt}) - E(\tilde{R}_{zt})] \tag{1}$$

where

R_{it} = return on asset i in period t,

R_{zt} = return on an asset whose returns are uncorrelated with R_{mt} in period t,

R_{mt} = return on the market portfolio in period t, and
β_i = relative risk of asset i.

Using (1), the effect of any new information on asset i becoming available in period t can be determined as:

$$\tilde{U}_{it} = \tilde{R}_{it} - E(\tilde{R}_{it} \mid \tilde{R}_{zt}, \tilde{R}_{mt}, \beta_i). \tag{2}$$

The procedure used to estimate the abnormal return ($\tilde{U}_{it}$) in (2) is based on the "companion portfolio" technique of Black and Scholes [1973]. Specifically, stocks are ranked on an estimate of beta in period $t-1$ and placed into one of twenty portfolios. The portfolio that stock i is placed in is termed the "companion portfolio" for that stock. The abnormal return on stock i in period t is estimated by "subtracting from the measured return [of stock i] the return on the 'companion portfolio' that has about the same dependence on $\tilde{R}_m$ and $\tilde{R}_z$ as the stock" (Black and Scholes [1973, p. 11]), that is:

$$\tilde{U}_{it} = \tilde{R}_{it} - \tilde{R}_{pt} \tag{3}$$

where R_{pt} = return on "companion portfolio" p in period t[5]. The abnormal returns for each security were then cumulated over the sixty-one-day period examined, to obtain the cumulative abnormal return (*CAR*):

$$CAR_{it} = \sum_{t=1}^{T} \tilde{U}_{it}. \tag{4}$$

The results are presented in two formats. In Figure 5.1, the average *CAR* behavior of the twenty-eight stocks is reported. In Figure 5.2, the average *CAR* behavior of the fifteen articles is presented; the average *CAR* of the stocks in each article is first calculated and then the averages of these *CAR*'s for the fifteen articles determined. The Figure 5.2 format avoids the possibility that the results in Figure 5.1 could be heavily influenced by one article in which a large number of companies were criticized (and whose stock prices were effected).

The results in Figures 5.1 and 5.2 are very similar. I will concentrate subsequent analysis on Figure 5.2 (which has the advantage that all observations are independent). All tests I report were also done on the Figure 5.1 data and yielded the same conclusions. The most noticeable feature of Figure 5.2 is the drop (of 0.086) in the average *CAR* on day 0, that is, the day Briloff's article was published. Is this drop a significant one? As a first step, the percent of the fifteen observations with negative abnormal returns on each day was computed. The days with the highest percents were:

> Day 0   : 93.3% Negative (14 out of 15)
> Day + 13 : 80%   Negative (12 out of 15)
> Day + 27 : 80%   Negative (12 out of 15)

Thus, based on the sign of the abnormal return, day 0 is the most extreme observation. If a binomial test is used and independence is assumed (see Siegel [1956]), the probability of fourteen out of fifteen negative observations is less than 0.01.[6] Days +13 and +27 were also significant at the 0.01 level. The drops in the *CAR* on days +13 and +27 were 0.017 and 0.014, respectively. Using a binomial test, day +4 exhibited a significant abnormal price increase — the increase in the *CAR* was 0.027, with twelve out of the fifteen observations

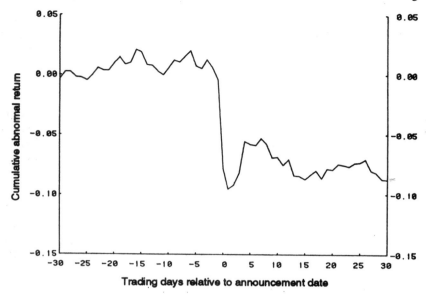

Figure 5.1 Market reaction for twenty-eight stocks

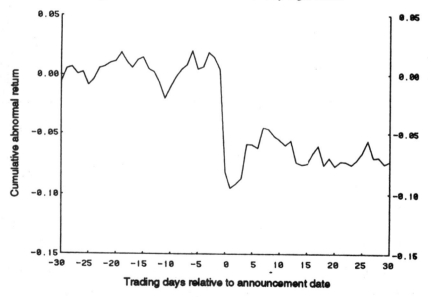

Figure 5.2 Market reaction for fifteen articles

positive. The *CAR* on day +30 is −0.073; this is not significantly different from the *CAR* on day 0 of −0.082. Thus, if a thirty-trading-day post-article announcement period is used, the significant drop on day 0 appears to be a permanent one.

A more powerful test of significance is the Kolmogorov–Smirnov (K–S) one-sample test, since it takes into account the size as well as the sign of the abnormal return on each day (see

Siegel [1956]). The test will be illustrated by reference to day 0. Under the null hypothesis of no negative effect on returns, there should be no clustering of observations with the lowest abnormal return at day 0; the probability of day 0 having the lowest return of the sixty-one returns examined is $\frac{1}{61}$. The number of observations with the lowest abnormal return during the -30 to $+30$ trading-day period at day 0 was first determined. Then the number of observations with the second lowest abnormal return during the -30 to $+30$ trading-day period at day 0 was determined. This procedure was repeated until all observations had been classified. Seven observations had the lowest abnormal return at day 0; one had the second lowest abnormal return; one the third lowest; two the fourth lowest.... The K–S test compares the actual cumulative distribution with the theoretical cumulative distribution and

Table 5.2   Results for Kolmogorov-Smirnov test: day 0

	# of Observations with ith lowest return	Cumulative % distribution of actuals	Cumulative % distribution under null	Difference between (2) and (3)
	(1)	(2)	(3)	(4)
Lowest return	7	0.467	0.016	0.451
Second lowest return	1	0.533	0.033	0.500
Third lowest return	1	0.600	0.049	0.551
Fourth lowest return	2	0.733	0.066	0.667
Fifth lowest return	0	0.733	0.082	0.651
Sixth lowest return	0	0.733	0.098	0.635
Seventh lowest return	1	0.800	0.115	0.685
Eighth lowest return	0	0.800	0.131	0.669
Sixty-first lowest return	0	1.000	1.000	1.000

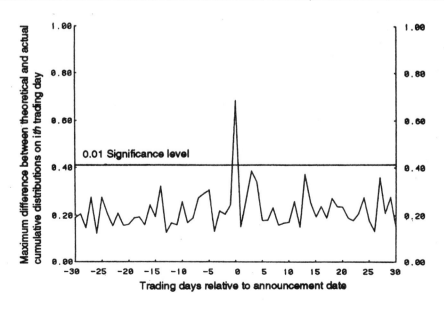

Figure 5.3   Kolmogorov–Smirnov test results for fifteen articles

concentrates on the maximum difference between the two. Summary results are presented in Table 5.2. The abnormal return at day 0 is at least within the seven lowest for twelve of the fifteen observations, that is, 80% of the cases examined. Under the null hypothesis, 0.115 $\left(\frac{7}{61}\right)$ of the cases would be expected to be in the seven with the lowest abnormal returns. This difference of 0.685 between the actual and theoretical cumulative distributions is the maximum difference for the sample. A difference of 0.404 between the two distributions is sufficient to reject the null hypothesis at the 0.01 level.

I applied the K–S test for each of the sixty-one trading days examined and observed the maximum difference between the actual and theoretical cumulative distributions for each day. A summary of these tests is presented in Figure 5.3. Only day 0 is significant at the 0.01 level. The results in Figures 5.2 and 5.3 suggest that associated with the publication of Briloff's articles is a significant negative and rapid capital market response.[7]

3. EXPLANATION OF THE RESULTS

What explanation can be given for the results in Section 2? At least five possible ones will be considered: (a) the capital market is inefficient; (b) Briloff, through his superior analytical insights, brings "new information" to the market; (c) Briloff, through his use of "nonpublic" information sources, brings "new information" to the market; (d) the exposés are cues for events such as increased government regulation of industry; and (e) the publication of Briloff's articles coincides with the release of other information about the cited companies.

Capital Market Inefficiency Explanation

The capital market inefficiency explanation raises the issue of what is meant by an efficient capital market. Definitions of efficiency with respect to a particular information set can be categorized into (a) those concerned with aggregate market variables such as security returns,[8] and (b) those concerned with aspects of individual investor decisions, such as the revision of portfolios.[9] At present, except for some highly specific results (e.g., Rubinstein [1974] and Ng [1975]), our knowledge of the relationship between individual investor behavior and security prices is limited. The implication is that our knowledge of the relationship between the various definitions of market efficiency is also limited. It is quite possible that one may infer (say) efficiency based on an aggregate market definition, but infer inefficiency based on an individual investor definition. When interpreting the results in Section 2, it is important for one to note that the variable examined was security prices. I will restrict my interpretation to a market efficiency definition related to this variable.

Fama [1976] defines a capital market as efficient, with respect to information set ϕ_t, if security prices "fully reflect" all the information in that set at time t. Notationally, this is expressed as:

$$f(P_{t+1} \mid \phi_t) = f_m(P_{t+1} \mid \phi_t^m) \tag{5}$$

where

$f(\cdot)$ = the "true" conditional probability distribution of security prices in period $t+1$,

ϕ_t = the information set available at period t,

$f_m(\cdot)$ = the market-assessed conditional probability distribution based on ϕ_t^m, and

ϕ_t^m = the information set used by the market at period t.

Several problems arise in testing whether the equality in (5) holds. First, $f(\cdot)$ is a construct that is not observable. The experimental control I use to proxy for $f(\cdot)$ is the asset-pricing model detailed in (1). Second, the equality in (5) does not specify what would constitute evidence consistent (or inconsistent) with capital market efficiency. It is necessary to assume something about the information set ϕ_t. Note that the definition of ϕ_t includes not only the specific signals in ϕ_t (what some call the "raw data"), but also the implications for $f(\cdot)$ of those signals. If we assume the information provided by Briloff is already costlessly available to all market participants (and the Black asset-pricing model is descriptively valid), then capital market efficiency implies there should be no price reaction to Briloff's articles.

That there is a significant price reaction of the kind detailed in Section 2, however, does not necessarily imply market inefficiency. The descriptive validity of the above-noted assumptions needs further investigation. The assumption that the information set provided by Briloff is already costlessly available to all market participants is an especially troublesome one. At a theoretical level, it is difficult to see what incentives there would be for information acquisition in such a world. Indeed, Grossman and Stiglitz [1975; 1976] argue that if information is costlessly available to all traders, it is possible that no market equilibrium would exist. At an empirical level, the analysis Briloff undertakes appears inconsistent with the information costlessly available to all investors assumption (see below).

"Superior Insight" Explanation

This explanation is based on the argument that Briloff possesses superior skills and is able to earn a (competitive) return from using these skills. The so-called information market, rather than the capital market, is seen as the key to the results (see Gonedes [1976]). Once one recognizes that individuals can earn economic rents from their information production activities, tests of capital market efficiency become more difficult to undertake. It is necessary to predict independently what is the "appropriate" price reaction to releases from such individuals, and then examine if the actual reaction is significantly different from the "appropriate" reaction. Only by independently predicting the "appropriate" price reaction can one devise a test that allows the alternative hypothesis of an inefficient market to be supported by the data. Two important attributes of an "appropriate" price reaction are its timing and its magnitude. To date, most tests have concentrated on the timing issue. A common hypothesis is that if a cue provides information to the market, the response to that cue should be rapid. Thus, once Briloff's articles are placed in the public domain (and are available to all market participations at a negligible cost), market efficiency predicts that any price reaction should be rapid. The data in Figures 5.1–5.3 generally support this prediction. On day -1, the average CAR in Figure 5.2 is 0.004. It drops to -0.082 on day 0 and is at -0.073 on day $+30$.

The other aspect of testing market efficiency is determining the magnitude (i.e., the direction and size) of the price effect one predicts, conditional on an efficient market. Frankly, I have difficulty making such a prediction. The returns to Briloff can take several forms not directly related to security prices (e.g., article and book royalties and an enhanced professional reputation). The readers of Briloff's articles also could find them newsworthy for factors such as their insights into the development of accounting and auditing standards. We can only conjecture whether, based on the information Briloff provides to the capital market, a price drop of 8% is (or is not) consistent with an efficient market.

It is important to note that this problem in ex ante predicting the magnitude of the price effect conditional on an efficient market is also apparent (although not always recognized) in many other empirical studies. For instance, Ball and Brown's [1968] study of annual accounting earnings is frequently cited as evidence supporting market efficiency. Though the study may support efficiency with regard to the timing of the price reaction, it is difficult to assert that it supports market efficiency with regard to the magnitude of the price reaction. We have little theory which tells us whether the composite CAR (API) of 8.3% which they reported should have been 5, 7, or 9%, etc., conditional on an efficient capital market.[10]

"Nonpublic" Information Source Explanation

Market efficiency (in the sense of (5)) is always defined with respect to a particular information set. One possible explanation for the results in Section 2 is that the data sources used by Briloff extend beyond the information set "publicly available" in period t. Unfortunately, there is no clear-cut distinction between "publicly available" and "nonpublicly" available information sets.[11] Rather, there is a continuum. At one end of the spectrum are items like annual reports and company announcements that appear to be publicly available at essentially zero cost. Briloff makes extensive use of such items. In nearly all cases they include those of the companies criticized. In some cases they also include those of other companies. For example, in the "Tomorrow's Profit" (*Barron's*, May 11, 1970) article the accounting practices of Telex (a seller of computer disc and tape drives) were criticized. One information source used was the prospectus of Hudson Leasing Corporation, "a Long Island concern instrumental in financing Telex's leasing activities." This prospectus revealed information about Telex's operations not disclosed in Telex's Annual Report, for example, about its continuing responsibility to maintain the equipment it leases throughout its useful lives.

Further along the information availability spectrum are items such as SEC filings which may be available only at restricted locations or by paying set fees. Briloff also uses these sources. For example, in "Out of Focus" (*Barron's*, July 28, 1969), Perfect Film and Chemical's accounting practices were examined. The use of pooling accounting for the acquisition of a 50.6% interest in Plume and Atwood by Perfect Film was criticized. In order to estimate the "net tangible assets" from the acquisition reported on Perfect's books, he used both the Plume and Atwood 1968 Annual Report and documents filed with "the SEC describing the proposed acquisition."

Even further along the spectrum of information availability are company memoranda, etc. Briloff also appears to use this source on occasion. For instance, in "You Deserve a Break ..." (*Barron's*, July 8, 1974), he quoted from an August 18, 1973 memorandum from the company's corporate counsel concerning the sale of shares that "McDonald's employees, executives and others" had received from Ray A. Kroc. The memorandum discussed the appropriate forms employees should file if they decided "to sell all or any part of the gift shares."

To gain some overall perspective of the information sources used by Briloff, a "source analysis" of each of the fifteen articles was made. The sources explicitly referred to in each article were noted and classified into one of eight categories.[12] The number of items referred to in each category over the fifteen articles was:

	# of items	
Annual and interim reports	32	39%
Prospectuses	15	18%
SEC documents	19	23%
Investment analyst/brokerage house reports	3	4%
Convention reports filed with State Insurance Commissioners	3	4%
Company news releases (letters, etc.) or reports thereof in *Wall Street Journal/Barron's*	7	9%
Company tax returns	1	1%
Company memorandum	2	2%
	82	100%

Based on this "source analysis," my judgement is that it is difficult to explain the drop on day 0 in Figures 5.1 and 5.2 by arguing that the major sources Briloff used were not previously readily available or were only available by incurring substantial acquisition costs.

Exposes as Cues for Other Events Explanation

This explanation assumes that due to the effective way Briloff writes (and the medium in which he writes), he acts as a catalyst to parties who can affect the future cash flows of firms (i.e., in addition to any capital market effect flowing from increased accounting disclosure). Consider the "Castles of Sand" (*Barrons's*, February 2, 1970) article where the financial reporting and management practices of land developers were criticized. This article could have increased the probability of congressional or SEC investigation into the operations of these companies in this industry.

It is difficult to collect data which directly examine whether this explanation is a major one. Information on how the criticisms of single individuals influence the decisions of congressmen, bureaucrats, etc., is not easily available. However, by examining the content of Briloff's articles, some indirect evidence appears possible. In many cases, Briloff's criticisms are of the accounting decisions of specific companies, without any attempt to elicit governmental, SEC, etc., restrictions on the decisions of these companies. For instance, in "You Deserve a Break," the accounting treatment of "gifts" of McDonald's stock by Ray Kroc to McDonald's employees was criticized. There was, however, no attempt to argue that such "gifts" should not have been made. In only three of the fifteen articles were the criticisms leveled more at the industry level than at the firm level, that is, in "All a Fandangle," "Castles of Sand," and "Gimme Shelter." In as much as criticisms leveled at an industry, rather than at an individual firm, are more likely to generate congressional movements for "reform," the fact that only three articles were exposited at the industry level is not very strong evidence for the "exposés as a cue for other events" explanation. Moreover, the average drop in the *CAR* on day 0 for these three articles (-0.072) was not significantly different from the average drop on day 0 (-0.089) for the other twelve articles.

Other Information Releases Explanation

There is always the possibility in any experiment that uncontrolled factors may cause the results observed. In Figures 5.1–5.3, day 0 is the date that each article is published. If the publication of each Briloff article coincides with the release of other information about the cited companies, then ambiguity would exist over the cause of the results. The *Wall Street Journal Index* was examined as a check on this possibility. For only four out of the twenty-eight companies examined was there an information item cited on day 0 in the *WSJ Index*. Moreover, for these four companies, it was difficult to make unequivocal inferences that the information item should have a negative effect. For instance, the news release for Great Southwest Corporation (on February 2, 1970—the day the "Castles of Sand" article was published) was "Entered into a joint agreement with C. Brewer and Co., a unit of International Utilities to develop 285,000 acres in Hawaii." An examination of the items released on day −2, day −1, day +1, and day +2 also revealed little support for this explanation. Thus, if we assume the *Wall Street Journal Index*'s summary of information releases about companies is reasonably comprehensive, the "other information releases" explanation does not appear to be a likely one.

4. CONCLUSION

Companies whose accounting practices are criticized by Briloff appear, on average, to suffer an immediate drop in price of approximately 8%. Using a thirty-trading-day postannouncement period, this drop is a permanent one. Five possible explanations for this result were examined in Section 3. I argued that three — the nonpublic information sources explanation, the exposés as cues for other events explanation, and the other information releases explanation — were not likely to be the major causes of the immediate price drop. Although the timing of the price reaction is consistent with an efficient market, I am unable (given existing data) to determine whether the magnitude of the price reaction is consistent with the capital market inefficiency explanation or the superior insight (information market) explanation.[13] I hope this analysis illustrates that when one goes beyond "publicly available information," tests of capital market efficiency raise difficult research issues that can leave the results subject to varying interpretations.

ENDNOTES

1. *Unaccountable Accounting* (New York: Harper & Row, 1972) and *More Debits than Credits* (New York: Harper & Row, 1976) illustrate both the breadth and style of his writings.

2. The appropriate journals were contacted to confirm the "chosen" date of publication. For instance, articles appear in *Barron's* dated on a Monday. *Dow Jones and Company* indicated that *Barron's* is published on Friday nights, for delivery to subscribers on Monday morning. Thus, the earliest date the security market could react to the article is the Monday dated on the journal. See endnote 6 for problems in deciding on day 0 for one article.

3. The basic data source was the *CRSP* daily security return file. Where data were not available from this source, the *ISL* books were used. In several cases, individual companies provided daily returns for the appropriate period.

4. See Foster [1978, chap. 11] for a survey of this research.

5. For *CRSP* stocks (twenty-four of the twenty-eight examined), the $\tilde{U}_{it}$'s were obtained from the "excess returns" tape. For the other four stocks, I assumed a relative risk of one and used the *S&P Composite 500 Stock Index* as the "companion portfolio."

6. The one article which was associated with a positive abnormal return on day 0 was "Kaufman & Broad — More Questions" (*Commercial & Financial Chronicle*, July 12, 1973). This is the only article for which there was some uncertainty over the centering of day 0. The July 12 date is when the article was first available in the *Commercial & Financial Chronicle*. However, the article was based on an address Briloff gave at the G. Tsai Institutional Investor Luncheon in New York City on July 9, 1973. The abnormal returns for Kaufman & Broad for July 9 were -0.017; for July 10, -0.055; and for July 11, -0.010. Thus, if one uses the address date as day 0, every one of Briloff's fifteen articles I examined was associated with a negative price change on day 0.

7. As a crude test of whether there is any difference in effect over time, I calculated the mean drop in the first eight articles (-0.074) and the mean drop in the last seven articles (-0.099). These means do not suggest a significant time effect.

8. For example, see the definition in Fama [1976], discussed subsequently in this note.

9. For example: "The market is action — efficient with respect to information set A if the optimal position of *any* investor, given the data in *any* information set B, the data in A, and the current price is equal to his optimal position given only the data in B and the price" (Beja [1976, p. 10]). See also Rubinstein [1975] and Beaver [1976] for further discussion of market efficiency definitions.

10. See Foster [1978, p. 357] for further discussion of this point relating to studies which examine the security market reaction to accounting changes.

11. This lack of a clear-cut distinction makes it difficult to classify studies into one of three forms of market efficiency (weak, semistrong, and strong) outlined in Fama [1970]. Sharpe foreshadowed these problems in his commentary on the Fama paper: ". . . the definition of semi-strong efficiency is open to dispute (when is information publicly available? which investors are in the public? how soon must the information be available? at what price?). . ." [1970, p. 418].

12. This "source analysis" is obviously not without problems, e.g. (a) I restricted myself to sources Briloff explicitly cited, which may only be a subset of all the sources he used, and (b) I only counted the sources rather than indicated their relative importance to his analysis.

13. Note: "Adjusting for the costs of information production activities involves a variety of heady problems in data collection. . . . It is not clear that any "real world" data are available for attacking these problems — not a very cheery thought for those interested in empirical work" (Gonedes [1976, p. 623]).

REFERENCES

Ball, R. and Brown, P. "An Empirical Evaluation of Accounting Income Numbers." *Journal of Accounting Research* (Autumn 1968): 159–78.

Beaver, W.H. "Market Efficiency." Working paper, Stanford University, 1976.

Beja, A. "The Limited Information Efficiency of Market Processes." Working paper, University of California, Berkeley, 1976.

Bernstein, L.A. "In Defence of Fundamental Investment Analysis." *Financial Analysts Journal* (January/February 1975): 57–61.

Black, F. "Capital Market Equilibrium with Restricted Borrowing." *Journal of Business* (July 1972): 444–54.

— — and Scholes, M. "The Behavior of Security Returns around Ex-Dividend Days." Working paper, University of Chicago, 1973.

Briloff, A.J. *Unaccountable Accounting*. New York: Harper & Row, 1972.

— —. *More Debits than Credits*. New York: Harper & Row, 1976.

Fama, E.F. "Efficient Capital Markets: A Review of Theory and Empirical Work." *Journal of Finance* (May 1970): 383–417.

— —. *Foundations of Finance*. New York: Basic Books, 1976.

Foster, G. *Financial Statement Analysis*. Englewood Cliffs, N.J.: Prentice-Hall, 1978.

Gonedes, N.J. "The Capital Market, The Market for Information, and External Accounting." *Journal of Finance* (May 1976): 611–30.

Grossman, S. and Stiglitz, J. "On the Impossibility of Informationally Efficient Markets." Working paper, Stanford University, 1975.

— —. "Information and Competitive Price Systems." *American Economic Review* (May 1976): 246–53.

Ng, D.S. "Information Accuracy and Social Welfare under Homogeneous Beliefs." *Journal of Financial Economics* (March 1975): 53–70.

Rubinstein, M. "An Aggregation Theorem for Securities Markets." *Journal of Financial Economics* (September 1974): 225–44.

— —. "Securities Market Efficiency in an Arrow-Debreu Economy." *American Economic Review* (December 1975): 812–24.

Sharpe, W.H. "Comments" on Fama [1970]. *Journal of Finance* (May 1970): 418–420.

Siegel, S. *Nonparametric Statistics*. New York: McGraw-Hill, 1956.

6
Stock Market Regularities: A Synthesis of the Evidence and Explanations
Donald B. Keim

1 INTRODUCTION*

The capital asset pricing model (CAPM) has occupied a central position in financial economics over the twenty years since its origins in the papers by Sharpe (1964), Lintner (1965) and Treynor. Given certain simplifying assumptions,[1] the CAPM states that the expected rate of return on any asset is related to the riskless rate and the expected market return as follows:

$$E(R_i) = R_Z + [E(R_M) - R_Z]\beta_i \tag{1}$$

where:

$E(R_i)$ is the expected rate of return on asset i;

R_Z is the rate of return on the riskless asset in the Sharpe–Lintner–Treynor model and is the rate of return of an asset with zero correlation with the market in Black's (1972) extension;

$E(R_M)$ is the expected rate of return on the market portfolio of all marketable assets; and

β_i (beta) is the asset's sensitivity to market movements.

If the model is correct and security markets are efficient (Fama, 1970), security returns will *on average* conform to the above relation. Persistent departures, however, represent violations of the joint hypothesis that both the CAPM and efficient market hypothesis are correct.[2]

The strict set of assumptions underlying the CAPM has prompted numerous criticisms. Although any model proposes a simplified view of the world, that is not sufficient basis for its rejection; the rejection or acceptance of the theory should rest on the scientific evidence.

Reprinted from: Keim, D.B. 1988: Stock Market Regularities: A Synthesis of the Evidence and Explanations. In Dimson, E. ed. 1988: *Stock Market Anomalies*. Cambridge: Cambridge University Press.

Sophisticated tests of the propositions of the CAPM were made possible by the creation of a computerized data base of stock prices and distributions at the University of Chicago in the 1960s. Numerous studies were conducted in the early 1970s, the most prominent being those conducted by Black *et al.* (1972), Blume and Friend (1973) and Fama and MacBeth (1973). The results of these studies were generally interpreted as supportive of the CAPM, although the coefficient on beta — representing an estimate of the market risk premium — was only marginally important in explaining cross-sectional differences in average security returns.

Although the early tests lend some credence to the CAPM in its basic form, Roll (1977) raises some legitimate questions regarding the validity of these tests. Very briefly, Roll argues that tests performed with any market portfolio other than the true market portfolio are not tests of the CAPM and that tests of the CAPM can be extremely sensitive to the choice of market proxy. He also points out that the need to specify an alternative model to the CAPM in some of the early tests — e.g. the Fama and MacBeth test of whether residual variance or beta squared are relevant for explaining returns — can lead to faulty inference. That is, the CAPM may be false, but if residual variance or beta squared do not explain the violation, the test will not reject the CAPM. In response to Roll's first point, Stambaugh (1982) constructs broader market indices that include, for example, bonds and real estate, and finds that such tests do not seem to be very sensitive to the choice of market proxy. The second point has been addressed in the work of Gibbons (1982), Stambaugh (1982) and others, which introduced the use of multivariate tests that do not require the specification of an alternative asset pricing model when testing the CAPM. These multivariate tests have not, however, yielded conclusive results regarding the validity of the CAPM.

Since the CAPM is not unambiguously supported by the tests, researchers have formulated alternative models. Many have developed equilibrium models by relaxing some of the CAPM assumptions. For example, Mayers (1972) allows for non-marketable assets such as human capital and Brennan (1970) and Litzenberger and Ramaswamy (1979) relax the no-tax assumption. Others have examined more *ad hoc* alternatives to the CAPM in the spirit of Fama and MacBeth. For example, Banz (1981) examines the importance of market value of common equity and Basu (1977) examines the importance of P/E ratios in explaining beta-risk-adjusted returns.

The remainder of this chapter discusses such alternatives to the CAPM. The next section addresses models that relax the no-tax assumption of the CAPM. Section 3 contains a discussion of the empirical evidence relating to the ability of market value of equity, E/P ratios and other *ad hoc* variables to explain violations of the CAPM. This evidence is followed by a rather lengthy section on potential explanations that addresses, among other issues, the exaggerated occurrence of these effects in January. Section 5 discusses other persistent patterns in security returns; the chapter ends with some concluding remarks.

2 AFTER-TAX ASSET PRICING MODELS

A well-known extension of the CAPM explicitly recognizes the complexity of the tax laws in many countries. For example, higher marginal tax rates of dividend income versus capital gains should make taxable investors prefer a dollar of pre-tax capital gain to a dollar of dividends. Under such conditions as exist in the U.S., Brennan (1970) and Litzenberger and Ramaswamy (1979) extend the CAPM to include an extra factor, dividend yield. The hypothesis is that, holding risk constant, the higher is a stock's dividend yield, the higher is the required before-tax return to compensate taxable investors for the higher tax liability.

There are, of course, counter-arguments. Miller and Scholes (1978) argue that the tax code has provisions that permit investors to transform dividend income into capital gains. If the marginal investors are using these or other effective shelters, then the before-tax rate on dividend-paying stocks may be no different from stocks that do not pay dividends even though the tax law appears to penalize dividends. Nevertheless, the tax differential has prompted some tax-exempt institutions to 'tilt' their portfolios toward higher yielding securities with the hope of capturing the benefits of the supposedly higher before-tax returns without bearing the costs of the higher implied taxes.

The effectiveness of such a strategy, of course, hinges on whether these after-tax models are supported by the evidence. The general form of the after-tax CAPM is

$$E(R_i) = a_0 + a_1\beta_i + a_2d_i \tag{2}$$

where d_i is the dividend yield for security i and a_2 is an implicit tax coefficient that is independent of the level of the dividend yield. The question is whether a_2 is reliably positive and consistent with realistic tax rates.

Empirical testing of the hypothesis that $a_2 = 0$ presents the researcher with a number of difficult problems. For example, since asset pricing models are cast in terms of expectations, the researcher needs to arrive at a suitable *ex-ante* dividend yield measure. Further, he must ask whether the tax effects that motivate the model occur at a single point in time (i.e. the ex date) or whether they are spread over a longer period. Finally, most researchers, based on the models of Brennan and of Litzenberger and Ramaswamy (1979), have assumed a linear relation between dividend yields and returns, even though the relation might be more complicated.

Studies have employed a variety of definitions of dividend yield and methodologies in addressing these issues. In the interest of brevity, we forego discussion of the methodological subtleties and simply summarize the major results. Table 6.1, adopted from Litzenberger and Ramaswamy (1982) and updated, reports estimates of the dividend yield coefficient a_2. In each instance the estimate of a_2 is positive indicating that, holding beta risk constant, the higher is the dividend yield the higher is the before-tax rate of return for common stocks. Although not all of the coefficients are significantly different from zero (e.g. Black and Scholes, 1974; Miller and Scholes, 1982) and not all authors attribute the positive coefficients to taxes (e.g. Blume, 1980; Gordon and Bradford, 1980), the evidence in many of the studies appears to be consistent with the after-tax models.

The story may not be as simple, though, as the models of Brennan (1970) and Litzenberger and Ramaswamy (1979) suggest. Blume (1980) and Litzenberger and Ramaswamy (1980) find that the yield-return relation is not linear for some definitions of dividend yield. They find that the average return for non-dividend paying firms is higher than for many dividend paying firms. Further, Keim (1985, 1986a) finds that this non-linear relation is primarily due to the exaggerated occurrence of the effect in January. Keim (1985) uses a definition of dividend yield similar to Blume and estimates dividend yield coefficients separately in January and non-January months. The estimated coefficients are positive and significant in January *and* non-January months, but the January coefficient of 1.15 $[t(a_2^{JAN} = 0) = 5.6]$ is significantly larger $[t(a_2^{JAN} - \alpha_2^{F-D}) = 4.6]$ than the non-January coefficient of 0.18 $[t(a_2^{F2-D} = 0)^2 = 3.3]$. Such a finding is not entirely consistent with the simple tax-related models and is suggestive of the possible manifestation of other anomalous effects that exhibit January seasonals, such as the size effect.

Table 6.1 Summary of implied tax rates from studies of the relation between dividend yields and stock returns

Author(s) and date of study	Test period and return interval	Implied tax rate (%) (t-statistic)
Black and Scholes (1974)	1936–66, monthly	22 (0.9)
Blume (1980)	1936–76, quarterly	52 (2.1)
Gordon and Bradford (1980)	1926–78, monthly	18 (8.5)
Litzenberger and Ramaswamy (1979)	1936–77, monthly	24 (8.6)
Litzenberger and Ramaswamy (1982)	1940–80, monthly	14–23 (4.4–8.8)
Miller and Scholes (1982)	1940–78, monthly	4 (1.1)
Morgan (1982)	1936–77, monthly	21 (11.0)
Rosenberg and Marathe (1979)	1931–66, monthly	40 (1.9)
Stone and Barter (1979)	1947–70, monthly	56 (2.0)

3 OTHER OBSERVED ASSET PRICING REGULARITIES

The Size Effect

Considerable interest has been generated in the financial and academic communities by the finding of a significant relation between common stock returns and the market value of common equity, commonly referred to as the size effect. Other things equal, the smaller is firm size the larger is the stock's expected return. Banz (1981) was the first to document this phenomenon. For the period from 1931 to 1975, Banz estimated a model of the form

$$E(R_i) = a_0 + a_1\beta_i + a_2 S_i \tag{3}$$

where S_i is a measure of the relative market capitalization ('size') for firm i. He found that the statistical association between returns and size is negative and of approximately the same magnitude as that between returns and beta, documented in, for example, Fama and MacBeth (1973).

Reinganum (1981, 1982), using daily data over the period from 1963 to 1977, found that portfolios of small firms had substantially higher returns, on average, than large firms. Table 6.2, adopted from Reinganum (1982), reports average returns and other characteristics for portfolios comprising the ten deciles of size for NYSE and AMEX firms. The difference in returns between the smallest and largest firms is about 30% annually. In response to Roll's (1981) conjecture that this size effect may be a statistical artifact of improperly measured risk due to the infrequent trading of small firms, Reinganum (1982) estimates betas according to methods designed to account for these problems (see Scholes and Williams, 1977; Dimson, 1979). He finds that the magnitude of the size effect is not very sensitive to the use of these estimates. (The Dimson estimator is reported in Table 6.2). Blume and Stambaugh (1983) demonstrate, however, that the portfolio strategy implicit in Reinganum's paper (requiring daily rebalancing of the portfolio to equal weights) produces upward-biased estimates of

Table 6.2 Mean daily returns (standard errors) and estimated betas for ten size portfolios of NYSE and AMEX firms, 1964–1978*

Portfolio	Mean daily mean (%)	Average median market value ($ million)	OLS beta	Dimson beta
Smallest	0.142 (0.015)	4.7	0.75	1.69
2	0.092 (0.015)	11.1	0.87	1.64
3	0.079 (0.014)	19.8	0.90	1.55
4	0.064 (0.140)	31.5	0.96	1.50
5	0.058 (0.014)	48.3	0.98	1.46
6	0.053 (0.013)	75.4	0.97	1.39
7	0.046 (0.013)	120.4	0.95	1.31
8	0.042 (0.013)	213.4	0.97	1.24
9	0.035 (0.012)	436.3	0.95	1.13
Largest	0.024 (0.012)	1086.0	0.98	0.97

*Table adapted from Reinganum (1982).

small-firm portfolio returns due to a 'bid-ask bias' that is inversely related to size. Blume and Stambaugh show that the size-related premium is halved in portfolio strategies that avoid this bias.

Two reservations are usually expressed regarding implementation of these findings — the market for the smallest capitalization firms is rather illiquid and the firms in this market do not meet minimum capitalization requirements for many institutional investors. The average market values reported in Table 6.2 demonstrate that such potential constraints may not be binding. The table shows that the effect is approximately linear in the decile of size, meaning that portfolios of securities with successively smaller firm values yield successively larger risk-adjusted returns. The evidence suggests a wide array of possible portfolios with higher average returns (in some cases, substantially higher returns) than a portfolio of large firms such as the S&P 500 — a typically-used performance benchmark in the investment industry.[3] In other words, the abnormal return opportunities presented by smaller firm stocks are not confined to the very smallest and least liquid stocks on the NYSE and AMEX.

The abnormal return opportunities presented by smaller firm stocks do not seem to be confined to the U.S. Analysis of stock returns on four major stock exchanges — Australia, Canada, Japan and United Kingdom — has revealed a distinct size-return relation.[4] The results are summarized in Table 6.3. It is difficult to draw comparisons about the relative magnitude of the size effect across the four countries because of differing time periods and research design (e.g. some studies use size quintiles, others use deciles). Nevertheless, in each country there is an inverse relation between stock returns and market capitalization.

Much of the subsequent research on the U.S. size effect has attempted to provide a more complete characterization of the phenomenon. For example, we know that among the firms

84

Table 6.3 The firm size effect: international evidence*

Australia (1958–81)[a]

Size portfolio	Return % (std error)
Smallest	6.75 (0.64)
2	2.23 (0.39)
3	1.74 (0.31)
4	1.32 (0.27)
5	1.48 (0.24)
6	1.27 (0.24)
7	1.15 (0.24)
8	1.22 (0.24)
9	1.18 (0.25)
Largest	1.02 (0.29)

Canada (1951–80)[b]

Size portfolio	Return % (std error) 1951–72	Return % (std error) 1973–80
Smallest	2.02 (0.27)	1.67 (0.58)
2	1.48 (0.22)	1.66 (0.56)
3	1.14 (0.22)	1.41 (0.59)
4	0.99 (0.23)	1.39 (0.56)
Largest	0.90 (0.23)	1.23 (0.58)

Japan (1966–83)[c]

Size portfolio	Return % (std error)
Smallest	2.03 (0.35)
2	1.50 (0.32)
3	1.38 (0.29)
4	1.17 (0.27)
Largest	1.14 (0.27)

United Kingdom (1956–80)[d]

Size portfolio	Return % 1956–65	Return % 1966–80
Smallest	1.27	1.00
2	1.18	0.89
Largest	0.98	0.84

Note: *Monthly returns are reported for each country.
Sources:
[a]Brown et al. (1983b).
[b]Berges et al. (1984).
[c]Nakamura and Terada (1984).
[d]Reinganum and Shapiro (1983).

that academic researchers consider 'small,'[5] those small firms with the largest abnormal returns tend to be firms that have recently become small (or that have recently declined in price), that do not pay a dividend or that have high dividend yields (Keim, 1986a) that have low prices (Stoll and Whaley, 1983; Blume and Stambaugh, 1983) and that have low P/E ratios (Reinganum, 1981; Basu, 1983).

Others have examined the time-related patterns of portfolio returns stratified by market capitalization. Brown et al. (1983a) find that when averaged over all months the size effect reverses itself for sustained periods; in many periods there is a consistent premium for small size, in (fewer) other periods there is a discount. In other words, there have been periods (one, for example, was 1969–73) when a small-capitalization strategy would have underperformed a large-capitalization strategy on a risk-adjusted basis.

The magnitude of the size effect also seems to differ across days of the week and months of the year. Keim and Stambaugh (1984) find that the size effect becomes more pronounced as the week progresses and is most pronounced on Friday. These tendencies are evident as you scan across the rows of Table 6.4. Reported in Table 6.4 is the average magnitude of the size effect as measured by the difference in returns between the smallest and largest deciles of firms on the NYSE and AMEX, cross classified by day of the week and month of the year

Table 6.4 Temporal behavior of the size effect. Average differences (t-statistics) in daily returns (percent) between portfolios constructed from firms in the top and bottom decile of size (measured by market value of equity) on the NYSE and AMEX over the period 1963–79

	Monday	Tuesday	Wednesday	Thursday	Friday	Mean daily return over all days
January	0.742	0.698	0.607	0.645	0.821	0.702
	(6.51)	(5.47)	(4.80)	(5.54)	(7.07)	(13.01)
February	0.288	0.150	0.181	0.217	0.240	0.212
	(2.80)	(1.78)	(2.15)	(2.41)	(2.46)	(5.18)
March	0.091	−0.006	0.171	0.175	0.127	0.112
	(1.31)	(−0.08)	(2.99)	(3.14)	(1.97)	(3.81)
April	−0.010	−0.096	0.008	0.047	0.159	0.018
	(−0.14)	(−1.64)	(0.10)	(0.81)	(3.00)	(0.62)
May	0.196	−0.093	0.052	−0.007	0.153	0.057
	(2.57)	(−1.21)	(1.00)	(−0.08)	(2.23)	(1.74)
June	−0.038	−0.135	0.081	0.011	0.171	0.018
	(−0.46)	(−1.80)	(1.71)	(0.17)	(2.62)	(0.57)
July	−0.027	0.151	−0.106	0.152	0.242	0.084
	(−0.38)	(2.35)	(−1.33)	(2.24)	(3.62)	(2.61)
August	0.034	−0.020	0.018	0.130	0.162	0.065
	(0.47)	(−0.28)	(0.27)	(1.68)	(2.28)	(2.00)
September	0.156	0.108	0.043	0.044	0.210	0.111
	(1.50)	(1.84)	(0.71)	(0.52)	(3.68)	(3.37)
October	−0.241	−0.159	−0.080	0.043	0.050	−0.077
	(−2.16)	(−1.90)	(−0.76)	(0.66)	(0.60)	(−1.87)
November	−0.110	−0.158	−0.069	−0.007	0.247	−0.016
	(−1.52)	(−1.61)	(−0.89)	(−0.07)	(4.41)	(−0.44)
December	−0.155	−0.182	−0.023	0.068	0.402	0.022
	(−1.81)	(−1.87)	(−0.20)	(0.90)	(5.44)	(0.52)
Mean return over all months	0.069	0.021	0.075	0.128	0.249	0.109
	(2.60)	(0.85)	(3.08)	(5.43)	(10.98)	(9.84)

over the period 1963–79. The bottom row which measures the average effect by day of the week, demonstrates the tendency for the size effect to increase as the week draws to a close.

The most dramatic seasonal pattern in the size effect is found at the turn of the year. Keim (1983) finds that the size effect is concentrated in January: approximately 50% of the return difference between small and large firm stocks found by Reinganum (1981) is concentrated in January. The January seasonal in the size effect is evident in the rightmost column of Table 6.4. Keim further reports that 50% of this January effect is concentrated in the first five trading days of the year. This turn-of-the-year return behavior is also found by Roll (1983a) who notes that, in addition, small firms have abnormally large returns on the last trading day in December.

The Price/Earnings Effect

Earnings-related strategies have a long tradition in the investment community. The most popular of such strategies, buying stocks that sell at low multiples of earnings, can be traced at least to Graham and Dodd (1940, p. 533) who proposed that 'a necessary but not a sufficient condition' for investing in a common stock is 'a reasonable ratio of market price to average earnings.' They advocated that a prudent investor should never pay as much as 20 times earnings and a suitable multiplier should be 12 or less.

Nicholson (1960) published the first extensive study of the relation between P/E multiples and subsequent total returns showing that low P/E stocks consistently provided returns greater than the average stock. Basu (1977) introduced the notion that P/E ratios may explain violations of the CAPM and found that, for his sample of NYSE firms, there was a distinct negative relation between P/E ratios and average returns in excess of those predicted by the CAPM. If one had followed his strategy of buying the quintile of smallest P/E stocks and selling short the quintile of largest P/E stocks, based on annual ranking, the average annual abnormal return would have been 6.75% (before commissions and other transaction costs) over the 1957 to 1971 period. Reinganum (1981), analyzing both NYSE and AMEX firms, confirmed and extended Basu's findings using returns data to 1975.

Some have argued that because firms in the same industry tend to have similar P/E ratios, a portfolio strategy that concentrates on low P/E stocks may indeed benefit from higher than average returns, but at a cost of reduced diversification. These arguments also suggest that the P/E effect may in fact be an industry effect. Peavy and Goodman (1983) address this potential bias and examine the P/E ratio of a stock relative to its industry P/E (PER). They find a distinct negative relation between PERs and abnormal returns over the 1970–80 period. A portfolio strategy that bought the quintile of lowest PER stocks and sold short the stocks in the highest PER quintile would have yielded an annualized abnormal return of 20.80% over the period. These results, in conjunction with the findings of Basu and Reinganum, suggest that the P/E ratio — or an underlying and perhaps more fundamental variable for which P/E is a proxy — is capable of explaining a considerable portion of the variation in cross-sectional security returns.

The Value Line Enigma

Investment advisory services often base their recommendations on earnings-related information. The largest and most consistently successful advisory service is the Value Line Investor Survey. Value Line forecasts the prospective performance of approximately 1700 common stocks on a weekly basis. Value Line separates these stocks into five categories of expected return based on historical and forecast information such as earnings momentum and *P/E* ratios.

The success of the Value Line system has been borne out by several academic studies. Black (1973), Holloway (1981) and Copeland and Mayers (1982) all find that, after adjusting for beta risk, investors can obtain abnormal performance by, for example, buying group 1 securities and selling short group 5 securities. Stickel (1985) finds that investors can earn abnormal returns by devising strategies based on rank changes (e.g. buying stocks upgraded from group 2 to group 1).

Value Line's successful performance is puzzling for the same reasons that the size and *P/E* effects are puzzling — predetermined variables are used to construct portfolios that have abnormal returns relative to the CAPM. It is possible that there is a high degree of association between a ranking produced by Value Line's system and a simple ranking based on *P/E* or size. Indeed, the evidence of Stickel suggests that much of Value Line's abnormal performance might be attributable to small firms. More research is necessary to sort out these issues.

Interrelation between the Effects

The literature discussed in the preceding sections documents a strong cross-sectional relation between abnormal returns and market capitalization, *P/E* ratios and dividend yields. Other effects have also been documented in the literature, perhaps most notably the relation between risk-adjusted returns and the ratio of price per share to book value per share (*P/B*) discussed most recently by Rosenberg *et al.* (1985). Few would argue that these separate findings are entirely independent phenomena, since market capitalization, *P/E* and *P/B* are computed using a common variable — price per share of the common stock. Further, results in Blume and Husic (1973), Stoll and Whaley (1983) and Blume and Stambaugh (1983) reveal a cross-sectional association between price per share and average returns.

To demonstrate the association among these variables, Table 6.5 reports average values of *P/B*, market capitalization, *E/P* and price for ten portfolios constructed of NYSE firms on

Table 6.5 Average values of price to book (*P/B*), market value, earnings to price (*E/P*) and price for ten portfolios of NYSE firms constructed on the basis of increasing price to book values[a] (1964–82)

Price/book portfolio	Average *P/B*	Average market value ($ million)	Average *E/P*	Average price ($)
Lowest	0.52	217.1	0.06	20.09
2	0.83	402.5	0.11	22.97
3	1.00	498.6	0.11	25.08
4	1.14	604.7	0.11	27.79
5	1.29	680.2	0.10	28.97
6	1.47	695.6	0.10	31.55
7	1.71	888.9	0.09	36.07
8	2.07	872.6	0.09	37.84
9	2.80	1099.2	0.07	44.80
Highest	7.01	1964.3	0.05	60.09

Note: [a]Portfolios are rebalanced at March 31. Prices and number of shares outstanding are March 31 values. Book values and earnings are year-end values. Only December fiscal closers are included in the portfolios.

the basis of increasing values of P/B. Portfolios are rebalanced annually over the 1964–82 period. It is apparent from Table 6.5 that the higher is the average P/B of the firms in a portfolio, the higher are the corresponding average values of market capitalization, P/E and stock price.[6]

Perhaps more direct evidence that the effects are associated with some common underlying factor lies in the finding that there are significant January seasonals in the dividend yield effect (Keim, 1985), P/E effect (Cooke and Rozeff, 1984) and price and P/B effects. Evidence on the last three effects is reported in Table 6.6 which contains average January and non-January returns for portfolios based on annual rankings on P/B, E/P and price over the 1964–82 period. The three time series of portfolio returns are created in a manner analogous to many previous studies. At annual intervals during the period, NYSE firms are ranked separately according to their P/E ratio, P/B ratio or price and sorted into ten portfolios. These portfolios are held for the next twelve months and equal-weighted portfolio returns are computed in each month. This process is repeated for each year of the sample period. The results are basically the same for each separate experiment. There is a strong inverse relation between the ranking variable and average returns in January, and not much of a relation in the other months.

From a practical perspective, the investor's objective is to isolate and use in a portfolio strategy the characteristic(s) that will result in the highest risk-adjusted returns for the portfolio. That is, the typical investor is less interested in the conjecture that all these effects are somehow related than he is in finding the ranking characteristic that works best. Recent studies have addressed this issue by trying to answer the following question: If an investor screens first on characteristic X, say P/E, can he further improve portfolio performance (on a beta risk-adjusted basis) by adding an additional screen based on characteristic Y, say market capitalization (or vice versa)?

Most of the studies in this area (Reinganum, 1981; Peavy and Goodman, 1982; Basu, 1983; Cooke and Rozeff, 1984) address the interrelation between the P/E and market capitalization effects. The results are less than conclusive: Reinganum argues that the size effect subsumes the P/E effect (i.e. there is no marginal value to P/E after first ranking on size); Basu argues just the opposite. Peavy and Goodman and Cooke and Rozeff, after performing meticulous replications of and extensions to the methodologies of Basu and Reinganum reach surprisingly different conclusions. Peavy and Goodman's results agree with those of Basu, but Cooke and Rozeff (1984, p. 464) conclude, 'it does not appear that either market value subsumes earnings/price ratio or the earnings/price ratio subsumes market value as has been claimed.'

The upshot of these studies is that if one constructs a portfolio based on high E/P stocks, there may still be some value added by considering the additional dimension of firm size, and vice versa. In a similar vein, Keim (1985, 1986a) analyzes the interrelation between the dividend yield and size effects and finds that the two effects are not mutually exclusive and that, over and above the benefits from discriminating along the size dimension, it may be beneficial to discriminate those firms that pay no dividends or that have high dividend yields. One interpretation is that market capitalization, E/P and dividend yield (as well as the other variables mentioned above) may be imperfect surrogates for an underlying and more fundamental 'factor' that is missing from the CAPM (see, for example, Ball, 1978).

Table 6.6 The *P/E, P/B* and price effects. Average monthly returns (standard deviations) for portfolios of NYSE firms over the 1964–1982 period

Decile of ranking variable	Price/earnings effect[a]		Price/book effect[a]		Price effect[b]	
	January	Feb–Dec	January	Feb–Dec	January	Feb–Dec
Lowest	6.65	1.04	9.14	0.87	12.02	0.96
	(9.39)	(5.34)	(10.32)	(5.64)	(14.07)	(7.15)
2	6.34	0.98	7.34	0.83	8.08	0.89
	(8.62)	(4.88)	(8.99)	(5.30)	(10.38)	(5.70)
3	5.06	0.95	5.96	0.87	6.00	0.83
	(7.44)	(4.49)	(7.81)	(4.78)	(9.06)	(5.17)
4	4.22	0.95	4.64	0.81	4.98	0.85
	(7.85)	(4.49)	(7.99)	(4.48)	(8.62)	(4.85)
5	4.01	0.62	3.97	0.67	3.93	0.78
	(7.49)	(4.53)	(7.49)	(4.30)	(7.70)	(4.70)
6	3.60	0.63	3.28	0.67	3.22	0.79
	(7.60)	(4.68)	(7.09)	(4.62)	(7.85)	(5.00)
7	3.32	0.48	3.21	0.79	2.69	0.83
	(7.18)	(4.67)	(7.13)	(4.84)	(7.29)	(4.70)
8	3.25	0.75	2.64	0.69	2.24	0.77
	(8.14)	(5.19)	(7.67)	(5.17)	(6.39)	(4.89)
9	2.39	0.89	2.93	0.87	1.27	0.85
	(7.07)	(5.15)	(7.39)	(5.37)	(6.59)	(5.02)
Largest	2.77	0.90	1.43	1.05	0.83	0.90
	(6.96)	(5.82)	(6.55)	(5.51)	(6.09)	(4.93)

Notes: [a]Portfolios are rebalanced at March 31 of each year. The *P/E* and *P/B* ratios used to create deciles are computed using the previous year-end earnings and book values and March 31 prices. Only December fiscal closers are included in the portfolios. [b]Portfolios are rebalanced annually at year-end. Year-end prices are used to create deciles.

4 CAN WE EXPLAIN THE SIZE EFFECT?

The lion's share of the effort expended in attempts to explain the above phenomena has been directed to the size effect. Some have argued that alternative asset pricing models may explain the cross-sectional association between risk-adjusted returns and size. For example, Chen (1983) and Chan et al. (1983) argue that most of the abnormal returns associated with the size effect are explained by additional risk factors in the context of the arbitrage pricing theory of Ross (1976). Others maintain that market imperfections assumed away by the CAPM are responsible. In this vein Stoll and Whaley (1983) argue that round-trip transactions costs are sufficient to offset the abnormal returns associated with the size effect. Schultz (1983) points out, however, that transactions costs would have to be larger in January than in other months to explain the January seasonal in abnormal returns, but he finds no evidence of seasonally varying transaction costs.

Others have addressed the possibility that the size effect is merely a statistical artifact. Roll (1981) suggests that large abnormal returns of small firms could be due to systematic biases (due to infrequent or nonsynchronous trading) in the beta estimates for these firms, but Reinganum (1982) demonstrates that this bias cannot explain the anomaly. Christie and Hertzel (1981) argue that the size effect could be due to non-stationarity of beta. A firm whose common stock price has recently declined—i.e. a firm that is becoming 'small'—has effectively experienced, other things equal, an increase in leverage and a concomitant increase in the risk of its equity. Thus, historical estimates of beta that assume such risk is constant over time are 'stale' and understate (overstate) the risk and overstate (understate) average risk-adjusted returns of stocks whose market capitalization has fallen (risen). Christie and Hertzel adjust for this bias, but the adjustment does not eliminate the size effect. Chan (1983) makes a similar adjustment and finds that 'the size effect is reduced to a magnitude whose economic significance is debatable.' Unfortunately, neither study differentiates between January and non-January returns. Finally, Blume and Stambaugh (1983) demonstrate that the portfolio strategies implicit in papers such as Reinganum (1982) and Keim (1983), which require daily rebalancing of the portfolio to equal weights, yield upward-biased estimates of small-firm portfolio returns due to a 'bid-ask bias' that is inversely related to market capitalization. Roll (1983b) presents similar arguments. The idea is that such strategies sometimes implicitly buy at the bid price and sell at the ask price. Blume and Stambaugh show that for portfolio strategies that avoid this bias, the size effect is substantially reduced and is significant only in January.

In light of these last findings, attempts to explain the size phenomenon have focused primarily on January. Rather than exploring alternative equilibrium models that may accommodate the seasonal, most explanations have instead focused on frictions in the market that represent violations of the CAPM assumptions. The most popular hypothesis attributes the effect to year-end tax-loss selling. The tax-loss hypothesis can be summarized as follows:

> The hypothesis maintains that tax laws influence investors' portfolio decisions by encouraging the sale of securities that have experienced recent price declines so that the (short-term) capital loss can be offset against taxable income. Small firm stocks are likely candidates for tax-loss selling since these stocks typically have higher variances of price changes and, therefore, larger probabilities of large price declines. Importantly, the tax-loss argument relies on the assumption that investors wait until the tax year-end to sell their common stock 'losers.' For example, in the U.S., a combination of liquidity requirements and eagerness to realize capital losses before the new tax year may dictate sale of such securities at year-end. The heavy selling pressure during this period supposedly depresses the prices of small firm stocks. After the tax year-end,

the price pressure disappears and prices rebound to equilibrium levels. Hence small firm stocks display large returns in the beginning of the new tax year. (Brown *et al.*, 1983b, p. 107)

Although popular on Wall Street, support for the tax-loss selling hypothesis has been less than overwhelming (on a priori grounds) in the academic community. Roll (1983b) has called the argument 'ridiculous' and Brown *et al.* (1983b) maintain that the tax laws in the U.S. do not unambiguously induce the year-end price behavior of small stocks as predicted by the hypothesis. Further, Constantinides (1984) claims that optimal tax trading of common stocks should produce a January seasonal pattern in stock prices only if investors behave irrationally.

The evidence on the tax-loss hypothesis is less than conclusive. Reinganum (1983) and Roll (1983b) both examine the hypothesis and their tests suggest that part, but not all, of the abnormal returns in January is related to tax-related trading. On the other hand, Schultz (1985) finds that prior to 1917 — before the U.S. income tax as we know it today created incentives for tax-loss selling — there was no evidence of a January effect.

The tax-loss selling hypothesis predicts a price rebound in the month of January immediately following price declines but makes no predictions regarding price movements for these stocks in subsequent turn-of-the-year periods. Chan (1985) and DeBondt and Thaler (1985) present evidence that the January abnormal returns of such 'loser' firms persist for as long as five years after the loser firms are identified. For example, Chan identifies 'losers' and 'winners' and constructs an 'arbitrage' portfolio (long losers, short winners) within each decile of market value for NYSE firms at December 31 of year t and tracks January abnormal returns in each of the following four years ($t + 1$ to $t + 4$). His results demonstrate a persistent January effect in each of the subsequent three years. Based on such evidence, both Chan and DeBondt and Thaler conclude that the January seasonal in stock returns may have little to do with tax-loss selling.

Others have tested the hypothesis by examining the month-to-month behavior of abnormal returns in countries with tax codes similar to the U.S. code but with different tax year-ends. The tax-loss selling hypothesis predicts that, in the month immediately following the tax year-end, abnormal returns of small firms will be large relative to both other months and larger firms. The hypothesis makes no predictions regarding the time series behavior of abnormal returns during other months. The studies that examine returns in countries with similar tax codes to the U.S. but different tax year-ends (Brown *et al.* (1983b) examine Australia (which has a June tax year-end); Reinganum and Shapiro (1983) examine the U.K. (which has an April tax year-end)) find seasonals after the tax year-end, but also find seasonals in January that are not predicted by the hypothesis. Further, Berges *et al.* (1984) find a January seasonal in Canadian stock returns prior to 1972, a period when Canada had no taxes on capital gains.

The inconsistent evidence regarding the tax-loss selling hypothesis argues for investigating other possibilities. One such possibility that has received attention on Wall Street is the notion that liquidity constraints of market participants may influence security returns, and these effects may have seasonal patterns. For example, periodic infusions of cash into the market as a result of, say, institutional transfers for pension accounts or proceeds from bonuses or profit-sharing plans, may impact the market. In fact, some evidence can be interpreted as supporting this idea. For example, Kato and Schallheim (1985), in an examination of the size effect in Japan, find January *and* June seasonals in small firm returns that coincide with traditional Japanese bonuses paid at the end of December and in June. Further, Rozeff (1985) finds a substantial *upward* shift in the ratio of sales to purchases of common stock by investors (who are not members of the NYSE) at the turn of the year that coincides with the dramatic increase in small firm returns in January (but Rozeff interprets this as evidence of a tax-loss selling effect). Ritter (1985) documents a similar pattern in the daily sale to purchase ratio for the retail customers of a large brokerage firm. Finally, Ariel (1988) finds a pattern in daily stock returns in *every month* but February that parallels precisely the pattern that occurs at the turn of the year. It would be easier to interpret such monthly patterns as liquidity or payroll effects than as tax effects.

5 OTHER 'SEASONAL' PATTERNS IN STOCK RETURNS

In addition to the January effect, recent studies have documented additional empirical regularities that are related to the day of the week or the time of the month. Research on the so-called 'weekend effect' finds that average stock returns tend to be higher on Fridays and negative on Mondays. Cross (1973) and French (1980) document the effect using the S&P Composite Index beginning in 1953 and Gibbons and Hess (1981) document it for the Dow Jones Industrial Index of 30 stocks (1962–78). Keim and Stambaugh (1984) extend the findings for the S&P Composite to include the period 1928 to 1982 and also find the effect in actively traded OTC stocks. Jaffe and Westerfield (1985) find the effect on several foreign stock exchanges. The average returns associated with this intra-weekly phenomena in the U.S. are shown in Figure 6.1 for the 1928 to 1982 period.

All of the above studies document negative Monday returns using Friday-close-to-Monday-close returns and thus cannot ascertain whether the negative returns are due to the week-end non-trading period or to active trading on Monday. The findings of authors who have investigated this appear to be period-specific. Harris (1988), for all NYSE stocks for the period 1981 to 1983, and Smirlock and Starks (1984), for the Dow Jones 30 for the period 1963 to 1973, examine intra-daily returns and show that negative Monday returns

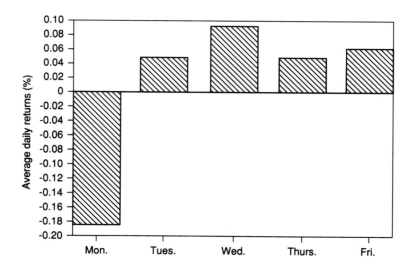

Figure 6.1 Day of the week effect, S&P Composite, 1928–1982. *Source*: Keim and Stambaugh (1984)

accrue from Friday close to Monday open, as well as during trading on Monday. On the other hand, Rogalski (1985) examines intra-daily data from 1974 to 1984 and finds that negative Monday returns accrue entirely during the weekend non-trading period.

Keim and Stambaugh (1984), noting results in Gibbons and Hess that suggest Friday returns vary cross-sectionally with market value, find that the return differential between small and large firms increases as the week progresses, and is largest on Friday (see Table 6.4). In addition, Keim (1986b) demonstrates that, controlling for the large average returns in January, the 'Friday effect' and the 'Monday effect' are no different in January than in the other months.

Although we do not yet have an explanation of the weekend effect, we do know that the effect is not likely to be a result of measurement error in recorded prices (Gibbons and Hess, 1981; Keim and Stambaugh, 1984; Smirlock and Starks, 1984), the delay between trading and settlement due to check clearing (Gibbons and Hess, 1981; Lakonishok and Levi, 1982) or specialist trading activity (Keim and Stambaugh, 1984).

The monthly effect was found by Ariel (1988) who showed that for the period 1963 to 1981 the average returns for common stocks on the NYSE and AMEX are positive only for the last day of the month and for days during the first half of the month. During the latter half of the month returns are indistinguishable from zero. Ariel (1988, p. 109) concludes that during his sample period '*all* of the market's cumulative advance occurred around the first half of the month, the second half contributing nothing to the cumulative increase.' Figure 6.2, which is drawn from Ariel (Table 3, 1988), illustrates the phenomenon for the total returns for the CRSP value-weighted index of NYSE and AMEX stocks. The figure clearly demonstrates that returns in the first half of the month are consistently larger than second-half returns (except for February); in fact, negative average returns occur only in

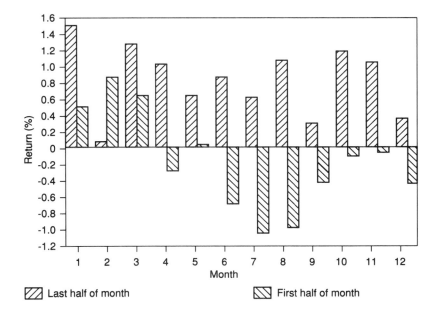

Figure 6.2 Monthly effect in stock returns, value-weighted CRSP index, 1963–1981. *Source*: Ariel (chapter 8)

the second half. The results given by Ariel (1988) also suggest that, with the exception of January, the difference between first-half returns of small firms and the first-half returns of large firms is not substantial. Although Ariel is unable to explain the effect, one potential explanation involves liquidity constraints of investors as discussed above.

6 CONCLUDING REMARKS

This chapter has presented a summary of evidence on empirical regularities that have persisted for quite a long time — in some instances for as long as fifty years. Many of these findings are inconsistent with an investment environment where the CAPM is descriptive of reality and argue for consideration of alternative models of asset pricing. Other findings, such as the day-of-the-week effect, do not necessarily represent violations of any particular asset pricing model, yet are still interesting for their regularity.

Of course, the bottom line for investors is the extent to which this information can be translated into improved portfolio performance. That strategies based on the evidence here can improve performance has, in fact, been borne out in actual 'real world' experiments. In addition, I have attempted in the above discussion to convey (whenever possible) some sense of the practical magnitude of these effects. However, several caveats regarding implementation of such strategies might form a fitting conclusion. First, that some effects have persisted for as many as fifty years in no way guarantees their persistence into the future. In other words, there is no sure thing. Second, even if the effects were to persist, the costs of implementing strategies designed to capture these phenomena may be prohibitive. For example, illiquidity of the market and transactions costs may render a small stock strategy infeasible. Day-of-the-week and other seasonal effects may have practical value only for those investors who were planning to trade (and pay transactions costs) anyway and, thereby, incur only the costs of timing the trade. Finally, one must be cautious when interpreting the magnitudes of the 'abnormal' returns reported in these studies. To the extent that alternative models of asset pricing may be more appropriate than the CAPM, studies that use the CAPM as a benchmark may not be adjusting for the relevant risks and costs in a complete way. In that case, superior performance relative to the CAPM may not be superior once these other costs and risks are considered.

ENDNOTES

* This is a substantially revised and expanded version of a paper that appeared in the *Financial Analysts Journal*.

1. The assumptions for the one-period CAPM are: (1) investors are risk averse and choose 'efficient' portfolios by maximizing expected return for a given level of risk; (2) no taxes or transactions costs; (3) identical borrowing and lending rates; (4) investors are in complete agreement with regard to expectations about individual securities; and (5) security returns have a multivariate normal distribution.

2. Such persistent departures are often referred to as 'anomalies.' The term anomaly, in this context, can be traced to Thomas Kuhn (1970) in his classic book, *The Structure of Scientific Revolutions*. Kuhn maintains that research activity in any normal science will revolve around a central paradigm and that experiments are conducted to test the predictions of the underlying paradigm and to extend the range of the phenomena it explains. Although research most often supports the underlying paradigm, eventually results are found that don't conform. Kuhn (1970, pp. 52–3) terms this stage 'discovery': 'Discovery commences with the awareness of *anomaly*, i.e., with the recognition that

nature has somehow violated the paradigm-induced expectations that govern normal science' (emphasis added).

3. The S&P 500, being a value-weighted index of primarily high-capitalization firms, behaves like a portfolio of very large firms (e.g. portfolios 9 and 10 in Table 6.2).

4. Nakamura and Terada (1984) also document a P/E effect on the Tokyo stock exchange.

5. For example, in 1980 the firms that comprised the smallest quintile of size for the NYSE had market capitalization of less than about $50 million.

6. One exception is the lowest P/B portfolio whose stocks on average have a low average E/P. This is due to the negative earnings firms that tend to be concentrated there. Note that firms with negative book values are excluded from the sample.

REFERENCES

Ariel, R.A. (1988) 'Evidence on intra-month seasonality in stock returns.' In E. Dimson (ed.) *Stock Market Anomalies*, Cambridge: Cambridge University Press.

Ball, R. (1978) 'Anomalies in Relationships between Securities' Yields and Yield-Surrogates,' *Journal of Financial Economics*, **6**, 103–26.

Banz, R.W. (1981) 'The Relationship Between Return and Market Value of Common Stock,' *Journal of Financial Economics*, **9**, 3–18.

Barone-Adesi, G. and Tinic, S. (1983) 'Seasonality in Stock Prices: A Test of the "Tax-Loss-Selling" Hypothesis,' manuscript, University of Alberta.

Basu, S. (1977) 'Investment Performance of Common Stocks in Relation to their Price/Earnings Ratios: A Test of the Efficient Market Hypothesis,' *Journal of Finance*, **32**, 3, June 663–82.

Basu, S. (1983) 'The Relationship Between Earnings' Yields, Market Value and the Returns for NYSE Stocks: Further Evidence,' *Journal of Financial Economics*, June, 129–56.

Berges, A., McConnell, J. and Schlarbaum, G. (1984) 'The Turn-of-the-Year in Canada,' *Journal of Finance*, March, 185–92.

Black, F. (1972) 'Yes, Virginia, There is Hope: Tests of the Value Line Ranking System,' *Financial Analysts Journal*, September/October, 10–14.

Black, F. and Scholes, M. (1974) 'The Effects of Dividend Yield and Dividend Policy as Common Stock Prices and Returns,' *Journal of Financial Economics*, **2**, 1–22.

Black, F., Jensen, M.C. and Scholes, M. (1972) 'The Capital Asset Pricing Model: Some Empirical Tests.' In M.C. Jensen (ed.) *Studies in the Theory of Capital Markets*, New York: Praeger.

Blume, M.E. (1980) 'Stock Returns and Dividend Yields: Some More Evidence,' *Review of Economics and Statistics*, **62**, 567–77.

Blume, M. and Friend, I. (1973) 'A New Look at the Capital Asset Pricing Model,' *Journal of Finance*, March, 19–33.

Blume, M.E. and Husic, F. (1973) 'Price, Beta and Exchange Listing,' *Journal of Finance*, **28**, 283–99.

Blume, M.E. and Stambaugh, R.F. (1983) 'Biases in Computed Returns: An Application to the Size Effect,' *Journal of Financial Economics*, November, 387–404.

Brennan, M. (1970) 'Taxes, Market Valuation and Corporate Financial Policy,' *National Tax Journal*, 417–27.

Brown, P., Kleidon, A.W. and Marsh, T.A. (1983a) 'New Evidence on the Nature of Size-Related Anomalies in Stock Prices,' *Journal of Financial Economics*, June, 33–56.

Brown, P., Keim, D.B., Kleidon, A.W. and Marsh, T.A. (1983b) 'Stock Return Seasonalities and the Tax-Loss Selling Hypothesis: Analysis of the Arguments and Australian Evidence,' *Journal of Financial Economics*, June, 105–28.

Chan, K.C. (1983) 'Leverage Changes and Size-Related Anomalies,' manuscript, University of Chicago, December.

Chan, K.C. (1985) 'Can Tax-Loss Selling Explain the January Seasonal in Stock Returns?' manuscript, Ohio State University, August.

Chan, K.C., Chen, N. and Hsieh, D. (1983) 'An Exploratory Investigation of the Firm Size Effect,' manuscript, University of Chicago, April.

Chen, N. (1983) 'Some Empirical Tests of the Theory of Arbitrage Pricing,' *Journal of Finance*, December, 1393–1414.

Christie, A. and Hertzel, M. (1981) 'Capital Asset Pricing Anomalies', University of Rochester Working Paper.

Constantinides, G.M. (1984) 'Optimal Stock Trading with Personal Taxes: Implications for Prices and the Abnormal January Returns,' *Journal of Financial Economics*, March, 65–90.

Cooke, T.J. and Rozeff, M.S. (1984) 'Size and Earnings/Price Ratio Anomalies: One Effect or Two?' *Journal of Financial and Quantitative Analysis*, **13**, 449–66.

Copeland, T.E. and Mayers, D. (1982) 'The Value Line Enigma (1965–1978): A Case Study of Performance Evaluation Issues,' *Journal of Financial Economics*, November, 289–321.

Cross, F. (1975) 'The Behavior of Stock Prices on Fridays and Mondays,' *Financial Analysts Journal*, November-December, 67–9.

DeBondt, W.F.M. and Thaler, R. (1985) 'Does the Stock Market Overreact?' *Journal of Finance*, July, 793–806.

Dimson, E. (1979) 'Risk Measurement when Shares are Subject to Infrequent Trading,' *Journal of Financial Economics*, **7**, 197–226.

Fama, E. (1970) 'Efficient Capital Markets: A Review of Theory and Empirical Work,' *Journal of Finance*, May, 383–417.

Fama, E. and MacBeth, J. (1973) 'Risk, Return and Equilibrium: Empirical Tests,' *Journal of Political Economy*, May/June, 607–36.

French, K. (1980) 'Stock Returns and the Weekend Effect,' *Journal of Financial Economics*, March, 55–69.

Gibbons, M. (1982) 'Multivariate Tests of Financial Models: A New Approach,' *Journal of Financial Economics*, **10, 1**, March, 3–27.

Gibbons, M. and Hess, P. (1981) 'Day of the Week Effects and Asset Returns,' *Journal of Business*, October, 579–96.

Gordon, R.H. and Bradford, D.F. (1980) 'Taxation and the Stock Market Valuation on Capital Gains and Dividends: Theory and Empirical Results,' *Journal of Public Economics*, 109–36.

Graham, B. and Dodd, D. (1940) *Security Analysis*, New York: McGraw-Hill.

Gultekin, M.N. and Gultekin, N.B. (1983) 'Stock Market Seasonality: International Evidence,' *Journal of Financial Economics*, December, 469–82.

Harris, L. (1988) 'Intra-day stock return patterns.' In E. Dimson (ed.) *Stock Market Anomalies*, Cambridge: Cambridge University Press.

Hess, P. (1983) 'Test for Tax Effects in the Pricing of Financial Assets,' *Journal of Business*, **56**, 537–54.

Holloway, C. (1981) 'A Note on Testing an Aggressive Investment Strategy Using Value Line Ranks,' *Journal of Finance*, June, 711–19.

Jaffe, J. and Westerfield, R. (1985) 'The Week-end Effect in Common Stock Returns: The International Evidence,' *Journal of Finance*, **40, 2**, June.

Kato, K. and Schallheim, J.S. (1985) 'Seasonal and Size Anomalies in the Japanese Stock Market,' *Journal of Financial and Quantitative Analysis*, **20**, 107–18.

Keim, D.B. (1983) 'Size-Related Anomalies and Stock Return Seasonality: Further Empirical Evidence,' *Journal of Financial Economics*, March, 13–32.

Keim, D.B. (1985) 'Dividend Yields and Stock Returns: Implications of Abnormal January Returns,' *Journal of Financial Economics*, **14**, September, 473–89.

Keim, D.B. (1986a) 'Dividend Yields and the January Effect,' *Journal of Portfolio Management*, **12**, December, 54–60.

Keim, D.B. (1986b) 'The Relation Between Day of the Week Effects and Size Effects,' *Journal of Portfolio Management*, forthcoming.

Keim, D.B. and Stambaugh, R.F. (1984) 'A Further Investigation of the Weekend Effect in Stock Returns,' *Journal of Finance*, July, 819–35.

Kuhn, T.S. (1970) *The Structure of Scientific Revolutions*, Chicago: University of Chicago Press.

Lakonishok, J. and Levi, M. (1982) 'Weekend Effects on Stock Returns: A Note,' *Journal of Finance*, June, 883–9.

Lintner, J. (1965) 'The Valuation of Risk Assets and the Selection of Risky Investments in Stock Portfolios and Capital Budgets,' *Review of Economics and Statistics*, February, 13–37.

Litzenberger, R. and Ramaswamy, K. (1979) 'The Effects of Personal Taxes and Dividends on Capital Asset Prices: Theory and Empirical Evidence,' *Journal of Financial Economics*, 7, 163–95.

Litzenberger, R. and Ramaswamy, K. (1980) 'Dividends, Short Selling Restrictions, Tax-Induced Investor Clienteles and Market Equilibrium,' *Journal of Finance*, 35, 2, May, 469–82.

Litzenberger, R. and Ramaswamy, K. (1982) 'The Effects of Dividends on Common Stock Prices: Tax Effects or Information Effects,' *Journal of Finance*, 37, 2, May 429–33.

Mayers, D. (1972) 'Nonmarketable Assets and Capital Market Equilibrium under Uncertainty.' In M.C. Jensen (ed.) *Studies in Theory of Capital Markets*, New York: Praeger.

Miller, M. and Scholes, M. (1978) 'Dividends and Taxes: Some Empirical Evidence,' *Journal of Financial Economics*, 90, 6, December, 333–64.

Morgan, I.G. (1982) 'Dividends and Capital Asset Prices,' *Journal of Finance*, 37, 4, September, 1071–86.

Nakamura, T. and Terada, N. (1984) 'The Size Effect and Seasonality in Japanese Stock Returns,' manuscript, Nomura Research Institute.

Nicholson, S.F. (1960) 'Price–Earnings Ratios,' *Financial Analysts Journal*, July/August, 43–50.

Peavy, J.W. and Goodman, D.A. (1982) 'A Further Inquiry into the Market Value and Earnings Yield Anomalies,' manuscript, Southern Methodist University.

Peavy, J.W. and Goodman, D.A. (1983) 'Industry-Relative Price–Earnings Ratios as Indicators of Investment Returns,' *Financial Analysts Journal*, July/August.

Reinganum, M.R. (1981) 'Misspecification of Capital Asset Pricing: Empirical Anomalies Based on Earnings' Yields and Market Values,' *Journal of Financial Economics*, 19–46.

Reinganum, M.R. (1982) 'A Direct Test of Roll's Conjecture on the Firm Size Effect,' *Journal of Finance*, 37, 27–35.

Reinganum, M.R. (1983) 'The Anomalous Stock Market Behavior of Small Firms in January: Empirical Tests for Tax-Loss Selling Effects,' *Journal of Financial Economics*, June, 89–104.

Reinganum, M.R. and Shapiro, A. (1983) 'Taxes and Stock Return Seasonality: Evidence from the London Stock Exchange,' manuscript, University of Southern California.

Ritter, J.R. (1985) 'The Buying and Selling Behavior of Individual Investors at the Turn of the Year: Evidence of Price Pressure Effects,' manuscript, University of Michigan, November.

Rogalski, R. (1984) 'New Findings Regarding Day of the Week Returns over Trading and Non-trading Periods: A Note,' *Journal of Finance*, December, 1603–14.

Roll, R. (1977) 'A Critique of the Asset Pricing Theory's Tests; Part I: On Past and Potential Testability of the Theory,' *Journal of Financial Economics*, March, 129–76.

Roll, R. (1981) 'A Possible Explanation of the Small Firm Effect,' *Journal of Finance*, 36, 879–88.

Roll, R. (1983a) 'Vas ist das? The Turn of the Year Effect and the Return Premium of Small Firms,' *Journal of Portfolio Management*, 9, 1, 18–28.

Roll, R. (1983b) 'On Computing Mean Returns and the Small Firm Premium,' *Journal of Financial Economics*, November, 371–86.

Rosenberg, B. and Marathe, V. (1979) 'Tests of Capital Asset Pricing Hypothesis.' In Haim Levy (ed.) *Research in Finance*, Greenwich, CT: JAI Press.

Rosenberg, B., Reid, K. and Lanstein, R. (1985) 'Persuasive Evidence of Market Inefficiency,' *Journal of Portfolio Management*.

Ross, S. (1976) 'The Arbitrage Theory of Capital Asset Pricing,' *Journal of Economic Theory*, 13, 3, December.

Rozeff, M.S. (1985) 'The Tax-Loss Selling Hypothesis: New Evidence from Share Shifts,' manuscript, University of Iowa, April.

Scholes, M. and Williams, J. (1977) 'Estimating Betas from Non-synchronous Data,' *Journal of Financial Economics*, 5, 309–27.

Schultz, P. (1983) 'Transactions Costs and the Small Firm Effect: A Comment,' *Journal of Financial Economics*, June, 81–8.

Schultz, P. (1985) 'Personal Income Taxes and the January Effect: Small Firm Stock Returns Before the War Revenue Act of 1917: A Note,' *Journal of Finance*, March, 333–43.

Sharpe, W.F. (1964) 'Capital Asset Prices: A Theory of Market Equilibrium under Conditions of Risk,' *Journal of Finance*, 19, 3, September, 425–42.

Smirlock, M. and Starks, L. (1984) 'Day of the Week Effects in Stock Returns: Some Intraday Evidence,' manuscript, University of Pennsylvania.

Stambaugh, R. (1982) 'On the Exclusion of Assets from the Two-Parameter Model: A Sensitivity Analysis,' *Journal of Financial Economics*, **10, 3**, November, 237-68.

Stickel, S.E. (1985) 'The Effect of Value Line Investment Survey Rank Changes on Common Stock Prices,' *Journal of Financial Economics*, **14**, 121-44.

Stoll, H.R. and Whaley, R.E. (1983) 'Transactions Costs and the Small Firm Effect,' *Journal of Financial Economics*, June, 57-80.

Stone, B.K. and Barter, B.J. (1979) 'The Effect of Dividend Yields on Stock Returns: Empirical Evidence on the Relevance of Dividends.' Manuscript, Georgia Institute of Technology.

Treynor, J.L. 'Toward a Theory of Market Value of Risky Assets,' (unpublished manuscript, undated).

7

The Long-Run Performance of Initial Public Offerings: The U.K. Experience 1980–88

Mario Levis

The empirical evidence accumulated during recent years for almost every capital market in the world, is unequivocal in its conclusion that initial public offerings (IPOs) provide significant abnormal returns on their first day of trading.[1] While there is considerable debate concerning the underlying rationale of such returns, the literature is almost unanimous in its conclusion that their presence constitutes evidence of deliberate underpricing.

More recently, however, Aggarwal and Rivoli [2] and Ritter [15] examine the long-run performance of new issues in the U.S. and report some degree of underperformance in the aftermarket. Aggarwal and Rivoli, on the basis of a sample of 1,598 IPOs issued during 1977–1987, document an abnormal return of −13.73% for investors purchasing all IPOs in the open market at the close of the first trading day and holding each for a period of 250 trading days. Ritter's study indicates that the underperformance of IPOs extends beyond the first year of trading; a sample of 1,526 IPOs issued during 1975–1984 underperformed similar size and industry firms by as much as 29% (excluding first day returns) by the third-year anniversary of their public listing. Similar results have been obtained for other countries as well. Uhlir [17], for example, shows that German IPOs underperformed the market by 7.41% (excluding first day returns) in their first year of trading while Aggarwal, Leal and Hernandez [3] report three-year market-adjusted returns of −47.0%, −19.6% and −23.7% for Brazil, Mexico and Chile, respectively; Keloharju [12] also reports similar patterns of long-run underperformance for Finnish IPOs.

The evidence of long-run underperformance, apart from the implications for the functioning of capital markets and the cost of raising funds for individual firms, is also central to the debate regarding the fundamental premise underpinning several explanations offered to account for the positive initial returns. If, for example, it is the case that firms choose to go public when "investors are irrationally over-optimistic about the future potential of certain

Reprinted from: Levis, M. 1993. The Long-Run Performance of Initial Public Offerings: The U.K. Experience 1980–88. *Financial Management*, 22, Spring, 28–41.

industries" (Ritter [15, p. 4]), then the significant returns in the early aftermarket may not necessarily be the result of intentional underpricing. Ritter, however, acknowledges that the relatively short time span of his study leaves open the possibility of alternative interpretations of these results. More specifically, he points to three questions that have been left unresolved by his work. First, is the documented underperformance a sample-specific phenomenon or does it apply to other offerings over different periods? Second, do IPOs ever recover from the relative decline or does their underperformance continue after the 36-month period? Third, is there a systematic relation between long-run performance and first-day returns? This last issue is important since it has implications for a large and well-established body of literature dealing with short-run underpricing phenomenon.

The purpose of this paper is to shed some further light on each of these questions. The availability of a sizable dataset (712 IPOs in 1980–1988) from a different major capital market (the London Stock Exchange is the third largest equity market in the world) offers a unique opportunity to test the robustness of Ritter's conclusions. Furthermore, the differences in institutional characteristics between the U.S. and U.K. markets allow for an independent test of the most prominent issues in the U.S. literature and also offer the opportunity to investigate the impact of the institutional setting on the performance of IPOs.

Section I describes the sample of IPOs used in this study, the main elements of the U.K. IPO market and the methodology used to evaluate short- and long-run performance. Section II presents cross-sectional and time-series evidence on initial and aftermarket performance, while Section III discusses the main conclusions of this study.

I. DATA AND METHODOLOGY

A company seeking admission to the London Stock Exchange, either the Official List or the Unlisted Securities Market (USM), will normally choose between an offer for sale (at a fixed price or tender) or a placement.[2] In an *offer for sale at fixed price*, the "sponsor" (issuing bank) fixes the price of the issue about two weeks before dealings in the issue begin and undertakes to distribute the shares at this price. Once the price of the issue is fixed, it can neither be changed in response to emerging demand nor can it be withdrawn. While applications for the issue at the fixed price are invited from the public, the issue is sub-underwritten at the same price, by a group of financial institutions. The remuneration of the sub-underwriters is related to the size of the issue. If there is excess demand, the issuing bank must allocate the shares according to some "fair" scheme.[3,4] In a placement, the sponsor also technically underwrites the entire issue for a short period but the sponsor's main function is to act as a distributor.[5] Normally, the sponsor buys the issue from the issuing company and arranges to place the majority of the shares with investors. The price of the issue is fixed about five days before the shares start trading. Placing of the shares is normally completed by the end of the first day of trading. Where a company is raising more than £2 million by this method, the sponsor also has to make one quarter of the issue available to the public either directly or by using a second distributor.[6]

The sample used in this study comprises 712 initial public offerings (offers for sale at fixed price and placements),[7] listed in the Main and Unlisted Securities Markets in 1980–1988.[8] The primary source of data is the KPMG Peat Marwick McLintock New Issue Statistics. Table 7.1 shows the annual distribution of the total population of new issues in the London markets (offers for sale and placements), during this period, and the equivalent distribution of the sample of 712 IPOs used in this study. A total of 94 IPOs were excluded

Table 7.1 Distribution of initial public offerings by year of issue, 1980–1988

Year	All IPOs			712 Sample			Sample coverage		
		Gross proceeds £ millions			Gross proceeds £ millions			% in the sample of 712	
	Number of issues	Including privatizations	Excluding privatizations	Number of issues	Including privatizations	Excluding privatizations	Number of issues	Including privatizations	Excluding privatizations
1980	12	26	26	6	13	13	50.0	50.0	50.0
1981	48	676	116	41	666	114	85.4	98.5	98.3
1982	48	202	100	40	186	84	83.3	84.0	84.0
1983	72	275	275	61	247	247	84.7	89.8	89.8
1984	102	5,530	341	87	5,487	338	85.3	99.2	99.1
1985	121	1,043	1,043	111	913	913	91.7	87.5	87.5
1986	141	9,587	1,481	126	9,467	1,376	89.4	98.7	92.9
1987	128	5,530	1,687	120	5,459	1,594	93.7	98.7	94.5
1988	134	3,916	1,393	120	3,752	1,252	89.6	95.8	89.9
All	806	26,785	6,462	712	26,190	5,931	88.3	97.8	91.8

Note: Initial public offerings include offers for sale at fixed price and placements only: offers for sale by tender, introductions and offers for sale by subscription are excluded. As a result of missing data on gross proceeds for a number of individual IPOs, estimates for gross proceeds for the entire population are based on 765 issues; the equivalent estimates for the sample of 712 IPOs are based on 696 issues. Gross proceeds are measured in constant end-1988 prices, using the U.K. GNP deflator. All columns reporting number of IPOs include the privatization issues.

from the sample because of either: (i) missing offer (placement) prices, (ii) missing first day of trading price, or (iii) unidentified company name in the London Share Price Database (LSPD). The sample of 712 IPOs covers 88.3% of the total number of new issues during the period (offers for sale at fixed price and placements) and 97.8% of the total amount of new equity raised. The 12 privatization issues[9] account for almost 76% of the total amount of new equity capital raised in IPOs in the London markets during the 1980–1988 period.[10]

Prices at the end of the first day of trading and the last day of the first trading month were obtained from Datastream.[11] Other details about individual characteristics of new issues (market value, amount raised and proportion of equity offered) were also obtained from KPMG. Inconsistencies in offer prices between these two sources were resolved with cross reference to the Extel Book of Prospectuses.

For each initial public offering, three measures of performance are calculated:

(i) The first day adjusted return for issue i is defined as the percentage change in price from the offering date to the close at the first day of trading (r_i) less the equivalent change in an appropriate benchmark (r_m).

$$ar_i = r_i - r_m \tag{1}$$

(ii) The first month adjusted return for issue i is defined as the return from the offering price to the last calendar day of the first trading month less the equivalent benchmark return;[12] the time interval of this measure of return varies from 1 to 30 calendar days.

$$ar_{it} = r_{i1} - r_{m1} \tag{2}$$

(iii) The long aftermarket return assesses share performance during the 36 calendar months following the first month of trading. Monthly returns are taken from LSPD;[13] they are based on prices at the last day of the month on which the stock is traded, incorporate dividend payments and, where applicable, are adjusted for rights and scrip offerings. For any new offering i, the monthly abnormal return is defined as:

$$a_{rt} = r_{it} - r_{mt}, \tag{3}$$

where r_{it} is the realized return in month t and r_{mt} is the benchmark return for the corresponding calendar month.

Measures of monthly abnormal returns used in this study do not explicitly adjust for systematic risk. The assumption, however, of a beta coefficient equal to 1.00 is unlikely to affect the essence of our results. A number of studies both in the U.S. and U.K. have demonstrated that the average beta of newly listed firms is higher than 1.00.[14] Thus, on the assumption of a positive market risk premium, measures of abnormal return based on IPO betas equal to 1.00 are likely to provide conservative estimates of IPOs' underperformance.

Ritter [15] shows that the measurement of the long-run performance of initial public offerings is sensitive to the benchmark employed. U.K. studies often use the Financial Times Actuaries All Share Index (FTA) to compute abnormal returns; this is a capitalization weighted index, analogous to the S&P 500 Index, representing about 650 stocks and embracing 90% of the U.K. stock market by value. Dimson and Marsh [6] demonstrate that the use of the FTA may lead to misleading assessments of abnormal performance when the composition of the sample of companies under investigation differs from the FTA in terms of company size and, at the same time, there are significant differences in the performance of small and large firms. A sample of IPOs is almost certain to include a markedly higher proportion of smaller companies than the FTA Index, and the size effect was pervasive during the period under consideration. To investigate the market size distribution of IPOs at the time of entering the market, all U.K. stocks, including the Unlisted Securities Market, are ranked by their market capitalization at the end of each calendar year and are assigned to deciles containing equal numbers of stocks. This procedure is repeated nine times — 1979 to 1987 — to determine the annual upper and lower market value boundaries for each decile. Each of the 712 IPOs is then assigned to the appropriate size decile.[15] Table 7.2 shows the average (over nine years) proportion of IPOs in the sample falling in each decile. The five smallest deciles (by market capitalization) contain more than 78% of the IPOs, although relatively few fall into the smallest decile; only 2.4% of the new issues in the 1980 to 1988 period belong in the two largest deciles. Thus, the sample of 712 IPOs is clearly very different from the FTA Index in terms of market capitalization.

The performance of smaller companies in the U.K. (both the Main and the Unlisted Securities Markets) is usually measured by the Extended Hoare Govett Smaller Companies (HGSC) Index.[16] Like the FTA, this is also a value weighted index; it comprises the lowest ten percent by capitalization of the Main and USM equity markets — about 1,600 firms — and is rebalanced annually. Although the HGSC Index is a better benchmark for measuring the performance of smaller companies, the sample of IPOs in this study is typical neither of the FTA Index nor the HGSC Index.

Table 7.2 also shows the average annual rates of return during the period January 1980 to December 1990 for each of the market size deciles, the FTA and the HGSC Indexes, as well as a specially constructed All Share Equally Weighted (ASEW) Index.[17] During the period 1980–1990, the ASEW Index outperformed the FTA and HGSC Indexes by an average 3.5% and 5.0% per annum, respectively. To account for the impact of the size effect on the long-run performance of IPOs, this study uses three alternative benchmarks: the capitalization

Table 7.2 Market value composition of 712 IPOs and annual average rates of return for size deciles and market indices

Firm size decile	% of IPOs in each decile	Cumulative % of IPOs in each decile	% Annual average rate of return		
			1980–1988	1989–1990	1980–1990
Smallest	6.3	6.3	64.7	−7.1	48.4
2	15.1	21.4	37.4	−13.4	26.4
3	20.8	42.2	35.8	−12.7	25.3
4	20.6	62.8	30.0	−10.2	21.5
5	15.4	78.2	27.2	−15.5	18.1
6	10.5	88.7	25.7	−9.8	18.3
7	5.9	94.6	25.3	−5.9	18.9
8	3.2	97.8	25.8	−2.1	20.2
9	0.6	98.4	24.5	1.4	20.2
Largest	1.6	100.0	24.4	7.7	21.2
All shares equally weighted index			32.1	−6.8	23.8
FTA Index (value weighted, inclusive of dividends)			22.5	−10.6	20.3
HGSC small firms index (value weighted)			26.1	−9.2	18.8

Note: The proportion of IPOs in each decile represents average estimates over a nine-year period. The average annual rates of return for market size deciles are averages of equally weighted portfolios rebalanced annually. The annual average returns for size deciles are equally weighted. The equally weighted all shares index is an average of the ten size deciles.

weighted FTA Index, the capitalization weighted extended (including USM securities) Hoare Govett Smaller Companies (HGSC) Index, and the all share equally weighted index.[18]

To facilitate direct comparability with existing empirical evidence, this study uses the same measures of long-run performance as Ritter [15]. Thus, the average benchmark-adjusted return on a portfolio of n IPOs for month t is the equally weighted arithmetic average of the benchmark adjusted returns:

$$AR_t = \frac{1}{n} \sum_{i=1}^{n} ar_{it} \tag{4}$$

The cumulative benchmark-adjusted aftermarket performance from the beginning of the first full calendar month of trading to event month s is the summation of the average benchmark-adjusted returns:

$$CAR_{1,s} = \sum_{t=1}^{s} AR_t. \tag{5}$$

The statistical significance of CARs is assessed by:

$$t(CAR_t) = \frac{CAR_t \cdot \sqrt{n}}{\sqrt{t \cdot \text{var} + 2 \cdot (t-1) \cdot \text{cov}}} \tag{6}$$

where t is the event month, var is the average (over 36 months) cross-sectional variance, and cov is the first-order autocovariance of the AR_t series.[19]

When a firm in portfolio p is delisted from the LSPD database, the portfolio return for the next month is an equally weighted average of the remaining firms in the portfolio. Thus, the estimation of CARs involves monthly rebalancing, with the proceeds of a delisted firm equally allocated among the surviving members of the portfolio p in each subsequent month.

The three-year holding period returns are computed as:

$$R_i = \prod_{t=1}^{36} (1 + r_{it}) - 1, \tag{7}$$

where r_{it} is the raw return on firm i in event month t. This measures the total return from a buy and hold strategy where an IPO is purchased at the first day of the first full calendar month and held until the earlier of either its third-year anniversary or its delisting. Performance measurement for a group of IPOs is assessed by the *wealth relative*, defined as:

$$WR = \frac{1 + \text{average 3 year total return on IPOs}}{1 + \text{average 3 year total on a market benchmark}}. \tag{8}$$

A *wealth relative* of greater than 1.00 indicates IPOs outperforming the market benchmark, while a value below 1.00 indicates IPO underperformance.[20]

II. EMPIRICAL FINDINGS

A. First Day Returns

Table 7.3 reports average first day and first partial-month returns for the entire sample of 712 IPOs and for offers for sale and placements separately. The sample mean first day return is

Table 7.3 First day market adjusted returns for initial public offerings, 1980–1988

	First day returns %			First partial-month return %
	Offers for sale	Placements	All issues	All Issues
Mean	11.50	15.28	14.30	14.75
t-statistic	(7.51)	(16.75)	(18.21)	(15.72)
Standard deviation	20.76	20.96	20.96	25.03
Third quartile %	20.00	20.87	20.68	22.81
Median %	7.00	8.99	8.57	8.14
First quartile	0.00	3.04	2.35	0.30
% issues with negative first day returns	28.26	13.45	17.28	
Total number of issues	184	528	712	712

Note: First day returns are based on Equation (1); first partial-month returns are based on Equation (2). The daily capitalization weighted FTA Index is used in the calculation of both measures.

14.3% with an associated t-statistic of 18.2.[21] The first partial-month returns (reported in the last column of the Table) are essentially the same with first day returns. Thus, in spite of the differences in the institutional framework, the level of initial returns of U.K. IPOs is virtually identical to the 14.1% reported in Ritter [15]. Initial returns are, however, significantly higher for placements (15.28%) in comparison to offers for sale (11.5%). Only 13.4% of the total number of placements (71 issues) started trading below their offer price as opposed to the 28.3% of the total number of offers for sale (52 issues). Given that placements are mainly available to institutional investors, the presence of some, albeit reduced, overpricing may be considered as rather surprising. In the context of information asymmetry underpricing models, it is usually understood that institutions are likely to be better informed about the true value of an issue. These results suggest that institutional investors also require a positive first day return incentive to encourage them to participate in the new issues' market.

The differences in average initial returns between offers for sale and placements may also be related to the degree of uncertainty about the true value of an issue. As a placement is traditionally the method of issuance used by smaller companies, it could be argued that the differences in initial returns between the two methods are related to the market value of the offerings. A number of studies have documented a negative and significant relation between market value (or gross proceeds from the issue) and initial returns.

In Table 7.4, IPOs are categorized according to the amount of funds raised and proportion of equity offered; the exhibit reports results for the entire sample and offers for sale and placements separately.[22] Panel A shows significant differences in initial returns for placements when categorized according to the gross proceeds of the issue.

The average first day return, for example, for issues raising a maximum of £1.2 million is 21.2%, while for issues raising more than £3.8 million, the average return is 12.78%. No significant differences in initial returns are observed for offers for sale. The average first day return of 18.43% for the 37 largest offer for sale issues is predominantly due to the high first day returns recorded for privatization issues. The average first day return for the 12 privatization issues in this study is 35.6%. Excluding these 12 issues from the largest size of issue quintile results in an average first day return of 9.8 for the remaining 25 issues in this group.[23] In Panel B, the sample is categorized in quintiles according to the proportion of equity offered (the ratio of gross proceeds over market value). The results suggest significant differences in average first day returns depending on the proportion of

Table 7.4 First day returns by method of issue, gross proceeds and proportion of equity retained, 1980–1988

Panel A. First day returns by the gross proceeds of the offer					
Offers for sale			Placements		
Gross proceeds (£000s)[a]	Number of issues	First day return	Gross proceeds (£000s)[a]	Number of issues	First day return
1–5,254	36	11.89	1–1,211	104	21.20
5,255–7,773	36	9.42	1,212–1,923	102	17.31
7,774–12,655	35	13.89	1,924–2,911	104	12.97
12,656–30,352	35	5.77	2,912–3,858	103	12.84
30,353 +	37	18.43	3,859 +	104	12.78
All issues	179	11.92	All issues	517	15.42
F-test		1.93	F-test		3.36
		(0.11)			(0.01)

Panel B. First day returns by the proportion of equity offered					
Offers for sale			Placements		
% of equity offered[b]	Number of issues	First day return	% of equity offered[b]	Number of issues	First day return
45.1 +	34	9.86	32.9 +	103	10.47
35.1–45.0	32	7.44	27.0–32.8	113	13.48
28.0–35.0	35	11.99	24.0–26.9	97	17.44
25.0–27.9	30	13.97	20.0–23.9	99	15.45
1.0–24.9	32	16.16	1.0–19.9	99	20.32
All issues	163	11.83	All issues	511	15.39
F-test		0.824	F-test		3.34
		(0.51)			(0.01)

Notes:

a. Gross proceeds on £000s is defined as the number of shares offered to the market multiplied by the offer (placement) price; they are in constant end-1988 prices using the GNP deflator. Significance levels of F-tests in parentheses.

b. Proportion of equity offered is defined as the gross proceeds of the offer divided by the market value at the offer. Significance levels of F-test in parentheses.

equity released to the market in placement issues. For example, the average first day return is 10.47% when more than 32.9% of the equity is offered via a placement, whereas the equivalent return when less than 20% is offered is 16.32%. A similar, but not statistically significant, pattern is also observed for offers for sale. This positive relation between equity retention and average first day returns is relevant to the debate regarding the implications of concentrated stock ownership and management control on firm value.

To investigate the pattern of returns over time, Table 7.5 reports initial returns for placements and offers for sale for each of the nine years under consideration. The results point to marked year-to-year variation in average initial returns. In full calendar year terms, the average first day returns for 1983 and 1987 are markedly higher (20.51% and 25.69%, respectively) than any other single year. In fact, the highest average first day returns are observed for the ten-month period leading up to the October 1987 Crash; the average return for the 102 IPOs issued between January 1987 and October 19, 1987 is 28.44%. In contrast to the U.S. findings, however, the annual distribution of IPOs in the U.K. provides no

Table 7.5 First day returns by year of issuance for initial public offerings, 1980–1988

Year	Offers for sales		Placements		All issues	
	Number of issues	First day return %	Number of issues	First day return %	Number of issues	First day return %
1980	2	16.00	4	21.41	6	19.60
1981	13	5.62	28	11.38	41	9.56
1982	7	2.53	33	19.96	40	16.91
1983	14	13.15	47	22.70	61	20.51
1984	23	20.03	64	16.14	87	17.17
1985	39	5.78	72	9.06	111	7.90
1986	47	8.86	79	10.08	126	9.55
1987	22	28.50	98	25.09	120	25.69
1988	17	5.25	103	9.71	120	9.08
All issues	184	11.50	528	15.28	712	14.30

clear evidence of a positive relation between the volume of issues and average first day returns.

B. Aftermarket Performance

Table 7.6 reports the cumulative average benchmark-adjusted returns (CARs), excluding first month returns, for the 36 months in the aftermarket. Separate results for the three different indexes are shown.[24] All three series exhibit a gradual but steady decline during the 36-month period following the first month of trading; they fall (excluding initial returns) to -11.38%, -8.31% and -22.96%, respectively, by the end of the third year of trading. Three findings stand out. First, consistent with U.S. results, the U.K. evidence shows that the level of IPO underperformance is economically and statistically significant. Second, its magnitude depends on the choice of the benchmark employed for calculating cumulative adjusted returns. The differences among the three CAR series reflect the pattern of the small firm effect at different points in time. Third, in contrast to the U.S. evidence, the plotting of the CAR series in Figure 7.1, demonstrates that the cumulative FTA and HGSC adjusted returns for U.K. IPOs are still positive by the third-year anniversary of their public listing when first month returns are included.

One of the issues left unresolved by Ritter's [15] study is the longer term (beyond 36 months) pattern of IPOs performance. The findings of Ibbotson [8] tend to suggest that underperformance does not extend beyond the three-year period. Evidence for the U.K. market, not reported in this paper, suggests that the relative underperformance probably continues beyond the third-year anniversary of their public listing. Using a sample of 346 IPOs covering the period 1980–1985, the average HGSC adjusted return, for example, falls to -19.95% and -27.14% (excluding initial returns) by the fourth and fifth year anniversaries of public listing; the equivalent return for this reduced sample of offerings at month 36 is -17.46.[25]

Table 7.6 Cumulative average adjusted returns for initial public offerings, 1980–1988, excluding initial returns

| Month of seasoning | Number of firms trading | FTA adjusted | | HGSC adjusted | | All share adjusted | |
		CAR %	t-statistic	CAR %	t-statistic	CAR %	t-statistic
3	712	0.98	1.10	−0.16	−0.15	−1.65	−1.49
6	710	2.08	1.62	0.20	0.15	−2.67	−1.91
9	709	1.48	0.94	−1.00	−0.63	−5.19	−3.26
12	705	1.57	0.85	−1.55	−0.86	−7.20	−4.01
15	697	0.69	0.33	−2.63	−1.32	−9.65	−4.85
18	688	−2.35	−1.03	−4.87	−2.23	−13.10	−6.01
21	676	−3.02	−1.21	−5.31	−2.24	−14.73	−6.17
24	656	−5.20	−1.92	−6.80	−2.69	−17.33	−6.87
27	611	−6.90	−2.32	−7.61	−2.75	−19.34	−6.99
30	579	−8.14	−2.52	−7.11	−2.37	−19.80	−6.61
33	518	−11.35	−3.18	−9.23	−2.80	−22.85	−6.93
36	483	−11.38	−2.95	−8.31	−2.35	−22.96	−6.49

Note: *t*-statistics are computed using Equation (6). The average (over 36 months) cross-sectional variance (*var*) of the AR_t series is 0.0165, 0.0157 and 0.0156 for the FTA, HGSC and All Share Indexes, respectively. The equivalent *cov* values are 0.0018, 0.0023 and 0.0020 representing autocorrelation coefficients of 0.110, 0.146 and 0.127 respectively. The marked decline in the number of firms trading after the 24th month of seasoning is predominantly due to data availability of monthly rates of return for 120 IPOs issued in 1988 (see footnote 24 for details).

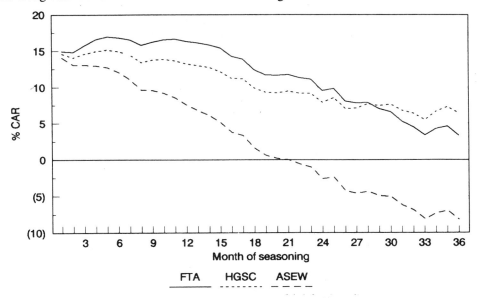

Figure 7.1 Cumulative average adjusted returns for 712 IPOs, 1980–1988 (including first partial-month returns)

Table 7.7 provides some further insight into the long-run underperformance of IPOs. It reports the distribution of three-year holding period returns for the 712 IPOs and the three indexes. The mean three-year holding period return of 55.72% for the sample of 712 IPOs is lower than the equivalent return of the individual benchmarks. This average holding period return is a rather "optimistic" estimate of long-run performance as it includes the exceptional returns of a small number of companies, including the Body Shop with a three-year holding period return of 1780.03%. Wealth relative ratios based on the median three-year holding period returns are notably lower than their mean-based counterparts. A direct comparison with Ritter's equivalent results in [15, Table III] demonstrates that the average underperformance of new issues in the U.K. is not as excessive as that recorded for their U.S. counterparts.

C. Aftermarket Performance by Year of Issuance

To investigate the relation between annual volume of issues, first day returns and aftermarket performance, firms are categorized by their year of issuance. Table 7.8 reports the average three-year holding period total return for the sample of 712 IPOs and wealth relatives based on the FTA, HGSC and ASEW benchmarks; the average first day returns are also reported.

Wealth relatives vary depending on the year of issuance and the benchmarks used for assessing long-run performance. In most years, however, they are less than one, confirming the widespread incidence of underperformance documented in the previous section. There are, however, notable occurrences of outperformance as well. IPOs issued in 1987 and 1988, for example, survived the sharp decline in prices of smaller companies during 1989–1990 relatively well; their wealth relatives, based on the HGSC Index, are 1.029 and 1.078, respectively. Further evidence of outperformance, in comparison to the FTA benchmark, is observed for IPOs issued in 1984 to 1986. This outperformance, however, is largely

Table 7.7 Distribution of three-year holding period returns for initial public offerings, excluding initial returns, and three indices, 1980–1988

Rank	Three-year holding period total returns, %			
	IPOs	FTA	HGSC	All shares
1 (lowest)	−94.48	−20.77	−34.00	−30.59
71	−61.62	18.52	−17.65	−16.91
144	−41.73	24.25	−11.04	−2.74
213	−18.49	29.05	12.69	27.45
284	−0.82	48.84	53.64	83.99
356 (median)	23.57	55.82	84.02	116.45
427	54.49	64.27	94.43	135.61
498	82.69	78.01	110.56	151.73
569	117.28	102.41	123.91	161.96
640	197.16	116.97	136.08	182.69
712 (highest)	1,780.03	186.34	255.24	336.42
Mean	55.72	62.49	69.37	97.83

Note: Three-year holding period returns are based on Equation (7). For initial public offerings that were delisted before the three-year anniversary, the total return is calculated until the delisting date. FTA is the Financial Times Actuaries value weighted index (analogous to the S&P 500), HGSC is the Extended Hoare Govett Smaller Companies value weighted index and the All shares is an equally weighted all shares index.

due to the presence of a pronounced small firm effect between January 1984 to December 1987; during this four-year period, smaller companies, as measured by the HGSC Index, outperformed the FTA Index by an average of 7.6% per annum. Thus, while there is evidence of variation in long-run performance, depending on the year of issuance, the results of Table 7.8, in contrast to the U.S. findings, do not demonstrate a systematic relation between annual volume of IPOs and aftermarket performance.

Table 7.8 Long-run performance by year of issuance for initial public offerings, 1980–1988, excluding initial returns

Year	Number of issues	Average first day return %	Average three-year holding period return IPOs %	Wealth relatives		
				FTA	HGSC	ASEW
1980	6	19.60	−1.22	0.506	0.487	0.457
1981	41	9.56	65.39	0.852	0.817	0.749
1982	40	16.91	59.49	0.781	0.729	0.654
1983	61	20.51	82.86	0.918	0.853	0.743
1984	87	17.17	146.12	1.098	0.930	0.778
1985	111	7.90	77.19	1.096	0.876	0.703
1986	126	9.55	72.47	1.116	0.999	0.822
1987	120	25.69	2.95	0.912	1.029	0.912
1988	120	9.08	−10.03	0.727	1.078	1.045
All issues	712	14.30	55.72	0.958	0.919	0.787

Note: Wealth relatives are defined in Equation (8). The average holding period for the 120 IPOs issued in 1988 is less than 36 months (see footnote 24 for details).

Table 7.9 Long-run performance (36 months) by first day return categories for initial public offerings, 1980–1988, excluding initial returns

% First day return category	Number of issues	Average three-year holding period return %	Wealth relatives		
			FTA	HGSC	ASEW
24.7+	143	42.07*	0.902*	0.886*	0.765*
12.2–24.6	143	50.55	0.934	0.898	0.762
5.8–12.1	142	72.04	1.066	1.029	0.879
0.01–5.7	161	60.58	0.976	0.930	0.798
<0	123	52.36	0.905	0.846	0.726
All issues	712	55.72	0.958	0.919	0.787

Notes: *Excluding the Body Shop, the average three-year holding period return for the highest first day return group falls from 42.07% to 29.83%; the respective wealth relatives fall to 0.825, 0.810 and 0.699. Wealth relatives are defined in Equation (8).

To provide some more direct evidence on the relation between initial and long-run performance, firms are categorized in five groups according to their level of first day returns. The pattern of the average wealth relatives in Table 7.9 suggests that initial return is not a good indicator of aftermarket performance. Nevertheless, when a single issue — the Body Shop — is excluded from the analysis, the average three-year holding period return for the 142 IPOs remaining in the highest initial return group (above 24.7%) falls from 42.07% to 29.83%; consequently, the respective wealth relatives also fall to levels noticeably lower — 0.825, 0.810 and 0.699 — than the equivalent wealth relatives of any of the four other quintiles. Thus, the evidence from the London market is again broadly consistent with the findings reported by Ritter [15] and lends some further support to the notion that investors are periodically overoptimistic about the earnings potential of at least some of the newly listed companies. It is important to note that the second worst performing group of firms in the aftermarket includes the IPOs that ended their first day of trading below their offer (placement) prices while IPOs with modest initial returns — between 5.8% and 12.1% — outperform both the FTA and the HGSC Indexes.

D. Aftermarket Performance by Industry, Market Value, Gross Proceeds and Proportion of Equity Offered

Table 7.10 reports the long-run performance for IPOs categorized by industry. The basic industry classifications used in this study are those prepared by the Stock Exchange and the British Institute of Actuaries and found in the LSPD dataset. Individual industries are listed separately if there are 15 or more IPOs in the sample; otherwise, they are merged into the broader industry classifications. In addition to the 15 industry groups formed by this procedure, the long-run performance of the 12 privatization issues is also reported under a separate heading. The average amount raised per industry, in constant 1988 prices, and the average first day returns are also shown in Table 7.10.

The wealth relatives point to marked differences in the long-run performance of individual industries. Five of the fifteen groupings — construction, leisure, publishing and printing, office equipment, and stores — have wealth relatives higher than 1.00, indicating superior performance relative to at least two of the three benchmarks. The high wealth relatives, however, for two of these sectors — construction and stores — are very sensitive to the year of issuance and the exceptional performance of individual issues. The average holding return

Table 7.10 Long-run performance (36 months) by industry for initial public offerings, 1980–1988, excluding initial returns

	Number of issues	Average gross proceeds £000s	Average first day return %	Average three-year holding period return %	Wealth relatives		
					FTA	HGSC	ASEW
Agencies	61	3,302	17.52	24.48	0.801	0.757	0.640
Capital goods	64	5,892	10.86	57.78	0.916	0.868	0.744
Consumer nondurables	55	5,741	15.56	65.91	1.054	0.999	0.849
Consumer durables	50	8,889	17.74	43.05	0.887	0.877	0.766
Construction	63	5,551	11.42	81.88	1.180	1.195	1.038
Electronics	82	4,981	16.43	52.95	0.876	0.812	0.692
Finance	30	20,606	14.27	52.65	0.937	0.919	0.786
Food manufacturing	25	5,875	18.59	33.51	0.782	0.709	0.603
Health & household	16	24,359	14.61	-2.95	0.629	0.700	0.589
Leisure	36	8,037	12.24	100.00	1.213	1.163	1.003
Publishing & printing	17	2,684	24.63	79.92	1.121	1.046	0.890
Property	44	8,203	12.59	43.30	0.892	0.891	0.769
Office equipment	15	3,594	4.37	114.36	1.270	1.228	1.035
Stores*	32	7,516	18.41	81.08	1.111	1.040	0.881
Other	110	16,139	10.81	44.33	0.896	0.855	0.729
Privatizations	12	1,694,103	37.25	96.91	1.157	1.125	0.963
All issues	712	37,537	14.30	55.72	0.958	0.919	0.787

Notes: *Excluding the Body Shop, the average three-year holding period return for stores falls to 26.27% and the three wealth ratios are 0.775, 0.725 and 0.614, respectively. Wealth relatives are defined in Equation (8). Average gross proceeds, in constant end-1988 prices, are based on a total of 696 IPOs.

Table 7.11 Long-run performance (36 months) by market listing and amount of funds raised for initial public offerings, 1980–1988, excluding initial returns

Panel A. All issues

Gross proceeds £000s	Number of issues	Average first day return %	Average three-year holding period return IPOs %	Wealth relatives		
				FTA	HGSC	ASEW
1–1,438	139	22.52	84.26	1.013	0.955	0.829
1,439–2,148	139	11.82	56.76	0.957	0.896	0.763
2,149–3,554	139	13.43	55.40	0.957	0.894	0.756
3,555–7,802	139	12.01	36.36	0.903	0.904	0.777
7,803+	140	12.82	49.58	0.975	0.967	0.823
All issues	696	14.52	56.46	0.963	0.924	0.790

Panel B. Main Market

Gross proceeds £000s	Number of issues	Average first day return %	Average three-year holding period return IPOs %	Wealth relatives		
				FTA	HGSC	ASEW
1–4,251	46	12.52	37.03	0.861	0.864	0.753
4,252–6,461	47	12.82	64.48	1.124	1.133	0.965
6,462–10,073	46	13.93	64.65	1.136	1.124	0.953
10,074–18,707	48	10.00	47.08	0.971	0.995	0.849
18,708+	47	16.21	68.91	1.120	1.098	0.931
All issues	234	13.08	56.44	1.042	1.046	0.894

Panel C. Unlisted Securities Market

Gross proceeds £000s	Number of issues	Average first day return %	Average three-year holding period return IPOs %	Wealth relatives		
				FTA	HGSC	ASEW
1–1,126	92	22.20	68.63	0.913	0.868	0.758
1,127–1,791	92	16.95	83.88	1.058	0.960	0.815
1,792–2,525	93	12.99	70.23	1.045	0.979	0.834
2,526–3,491	92	13.96	46.86	0.881	0.820	0.695
3,492+	93	10.22	13.57	0.727	0.712	0.611
All issues	462	15.25	56.47	0.927	0.872	0.746

Note: Gross proceeds are in constant end-1988 prices using the GNP deflator.

for the construction industry, for example, is driven by the large number of contracting firms listed during the property boom in 1985–1988; the three-year average holding period return of 81.08% for stores falls to 26.27 when one single issue—the Body Shop—is excluded from the sample. Thus, the only evidence of superior performance is concentrated on a relatively small sample of firms. It is also interesting to note that some of the industries with the highest average first day returns—agencies, consumer durables, electronics, food manufacturing, and health and household—are also among the worst long-run performers. The average first day return and average wealth relatives for the publishing and printing industry do, however, provide a notable exception to this pattern. Although the results in Table 7.10 also indicate some differences in the average amounts of funds raised by firms in the various industrial sectors, there is no evidence of a direct relation between size of the issue and long-run performance.

Table 7.11 provides a closer investigation into this issue by segmenting the firms into five equal number groups according to the amount of funds raised. The wealth relatives for the entire sample of IPOs in Panel A show no evidence of a cross-sectional variation in the long-run performance among the five groups. Except for the FTA-based wealth relatives, for the first quintile, all other ratios are less than 1.00, providing even further support to the generality of the conclusion regarding long-run underperformance.

These average results, however, mask important differences in the long-run performance of IPOs listed in each of the two London markets. Panels B and C show wealth relatives according to the size of the issue for the Main and USM markets separately. In contrast to our previous findings, the size of the issue emerges as an important determinant of long-run performance. Its impact, however, is rather ambiguous. First, the average wealth relatives for the 234 issues in the Main market are consistently higher — across all three benchmarks — than their USM counterparts. Given that the average amount of funds raised by a firm listed in the Main market is about seven times higher (excluding privatization issues) than an issue in the USM, it could be argued that there is a positive relation between size of issue and long-run performance. Such a conclusion is supported by the apparent differences in the wealth relatives among the size quintiles within the Main market. The performance of the bottom 20% of the firms, in terms of amount raised, is clearly inferior to that of their larger counterparts. This positive relation between size of issue and long-run performance is consistent with U.S. findings. For issues originally listed in the USM, however, exactly the reverse pattern is observed. The average wealth relatives for the 93 largest issues in this market are lower than the average wealth relatives for the entire population of 462 USM listings. These results are a little difficult to interpret in trying to reach any conclusions on the impact of issue size on long-run performance. It appears that some public offerings that could have been suitable for a listing in the Main (USM) market have chosen instead the USM (Main) market; the long-run performance of such firms is markedly different from the remainder of the IPOs in the sample.[26]

III. CONCLUSIONS

Using a sample of 712 IPOs listed on the London Stock Exchange in 1980 to 1988, this study documents an average first day return of 14.3%. Placements start trading at significantly higher returns than offers for sale; such differences are broadly consistent across various issue sizes, across proportion of equity offered, and across different time periods. This study also shows that initial public offerings in the U.K. underperformed a number of relevant benchmarks in the 36 full months of public listing following their first day of trading. The magnitude of underperformance is more pronounced when account is taken of the superior performance of smaller companies during the period 1980–1988.

The U.K. evidence sheds light on a number of issues left unresolved by the studies of Aggarwal and Rivoli [2] and Ritter [15]. First, it demonstrates that the long-run underperformance of initial public offerings is not a phenomenon unique to U.S. new issues. Poor aftermarket performance emerges as a persistent feature of initial public offerings in at least one other market — the world's third largest capital market during the 1980s. Second, our results for IPOs in 1980–1985 suggest that the long-run underperformance extends beyond 36 months. This evidence, however, has to be interpreted with caution because of the marked changes in the actual composition of the sample that take place during prolonged test periods. A detailed analysis of subsequent changes in listing details (takeovers, bankruptcies, suspensions, transfers, etc.) may provide useful insight into the causes of the long-run underperformance of initial public offerings. Third, the apparent tendency for the firms — excluding the Body Shop — with the highest initial returns to have the worst aftermarket performance, together with the marginal long-run out-performance of firms with moderate first day returns, casts further doubts on the conventional belief that positive initial returns are entirely due to deliberate underpricing. The emerging evidence is more consistent with the proposition that while a certain level of first day returns is the result of intentional underpricing, marked deviations from this baseline level represent some form of market overreaction.

ENDNOTES

1. For a summary of the international evidence on first day IPO returns, see Aggarwal, Leal and Hernandez [3] and Ibbotson and Ritter [10]. Dimson [5] presents a comprehensive review of the early literature on U.K. IPOs, while the Bank of England [4] provides an update of the British new issues market in the 1980s.

2. If a company simply wishes to obtain a stock exchange quotation for its existing shares rather than linking its admission to the market with the issue of new shares to the market as a whole, it can enter the market by *introduction*. Investment trusts (the equivalent of closed end funds) often use an *offer for sale by subscription*. According to this method, the company itself (rather than the issuing house or broker) offers the shares directly to the public.

3. For further details on allocation procedures and their implications on first day "effective" returns earned by new issues' investors, see Levis [14].

4. The *offer for sale by tender* differs from the offer for sale at fixed price in that the public is invited to tender for the shares at any price over a stated minimum. A single striking price is set to ensure that the issue is sold. Investors who tendered for shares at this price, or above it, receive shares at the striking price.

5. Before October 1986, for issues larger than £3 million the offer for sale at fixed price or by tender were the only methods available. On the date of the Big Bang (October 27, 1986), the London Stock Exchange changed its rules to allow placements to be used for larger issues — up to £15 million in the listed market and up to £5 million in the Unlisted Securities Market.

6. For further details of the U.K. institutional framework, see Bank of England [4].

7. Offers for sale by tender are excluded from the sample. During the period 1980–1986, only 26 offers for sale were on a tender basis. Since 1986, no tender offers have taken place.

8. The choice between the Main and USM markets depends on market size and trading requirements. Of the total sample of 712 initial public offerings, 241 started trading in the Main market and 471 in the USM.

9. The 12 privatization issues (offers for sale at fixed price) during the period 1980–1988 are: British Aerospace, Cable & Wireless, Amersham International, Associated British Ports, Jaguar, British Telecom. British Gas, British Airways, Rolls Royce, and British Airport Authority.

10. Gross proceeds are measured in pounds of 1988 purchasing power using the U.K. GNP deflator.

11. Datastream is an on-line financial database of daily share prices for all U.K. quoted and unquoted companies. In a large number of cases, this service was also used as a cross reference for the exact offer price. It often records the offer price of a new issue for a few days before the first day of trading.

12. Both first day and first month adjusted returns are calculated using the daily FTA value weighted index as the benchmark.

13. Monthly rates of return in LSPD are recorded in log (continuously compounded) form; for the purposes of this study, they have been transformed to simple arithmetic returns.

14. See, for example, Ibbotson [8] and Affleck-Graves, *et al* [1] for the U.S. and Sudarsanam [16] for the U.K. market.

15. The market value of an IPO at the time of entering the market is defined as the total number of shares multiplied by the offer (placement) price.

16. For details of the Hoare Govett Smaller Companies Index, see Dimson and Marsh [7].

17. For details on the size effect on the London market and details on the construction of market size portfolios, see Levis [13].

18. The returns for the extended HGSC Index are taken from Dimson and Marsh [7]. The ASEW was calculated for the purposes of this study. In addition to these three benchmarks, I have also estimated long-run performance using the smallest and the medium size deciles, as well as a value weighted index, whose weighting corresponds to the size composition of the 712 IPOs in the sample. These results are available from the author on request.

19. Although an adjustment is made to the t-statistic to compensate for the lack of independence of *AR* series, these statistics should still be interpreted as upper-bound estimates.

20. For IPOs that are delisted prior to their three-year anniversary, the total return is computed up to the delisting date for both the IPO and the market benchmark.

21. The t-statistics on initial returns must be interpreted with caution since the distribution on initial returns is positively skewed.

22. Data availability restricts tests using market value at offer to a sample of 695 initial public offerings. Market value is defined as the post-issue number of shares multiplied by the offer (placement) price. Gross proceeds are defined as the number of shares offered to the market multiplied by the offer (placement) price.

23. For details of the privatization process in the U.K., see Jenkinson and Mayer [11]. For issues purchased in installments, the first day return is based on the partly paid price.

24. As the latest available version of LSPD provides monthly rates of return data up to December 1990, the estimates of long-run performance for the 120 IPOs issued in 1988 are based on less than 36 monthly observations. The effective number of available monthly returns for these firms ranges from 24 to 35 months. As a result of the concentration of issuing activity during the first six months of 1988, 71 of the 120 IPOs have monthly returns for at least 30 months; 13 of the 1988 IPOs were issued during December 1988; they have a maximum of 24 months of returns data. The average holding period for the 120 IPOs issued in 1988 is 29 months, while the equivalent period for the remaining 592 IPOs in 1980–1987 is 34 months.

25. The number of firms trading after 36, 48 and 60 months drops from an initial sample of 346 IPOs to 288, 250 and 223, respectively.

26. In contrast to the evidence related to first day returns, the long-run performance of IPOs is not directly related to the method of issue and the proportion of equity offered.

REFERENCES

[1] Affleck-Graves, J., Hegde, S. and Miller, R.E. "The Relationship Between the First Day Return and the Aftermarket Performance of Initial Public Offerings," Unpublished Manuscript, Northern Illinois University, October 1991.

[2] Aggarwal, R. and Rivoli, P. "Fads in the Initial Public Offering Market?" *Financial Management* (Winter 1990), pp. 45–67.

[3] Aggarwal, R., Leal, R. and Hernandez, F. "The Aftermarket Performance of Initial Public Offerings in Latin America," *Financial Management* (Spring 1993), pp. 42–53.

[4] Bank of England, "New Equity Issues in the U.K.," *Bank of England Quarterly Bulletin* (May 1990), pp. 243–252.

[5] Dimson, E. "The Efficiency of the British New Issue Market for Ordinary Shares," Doctoral Thesis, London Business School, 1979.

[6] Dimson, E. and Marsh, P. "Event Study Methodologies and the Size Effect: The Case of U.K. Recommendations," *Journal of Financial Economics* (June 1986), pp. 113–142.

[7] Dimson, E. and Marsh, P. *The Hoare Govett Smaller Companies Index*, 1991, Hoare Govett Investment Research Limited, London, 1991.

[8] Ibbotson, R. "Price Performance of Common Stock New Issues," *Journal of Financial Economics* (September 1975), pp. 235–272.

[9] Ibbotson, R., Sindelar, J. and Ritter, J. "Initial Public Offerings," *Journal of Applied Corporate Finance* (Summer 1988), pp. 37–45.

[10] Ibbotson R. and Ritter, J. "Initial Public Offerings," in *Handbooks of Operations Research and Management Science*, Jarrow R.A., Maksimovic V. and Ziemba W.T. (eds.), North Holland, 1993.

[11] Jenkinson, T. and Mayer, C. "The Privatization Process in France and the U.K.," *European Economic Review* (March 1988), pp. 482–490.

[12] Keloharju, M. "Winner's Curse, Legal Liability, and the Long-Run Price Performance of Initial Public Offerings in Finland," Unpublished Working Paper, Helsinki School of Economics, 1992.

[13] Levis, M. "Stock Market Anomalies," *Journal of Banking and Finance* (September 1989), pp. 675–696.

[14] Levis, M. "The Winner's Curse Problem, Interest Costs and the Underpricing of Initial Public Offerings," *Economic Journal* (March 1990), pp. 76–89.

[15] Ritter, J. "The Long-Run Performance of Initial Public Offerings," *Journal of Finance* (March 1991), pp. 3–27.

[16] Sudarsanam, S. "Initial Public Offerings in the U.K. Unlisted Securities Market," Unpublished Manuscript, City University Business School, London, 1992.

[17] Uhlir, H. "Going Public in F.R.G.," in *A Reappraisal of the Efficiency of Financial Markets*, Guimaraes R.M., Kingsman B. and Taylor S. (eds.), New York, Springer-Verlag, 1989.

8

The Psychology of Investor Decision Making

Harvey A. Pines

Psychology is enjoying a bull market. It is difficult these days to find an analysis of Wall Street happenings that does not at some point refer to "market psychology," "investor sentiment," "contrary opinion" or some other term related to psychology. In this article I want to bring to your attention a new psychological perspective, one that until now has received relatively little notice outside of the academic milieu. Drawing on recent research findings defining this perspective, I will identify several important, but non-obvious, ways in which the individual investor's judgment and choices may be biased or erroneous. Then, several suggestions will be made for tactics to counter these sources of bias and error.

The psychological perspective I shall present arises from the relatively new field of *cognitive psychology*. In contrast to earlier work, cognitive psychology does not speak to the social influences on investor behavior emphasized by David Dreman in his important work on contrarian investing, or to the effects of motivation and personality eccentricities discussed by other writers. The field of cognitive psychology is based on an analogy between *information processing* in computers and the same processes in human beings. How we acquire and remember information, and how we process that information to arrive at judgments and decisions, are the focal point for cognitive psychologists. This concern with information processing activity is especially appropriate in an investing environment in which the dominant academic hypothesis about the dynamics of the stock market — the efficient market hypothesis — is couched in terms of the dissemination of and responsiveness to information.

Among the most fundamental information processing activities for investors are assessing probabilities, judging values and combining this information into an overall evaluation leading to a choice from among different courses of action. These behaviors ultimately rely on subjective judgments, even when performed in the context of formal models of security evaluation and portfolio management.

Reprinted from: Pines, H.A. 1983: A New Psychological Perspective on Investor Decision Making. *AAII Journal*, 5, September, 10–17. Reprinted with permission of The American Association of Individual Investors, 625 N. Michigan, Chicago.

What does cognitive psychology tell us about our ability to carry out these judgments, to process the vast amount of information that daily impacts investors? It is becoming abundantly clear that there are several facts about us as human decision makers.

- We have a limited capacity to process large amounts of complex information.
- We try to cope with that limited capacity by using a variety of simplifying rules-of-thumb or *heuristics* which, while effective in economizing on the information processing activity, are fallible guides to action and, under certain circumstances, become a liability rather than an asset.
- In assessing probabilities of events, we tend to overweigh information that is either minimally relevant or completely irrelevant, and to underweigh information which should form the basis of our assessments.
- We regularly underestimate important statistical influences on events.
- Our judgments and choices exhibit important inconsistencies.
- Our assessment heuristics lead us to beliefs about the predictability and control of events which may not be true in the uncertain world of investing.
- We are measurably *overconfident* in our judgments, in spite of all of the above.

From what evidence does the cognitive psychologist draw such pessimistic conclusions? Being committed to empirical investigation, these psychologists often construct decision environments in the laboratory to test their hypotheses. Efforts are then made to validate these observations by studying decision making behaviors in more natural settings, with experts in the field as subjects of study. I shall present a few examples of the judgmental and decision tasks that have been used by cognitive researchers. While these tasks often do not involve investment judgments directly, their relevance to such judgments will be made clear.

HEURISTICS: SIMPLIFYING A COMPLEX WORLD

Consider the following two questions, both of which involve an assessment of frequency or likelihood:

Question 1. John and Mary are part of a family with six children, three boys and three girls. The following are three of several possible orders in which they might have had their children: a) GBBGBG b) BBBGGG c) BGGBGB. Is one of these sequences more likely to have occurred than the other two? Why?

Question 2. Does the letter k appear more often as the first letter of a word or as the third letter?

The well-known cognitive researchers, Professors Daniel Kahneman and Amos Tversky, have proposed that in an effort to reduce the complexity and demands of exhaustively calculating the likelihood of an event, we seek to use heuristics to arrive at our probability estimates. Two important and commonly used heuristics are the *representativeness heuristic*, according to which estimated probability is a function of the similarity of two events, and the *availability heuristic*, according to which estimated probability is a function of the availability of information in our memory.

To illustrate the *representativeness heuristic*, consider the first question. Most people believe that either GBBGBG or BGGBGB is more likely to occur than BBBGGG. This judgment is made, according to Kahneman and Tversky, because we employ the following heuristic reasoning: since a child's sex is randomly determined, we should observe a sequence that is representative of (typical of or similar to) the occurrence of a random process. The irregularly mixed sequences appear to be more representative of a random process than the regular sequence, so we judge the regular sequence as least likely. In fact, each of the above sequences is equally likely to occur. Thus, our seemingly plausible rule-of-thumb has, in this case, led us to an erroneous conclusion.

How might the representativeness heuristic lead our investing judgment astray? One closely related example would be predictions by technical analysts based on patterns of short-run price changes. Here the heuristic might be: Because there are apparent systematic or orderly patterns to short-run price changes, judge the underlying market process also to be orderly. In fact, the apparently regular sequence of price changes may be randomly generated. Use of the representativeness heuristic makes it very difficult to "see" or acknowledge this randomness, even if present. A second example of representativeness-induced bias might arise in evaluating a newly formed company's business prospects. In today's economic environment, we might intuitively, but erroneously, predict a high technology firm as more likely to succeed than, say, a company that makes baby products. This judgment would be arrived at, not by a careful analysis of the firm's business environment, but because the technology company is more representative of companies that are visibly successful in today's markets. Other applications of the representativeness heuristic will be identified below.

To see how the *availability heuristic* affects our likelihood judgments, examine question two. Although most people judge the letter k to occur more frequently as a first letter (know), it is actually three times as likely to appear as a third letter (acknowledge). This error in frequency estimation can be accorded to our tendency to search our memory for relevant instances of what we are trying to estimate and then judge their probability by the ease with which we find such instances. Normally, more frequent events are more available in memory. In applying the availability heuristic, we appear to reverse this association and assume that if an event is more easily recalled it must have occurred more frequently. However, availability of information in our memory is influenced by many factors unrelated to the frequency of an event, e.g., its recency, its interest, its importance or emotional significance to us, or simply the attention given to it. Words beginning in k may be more readily noticed and thus remembered, but they are not more frequent.

The impact of the availability heuristic on investors' judgments is widely visible. A somewhat unusual example comes from a study of the purchase of disaster insurance. It has been documented that right after an earthquake there is a sharp increase in the purchase of earthquake insurance, but that the purchase rate soon drops back to normal as the earthquake ceases to be a recent event. Although one earthquake does not significantly alter the objective probabilities of earthquake occurrence, its increased availability in memory temporarily changes our subjective probability assessment. The availability heuristic also explains why our investment judgments are unduly affected by the most recent change in stock market prices; yesterday's price activity tends to stand out in our memory, and, as a result, it disproportionately influences our estimate of future price changes. More generally, our estimates of the likelihood that prices will appreciate or decline may be significantly influenced by the ease with which we can retrieve bullish or bearish information from our memory. Therefore, memorable events like a dramatic daily rise or fall in the market averages, pronouncements by well-known, but not necessarily expert public figures, or vivid coverage by the media, are all likely to unjustifiably alter our individual, subjective estimates of future price changes.

Even the wording of a question may affect our probability estimates because of the availability heuristic. Consider the following example:

a) How likely is it that there will be a resurgence of inflation?
b) How likely is it that, with the present expansion of the money supply, there will be a resurgence of inflation?

The second question may induce a narrow focus, making information about past instances of money supply growth especially available in memory. The first question may lead instead to the recall of available facts about the more general condition of inflation. The resulting probability estimates may vary considerably, depending upon which of these sets of information becomes available to the decision maker.

The availability heuristic also affects our probability estimates when we construct a *causal scenario*. Let us say that you are asked to indicate the likelihood that there will be increased earnings in the forest products industry next year. We may try to imagine a series of events which would lead to such an increase in earnings, a causal scenario. We then make a judgment about the likelihood of an increase in earnings, by the *ease* with which we were able to imagine the scenario. Here is one way this might occur. Let us say that you were watching the PBS television show, "Wall Street Week," and a reputable analyst explains why she believes the forest products industry will post record earnings next year. She constructs a cogent scenario leading to this event, a scenario including a period of declining interest rates. Several days later you read in the paper that there was a downtick in interest rates. The analyst's well-constructed scenario easily comes to mind and suddenly it seems as if the forest products industry is on the verge of an earnings explosion. In this example, the causal scenario was "pre-constructed" by the analyst, but if we were trying to construct the scenario ourselves, the same principle would apply: the easier it is to imagine a chain of events leading to an end state, the more likely that end state will appear to be.

BIASES IN THE SELECTION AND EFFECT OF INFORMATION

Modern cognitive psychology suggests that our probability estimates tend to be more influenced by some kinds of information than by others. To experience this process, try answering the next two questions:

Question 3. A recent survey of occupations in a large midwestern city found that among its inhabitants were approximately 1250 long-haul truck drivers and about 30 professors of classical literature. Consider Bill, a resident of that city. Bill is short, slim, and likes to read poetry. Is Bill more likely a professor of classical literature or a long-haul truck driver?

Question 4. A panel of psychologists interviewed a sample of 30 engineers and 70 lawyers, and summarized their impressions in thumbnail descriptions of these individuals. The following description has been drawn at random from the sample of 30 engineers and 70 lawyers:

"Jack is 39 years old. He is married with no children. A man of high ability and motivation, he promises to be quite successful in his field. He is well liked by his colleagues." Is Jack more likely to be an engineer or a lawyer?

In both questions there are two kinds of information available: singular or *case data*, consisting of evidence about the unique case under consideration (Bill, Jack), and distributional information or *base-rate data*, consisting of knowledge about the distribution of relevant events (numbers of truck drivers, lawyers, etc.). Considerable research has shown that in making these judgments we tend to focus on the unique qualities of the case data and fail to give sufficient weight to the base-rate data. In answering question 3, we tend to focus on Bill's personal characteristics, and then employ the *representativeness heuristic* to arrive at a decision. Since most people believe that "slim, short, and reads poetry" are characteristics representative of classics professors, they assign Bill to that category. The fundamental error here, however, is the inappropriate neglect of the fact that there are far more truck drivers than classics professors. Indeed, when people know only the base rate and nothing about Bill they most often, and correctly, conclude that Bill is more likely to be a truck driver. The addition of case data, however, causes them to almost completely ignore the base rate.

It is not inappropriate to factor case data into our assessments. However, in comparison to normative statistical models, models that may sometimes be used to estimate how much we should adjust for the case data, we appear to weigh this kind of specific information far too heavily. The same bias affects answers to question four. Here the case data is intentionally neutral in its implications for classifying Jack as a lawyer or engineer. As a result, most people neglect the base rate showing more than twice as many lawyers in the sample from which Jack was randomly drawn, and erroneously conclude that Jack is equally likely to be a lawyer or engineer. Kahneman and Tversky believe that this prevalent tendency to insufficiently consider information about the distribution of similar events is perhaps the major error of intuitive predictions. They also suggest that this error is likely to be magnified the better one is acquainted with the specific case or the more intensely involved one is with it.

Consider an example of how this bias might operate in an investment decision context. Widget-Tech is going public. Let us imagine a base-rate distribution such that 70% of new issues are lower in price 12 months after they are on the market and 30% are higher in price. What is the likelihood that Widget-Tech will end the next 12 months higher in price? Using the base-rate information alone you might be inclined to let other investors subscribe to this new issue. Now, consider the unique case data your broker provides you about Widget-Tech. It makes rapid pulse lasers for storing data on optical disks. Lasers. Optical disks. Data storage. There goes the base-rate; here comes the representativeness heuristic. Furthermore, if your source of this information is someone you "know" inside the company, you are even more likely to neglect the base-rate data.

Why do we neglect base-rate data and overemphasize case data? While research is still continuing into this question, there are some useful clues. To begin with, the delivery system for these two kinds of information is different: base-rate data is typically obtained from printed tables or figures while case data is often received in the context of a "personal" encounter, e.g., from a friend, broker, TV commentator, etc. Cognitive research suggests that our information processing system is more readily attuned to vivid, concrete, often emotionally laden case information than it is to pallid, dry, statistical data. In other words, vivid case information may be more available in memory and, in accordance with the *availability heuristic*, will be more likely to affect our probability judgments. To illustrate, consider:

Question 5. Which of the following causes a greater percentage of deaths in the United States each year?

a)   accidents *or* cardiovascular disease (e.g., strokes, heart attacks)

b)   suicide *or* homicide

Most people estimate that accidents kill as many or more persons each year as cardiovascular disease and that homicide is a more frequent cause of death than suicide. In fact, there are 10 times as many deaths due to cardiovascular disease than accidents and 30% more deaths are due to suicide than homicide. Moreover, contrary to most people's estimates, asthma causes more deaths than tornadoes, and diabetes more deaths than breast cancer. Professors Slovic, Fischoff and Lichtenstein, who have gathered these observations, believe that the vivid portrayal in the media of homicide, accidents, tornadoes, etc., make these causes of death more available in memory. When we make use of the availability heuristic to estimate these events' probabilities, the more vivid ones are judged as more likely to happen.

We can understand now why a stock market "tip" from a friend, broker or the media may have a far greater impact on our choice of investments than duller, but presumably more reliable, investment data obtained from statistical tables or charts. A vivid, perhaps even dramatic, tip will be more available in our memory. Then, when we apply the availability heuristic, the events promised in the tip will seem most likely to occur.

INCONSISTENCIES IN JUDGMENT

There are two kinds of judgmental inconsistency that an investor should be concerned about: *random inconsistency*, in which we make randomly different judgments of the same event, usually because of transitory conditions such as boredom, fatigue, distraction, etc., and *systematic inconsistency*, in which we make different judgments of the same event, because of some systematic bias in the way we think about the event. Random inconsistency was manifested when expert radiologists, observed as they attempted to detect the presence of lung disease on x-ray films, changed their minds in about 20% of the cases when reading the same film on two separate occasions. In another study, this one of horse race predictions, expert handicappers changed their mind on between 22% and 39% of their judgments during repeated appraisals of several races. Surprisingly, the more information the handicappers had to work with, the greater their inconsistency! No wonder we adopt heuristics to simplify our decision making. If you have ever wondered "How could I have decided to buy that?" part of the reason may have to do with the random inconsistency of our judgments.

One factor that may produce random inconsistency seems especially worthy of note. Recent research conducted by Professor Gordon Bower of Stanford University suggests that our moods or feelings may influence our probability estimates. According to Dr. Bower's data, people who are happy or in a good mood tend to think it more likely that good things will happen to them and less likely that bad things will befall them. People in a depressed or unhappy mood view the likelihood of good and bad events befalling them in the reverse manner. Thus, depending on your emotional state of mind, it may seem that the security whose purchase you are considering is either about to double in price or to lose half of its market value. Professor Bower speculates that the basis of this mood-probability estimation effect may be the *availability heuristic*: When we are in a good mood we tend to retrieve positive or bullish facts from memory; when we are in a bad mood, we tend to recall negative facts. As we have already seen, the information available in our memory influences our probability judgments.

Random inconsistencies tend to cancel each other out over time. Of greater concern is investment judgment that displays systematic biases that lead to logically inconsistent choices. Consider the following question:

Question 6. Do you prefer a sure gain of $80 *or* a risky choice that offers an 85% probability of winning $100 and a 15% probability of winning nothing?

Most people prefer the sure $80, in spite of the fact that the uncertain choice has a higher "monetary expectation." (The monetary expectation or "expected value" of an alternative is the sum of its outcomes weighted by their probabilities. Hence, 100×0.85 plus $0 \times 0.15 =$ $85 [versus $80 \times$ certainty $= $80]. The monetary value is what one would expect to get if the uncertain alternative were taken many times, i.e., the average gain.) Most investment theory assumes that investors are "risk averse," that they prefer a certain outcome to a risky alternative with an equal monetary expectation. Investors would be "risk seeking" if they reject the certain outcome in favor of the uncertain one. Economists generally assume that the rational investor is risk seeking only when the expected monetary gain of the risky alternative is large enough to compensate for taking a risk and foregoing the certain gain. Now consider the following choice:

Question 7. Do you prefer a sure loss of $80 *or* a risky choice that involves an 85% chance of losing $100 and a 15% chance of losing nothing?

Here, the risky alternative does *not* offer a greater monetary expectation (greater gain or lesser loss) to compensate for the risk. Rather, it offers the prospect of a greater loss. Thus, the rational investor should logically, and consistently, be risk averse and choose the certain loss. However, many studies indicate that a large majority of persons faced with this choice select the uncertain loss, i.e., they are risk seeking. In other words, our risk preferences are systematically inconsistent: we are risk averse in the face of gains, but risk seeking in the face of losses.

Many economists, decision theorists and psychologists have grappled with the theoretical implications of this inconsistency, and it is not our intention here to delve into these theoretical issues. Rather, let us consider the implication of this inconsistency for helping us to understand what appears to be a widespread bias in investor decision making.

In a fascinating volume, titled *Winning: The Psychology of Successful Investing*, Srully Blotnick reported the results of a 10-year study of over 1,100 investors. This report, published by McGraw-Hill in 1979, constitutes one of the few publicly available surveys of actual, ongoing investor behavior. In his book, Blotnick notes that many investors at one time or another owned a stock that had either a spectacular rise or decline. What was especially notable, however, was that in these cases an investor was almost 21 times more likely to "ride a spectacular stock all the way down than to ride it all the way up." This pattern of behavior, points out Blotnick, is in direct contradiction to one of the most widely given pieces of advice on Wall Street: to wit, cut your losses and let your profits run. Why do so many investors appear to behave in a manner opposite to this dictum? Blotnick suggests that a rising stock creates a state of tension in the investor, tension that can be relieved by the sale of the security; a declining stock leads to a state of depression and helplessness that effectively paralyzes the investor into inaction.

From a cognitive perspective, however, something else may be going on as well. Consider the investor who owns a stock that has appreciated in price. That investor is now faced with the choice of a certain gain from the sale of the security or the prospect of holding the stock for a greater but uncertain gain. As we have just seen, for the risk averse investor it "makes sense" to take the certain gain. Now consider the investor who is holding a security that has declined in price. That investor is faced with the choice of a certain loss or the uncertain prospect of an even greater loss. Again, as we have just seen, when faced with losses investors appear to act as risk seekers. Under loss conditions, in other words, it appears to "make sense" to select the risky alternative and hold the security. The result of this systematic inconsistency is to suggest that we sell our winning stocks and hold our losers.

The bias in our decision making induced by this inconsistent risk preference is aggravated by the way we define or "frame" the consequences of choice. Consider two securities. Security A, let us say, has a 70% chance of bringing a profit, security B a 60% chance. We could just as well say that security A has a 30% chance of bringing a loss and security B a 40% chance. Whether we compare the securities in terms of potential gains or potential losses logically should have no effect on our decision, since the two frames are merely opposite sides of the same coin. Psychologically, however, the choice of frame can produce a considerable effect. Professors Tversky and Kahneman asked a large number of physicians to choose one of two programs of treatment for "an outbreak of an unusual Asian disease expected to kill 600 persons." In one frame, the choice was presented in terms of gains, i.e., in terms of lives potentially saved. Here the choice was given as between program A that would certainly save 200 lives *or* program B that offered a one-third probability that 600 lives would be saved coupled with a two-thirds probability that no lives would be saved. When the programs were presented in these terms, the majority of the physicians were risk averse; they preferred program A that offered a certain saving of 200 lives. Then the two *identical programs* were presented to another group of physicians in terms of lives lost, i.e., program A which would certainly result in 400 deaths *or* program B with a two-thirds probability that all 600 would die coupled with a one-third probability that nobody would die. When the choice of programs was presented in terms of lives to be lost, the majority of physicians chose the uncertain or risky program B. In other words, the physicians were risk averse in the face of gains, and risk seekers in the face of losses. But, the perception of gain and loss was induced entirely by the framing of the problem; the "real" choice was always the same.

Once again, the implications for investors are clear. Comparing choices in terms of profits or positive rates of return is likely to induce a different risk perspective, and consequently a different decision, than might occur if the same choice was framed in terms of losses. Whether we view the cup as half full or half empty is entirely in the eye of the beholder, but it appears to have an important effect on our decisions.

SUMMARY THOUGHTS AND SOME CORRECTIVE PROCEDURES

In this article, we have looked at investor decision making through the eyes of the cognitive psychologist. We have seen that man has limited capacities as a processor of investment information. Like all human decision makers, investors operate according to what Herbert Simon called "the principle of bounded rationality." Professor Simon, recipient of the Nobel Prize for his studies of organizational decision making, believes that we develop a much more simplified and personally biased view of decision problems than is typically assumed in the formalized, normative models employed by economists.

Not that Professor Simon, or other students of human cognition, view their research as deprecating the extraordinary cognitive skills possessed by man — quite the contrary. Expanding knowledge about how we learn and remember, about how we make inferences and judgments, makes clear that our abilities in these domains are marvelously complex. However, the same skills and heuristic strategies that allow our greatest achievements also can lead to errors in judgments with important consequences for investors. Baruch Fischoff expressed this point eloquently. Our judgment skills, he noted, "are good enough to get through life, poor enough to make predictable and consequential mistakes; they are clever enough to devise broadly and easily applicable heuristics..., unsophisticated enough not to realize the limitations of these heuristics."

Many readers were probably familiar with the concept of heuristics before reading this article, if not with the term itself. Consider some of the rules of thumb that abound on Wall Street: "concentrate on emerging growth stocks;" "buy low PE stocks;" "cut your losses and let your profits run;" "buy the strongest stocks in the strongest groups." These "rules-for-investing" are heuristics, and one of their values is that they keep us from being overwhelmed with information. Cognitive psychology is now making us aware that we use similar rules of thumb at a much more fundamental level of investment decision making: in assessing the likelihood that an event will occur, in judging the risks and benefits of alternative courses of action, even in selecting information to attend to. At this more basic level, however, we may be unaware of our reliance on heuristics and unsuspecting of the biases and errors to which these useful strategies can lead.

Are there any tactics we can use to counter these biases? Recognizing that increased awareness is itself an important first step toward "debiasing" efforts, and with a caveat that the correctives offered here are only suggestive, what follows are a few possibly useful tactics.

1) Altering Availability

One technique for countering the biases induced by our use of the availability heuristic owes its inspiration to Louis Rukeyser, host of "Wall Street Week." As discussed earlier, guests on this program often construct persuasive and easily remembered causal scenarios to support their predictions about some future event, e.g., improved industry conditions, higher market averages, etc. After such a presentation, Rukeyser may ask his guest, "What could happen to change your mind?" From the perspective of cognitive psychology, this question forces the guest to provide the audience with an alternative causal scenario, one that makes an alternative forecast equally probable because it is now equally available in our memory. Try this tactic the next time a broker or financial adviser paints a particularly rosy picture for an investment. We can also apply this technique to our own forecasts. After constructing a scenario to explain why Widget-Tech's earnings are going to increase 20% a year for the next five years, construct another scenario that would lead to flat or even declining earnings. You will find that the 20% a year gain no longer seems quite so certain. Additionally, you will be in a more unbiased position to evaluate the causal chain that led to the initial forecast.

2) Doing Contrarian "Exercises"

Being on guard against the availability heuristic is also important in combating inconsistency in our judgment, especially that induced by extremes of emotion. Recall Professor Bower's finding about emotion's effects on judgments of the likelihood that good or bad things will happen to us. It is easy to see how the euphoria occurring at market tops and the gloom and depression that are prevalent at market bottoms can bias our forecasts. These extreme emotional conditions would make bullish or bearish thoughts more readily available in our memory in a particularly undiluted form. At such times the ability to act contrary to the prevailing mood may be facilitated by contrarian "exercises;" development and rehearsal of causal scenarios with outcomes opposite to that which everyone else is expecting. The increased strengthening or availability of these "contrary cognitions" may serve as an anti-dote to the highly available news supporting the prevailing psychological environment. Beware if you find that you "can't think of anything that could turn this market around;" that "can't think of" means your availability heuristic is hard at work against you!

3) Fixing the Frame

This next suggestion is a bit more demanding. We have seen that how we frame an invest-ment decision, e.g., whether in terms of future gains or future losses, may bias our risk preference. The dangers of this bias are probably less when applying a formal model of investment decision making, e.g., modern portfolio theory, where risk and reward are framed in more abstract, quantitative terms. More typically, however, we tend to think in terms of vivid, concrete, dollar denominated gains and losses, especially when confronting decisions about assets that have advanced or declined in price. How might we deal in a less biased manner with the decision over whether to hold these assets or sell them to realize a gain or loss? One useful tactic may be to "reframe" the sell alternative. Rather than thinking of the sale as resulting in a certain gain or loss, think of the proceeds of that sale as being invested in another risky asset, along with its attendant uncertain outcomes. Instead of being confronted with the alternatives of an uncertain hold versus a certain profit or loss, a condition that seems to produce significant biasing, the decision is "reframed" as a choice between two uncertain holds. In effect, this tactic frames the investment decision more clearly and appropriately as one of relative risk management, rather than as a choice guided by a dubiously applicable heuristic like "a bird in the hand is worth two in the bush."

4) Basing Forecasts on the Base Rate

If Professors Kahneman and Tversky are correct in their belief that overweighing the unique aspects of a case is the major error behind our intuitive predictions, then we need to be on guard not to neglect information about other cases of the same general class, i.e., not to ignore base-rate data. Analysts who prognosticate about future market directions provide examples of both the use and abuse of base-rate information. A positive example of using base-rate data is afforded by the commentator who evaluates the present market advance (or decline) by comparing it to a statistical summary of past market advances. For example, if the analyst provides data on the *average* duration or magnitude of previous bull markets, along with the *range* of those figures, i.e., the lengths of the shortest and longest advances, then she is providing useful base-rate information against which to judge present market conditions. However, the analyst who says "this advance reminds me of the 1951–53 market runup" is committing a double heuristic error: he is relying on *availability* of past instances in memory ("reminds me of") and is selecting some particularly salient, *representative* features of the present market to define a comparison. This error is the same as that committed in judging whether Bill was a classics professor or a truck driver by using the representative case information, "short-slim-reads poetry," and ignoring base-rate information about the number of professors and truckers. Of course, using base-rate information about past markets does not guarantee accurate predictions about future markets. It does, however, provide some protection against completely unrealistic expectations based on the current "case" and our involvement with it.

Indeed, none of the psychological insights or tactics presented in this article can give assurance of forecasting success. Furthermore, they certainly do not guarantee increased profits or rates of return. Their importance is best indicated by a line from *The Money Game*, Adams Smith's witty and literate survey of Wall Street and its psychology: "If you don't know who you are, the stock market is an expensive place to find out." Knowing who you are, whether in terms of your investment goals, your personality and motivations or the cognitive processes described in this article, may not result in larger profits, but such self-awareness may lead to smaller losses.

Finally, I would offer a caution to the reader who is provoked to conclude from this article that the biases and errors of individual investors "disprove" the thesis that the market acts as an efficient and rational price setting mechanism. Quite the opposite conclusion could be drawn. It can be shown on statistical grounds that when a reasonably large number of independent biases are operating together, a kind of "cancelling out" occurs. Consistent with the efficient market hypothesis, the collective, or *net*, effect of our individual cognitive biases and errors may be a market judgment that is more correct, more of the time, than any single one of us.

Cognitive Sources of Common Errors in Investor Judgment

Judgmental Bias or Error	Cognitive Source
1. Being bearish at market bottoms and bullish at market tops	Unavailability of a "contrarian," causal scenario
2. Selling winners and holding losers	Inconsistent risk preference and the biasing effects of decision frames
3. Over-optimistic appraisal of a security	Applying the representativeness heuristic to case data while neglecting base-rate data
4. Acting on unreliable "tips"	Vivid, "personal" information is more memorable than statistical data
5. Indecision and/or inconsistency	Effect of emotion on information availability and probability judgments
6. "It's the 1960s again!": misleading market metaphors	Misapplying the availability and representativeness heuristics
7. The "sure thing" that wasn't	Over-reliance on one available, causal scenario

9

The Bernstein Multifactor Optimization Model

Michael L. Goldstein, Michael Sommer and Robert A. Pari

SIGNIFICANT RESEARCH CONCLUSIONS

1)   Some years ago the *New Yorker* published a cartoon that captures the thought underlying our multifactor optimization model, and to some degree our view of investing in general. The cartoon portrays two men in conversation at a cocktail party, with the caption: "My feeling is that while we should have the deepest respect for reality, we should not let it control our lives." The idea behind our model is to systematically balance reality, as represented by recent trends in analysts' revisions of earnings estimates, against our own subjective view of the long-term value of each company quantified through our dividend discount model. The output is risk-optimized portfolios and stock rankings formed using a varying combination of our valuation view and earnings revision data.

2)   Our model attempts to capitalize on the fact that undervalued stocks are less sensitive to bad news, here in the form of downward earnings estimate revisions, than the average stock, and more sensitive to good news (see Table 9.1).

Earnings estimate revisions, which are quite predictive of stock price performance in general (see Table 9.2), are of even greater benefit when systematically combined with valuation data. Our model hinges upon this synergistic interaction between valuation and expectation. The combination of these factors produces results that exceed the sum of the parts. The results of our backtest, using 15 years of monthly data are shown in Table 9.3. It consistently outperforms, with moderate risk and turnover. The performance results are quite similar whether following a sector overweighted or sector neutral strategy. The sector neutral approach produces only one-third the volatility of an overweight strategy.

3)   The returns produced by a multifactor model depend, in part, upon how one weights the factors. Our research suggests that, on average, our viewpoint on valuation and recent trends in revisions should be about equal-weighted. Specifically, based on the experience

Reprinted from: Goldstein, M.L., Sommer, M. and Pari, R.A. 1991: *The Bernstein Multifactor Optimization Model*. New York: Sanford C. Bernstein

Table 9.1 Relative performance of the intersection between valuation and earnings revisions. Subsequent quarter annualized. (1976–1991)

Revision category	Valuation ranking		
	Most under-valued quintile	Average	Most over-valued quintile
Most upward	14.6%	10.2%	2.7%
Neutral	2.9	0.2	(2.2)
Most downward	(4.3)	(8.3)	(15.4)

Source: Bernstein research.

Table 9.2 Relative performance of our earnings revision model: mid-1976–mid-1991

	Annual relative[1] performance
Top quintile	+7.9%
Bottom quintile	(6.0)

1. Monthly rebalancing. After transaction costs.
Source: Bernstein research.

Table 9.3 Multifactor model relative performance, risk, and turnover: mid-1976–mid-1981

	Sector overweights	Sector neutral
Annual relative performance[1]	+8.7%	+7.0%
Standard deviation	8.9	3.0
Annual turnover	131	84
Share of months underperforming	37	36

1. Before transaction costs based on an out-of-sample test design.
Source: Bernstein research.

of the past 15 years, the average optimal weight for valuation would be 45% and revisions 55%. Of course, times are rarely average and therefore a static weighting scheme is less than ideal. We found that varying the weightings according to the degree of undervaluation found in the cheapest stocks when compared to history, comprises a major portion of total returns (see Table 9.4). When uncertainty is elevated, the odds and payoff of betting on a return to normal are high and, as such, value criteria should be preeminent. Figure 9.1 [p. 146] portrays the relationship between our measure of investor uncertainty and factor weightings. It should also be noted that revisions aided performance in 70–75% of all months in the last fifteen years. Many of those months in which revisions failed occurred when the Fed was initially easing credit at or near recession troughs. At those times, current changes in earnings expectations are dismissed by the market and the focus is shifted to earnings power. Our model, in part, accounts for this sensitivity to the economic cycle by varying weights based on the degree of misvaluation. Misvaluation is typically most

Table 9.4 Impact of varying the factor weights on the performance of our multifactor model: mid-1976–mid-1991

	Weights varied	Weights fixed
Annual relative performance[1]	8.7%	5.7%
Standard deviation	8.9	5.8
Annual turnover	131	85
Share of months underperforming	37	42

1. Before transaction costs. Reweighting of factors is guided by the historical range of valuation spreads and therefore has an element of hindsight. *Source*:Bernstein research.

severe at troughs, thereby overweighting value criteria when they should have the greatest effectiveness and revisions its least effectiveness.

4) The current year began with our multifactor model weighting undervaluation heavily and earnings revisions barely at all. This degree of skewing is quite unusual. As the Fed eased credit and the economy began to respond, the weight shifted towards revisions — the value opportunity was largely exhausted by June. The subsequent weakness in the economy has begun to again create compelling value opportunities, and today the relationship between the factors again slightly overweights value criteria.

Our model at this time suggests overweighting financials (New England banks, insurance companies), defense, forest products and housing, long-distance carriers, photography, and a few drug stocks. Electric utilities, energy, and technology are moderately underweighted. Given only average uncertainty, the payoff for large sector bets is absent and, therefore, most sectors should receive weights close to the S&P benchmark, with the exception of financials which should be overweighted by more than two times.

Table 9.5 presents our current optimized portfolio and Table 9.6 presents a sector neutral version using the same methodology. A ranking of the S&P 500 stocks, based on our multifactor approach by quintile and in alphabetical order, is [contained in the original article].

WHY A MULTIFACTOR MODEL?

Investing is an ongoing war between the short and long term. Stocks which appear undervalued compared to their long-term prospects are almost always experiencing some type of problem today. Conversely, stocks that currently exceed expectations rarely are strongly undervalued. The intent of our multifactor model is to address this dichotomy in a systematic way. We seek to quantify the amount by which each stock is under- or overvalued and the degree to which current expectations are either rising or falling. The process of quantification allows us to appropriately trade-off the short and long term across a broad universe of stocks. We also seek to capitalize on the asymmetric response to revisions characteristic of cheap stocks. Downward revisions create lesser performance penalties for undervalued stocks than the average stock, upward revisions greater outperformance. Finally, the investment horizon of the market is highly variable and therefore the returns attributable to undervaluation or rising expectations are unstable. It is, therefore, necessary to adjust the weighting between valuation and current trends based on the degree of miscalculation as measured in a historic perspective. The willingness to trade the portfolio should also relate to the magnitude of

Table 9.5 Multifactor optimized with sector overweights allowed: end-of-November 1991

	S&P weight	Representative stocks	Suggested weight	Price 11/30/91
Forest products & housing				
Forest products		Weyerhaeuser Co.	0.5%	$23.50
		Georgia Pacific**	0.5	47.50
		Louisiana-Pacific Corp.	0.8	37.75
Home building		P.H.M. Corp.	1.0	18.38
	1.3%		2.8%	
Financials				
Banks-NYC		Chase Manhattan Corp.*	2.0%	$15.00
		Chemical Banking Corp.*	1.5	21.13
Major regional banks		Shawmut National Corp.*	1.0	9.00
		Bank of Boston Corp.*	2.7	11.75
		First Chicago Corp.*	0.5	23.25
		First Union Corp.*	0.5	26.13
Misc. financial		Merrill Lynch & Co.*	0.5	48.00
		Primerica Corp.*	0.5	32.63
		Federal National Mortgage Assn**	2.0	56.00
Multi-line insurance		Household International**	0.5	40.88
		Aetna Life & Casualty Co.*	1.5	37.50
		American General Corp.	2.0	41.00
		Cigna Corp.*	3.0	52.13
Property-casualty ins.		American International Group	0.5	86.38
Savings & loan		Ahmanson (H.F.) & Co.*	0.5	13.75
	8.5%		19.2%	
Utilities				
Electric companies		Houston Industries Inc.	2.0%	$41.25
		Niagara Mohawk Power	0.5	17.50
		American Tele & Telegraph*	4.0	36.38
Telephone		MCI Communications*	2.0	27.88
	11.4%		8.5%	
Consumer growth				
Drugs		Bristol Myers Squibb*	2.0%	$78.50
		Lilly (Eli) & Co.*	1.5	73.50
		Schering Plough Corp.	1.0	59.00
		Warner-Lambert Co.*	1.0	69.63
		Upjohn Co.*	1.0	39.63
Entertainment		Disney (Walt) Company	1.5	104.15
Hospital management		Beverly Enterprises	0.5	8.13
		Manor Care Inc.	0.5	20.13
Photography		Eastman Kodak Co.	2.0	46.63
		Polaroid Corp.	0.5	24.88
Publishing		DeLuxe Check	1.0	37.25
		Time Warner Inc.	2.0	83.00
	15.4%		14.5%	
Consumer staples				
Auto parts aftermarket		Genuine Parts*	0.5%	$43.00
Beverages-soft, light & hard		Pepsico Inc.*	1.0	29.63
		Brown-Forman	0.5	77.13

Table 9.5 (*continued*)

	S&P weight	Representative stocks	Suggested weight	Price 11/30/91
Foods		Ralston Purina Co.	1.0	$52.88
		Archer-Daniels-Midland Co.	1.0	27.38
Restaurants		McDonalds Corp.	1.0	33.63
Retail stores-drugs		Rite Aid Corp.	1.0	18.13
Soaps		Unilever NV	2.0	91.38
Tobacco		Philip Morris Cos Inc.*	2.0	68.68
	15.0%		10.0%	
Consumer cyclicals				
Autos & auto parts OEMS		Chrysler Corp.*	1.5%	$11.63
Home furnishings		Bassett Furniture Inds	0.5	34.88
Misc. consumer cyclicals		Brunswick Corp.	1.0	11.63
		Outboard Marine Corp.	1.0	16.38
Retailers		May Department Stores Co.*	0.5	50.75
		Toys R Us, Inc.*	0.5	28.00
		Limited Inc.*	0.5	24.88
Textiles/shoes-apparel mfg		Russell Corp.	0.5	26.88
		Reebok International Ltd	0.5	26.88
Tires & rubber goods		Goodyear Tire & Rubber Co.	2.0	47.87
	9.7%		8.5%	
Industrial commodities				
Chemicals		Allied Signal Inc.	2.0%	$38.88
Containers-metal/glass/paper		Stone Container	2.0	20.00
Paper		International Paper Co.	1.0	66.75
Steel		Birmingham Steel Corp.**	0.5	18.38
		Chapparral Steel Company**	0.5	9.88
	6.8%		6.0%	
Capital equipment				
Aerospace-defense		General Dynamics Corp.	2.0%	$48.75
		United Technologies Corp.	1.5	47.63
		Grumman Corp.	0.5	17.50
		Northrop Corp.	0.5	21.13
		McDonnell Douglas Corp.	3.0	70.25
Auto trucks-parts		Eaton Corp.*	0.5	56.63
		Harnischfeger Inds Inc.	0.5	17.63
Electrical equipment		General Electric Co.	2.5	64.75
	7.9%		11.0%	
Technology				
CAD/CAM/CAE		Intergraph Corp.	0.5%	$16.88
Computer services/software		Lotus Development Corp.*	0.5	20.00
Computer/instrumentation		Amp Inc.	1.0	51.25
Computers		Sun Microsystems Inc.	0.5	24.00
		Intl Business Machines Corp.*	2.0	92.50
Miscellaneous		Minnesota Mng & Mfg Co.	0.5	86.75
	8.8%		5.0%	

continued overleaf

Table 9.5 (*continued*)

	S&P weight	Representative stocks	Suggested weight	Price 11/30/91
Transportation				
Airlines		American Airlines**	1.0%	$59.00
Misc. industrial/transportation		Waste Management Inc.	1.0	36.63
Railroads		Burlington Northern Inc.	2.5	35.75
	2.7%		4.5%	
Energy				
Gas pipelines		Sonat Inc.	0.5%	$34.38
		Enron Corp.	0.5	71.88
Oil-crude products		Louisiana Land & Exploration	2.0	32.88
		Halliburton Co.	0.5	29.88
Oils-integrated domestic		Amoco Corp.*	1.0	47.38
		Ashland Oil Inc.	1.0	28.00
		Unocal Corp.*	0.5	22.25
Oils-integrated international		Exxon Corp.*	3.0	58.63
		Mobil Corp.*	1.0	65.00
	12.5%		10.0%	
Total	100.0%		100.0%	

* Securities which are followed by Institutional Research Industry Specialists of Sanford C. Bernstein & Co., Inc. (SCB).
** Strategist additions. The strategist additions and all remaining securities are presented for illustrative purposes only on the understanding that SCB will not provide information with respect to these securities. The principal portfolio themes are determined by SCB's internal investment management process and take into account a combination of forecast information provided by SCB's Institutional Research industry specialists, internal Investment Management Research analysts, and purchased research services. Accordingly, they may differ from the estimate of earnings and dividends provided by our institutional research industry specialists. Institutional investment recommendations made by our institutional research industry specialists and by our Institutional Investment Strategist may differ from those indicated by our Investment Management valuation rankings. Additionally, our institutional clients very often have investment philosophies which differ significantly from that reflected in our investment management process. Accordingly, our institutional investment recommendations made to institutional clients may differ from the actions taken by our Investment Management Department.
Source: Corporate reports and Bernstein estimates.

misvaluation — the cheaper we believe the stock is, the less willing we should be to sell it, even in the face of very adverse current news. The singular advantage of this type of model is the ability to consistently compare a large number of stocks simultaneously.

What Factors?

The array of factors that can go into a multifactor model is virtually limitless. We have chosen just two — expected returns derived from our dividend discount model and smoothed recent changes in earnings estimates (revisions). By incorporating only two factors we have excluded explicit consideration of many traditional measures such as *P/E*, price-to-book, dividend yield, sustainable growth, size, price momentum, liquidity, price volatility and estimate risk. Our dividend discount model acts as a proxy for some of these factors (*P/E*, price-to-book, dividend yield, sustainable growth); our earnings revision model is, to a degree, a proxy for price momentum, and the optimization process addresses liquidity concerns. Philosophically, we have chosen these factors because they are comprehensible

Table 9.6 Multifactor optimized sector neutral end-of-November 1991

	S&P weight	Representative stocks	Suggested weight	Price 11/30/91
Forest products & housing				
Forest products		Georgia Pacific**	1.0%	$47.50
Home building		P.H.M. Corp.	1.0	18.00
	1.3%		2.0%	
Financials				
Banks-NYC		Chase Manhattan Corp.*	1.5%	$15.00
		Chemical Banking Corp.*	0.5	21.13
Major regional banks		Shawmut National Corp.*	1.0	9.00
		Bank of Boston Corp.*	1.0	11.75
		First Chicago Corp.*	0.5	23.25
		First Union Corp.*	0.5	26.13
		Federal National Mortgage Assn**	1.0	56.00
		Aetna Life & Casualty Co.*	1.0	37.50
		Cigna Corp.*	1.5	52.13
		American International Group	0.5	86.38
Savings & Loan		Ahmanson (H.F.) & Co.*	0.5	13.75
	8.5%		9.5%	
Utilities				
Electric companies		Houston Industries Inc.	3.0%	$41.25
		Niagara Mohawk Power	1.0	17.50
		American Tele & Telegraph*	4.0	36.38
Telephone		MCI Communications*	1.5	27.88
		Ameritech**	1.0	59.75
	11.4%		10.5%	
Consumer growth				
Drugs		Bristol Myers Squibb*	3.0%	$78.50
		Lilly (Eli) & Co.*	1.5	73.50
		Schering Plough Corp.	1.5	59.00
		Warner-Lambert Co.*	1.0	69.63
		Upjohn Co.*	1.0	39.63
Entertainment		Disney (Walt) Company	1.5	104.15
Hospital Management		Beverly Enterprises	0.5	8.13
		Manor Care Inc.	0.5	20.13
Photography		Eastman Kodak Co.	2.0	46.63
		Polaroid Corp.	0.5	24.88
Publishing		DeLuxe Check	1.0	37.25
		Time Warner Inc.	2.0	83.00
	15.4%		16.0%	
Consumer staples				
Auto parts aftermarket		Genuine Parts*	0.5%	$43.00
Beverages-soft, light & hard		Pepsico Inc.*	1.0	29.63
		Brown-Forman	0.7	77.13
Foods		Ralston Purina Co.	2.0	52.88
		Archer-Daniels-Midland Co.	1.0	27.38
Restaurants		McDonalds Corp.	1.5	33.63
Retail stores-drugs		Rite Aid Corp.	1.0	18.13
Soaps		Unilever NV	2.5	91.38

continued overleaf

Table 9.6 *(continued)*

	S&P weight	Representative stocks	Suggested weight	Price 11/30/91
Tobacco		Philip Morris Cos Inc.*	4.0	$68.68
		American Brands Inc.	0.5	38.63
	15.0%		14.7%	
Consumer cyclicals				
Autos & auto parts OEMS		Chrysler Corp.*	1.5%	$11.63
Home furnishings		Bassett Furniture Inds	0.5	34.88
Misc. consumer cyclicals		Brunswick Corp.	1.5	11.63
		Outboard Marine Corp.	0.5	16.38
Retailers		May Department Stores Co.*	1.0	50.75
		Melville Corp.	1.0	41.63
		Toys R Us, Inc.*	0.5	28.00
		Limited Inc.*	0.5	24.88
Textiles/shoes-apparel mfg		Russell Corp.	0.5	26.88
		Reebok International Ltd	0.5	26.88
Tires & rubber goods		Goodyear Tire & Rubber Co.	2.0	47.87
	9.7%		10.0%	
Industrial commodities				
Chemicals		Allied Signal Inc.	2.5%	$38.88
Containers-metal/glass/paper		Stone Container	2.0	20.00
Paper		International Paper Co.	1.0	66.75
Steel		Birmingham Steel Corp.**	0.5	18.38
		Chapparral Steel Company**	0.5	9.88
	6.8%		6.5%	
Capital equipment				
Aerospace-defense		General Dynamics Corp.	1.5%	$48.75
		United Technologies Corp.	1.0	47.63
		Grumman Corp.	0.5	17.50
		Northrop Corp.	0.5	21.13
		McDonnell Douglas Corp.	2.0	70.25
Auto trucks-parts		Eaton Corp.*	0.5	56.63
		Harnischfeger Inds Inc.	0.5	17.63
Electrical equipment		General Electric Co.	1.5	64.75
	7.9%		11.0%	
Technology				
CAD/CAM/CAE		Intergraph Corp.	0.5%	$16.88
Computer services/software		Lotus Development Corp.*	0.5	20.00
		Oracle Systems Corp.	1.0	13.5
Computer/instrumentation		Amp Inc.	1.5	51.25
Computers		Sun Microsystems Inc.	0.5	24.00
		Intl Business Machines Corp.*	2.5	92.50
Miscellaneous		Minnesota Mng & Mfg Co.	1.0	86.75
	8.8%		7.5%	
Transportation				
Airlines		American Airlines**	1.0%	$59.00
Misc. industrial/transportation		Waste Management Inc.	1.0	36.63
Railroads		Burlington Northern Inc.	1.0	35.75
	2.7%		3.0%	

Table 9.6   (*continued*)

	S&P weight	Representative stocks	Suggested weight	Price 11/30/91
Energy				
Gas pipelines		Sonat Inc.	0.5%	$34.38
		Panhandle Eastern	1.0	15.98
		Enron Corp.	0.5	71.88
Oil-crude products		Louisiana Land & Exploration	2.0	32.88
		Halliburton Co.	0.5	29.88
Oils-integrated domestic		Amoco Corp.*	2.3	47.38
		Ashland Oil Inc.	1.0	28.00
		Unocal Corp.*	0.5	22.25
Oils-integrated international		Exxon Corp.*	3.0	58.63
		Mobil Corp.*	1.0	65.00
	12.5%		12.3%	
Total	100.0%		100.0%	

* Securities which are followed by Institutional Research Industry Specialists of Sanford C. Bernstein & Co., Inc. (SCB).
** Strategist additions. The strategist additions and all remaining securities are presented for illustrative purposes only on the understanding that SCB will not provide information with respect to these securities. The principal portfolio themes are determined by SCB's internal investment management process and take into account a combination of forecast information provided by SCB's Institutional Research industry specialists, internal Investment Management Research analysts, and purchased research services. Accordingly, they may differ from the estimate of earnings and dividends provided by our institutional research industry specialists. Institutional investment recommendations made by our institutional research industry specialists and by our Institutional Investment Strategist may differ from those indicated by our Investment Management valuation rankings. Additionally, our institutional clients very often have investment philosophies which differ significantly from that reflected in our investment management process. Accordingly, our institutional investment recommendations made to institutional clients may differ from the actions taken by our Investment Management Department.
Source: Corporate reports and Bernstein estimates.

and seem to represent the heart of portfolio management as practiced by many active managers.

The Bernstein Dividend Discount Model

Dividend discount models are inherently highly subjective. By definition, the more undervalued a stock appears the greater the disagreement between the analyst providing input to the model and the market. It is this fundamental point of view that forms the character and much of the value-added of our multifactor model.

Our firm maintains a three-phase dividend discount model which ranks S&P 500 stocks based on long-term valuation criteria. An explicit five-year earnings and dividend forecast is created by an analyst for each stock in the model. This is the first phase of forecast growth. Earnings estimates for the next two calendar years are monitored versus the IBES consensus. A second phase transition growth rate is also specified for a subsequent period of two to six years. The default value for the second growth phase is 7%, with a specified range of 4.5% to 15%. In the third phase of growth, all companies are assumed to grow at 7%. An internal rate of return is computed for each stock, which is the discount rate which equates the current stock price to the projected dividend stream. These forecast annual IRRs are then transformed into long-term expected returns based on research we have done on duration.

The model includes a number of data control elements. Long-term ROEs (e.g., 1969–1989, 1969–1995E) are compared to the average ROE of the forecast period and to the forecast value for the final explicit forecast year (currently 1995). Similarly, growth rates are compared to the history forecast of the 1969–1995 period and the most recent peak-to-peak growth experience. Industry and sectoral ROEs and growth rates are also compiled and compared to historical values. The expected returns on individual stocks are a major input to our multifactor model.

Quantitative Characteristics of our Dividend Discount Model Output

Dividend discount models are inherently very flexible tools. Many, including ours, are applied using the principle that extreme growth rates, on average, regress to the mean. The application of this idea produces a ranking of stocks with strong value overtones. Table 9.7 compares the *P/E*, price-to-book, and dividend yield of the top quintile of this model to the market as represented by the S&P 500.

Today the price-to-book discount to the market exceeds the norm mostly due to the large overweighting in the financial sector. The price-to-book discount is currently 56%, while the dividend yield premium is 22%. Large losses in the auto stocks have rendered meaningless the current year *P/E* by distorting earnings of the top quintile of the dividend discount model.

Qualitative Characteristics of our Dividend Discount Model Output

Since the dividend discount model is a relative valuation tool it needn't always adhere to the quantitative restrictions of absolute value (i.e., dividend yield above 3.6%). During the last two economic booms (1984 and 1988), higher growth stocks were relatively more attractive than had been the case at other points in time, and as a result, the price-to-book discount and dividend yield premium were about half the average of the last decade.

The absence of meaningful economic growth in 1989–1991, combined with the deflationary cycle underway in commercial real estate, has made the financial sector a major investment theme. Table 9.8 shows the share of each sectors' stocks which were resident in the top quintile of the dividend discount model over the past three years. In interpreting this table large deviations from the benchmark weight of 20% are notable. While peaking in October 1990, today the model still has a strong pro-financials theme and a small procyclical theme. Since the dividend discount model weights long-term earnings estimates heavily in assessing valuation, themes are slow to change; the market's (or the analyst's) view of the long term must change first.

Table 9.7 Value characteristics of the top quintile of the dividend discount model compared to the S&P 500

	Long-term averages: mid-1980–1991		
	DDM Top quintile	S&P 500	(Discount)/ premium
P/E ratio-current year	9.6x	11.1x	(14)%
Price-to-book	1.16	1.62	(28)
Dividend yield	5.1%	4.2%	+23

Source: Corporate reports and Bernstein estimates.

Table 9.8 Share of stocks by sector in the top quintile of our dividend discount model

	Year-end 1989	9/30/90	Year-end 1990	6/30/91	Today
Forest products & housing	21.7%	46.0%	45.5%	23.8%	33.3%
Financials	51.8	60.0	55.4	50.8	47.5
Utilities	0.0	0.0	2.5	7.5	4.9
Consumer growth	9.1	7.8	3.6	9.1	7.4
Consumer staples	1.8	0.0	0.0	0.0	5.5
Consumer cyclicals	30.4	38.6	34.5	25.5	20.0
Commodities	13.6	11.7	13.3	13.6	18.3
Capital equipment	22.2	14.3	19.6	21.1	19.6
Technology	31.0	27.5	30.0	17.5	22.5
Transportation	28.6	14.3	19.0	20.0	35.0
Energy	2.6	2.6	2.6	28.9	16.2
Average	20.0%	20.0%	20.0%	20.0%	20.0%

Source: Bernstein research.

It is noteworthy that utilities and energy stocks, often associated with value because of their yields, are disfavored today by the dividend discount model. This illustrates the difference between a dividend growth approach such as our dividend discount model and one based upon current dividend yield.

Performance of the Dividend Discount Model

In the long term, the dividend discount model yields outperformance. The top quintile of the model has outperformed the market by about 3% a year on average since 1980. Using a longer 20-year period the premium is about 4%.

The Bernstein Earnings Revision Model

Earnings revisions are among the most powerful and consistent factors in explaining near-term stock price behavior. Upward earnings revisions predict outperformance and downward revisions underperformance. This prediction is most powerful in the first month but clearly persists even four months into the future (see Table 9.9).

The effect exists because changes in consensus estimates are autocorrelated — one change in a given direction predicts another in the same direction. Table 9.10 portrays the correlation in earnings revisions, computed on a monthly basis.

Table 9.9 Correlations between an earnings revision and future performance — 1976–1991

	Coefficient	Significant at the level of:
Next month	3.8%	0.01%
Two months hence	1.5	0.03
Three months hence	1.4	0.08
Four months hence	0.9	2.74

Source: Bernstein research.

Table 9.10 Correlations between an earnings revision and subsequent revisions — 1976–1991

	Correlation coefficient
Next month	56.3%
Two months hence	50.0
Three months hence	44.0
Four months hence	37.4
Five months hence	33.6

Source: Bernstein research.

The autocorrelation exists for several reasons:

1) Not all analysts have access to the same information or react at the same time. As a result, revisions to the consensus estimate occurring over multiple months are reactions to the same fundamental data. Nonetheless, the structural lag does matter and influence the behavior of stocks.

2) Systematic biases seem to exist in analysts' forecasts. As has been well-documented, analysts' estimates are almost always too high. Two-thirds of all earnings revisions are downward. The fact that estimate changes are trended suggests that initial revisions in response to changing reality are systematically inadequate.

Our earnings revision model is designed to monitor changes in earnings expectations across a universe of about 1,200 stocks. To be included a stock must be followed by at least three analysts. Stocks are ranked based upon relative changes in expected earnings yield (earnings change divided by current stock price). Changes in earnings expectations are measured on a monthly basis, with revision ranks computed by weighting the past four months' changes. The weighting places about half the weight on the current month. This smoothing is done to eliminate the underlying instability of revisions and to reduce turnover. While a smoothed revision series is statistically slightly less powerful than a pure one month revision index (see Table 9.11) the gain in stability and reduction in turnover makes this compromise worthwhile. The differential between the performance of one month and smoothed revisions is greater for downward revisions. This finding is sensible: the market believes bad news immediately but is skeptical of good news. Smoothing, in essence, capitalizes on the fact that revisions are trended in their character, and we are willing to wait for part of the trend to develop before acting.

Quantitative Characteristics of our Earnings Revision Model

We have evaluated the effectiveness of the earnings revision model across economic cycles, market sectors, valuation quintiles, and over time. We have found the revisions effect to be quite robust, adding significant performance across all these dimensions. Some distinctions in performance do exist though, which merit comment:

1) *Economic cycles matter.* The top quintile of the earnings revision model outperforms the bottom quintile in about three-quarters of all months. Many of those months in which the model failed, and in fact worked perversely, occurred in the early stages of Fed easings at the troughs of recessions (see Table 9.12). The reason revision information is harmful

Table 9.11 Correlations between one-month and smoothed revisions and subsequent performance — 1976–1991

	Correlation coefficients	
	Current month revision only	Last four months[1] revisions smoothed
Next month	6.6%	5.6%
Two months hence	8.4	7.8
Three months hence	9.0	7.9
Four months hence	9.9	9.1

1. With about half the weight assigned to the current month.
Source: Bernstein research.

Table 9.12 Relationship between Fed funds changes and the effectiveness of valuation and earnings revision model: 1976–1990

	Lagged one month Factor effectiveness[1]				
Monthly change in Federal funds rate	Dividend discount model (valuation)	Earnings revision model (earnings)	Average change in Fed funds rate (basis pts)	Frequency	Memo: Bernstein uncertainty index
< 100+ > Basis Points	26	(43)	(217)	6%	114
< 50 > − < 99 >	28	(41)	(83)	4	135
< 25 > − < 49 >	4	(21)	(34)	14	102
0− < 24 >	(19)	2	(10)	17	96
25–49	26	2	38	14	88
50–99	0	36	68	5	109
100+	22	20	223	5	127
Average: 1976–1990	0	0	12	100%	100

1. 0 = neutral, > 0 = more helpful than usual, 0 <= less helpful than usual.
Source: Bernstein research.

at such times is that investors are largely ignoring the near-term and focusing on earnings potential. As it would defeat the purpose of the model to require a forecast or even interpretation of the Fed's actions, we do not try to explicitly correct for this inherent shortcoming. Rather, our multifactor model weights its valuation factor in accordance with the degree of misvaluation, and misvaluation of economically sensitive stocks peaks at economic troughs. Therefore, the design of the model, in part but certainly not in total, accounts for the economic sensitivity of revisions.

2) *Revisions work across most market sectors.* We have found the earnings revision model effective across market sectors. The exception to the rule is in transportation where the erratic nature of earnings seems to render this variable impotent. Table 9.13 illustrates the relative performance of the top decile of revisions by sector versus the performance of that sector. In some months certain sectors would produce no top decile revision stocks. The payoff from revisions is stronger in the more volatile cyclical sectors.

Table 9.13 Performance of the top decile of earnings revisions[1] by market sector versus sector benchmark: 1978–1990

	Annual relative performance
Forest products and housing	14.8%
Consumer cyclicals	13.0
Technology	12.5
Utilities	11.9
Capital equipment	11.1
Industrial commodities	10.8
Energy	10.3
Consumer growth	8.2
Financial	7.4
Consumer staples	6.4
Transportation	0.8
Average	9.7%

1. Computed as One-Month Change in Mean EPS Estimate/Price; Performance measured in next calendar month.
Source: Bernstein research.

3) *The payoff from revisions is influenced by expectations and valuation.* Undervalued stocks are less sensitive to negative revisions and more sensitive to positive changes than the average stock (see Table 9.1). Overvalued stocks are more sensitive to negative revisions and less sensitive to positive changes; the latter are anticipated.

In addition, the probability of outperformance in reaction to upward revisions is meaningfully higher for undervalued stocks, and the chance for underperformance in response to downward revisions is lower. This constructive interaction between valuation and revisions forms the foundation for our approach.

4) *The power of revisions as an investing tool has not declined over time.* The performance spread between the top and bottom quintile of our revisions model has not diminished in the 1978–1991 period. To the contrary, 1990 and 1991 are among the best of the past fifteen years (see Table 9.14).

Performance of the Earnings Revision Model

The top quintile of our earnings revision model outperformed the market by 8.2% per year in a backtest for the 1978–1990 period. Outperformance occurred every year. The bottom quintile underperformed by 6.8% per year on average, but did beat the market in the economic recovery year of 1983 and the economic boom year of 1988. These results assume monthly rebalancing. Since, in practice, portfolios are not rebalanced monthly, we examined the correlation between revisions and subsequent stock performance for holding periods ranging from one-to-four months (see Table 9.9). The significance of revisions to stock price performance, even four months later, means just one upward revision predicts a multimonth period of compounding outperformance.

Table 9.14 Performance differential between top and bottom quintiles of our earnings revision model

	Revision Q1/Q5 performance spread
1978	15.5%
1979	17.2
1980	20.0
1981	7.3
1982	10.1
1983	5.1
1984	8.9
1985	12.0
1986	20.8
1987	18.4
1988	3.7
1989	19.6
1990	27.8
1991 YTD	16.5
1978–1991 Average	13.2%
1990–1991 Ann.	21.6%

Source: Bernstein research.

Combining the Factors: Considering Uncertainty Helps

Our analysis of the explanatory power of each factor (valuation and revisions) over the past 15 years suggests that an average weighting of roughly 55% on revisions and 45% on valuation is optimal if one chooses a one-year investment horizon. The dividend discount model has stronger autocorrelations and, as a result, a higher weight the longer the horizon chosen. Results from the first half of the era favor the dividend discount model, while the second half favors the earnings revision model. As we shall discuss subsequently, even a static combination of the factors yields outperformance.

We explored the idea of dynamically weighting the factors based on the concept of uncertainty. Figure 9.1 illustrates the relationship between factor weights and our uncertainty index. When uncertainty is high (as represented by an abnormally large misvaluation of the cheapest stocks or an abnormal overvaluation of the most prized stocks) a greater weight is placed on the dividend discount model and the cost of turnover is raised. At extremes either factor can warrant a negative weight. As uncertainty falls to or below its norm the greater weight shifts to the revisions input and the trading threshold is reduced. The premise of this work is that the past range of uncertainty and misvaluation can be reliably used to assess the current behavior of these variables. We found dynamically weighting factors based upon the degree of misvaluation adds greatly to returns, as outlined in our backtest results, discussed below.

Optimization

To make appropriate tradeoffs between excess returns derived from the two factor inputs discussed previously and risk, we have employed our portfolio optimizer. This system constructs risk-adjusted portfolios considering the forecasted two factor excess return, the

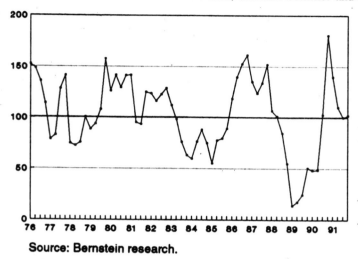

Source: Bernstein research.

Figure 9.1a   Bernstein uncertainty index

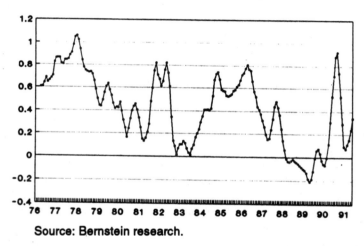

Source: Bernstein research.

Figure 9.1b   Weight assigned to valuation factor: smoothed 3 month rolling average

degree of diversification sought, the trailing three-year correlations between individual stock returns and turnover costs.

We have selected two alternative diversification schemes: the first, a broadly diversified stock portfolio; the second, a sector neutral portfolio. Since our optimizer varies the cost of turnover according to stock liquidity and position size, the size of the portfolio is relevant. We have assumed about $2.5 billion today.

Results of Our Backtest Simulations

Data Considerations

We have simulated a variety of multifactor approaches for the period from mid-1976 to mid-1991. The universe of stocks consisted of all those in the Bernstein Dividend Discount

Model, which for most of the test period approximated the S&P 500. The data base includes stocks which were subsequently merged or went bankrupt. All simulations began with $100 million under management which compounded to about $2.5 billion by 1991. Turnover and liquidity costs reflect this asset progression. Stocks which encounter data problems, such as the absence of earnings estimates, are sold if owned. Similarly, stocks whose price dips below $2.50 are liquidated if owned.

The portfolio is reoptimized at the beginning of each month using only data available at that time. The revisions data used in the simulations are from IBES, rather than the First Call/IBES combination used in production, and were incorporated only after a ten-day lag from time of release. We do not believe the test suffered from either survivorship or hindsight biases. It is, however, a large capitalization universe.

Out-of-Sample Test Design

Factor weightings are critical to this model. To eliminate the hindsight inherent in using the optimal weights for the entire backtest period on that same period, we conducted an out-of-sample test. The overall time period (1976–1991) for the simulation was partitioned into two subperiods, where weights derived from the first subperiod are used in the second subperiod simulation. This process is reversed to simulate investment behavior during the first subperiod. In essence, this resulted in a slightly higher dividend discount model weighting during the second subperiod (when value tended to underperform), and a much smaller dividend discount model weighting in the first subperiod (when value tended to outperform). Therefore, our results and conclusions are tempered with a fairly large dose of conservatism.

The results of our out-of-sample test are presented in Table 9.15. All performance statistics are presented before transaction costs.

Reweighting the value and earnings revision data dynamically accounts for just over one-third of the relative performance of the model in this test. It also boosts volatility by one-half and turnover by a like amount. It should be noted that the process of dynamic reweighting incorporates a degree of hindsight for the historic parameters if misvaluations are known. In retrospect we know when cheap was cheap. But even without this benefit the stable factor backtest shows strong outperformance.

In-Sample Backtest Results

Surprisingly, the in-sample test shows worse performance for the stable weight scenario than the out-of-sample test, but better performance for the dynamic weighting approach

Table 9.15 Relative performance, standard deviation and turnover of our out-of-sample backtest: mid-1976–mid-1991

	Dynamic factor reweighting?	
	Yes	No
Annual relative performance	+8.7%	+5.7%
Standard deviation	8.9	5.8
Annual turnover	131	85
Share of months underperforming	37	42

Source: Corporate reports and Bernstein estimates.

Table 9.16 Relative performance, standard deviation and turnover of our in-sample backtest: mid-1976–mid-1991

	Dynamic factor reweighting?	
	Yes	No
Annual relative performance	+9.6%	+4.3%
Standard deviation	4.6	5.6
Annual turnover	132	50
Share of months underperforming	33	41

(see Table 9.16). The standard deviation under the dynamic weighting scenario is lower, likely reflecting the hindsight benefit.

We conclude the out-of-sample and in-sample backtests produced essentially similar results.

Sector Neutral Backtest Results

We also tested a sector neutral (neutral to the S&P 500) approach on both an in-sample and out-of-sample basis. As shown in Table 9.17, the sector neutral results are 80–85% that of the sector optimized portfolio with much lower variation and turnover, an appealing combination.

Table 9.17 Relative performance, standard deviation and turnover of a sector neutral backtest

	Out-of-sample	In-sample
Annual relative performance	+7.0%	+8.1%
Standard deviation	3.0	3.6
Annual turnover	84	83
Share of months underperforming	36	35

Source: Corporate reports and Bernstein estimates.

[...]

10

How to Screen Using
High-Performance Generic Stocks[1]

Avner Arbel

[...] Once you have identified and confirmed a set of generic stocks, you are ready to consider the screening process. The term "consider" is appropriate here because you first have to decide how rigorous you want to be with the screening. One might correctly prefer to avoid a full screening and just do some "pruning." Surprisingly, under certain conditions this approach can be just as effective. This is why the Generic Stock Investment Strategy is so appealing: it is easy to implement. First, let's try to understand what the role of the screening process is within the specific context of the Generic Stock Investment Strategy. Then we'll consider the choices.

THE ROLE OF THE SCREENING

The screening serves two main purposes. The first is to exclude stocks that are neglected for good reasons. That is, stocks with a high risk of financial failure or even bankruptcy, which any rational investor should avoid. The objective here is to distinguish between neglect and rejection. Some stocks are not really neglected but are actually rejected by financial institutions and analysts for good reasons. We simply want to identify the lemons.

The second objective is to exclude companies that will not go bankrupt but will not do anything positive, either. The objective here is to identify and exclude the nebbishes, the permanent sleepers that will never move anywhere.

Given the time value of money, once we buy a neglected stock the shorter its discovery period by the rest of the world, the better. The whole idea of the Generic Stock Investment Strategy is to buy neglect and sell a darling. In fact, the best generic stock is a neglected stock of a solid company that will stop being neglected immediately after we have bought it. In the ideal case, we want to just precede the popularity flow. Clearly your objective should be to avoid both the *lemons* and the *nebbishes*.

This can be accomplished by using a combination of two tools: (a) screening and (b) diversification, which can, within limits, be substituted for each other. That is to say,

Reprinted from: Arbel, A. 1985: *How to Beat the Market with High-Performance Generic Stocks*. New York: Morrow

the more you diversify the less you have to screen, and vice versa. But this trade-off is imperfect. Even if you apply most rigorous and extensive screening, it is still a good idea to diversify — at least on a limited scale. Similarly, even if you diversify extensively, it is always beneficial to try to avoid securities of high financial risk by doing at least some minimal basic screening. In the area between these two extremes there is a trade-off between diversification and screening: to a large extent one can replace the other. More specifically, this suggests that there are two different approaches to generic stock selection:

1. *The Minimum Screening-Broad Diversification Approach.* Here the idea is to reduce risk by broad diversification within the opportunity set of neglected stocks that have passed a very minimal screening for high financial risk of bankruptcy. The rest of the risk is expected to be diversified away. . . .

2. *The Broad Screening-Limited Diversification Approach.* Here the idea is to reduce risk by screening each stock as carefully as possible and then to diversify just within the limited set of stocks that pass.

I don't understand, the perfectionist in you might be thinking at this point:

Surely a fully diversified portfolio of thoroughly screened stocks will do better than a portfolio of half-screened, half-diversified stocks?

This is correct, provided you have the resources (and time) to create a sufficiently diverse set of fully screened stocks to use in forming the portfolio. Remember, what might be ideal under theoretical conditions is often unfeasible in real-life situations. So we have to compromise in order to be realistic about it.

Does this mean that the broad screening approach is better than the broad diversification approach? Not necessarily. We should not ignore the fact that even with the maximum money, time, and effort invested in screening, some uncertainty will still remain. This is especially true for generic stocks because they suffer from information deficiency. Furthermore, given the benefit of diversification as a partial substitute for screening in reducing risk, extensive screening might be redundant.

If diversification is so wonderful why can't we just diversify a lot among a large number of neglected stocks without any screening at all? For two reasons. First, most investors do not have the resources to diversify among a sufficient number of securities to completely get rid of the company-related risk. This is specifically true of small investors. It is simply impractical.

Second, and more important, not all the specific risk associated with generic stocks can be diversified away. Remember, we are dealing here with a special segment of stocks that have a lot in common. For one thing, by being neglected, they all suffer from information deficiency and the resulting estimation risk. By diversification within the generic group, this risk can be reduced but not eliminated. The group as a whole is too homogeneous in this respect to benefit fully from the offsetting effect required for complete elimination of risk by diversification. . . . There is no doubt that even if you invested in all neglected stocks available in the market — creating a huge, well-diversified portfolio of thousands of stocks — a high level of information deficiency and estimation risk would still exist for this portfolio as a whole. The only way to reduce the bite of this deficiency is to do at least some screening. Remember, the generic premium is not free. You do have to earn it!

So, the best approach for selecting an effective portfolio of generic stocks is a mix between the two extreme alternatives, i.e., minimum screening-broad diversification, and broad screening-limited diversification. The ideal mix depends upon the availability of information, the investor's expertise, the resources available, and personal preference. It should not be forgotten, however, that while the relative emphasis depends on the specific situation in each case, it is important that at least some combination of screening and diversification is applied, keeping in mind the incomplete trade-off that exists between the two.

How can I tell what the right mix is? asks the pragmatist. To answer this question we have to remember that the reduction in risk associated with some diversification on the one hand, and some basic screening on the other, is very large. That is to say, the initial contribution of even very limited diversification or very minimal screening is considerable. Conversely, the risk reduction benefits from both screening and diversification drop off sharply once you pass a certain point. This is like a good wine that improves a lot by aging in the first years and less in the following years. Several studies have shown that a randomly diversified portfolio of about twelve stocks gets rid of well over 90% of all the risk that could be diversified away with a much larger portfolio. Similarly, after screening a portfolio of generic stocks for the clear losers, the benefit in relation to cost of additional screening on the margin becomes more and more questionable.

The practical question is, What specific screens should you use for each level of diversification and how far should you go with them. Let's try to answer these questions for the two basic alternative approaches that are presented here. Any combinations are up to you.

BASIC SCREENS FOR THE MINIMUM SCREENING-BROAD DIVERSIFICATION APPROACH

The objective of the screening in this case is to eliminate companies with a high risk of financial failure. There are several established methods for assessing bankruptcy potential. Most of them rely on a historical analysis of various financial ratios.

Two kinds of financial failure prediction models are widely used: multivariate models and univariate models.

The multivariate approach is pretty complicated, but not really necessary for our purposes. It uses several financial ratios that in combination are expected to predict bankruptcy. The best known is probably Altman's Z-score, which is a weighted average of five accounting ratios.[2] Different values of the Z-score correspond to different historically determined chances of bankruptcy. A company's Z-score below a certain level is supposed to indicate a high probability of failure. How is the Z-score calculated? First, take five financial ratios like the following:

1. Working capital to total assets
2. Retained earnings to total assets
3. Earnings before interest and taxes to total assets
4. Market value of equity to book value of total debt
5. Sales to total assets

Then assign weights to each of the ratios and calculate an index, Z, that is a weighted average of all the ratios found to be the best predictors. By using analytical techniques like discriminant analysis on data of past success and failure for a large number of companies, one can determine (a) which financial ratios to use, (b) which weights to choose, and (c) which is the appropriate cutoff point for the weighted average index, Z, to determine which companies pass or fail the test of financial solvency.

The multivariate approach is not simple. Luckily, univariate models, which are much simpler to implement, can be used—yielding results that are a good approximation for those of the more complicated approach. The univariate model, as the name implies, uses just one financial ratio instead of many, but it performs almost as well in bankruptcy prediction as the Z-score and other more complicated indicators. This is the ratio of cash flow to total debt. Cash flow is defined as the firm's net profits after taxes plus noncash cost items (primarily depreciation) minus capital expenditure paid in cash but not charged against profit. Total debt includes all borrowing: both short-term and long-term. Several studies show that companies with a cash flow to total debt ratio of less than 15% face a high probability of bankruptcy, while those with ratios above 15% are basically safe. The higher the ratio, the better in this respect.

The reason cash flow to total debt works so well as a bankruptcy predictor is that it reflects the ability of the company to repay its outstanding liabilities without refinancing. Companies approaching bankruptcy have usually exhausted all their financing options, so that cash flow is their only source of funds for repayment of debts. For example, a company with a ratio of 10% could only pay back its liabilities within an average period of ten years (if it survived that long).

Where does the cutoff point of 15% come from? you wonder.

It comes from historical analysis of the many firms that went bankrupt compared to similar firms that did not fail. But, the cutoff number is not cast in stone. Being based on historical data, there is no guarantee that the same cutoff figure will hold in the future. Also, it might be different for companies in different industries. In accuracy tests it has been found that it works better at predicting which firms will survive than which ones will go bankrupt. Thus, when this ratio is used as a screen for neglected firms, the chances of a lemon slipping through are pretty small, based on past evidence. Figure 10.1 summarizes the steps involved in this simple basic screen.

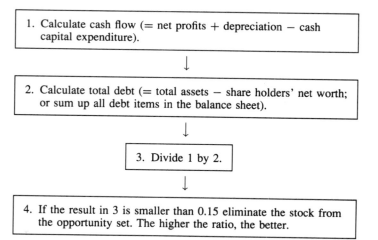

Figure 10.1 An example of univariate financial failure risk screen: the ratio of cash flow to total debt

There are many other simple univariate measures that can be used as predictors of financial failure to supplement the cash flow to total debt ratio. Note that by using additional ratios you in fact create your own *multivariate* model.

Other Screens for Financial Failure

1. The *current-ratio* (current assets divided by current liabilities) measures the ability to meet current debts with current assets. The particular ratio found for the company in question should be compared with the average for the industry, or a subindustry group. If the ratio is substantially below the average, this suggests a high short-term risk or liquidity problems. Such a stock should be rejected. *Industriscope* [3] is a handy source of data for this comparison.

2. Several other *liquidity ratios*, such as working capital to total assets; and coverage ratios, such as earnings before depreciation, interest, and taxes to debt interest can be used to measure the short-run ability to meet interest payment.

3. Also, as a single ratio, *net income* to total assets has been found to be an excellent predictor (the higher the better).

Two more approaches to determine the financial failure risk of companies are to consider the overall *financial strength* and the *safety ranking* of a company — as determined by different financial information services like Standard and Poor's, Moody's, Value Line, and several others. The most convenient services, with excellent records of predicting financial failure, are described below:

4. Value Line's financial strength ratings [6] measure the financial strength of each of the seventeen hundred companies in the Value Line data base relative to all other companies, in a declining scale starting with $A + +$ for the strongest companies, $A+$, A, $B + +$, $B+$, etc., all the way to C for the weakest companies. A rating of $C+$ is considered to be well below average, and C indicates very serious financial problems. The rating is based on a wide range of financial ratios as well as the judgment of Value Line's analysts regarding several relevant risk factors that cannot be quantified across the board for all stocks.

Among the main factors considered are financial leverage, equity coverage of debt, equity coverage of intangibles, the quick ratio, variability of return, fixed charges coverage, stock price stability, company size, and reliability of the accounting method.

In using this financial strength rating, your objective should be to identify neglected companies, as previously defined, with the highest possible rating. As a rule, a company with a rating below $C + +$ should be excluded as too risky.

5. Another convenient overall measure of risk is the *safety rankings*, also provided by Value Line [6]. It is similar but not identical to the previous measure. Therefore, both may be considered as a double check. The safety ranking ranges from 1 (safest) to 5 (most risky), and 3 represents an average risk. The ranking is based on several factors like stock price stability, the penetration of the company's market, product market volatility, financial leverage, earning quality, and the overall condition of the balance sheet, as assessed by Value Line analysts. Again, one should try to find neglected stocks with a safety ranking as high as possible and avoid stocks with a safety ranking over 3.

The main advantage of the Value Line *financial strengths* and *safety rankings* is their credibility. In addition, they are easy to interpret, straightforward and nonambiguous in their message, as well as easy to get. Value Line's publications are available in most libraries, and practically all brokers have access to them. Recently, these ratings as well as thirty other important variables for security analysis have been available on a current basis on disks for personal computer users. This state-of-the-art computerized system called Value/Screen [7] allows immediate and updated applications of various screening criteria simultaneously, using the large Value Line data base.

6. Still another excellent overall default-risk indicator for a company is its *bond rating*, which can be found for a large number of companies in Standard and Poor's [5] or Moody's [4] bond guides. The bond guides are also easy to get and their message is clearcut. In fact, a single call to your broker will give you the information.

Unfortunately, bonds of the really highly neglected companies are not rated. This is another example showing that if you want a real generic for a real bargain price, you'll have to do a lot of the investigating yourself. Good, reliable secondary sources are often not available. And don't forget that one of the most important characteristics of the generic stock investment concept is the do-it-yourself aspect. But an important point should not be overlooked. You don't have to take the generic trip all the way to its extreme, and go for the supergeneric stocks or the most neglected companies. Remember, the further you go, the more difficult it is to find reliable information, and the larger the do-it-yourself component. Luckily, however, neglect, like most other things, is a question of degree. In our research we found again and again that the generic frontier starts, in fact, close to home.

Clearly many generic-neglected companies can be found even among the companies included in the Standard and Poor's 500 index. This is true for every year without exception in the last ten years. Recall that the relatively neglected companies within the S&P 500 universe have markedly outperformed the S&P 500 index as a whole and have shown several times higher returns than the popular stocks in the same universe.

This also applies to the Value Line data base. It covers about 95% of the volume of trade of all stocks. While less than complete, it includes at any given time hundreds of relatively neglected stocks.

What about the other 5%? you might ask. As in the case of bond rating, aren't the *missing* companies the really neglected ones, which therefore represent even better opportunity?

The answer is yes, no doubt. But, as always, a trade-off exists here, and the question is how far do you want to go, and can you afford to go into the neglected domain. Within limits, the further you go, the higher the return is expected to be. But so are the costs, in the broad sense of the term; the cost of collecting, verifying, and monitoring information (and, in some extreme cases, even the cost of generating the relevant information practically from scratch), not to mention the guts it takes to be an entrepreneur and operate on your own.

But you don't have to go that far. You might decide to take, for example, the Value Line data base and/or the Standard and Poor's as your relevant universe (as far as the generic idea is concerned, this is a compromise but not necessarily a bad one: you're being realistic). This universe *admittedly* does not represent the *most* obscure set — the ultimate generic universe — but, still, it contains enough generic stocks to explore, hundreds at any given time. This is the ideal universe for a person who is beginning to experiment with the generic stock strategy. While the return here over the long run is not expected to be as high as for more neglected companies outside this universe, it is still expected to be higher than for less neglected companies and, most important, it is a feasible strategy to implement for most investors.

So, the message here is clear: Don't go to Spokane [...]: there is enough to pick not so far from your own backyard.

Finally, as general advice for the Minimum Screening-Broad Diversification Approach, I recommend a conservative attitude throughout. That is, in the process of eliminating the high financial risk companies, it is better to take a cautions approach. When you have a doubt, you would be better off rejecting a company and looking for another more solid generic stock. There are enough of them around.

Remember, risk taking may be good or bad depending upon the expected risk/reward ratio and the investor's preference. But it is *always* bad to take needless risk. The basic screens for financial failure, as discussed above, are so easy to implement and yield a reward that is expected to be so high that it's well worth the effort. So check and recheck and don't compromise.

Recall that broad diversification is a must for the limited screening approach. How much is "broad"? [This point is covered later in Arbel's book.] But first let's cover the second screening option.

THE BROAD SCREENING-LIMITED DIVERSIFICATION APPROACH

If for some reason you choose not to apply a broad diversification approach and select instead to invest in just a small number of stocks, you obviously lose some of the benefit of diversification in reducing risk. Consequently, you have to be more careful in the screening process and apply additional screens to those just mentioned.

The objective of the additional screens is to avoid the generic trap.

The Generic Trap

The generic trap is not unique to the stock market. It often exists in the product market, and the smart shopper tries to identify and avoid it. One can find generic products that deliberately or unintentionally are over-priced. Sometimes shrewd sellers dress up products this way and create generic traps for naïve shoppers who think that they are buying a bargain but in fact would be better off buying brand-name or another generic product. The notion that the poor usually pay more is probably partially related to the generic trap.

Recall where we stand now in the generic stock selection process. Presumably the lemons have already been eliminated by applying the screens for bankruptcy and financial risk discussed above. We are left now with a subset of generic stocks that are most probably financially solid. They are not going to die soon. This is fine, and clearly a necessary condition for all that follows. But we are in the market not just to avoid disasters, but to make money. Therefore, the next step is to unveil the two components of the generic trap. These are (a) the overpriced stocks, which are the most probable candidates for decline in price, and (b) the permanent sleepers, or the nebbishes that are correctly priced but, given their underlying business situation, cannot be expected to go anywhere in the foreseeable future. Remember, there is nothing more frustrating for an entrepreneurial investor than to be stuck with a nebbish stock. It puts you in the position of a dinosaur waiting for the weather to get warmer.

Broad diversification can help in this respect. When you diversify correctly, the traps are at least to a large extent automatically canceled out and diversified away (see detailed discussion coming soon). In this case you don't even have to identify the traps. But what if you are not ready, willing, or able to split your investment among the required number of stocks for effective diversification? Then the only way to reduce the chances of generic trap is by careful screening.

That is, you have first to uncover the traps and then make sure that you bypass them — this is the double role of the broad screening process. It is easier said than done. Unfortunately, many of the generic traps, like most other traps, are very tempting.

Screens for the Broad Screening-Limited Diversification Approach

The screening is done in steps starting with the more critical screens (which also happen to be easier to implement) and moving to broader, less critical tests. The idea is to apply a *stepwise elimination process* by which stocks that do not meet certain criteria are eliminated. The remaining set is screened again for another criterion and the stocks not passing this second screen are eliminated. This process continues in consecutive steps for several criteria until finally you are left with a subset of stocks that have passed all screens. If the number of the selected stocks is too small for even limited diversification, you may either decide not to invest at this time or you can relax your cutoff points for some, or all, screening criteria — implying acceptance of a higher (and perhaps more realistic) level of risk. Conversely, if you end up with too many stocks in the final stage, you might decide to do the opposite and raise your cutoff points by applying more rigorous acceptance criteria to select only the best of the best.

A "what-if" analysis of checking the sensitivity of the end results to marginal changes in the screening criteria (or perhaps just one of them) is always helpful.

The proposed screens for the Broad Screening-Limited Diversification approach are listed and explained below. It is recommended that you implement them stepwise in the order listed here.

Screen 1: Select Neglected (Generic) Stocks

The first step is to eliminate all stocks that are closely followed by analysts and/or extensively held by financial institutions. ... Your objective is to come up with a large number of truly neglected stocks. ... When completed, apply screen 2 for the remaining set.

Screen 2: Test for Financial Risk, Default, and Bankruptcy

Eliminate stocks of companies whose financial risk is too high to be included in the generic portfolio. Follow the procedures discussed in the "Minimum Screening-Broad Diversification Approach" section (p. 151), and apply the tests explained there. Remember, this screen is easy to implement and highly cost-effective. So, don't compromise. Now, proceed to screen 3.

Screen 3: The Growth Potential Test

The purpose of this screen is to eliminate stocks of companies with insufficient growth potential. Such stocks are good candidates to stay neglected forever. Conversely, high growth in earnings per share eventually attracts attention and starts the popularity flow, so that's what you are looking for.

The underlying idea of this test is pretty simple: compare the predicted growth in earnings per share for the company with a relevant reference group.

A stock will pass this screening if its expected growth rate is larger by a certain percentage (cutoff parameter) than those of the reference group. For example, using a cutoff parameter of 20% larger growth for the company in question than for the reference group, if the earnings per share of company Z is expected to grow in the next three to five years by 15% annually, while the growth rate of the reference group is 10%, company Z has passed the screen (since 15% is more than 20% larger than 10%).

This cutoff parameter can be changed based on the "survival count" of number of companies that have passed this screen (in combination with the previous and following screens). This is the "what-if" analysis mentioned before. Play with it by moving the parameter up and down (for example, try a required growth rate of 18% or 22% above the reference point) and see how the number of passing companies is affected.

What can be an appropriate reference group to use as a standard for comparison? This can be any of the following:

1. The relevant industry/subindustry group (e.g., electronics/consumer-electronics, auto-parts/autoparts replacement, office equipment/computers and peripherals)

2. A concept group (for example, cyclical companies whose earnings rise and fall with the economic cycle like metals, papers, machinery, autos. Other examples of concept groups include high tech, services, basic goods, recreation, interest sensitive, international, etc.)

3. Some broader universe like average growth for the market portfolio as a whole (all stocks or a representative sample like the S&P 500 index stocks). Being so broad, however, this reference group is less recommended.

Sometimes, especially when you face borderline cases, it is a good idea to double-check and use more than one reference group, like subindustry group *and* the relevant concept group. This can give you not only a cross-checking but also a better focus on the specific universe most relevant for the screened company. For example, computers *and* international, if the company in question is strongly involved in computer exports.

How can you arrive at reliable earnings predictions?

You can use your own earnings per share growth estimates for the company based upon data received directly from the company, other direct sources (e.g., government sources for defense contracts, when relevant; suppliers, buyers, people who work for the company, etc.), and your own personal knowledge of the company. Another approach is to use *secondary sources* on growth estimates as prepared, or compiled, by security analysts and financial services. Three excellent sources are described here.

1. Value Line [6] publishes predicted rate of growth in earnings per share for the next three to five years for about seventeen hundred companies on a current, updated basis. Value Line also estimates projected, for three to five years, book value per share, and dividend per share. In addition, as reference information you can check the actual earnings growth rate for the last five years.

2. Institutional Brokers Estimate System (IBES) Monthly Summary Data [2] compiles and publishes growth estimates for more than three thousand companies as prepared by thousands of security analysts. IBES offers not only the average growth rate based on predictions of practically all analysts across the country but also the range of their

estimates — high and low, a measure of consensus among analysts, recent changes in estimates — as well as several other relevant pieces of information relating to growth and how it is perceived by analysts.

3. Zacks Investment Research: The Icarus Service [8]. This source is very similar to IBES. The information can be obtained directly from the company, or now also through the Dow Jones News Retrieval Data Base [1] if you have access to a personal computer.

In addition, your broker can get growth estimates from other sources through his or her own files or the company research department.

Remember, however, that the further you go to the neglected ground, the more difficult it will be to find secondary sources for the growth estimates, the less consensus there will be, and the more you will have to do yourself.

This growth potential test (following the previous screens just described) when completed results in a sub-set of stocks that are neglected, financially sound, and have a growth potential larger than the relevant reference group or groups.

But this is not yet the end of the screening. A good, solid growth potential is not enough for a company to be included in your generic portfolio. Growth is great. But how much should you pay for it? That's why we need screens 4 and 5 — designed to check whether the growth potential is not already impounded in the stocks' price; testing, in fact, whether the Rolls-Royce is not too expensive.

Screen 4: The Normalized Price/Earnings Test

The purpose of this test is to make sure that the popularity flow has not yet started. We know by applying screen 1 that the stock is still relatively neglected. But what if without attracting wide attention some investors have discovered the stock before you and started to buy and consequently the price has gone up? This might be good for them but not for you. Again, such a stock could be an excellent candidate to become a nebbish from now on, or even worse, since it might be overpriced because of overreaction, its price may go down.

One way to check for this is to compare the current price of the stock with its normal price. Given, however, that stock prices are meaningless without reference to earnings, a better test is the normalized price/earnings (*P/E*) test.

This test will tell us how the current *P/E* of the stock compares with its normal historical level. If it is now considerably higher we had better eliminate the stock because this Cinderella might have a prince or two already. A typical generic trap.

The procedure for using the normalized price/earnings screen is as follows:

1. Compute current *P/E* ratio (by dividing the share price by the most recent annual earnings per share). Or simply take the current *P/E* ratio from a newspaper.

2. Compute the normal *P/E* ratio for each of the last three to five years by using the average price (one half of the high price-plus-the-low-price for the year) divided by the annual earnings per share. Then, calculate the average of these numbers for the last three to five years. This is the normalized *P/E* ratio.

3. Divide the current *P/E* ratio by the normalized *P/E* ratio as calculated in step 2.

4. If the result in 3. is much larger than 1, eliminate the stock from the investment opportunity set. This means that either the stock is overpriced or the popularity flow has already started. Conversely, if the current *P/E* ratio is equal to or lower than the historical norm,

you can be sure that the popularity flow has not yet started. Moreover, if reestablishment of the norm is considered likely, then a low *P/E* ratio is bullish.

Please note that in this test we compare the stock's present *P/E* ratio with its *own P/E* ratio over time. This is an important screen to capture the dynamic of the price changes. But, important as it is, this test by itself does not ensure that indeed we have avoided completely the generic trap. What if both the normalized *and* the current *P/E* ratio are relatively high? If this is the case we might be trapped with a stock that was and still is overpriced. This expensive wallflower should also be eliminated. Another, final test is therefore needed to check whether the stock with all its built-in attractions (neglected, financially sound, high growth potential, popularity flow not yet started) is not overpriced relative to *other relevant stocks*. To do so, we take our subset of survivors (which is now probably very thin and tired of tests) and apply screen 5.

Screen 5: The Growth Multiple Test

While the purpose of the previous test was to compare prices of the screened subset stocks across time (compared with their past normal price), the purpose of the growth multiple test is to compare prices across stocks of other companies.

Comparison of price/earnings ratios between companies is often used to identify over- or underpriced stocks. The lower the *P/E*, the smaller is the chance that the stock is overpriced, and vice versa. The problem with this approach is that it assumes "other things being equal." Of course in real life things are never equal and the level of the *P/E* is affected by several factors.

As a rule, (a) the higher the company's growth potential, (b) the more dividend it pays, and (c) the smaller the risk, the higher the *P/E* ratio of its stock should be and usually is. When you compare two stocks and one has a higher *P/E* than the other, this does not necessarily imply that the stock is overpriced. The higher price per unit of current earnings might well be justified by a larger growth potential, a higher dividend yield, or overall lower level of risk. In addition, there could be other distinct characteristics of the two companies, and their potential, that justify differences in the price that investors are willing to pay for a unit of current earning. This clearly indicates that *P/E* comparisons can be meaningful for detecting over- or underpriced stocks only if correct adjustments are made for other factors, mainly those mentioned above. We are dealing here with multidimensional comparisons, which are not easy to make.

Keeping this in mind, we propose to apply for the last screen a *growth multiple test* that adjusts for the relative growth potential of the company compared with other companies, but not for dividend yield and risk or other factors that might be relevant here. We have intentionally selected this simplified approach, not only because it is extremely difficult to specify and apply a single measure that is capable of making stock price comparisons simultaneously adjusted for more than one factor, but mainly because a growth-adjusted measure seems to be sufficient for our purposes.

Recall that we have already screened for risk. If indeed we have done a good job, the stocks that have passed this test are of an acceptable risk level. Furthermore, remember also that by deciding to adopt the Generic Stock Investment Strategy, we have accepted right at the outset a low or no dividend income, at least for the foreseeable future. Low payout is clearly one characteristic of generic stocks that the investor has to accept and live with. Consequently, it is an irrelevant factor in the analysis. We of course know that a stock that will never pay dividends, if so recognized by investors, should have a current price of zero. The underlying assumption here is that the lack of current dividend will be compensated by higher capital gains generated by expectations for high dividend in the future.

Clearly, the potential growth in earnings per share is extremely important for generic stocks and it should be taken into consideration when the price of the stock per unit of current earnings (the usual *P/E* ratio) is compared with that of other companies. Consequently, the growth multiple test is designed to measure whether the price/earnings ratio of the surviving set of generic stocks (which have already passed all the previous four screens) is not too high *per unit of expected growth*. If a stock has a *P/E* ratio per unit of expected growth, i.e., a growth multiple, that is relatively high, the chances of overpricing are correspondingly high.

The growth multiple for a stock is defined as

$$\text{Growth multiple} = \frac{\text{Current } P/E \text{ ratio}}{\text{Predicted growth in earnings per share (\%)}}$$

For example, if the current *P/E* ratio of Yatom Corp. [...] is 14 and its average annual predicted growth in EPS for the next three to five years is 10%, the growth multiple is 1.4 (= 14/10). Other things being equal, the lower the growth multiple, the better. A stock will pass the growth multiple test if its growth multiple is substantially lower than that of a relevant reference group.

The relevant reference group (or groups) can be selected in the same way as previously explained when the growth potential test was discussed (see p. 106). Namely, you can choose as a benchmark a relevant subindustry group, a concept group, or some broad market portfolio like the S&P 500 stocks.

The information sources for the predicted growth estimates are the same as for the growth potential test (see p. 156).

In summary, the procedure for applying the final growth multiple test is as follows:

1. Take the current *P/E* ratio from a newspaper (or calculate it yourself by dividing the share's most recent price by the most recent annual earnings per share).

2. Get the best estimate for the expected annual growth rate in earnings per share in percentage points (by using such sources as those listed on pp. 157–8).

3. Calculate the growth multiple by dividing 1 by 2, i.e., the current *P/E* ratio by the predicted growth. This will give you the *P/E* multiple per unit of expected growth.

4. Repeat points 1, 2, and 3 for a relevant reference group as explained on p. 157. The growth multiple for a reference group is calculated in the exact same way as it is for individual stock.

5. Compare the growth multiple for the stock (3) with the growth multiple for the reference group (4).

6. If the result in 5 indicates that the stock's growth multiple is substantially lower (say by 20%) than that for the reference group, include the stock as a candidate for the generic investment portfolio. If the stock multiple is not substantially lower or, even worse, is higher than the reference group, eliminate the stock from the investment opportunity set.

The threshold of 20% below reference is not cast in stone. That's the cutoff that I typically use and it seems to work well. However, you can select another cutoff point or just accept all stocks whose growth multiple is equal to or lower than that of the reference group. In fact, the threshold can be changed relative to your own preference (which might change over time as you gain more experience) and the characteristics of the specific universe of stocks that you screen. In any case, a "what-if" analysis (of changing the cutting criterion and checking the results) is always valuable and highly recommended.

Finally, a note about flexibility and judgment. Remember that the screening process as a whole refers to several variables. You can relax your requirements a bit on one screen if the results of the others for a certain stock are highly positive, and vice versa. For example, if the firm shows much above-average growth potential, and in addition the financial risk is well below average, you can probably accept a higher growth multiple. No doubt, some trade-off between the screening criteria can be allowed. They should be considered in combination.

This completes the screening process for the Broad Screening-Limited Diversification Approach.

If you did a good job you have now a subset of generic stocks that has a high probability of being free of lemons, nebbishes, and overpriced stocks. The chances of falling into the generic trap are small. More specifically, the screened set includes stocks that

— Are confirmed to be really neglected.

— Are financially strong and are not expected to default in the foreseeable future.

— Have above average growth potential.

— Have a current price/earnings ratio not above the stock's normal historical level — indicating that the popularity flow has not yet started; and finally.

— Are not overpriced compared with other relevant stocks — taking into consideration the company's current earnings and its expected growth.

Remember that all of the above are needed for the Broad Screening-Limited Diversification Approach, while only the first two screens, which are quite simple to perform, are needed for the Minimum Screening-Broad Diversification Approach. . . .

ENDNOTES

1. Arbel assumes that investors will apply their screening to a universe of generic, i.e., neglected, stocks. [Note added by editor.]

2. See Edward Altman, "Financial Ratios, Discriminant Analysis, and the Prediction of Corporate Bankruptcy," *Journal of Finance*, (September 1968).

REFERENCES

[1] Dow Jones & Company. *Dow Jones News/Retrieval*. P.O. Box 300, Princeton, NJ 08540. Tel.: 1-800-257-5114.

[2] Institutional Brokers Estimate System (IBES). *Monthly Summary Data*. Lynch, Jones & Ryan, 325 Hudson Street, New York, NY 10013. Tel.: 212-243-3137.

[3] Media General Financial Services, Inc. *Industriscope*. P.O. Box C-32333, Richmond, VA 23293. Tel.: 804-649-6569.

[4] Moody's Investors Service, Inc. *Moody's Bond Record*. 99 Church Street, New York, NY 10007. Tel.: 212-553-0300.

[5] Standard & Poor's Corp. *Standard and Poor's Guide*. 25 Broadway, New York, NY 10004. Tel.: 212-208-8769.

[6] Value Line, Inc. *Value Line Investment Survey*. 711 Third Avenue, New York, NY 10017. Tel.: 212-687-3965.

[7] ——. *Value/Screen*. 711 Third Avenue, New York, NY 10017. Tel.: 212-687-3965.

[8] Zack's Investment Research. *The Icarus Service*. 2 North Riverside Plaza, Chicago, IL 60606. Tel.: 312-559-9405.

11

Index Funds

Stephen Lofthouse

The first equity index fund was created by Wells Fargo in the U.S. in 1971. Since then indexing has grown rapidly, especially in the U.S. and the U.K. Indexing is generally associated with institutional investment: although a number of retail unit trust products are available, these have a small market share. Greenwich Associates conducts research on the institutional investment market and examines mainly large funds. For its universe (Greenwich Associates, 1991 and 1992), more than 18% of U.K. institutional funds' U.K. equities were indexed. In the U.S. the comparable figure for U.S. equities was nearly 35%. About 25% of U.S. institutional funds' international equities were indexed and about 14% of their bond portfolios.

What has accounted for the rapid growth of index funds? First, a growing acceptance of aspects of modern portfolio theory. Second, the increasing power and decreasing cost of computer facilities. Third, the introduction of negotiated commissions in the U.S. and U.K. which enabled index fund managers, who do not require brokers' research, to deal at low cost.

SELECTING AN INDEX TO TRACK

When setting up an index fund the first issue that has to be tackled is which index will be the benchmark. This will depend upon the objective of the investor. For example, investors who wished to index their entire U.K. and U.S. equity investments would probably choose broad indexes such as the FT-A All-Share and the S&P 500. The former index covers over 800 shares while the latter covers 500. Indeed it might be felt that 500 shares is not a very broad coverage for an economy as large as the U.S. and involves too much of a big company bias. In that case the Wilshire 5000 might be thought appropriate. If an investor thought he had skill in selecting large stocks he might wish to actively manage the large stocks and only index small stocks. In the U.K. such an investor might choose a smaller companies index such as the Hoare Govett Smaller Companies Index, or the FT-SE SmallCap Index, as the benchmark.

Reprinted, with minor changes, from Chapter 35 of: Stephen Lofthouse, 1994: *Equity Investment Management*. Chichester: Wiley.

Clearly there is no correct answer to the question of which index to track. It depends on the objective. But some indexes are better for tracking than others. Some indexes have a large number of non-investable stocks. A non-investable stock is one in which the index fund cannot invest. For example, some countries do not allow foreigners to buy certain types of stocks or certain classes of equity. If the non-investable stock is included in the index, an index fund run by a foreigner will inevitably be subject to tracking error. The size of the inevitable tracking error can be calculated and allowed for, but it might be thought better to select a different index that does not have this problem — e.g. the FT-Actuaries World group of indexes.

METHODS OF INDEXATION

Having chosen an index, the next step is to select a method of indexation. There are four main methods, listed below, and each will be discussed in turn:

- full replication
- stratified sampling
- optimization
- synthetic funds

Full replication. Full replication involves buying all the stocks in the index, and in the same proportion. This can involve tedious administrative chores. A large number of stocks may have to be bought (and some of the smaller ones may be difficult to buy) and a large number of dividends handled. These dividends have to be reinvested in the correct proportions. The fund has to be adjusted for rights issues, acquisitions and changes in the index.

A fully replicated fund will track an index closely, but not exactly, because the index does not have the costs associated with setting up the fund, re-investing dividends and custody. Moreover, calculations of the index with dividends re-invested usually assume that dividends are reinvested on the ex-dividend date although the income will not be received by a fund for some time.

Stratified sampling. Instead of holding all the stocks in an index, the stratified sampling approach aims to track the index by holding only a sample of stocks in the index. There are a variety of sampling techniques.

If an investor aimed to track the FT-A All-Share Index, all stocks above a certain size, say 0.25% of the index, might be purchased, and in proportion to their market capitalization. Further stocks might then be purchased to bring the sector distribution of the sample into line with the index. This approach will inevitably have a large stock bias and, if there is a small stock effect, lead to large tracking errors.

An alternative approach is to set each sector weight in the sample equal to the index sector weight. Each sector then might be split into large, medium and small stocks and samples drawn from each of these subcategories. One could go even further and try to ensure that the sector samples broadly match the index with regard to a few variables such as price–earnings ratio, yield and beta. This introduces a modest degree of optimization, which is discussed below.

Generally the tracking error from stratified sampling will be good, albeit a little worse than full replication, although if some individual stocks or small stocks as a group do exceptionally well the tracking error can be substantially greater. For example, the small stock effect was a particular problem for funds tracking the FT-Actuaries Japan Index in 1989. If all costs are allowed for in calculations of tracking errors, a stratified sample index fund could track better than a fully replicated fund if brokerage commissions or custody costs have a sliding scale (i.e., higher proportionate fees for small deals) or include a fixed sum per transaction.

Optimization. Optimization is a sample method based on the view that the return from a stock is determined by its exposure to certain attributes such as size, price–earnings ratio, volatility, growth etc. In the U.K., proprietary optimization models sold by BARRA use about 40 variables in the optimization procedure, which attempts to ensure that the sample has the same characteristics as the index with regard to these variables.

This seems rather hard conceptual work compared to stratified sampling, but optimization adherents argue that stratified sampling "is unsophisticated in that the only control of tracking error is by minimizing the deviations of portfolio holdings from index holdings along the two dimensions of, usually, capitalization and industry groups. Unfortunately, the intuition that keeping the differences in holdings small will cause the tracking error also to be small is frequently erroneous." (Rudd, 1980, pp. 60–61). Stratified sampling adherents criticize optimization, in turn, on the grounds that it involves some data interpretation so that there is a blurring of the distinction between passive and active management. Moreover the optimization model assumes that historical risk and return relationships will hold in the future, which is not necessarily true. Also, as the characteristics of the market and stocks change, portfolio rebalancing will be required. Tracking errors can vary from year to year and user to user.

Despite these concerns, in the U.K. optimization dominates the indexation market. About 75% of the indexation market uses optimization techniques against about 10% in the US. This U.K. bias towards optimization is probably a result of the ready availability of off-the-peg optimization software rather than a result of intellectual arguments.

Synthetic index funds. It is possible to construct synthetic index funds by using a derivative product, a stock index future. A future is a contract that requires investors to buy or sell a given quantity of a specified asset on a specified future date at a specific price. Futures have traditionally been important for agricultural products but now cover financial instruments and stock market indexes. A rapidly increasing number of indexes are now traded on futures markets, both on their local market and in the U.S. (for a list, see, e.g., Abbott, 1991). Because no physical commodity underlies an index, stock index futures are settled by cash when the contract expires.

Futures are bought and sold on margin. Only a small part of the total value of the future changes hands when the trade is made. The price of a future will be the current index value plus an allowance for interest earned on the cash that can be deposited because of the margined nature of the transaction, less the value of dividends that would be received on the underlying stock. Futures trade at close to the theoretical value, but not always exactly at it.

It is possible to construct an index fund by buying futures. A single transaction would suffice to index the S&P 500 by stock index futures. Apart from the simplicity, futures involve much lower costs. Bid/ask spreads are lower, commissions are lower and stock exchange taxes are often avoided. Liquidity is often better in the futures markets than the underlying markets and execution may be easier. For funds with inflows and outflows of money, it is easier to adjust exposure in the futures market than in the equity market. (For more details of the advantages of futures, see Bruce and Eisenberg, 1992.)

Against these advantages it must be noted that futures are not available for all indexes — for example there is a future on the FT-SE 100 but not on the FT-A All-Share. However it would be possible to track reasonably well a broad index such as the MSCI EAFE or the FT-Actuaries World Index by combining various local indexes (see Meier, 1991).

There are a number of tracking risks with synthetics. First there is the possibility that the future will be mispriced against stocks at the time of purchase. The FT-SE 100 future has been mispriced by as much as 2% although the S&P 500 has seldom been more than 1/2% mispriced. Second, futures contracts are short-dated and managers wanting to buy large positions will have to operate with the most liquid contracts which usually are those expiring in three to six months. This means the manager must roll-over the contracts periodically to a longer date. At each roll-over there is a pricing risk. Third, in calculating the theoretical price for a future, both dividends and interest rate assumptions have to be made. If the forecasts are incorrect, there will be tracking error. Fourth, cash-settled stock index futures are on a daily market-to-market basis, i.e., any gain or loss on a future must be settled daily. This means that in a falling market the futures investor will have to pay away cash, thereby earning less interest than anticipated. This will lead to underperformance. In a rising market the fund will outperform.

In practice, there are few synthetic index funds outside the U.S.

THE MISPLACED EMPHASIS ON TRACKING ERROR

It is worth saying a little about tracking error, that is the amount an index fund deviates from its benchmark index. Many investors become obsessed with tracking error — the smaller, the better, they argue. However it should be noted that for a sampling approach the tracking error can be reduced by increasing the sample size. There will always be a trade-off between administrative chores and tracking error and the investor must decide the optimal blend.

Further, it is worth asking whether the size of the tracking error, within reason, really matters. Is the real objective of an index fund exactly to match the index or to avoid the unpleasant surprises that can result from an active manager underperforming by a very large amount? If the latter, a tracking error of, say, 0.5% rather than 0.35%, does not seem very important.

The tracking error is important as a control measure. If the change in the index and the change in the portfolio are measured daily, one can check whether the tracking error is behaving randomly. Some days the fund should outperform the index and some days it should underperform. Based on historical data, the standard deviation of the historical tracking error can be calculated and the size of the tracking error can be related to historical experience. If the tracking error is behaving non-randomly, or growing in size, the index fund should be re-balanced, that is to say stocks should be bought and sold to get a closer match to the index.

There is an important point here. The tracking error based on market prices and ignoring costs is the best way of seeing if the fund is correctly structured. However what interests the investor is the tracking error after costs and this may affect indexing tactics, especially for smaller company funds. Sinquefield (1991) shows that in practice it may be better to be as much concerned with achieving good trades as attempting to always have the exact index weights. It is important that the quantitative staff and the traders for an index fund work closely together.

THE FUTURE

What of the future? The U.K. will probably follow the U.S. in developing a number of "enhanced" index funds. Such funds are tilted to stress attributes thought to lead to outperformance, such as low price–earnings ratios. Funds may also engage in arbitrage by holding stocks or futures depending on which is cheap relative to the other. Passive funds are also likely to be held alongside active funds to gain exposure to areas where the manager lacks expertise, such as small stocks or emerging markets, or for practical reasons.

A good example of a practical reason for indexing concerns small overseas stocks. Many fund managers' foreign holdings have underperformed the local indexes. There may be many reasons for this but one is surely the small company effect. A manager running a U.K. pension fund might invest, say, 8% of the fund in Continental Europe. With the prospect of investing in perhaps 10 countries, the number of holdings in each country is going to be fairly limited if the pension fund is small. Even in France and Germany no more than five or six stocks might be held and fewer in the other, smaller, countries. Where a manager holds one to six stocks in a country it is unlikely that a top-down manager will invest in small stocks: to do so would be to take a stock rather than a country bet. Moreover the manager may not have the time to follow smaller stocks in ten markets. Inevitably, such a manager's fund will have a rather blue chip bias. This could kill performance. One solution would be to invest part of this European exposure in a European smaller companies index fund. This would seem to be a sensible blend of active and passive management.

CONCLUDING COMMENTS

Index funds are here to stay. They give up the chance to outperform an index for the security of not underperforming. In practice, index funds have often outperformed the average active fund manager. There are four main methods of managing an index fund: each has advantages and disadvantages. Somewhat oddly, the U.K. market is dominated by the optimization approach, which has a small U.S. market share. Managers tend to be either for or against index funds yet there is no reason why a predominantly active manager should not hold index funds for areas where he lacks expertise or for practical reasons.

REFERENCES

Abbott, S. 1991: Stock Market Indexes Opening in Every Direction. *Futures*, **20**, August, 40–42.
Bruce, B. and Eisenberg, A. 1992: *Global Synthetic Index Funds*. Chicago: Chicago Mercantile Exchange Strategy Paper Series.
Greenwich Associates, 1991: *Coming Challenges, Growing Sophistication*. Greenwich: Greenwich Associates.
Greenwich Associates, 1992: *Strengthening Relationships, Improving Performance*. Greenwich: Greenwich Associates.
Meier, J.P. 1991: Tracking Global Equities With Stock Index Futures. *Futures*, **20**, January 34, 36.
Rudd, A. 1980: Optimal Selection of Passive Portfolios. *Financial Management*, **9**, 57–66.
Sinquefield, R.A. 1991: Are Small-Stock Returns Achievable? *Financial Analysis Journal*, **47**, January-February, 45–50.

PART THREE
The Bond Market

In this Part we examine some aspects of the bond markets and bond management.

As a general principle in this book I have not included articles on concepts that are covered clearly in the textbooks. In Chapter 12, however, I have made an exception for duration and convexity. Outside of the U.S., many equity managers and private investor managers still think of maturity as the usual measure of the interest rate risk of a bond. Bond professionals, however, think in terms of duration and convexity. On the basis that some equity and generalist investment professionals will read this section, it seems worth giving a brief review of the concepts. Moreover, duration is used in another reading in this book (Chapter 13), so a little revision may be useful. Mark Kritzman, of Windham Capital Management, is our instructor. Kritzman is a regular contributor to the "What Practioners Need to Know. . ." column in the *Financial Analysis Journal*, useful reading for both students and practioners.

Given that most bond funds are managed actively, textbooks spend a disproportionately large amount of space on passive bond management techniques such as portfolio immunization and a disproportionately small amount on active bond management. And what they say on active management is generally unhelpful as it does not really give much of a feel for how one would implement the analysis. I try to redress the imbalance I perceive by concentrating here on active management (although Kritzman says a few words on immunization in Chapter 12).

As the textbooks explain, investors can make active bond market decisions on the basis of interest rate forecasts, credit analysis, sector switches (e.g., from corporate issues into Treasuries), yield pick-up, and so forth. We can describe all the non-interest rate forecast items as bond analytics. Forecasting interest rates accurately is probably the way to achieve the largest abnormal returns — positive and negative. As a result some bond managers concentrate on interest rate forecasts. In some markets, for example in the U.K., the paucity of corporate issues has generally led investors to take this stance by default, although many U.K. managers continue to take this approach in the international markets where sector and credit analysis can be carried out. But there are two types of question that we might raise about concentrating on interest rates. First, how good are investors at calling moves in interest rates? And how exactly do they do it? Do they have a specific forecasting model? If there is no proven track record and no systematic method of forecasting, one might argue that investors should not be taking big interest rate bets. Second, are big interest rate bets in clients' interests? Of course, if they always come off, they are. But even good forecasters make mistakes. Betting on interest rates is likely to add to the volatility of returns.

Since equities offer higher returns than bonds over the long term but with greater volatility, anybody who has a bond portfolio is presumably more concerned about volatility than returns. Does it make sense to manage bonds in such a way as to increase their volatility? If it doesn't, maybe this again argues for taking modest interest rate bets and trying to add to returns by other strategies. In this view investors or their managers should not stray too far from some benchmark duration. I happen to be in general sympathy with this view of not making big interest rate bets for pure bond portfolios, but investors sometimes hold bonds not because they have defined themselves as bond investors, for whatever reason, but as an alternative to cash or equities. In that case they are presumably holding bonds on the basis of relative expected returns (after allowing for risk). It might be argued that in such a case a benchmark bond duration is not especially meaningful.

Clearly investors can legitimately disagree as to how much weight to put on interest rate forecasting and bond analytics. Differences in abilities will also justify different approaches. In Chapter 13, Francis Trainer and Jonathan Reiss describe one bond analytical approach. The original article is too long to reproduce here and I have omitted sections on callable bonds, mortgage pass-throughs, financial futures and other complex securities, as well as some mathematics relating to duration. Omitted sections are indicated by ellipses. Trainer is a fixed income manager and Reiss a quantitative analyst: both are at investment managers Sanford C. Bernstein.

I have not included anything on interest rate forecasting as I think useful articles on this demand more economic knowledge than the typical reader will possess.

Chapter 13 was wide-ranging. The next three chapters deal with more narrowly focused issues. The first looks at the shape of the yield curve (which was also discussed in Chapter 12). Bonds with different maturities, but otherwise similar characteristics, usually offer different yields. The relationship between maturity and yield is known as the term structure of interest rates or as the yield curve. Every investor knows that the yield curve can be upward sloping, downward sloping, flat or hump-shaped. Despite this, there is a tendency among many investors to believe, and some textbooks to imply, that the "normal" yield curve is upward sloping, i.e., longer maturity bonds yield more than short-dated. The evidence is that this is indeed the most frequently observed curve, but it is a much closer call than usually thought — in the U.S. between 1900 and 1929, for example, the yield curve sloped upwards in only two years.

In Chapter 14, John Wood, a professor at Wake Forest University (and at Northwestern University when the article was written) shows the shape of yield curves for the U.S. for 83 years and reports on the shape for an even longer period. He finds that yield curves tend to be positively sloped when yields are low and negatively sloped when yields are high. These findings are consistent with: (1) expectations theory, which argues that the shape of the yield curve reflects investors' expectations of future interest rate levels; and (2) expectations being formed on the basis of regressive, rather than extrapolative, expectations, i.e., recent interest rate trends are expected to reverse and not continue in the same direction. This argument requires some notion of a "normal" level of interest rates to which rates regress, and this normal level can change over time. Wood relates changes in the normal level to changes in the monetary standard. This article is by no means the last word on yield curves, and the textbooks contain expositions of other theories, but the article does discuss a major theory and provides a large amount of useful historical information on the shape of yield curves. A more detailed discussion of the same material may be found in Chapter 19 of Wood and Wood (1985).

In Part Two we saw that Arbel tried to screen out stocks that might become bankrupt. Lakonishok, Schleifer and Vishny (1993) note that one reason value stocks perform well may be that investors are willing to pay too much for glamour stocks because of the perceived prudence of holding such stocks. One aspect of this is avoiding stocks that might become bankrupt or have recently received some adverse news or are unattractive in some other way. Clearly there are conflicting pressures. Holding stocks that go bust is not profitable; holding "distressed" stocks that turnaround will be profitable. In the bond markets this conflict can be seen in extreme form in the defaulted bonds market. Many investment portfolios will not, or are not permitted to, hold bonds that have defaulted. Defaulted bonds are clearly the issues of companies that could become bankrupt but, since the bonds will have suffered large price falls when they defaulted, they may well make rewarding investments. While it is unusual for defaulted interest payments to be made good, a part of the principal is usually recovered in the form of new securities when the issuer is reorganized. This may exceed the market price immediately following default.

In Chapter 15, David Ward and Gary Griepentrog, professors at the University of Wisconsin-Oshkosh, look at the risk and returns from defaulted bonds. They note the classic study by Hickman covering the period 1900–43, which showed that buying defaulted bonds was a worthwhile strategy. Ward and Griepentrog examined the period 1972–91 and found that investments in defaulted bonds produced excess returns; however, the returns fell over the period. Either the market was getting more efficient — several mutual funds specialize in buying distressed securities — or there were special factors at play in the second half of the 1980s. Over the entire period, defaulted bonds produced returns similar to those from small capitalization stocks, but with a total risk similar to that of the S&P 500. However, defaulted bonds had very high unsystematic risk, suggesting the desirability of good diversification, and systematic risk more akin to that of bonds than equities. It would seem that there is a case for holding defaulted bonds.

We have seen in Part Two the substantial evidence of empirical regularities in the equity market, for example, January effects, day-of-the-week effects, earnings revision effects and so forth. Regularities have been found in the bond markets too. In the bond markets there is also considerable interest in the returns from bonds of various quality levels and whether junk bonds are the issues of the rising stars of tomorrow or really are just junk — ticking time bombs. Chapter 16, by Edward Altman and Duen Li Kao, links both types of research. They find that bonds that are issued with non-investment-grade ratings tend neither to be upgraded or downgraded. However, echoing the earnings revision findings of the equity market, high-yield bonds that are re-rated tend to be next re-rated in the same direction, i.e., upgrades continue to be upgraded and downgrades continue to be downgraded. AAA/AA/A original issues that are downgraded tend to continue to decline. Altman is a professor at New York University and Kao is Director of Investment Research at General Motors Investment Management Corporation.

REFERENCES

Lakonishok, J., Shleifer, A. and Vishny, R.W. 1993: *Contrarian Investment, Extrapolation, and Risk.* Faculty Working Paper No. 93–0128, College of Commerce and Business Administration, University of Illinois at Urbana-Champaign.

Wood, J.H. and Wood, N.L. 1985: *Financial Markets.* San Diego: Harcourt Brace Jovanovich.

12

The Essentials of Duration and Convexity

Mark Kritzman

In 1938, Frederick Macaulay published his classic book, *Some Theoretical Problems Suggested by the Movements of Interest Rates, Bond Yields and Stock Prices in the United States Since 1865*.[1] Although Macaulay focused primarily on the theory of interest rates, as an aside he introduced the concept of duration as a more precise alternative to maturity for measuring the life of a bond. As with many of the important innovations in finance, the investment community was slow to appreciate Macaulay's discovery of duration. It was not until the 1970s that professional investors began to substitute duration for maturity in order to measure a fixed income portfolio's exposure to interest rate risk.[2] Today, duration and convexity — the extent to which duration changes as interest rates change — are indispensable tools for fixed income investors. In this column, I review these important concepts and show how they are applied to manage interest rate risk.

MACAULAY'S DURATION

A bond's maturity measures the time to receipt of the final principal repayment and, therefore, the length of time the bondholder is exposed to the risk that interest rates will increase and devalue the remaining cash flows. Although it is typically the case that, the longer a bond's maturity, the more sensitive its price is to changes in interest rates, this relationship does not always hold. Maturity is an inadequate measure of the sensitivity of a bond's price to changes in interest rates, because it ignores the effects of coupon payments and prepayment of principal.

Consider two bonds, both of which mature in 10 years. Suppose the first bond is a zero-coupon bond that pays $2000 at maturity, while the second bond pays a coupon of $100 annually and $1000 at maturity. Although both bonds yield the same total cash flow, the bondholder must wait 10 years to receive the cash flow from the zero-coupon bond, while he receives almost half the cash flow from the coupon-bearing bond prior to its maturity. Therefore, the average time to receipt of the cash flow of the coupon-bearing bond is significantly shorter than it is for the zero-coupon bond.

The first cash flow from the coupon-bearing bond comes after one year, the second after two years, and so on. On average, the bondholder receives the cash flow in five and one-half years $((1 + 2 + 3 + \cdots + 10)/10)$. In the case of the zero-coupon bond, the bondholder receives a single cash flow after 10 years.

This computation of the average time to receipt of cash flows is an inadequate measure of the effective life of a bond, because it fails to account for the relative magnitudes of the cash flows. The principal repayment of the coupon-bearing bond is 10 times the size of each of the coupon payments. It makes sense to weight the time to receipt of the principal repayment more heavily than the times to receipt of the coupon payments.

Suppose we weight it 10 times as heavily as each coupon payment and compute the weighted average of these values. This approach yields a weighted average time to receipt of 7.75 years. But this measure too is deficient because it ignores the time value of money. A $100 coupon payment to be received two years from today is less valuable than a $100 coupon payment to be received one year hence.

Macaulay recognized this distinction and determined that the time to receipt of each cash flow should be weighted, not by the relative magnitude of the cash flow, but by the present value of its relative magnitude. Macaulay's duration, therefore, equals the average time to receipt of a bond's cash flows, in which each cash flow's time to receipt is weighted by its present value as a percentage of the total present value of all the cash flows. The sum of the present values of all the cash flows, of course, equals the price of the bond.

Assume that the yield to maturity of a 10-year bond equals 10%. The duration of the zero-coupon bond maturing in 10 years is the same as its maturity, because the time to receipt of the principal repayment is weighted 100%. The duration of the coupon-paying bond, though, is significantly shorter. It is not, however, as short as 5.5 years, the average time to receipt of the cash flow ignoring the relative sizes of the payments. Nor is it as long as 7.75 years, the estimate that accounts for the relative sizes of the cash flows but ignores their present values. The duration of the coupon-bearing bond equals 6.76 years, as Table 12.1 shows.

Table 12.1 Macaulay's duration (yield to maturity = 10%)

Cash flow	Time to receipt (years)	Present value of cash flow	Weight	Weighted-value time to receipt
100	1	90.91	0.0909	0.0909
100	2	82.64	0.0826	0.1653
100	3	75.13	0.0751	0.2254
100	4	68.30	0.0683	0.2732
100	5	62.09	0.0621	0.3105
100	6	56.45	0.0565	0.3387
100	7	51.32	0.0513	0.3592
100	8	46.65	0.0467	0.3732
100	9	42.41	0.0424	0.3817
1100	10	424.10	0.4241	4.2410
2000	55	1000.00	1.0000	6.7591

In general, we can write the formula for Macaulay's duration as follows:

$$D = \frac{\displaystyle\sum_{t=1}^{n} \frac{t \cdot C}{(1+r)^t}}{\displaystyle\sum_{t=1}^{n} \frac{C}{(1+r)^t}}$$

where

D = duration,
n = number of cash flows,
t = time to receipt of the cash flow,
C = cash flow amount and
r = yield to maturity.

PROPERTIES OF DURATION

It is apparent from the formula for Macaulay's duration that its value depends on three factors — the final maturity of the bond, the coupon payments and the yield to maturity.

If we hold constant the size of the coupon payments and the yield to maturity, duration in general increases with a bond's maturity. But it increases at a slower rate than the increase in maturity, because later cash flows are discounted more heavily than earlier cash flows. If we extend the maturity of the coupon-bearing bond described earlier from 10 years to 15 years, for example, its duration increases by only 1.61 years, from 6.76 years to 8.37 years. Of course, in the case of zero-coupon bonds, duration increases exactly with maturity, because these values are equal to each other.

Deep-discount bonds are another exception to the general rule. They increase in duration as maturity increases up to a distant threshold and then decrease in duration as maturity increases beyond this threshold. This peculiar result arises because deep-discount bonds with sufficiently long maturities behave like perpetuities (bonds that pay coupons forever). Perpetuities have an infinite maturity but a finite duration, because the weight of the principal repayment is inconsequential by the time it is discounted to present value.

At a given maturity and yield to maturity, duration declines with increases in the coupon payments or principal prepayments. This is because a larger percentage of the total cash flow is received earlier; stated differently, the times to receipt of the coupon payments or principal prepayments are weighted more heavily relative to the final repayment of principal. If the coupon payments from our earlier example were $120 rather than $100, the bond's duration would equal 6.54 years instead of 6.76 years.

Finally, if we increase yield to maturity while holding the coupon payments and maturity constant, duration will fall, because the discount factors for the later cash flows increase

Table 12.2 Properties of duration

Maturity increases:	Duration increases*
Coupon payment increases:	Duration decreases
Yield to maturity increases:	Duration decreases

*For par and premium bonds. For deep-discount bonds, duration increases up to a distant threshold and then decreases.

more than the discount factors for the earlier cash flows. The duration of the coupon-bearing bond in our example, for instance, declines to 6.55 years as the yield to maturity rises to 12%. Table 12.2 summarizes these properties of duration.

MODIFIED DURATION

Although Macaulay conceived of duration as a measure of the effective life of a bond, it can be modified to measure the sensitivity of a bond's price to changes in the yield to maturity. The modification simply requires dividing Macaulay's duration by the quantity one plus the yield to maturity, as shown below:[3]

$$D_m = \frac{D}{(1 + r)}$$

where

D_m = modified duration,
D = Macaulay's duration and
r = yield to maturity.

We can estimate the percentage change in the price of a bond by multiplying the basis-point change in yield to maturity by minus one times the bond's modified duration. Again, suppose that we have a 10-year bond that pays a $100 coupon annually and $1000 at maturity; its yield to maturity is 10%. The Macaulay duration of this bond equals 6.76 years. Its modified duration thus equals 6.14 years, which we derive by dividing 6.76 by 1.10.

If yield to maturity increases 10 basis points to 10.1%, modified duration predicts that the bond's price will decline 0.614%, to $993.86. And if yield to maturity declines 10 basis points to 9.90%, modified duration predicts that the bond's price will *increase* 0.614%, to $1006.14.

Although these predictions are close to the true answer, they are not exact. If yield to maturity does increase by 10 basis points, the price of the bond will actually decline by

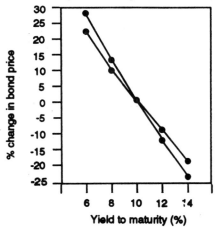

Figure 12.1 Pricing Error of Modified Duration (10-year bond with $100 annual coupon, $1000 principal and 10% initial yield to maturity)

0.612%, to $993.88, and if yield to maturity falls 10 basis points, the bond's price will increase by 0.617%, to $1006.17. Modified duration apparently overestimates price declines and underestimates price increases with respect to changes in yield to maturity.

One might argue that the errors are so tiny as to be inconsequential. For larger changes in yield to maturity, however, the percentage change in price predicted by modified duration can be significantly wrong. For example, modified duration predicts a 6.14% change in price for a 100-basis-point change in yield to maturity, given our particular example. In fact, the bond's price would decline by only 5.89% if yield to maturity rose by 100 basis points, and it would rise by 6.42% if yield to maturity fell by 100 basis points. Figure 12.1 shows the change in price predicted by modified duration for given changes in yield to maturity (the straight line) compared with the change in price that would actually occur (the curved line).

CONVEXITY

In Figure 12.1, the line that represents the actual price response to a given change in yield to maturity is convex. The larger the increase in yield to maturity, the greater the magnitude of the error by which modified duration will overestimate the bond's price decline; the larger the decrease in yield to maturity, the greater the magnitude of the error by which modified duration will underestimate the bond's price rise.

This phenomenon is called convexity, and it arises for the following reason. As yield to maturity changes, a bond's duration changes as well. Modified duration is thus an accurate predictor of price change only for vanishingly small changes in yield to maturity. If yield to maturity is 10%, for example, modified duration equals 6.14, which implies that a 100-basis-point change in yield to maturity will result in a 6.14% change in bond price. However, as yield to maturity increases to 10.25%, modified duration falls to 6.02, which implies smaller price changes for subsequent changes in yield to maturity.

The price response of a bond to changes in yield to maturity is consequently a function not only of the bond's modified duration, but of its convexity as well. Whereas modified duration measures the sensitivity of bond prices to changes in yield to maturity, convexity measures the sensitivity of duration to changes in yield to maturity.

Convexity is more pronounced, the farther apart the cash flows are. Imagine a bond that has 10 annual cash flows. If yield to maturity increases, the present value of the 10th cash flow will decrease the most, the present value of the ninth cash flow will decrease by a smaller amount, the present value of the eighth cash flow will decrease by yet a smaller amount, and so on. Duration will decrease as the more distant cash flows are assigned less and less weight. To the extent the cash flows are not far apart from each other, however, duration will not decrease that much because the changes in the weights associated with successive cash flows will be similar to each other.

Now consider a bond that has only two cash flows, one after the first year and one after the 20th year. If yield to maturity increases, the present value of the first cash flow will change by a significantly smaller amount than the change in the present value of the second cash flow. The weight assigned to the time to receipt of the first cash flow will thus decline only slightly, whereas the weight assigned to the time to receipt of the second cash flow will decline meaningfully, resulting in a more substantial change in the bond's duration.

APPLICATIONS OF DURATION AND CONVEXITY

Duration and convexity are essential tools for fixed income portfolio management. Duration enables portfolio managers to act upon their convictions about interest rate shifts. If a manager expects interest rates to fall, she should increase the duration of her portfolio in order to leverage the price appreciation that will occur if she is correct. If she expects an increase in rates, she should of course reduce duration to protect her portfolio from price losses.

Duration and convexity are also useful for hedging a stream of liabilities. A portfolio manager can hedge a liability stream by constructing a portfolio of equal duration and convexity, as long as its present value equals the present value of the liabilities at the outset. If the present value of the liabilities exceeds the present value of the assets available for hedging, the duration of the portfolio must exceed the duration of the liabilities. The converse is true if the value of the portfolio exceeds the value of the liabilities. Moreover, modified duration relates the *percentage* change in price to absolute changes in yield to maturity. In order to hedge a portfolio of liabilities with a different value, duration must be adjusted to relate the *dollar* change in price to changes in yield to maturity.

Finally, a portfolio can be immunized from interest rate shifts by setting its duration equal to the investor's holding period. If interest rates rise, the capital loss will be offset by the gain from reinvesting the cash flows at higher yields. Conversely, if interest rates fall, the reduction in income resulting from reinvestment of cash flows at lower rates is offset by the capital gain. Of course, capital gains and losses are balanced by reinvestment gains and losses only to the extent that short-term rates and long-term rates move together. If long-term rates increase but short-term rates remain unchanged, the portfolio's income will not increase sufficiently to offset the capital loss; in this case, immunization will fail.

CONCLUSION

This column is intended to provide some elementary insights into the notions of duration and convexity. As such, I have ignored many of the complexities associated with these notions. For example, I have implicitly assumed throughout that a bond's cash flows are perfectly predictable. In fact, many bonds have call or put provisions that introduce an element of uncertainty to the cash flows. Moreover, the cash flows of mortgage-backed securities are uncertain because mortgage borrowers usually have the right to prepay their loans. These complexities can have a significant impact on the measurement of duration and convexity and their application to risk control. Those who are interested in interest rate risk should consult more advanced sources.[4]

ENDNOTES

1. Macaulay, F. *Some Theoretical Problems Suggested by the Movements of Interest Rates, Bond Yields and Stock Prices in the United States Since 1865* (New York: National Bureau of Economic Research, 1938).

2. For example, see Leibowitz, M. "How Financial Theory Evolves in the Real World — Or Not: The Case of Duration and Immunization," *The Financial Review*, November 1983.

3. This formula assumes that coupons are paid annually. If coupon payments occur more frequently, the yield to maturity should be divided by the number of discounting periods per year.

4. For a more thorough review of these issues, see Fabozzi, F. and Pollack, I. eds., *The Handbook of Fixed Income Securities* (Homewood, IL: Dow Jones-Irwin, 1987), and Platt, R. ed., *Controlling Interest Rate Risk: New Techniques and Applications for Money Management* (New York: John Wiley & Sons, 1986).

13

Active Bond Portfolio Management

Francis H. Trainer and Jonathan A. Reiss

Active bond management presupposes that managers can identify a particular bond or set of bonds that will outperform the universe of fixed-income securities. Most active bond management strategies are heavily influenced by the manager's forecast for interest rates. Individual securities may be classified on a continuum from most aggressive to most defensive, principally according to their maturities (or durations).[1] Once the outlook for interest rates has been assessed, the manager constructs a portfolio that reflects the magnitude of the expected change in interest rates, the degree of confidence in the forecast, and the willingness of the manager and client to bear risk.

There are, however, a great many other factors that influence bond price behavior. These include sector, quality, call and sinking fund provisions, coupon, maturity mix, and the financial position of specific issuers. Although none of these *individual* factors is as significant as interest rate change, collectively they exert a profound influence on bond portfolio performance.

Thus, we can distinguish two basic approaches to bond management. The interest rate forecasting approach is largely based upon economic analysis and Fed watching. It offers the possibility of substantially outperforming the market (and competing managers) but opens up the possibility of substantial *underperformance* as well. It is a risky strategy because it depends on the accuracy of a single judgment.

By way of contrast, what we may call the bond-analytical approach is based on quantitative techniques that evaluate the various attributes of bonds that were mentioned above. Inasmuch as some of these factors will help performance in a given year while others will hurt, the potential deviation from market performance is more limited. But to the extent that skilled managers are capable of making correct judgments, the bond-analytical approach represents a much more reliable path to superior performance than interest rate forecasting.

How does the manager decide which strategy to use and how aggressively to pursue it? The answer depends upon what the manager and the client are trying to accomplish. If the client has no clearly defined goals, then it does not really matter which technique is used. (Actually, it matters, but it will be very difficult to assess what was or was not accomplished.)

Reprinted from: Trainer, F.H. and Reiss, J.A. 1988: Active Bond Portfolio Management. In: Levine, S.N., ed. *The Financial Analyst's Handbook*. Second Edition. Homewood: Dow Jones-Irwin. © Dow Jones-Irwin, 1975 and 1988.

If the aim is to maximize performance, then interest rate forecasting offers the greatest opportunity. But the riskiness of this strategy lessens its relative attractiveness. Interest rate forecasting also seems to be an inefficient tool for achieving superior returns. Bonds produce lower returns than equities over the long run. The reason, then, that assets are allocated to fixed-income securities is that the resulting reduction in volatility is worth the give-up in return. It would seem to be self-defeating to allocate assets to fixed income in order to reduce risk, only to invest the assets according to a highly risky interest rate forecasting strategy.

For most purposes, we favor the bond-analytical approach. The correct strategy is to try to maximize performance for a *given degree* of interest rate exposure — one that is permitted to vary relatively little or, even, not at all.

Once this strategy is selected, the focal point of the investment process should be a benchmark portfolio that has a clearly defined level of interest rate exposure. The choice of a broad market index, such as the Shearson Lehman Aggregate Index or the Salomon Brothers Broad Index, will serve this purpose well in most cases. In instances where the overall goals of the fund would be better served by a bond portfolio that is either more sensitive or less sensitive to interest rates than the fixed-income market as a whole, a different benchmark may be chosen. In either case, however, it is important to select a benchmark for it provides a standard against which the manager's performance may be judged.

A central premise of the bond-analytical approach is that superior performance can be achieved through the identification of undervalued bonds. The notion that misvalued bonds can be uncovered is predicated upon a belief that the market is inefficient — that there are always opportunities available. Such opportunities may be identified through the systematic evaluation of the components of a bond's value and the performance of this analysis in a consistent fashion across a broad spectrum of the market. If the bond market is, in fact, inefficient and if these analytical tools are sufficiently robust, then active bond management will earn substantial incremental returns.

Once undervalued bonds are identified, a method must be devised that allows one to construct a portfolio that capitalizes on the opportunities in a manner consistent with the overall objectives of the portfolio.

In the first part of this chapter we introduce the valuation framework and tools we use to identify undervalued bonds. The second part of this chapter discusses the portfolio construction process and the techniques we use to maintain optimal portfolios over time.

PART ONE — A FRAMEWORK FOR VALUING BONDS

WHY OPPORTUNITIES OCCUR

An active bond management strategy is based on the belief that bonds do not always sell at their fair value, that the differences are material, and that such bonds can be identified.[2] Several factors account for the inefficiency of the bond market. First, bonds are complex securities. The yield on a bond is a function of its quality, coupon, maturity, and any options that are part of the bond (such as call exposure). Valuation of a bond, therefore, requires an analysis of each of these features. While the processes for analyzing quality are well developed, there have been very few attempts at rigorous quantification of the remaining factors. For example, there is no analytical formula for the value of the call option on corporate bonds and mortgage pass-through securities. While option theory is well developed for short-term options on equities, the assumptions that underlie this model are not acceptable for valuing a long-term option on a bond.

A second reason that bonds deviate from their fair value is the paucity of reliable pricing information. Unlike the equity market, where bids and offers are continuously available, there is virtually no information on the prices of bonds. With the exception of on-the-run Treasuries and recently issued corporates, there are no quote machines to punch up the latest trade or the bid and asked price.[3] In fact, it is extremely difficult to get high-quality pricing information even on a monthly basis. Without the anchor of continuous quality pricing, it is difficult to know where a bond has traded lately. As a result, the potential for a bond to deviate from its fair value is considerable.

A third cause of inefficiency in the bond market arises from supply-and-demand imbalances. For example, the interest rate differential between industrial bonds and Treasuries was fairly constant throughout 1985. Yet as may be seen in Table 13.1, the yield spreads on the debt of Chrysler Corporation widened dramatically.

While at first blush one might attribute this widening of spreads to a deterioration of credit, Chrysler established record pretax earnings in 1985, and its common stock appreciated by 46% — 20% more than the market.

Chrysler spreads widened because the company issued a massive amount of debt. During 1985 Chrysler raised $1.6 billion, or more than 6% of all new industrial debt. While this did result in an increase in leverage — from 17% to 33% — the company's degree of leverage is far below that of the average BBB corporation. In fact, Chrysler's debt/equity ratio and other financial characteristics make it appear comparable in quality to a typical AA industrial. But it sells closer to a BBB company, not so much because it is rated BBB but because the massive supply of Chrysler paper led to congestion in the marketplace. Investors who were interested in Chrysler already felt they owned enough. As a result, additional investors had to be enticed with incremental yield. Thus, the market clearing process led to a distortion in the yield relationship of Chrysler versus the rest of the market.

Finally, there is one additional factor that contributes to the inefficiency of the bond market. It is the fact that a single correct interest rate decision (provided the bet is large enough) can be worth more to performance than the cumulative effect of correct decisions on all of the other aspects of bonds.

To illustrate the power of accurate forecasting, we have computed the return that would have resulted if one had been able to earn the higher of the returns available from (a) one-month Treasury bills or (b) 30-year Treasury bonds in each month over the past five years.[4]

As may be seen in Figure 13.1, our omniscient manager would have earned a 38% compound annual return — 21% higher than the return on the market! This potential is so large that perfect forecasting hardly seems necessary. One can easily imagine a manager saying to himself, "If I can just be right on the direction of interest rates 60% of the time (thereby earning one fifth of the excess return), I will outperform virtually all of my competitors." As a result, many fixed-income portfolio managers expend a great deal of

Table 13.1 Comparative yield spreads versus Treasuries

	12/31/84	12/31/85	Change
AA industrials	78	75	−3
BBB industrials	178	173	−5
Chrysler Corporation	112	156	44

Source: Salomon Brothers and Bernstein estimates.

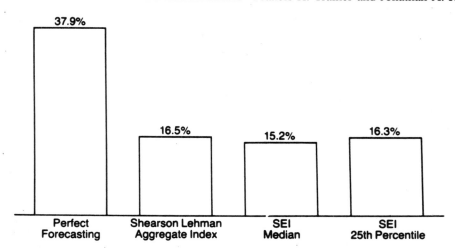

Figure 13.1 The lure of interest rate betting — compound annual rates of return (31 December 1980–31 December 1985).

effort trying to forecast the future course of interest rates. Furthermore, since their forecasts may change at any time, these managers usually require a level of liquidity that can only be found in on-the-run Treasuries and a handful of recently issued corporates.

Since maturity and liquidity requirements are dominant, valuation distortions, *even if perceived*, are not worth worrying about. It doesn't really matter if a bond is overpriced — the error of the purchase will be overwhelmed by the expected positive returns from the interest rate forecast.

For all of these reasons, there are always misvaluations in the bond market. The fundamental challenge of active bond management is to uncover and exploit these opportunities.

ESTIMATING FAIR VALUE

The value of a fixed-income security is dependent on its specific characteristics — i.e., its coupon, maturity, sector, quality, and embedded options such as call exposure. We use three different bases for estimating the value of a bond's attributes.

1. What is its *intrinsic value*?
2. What has been the *historical price* of the attribute under similar economic conditions?
3. What is *today's market price* for that attribute?

Different methods are used for different characteristics. For example, we have estimated the intrinsic value of call options on bonds by using a binomial process similar to that used for valuing other types of options. This tells us what the option is worth given the current yield curve and our estimates of future volatility. On the other hand, to determine what yield spread we should demand to buy an industrial bond instead of a Treasury, we utilize a regression analysis that estimates industrial/Treasury yield spreads as a function of the change in economic conditions. Finally, for quality spreads — BBB bonds versus AA bonds, for instance — we use an estimate of the prevailing average spread in today's market.

All three of these approaches are attempts to find securities that are underpriced and will, therefore, outperform other bonds of the same duration *regardless of the direction of change in interest rates.*

VALUING TREASURY BONDS

The least complicated bonds to value are Treasury bonds. They have no credit risk and little or no call exposure. Moreover, they are very actively traded, and so they do not become misvalued because of a dearth of accurate price information. The only characteristics that differ materially from one Treasury note or bond to another are coupon and maturity.

Coupon Analysis

Although bonds are usually issued at par ($100), they rarely sell at this price. As interest rates change, they become either discount or premium bonds. Prior to mid-1984, the yields on discount bonds were always lower than the yields on comparable maturity par and premium bonds for two reasons: First, the portion of the yields to maturity that derived from the accretion of the discount was taxed as capital gains. Second, the tax on such gains was deferred until sale or maturity.

To illustrate the magnitude of these effects and their relationship with maturity, we have calculated the after-tax yield on a bond with a 9% coupon that is priced to yield 10% to maturity, assuming an income tax rate of 35% and a capital gains tax rate of 14%. (See Table 13.2.)

The tax benefits of discount bonds are greatest for the one-year maturity and decline as maturity lengthens. Moreover, the portion of the tax benefit that derives from capital gains treatment (as opposed to tax deferral) varies with maturity. To separate these components, we calculate the after-tax yield of a discount bond when the capital gains and income tax rate are *both* 35%. (See Table 13.3.)

The value of the deferral rises with maturity and peaks at 20 years. The reason for the subsequent decline in the deferral's value is that the portion of the yield to maturity that is attributable to the appreciation of the bond to par at maturity declines as the maturity lengthens and eventually overwhelms the benefit of deferred taxation.

Table 13.2 Effect of maturity on after-tax yield (35% income tax, 14% capital gains tax)

1	2	3	4 (3−2)
	After-tax yield to maturity		
Maturity	10% coupon at a 10% yield to maturity	9% coupon at a 10% yield to maturity	After-tax benefit of discount
1	6.50%	6.70%	0.20%
3	6.50	6.69	0.19
5	6.50	6.68	0.18
10	6.50	6.65	0.15
20	6.50	6.60	0.10
30	6.50	6.56	0.06

Table 13.3 Quantifying the benefit of deferral (35% income tax, 35% capital gains tax)

1	2	3	4
	After-tax yield to maturity		(3-2)
Maturity	10% bond at a 10% yield	9% bond at a 10% yield	Benefit attributable to deferral
1	6.50%	6.51%	0.01%
3	6.50	6.52	0.02
5	6.50	6.54	0.04
10	6.50	6.55	0.05
20	6.50	6.55	0.05
30	6.50	6.54	0.04

The portion of the after-tax benefit of a discount bond that is attributable to the lower capital gains rate is the differential between the total discount effect and the deferral benefit. (See Table 13.4.)

At the one-year maturity, 95% of the discount effect — 19 basis points out of the total of 20 basis points — arises from the lower capital gains tax rate. As the maturity lengthens, this effect declines and explains a decreasing amount of the total benefit of a discount bond. At the 30-year maturity, 67% of the value of a discount derives from the deferral provision of the tax law.

Premium bonds do not have any direct tax benefits or penalties because taxpayers are permitted to amortize the premium, thereby offsetting the extra income provided by the high coupon. However, because their coupons are higher than those of par bonds, it is less likely they will become discount bonds. Since it is less likely that premium bonds will ever receive the beneficial tax effect afforded discount bonds, they should be expected to sell at higher yields than par bonds.

On the basis of tax law, we would expect discounts to trade at lower yields than par bonds — the deeper the discount, the lower the yield. Conversely, we would expect premium bonds to trade at slightly higher yields than par bonds — the larger the premium, the higher the yield. Finally, since the total discount effect decreases with maturity, we would expect shorter discounts to trade at a lower yield relative to par bonds than longer discounts.

Table 13.4 Decomposition of the discount effect (35% income tax, 14% capital gains tax)

1	2	3	4 (2-3)	5 (3/2)	6 (4/2)
Maturity	Total discount effect	Benefit attributable to deferral	Benefit attributable to capital gains treatment	Percent of benefit attributable to deferral	Percent of benefit attributable to capital gains treatment
1	0.20%	0.01%	0.19%	5%	95%
3	0.19	0.02	0.17	11	89
5	0.18	0.04	0.14	22	78
10	0.15	0.05	0.10	33	67
20	0.10	0.05	0.05	50	50
30	0.06	0.04	0.02	67	33

Table 13.5 Calculation of the coupon effect

1	2	3 (1–2)	4	5 (3 × 4)	6 (2 + 5)
Coupon	Par bond yield	Differential from par bond yield	Adjustment per percent in coupon	Adjustment	Expected yield
8%	10%	−2%	0.05	−0.10%	9.90%
9	10	−1	0.05	−0.05	9.95
10	10	0	0.00	0.00	10.00
11	10	+1	0.03	+0.03	10.03
12	10	+2	0.03	+0.06	10.06

Source: Bernstein estimates.

While analysis of the 1954–1983 period confirms that discounts have always sold for lower yields than par bonds, the historical data also suggest that the discount effect is slightly greater at longer maturities than it is at shorter maturities. Moreover, premium bonds have historically traded at much higher yields relative to par bonds than a tax-based analysis would suggest.[5]

Our historical analysis, in fact, indicates that a (rational) tax-based analysis of the relationship between coupon and yield to maturity has less predictive power than simpler rules of thumb that are based on how bonds with different coupons have actually sold relative to one another. We found that there seems to be a fairly consistent relationship between the magnitude of the discount or premium in the coupon of a bond and its yield relative to that of a bond selling at par. The larger the coupon discount (coupon minus yield), the lower the yield, and the larger the coupon premium, the higher the yield. The size of this effect was independent of maturity. Additionally, the coupon effect was larger for discount bonds than it was for premium bonds.

To illustrate our findings, let us assume that we have a flat par bond yield curve at 10%. If there were no coupon effect, both a 9% and an 11% bond would sell at a 10% yield. What we found historically is that there is, on average, a five basis point adjustment per 1% in coupon for discount bonds and a three basis point adjustment for premium bonds. Thus, a 9% bond that is yielding 10%, has a coupon/yield differential of 1%. Using our discount rule of thumb of five basis points per 1%, we would expect this bond to sell at a yield of (10.00%–0.05%), or 9.95%. Our rule for premium coupons is three basis points per 1% differential. Table 13.5 illustrates these adjustments.

New Bonds versus Old Bonds

The 1984 tax reform bill changed the tax treatment of bonds issued on or after July 19, 1984. If an old bond—i.e., a pre-July 19, 1984, issue—is bought at a discount to par, the locked-in appreciation to par is not taxed until it is realized at maturity (or upon sale) and is treated as a capital gain. Although the comparable appreciation on a new bond is also deferred (i.e., not taxed until it is realized), the gain is now taxed as ordinary income.

As a result, only a fraction of the advantage of discounts remains for new bonds—the portion due to the deferral of taxation. This fraction increases from near zero for short bonds (since there is virtually no benefit from deferral) to one half of the old effect for long bonds (see Table 13.6).

Table 13.6 Summary of coupon adjustments (in basis points per 1% of coupon/yield differential)

	Old bonds	New bonds			
	All maturities	1 year	5 years	10 years	20 years
Discount	5.00	0.25	1.10	1.65	2.50
Premium	3.00	0.15	0.66	0.99	1.50

Source: Bernstein estimates.

The foregoing discussion illustrates two of the approaches we use to determine fair value. The size of the tax effect was estimated simply by measuring the historical average. This must be done with caution because we are implicitly assuming that the historical average will be the central tendency for the future. Therefore, we must choose the *relevant* history carefully and try to determine if there is any reason that the future should differ from the past. The second approach was theoretical rather than empirical, for we have spent very little time under the new tax regimen.

In addition to reflecting historical relationships, coupon adjustments must also incorporate changes in tax legislations. For example, the Tax Reform Act of 1986 eliminated the capital gains/ordinary income differential for 1988 and beyond. Under this provision, the only benefit of discounts arises from deferral and the treatment is the same for old and new bonds.

Estimating the Yield Curve

We use these coupon adjustments to estimate the par equivalent yield of a bond. When the outstanding Treasuries are adjusted for these effects, we are left with a set of yields on bonds which differ only in maturity. These yields are listed in column 5 of Table 13.7. As may be seen, they are fairly consistent but not perfectly so. We find a best-fit curve through these yields to determine what we call the par bond yield curve — column 7.[6]

The adjusted yield of any non-callable Treasury bond should equal the par bond yield of the same maturity. That is, if the market priced all Treasury bonds consistently with one another, column 5 of Table 13.8 would be identical to column 7. As may be seen, it is not — the differences are listed in column 8.

Whether column 8 actually measures what it purports to measure (i.e., yield misvaluation) can be tested by examining the subsequent performance of Treasury bonds. Those bonds for which column 8 is positive (i.e., underpriced) should systematically outperform those for which column 8 is negative. We performed this test over the past three years and found consistent outperformance by the bonds identified as underpriced.

Although our particular method of yield curve smoothing is proprietary, similar estimations are available from a variety of consulting firms, such as BARRA, Capital Management Sciences, and Gifford Fong Associates.[7]

VALUING A CORPORATE BOND

The estimation of a par bond Treasury yield curve is the foundation of our analysis of corporate bonds. Since all corporate bonds are of lower quality than Treasuries and most corporates have substantially less call protection, they should offer higher yields to maturity.

Table 13.7 Derivation of the treasury par bond yield curve — December 31, 1985

1 Coupon	2 Maturity	3 Price	4 Yield to maturity	5 Adjusted yield to maturity	6 Adjusted yield to call	7 Smoothed par bond yield	8 Memo: yield misvaluation
9.750%	01/31/87	$101.97	7.81%	7.75%	—	7.76%	(0.01)%
9.000	02/15/87	101.28	7.77	7.74	—	7.75	(0.01)
10.875	02/15/87	103.19	7.84	7.75	—	7.75	0.00
12.750	02/15/87	105.16	7.85	7.70	—	7.75	(0.05)
10.000	02/28/87	102.31	7.86	7.79	—	7.74	0.05
10.250	03/31/87	102.81	7.82	7.75	—	7.73	0.02
10.750	03/31/87	103.41	7.81	7.72	—	7.73	(0.01)
9.750	04/30/87*	102.34	7.84	7.84	—	7.74	0.10
12.000	05/15/87	105.47	7.71	7.58	—	7.74	(0.16)
12.500	05/15/87	106.09	7.72	7.58	—	7.74	(0.16)
14.000	05/15/87	108.06	7.68	7.49	—	7.74	(0.25)
9.125	05/31/87*	101.66	7.86	7.85	—	7.75	0.10
8.500	06/30/87*	100.88	7.87	7.87	—	7.77	0.10
10.500	06/30/87	103.66	7.86	7.78	—	7.77	0.01
8.875	07/31/87*	101.44	7.88	7.88	—	7.80	0.08
12.375	08/15/87*	106.59	7.95	7.94	—	7.81	0.13
13.750	08/15/87	108.69	7.93	7.76	—	7.81	(0.05)
8.875	08/31/87*	101.41	7.94	7.94	—	7.82	0.12
9.000	09/30/87*	101.69	7.93	7.93	—	7.85	0.08
11.125	09/30/87	105.03	7.96	7.87	—	7.85	0.02
8.875	10/31/87*	101.44	8.00	8.00	—	7.88	0.12
7.625	11/15/87	99.53	7.89	7.90	—	7.89	0.01
11.000	11/15/87*	105.06	8.02	8.02	—	7.89	0.13
12.625	11/15/87	107.81	8.03	7.90	—	7.89	0.01
8.500	11/30/87*	100.91	7.97	7.97	—	7.90	0.07
7.875	12/31/87*	99.84	7.96	7.96	—	7.93	0.03
11.250	12/31/87	105.88	8.01	7.92	—	7.93	(0.01)
12.375	01/15/88	108.09	7.99	7.86	—	7.95	(0.09)
10.125	02/15/88	104.03	8.01	7.95	—	7.97	(0.02)
10.375	02/15/88*	104.44	8.05	8.04	—	7.97	0.07

continued overleaf

Table 13.7 (continued)

1	2	3	4	5	6	7	8
Coupon	Maturity	Price	Yield to maturity	Adjusted yield to maturity	Adjusted yield to call	Smoothed par bond yield	Memo: yield misvaluation
12.000	03/31/88	107.88	8.09	7.97	—	8.01	(0.04)
13.250	04/15/88	110.53	8.10	7.95	—	8.03	(0.08)
8.250	05/15/88	100.56	7.98	7.97	—	8.05	(0.08)
9.875	05/15/88	103.72	8.11	8.06	—	8.05	0.01
10.000	05/15/88*	104.00	8.10	8.10	—	8.05	0.05
13.625	06/30/88	112.16	8.15	7.98	—	8.09	(0.11)
14.000	07/15/88	113.25	8.12	7.94	—	8.10	(0.16)
9.500	08/15/88*	103.03	8.19	8.18	—	8.13	0.05
10.500	08/15/88	104.00	8.21	8.15	—	8.13	0.02
11.375	09/30/88*	107.53	8.24	8.23	—	8.16	0.09
15.375	10/15/88	117.41	8.25	8.03	—	8.18	(0.15)
8.625	11/15/88*	101.47	8.04	8.03	—	8.20	(0.17)
8.750	11/15/88	101.09	8.31	8.29	—	8.20	0.09
11.750	11/15/88	108.75	8.26	8.15	—	8.20	(0.05)
10.625	12/31/88*	106.09	8.29	8.28	—	8.23	0.05
14.625	01/15/89	116.53	8.35	8.16	—	8.24	(0.08)
11.375	02/15/89	108.13	8.36	8.27	—	8.26	0.01
11.250	03/31/89*	108.06	8.35	8.34	—	8.29	0.05
14.375	04/15/89	116.69	8.44	8.27	—	8.30	(0.07)
9.250	05/15/89	102.97	8.22	8.18	—	8.32	(0.14)
11.750	05/15/89	109.59	8.42	8.32	—	8.32	(0.00)
9.625	06/30/89*	103.63	8.41	8.40	—	8.35	0.05
14.500	07/15/89	117.84	8.55	8.37	—	8.36	0.01
13.875	08/15/89	116.16	8.59	8.43	—	8.38	0.05
9.375	09/30/89*	103.03	8.41	8.40	—	8.40	0.00
11.875	10/15/89	110.66	8.52	8.41	—	8.41	0.00
10.750	11/15/89	107.38	8.47	8.40	—	8.42	(0.02)
12.750	11/15/89*	113.31	8.63	8.61	—	8.42	0.19
8.375	12/31/89	100.06	8.36	8.36	—	8.45	(0.09)
10.500	01/15/90	106.56	8.54	8.48	—	8.46	0.02
11.000	02/15/90*	108.13	8.61	8.60	—	8.47	0.13

10.500	04/15/90	106.63	8.61	8.56	—	8.50	0.06
8.250	05/15/90	102.09	7.67	7.66	—	8.51	(0.86)
11.375	05/15/90*	109.72	8.65	8.64	—	8.51	0.13
10.750	07/15/90	107.81	8.63	8.57	—	8.54	0.03
9.875	08/15/90*	104.78	8.59	8.59	—	8.55	0.04
10.750	08/15/90	108.00	8.61	8.55	—	8.55	(0.00)
11.500	10/15/90	110.78	8.69	8.61	—	8.58	0.03
9.625	11/15/90*	104.06	8.58	8.57	—	8.59	(0.02)
13.000	11/15/90	116.69	8.72	8.59	—	8.59	(0.00)
11.750	11/15/90	112.09	8.73	8.64	—	8.61	0.03
9.125	01/15/91	102.50	8.51	8.50	—	8.63	(0.13)
12.375	02/15/91*	114.91	8.78	8.68	—	8.65	0.03
14.500	04/15/91	124.16	8.76	8.59	—	8.66	(0.07)
13.750	05/15/91	121.03	8.86	8.72	—	8.68	0.04
14.875	07/15/91	126.16	8.86	8.68	—	8.69	(0.01)
12.250	08/15/91	115.12	8.85	8.82	—	8.71	0.11
14.250	10/15/91*	124.09	8.89	8.73	—	8.72	0.01
11.625	11/15/91	112.72	8.86	8.84	—	8.74	0.10
14.625	01/15/92*	126.44	8.92	8.75	—	8.75	0.00
11.750	02/15/92	113.50	8.89	8.87	—	8.76	0.11
13.750	04/15/92*	122.91	8.95	8.81	—	8.77	0.04
10.375	05/15/92	107.25	8.89	8.88	—	8.79	0.09
7.250	07/15/92*	93.69	8.51	8.58	—	8.80	(0.22)
9.750	08/15/92	104.50	8.85	8.84	—	8.81	0.03
10.500	10/15/92*	108.47	8.83	8.78	—	8.82	(0.04)
6.750	11/15/92	90.25	8.61	8.70	—	8.84	(0.14)
7.875	02/15/93	95.94	8.65	8.69	—	8.84	(0.15)
10.875	02/15/93	110.19	8.91	8.85	—	8.84	0.01
10.125	05/15/93	106.69	8.87	8.83	—	8.87	(0.04)
7.500	08/15/93	93.75	8.63	8.69	—	8.89	(0.20)
8.625	08/15/93	99.84	8.65	8.65	—	8.89	(0.24)
11.875	08/15/93	115.69	8.98	8.90	—	8.89	0.01
8.625	11/15/93	99.75	8.67	8.67	—	8.91	(0.24)
11.750	11/15/93	115.25	9.00	8.92	—	8.91	0.01
9.000	02/15/94	101.59	8.72	8.71	—	8.92	(0.21)

continued overleaf

Table 13.7 (*continued*)

1 Coupon	2 Maturity	3 Price	4 Yield to maturity	5 Adjusted yield to maturity	6 Adjusted yield to call	7 Smoothed par bond yield	8 Memo: yield misvaluation
13.125	05/15/94	123.28	9.09	8.97	—	8.94	0.02
8.750	08/15/94	100.00	8.75	8.75	—	8.96	(0.21)
12.625	08/15/94*	120.78	9.09	9.05	—	8.96	0.09
10.125	11/15/94	107.94	8.81	8.77	—	8.98	(0.21)
11.625	11/15/94*	115.37	9.06	9.04	—	8.98	0.06
10.500	02/15/95	108.91	9.04	9.00	—	8.99	0.01
11.250	02/15/95*	113.28	9.07	9.05	—	8.99	0.06
10.375	05/15/95	108.72	8.98	8.98	—	9.01	(0.03)
11.250	05/15/95*	113.34	9.10	9.08	—	9.01	0.07
12.625	05/15/95	121.81	9.11	9.01	—	9.01	(0.00)
10.500	08/15/95*	109.13	9.06	9.04	—	9.02	0.02
9.500	11/15/95*	103.28	8.99	8.98	—	9.04	(0.06)
11.500	11/15/95	115.66	9.06	8.99	—	9.04	(0.05)
7.000	05/15/98	85.19	9.01	9.10	10.01%	9.16	(0.05)
8.500	05/15/99	94.84	9.17	9.21	9.44	9.20	0.01
7.875	02/15/00	89.31	9.24	9.31	9.75	9.23	0.08
8.375	08/15/00	93.00	9.26	9.30	9.55	9.25	0.05
11.750	02/15/01	118.09	9.47	9.40	—	9.27	0.13
13.125	05/15/01	128.62	9.54	9.43	—	9.28	0.15
8.000	08/15/01	89.81	9.24	9.31	9.62	9.28	0.03
13.375	08/15/01	130.56	9.56	9.45	—	9.28	0.17
15.750	11/15/01	150.25	9.54	9.35	—	9.29	0.06
14.250	02/15/02	138.84	9.49	9.35	—	9.30	0.05
11.625	11/15/02	117.16	9.55	9.49	—	9.32	0.17
10.750	02/15/03	110.53	9.49	9.45	—	9.33	0.12
10.750	05/15/03	110.53	9.50	9.46	—	9.34	0.12
11.125	08/15/03	110.28	9.55	9.50	—	9.34	0.16
11.875	11/15/03	119.47	9.58	9.51	—	9.35	0.16
12.375	05/15/04	123.94	9.58	9.49	—	9.36	0.13
13.750	08/15/04	135.97	9.57	9.46	—	9.37	0.09
11.625	11/15/04*	118.75	9.47	9.44	—	9.38	0.06

8.250	05/15/05	90.59	9.30	9.36	9.52	9.39	(0.03)
12.000	05/15/05*	122.31	9.46	9.43	—	9.39	0.04
10.750	08/15/05*	111.06	9.49	9.48	—	9.40	0.08
7.625	02/15/07	85.06	9.24	9.33	9.54	9.43	(0.10)
7.875	11/15/07	87.59	9.20	9.27	9.42	9.45	(0.18)
8.375	08/15/08	91.94	9.23	9.27	9.36	9.46	(0.19)
8.750	11/15/08	95.13	9.26	9.29	9.34	9.47	(0.18)
9.125	05/15/09	98.13	9.32	9.33	9.35	9.48	(0.15)
10.375	11/15/09	108.06	9.51	9.49	9.42	9.49	(0.00)
11.750	02/15/10	119.06	9.69	9.48	9.49	9.38†	0.11
10.000	05/15/10	104.78	9.49	9.48	9.44	9.50	(0.02)
12.750	11/15/10	127.87	9.75	9.66	9.49	9.40†	0.09
13.875	05/15/11	137.91	9.80	9.68	9.47	9.41†	0.06
14.000	11/15/11	139.06	9.81	9.69	9.49	9.43†	0.06
10.375	11/14/12	107.97	9.54	9.52	9.47	9.54	(0.02)
12.000	08/15/13	122.03	9.69	9.62	9.52	9.46†	0.06
13.250	05/15/14	133.78	9.72	9.62	9.49	9.48†	0.01
12.500	08/15/14*	127.12	9.68	9.64	9.53	9.48†	0.05
11.750	11/15/14*	117.97	9.86	9.83	9.76	9.57	0.19
11.250	02/15/15*	117.97	9.43	9.40	—	9.58	(0.20)
10.625	08/15/15*	112.34	9.38	9.36	—	9.58	(0.24)
9.875	11/15/15*	106.09	9.27	9.26	—	9.59	(0.34)

*Issued after July 18, 1984.
†Price on a yield to call basis.
Source: The Wall Street Journal and Bernstein estimates.

Table 13.8 Estimation of a corporate yield

Par bond yield on a comparable maturity Treasury	+	Effect of [Coupon + Quality + Call + Sector]	=	Estimated fair value of corporate

The estimated fair value of a corporate bond is a function of the yield on the comparable maturity par bond Treasury and the value that should be attached to those features that make a corporate bond different from a Treasury. (See Table 13.8.)

If the estimated yield is a reasonable approximation of fair value, those bonds that appear to be cheap (offering a higher yield than fair value) should outperform bonds that are rich or fairly priced. The better our estimate of fair value, the more confidence we have in our ability to produce incremental returns.

Coupon and Quality

The valuation of the coupon effect that we use for corporate bonds is identical to the process explained above for Treasury bonds. To estimate the spread attributable to rating, we use the work of BARRA.

BARRA has developed a bond analysis model that explains the current pricing of Treasuries and corporates by a variety of factors — similar to the concept we introduced above. The difference between their work and ours is that BARRA's model finds the parameters that best fit current pricing, while we make assertions about fundamental value whenever possible.

For quality, we do not yet have a fundamental valuation, and so we use BARRA's estimates as an indication of the market's valuation. For example, as of December 31, 1985, the incremental yield that was attributed to quality — holding every other consideration constant — was as shown in Table 13.9.

The estimates for AA, A, and BBB bonds represent the yield spreads within the corporate market over AAA bonds of the same sector. The spread for AAA bonds versus Treasuries is the "sector spread" (for a discussion see p. 195).

BARRA's estimates are constant across maturity — i.e., both short-term and long-term bonds are assumed to sell at the same quality spread. Our analysis indicates that for higher quality ratings — AA and A — the spread increases with maturity while for BBB bonds it is flat. Thus, we have adjusted BARRA's ratings as shown in Table 13.10.

These adjustments for quality are based upon the published ratings of Moody's and Standard & Poor's. In assigning a rating these agencies rely upon the historical operating results of a corporation, with (in our opinion) a disproportionate emphasis on recent results. While a historical perspective is valuable, we believe it is more important to understand where a corporation is headed. How strong will its financial statements be in five years?

Table 13.9 BARRA's rating estimates

AAA	0
AA	11
A	36
BBB	89

Source: BARRA.

Table 13.10   Adjusted rating estimates

Maturity	AAA	AA	A	BBB
Short	0	7	24	89
Intermediate	0	11	36	89
Long	0	15	48	89

Source: BARRA and Bernstein estimates.

To gain this insight, it is necessary to forecast the firm's balance sheet and income statement. From these forecasts we can calculate the critical analytical ratios such as debt service coverage and leverage. When these ratios are compared to those of the recent past, as well as to other corporations, we are able to assess the appropriateness of the current rating and the likelihood that it will be changed. If we disagree with the current rating, we use our estimate in the evaluation of the company. Furthermore, we use our assessment of the future as a qualitative overlay to the entire valuation process. All other things being equal, we prefer to own an improving credit to one that is likely to be stationary.

Evaluating the Call Option

While the need to have a method for valuing call options on corporate bonds is great, few have even attempted to tackle this problem. One reason may be that the valuation models that have been developed for call options on equity securities are not applicable to bonds.

For example, most option models assume that the variability of prices is constant over time. While this may represent an acceptable simplification for the purpose of valuing options on equities, it is totally inappropriate for options on bonds. Since bonds mature at known prices (usually $100) on known dates in the future, their price variability declines with the passage of time. Moreover, since bonds shorten over time, we need to estimate the volatility of the entire yield curve, not just the interest rate of one particular maturity.

Furthermore, the common assumption that the level of interest rates is stationary is clearly false. Not only are interest rates not constant, but it is very difficult to model the distribution of interest rates. Over the 1973–1985 period, for example, the entire Treasury yield curve was higher than it had ever been prior to 1966. Thus, it is not sufficient to be concerned solely with month-to-month volatility when valuing call options. Finally, bond options are typically exercisable for long periods of time. For example, the typical 30-year utility bond has 5 years of call protection and 25 years of call exposure. Thus, existing analytical solutions that evaluate calls as if they were options exercisable on a single date (i.e., like the so-called European option) are of limited usefulness.

As a result of these problems, the call option on bonds is difficult to analyze and is frequently mispriced. We have been able to relax some of the limiting assumptions presented above and have developed a methodology for valuing call options on bonds. . . .

Sector Analysis

Since corporate bonds are of lower quality than Treasuries and generally have greater call exposure, it is logical to assume that the spreads between corporates and Treasuries should be dependent upon the market's evaluation of their quality and of the call option. The general perception of quality should be related to the current and prospective financial condition of the specific industry. The call value of bonds should be a function of expected volatility and the current level of interest rates.

Table 13.11 Decomposition of sector spread — long AA utilities versus Treasuries (basis points)

SCB spread estimate	Rating	Call	Pure sector estimate
99	15	69	15

Source: BARRA and Bernstein estimates.

Table 13.12 Historical long-term utility spread analysis (basis points)

1	2	3	4	5	6
		Components		(2 + 3 + 4)	
Date	AA rating	Call	Sector	Composite	Memo: actual spread
12/31/79	20	63	40	123	172
12/31/80	40	106	39	185	259
12/31/81	39	125	116	280	299
12/31/82	29	110	50	189	196
12/31/83	25	93	53	171	114
12/31/84	16	71	22	109	81
12/31/85	15	69	15	99	112

Source: BARRA, Salomon Brothers, and Bernstein estimates.

In order to determine where spreads should be at any point in time, we performed a regression analysis of spreads from 1970 to 1985 that sought to explain yield spreads versus Treasuries on the basis of industry-specific and general economic variables as well as market conditions — i.e., interest rate volatility and the yield curve slope. The sectors studied were intermediate- and long-term agency, utility, and industrial bonds.

By way of example, Table 13.11 presents our analysis of the spread between newly issued AA utilities and 30-year Treasuries. The spread is a composite of rating, call protection, and sector. Since we already have an estimate of the market's pricing of rating (from BARRA) and the theoretical value of the call option, the residual is the pure sector spread.

To see how each of these components has varied over time, we have decomposed our long-term utility sector spread from 1979 to 1985, as shown in Table 13.12.

BRINGING IT ALL TOGETHER

Having separately analyzed each of the factors that influence a bond's price, evaluating an actual bond is a relatively straightforward process. To illustrate, consider an 8%, 17.5-year, AA utility, callable in two years at $104 and selling at $82.06 to yield 10.25%. The starting point is the 17.5-year yield from the par bond yield curve (Table 13.7) — 9.34%. This base yield is then adjusted for the specific characteristics of the bond. Table 13.13 displays the estimates for each component.

When the components of value are added to the yield on a comparable maturity Treasury, we would expect a yield of 9.93%. The yield on our hypothetical bond is 10.25%. In terms of yield misvaluation, the bond is attractive by 32 basis points.

The other way to quantify misvaluation is to look at the actual and predicted price. A yield of 9.93% is equivalent to a price of $84.31, which is 2.74% higher than the actual price of $82.06.

Table 13.13 Composition of a predicted corporate yield

1 Comparable Treasury yield	2 Coupon	3 Components of value Rating	4 Call	5 Sector	6 $(1 + 2 + 3 + 4 + 5)$ Predicted yield
9.34%	−0.11%	0.15%	0.40%	0.15%	9.93%

Source: BARRA and Bernstein estimates.

In this analysis, we used the 17.5-year par bond Treasury yield to derive the spread. This methodology differs from industry practice where the yield on a bond is compared to the nearest on-the-run Treasury. If the yield curve is sloped (positively or negatively) or if there are anomalies in the pricing of the on-the-run issue, it is difficult to evaluate a broad range of maturities on a consistent basis. This problem is avoided by utilizing a smoothed par bond Treasury yield curve.

The yield and price misvaluations illustrated above are the synthesis of five separate valuation analyses—yield curve, quality, sector, coupon, and call. It is, of course, true that the quality of the valuation process is only as good as the quality of its parts. If one or more of the valuation techniques is faulty, the usefulness of the summary estimate is reduced. However, we believe that even if the estimates are not perfect, the fact that rigorous, logical valuation methodologies are applied *consistently* over a wide base of securities allows for the identification of anomalies and the generation of incremental returns. Furthermore, we establish high misvaluation hurdles that increase our confidence that we have uncovered a truly mispriced security. . . .

PART TWO—PORTFOLIO CONSTRUCTION

It is not sufficient to identify undervalued bonds. We must construct portfolios that translate this knowledge into incremental returns. While added return is the primary goal of active bond management, the client's other objectives must be considered as well. Most of our clients use bonds to reduce the risk of their overall portfolio, and they want their fixed-income portfolios to exhibit less year-to-year variability than their equity portfolios. It is important that the clients and their manager make explicit the level of risk that is desired and the amount of variation around this target that is acceptable. We have found that the easiest way to make these objectives tangible is through the selection of a published index as a benchmark for the portfolio.

These indexes' past returns can be reviewed so the plan sponsor can see the distribution of returns that can realistically be expected. The most important factor is the index's interest rate sensitivity—i.e., its duration. A portfolio with a high duration will be more sensitive to swings in interest rates and, therefore, more volatile, than an index with a low duration.

Once a benchmark has been chosen, the client has something to measure our returns against. Our goal is unambiguous—to outperform the benchmark. In addition, while we cannot be expected to outperform every quarter, our return should never deviate too greatly from that of the benchmark. If it does, it indicates that we are permitting the duration of the portfolio to vary too far from the benchmark.

We use the duration of the index as our neutral target. If we think interest rates will decline, we position the duration of our portfolios somewhat longer than that of the index.

Since we want to limit the influence of interest rate betting on our returns, we constrain the amount of variance in duration from our benchmark. In almost all circumstances, we will be within a year of our benchmark.

We have used the term *duration* several times already. This is because it is an invaluable measure of interest rate sensitivity. Even if you choose not to bet on interest rates — in fact, *especially* if you decide not to bet on interest rates — it is essential to know how interest rates will affect your portfolio.

DURATION

Duration measures the weighted average life of the cash flows from a fixed-income security — discounting those cash flows by the interest rate on the instrument. The value of the duration statistic is that it provides an excellent measure of the interest rate risk of individual securities and of portfolios. For this reason, it has supplanted the use of average maturity — which is a very poor measure of interest rate risk — in the lexicon of bond managers.

For zero-coupon securities, the calculation of duration is straightforward. Since all of the cash flow is received at maturity, its duration is its maturity. Furthermore, as may be seen in Table 13.14, when interest rates change, the percentage change in the price of a zero-coupon bond is approximately equal to its duration times the interest rate change. . . .

To understand the calculation of duration for a bond with semiannual coupon payments, it is helpful to think of a bond as a combination of several zero-coupon bonds — i.e., to treat each coupon payment as a separate instrument. Thus, a two-year bond can be thought of as the combination of four zero-coupon bonds. The durations of these four bonds are 0.5, 1.0, 1.5, and 2.0 years, respectively. (See Table 13.15.)

Table 13.14 The price sensitivity of zero-coupon bonds

1 Maturity	2 Price at a 10% yield	3 Price at a 9% yield	4 Percentage change in price
1	$90.703	$91.573	0.96%
2	82.270	83.856	1.93
3	74.622	76.790	2.90
5	61.391	64.393	4.89
10	37.689	41.464	10.01
20	14.205	17.193	21.04

Table 13.15 Source of present value of a two-year 10% bond

Maturity (years)				
0.5 Cash flow	1	1.5	2.0	Present value
$5.00				$ 4.76
	$5.00			4.54
		$5.00		4.32
			$105.00	86.38
$5.00	$5.00	$5.00	$105.00	$100.00

Table 13.16 Calculation of duration for a two-year 10% bond

1	2	3 Weighting = present value/ price ($100)	4 (1 × 3) Duration (weighted maturity)
Maturity	Present value		
0.5	$ 4.76	0.0476	0.0238
1.0	4.54	0.0454	0.0454
1.5	4.32	0.0432	0.0648
2.0	86.38	0.8638	1.7276
	$100.00		1.8616

Table 13.17 Portfolio duration calculation

1	2	3	4 (2 × 3)
Maturity	Duration	Weighting	Weighted duration
1	0.98	25.0%	0.25
5	4.05	25.0	1.01
10	6.54	25.0	1.64
20	9.01	25.0	2.25
		100.0%	5.15

How do we meld these four durations to calculate the duration of the two-year instrument? We do this by weighting them according to their importance to the combined value of the bond — i.e., the percentage they represent of the total present value. Table 13.16 calculates the duration of the bond by weighting each component of present value by its maturity.

Since duration and maturity are identical for zero coupons, the weighted average maturity of the cash flows is the bond's duration. Thus, the duration of a bond is the weighted average maturity of all of the cash flows, where the cash flows are weighted by their contribution to the bond's value. In the example presented in Table 13.16, the duration is 1.86 years. This duration value is called Macaulay's duration, after the economist who first defined this relationship in 1938.[8]

The duration of a portfolio is simply a weighted average of the duration of the individual bonds. (See Table 13.17.)

The reason we use duration as the cornerstone of an investment program is that it is a reasonably accurate measure of the volatility of the portfolio. However, if duration is calculated by using the stated maturity of a bond, it can seriously overstate the risk of bonds that have call exposure.

The "true" duration of a callable bond lies somewhere between its duration to call and its duration to maturity. . . .

SETTING A DURATION TARGET

As we discussed above, the focal point of the portfolio management process should be a benchmark portfolio, and the most suitable candidates for this role are the major bond indexes. However, the durations of these indexes cover the full maturity spectrum — from short term to long term. Which one should be used? The answer depends upon the goals of the client.

We believe that most investors choose bonds to mute the volatility of their total portfolio — to act as an anchor to the windward. Therefore, the bond portfolio should have a modest level of volatility relative to equities. Since most of a bond portfolio's volatility is due to changes in interest rates, setting a duration target is essentially a question of identifying an acceptable level of exposure to interest rate changes.

Unfortunately, it is not possible to know for sure just how much exposure there is at any given duration target. To be sure, we know how much price risk there is for any given change in interest rates. The problem is, we are uncertain about the future volatility of interest rates. There is no central tendency of interest rates. Rather, they depend upon the Federal Reserve's response to current and expected economic conditions. Moreover, the volatility of interest rates has increased dramatically with the deregulation of the financial markets and shifts in the operating philosophy of the Federal Reserve. It may increase further in future years — or it may decline. As a result, the possible range of interest rates is quite wide, and the probability that interest rates will reach toward the extremes of this range is far higher than would be suggested by a normal distribution. Therefore, the risk of a bond portfolio cannot be precisely defined, and the choice of an optimal duration level for bonds is more of an ad hoc judgment based upon some practical considerations.

For example, if the duration target is very short — i.e., one year — an active bond manager will be precluded from participating in any meaningful way in the intermediate- or long-term markets that are so often rich in misvaluation. By contrast, a long-term target will result in highly volatile returns. An alternative target that offers maximum flexibility is to use the duration of the market itself — 4.9 years as of December 31, 1985, as measured by the Shearson Lehman Aggregate Index. Not only does this target afford the active manager the full maturity range of securities, it has the desirable property of yielding a high probability of positive annual returns.

Since the inception of the Shearson Lehman Aggregate Index in 1976, there have been 109 overlapping 12-month periods. The rate of return on the index was positive in 97, or 89%, of these periods. Since this is consistent with what most of our clients are interested in achieving with their bond portfolios, it is appropriate to adopt the duration of the index as a target duration.

However, there is a problem with using the published duration of the index as a target. Because its duration is calculated on the basis of maturity, its true duration is overstated. This stems from the fact that mortgage backed securities and corporate bonds (most of which are callable) represent 38% of the index (as of December 31, 1985). We estimate that the overstatement is currently 0.8 years and that the true duration is more on the order of 4.1 years.[9]

Once a duration target is selected, there is an additional question: Should we alter this target to incorporate our interest rate forecast? The answer depends upon our confidence in our forecast and the goals we are trying to achieve with the bond portfolio.

While it is relatively easy to have an opinion on interest rates, it is quite difficult to accurately forecast rates on a consistent basis. Not only is it difficult to forecast interest rates but it is also dangerous. Unfettered interest rate betting will often call for positioning the entire portfolio in long-term bonds. Yet in 8 out of the past 26 years, the returns on long-term Treasury bonds have been negative — a result that is inconsistent with the risk reduction role that most clients seek from bonds.

We believe that a portfolio manager has two acceptable courses of action — to avoid interest rate betting altogether or to severely limit its scope. If a portfolio manager does not believe he can forecast the future course of interest rates, then he should maintain the duration of his portfolio at the duration of the appropriate index. If a manager feels that over time his forecast can add value, then he should alter the duration of his portfolio. However, to prevent these interest rate bets from dominating the portfolio's return, the duration should be maintained within a narrow band around the index's duration. By restricting the potential shifts in duration, interest rate betting becomes simply another component in the portfolio management process.

MAXIMIZING MISVALUATION IN PORTFOLIO CONSTRUCTION

The valuation process described in Part One estimates the yield misvaluation and the percentage price misvaluation of a bond. How do we use this information to construct a portfolio? How do we determine the sector distribution of Treasuries, agencies, mortgages, and corporates?

In deriving the sector distribution, a simple percentage delineation is inadequate. For example, knowing that we have 20% of our portfolios in agencies does not tell us how our portfolios will fare if the pricing of agencies changes relative to the rest of the market. Why not?

A percentage breakdown of a portfolio ignores the importance of the duration of that sector to the duration of the portfolio. We are interested in identifying those sectors of the market that will earn incremental returns vis-à-vis the market. In this context, if a 20% agency position is invested in very short maturities, a change in relative yield spreads will not materially influence returns. If, on the other hand, the 20% position is in long-term agencies, a change in yield spreads will have a significant impact on return.

The greater the duration of an agency position, the greater will be the impact on the market value of a portfolio from a change in yields relative to the rest of the market. Consequently, the *exposure* to a sector is a combined function of the percentage invested as well as the average duration of the sector.

To illustrate, we have calculated the sector distribution and exposure of the Shearson Lehman Aggregate Index in Table 13.18.

We can see from column 3 that agencies make up 10% of the market value of the index. However, the average duration of the agency component is 3.35 years — substantially shorter

Table 13.18 Derivation of market exposure

1	2	3	4	5	6
Sector	Market value* (billions)	Distribution	Call adjusted duration (years)	(3 × 4) Weighted duration	Contribution to portfolio duration
Treasuries	$ 818	49%	4.35	2.13	52%
Agencies	171	10	3.35	0.34	8
Mortgages	307	19	3.00	0.57	14
Corporates	316	19	5.00	0.95	24
Yankees	46	2	4.65	0.09	2
	$1,658	100%		4.08	100%

*As of December 31, 1985. *Source*: Shearson Lehman Brothers and Bernstein estimates.

than the 4.08-year average of the entire index. Since agencies are 10% of the total, they contribute 0.34 years (3.35 × 10%) of duration to the index, which is 8% (0.34/4.08) of the total duration. Corporates, on the other hand, have a long duration relative to the market and, therefore, represent 24% of the duration of the index even though they constitute only 19% of the index's value. Thus, a "market" weighting of corporates, from a portfolio management standpoint, would be the percentage that contributes 24% of the portfolio's duration. Depending on the maturities and callability of the corporates actually purchased, this could entail placing considerably more or less than 19% of the portfolio in corporate securities.

This same principle applies to coupon strategies, to decisions regarding the optimal maturity mix, to virtually all portfolio decisions. The impact that any projected shift in the market will have upon a portfolio depends upon how important the duration of the securities in question is to the duration of the total portfolio.

Yield Misvaluation versus Price Misvaluation

When we construct a portfolio, our objective is to maximize expected return. To obtain this result, we should construct the portfolio that maximizes misvaluation. One way to do this is to rank bonds by percentage price misvaluation and select securities in descending order. The problem with this approach is that it results in a preponderance of long-term bonds. Why?

Since long-term bonds have long durations, for a given level of yield misvaluation they will have the largest percentage price misvaluation. (Duration times yield misvaluation is equal to price misvaluation.) Therefore, long-term bonds will *appear* to be the most attractive and will dominate the selection process.

A second way to maximize misvaluation is to rank bonds by yield misvaluation and to select in descending order. The advantage of this approach is that it is not biased to any maturity and is straightforward to implement.

To illustrate the difference between these two selection methods, let's assume that we have three groups of bonds — short, intermediate, and long term — with the *same* yield misvaluation — 100 basis points. (See Table 13.19.)

Table 13.19 Comparable risk portfolio

1	2	3	4	5	6 (4 × 5)
Composition	Maturity	Duration (years)	Weighting	Price misvaluation	Weighted price misvaluation
Single maturity	Intermediate	4	100%	4.0%	4.0%
Laddered	Short	1	33%	1.0%	0.3%
	Intermediate	4	33	4.0	1.3
	Long	7	33	7.0	2.3
			100%		4.0%
Barbelled	Short	1	50%	1.0%	0.5%
	Long	7	50	7.0	3.5
			100%		4.0%

If our target portfolio duration is 4.0, then every combination of maturities that has a duration of 4.0 will have the same percentage price misvaluation — 4%. Why?

Since each of the bonds has the same yield misvaluation, they are equally attractive. Any combination of these bonds will have an average yield misvaluation of 100 basis points. Therefore, any portfolio with a duration of 4.0 will have a price misvaluation of 4% and be equally attractive.

The choice between these two methods of ranking misvaluation can be seen more clearly if we assume unequal yield misvaluation as in Table 13.20.

Which security or combination of maturities is the most attractive? If we use percentage price misvaluation, we would pick the long bond and then add sufficient short-term bonds to hit the duration target. If we look at yield misvaluation, we would choose the intermediate alone. To determine which is more attractive, we have repeated the format of Table 13.19 in Table 13.21.

As may be seen, the long and the short bonds have lower yield misvaluations than the intermediate bonds. As a result, any combination of these bonds with any other maturity is not as attractive as a single intermediate maturity. Thus, the most attractive security is the one with the greatest yield misvaluation. The portfolio construction process is one of maximizing the investment in the most attractive bonds while maintaining the target duration.

Controlling Exposure

In the hypothetical case of a perfectly priced bond market, we would invest our entire portfolio in Treasuries. The coupon and maturity structure would be roughly in line with

Table 13.20 Securities with unequal yield misvaluation

1	2	3	4
		Yield	(2×3)
		misvaluation	Price
Maturity	Duration	(basis points)	misvaluation
Short	1.0	90	0.9%
Intermediate	4.0	100	4.0
Long	7.0	90	6.3

Table 13.21 Effect of unequal yield misvaluations on comparable risk portfolios

1	2	3	4	5	6
					(4×5)
					Weighted price
Composition	Maturity	Duration	Weighting	Price misvaluation	misvaluation
Single	Intermediate	4	100%	4.0%	4.0%
Ladder	Short	1	33%	0.9%	0.3%
	Intermediate	4	33	4.0	1.3
	Long	7	33	6.3	2.1
			100%		3.7%
Barbell	Short	1	50%	0.9%	0.4%
	Long	7	50	6.3	3.2
			100%		3.6%

the market. As misvaluations are identified, we replace the Treasury with the maximum percentage that we can invest in the cheap bond. There are several considerations. First, prudence requires diversification limits on the maximum investment in any one company or industry. In addition, all misvaluations are not created equal. We are not indifferent to the choice between a corporate and a Treasury that are equally misvalued.

To establish our corporate weighting rules, we asked the following question: At what level of misvaluation are we interested in holding?

1. A market weighting (24% exposure from Table 13.18).
2. One hundred percent in corporates.
3. No corporates at all.

Table 13.22 shows the schedule we have adopted.

At misvaluations of 20 basis points or lower we do not want to own any corporates — we can routinely buy Treasuries that are 10 to 20 basis points cheap. Furthermore, at this distortion level, we are vastly more certain that Treasuries are mispriced than we are that corporates are mispriced.

At the opposite end of the spectrum is the yield misvaluation that would induce us to invest 100% of a portfolio in corporates. The number that we chose was 200 basis points. Since this is extreme by historical standards, we do not expect to be fully invested in corporates except under very unusual circumstances. Finally, we require a misvaluation of at least 40 basis points to reach an approximate market weighting of 25%.

Once the corporate exposure schedule has been established, an iterative portfolio construction process is triggered. To illustrate the process, we will make the following assumptions:

1. The portfolio is initially 100% in cash.
2. The bonds listed in Table 13.23 are the most undervalued securities that are available and approved.
3. The target duration is four years.

From Table 13.22 we know how much yield misvaluation we need to support a given level of corporate exposure. As we add corporates, the yield misvaluation that is available drops, and, therefore, our desired exposure drops. At some point, we are not interested in owning any more corporates.

Table 13.22 Corporate exposure schedule

Yield misvaluation (basic points)	Contribution to portfolio duration
20	0%
28	10
36	20
45	30
60	40
80	50
100	60
120	70
145	80
170	90
200	100

Table 13.23 Determination of corporate exposure — target duration of four years

1		2	3	4	5	6	7
Description		Yield misvaluation	Weight	Duration	Weighted duration	Contribution to portfolio duration	Cumulative contribution to portfolio duration
Armco Steel	$8\frac{1}{2}\%$ 9/1/01	281	0.05	7.1	0.36	8.9%	8.9%
Public Service of Indiana	$7\frac{5}{8}$ 1/1/07	149	0.05	7.4	0.37	9.3	18.2
Chrysler	$12\frac{3}{4}$ 3/1/92	109	0.05	4.5	0.23	5.6	23.8
Philip Morris	6 1/1/99	95	0.05	7.3	0.37	9.1	32.9
GMAC	11 4/1/88	86	0.05	2.1	0.11	2.6	35.5
NCNB	$8\frac{3}{8}$ 3/1/99	61	0.03	6.3	0.19	4.7	40.2
Chemical	$8\frac{1}{4}$ 8/1/02	54	—	7.1	—	—	—
Household Finance	$7\frac{1}{4}$ 1/1/90	50	—	3.0	—	—	—

Source: Bernstein estimates.

Table 13.24 Non-Treasury exposure schedule

Yield misvaluation			Cumulative contribution to portfolio duration
Agencies	Mortgages	Corporates	
10	15	20	0%
18	21	28	10
28	27	36	20
40	34	45	30
58	45	60	40
80	60	80	50
N/A	75	100	60
N/A	90	120	70
N/A	105	145	80
N/A	120	170	90
N/A	135	200	100

This point is reached in Table 13.23 with the addition of NCNB, which is misvalued by 61 basis points and raises the exposure to 40%. To add more bonds, we need more than 60 basis points misvaluation. Since Chemical's misvaluation is only 54 basis points, the process ends. Generally, we will hold these bonds in this portfolio until the yield misvaluation on any one of them falls to zero. If another corporate bond becomes available with a yield misvaluation of more than 60 basis points, we will buy it.

We utilize the same methodology for agencies and mortgages. However, as may be seen in Table 13.24, the amount of yield misvaluation we require for similar degrees of exposure varies from sector to sector.

The difference in scaling between sectors reflects our confidence in our ability to identify misvaluations. The agency sector tops out at 50% exposure because there are only three agencies and they are not guaranteed by the federal government. With mortgages and corporates, there is far greater diversification potential, and we are willing to invest 100% in a sector if there are extremely large opportunities.

CONCLUSION

The goals of an active bond portfolio management process should be to maximize performance while, at the same time, maintaining a low level of volatility relative to equities. One way (we would argue, the best way) to achieve these goals on a consistent basis is to pursue a bond-analytical approach—an approach that seeks to identify the *fair* value of a bond. The value of a bond is a function of its coupon, maturity, quality, and call exposure. To properly evaluate a bond, the value of each of these components must be estimated. We have outlined some solutions to these analytical problems and hope that our work will stimulate further research in this area.

The volatility of a portfolio should be controlled by constraining the duration of a portfolio to a narrow band around an appropriate index. While more dramatic interest rate betting *may* produce higher returns, it is more likely to introduce an unacceptable level of volatility.

ENDNOTES

1. Duration is a measure of interest rate risk....

2. A material difference is defined as one in which the misvaluation exceeds transaction costs.

3. While it is possible to get the bid and asked price on bonds traded on the New York Stock Exchange, these markets are usually for odd-lot trades (less than $100,000 in par value).

4. Perfect forecasting is the return that would have resulted if one had been able to earn the higher of the returns available from the one-month Treasury bill or the 30-year Treasury bond in each month. The yield information was drawn from Ibbotson and Sinquefeld, "Stocks, Bonds, Bills and Inflation," Ibbotson Associates, Inc. (Chicago, Ill.) and *The Wall Street Journal*. Shearson Lehman Index is the *Shearson Lehman Aggregate Bond Index*. SEI Median is the *Bond Funds Background: Total Fund Rates of Return*, provided by the SEI Funds Evaluation Service.

5. For those readers who might question the potential mispricing of coupons, in the fall of 1983 the yields on premium, non-callable Treasuries rose 40 to 60 basis points (!) above the yield on similar maturity Treasuries priced at par.

6. Since duration is a better measure of the life of a bond, we would expect a fit based on duration to be superior to our maturity fit. While this is clearly the case theoretically, we have tested both processes and found that misvaluations off of the fit by maturity are better indicators of value than those off of the duration fit.

7. Wherever it is relevant, we will provide the names of vendors of bond analysis that we have found to be useful. Bernstein has no business relationship with any of these firms other than (in some cases) as a subscriber and derives no benefit from the references.

8. Frederick R. Macaulay, *The Movements of Interest Rates, Bond Yields and Stock Prices in the United States since 1856* (New York: National Bureau of Economic Research, 1938).

9. Capital Management Sciences provides estimates of the effective durations of individual corporate bonds as well as the Shearson Lehman and Salomon Brothers indexes.

—— 14 ——

Do Yield Curves Normally Slope Up? The Term Structure of U.S. Interest Rates, 1862–1982

—— John H. Wood ——

The downward-sloping yield curves of recent years have been called *perverse*, but an examination of the history of American interest rates reveals that, at least since the Civil War, falling yield curves have been nearly as common as those with upward slopes. This article summarizes yield curve patterns since 1862 and suggests that (1) the traditional expectations theory remains a viable explanation of observed yield curves and (2) yield curves since the abandonment of the gold standard in 1971 have much in common with those of the greenback era of 1862–78 but are distinct from those of the gold standard years of 1879–1970. The slopes of yield curves appear to depend upon expectations of future yields as determined by expectations of inflation, which, in turn, depend upon the prevailing monetary standard.

U.S. YIELD CURVES IN THE 20TH CENTURY

Yield curves for high-grade corporate bonds from 1900 to 1982 are shown in the two panels of Figure 14.1.[1] Each curve shows the term structure of yields in a particular year, i.e., the relationship between bond yields and terms to maturity at a point in time. Figure 14.1a shows yield curves for the period prior to 1930. Yield curves for 1930 through 1982 are shown in Figure 14.1b. Curves since 1966 have been identified by year of occurrence.

A striking feature of the yield curves in Figure 14.1 is their tendency to be positively sloped when yields are "low" and to be negatively sloped when yields are "high". Suppose, for example, that between 1900 and 1970 one-year bond yields above 4.40% were considered high and yields below 3.25% were thought to be low. The upper portion of Table 14.1 shows that if "high" and "low" are distinguished in this manner all yield curves had negative slopes

Reprinted from: Wood, J.H. 1983: Do Yield Curves Normally Slope Up? The Term Structure of Interest Rates, 1862–1982. *Economic Perspectives: Federal Reserve Bank of Chicago*, 7, July–August, 17–23.

when short-term yields were high and all yield curves had positive slopes when short-term yields were low.

This observation applies throughout the 1900–1970 period, but breaks down after 1970. In order to understand yield patterns since 1970, it is first necessary to examine a popular and persuasive explanation of the shapes of observed yield curves.

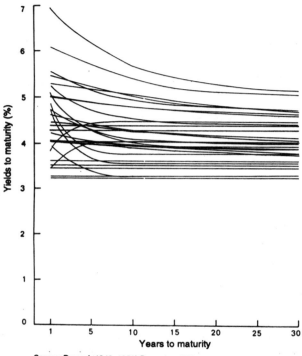

(a)

Figure 14.1 a) Yield curves for high-grade corporate bonds, 1900–1929 and b) Yield curves for high-grade corporate bonds, 1930–1982 [shown on page 211]

Table 14.1 Frequencies of rising, flat, and falling yield curves, 1900–1982

One-year corporate bond yield (% per annum)	Slope of yield curve		
	Positive	Flat	Negative
	1900–1970		
Above 4.40	0	0	20
3.25–4.40	10	10	5
Below 3.25	26	0	0
	1971–1982		
Above 8.00	1	0	3
Below 8.00	8	0	0

Sources: Durand, Durand and Winn and Scudder, Stevens and Clark.

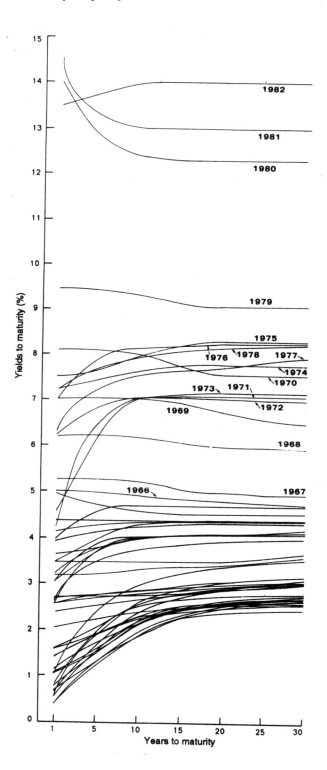

(b)

AN EXPLANATION: THE TRADITIONAL EXPECTATIONS THEORY WITH REGRESSIVE EXPECTATIONS[2]

Any theory of equilibrium relations among bond yields must specify (1) the criteria by which investors select bonds *given their expectations of future yields* and (2) how those expectations are formed. With regard to (1), the traditional expectations theory of the term structure of interest rates asserts that bond-market equilibrium requires equal expected returns on bonds of all maturities.[3] For the simple case of pure discount (zero-coupon) bonds, this implies long-term yields that are averages of current and expected short-term yields (see Box 14.1).

To convert the expectations theory into an operational explanation of the term structure, a mechanism for determining expected short-term yields must be specified. Only two of the simplest and most common types of expectations — extrapolative and regressive — are considered here.

Box 14.1: The traditional expectations theory of the term structure

The equilibrium term structure is

$$(1 + R_n)^n = (1 + R_1)(1 + {}_1R_1^e)(1 + {}_2R_1^e) \ldots$$
$$(1 + {}_{n-1}R_1^e), \qquad (1)$$

where R_1 and R_n are the yields-to-maturity currently prevailing on bonds maturing after one and n periods, respectively, and ${}_1R_1^e, {}_2R_1^e, \ldots, {}_{n-1}R_1^e$ are the one-period yields currently expected by investors to prevail one, two, ..., and $(n - 1)$ periods in the future.

A convenient linear approximation of the equilibrium term structure describes long-term yields as arithmetic averages, instead of geometric averages as in equation (1), of current and expected short-term yields:

$$R_n = \frac{R_1 + {}_1R_1^e + {}_2R_1^e + \cdots + {}_{n-1}R_1^e}{n} \qquad (2)$$

This approximation deteriorates as short and long yields diverge. For example, let R_2^a be the approximate two-period yield given by equation (2). Then comparing R_2^a with R_2 from equation (1).

$$R_2^a = R_2 = 0.10 \text{ if } R_1 = {}_1R_1^e = 0.10;$$

$R_2^a = 0.10$ and $R_2 = 0.0997$ if $R_1 = 0.075$ and ${}_1R_1^e = 0.125$; and $R_2^a = 0.10$ and $R_2 = 0.0989$ if $R = 0.05_1$ and ${}_1R_1^e = 0.15$.

Equation (1) is itself an approximation of observed yield curves even if all the usual assumptions of the traditional expectations theory are satisfied. One reason is that equation (1) neglects uncertainty and is therefore valid only under conditions of perfect foresight. (This point has been made ·in different ways by Nelson [1972, pp. 21–28] and Cox, Ingersoll and Ross [1981].) Second, equation (1) strictly applies only to zero-coupon bonds — whereas most yield curves, including those in Figure 14.1, are for coupon bonds. Garbade [1982, pp. 293–99] and others have shown that the effect of coupons is to moderate the slopes of yield curves implied by equation (1).

Although it would be difficult to assess the empirical importance of these deficiencies, it is shown in the text that the traditional expectations theory with regressive expectations is at least roughly consistent with observed yield curves.

Extrapolative expectations mean that investors expect short-term yields to continue to move in the same direction as recent yield movements. If yields have been rising, they are expected to continue to rise in the future. If yields have been falling, they are expected to fall further.

Regressive expectations imply just the opposite of extrapolative expectations. If yields have been rising, they are expected to reverse course, or regress, towards what are considered "normal" levels. If yields are below "normal," they are expected to rise.

Now, suppose that yields have fallen to low levels such that the current short-term yield is $R_1 = 0.02$ and, because investors extrapolate recent events into the future, the short-term yield expected to prevail in the next period is $_1R_1^e = 0.01$. Using the approximation provided by equation (2) in Box 14.1, this means a two-period yield of $R_2 = (0.02+0.01)/2 = 0.015$, and the yield curve has a negative slope.

Considering another example, suppose yields have risen to high levels such that $R_1 = 0.20$. If expectations are formed extrapolatively, so that, perhaps, $_1R_1^e = 0.21$, we have $R_2 = 0.205$ and the yield curve is rising. Thus, the traditional expectations theory with extrapolative expectations suggests that yield curves will tend to have positive slopes when yields are high and negative slopes when yields are low. This is inconsistent with the data in Figure 14.1 and Table 14.1, at least for 1900–1970.

On the other hand, suppose short-term yields are expected to regress toward some "normal" value denoted by R_1^*. Assume $R_1^* = 0.06$ and that the change in each later period is expected to be one-half the difference between the normal yield and the short-term yield prevailing in the preceding period. Given $R_1 = 0.02$ and $R_1^* = 0.06$, these assumptions imply that

$$_1R_1^e = R_1 + s(R_1^* - R_1) = 0.02 + 0.5(0.06 - 0.02) = 0.04,$$

where $s = 0.5$ is the expected speed of adjustment. The resulting yield curve has a positive slope because $R_2 = (0.02 + 0.04)/2 = 0.03$. Following the same procedure and letting $R_1 = 0.20$, we obtain

$$_1R_1^e = 0.13 \text{ and}$$

$R_2 = 0.165$, so that the yield curve has a negative slope when $R_1 = 0.20$. These examples support the view that the traditional expectations theory supplemented by regressive expectations is consistent with observed yield curves, at least during 1900–1970.[4]

AN UPWARD REVISION OF EXPECTATIONS IN THE 1970s?

The upper portion of Table 14.1 suggests that yield curves between 1900 and 1970 were consistent with the traditional expectations theory with regressive expectations, if the normal one-year, high-grade corporate bond yield was thought by investors to be between 3.25 and 4.40%. But notice the high and rising yield curves for 1971–1978 and 1982 in Figure 14.1. Either (1) the explanation that is so effective for 1900–1970 has failed in recent years because investors no longer behave according to the tenets of the traditional expectations theory and/or they no longer form expectations regressively, or (2) they have revised their estimates of the normal rate.

The extrapolative expectations version of the traditional expectations theory appears broadly consistent with the generally rising yields and positively sloped yield curves of 1971–78. But it does not look as promising in light of the yield curves of 1979–81, which had negative slopes during a period of rapidly rising yields. A variety of other explanations of the events of 1971–82 might be worth pursuing, but the analysis of this paper will remain with the explanation emphasized thus far — the traditional expectations theory with regressive expectations. That is, we will examine the extent to which alternative (2) in the preceding paragraph is capable of explaining yield curves since 1971. But this approach requires an additional hypothesis, one that supplies a rule by which investors revise their estimates of the normal rate. However, such a rule, whatever it is, cannot be subjected to any kind of test on the basis of data considered so far because the only unambiguous 20th century revision or revisions have occurred since about 1970. For other possible revisions we must go to the 19th century.

THE 19TH AND 20TH CENTURIES COMPARED

No complete yield curves such as those in Figure 14.1 are available for the 19th century. However, the slopes of yield curves may be inferred from data on the prime commercial paper rate (the short-term yield) and Frederick Macaulay's railroad bond yield index (the long-term yield).[5] Annual averages of commercial paper and railroad bond yields for 1862–1929 are shown in Figure 14.2. This figure tells, in a different way, essentially the same stories as Figure 14.1: first, that yield curves tended to be positively sloped when yields were low and negatively sloped when yields were high and, second, that there was apparently a revision of the notions of "high" and "low".[6] However, instead of an upward revision, as in the early 1970s, Figure 14.2 suggests a downward adjustment of the normal rate in the late 1870s. Notice, for example, that the seven short-term yields between 5.58% and 7.55% during 1866–1875 were all associated with rising yield curves, while after those years all short-term yields above 5.40% were associated with falling yield curves.

No precise dating of the normal rate's revision, which may have occurred over several years, is immediately obvious from the data. (This is also true of the shift in the 1970s, or perhaps the late 1960s.) But suppose, for simplicity of exposition, that most of the adjustment took place early in 1879. Using this date to divide 1862–1929 into two periods, Table 14.2 suggests that the normal rate may have been in the vicinity of 7.50% during 1862–1878 and between 4 and 5.50% during the 1879–1929 period.

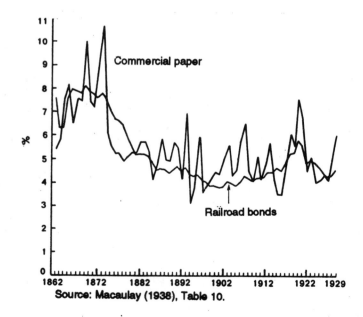

Figure 14.2   Long and short rates 1862–1929

Table 14.2 Frequencies of rising and falling yield curves, 1862–1929

Commercial paper yield (% per annum)	Slope of yield curve	
	Positive	Negative
1862–1878		
Above 7.57	0	5
Below 7.56	12	0
1879–1929		
Above 5.40	0	16
4.21–5.40	4	17
Below 4.21	14	0

Source: Macaulay, Table 10.

What events triggered these upward and downward revisions in investors' expectations of normal rates? A look at the history of U.S. monetary standards since 1862 may provide an answer.

THE MONETARY STANDARD AND THE YIELD CURVE

The American monetary standard has undergone the following changes since early in the Civil War. The gold standard was abandoned when banks suspended specie payments on December 30, 1861.[7] In February 1862, Congress authorized the first of several issues of legal tender currency (the famous greenbacks). After a period of monetary expansion accompanied by depreciation of the dollar, followed by prolonged monetary controversy, a bill for the resumption of the gold standard at the prewar exchange rate was passed in January 1875. Resumption was achieved on the target date of January 1, 1879, although success was not assured until late in 1878.[8]

The monetary standard remained unchanged until banks were legally prohibited from paying out gold in March 1933. The *international* gold standard was resumed in January 1934,[9] although the gold value of the dollar was reduced to 59% of that prevailing between 1879 and 1933. Finally, in August 1971, the United States suspended the international convertibility of the dollar and embarked on a paper standard identical in all important respects to the greenback era of 1862–1878.

The following line of reasoning suggests that the monetary standard should be expected to be an important, perhaps the dominant, influence on the normal rate. First, define the normal rate on securities of a particular risk class as the yield expected by investors to apply to those securities in long-run equilibrium. (References from this point are to normal rates instead of to a single normal rate.) Second, the available evidence strongly suggests that interest rates are to a considerable extent determined by inflationary expectations, which in turn depend on actual inflation.[10] Finally, inflation has for centuries been highly correlated, and generally believed to be highly correlated, with the choice of monetary standard.[11]

These arguments are supported by the data in Figures 14.1a and 14.1b and Tables 14.1 and 14.2, which are consistent with a downward revision in the 1870s and an upward revision in the 1970s of investor estimates of normal rates. The rising 1982 yield curve suggests that the latter revision may not yet be complete. It is not clear from the data whether another revision occurred in the 1930s because the steeply rising yield curves of that decade (and of the 1940s and 1950s) were, in view of the record-low yields prevailing at the time, consistent with normal rates based on experience of both gold and paper standards.[12]

The values in Table 14.2 are not directly comparable with those in Table 14.1, because the yields in the two tables apply to different securities. Nevertheless, these tables and the figures upon which they are based combine to tell a single story—that American yield curves since 1862 are at least roughly consistent with the traditional expectations theory supplemented by regressive expectations *where the normal rate is a function of the monetary standard*. That is the hypothesized rule for revising the normal rate that earlier was declared to be required for a complete explanation of observed yield curves.

CONCLUDING COMMENT: INFLATION AND THE MONETARY STANDARD AS PARTS OF THE SAME POLITICAL DECISION

The data presented above suggest that changes in inflationary expectations are associated with, and perhaps influenced by, changes in the monetary standard. But it is important to stress that the monetary standard is not imposed upon an economic system from outside. A shift from a fixed-rate to a flexible-rate system, for example, may be viewed as merely one of several reflections of a decision by one or more countries to abandon long-run price stability as a goal. This means that the data contain no implications for monetary policy. The monetary authority is not free to attempt to influence inflationary expectations by manipulating the monetary standard. Both are chosen and imposed upon the central bank by the political process.

ENDNOTES

1. Data are David Durand's "basic yields on high-grade corporate bonds," first published in 1942, updated by Durand and Winn to 1959, and updated since 1959 by Scudder, Stevens and Clark. Selected data are available for 1900–1970 in the U.S. Department of Commerce, *Historical Statistics of the United States*, Vol. 2, p. 1004, and more recently in the annual *Statistical Abstract of the United States*. Ruth Heisler of Scudder, Stevens and Clark has kindly supplied data for 1982. A detailed account of the method by which the yield curves in Figure 14.1 were constructed is given in Durand [1942].

2. The "traditional" and other expectations theories, most notably the "modern" expectations theory, are compared in Cox, Ingersoll and Ross [1981]. An early statement of the traditional expectations theory with regressive expectations was that of Lutz [1937].

3. This statement may be illustrated as follows for 1-and 2-period bonds and a 1-period holding period. The 1-period rate-of-return on a 2-period zero-coupon bond worth $1 at maturity is

$$\frac{{}_1P_1^e - P_2}{P_2} = \frac{\dfrac{\$1}{(1 + {}_1R_1^e)} - \dfrac{\$1}{(1 + R_2)^2}}{\dfrac{\$1}{(1 + R_2)^2}} = \frac{(1 + R_2)^2}{(1 + {}_1R_1^e)} - 1.$$

where P_2 is the current price of the 2-period bond and ${}_1P_1^e$ is the price currently expected to prevail next period on a 1-period bond. If the expectations theory holds, (see equation (1) in Box 14.1) this rate-of-return equals R_1—i.e., the expected 1-period returns on 1- and 2-period bonds are equal. As indicated in the Box, these results hold precisely only under conditions of certainty.

4. Both extrapolative and regressive expectations may be rational in an economy in which yields fluctuate cyclically about "normal" levels, with short-term expectations being formed extrapolatively and long-term expectations being formed regressively. Possible examples of the interaction of extrapolative and regressive expectations are the hump-backed yield curves that are common when yields are high. These humps tend to occur at maturities of 3 to 6 months and thus do not appear in the yield curves of Figure 14.1, in which the shortest maturity is one year.

5. See Macaulay (1938, Table 10) for data on the unadjusted index of railroad bond yields. "Choice" and "prime" commercial paper rates, reported on a discount basis, have been converted to bond equivalent yields. Macaulay tried to construct yield curves for railroad bonds like those later reported by Durand, but he found the correlation between yield and maturity too small. However, the use of Macaulay's data in Table 14.2 is consistent with the use of Durand's yield curves in Table 14.1 because Macaulay found that longer-term bonds tended to have higher yields when short-term rates (such as the commercial paper rate) were low and that shorter-term bonds tended to have higher yields when short-term rates were high (p. 80).

6. During 1900–1929, when Figures 14.1 and 14.2 overlap, the yield curves implied by the latter figure have the same sign as those in the former on three-quarters of the occasions on which Durand's yield curves are not flat. Furthermore, the slopes implied by Figure 14.2 tend to be smaller in absolute value when Durand's curves are flat than when they have non-zero slopes.

7. The official standard was bimetallic, but silver had long ceased to circulate because it had been undervalued by the official gold-silver exchange rate.

8. For example, see Dewey (1936) and Friedman and Schwartz (1963) for histories of American monetary standards.

9. The domestic circulation of gold was ended by the Gold Reserve Act.

10. Most observers, including Fisher (1930) and Fama (1975) would agree with this statement see Wood (1981) for a review of empirical work on the connections between interest rates and inflation.

11. See Attwood (1819), Lester (1939), Dewey (1936), Friedman and Schwartz (1963), Barro (1980) and Bordo (1981) for discussions of evidence and attitudes regarding inflation under gold and paper standards.

12. In annual averages, American commercial paper yields have not, except during 1935–46, been less than 1% and have not, except during 1931–58, been less than 3%. They were continuously less than 1% during 1935–46 and continuously less than 3% during 1931–55. These statements are based on data available since 1819 in Homer (1977).

REFERENCES

Thomas Attwood, *A Second Letter to the Earl of Liverpool on the Bank Reports as Occasioning the National Dangers and Distresses*, R. Wrightson, Birmingham, 1819.

Robert J. Barro, "U.S. Inflation and the Choice of Monetary Standards." NBER Conference on Inflation, Washington, October 1980.

Michael D. Bordo, "The Classical Gold Standard: Some Lessons for Today," Federal Reserve Bank of St. Louis *Review*, May 1981, 2–17.

John C. Cox, Jonathon E. Ingersoll and Stephen A. Ross, "A Reexamination of Traditional Hypotheses About the Term Structure of Interest Rates," *Journal of Finance*, September 1981, 769–99.

Davis R. Dewey, *Financial History of the United States*, 12th ed., Longmans, Green, and Co., New York, 1936.

David Durand, "A Quarterly Series of Corporate Bond Yields, 1952–1957, and Some Attendant Reservations," *Journal of Finance*, September 1958, 348–56.

— —, *Basic Yields of Corporate Bonds*, 1900–1942, National Bureau of Economic Research, Technical Paper 3, 1942.

David Durand and Willis J. Winn, *Basic Yields of Bonds, 1927–1947: Their Measurement and Pattern*, National Bureau of Economic Research, Technical Paper 6, 1947.

Eugene F. Fama, "Short-Term Interest Rates as Predictions of Inflation," *American Economic Review*, June 1975, 269–82.

Irving Fisher, "Appreciation and Interest," *Publications of the American Economic Association*, Vol. II, August 1896.

—— ——, *The Theory of Interest*, Macmillan, New York, 1930.

Milton Friedman and Anna J. Schwartz, A *Monetary History of the United States, 1867–1960*, Princeton University Press, Princeton, N.J., 1963.

Kenneth Garbade, *Securities Markets*, McGraw-Hill, New York, 1982.

Sidney Homer, *A History of Interest Rates*, 2nd ed., Rutgers University Press, New Brunswick, N.J., 1977.

Richard A. Lester, *Monetary Experiments*, Princeton University Press, Princeton, N.J., 1939.

F.A. Lutz "The Structure of Interest Rates," *Quarterly Journal of Economics*, November 1940, 36–63.

Frederick R. Macaulay, *Some Theoretical Problems Suggested by the Movements of Interest Rates, Bond Yields and Stock Price in the United States Since 1856*, National Bureau of Economic Research, New York, 1938.

Charles R. Nelson, *The Term Structure of Interest Rates*, Basic Books, New York, 1972.

John H. Wood, "Interest Rates and Inflation," Federal Reserve Bank of Chicago *Economic Perspectives*, May/June 1981, 3–12.

— 15 —

Risk and Return in Defaulted Bonds
David J. Ward and Gary L. Griepentrog

In the last 20 years, investors have faced levels of defaults on publicly held debt not experienced since the Great Depression. For example, in the 1970–91 period, over $63 billion in publicly held debt defaulted.[1] The volume of defaults in 1990–91 alone was over $37 billion. Corporate restructuring and the excessive leveraging of corporations that accompanied the LBO frenzy in the 1980s were primary factors in the accelerating level of defaults.

The unprecedented volume of defaults on publicly held debt, particularly defaults of high-yield corporate bonds, has had a serious impact on financial institutions and investors. Defaults on high-yield corporate bonds were a major factor in the collapse of several large S&Ls. Bond defaults have also contributed to serious problems and financial failures among life insurance companies. In addition to these problems, institutional and individual investors have been faced with large losses of principal and interest on bond holdings.

The political reaction to these default problems has been a series of legislative and regulatory changes mandating the liquidation of current high-yield and defaulted bond holdings in the portfolios of S&Ls and other financial institutions. Unfortunately, most of this regulatory action has not been informed by a comprehensive view of the risk and return characteristics of defaulted debt.

BACKGROUND

The most comprehensive study of the investment characteristics of defaulted bonds was done by Hickman.[2] Hickman's findings, summarized in Table 15.1, show robust average returns on defaulted debt from the time of default to the extinguishment of the default. The performance of industrial bond defaults after 1930 was particularly striking. He also found a significant difference between pre and post-Depression default returns. Hickman concluded:

> On the average, investors who sold at default suffered unnecessarily large losses, and those who purchased obtained unusually large gains. It is unfortunate that many financial intermediaries were forced by their directors or by regulatory authorities to sell at that time.

Table 15.1 Average simple yield on defaulted bonds from default to extinguishment (issues with par values of $5 million or more)

Category	1900–1943	1900–1929	1930–1943
All issues	20.0%	6.4%	26.4%
Railroads	18.6%	6.4%	24.4%
Public utilities	17.0%	6.2%	22.7%
Industrials	25.8%	6.7%	33.6%

Source: W. Braddock Hickman, *Corporate Bond Quality and Investor Experience* (Princeton: Princeton University Press, 1958).

More recent studies by Altman, Hradsky and Long, and Warner provide contemporary data on the risks and returns of defaulted bonds.[3] For the 1987–91 period, Altman reported an arithmetic average annual return of 13.5% and a compound average annual return of 9.8% on a portfolio of over 160 defaulted bond issues. Hradsky and Long examined cumulative excess returns for 384 bond defaults in the 1977–89 period and found a post-default pattern of excess returns that suggested a strategy of buying defaulted bonds five months after default and selling them 24 months after default. Finally, Warner studied 73 defaulted railroad bonds in the 1930–55 period and found that the risk of defaulted bonds was similar to that of common stocks and that significant profits could be made by buying defaults in the month after a firm files for bankruptcy.

DATA

Obtaining the data needed to provide a comprehensive overview of the risk and return characteristics of defaulted bonds was a major part of this research. Data required included a list of defaulted bonds, monthly returns for defaulted bonds, and monthly returns of basic equity and debt investments.

Measures of monthly returns for basic debt and equity investments were obtained from the publications of Ibbotson Associates.[4] Returns for Treasury bills, long-term government bonds, high-grade corporate bonds, small-company stocks and the S&P 500 were used to provide comparative risk and return measures.

Listings of defaulted securities and the monthly return data for defaulted bonds were obtained from the Ward-Niedermeier Defaulted Bond Project. This project tracked over 750 defaulted bond issues in the 1944–91 period. These issues were identified by researching *Moody's Bond Record, Standard & Poor's Bond Guide* and the *Wall Street Journal*. Monthly price quotes for each issue were obtained from the *Bond Record*, the *Bond Guide* and other bond price databases. Successive monthly returns were computed for the market-weighted aggregate portfolio of all defaulted issues with a recorded monthly sale or bid price. Over the period of this research, an average of 150 bonds were used to compute the monthly portfolio return.

Methodology

We report here rates of return and systematic and unsystematic risk measures for defaults in 1972–91 and the subperiod 1987–91. Risk and return measures for defaults are compared with returns on investments in bonds and equities. Measures of return include a geometric mean and an arithmetic mean. Risk is measured by both the standard deviation and the coefficient of variation. Measures of skewness and kurtosis are also calculated to assess the distribution of returns for defaulted bonds compared with returns on other assets and with the normal distribution.

A second view of the investment characteristics of defaulted bonds is provided by characteristic line estimates. We calculated measures of systematic and unsystematic risk from the risk-premium form of the characteristic line introduced by Jensen.[5] Jensen's alpha (the estimated alpha of the characteristic line) measures excess return for a given amount of systematic risk as measured by beta.

RESULTS

Table 15.2 shows how defaulted bond returns compare with other basic debt and equity returns. It reveals that defaulted bonds are not clearly similar to either debt or equity. Over the entire period of the study, the geometric and arithmetic mean returns of defaulted bonds exceeded those of bonds or equities. However most of the dominance of the defaulted bonds' returns is due to unusually high returns in the late 1970s and early 1980s. Returns on defaulted bonds in later years, as reported in Table 15.2 for the subperiod 1987–91, are more typical of the lack of consistent dominance over the entire period of the study.

Further analysis of Table 15.2 reveals that the standard deviation of defaulted bond returns is greater than the standard deviation of all other asset categories except that of small-company returns. When relative risk is considered, the coefficient of variation presents a slightly different result. When compared with long-term government bond, corporate bond

Table 15.2 Monthly returns

| | January 1987 to December 1991 | | | | | | |
Asset	Geometric mean (%)	Arithmetic mean (%)	Standard deviation (%)	Coefficient of variation (%)	Skewness	Kurtosis	First-order auto-correlation
Treasury bills	0.54	0.54	0.11	21	0.03	2.05	0.81
Long-term government	0.78	0.81	2.57	315	0.08	2.69	0.15
High-grade bonds	0.83	0.85	2.11	248	−0.31	3.13	0.14
S&P 500	1.20	1.34	5.33	397	−1.18	7.30	0.15
Small company	0.55	0.75	6.03	803	−2.16	11.39	0.30
Defaulted bonds	0.75	0.84	4.36	520	0.56	3.85	0.39

| | January 1972 to December 1991 | | | | | | |
Asset	Geometric mean (%)	Arithmetic mean (%)	Standard deviation (%)	Coefficient of variation (%)	Skewness	Kurtosis	First-order auto-correlation
Treasury bills	0.62	0.62	0.22	35	1.07	4.08	0.91
Long-term government	0.72	0.77	3.28	424	0.66	5.33	0.08
High-grade bonds	0.75	0.80	3.06	383	0.58	5.72	0.14
S&P 500	0.94	1.05	4.69	446	−0.27	5.34	0.01
Small company	1.14	1.35	6.44	477	−0.30	7.25	0.14
Defaulted bonds	1.29	1.39	4.90	352	1.05	7.58	0.31

Table 15.3 Compound average annual returns on defaulted bonds, 1972–1991

Base period (Jan. 1)	Terminal period (December 31)																			
	1972	1973	1974	1975	1976	1977	1978	1979	1980	1981	1982	1983	1984	1985	1986	1987	1988	1989	1990	1991
1972	−22.28	−3.79	−11.58	−2.27	2.34	9.68	16.11	15.09	15.41	20.28	20.67	22.01	20.02	20.28	19.15	20.19	20.05	18.78	15.50	16.62
1973		19.08	−5.69	5.49	9.62	17.51	24.14	21.73	21.25	26.26	26.10	27.12	24.45	24.39	22.84	23.73	23.36	21.78	18.07	19.14
1974			−25.31	−0.71	6.64	17.11	25.18	22.18	21.57	27.19	26.90	27.95	24.95	24.85	23.14	24.07	23.65	21.95	18.01	19.14
1975				31.98	27.42	36.06	42.43	34.81	31.85	37.24	35.59	35.84	31.54	30.81	28.38	29.01	28.18	26.01	21.44	22.46
1976					23.03	38.14	46.10	35.53	31.82	38.13	36.12	36.33	31.50	30.70	28.05	28.77	27.90	25.59	20.76	21.88
1977						55.12	59.21	39.97	34.11	41.37	38.43	38.34	32.59	31.58	28.57	29.30	28.31	25.79	20.60	21.81
1978							63.40	32.97	27.76	38.13	35.32	35.73	29.66	28.90	25.91	26.97	26.12	23.61	18.29	19.72
1979								8.20	12.97	30.60	29.08	30.78	24.75	24.61	21.88	23.46	22.89	20.52	15.15	16.89
1980									17.96	43.49	36.90	37.13	28.35	27.57	23.97	25.52	24.64	21.82	15.80	17.65
1981										74.54	47.49	44.19	31.09	29.59	25.00	26.63	25.50	22.26	15.59	17.62
1982											24.63	31.06	19.16	20.29	16.93	20.04	19.73	16.94	10.41	13.07
1983												37.81	16.52	18.88	15.08	19.14	18.93	15.88	8.76	11.85
1984													−1.48	10.41	8.36	14.88	15.48	12.58	5.14	8.97
1985														23.73	13.65	20.92	20.15	15.62	6.28	10.55
1986															4.39	19.54	18.98	13.68	3.10	8.49
1987																36.90	27.03	16.95	2.78	9.33
1988																	17.87	8.10	−6.58	3.36
1989																		−0.86	−16.84	−1.07
1990																			−30.24	−1.18
1991																				40.00

Table 15.4 Compound annual return spreads between defaulted bonds and long-term government bonds, 1972–1991

Base Period (Jan. 1)	Terminal Period (December 31)																			
	1972	1973	1974	1975	1976	1977	1978	1979	1980	1981	1982	1983	1984	1985	1986	1987	1988	1989	1990	1991
1972	−27.95	−6.02	−14.51	−6.73	−4.47	4.16	11.57	11.29	12.50	17.48	14.92	16.70	13.96	12.61	10.43	12.22	11.98	10.18	7.03	7.63
1973		20.19	−7.27	1.43	2.53	12.01	19.79	18.20	18.69	23.77	20.34	21.83	18.35	16.56	13.90	15.61	15.14	13.01	9.44	9.97
1974			−29.66	−7.46	−3.34	9.90	19.70	17.85	18.46	24.24	20.35	22.01	18.17	16.23	13.38	15.26	14.78	12.53	8.78	9.37
1975				22.79	14.51	27.88	36.67	30.49	28.95	34.49	28.76	29.71	24.52	21.81	18.16	19.84	18.98	16.23	11.89	12.36
1976					6.26	30.47	41.45	32.39	30.14	36.42	29.62	30.58	24.71	21.71	17.74	19.60	18.69	15.77	11.19	11.73
1977						55.82	60.14	41.01	35.89	42.43	33.56	34.08	26.99	23.42	18.88	20.80	19.71	16.49	11.53	12.08
1978							64.57	34.18	29.89	39.28	29.29	30.62	23.12	19.58	15.00	17.51	16.63	13.43	8.43	9.21
1979								9.45	15.58	31.75	21.18	24.37	16.88	13.70	9.36	12.75	12.28	9.24	4.31	5.43
1980									21.91	44.58	25.76	28.71	18.56	14.50	9.33	13.20	12.63	9.21	3.79	5.05
1981										72.70	27.93	31.30	17.56	12.77	6.93	11.78	11.32	7.64	1.85	3.39
1982											−15.72	12.20	1.45	−0.61	−4.69	2.87	3.66	0.62	−4.73	−2.49
1983												37.16	8.71	3.84	−2.26	6.12	6.48	2.64	−3.58	−1.23
1984													−16.95	−12.57	−15.12	−1.46	0.50	−2.91	−8.97	−5.77
1985														−7.24	−14.06	4.29	5.30	0.13	−7.60	−4.09
1986															−20.13	9.48	9.05	1.76	−7.64	−3.63
1987																39.61	23.74	8.95	−4.76	−0.46
1988																	8.20	−5.70	−17.78	−9.81
1989																		−18.96	−28.81	−15.42
1990																			−36.41	−13.70
1991																				20.73

and S&P 500 stock returns, the defaulted bond returns have a lower coefficient of variation over the entire period.

In terms of extreme returns, Table 15.2 shows that defaulted bond returns have greater positive skewness than the returns on other assets. For the entire period, the kurtosis value for the defaulted bond returns is largest. Combining the skewness and kurtosis information suggests that defaulted bond returns have more large positive returns than the other asset groups. An inspection of the extreme values results in a similar conclusion. Finally, the first-order autocorrelations for the defaulted bond returns are significantly larger than the autocorrelations for the other debt and equity returns. This suggests that the market for defaulted bonds is less weak-form efficient and adjusts to new information less rapidly than the other markets.

Table 15.3 presents a matrix of geometric mean annual returns for defaulted bonds. There were only five negative annual return periods (1972, 1974, 1984, 1989 and 1990), and returns were mostly in the double-digits in the remaining 15 years.

Table 15.4 gives the compound annual return spreads between defaulted bonds and long-term government bonds. Positive spread intervals are about four times more frequent than negative spreads. Negative spreads occurred most frequently in the 1980s.

If investors were to include the defaulted bond returns in a portfolio, then the risk and return measures of Table 15.2 would not be appropriate. Table 15.5 presents appropriate measures of risk and return when defaulted bonds are included in a diversified portfolio. The beta measures in Table 15.5 describe the systematic risk and the standard error of the estimate describes unsystematic risk. These risk measures suggest two conclusions. First, the beta of defaulted bond returns is closer to the beta of debt than to the beta of equity. Second, defaulted bond returns clearly have the largest amount of unsystematic risk. Thus, while the total risk measure of defaulted bonds closely resembles that of the S&P 500, the proportion of unsystematic risk in defaulted bonds is much higher, indicating the need for substantial portfolio diversification.

Jensen's alpha measure of excess return adjusts for the amount of systematic risk. The alpha measure of excess return for the defaulted bonds was greater than the excess return for all other assets except high-grade bonds in 1987–91. The excess return of defaulted bonds (alpha) is closer to that of equity (small-company returns), while the systematic risk (beta)

Table 15.5 Characteristic line estimates*

January 1987 to December 1991

Asset	Alpha (%)	Standard error (%)	Beta	Standard error	R^2	Standard error of the estimate (%)
High-grade bonds	0.23	0.27	0.10	0.05	0.06	2.05
Small company	−0.59	0.37	1.00	0.07	0.77	2.91
Defaulted bonds	−0.01	0.52	0.37	0.10	0.21	3.94

January 1972 to December 1991

Asset	Alpha (%)	Standard error (%)	Beta	Standard error	R^2	Standard error of the estimate (%)
High-grade bonds	0.07	0.18	0.25	0.04	0.14	2.83
Small company	0.26	0.25	1.09	0.05	0.63	3.93
Defaulted bonds	0.62	0.30	0.34	0.06	0.10	4.65

*Computed from $(R_p - R_f) = \alpha + \beta(R_m - R_f) + \mu$.

Table 15.6 Correlations between asset returns (January 1972 to December 1991)

Asset	S&P 500	Small company	High-grade bonds	Long-term government
Defaulted bonds	0.32	0.48	0.09	0.07
S&P 500		0.79	0.38	0.36
Small company			0.23	0.21
High-grade bonds				0.93

of defaulted bonds is closer to that of debt (high-grade corporate bond returns). The correlations in Table 15.6 support the conclusion that defaulted bond returns are more closely correlated with equity returns than with bond returns. Defaulted bonds have a systematic risk similar to that of bonds and an excess return that moves with the excess return of small-company equity.

CONCLUSIONS

Investors who hold or are interested in speculating in defaulted bonds should examine the risk and return characteristics of this asset carefully. Compared with standard bond and equity investments, defaults provide returns somewhat larger than those on equity and generally have total risk measures approximating those of the S&P 500. However, the high levels of unsystematic risk suggest that investment portfolios of defaulted bonds must be well diversified to take advantage of favorable return levels.

The wisdom of speculating in defaults should also be carefully examined. It appears that defaults had large returns in 1975–83. However, excess returns in defaults have virtually disappeared in later years. Measures of the dispersion of returns suggest that defaulted bonds have a high proportion of big winners and a lower proportion of big losers than other investments. This, coupled with indications of market inefficiency, may offer the best rationale for speculation in defaults and may suggest the need to reexamine policies that call for the liquidation of defaulted bonds at the time of default.

ENDNOTES

1. "Corporate Bond Defaults and Default Rates, 1970–1991," *Moody's Special Report*, January 1992, p. 3.

2. Hickman, W.B. *Corporate Bond Quality and Investor Experience* (Princeton: Princeton University Press, 1958).

3. Altman, E. "A Performance Review of Defaulted Debt Securities, 1987–1991" (Merrill Lynch & Co., March 20, 1992); Hradsky, G.T. and Long, R.D. "High Yield Default Losses and the Return Performance of Bankrupt Debt," *Financial Analysts Journal*, July/August 1989; and Warner, J.B. "Bankruptcy, Absolute Priority, and the Pricing of Risky Debt Claims," *Journal of Financial Economics*, May 1977.

4. *Stocks, Bonds, Bills and Inflation, 1992 Yearbook* (Chicago: Ibbotson Associates, Inc., 1992).

5. Jensen, M.C. "Risk, the Pricing of Capital Assets, and the Evaluation of Investment Portfolios," *Journal of Business*, April 1969.

16

Rating Drift in High-Yield Bonds

Edward I. Altman and Duen Li Kao

Most of the literature on high-yield, low-rated bonds has concentrated on default rates and losses to investors within a total return context. An example is Altman and Nammacher [1987], who examine defaults and performance using the traditional average annual rate approach. Altman [1989] and Asquith, *et al.* [1989] use mortality/aging approaches to assess default risk and return (the latter study did not analyze returns) on a cumulative basis.

In virtually all such studies, the general assumption is that a bond will either survive to maturity, be called prior to maturity, or default at some point after issuance. The last scenario involves the extreme rating "drift" of an issue from its original rating to its final default status (a *D* rating by Standard & Poor's).

Two recent studies enable us to analyze bond performance for less dramatic but still important credit quality changes. Lucas and Lonski [1992] describe changes across the full spectrum of original Moody's ratings. Altman and Kao [1991] analyze both the descriptive and predictive aspects of rating changes on the population of 1970–1988 new issues rated by Standard & Poor's, using a Markov chain approach to model future rating changes based on past experience.

Our 1991 monograph concentrates on original ratings from AAA to CCC, for up to ten years after issuance. This article focuses primarily on the high-yield debt population, with a careful analysis of differences in experience between original issue high-yield (or "junk" bonds) and those that declined from investment-grade ("fallen angles"). We analyze the serial correlation of high-yield bond rating changes with respect to credit quality changes subsequent to initial rating changes, concentrating on these subsequent rating changes, rather than total return.

SAMPLE CHARACTERISTICS

This study analyzes a subsample from the over 7,000 rating changes reported on in our original study.[1] We concentrate on 1,548 issues, of which 1,112 (72%) were issued originally as below investment-grade securities, and 436 (28%) reached this state via the fallen angel route.

Our analysis covers the entire nineteen-year new issue period, 1970–1988. The results, however, are virtually identical to the experience of high-yield bonds for the shorter period 1977–1989, when new low-grade issuance increased dramatically. Indeed, of the 1,112 new low-grade bonds issued during 1970–1988, more than 94% were issued from 1977 onward, while an even greater proportion of fallen angels (96%) entered the non-investment-grade universe during or after 1977. We use the entire observation period in our analysis in order to maximize the sample size.

The number of observations diminishes as the post-issuance observation period lengthens. This is attributable partly to redemptions of debt prior to maturity and capital restructurings during bankruptcy. In addition, bonds issued in the 1980s could not be tracked beyond 1989, the last year of our analysis.

While our analysis concentrates on low-grade issues, we also present some comparative statistics for investment-grade bonds, particularly noting the differences between the BBB and higher-quality (AAA, AA, and A) categories. Finally, we distinguish between utility and non-utility fallen angels in our analysis, a distinction that proved to be extremely significant.

Key findings are:

- Bonds that originally come to market with non-investment-grade ratings have neither a tendency to be upgraded nor a tendency to be downgraded subsequent to issuance.

- If an original issue high-yield bond is downgraded, however, the direction of the next rating change is likely to be negative. Conversely, if an original issue high-yield bond is upgraded, its next change is likely to be positive, although this tendency is not as strong as the link between two or more downgrades.

- Among the fallen angels, utilities have a superior record for upgrading subsequent to their initial descent into the non-investment-grade category.

EMPIRICAL RESULTS

The one-, three-, five-, and ten-year post-issuance rating transition results for our original issue low-grade bond population appear in Table 16.1. In Table 16.2, Panel A, we observe aggregate upgrade and downgrade experience; Panel B further distinguishes between public utilities (mainly electric power companies) and non-utilities (industrials and finance companies) in a breakdown of fallen angels.

We stratify the sample in this manner based on our earlier observation (Altman [1991]) that public utilities outperformed non-utilities on a total return basis in the period following downgrading to below investment-grade. We conjecture that this superior performance resulted from a general improvement in credit quality of utilities. (Note that the 1991 study covers the 1984–1988 period only.)

Original Issue Low-Grade Bonds

We find that original issue high-yield bonds have essentially an equal incidence of upgrades and downgrades after issuance. Upgrades were slightly greater (4.1%) than downgrades (3.8%) after one year, but the incidence was identical after ten years (28.1% versus 28.1%). Downgrades were slightly greater than upgrades for the three- and five-year horizons, although the differences are not statistically significant.

Table 16.1 Rating transitions for original issue low-grade bonds (1970–1989)

No. bonds 1 Yr	Original rating	Subsequent rating									
		AAA	AA	A	BBB	BB	B	CCC	CC	C	D
237	BB	0.0	0.0	0.0	6.8	**86.1**	6.3	0.8	0.0	0.0	0.0
702	B	0.0	0.0	0.1	1.6	1.7	**94.0**	1.7	0.3	0.0	0.0
173	CCC	0.0	0.0	0.0	0.0	0.0	2.9	**92.5**	0.0	2.3	2.3
13	CC	0.0	0.0	0.0	0.0	0.0	0.0	0.0	**84.6**	15.4	0.0
3 Yrs		AAA	AA	A	BBB	BB	B	CCC	CC	CD	D
170	BB	0.6	0.6	1.8	17.1	**62.9**	11.8	2.9	0.6	0.0	1.8
431	B	0.2	0.2	1.2	1.9	4.2	**74.5**	10.7	1.2	1.4	3.7
77	CCC	0.0	0.0	1.3	0.0	2.6	14.3	**66.2**	1.3	2.6	11.7
9	CC	0.0	0.0	0.0	0.0	0.0	11.1	11.1	**44.4**	0	33.3
5 Yrs		AAA	AA	A	BBB	BB	B	CCC	CC	CD	D
103	BB	0.0	0.0	7.8	20.4	**40.8**	16.5	6.8	1.0	0.0	6.8
222	B	0.5	0.0	2.7	4.5	8.6	**59.9**	13.5	0.5	0.9	9.0
28	CCC	0.0	0.0	3.6	3.6	0.0	35.7	**28.6**	7.1	0.0	21.4
10 Yrs		AAA	AA	A	BBB	BB	B	CCC	CC	CD	D
37	BB	0.0	0.0	10.8	27.0	**21.6**	13.5	18.9	2.7	0.0	5.4
52	B	1.9	0.0	7.7	9.6	5.8	**53.8**	9.6	0.0	0.0	11.5
7	CCC	0.0	0.0	0.0	0.0	0.0	0.0	**85.7**	0.0	0.0	14.3

Table 16.2 Panel A: rating transitions for original issue low-grade bonds (1970–1989)

Year(s) after issuance	Total issues	Unchanged		Upgrades		Downgrades	
		No.	%	No.	%	No.	%
1	1112	1024	92.1	46	4.1	43	3.8
3	678	483	71.2	82	12.1	113	16.7
5	353	183	51.8	77	21.8	93	26.4
10	96	43	45.1	27	28.1	27	28.1

Panel B: fallen angel low-grade bonds

Year(s) after becoming fallen angel	Type of bond	Total issues	Unchanged		Upgrades		Downgrades	
			No.	%	No.	%	No.	%
1	Utilities	186	122	65.5	58	31.2	6	3.2
	Nonutil.	250	199	79.6	6	3.6	42	16.8
3	Utilities	161	83	51.6	60	37.3	18	11.1
	Nonutil.	159	64	40.2	49	30.8	46	29.0
5	Utilities	89	9	10.1	76	85.4	4	4.5
	Nonutil.	59	14	23.8	18	30.5	27	45.7
10	Utilities	8	0	0.0	7	87.5	1	12.5
	Nonutil.	16	2	12.5	7	43.8	7	43.8

At every non-investment-grade rating level and for all observation periods, the majority of issues held steady or improved in quality. As an example, of bonds initially rated B, 59.9% remained in that category after five years, and another 16.2% were upgraded. At the same time, however, downgrades exceeded upgrades for the five-year horizon, and 9% of the Bs dropped all the way to D (default). This latter percentage is slightly less than the cumulative mortality rate for five years (Altman [1989]). The ten-year rating drift results (in Table 16.1) for Bs dropping to D rating are, however, quite a bit below the ten-year mortality rates because of a much smaller sample size for the rating drift study.

Fallen Angels

The aggregate fallen angel population demonstrated a greater propensity for upgrades than for downgrades for every horizon. This result, however, was wholly attributable to the exceptional performance of the public utility segment. For utilities, upgrades dominated downgrades by 31.2% versus 3.2% after one year, by 85.4% versus 4.5% in five years, and by 87.5% versus 12.5% for ten years.

Meaningful rate relief over the period was accorded the vast majority of low-grade utilities. More recently, there has been a greater incidence of further deterioration by utilities following their demotion to the fallen angel category. For example, Columbia Gas System and El Paso Electric defaulted during 1991. Nevertheless, the experience of fallen angel utilities in the 1970s and 1980s is, in our opinion, an important indicator for the future.

Non-utility fallen angels had a different experience, ranging from virtually equivalent numbers of upgrades and downgrades among their subsequent rating changes (i.e., in years 3 and 10 after the drop to lowgrade status) to a greater incidence of further downgrades in years 1 and 5 after the initial downgrade (Table 16.2, Panel B). And while the aggregate experience was balanced or slightly favoring future downgrades, the magnitude of the subsequent rating change was dramatic. Defaults occurred in at least twenty-three cases (out of 320) within three years after the initial downgrade. These dramatic cases no doubt resulted in significant losses to investors, far greater than the small gains from upgrades.

Investment-Grade Bond Results

Unlike low-grade issues, investment-grade bonds as a whole experienced considerably more downgrades than upgrades. Table 16.3 lists the initial rating change results for investment-grade issues, with a further breakdown between the AAA/AA/A categories and the BBB category. While the AAA/AA/A original issues had a predominantly negative first rating

Table 16.3 Aggregate first rating change experience: Original issue investment-grade bonds (1970–1989)

| Year(s) after issuance | AAA/AA/A bonds | | | | | | | BBB bonds | | | | | | |
| | Total issues | Unchanged | | Upgrades | | Downgrades | | Total issues | Unchanged | | Upgrades | | Downgrades | |
		No.	%	No.	%	No.	%		No.	%	No.	%	No.	%
1	4976	4607	97.6	76	1.5	293	5.9	1090	982	90.1	60	5.5	48	4.4
3	3989	3142	78.8	170	4.3	677	17.0	807	592	93.4	126	15.6	89	11.0
5	2927	2061	70.4	163	5.6	703	24.0	514	338	65.7	111	21.6	65	12.7
10	1645	904	55.0	131	8.0	610	37.1	217	94	43.3	86	39.6	37	17.1

change performance for all horizons, the BBB category posted a definite propensity toward upgrades vis-à-vis downgrades. This phenomenon is discussed in Altman and Kao [1991] and is consistent with the superior performance of BBB bonds during the 1980s (Altman [1990]).

SERIAL CORRELATION TESTS

One of the more intriguing questions regarding bond rating changes is whether an investor can learn anything from past changes. In our earlier monograph, we constructed several Markov chain models to assist us in modeling future changes, with considerable success. In this article, we ask two questions:

1. After the original issue low-grade bonds experience a rating change, does the next change (if any) tend to be in the same direction?

2. For our fallen angel population, do subsequent changes tend to continue in the downgrade direction?

We can also examine whether two changes in the same direction are accurate predictors of any further changes. Note that for all these rating change serial correlation tests, a change can be as small as a single "notch" within a major letter rating (e.g., BB to BB−). Finally, in addition to testing the low-grade, high-yield population, we again split the investment-grade issues into the AAA/AA/A and BBB categories.

Table 16.4 lists the first rating change for our three major categories as well as breaking down the fallen angels by utilities and non-utilities and the investment-grades by AAA/AA/As and BBBs. With respect to the fallen angel population, the first rating change after becoming a fallen angel of course is really a second change, which can therefore be tested for serial correlation.

Our observations are for new issues covering the period 1970–1985 rather than through the entire period ending in 1989. This is necessitated by the fact that the vast majority of issues took up to four years to experience their first rating changes.

Our first result concerns original issue low-grade bonds. We find that the first rating change after issue has an equivalent probability of being an upgrade (U) as it has of being a downgrade (D). In the notation we use for this research, the D/U ratio = 1.00. We will not comment upon the result for the aggregate fallen angel population, which would be misleading until it is broken down by utilities and non-utilities.

Table 16.4   First rating change experience (1970–1985 new issues)

Type of bond	Total	Unchanged	Downgrade (D)	Upgrade (U)	D/U
Original issue high-yield	620	142	239	239	1.00
Investment-Grade					
AAA,AA,A	3733	1139	1859	735	2.53*
BBB	732	157	252	323	0.78
Fallen angels	Total	Unchanged	DD	DU	DD/DU
Utilities	193	20	32	141	0.23*
Non-utilities	151	15	86	50	1.72*

*Significant at 0.01 level.

For investment-grade original issues, the AAA/AA/A categories experienced a far greater proportion of downgrades than upgrades; D/U = 2.53. BBB bonds, however, experienced a greater proportion of upgrades (323 versus 252, D/U = 0.78), again showing the group's distinctively attractive characteristics vis-à-vis the rest of the higher-rated issues.

The figures for fallen angels in Table 16.4 actually reflect a subsequent rating change after each downgrade. Results show that public utility fallen angels demonstrate strong negative serial correlation, i.e., reversal of direction. For issues that do experience a second change, the proportion of upgrades following the original downgrade (DU) is 81.5% (141/173), compared to only 18.5% for two consecutive downgrades (DD). The ratio of DD/DU is therefore 0.23, significantly different from 1.0 at the 0.01 level.[2]

The opposite result is realized for the non-utility fallen angels. That is, the number of subsequent downgrades after dropping to fallen angel status (DD) far exceeds the number of subsequent upgrades. The ratio of DD/DU for non-utilities is 1.72 (86/50). Again the test is significant at the 0.01 level, but this time it indicates significant *positive* serial correlation.

In Table 16.5, we proceed to the next level of rating changes. In order to be tested for serial correlation, an original issue low-grade bond must have a second rating change. Recall that the initial changes for these issues represent equivalent proportions of upgrades and downgrades (Table 16.4). If the initial change is a downgrade, though, the second change is usually in the same direction, i.e., DD. Indeed, the ratio of DD/DU, assuming a second change does take place, is 2.58. This results in a sign-test of 10.5, easily significant at the 0.01 level.

On the other hand, if the initial change is an upgrade, the next change is also more often than not in the same direction (UU/UD = 1.33, with a sign-test = 3.5). Positive serial correlation in upgrades is not nearly as significant as the downgrade positive serial correlation, however.

Investment-grade AAA/AA/A downgrades are also usually followed by subsequent downgrades, with a DD/DU ratio of 2.86 and a very significant sign-test of 35.9. Initial upgrades of these groups show subsequent rating changes that favor a reversal of direction (UU/UD = 0.78). If we observe the BBB investment grades, however, we again find positive performance (UU/UD = 1.47).

Our final tests involve fallen angels with at least three rating changes. We find that the limited number of utilities that experienced two consecutive downgrades had a very small chance of experiencing a third downgrade (DDD) rather than a reversal (DDU). On the other hand, utility fallen angels that had reversals (i.e., that were upgraded) just after falling to

Table 16.5 Subsequent rating change experience (1970–1985 new issues)

	First change downgrade				First change upgrade			
	DD	DU	DD/DU	Sign-test	UU	UD	UU/UD	Sign-test
Original issue high-yield	103	40	2.58	10.5*	84	63	1.33	3.5*
Fallen angels								
Utilities	5	25	0.20	−7.3*	23	6	3.83	6.3*
Non-utilities	40	27	1.48	3.2*	74	41	1.80	6.2*
Investment-grade								
AAA, AA, A	1028	360	2.86	35.9*	193	247	0.78	−5.1*
BBB	101	85	1.19	2.3*	125	85	1.47	5.5*

*Significant at 0.01 level.

"junk" status had a strong likelihood of continuing to be upgraded (DUU), if further rating changes took place.

CONCLUSIONS

A number of practical investment conclusions emerge from our results. One finding that is particularly pertinent for high-yield investors is that original issue speculative-grade companies display no tendency either to rise or to decline in quality over time. This result contrasts with pronouncements made by both advocates and critics of high-yield bonds.

Boosters of such debt sometimes claim these securities represent borrowings by "rising stars" of American industry, those headed for inevitable upgrading. Detractors argue, quite the contrary, that over-leveraged junk bond companies are ticking time bombs for which credit deterioration is preordained. While this may have been the case for certain corporate restructuring bonds issued in 1986–1989, our results show this was decidedly not the case for the average low-grade bond issued prior to 1986. And we expect this will not be the case for new issues after 1990.

For original issue low-grade bonds that do experience an initial downgrade, however, the outlook is much bleaker. Our results indicate that investors must be careful to assess the credit prospects of these issues thoroughly before they make a portfolio decision. The opposite outlook look pertains to issues experiencing an initial upgrade.

Another instructive finding is the contrast between the public utility and the non-utility fallen angels. The numbers say that, for non-utilities, the better course for investors is generally to cut their losses at the point of downgrading to speculative-grade. Further deterioration occurs in the vast majority of cases. Utility fallen angels show a decidedly more positive outlook, however, with as much as an 80% frequency of subsequent upgrading.

Finally, AAA/AA/A original issues that are downgraded display continued downgrading in the great majority of cases. BBB original issues, however, not only show a greater likelihood of being initially upgraded than downgraded, but also an upgrade bias that continues for subsequent changes.

ENDNOTES

1. In Altman and Kao [1991], we analyze 7,195 rating changes for all new issues of 1970–1988, where only major letter changes, e.g., AA to A, B to BB, are covered.

2. The test for significance is the sign-test, whereby we assess whether the initial rating change (in this case, D) is followed by one in the same direction. The test is of the form:

$$Z = \frac{N_{SD} - N_{RD}}{1/2\sqrt{N}}$$

where

N_{SD} = Number of rating changes in same direction;

N_{RD} = Number of rating changes in the reverse direction; and

N = Total number of observations.

REFERENCES

Altman, E.I. "Default Risk, Mortality Rates, and the Performance of Corporate Bonds." The Research Foundation of the Institute of Chartered Financial Analysts, Charlottesville, Virginia, 1989, and *Journal of Finance*, September 1989.

— —. *Distressed Securities: Analyzing and Evaluating Market Potential and Investment Risk.* Chicago: Probus Publishing, 1991.

— —. "How 1989 Changed the Hierarchy of Fixed Income Security Performance." *Financial Analysts Journal*, May-June 1990.

Altman, E.I. and Kao, D.L. "Corporate Bond Rating Drift: An Examination of Rating Agency Credit Quality Changes." Association for Investment Management Research, Charlottesville, Virginia, 1991.

Altman, E.I. and Nammacher, S. *Investing in Junk Bonds.* New York: John Wiley & Sons, 1987.

Asquith, P., Mullins, D. and Wolff, E. "Original Issue High Yield Bonds: Aging Analysis of Defaults, Exchanges and Calls." *Journal of Finance*, September 1989.

Lucas, D. and Lonski, J. "Changes in Corporate Credit Quality 1970–1990." Moody's *Special Report*, February 1991, and *Journal of Fixed Income*, March 1992.

———————————— PART FOUR ————————————
⌈ Strategic and Tactical Asset Allocation ⌋

When an investor has decided on the types of assets to be included in a portfolio, a decision must be made on the strategic asset weights. These weights can be viewed as those which would be applicable if the manager had no views about likely short-term market performance. They can also be viewed as the weights that the fund will actually have, on average, over a five-to-ten year period, assuming there is no reason to change them during that period. The strategic asset class weights are often set with a central value, and a range around that to set the bounds for short-term tactical deviations. The tactical asset allocation decision determines what departure, based on current market valuations, should be made from the strategic asset allocation.

I shall begin with strategic asset allocation. When making strategic asset allocation decisions, investors have to forecast asset returns over a long period. Most investors will do this by looking at the historical returns and assuming that these will apply in the future, or they may modify the historical returns if they think it appropriate to do so. We begin Part Four with a look at the historical returns. Because equities are more volatile than bonds, we would expect them to produce a higher return over long periods. In Chapter 17, Jeremy Siegel, a professor at the University of Pennsylvania, shows that this indeed has been the case. U.S. equities have produced around a 6% real return in each of the periods 1802–70, 1871–1925 and 1926–90. U.S. bonds have produced a lower real return but, more interestingly, a declining real return over the same periods. The figures for long-term bonds are 5.2%, 4.0% and 1.8%. For short-term bonds the figures are 5.1%, 3.1% and 0.5%. Siegel argues that equities have earned an excessive premium over bonds over the last 50 years, and that bonds are likely to offer better real returns in the future. Siegel offers a lot of interesting material, but is it true that the return gap between bonds and equities will be narrowed? Investors will have to take a view if they are to be able rationally to reach a strategic asset allocation decision. Readers interested in long-term rates of return for international markets should consult Ibbotson and Brinson (1993).

Given a view on future returns, how does one decide the appropriate strategic asset allocation? This is a very complex issue and a very much simplified approach will be taken here. One wishes to relate the decision to the circumstances of the investor, and this is difficult. It will simplify matters if we consider just one example, so I have chosen a pension fund. Here the task would seem to be to relate the liability structure of the fund, and the circumstances of the sponsoring company, to the asset allocation. One method of relating the assets and liabilities is by means of statistical simulation. A complete analysis would require:

- expected returns for each asset class;
- standard deviations for each asset class;
- correlation coefficients between each asset class;
- expected level of pension payments each year;
- standard deviation of pension payments;
- correlation coefficients between asset class returns and changes in pension payments.

Such analysis is beyond the scope of this book, and indeed real-world practice. However, Chapter 18, by Irwin Tepper, gives a good idea of the basic issues. Tepper, proprietor of a financial consulting firm, and formerly a professor at Harvard University, outlines by means of a case study how a computer model simulates the way in which a pension plan fares with a range of investment policies and actuarial conditions. He discusses how a decision as to the correct strategy might be made. Tepper's article is much older than most of the material in this book, but it is clear, and a useful starting point for readers who are not quantitatively orientated. The article reflects legislation at the time it was written. Tepper mentions vesting and the interest rate assumption, both of which may need explaining. Employees may be in a firm's pension plan but lose their rights if they leave the company before, say, two years of employment. Once they have served their qualifying period they are said to be vested. The interest rate assumption relates to the fact that in valuing the liabilities of a fund, actuaries will make an interest rate assumption to convert the future liabilities into today's money. The abbreviation ERISA, used in the article, refers to the United States' Employee Retirement Income Security Act of 1974.

The recognition of some institutional details could greatly modify the conclusions of asset-liability modelling. Some analysts have argued for greater equity positions than conventional analysis might suggest. For example, in the U.S., the Pension Benefit Guaranty Corporation (PBGC) is a pension insurance fund operated by the Department of Labor. Firms pay a fixed sum to the PBGC for each employee in a pension plan and in return are guaranteed that pension benefits will be paid even if the plan fails. Why not adopt a high return/high risk strategy and invest solely in equities? If things work out, the plan sponsor gains, but if they do not, the PBGC picks up 70% of the tab. On the other hand some analysts have argued for a more pro-bond stance. Assets within the pension plan are tax exempt. Borrowed money incurs interest that is a charge against tax, while money invested in the pension plan in bonds can obtain interest that is not taxed. This suggests scope for a firm that views its pension plan as part of its total cash flows to undertake tax arbitrage. These complex issues, that make even an asset-liability model too simple, will not be discussed further here.

I turn now to tactical asset allocation. In Part Two some issues bearing on the efficiency of markets were discussed. The readings related to the pricing of stocks. In this Part, we look at whether the efficient market analysis applies at the level of the entire market. If the various asset class markets are always efficiently priced, investors should determine their strategic allocation, implement it, and review it only when their circumstances change. If markets are inefficient, there is scope for tactical asset allocation, although it may be that investors lack the skills to be able to successfully exploit the opportunities available.

Before we look at some evidence relating to tactical asset allocation, it is worth making a general point. It is frequently asserted that asset allocation is *the* investment decision. Hence the interest in tactical asset allocation. But we have to be careful here. It is clear that over the long-run, equities have handsomely outperformed bonds and cash. It is therefore important to decide just how much risk you are willing to bear for extra return: the more equities you hold, the higher your returns are likely to be. The strategic asset allocation decision is indeed the most important decision in this sense. However, once the liability structure, income requirements and so forth have been determined, and the appropriate strategic asset allocation for a fund determined, with a range for each asset class for tactical timing purposes, the position changes.

Imagine that a manager has a strategic target of 60% equities and 40% bonds, with permitted ranges of 70%–50% and 50%–30% respectively. Now let us assume an investor believes that equities will outperform bonds by 10% over a year and moves from a 60/40 weighting to 70/30. Even if the forecast is correct, that asset allocation move will have added only an extra 1% to the value of the fund. Now this is precisely the sort of added value that might be achieved by good stock selection. Thus, once the strategic decision has been made, given the limited asset allocation moves that are then likely to be made in response to market opportunities, the added value from good asset allocation may not be the most important decision. Strategic asset allocation is indeed *the* decision for a fund's sponsor, but for the investment manager's day-to-day activities, stock selection is likely to be just as important as tactical asset allocation. In Chapter 19, Chris Hensel, Don Ezra and John Ilkiw develop these ideas in more detail. Depending on the naive alternative, even strategic asset allocation's value may be overstated. The first two authors are with the U.S. consultants Frank Russell Company, and the third is with Frank Russell Canada.

I have included a number of articles that shed some light on how efficient the market is at a macro level. This may affect an investor's decision as to whether it is likely to be worth attempting tactical asset allocation. In Chapter 20, Andrei Shleifer and Lawrence Summers argue that the limited arbitrage opportunities available at the asset class level, make it unlikely that markets are efficient. They argue that their approach—the noise trader approach—better accords with the evidence than does the efficient market theory. Further, they argue that their approach is not an empty one capable of explaining anything, but only after the event, but rather one which generates testable hypotheses. Chapter 20 is a very clear statement of this alternative model to the efficient market approach. Shleifer is a professor at the University of Chicago and Summers is U.S. Under-Secretary for International Affairs at the U.S. Treasury: at the time the article was written, Summers was a professor at Harvard University.

Shleifer and Summers mention, albeit briefly, some statistical findings using long runs of data relating to excess volatility of the market level and mean reversion of returns. Good textbooks discuss these findings. The textbooks give less space to a different type of information relating to market efficiency, that concerning extreme events such as market panics and manias. These may help us understand both extreme behaviour and also better understand more normal behaviour. Of course, we may end up as baffled as when we began our study.

I have included three articles on panics and mania (plus the coverage in Shleifer and Summers). To remind readers of some recent stock market history, I have included four charts. Figure 1 shows the rise and fall of the MSCI World Index in 1987. Figure 2 shows S&P 500 during October 1989, when there was a short-lived mini-crash. Figure 3 shows the rises and falls of the Japanese stock market over the last 21 years and Figure 4 shows the price–earnings ratio for the Japanese market over the same period.

In Chapter 21, William Schwert, a professor at the University of Rochester, looks at possible reasons for the crash of the U.S. stock market in 1987. He thinks the causes of the crash remain uncertain. Schwert believes in efficient markets and does not consider

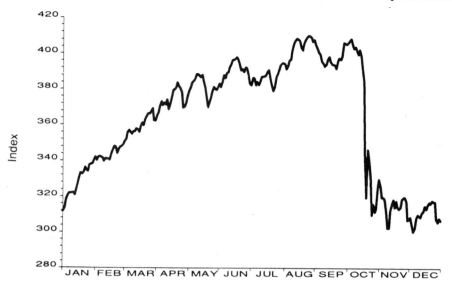

Source: DATASTREAM

Figure 1   MSCI world stock market index: 1987

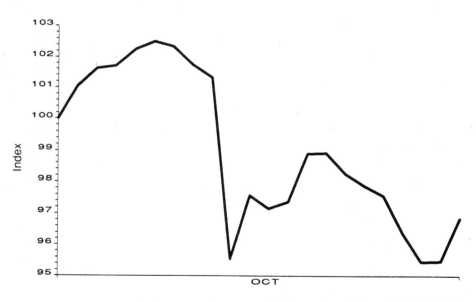

Source: DATASTREAM

Figure 2   U.S. stock market index: October 1989 (Rebased: October 2 = 100)

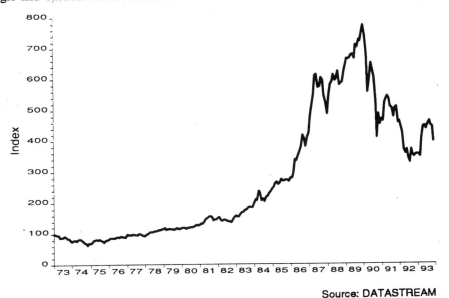

Figure 3 Japanese stock market index: 1973–93

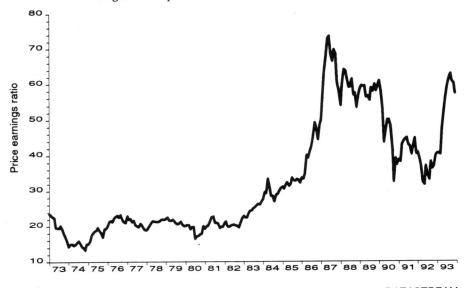

Figure 4 Japanese stock market price–earnings ratio: 1973–93

the possibility of irrational behaviour. Robert Shiller on the other hand, a professor at Yale University, and well known for his research which suggests that the markets move "too much", is willing to accept psychological factors as an important aspect of market behaviour. Chapter 22 is an extract from a conference paper in which Shiller uses survey data to suggest that some investors buy and sell for no reason other than the fact that other investors are buying or selling or are expected to do so. Of course, since the markets don't experience boom or bust all the time, even if we accept a psychological component to market pricing, we still face the problem of knowing when the psychology of the crowd will lead to extreme behaviour. Not every sell-off leads to a market panic.

In Chapter 23, Kenneth French and James Poterba, professors at the University of Chicago and the Massachusetts Institute of Technology respectively, ask whether the bull market in Japanese stocks in the 1980s can be explained by fundamental factors. They point out that Japanese ratings can be misleading because of the different accounting standards of U.S. and Japanese firms. They then approach the change in equity market ratings in terms of a dividend discount model. They note that part of the rise in the Japanese market can be explained, but part cannot. Many financial practitioners value a market in terms of the visual relationship between the long bond yield and the earnings yield, i.e., the reciprocal of the price–earnings ratio, or a short rate and the earnings yield, rather than in terms of a mathematically specified dividend discount model. (These approaches are mathematically related.) The relationships which practitioners often look at are shown in Figures 5 and 6. On the basis of these charts, was the Japanese market massively overvalued in the second half of the 1980s?

Schwert, and French and Poterba, try to use various measures to explain retrospectively the course of the U.S. and Japanese markets. Most investors, of course try to anticipate market moves. I now switch to how investors make tactical decisions and decide where to be in their tactical ranges. There are a number of ways of approaching this: methods commonly used include business cycle anticipation, valuation and comparative valuation (e.g., price–earnings ratio level, dividend yield level, aggregate dividend discount model, bond yield versus earnings yield, foreign versus domestic markets), liquidity and flow of funds (money supply, cash reserves) and technical analysis. Some of these methods allow investors to make quantitative estimates of returns whereas others allow only qualitative judgements. I can only give a brief sample of these methods here. I shall give two examples of comparative valuation. One looks at price–earnings ratios in relation to past history and another looks at expected returns from equities in relation to expected returns from bonds.

In Chapter 24, Steven Bleiberg asks whether it makes sense to buy the market when it is on a low price–earnings ratio. The answer is that it does, although it isn't an infallible strategy. But there is a snag. How do we know what the definition of low is? One way, and the basis of many popular strategies, is to look at past data and use that data to construct the decision rule. But, if you use all the available data, it is not surprising you often get a rule that works *on that data*. It will not necessarily work in the future. In reaching his initial conclusion, Bleiberg uses all his data in his analysis, but then he reworks his analysis, this time only using half the data to determine what constitutes high and low price–earnings ratios which he then uses as the basis of an investment strategy on the second half of the data. The results are quite different. Bleiberg offers a thoughtful conclusion that would apply to many asset allocation tools. Bleiberg is with investment managers BEA Associates.

In Chapter 25, Peter Carman, of investment managers Sanford C. Bernstein, discusses the equity risk premium approach. He equates this approach with tactical asset allocation. There is a tendency for firms which offer tactical asset allocation on a commercial basis to use the equity risk premium approach, but tactical asset allocation is much more general than this one tool. Carman provides a useful overall discussion of the advantages and disadvantages of the premium approach but is very brief in his comments on assessing fair value for the equity market. It may be useful to add a little background.

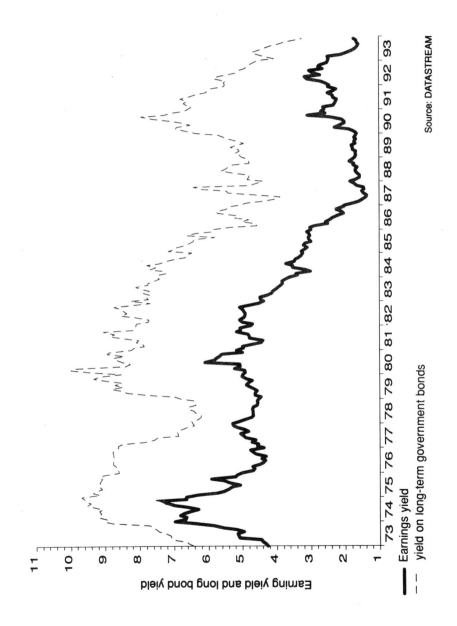

Figure 5 Earnings yield and the yield on long-dated Japanese government bonds: 1973–93

Source: DATASTREAM

242

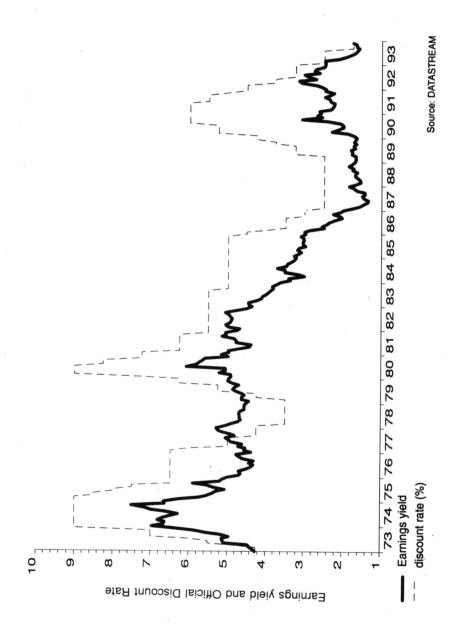

Figure 6 Japanese earnings yield and the Official Discount Rate: 1973–93

The basic constant growth dividend discount model is mentioned in Chapter 23. Using that approach for assessing the equity market, we would find that the expected return for the market will simply be its dividend yield and the expected dividend growth rate, i.e.:

equity market expected return = dividend yield + dividend growth rate

In equilibrium, we would expect the returns from equities to equal the return from bonds (i.e., the yield to maturity) plus an equity risk premium to compensate for the greater risk of equities, i.e.:

dividend yield + dividend growth rate = bond yield + equity risk premium

Swapping terms around we see that:

equity risk premium = dividend yield + dividend growth rate − bond yield

This is the basis of all equity risk premium approaches. Of course investors may wish to use a three stage dividend discount model rather than the simple constant growth model, but that merely complicates the calculation rather than affecting the basic form of the approach.

Carman gives a good overview of the equity risk premium approach but only briefly relates it to inflation. Many participants in the financial markets believe that equities sell on a higher rating during periods of low inflation. Davies and Wadhwani (1988), of stockbrokers Goldman Sachs, looked at the equity risk premium for the U.K. for the period 1923–88. It was clear that the premium was very variable over the entire period but part of the variability was explained by the rate of inflation. The average equity risk premium over the entire period was about 6%. Allowing for the rate of inflation, the average risk premium was about 2.8% plus half the forward-looking inflation rate. In terms of investment decision-making, Davies and Wadhwani suggested that the equity risk premium should be compared not with the historical average risk premium, but instead with the historical average for the expected inflation rate.

Optimizers were mentioned in Part One. If, for various assets, we have expected returns, standard deviations of returns, and correlations of returns between the assets, we can construct the portfolio with the highest return for a given level of risk by using an optimizer. Then we can calculate, for example, the optimal combination of cash, bonds, domestic equities, international equities and real estate based on our forecasts and for a specified level of portfolio risk. The textbooks tend to imply that an optimizer is the beginning and end of the asset allocation task. While optimizers are used by some investors for asset allocation, they are not widely used, and many investors who do use them are sceptical of the optimizer's output. Why is this? One reason is that managers do not always produce quantitative forecasts that can be used in an optimizer. While historical data can be used for the standard deviations and correlations required by an optimizer, it would be usual to forecast the returns. But not all investors forecast returns. For example an investor may use a measure such as a yield ratio to assess whether equities are cheap or expensive relative to bonds, without generating a quantitative returns forecast.

In Chapter 26, Richard Michaud, of Acadian Asset Management, but with stockbroker Merrill Lynch when the article was written, discusses a large number of problems that have to be faced when optimizers are used. His points range from organizational politics and the effect of introducing quantitative techniques into an investment organization to the basic mathematics of optimizers. For example, optimizers emphasize assets with extreme features, for example a negative correlation of returns, a low standard deviation of returns or high forecast returns. Assets with extreme characteristics may frequently be those with the largest forecast errors: by focusing on these, the optimizer becomes, in effect, an error maximizer. In practice, many investors impose constraints on the optimizer (for example, no more than 3% in Hong Kong) to minimize this type of problem. While this improves the technique, if many constraints are introduced, one wonders whether there is any improvement over simply eye-balling the problem. Some readers may not understand all of Michaud's article—no matter, the key points should be accessible to all.

REFERENCES

Davies, G. and Wadhwani, S. 1988: *Valuing UK Equities Against Gilts—Theory and Practice*. London: Goldman Sachs, April 28.

Ibbotson, R.G. and Brinson, G.P. 1993: *Global Investing*. New York: McGraw-Hill.

The Equity Premium: U.S. Stock and Bond Returns Since 1802

Jeremy J. Siegel

Since 1926, the compound real value-weighted return on all stocks listed on the New York Stock Exchange has averaged 6.4% per year, while the real return on Treasury bills has averaged only 0.5%.[1] This means that the purchasing power of a given sum of money invested (and reinvested) in stocks from 1926 to 1990 would have increased over 50 times, while reinvestment in bills would have increased one's real wealth by about one-third. Using these historical returns, it would take 139 years of investing in Treasury bills to double one's real wealth while it would take only 11 years of stock investment. Money managers often use these figures persuasively to convince investors that, over long periods of time, equity has no match as a wealth builder.

The return on stocks in excess of the return on short-term bonds is called the equity premium. Because stocks are generally riskier than fixed income investments, it is to be expected that the return on stocks would exceed that on bonds. However, in 1985 Rajnish Mehra and Edward Prescott demonstrated that stocks, despite their risk, appear to offer investors *excessive* returns, while bonds offer puzzlingly low returns.[2] The *excessive* return on equity is termed the "equity premium puzzle." Investors would have to be extraordinarily risk-averse, given the documented growth and variability of the economy, to accept such low returns on bonds while equity offered such superior returns. Such extreme risk-aversion appears to be inconsistent with data that reveal investor choice under uncertainty.

Many theories have been offered to explain the equity premium puzzle.[3] The data that Mehra and Prescott analyzed covered a sufficiently long period of time and were derived from well documented sources. Thus no one questioned the validity of their return data.

I extended the time period analyzed by Mehra and Prescott back to 1802, while updating the returns on stocks and bonds to 1990. My analysis demonstrates that the returns from bonds during most of the 19th century and after 1980 were far higher than in the period analyzed by Mehra and Prescott. The equity premium is not nearly as large when viewed over this extended time span as it is in the post-1926 period. These data suggest that the excess return of stocks over bonds may be significantly smaller in the future than it has been over the past 65 years.

LONG-TERM ASSET RETURNS

William Schwert has developed historical stock price series dating back to 1802; there are also some fragmentary data on stock returns dating to 1789.[4] In order to analyze asset returns since 1802, I divided the data into three subperiods. The first period, running from 1802 through 1870, contains stocks of financial firms and, later, railroads. The second period, running from 1871 through 1925, comprises the period studied by the Cowles Foundation.[5] The last subperiod, from 1926 to the present, coincides with the development of the S&P 500 stock index and contains the most comprehensive data on stock prices and other economic variables.[6] I use the Schwert data for the first subperiod and a capitalization-weighted index of all NYSE stocks for the second and third subperiods.

The early stock indexes were not as comprehensive as those constructed today. From 1802 to 1820, the stock index consisted of an equally weighted portfolio of stocks of several banks in Boston, New York and Philadelphia. An insurance company was added later, and in 1834 the portfolio became heavily weighted toward railroad stocks. The Cowles index consisted of all stocks listed on the New York Stock Exchange and recorded, for the first time, dividend payments. The Cowles index is spliced to modern indexes, which calculate averages for all classes of common stock.

Stock Returns

Figure 17.1 displays what one dollar invested in various asset classes in 1802 would have accumulated to by the end of 1990. These series are referred to as total return indexes, because they assume that all cash flows, including interest and dividends as well as any capital gains, are continually reinvested in the relevant asset. Total return indexes differ from standard stock market indexes such as the S&P 500, which do not include the reinvestment of cash flows. These standard indexes are called capital appreciation indexes.[7]

Figure 17.1 indicates that, in terms of total return, stocks have dominated all other asset classes since 1802. Over the entire period, equities achieved a compound annual nominal rate of return of 7.6% per year; at this rate, the nominal value of equity approximately doubles every 9.5 years. Figure 17.1 also demonstrates that nominal stock returns have also increased over time. The average compound rate of return on stocks was 5.8% from 1802 through 1870, 7.2% from 1871 through 1925 and 9.8% from 1926 through 1990.[8] Table 17.1 gives the stock returns in each subperiod.

The average nominal *arithmetic* (or mean) return on stocks is 9.0% per year over the entire period. Although this can be interpreted as the expected return on stocks over a 12-month period, it cannot be converted into a compound annual rate of return over periods longer than one year. Because of the mathematical properties of return calculations, the compound rate of return to a buy-and-hold strategy is measured by the geometric, rather than the arithmetic, return.[9]

The power of compound returns is clearly evident in the stock market. One dollar invested in 1802, with all dividends reinvested, would have accumulated to nearly $1 million by the end of 1990. Hypothetically, this means that $3 million, invested and reinvested over these

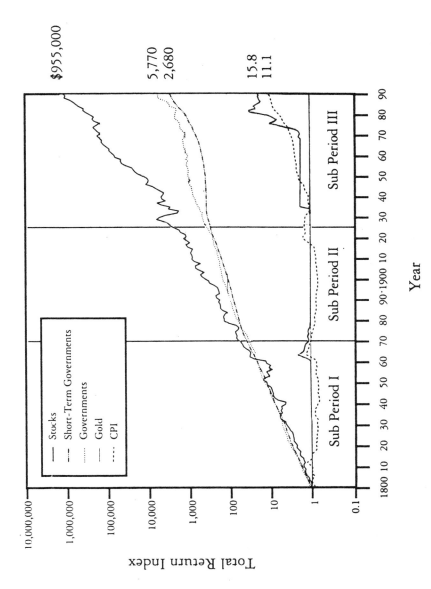

Figure 17.1 Total nominal return indexes, before taxes, 1802–1990

Table 17.1 Stock market returns (standard deviations in parentheses)*

Period	Total nominal return (%)		Total real return (%)		Nominal capital appreciation (%)		Real capital appreciation (%)		Dividend income (%) A	Average tax rate (%) A	Total real after-tax return (%)	
	A	G	A	G	A	G	A	G			A	G
1802–1990	9.0 (17.8)	7.6	7.8 (18.4)	6.2	4.0 (17.6)	2.5	2.8 (18.1)	1.2	5.0 (1.0)	6.8	7.3 (18.1)	5.8
1871–1990	10.3 (18.9)	8.6	8.3 (19.3)	6.5	5.3 (18.6)	3.6	3.3 (19.0)	1.6	5.0 (1.3)	10.8	7.6 (18.9)	5.9
1802–1870	6.8 (15.4)	5.8	6.9 (16.6)	5.7	1.8 (15.4)	0.7	1.9 (16.5)	0.6	5.0 (0.0)	0.0	6.9 (16.6)	5.7
1871–1925	8.4 (15.6)	7.2	7.9 (16.6)	6.6	3.1 (15.9)	1.9	2.7 (16.9)	1.3	5.2 (1.1)	0.7	7.9 (16.6)	6.6
1926–1990	11.9 (21.1)	9.8	8.6 (21.2)	6.4	7.1 (20.4)	5.0	3.9 (20.5)	1.8	4.8 (1.4)	19.3	7.4 (20.7)	5.3
1946–1990	12.0 (14.6)	11.1	7.4 (15.6)	6.2	7.4 (13.8)	6.5	3.0 (14.8)	1.9	4.6 (1.4)	24.4	6.0 (14.8)	4.9
1966–1981	7.3 (15.1)	6.2	0.4 (14.3)	-0.7	3.1 (14.3)	2.1	-3.5 (13.8)	-4.6	4.2 (1.3)	26.4	-0.9 (13.5)	-1.8
1966–1990	10.7 (15.1)	9.6	4.6 (15.2)	3.5	6.3 (14.4)	5.3	0.6 (14.6)	-0.6	4.3 (1.2)	25.9	3.3 (14.3)	2.2
1982–1990	16.7 (13.1)	15.9	12.3 (13.5)	11.4	12.1 (12.7)	11.3	7.9 (13.0)	7.0	4.6 (1.0)	25.1	10.5 (12.7)	9.8

*A = arithmetic mean; G = geometric mean.

past 188 years, would have grown to the incredible sum of $3 trillion — nearly equal to the entire capitalization of the U.S. stock market in 1990!

Three million 1802 dollars — equivalent to about $35 million in today's purchasing power — was a large — but certainly not over-whelming — sum of money to the industrialists and landholders of the early 19th century.[10]

Long-Term Bonds

In comparing past with future bond returns, it is important to choose securities whose risk characteristics match closely. There was an active market for long-term U.S. government bonds over most of the 19th century except for the years 1835 through 1841, when prior budget surpluses eliminated all federal government debt outstanding. Sidney Homer presented a series of long-term government yields in his classic work, *A History of Interest Rates.*[11] Long-term government bond issues were not numerous during the 19th century; maturities generally ranged from three to 20 years, although some bonds had no fixed duration.[12] Figure 17.2 displays the interest rates on long-term U.S. government bonds, joining the Homer series with the Ibbotson and Sinquefield series, which begins in 1926.[13]

Despite the good data on federal government bond yields, there are persuasive reasons why high-grade municipal bonds may be more representative of high-quality bonds during much of the 19th and early 20th centuries. Some of the municipal bonds issued during the early 19th century, particularly those of the Commonwealth of Massachusetts and the City of Boston, were considered of higher quality than those of the federal government and thus traded at lower yields.[14] Risk of default on federal government bonds increased during both the War of 1812 and the Civil War, hence yields on federal debt rose above the yields on comparable high-grade municipals.[15] Furthermore, these high-grade municipals promised to pay interest and principal only in gold, thereby avoiding the "bimetal" option, which gave the federal government the right to redeem the principal in either gold or silver. This option may have biased the yields on federal government bonds upward.[16]

There is another reason why municipal bond yields should sometimes be substituted for federal government bonds. From the Civil War to 1920, the yields on federal government bonds were biased downward because banks were permitted to issue circulating bank notes against government bonds held as reserves. These rights, called "circulation privileges," motivated banks to bid the prices of federal bonds up above the prices of comparable high-grade securities. The effect of this bias is evident in Figure 17.2. In 1920, circulation privileges were abolished, and the yield on federal government bonds jumped to the level of high-grade municipals.[17]

To avoid the noted problems with federal government bond yields, I constructed a high-grade series that uses the minimum yield on Treasury bonds and high-grade municipal bond yields from 1800 to 1865 and high-grade municipal yields from 1865 to 1917. This is the high-grade bond series depicted in Figure 17.1. Table 17.2 summarizes the statistics.

Short-Term Bonds

Treasury bills, or short-term governments, did not exist before 1920. Data on commercial paper rates dating back to the 1830s are available from Macaulay, but during the 19th century commercial paper was subject to a high and variable risk premium, as Figure 17.3 shows.[18] These premiums often developed during or just prior to liquidity and financial crises (marked by NBER-designated recessions). There were also defaults on this paper,

250

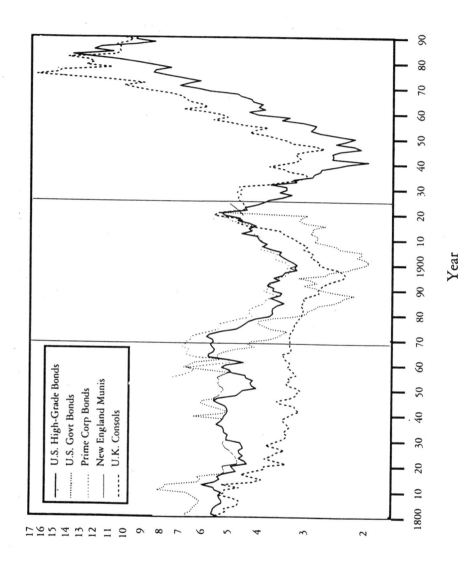

Figure 17.2 Long-term interest rates, 1800–1990

Table 17.2 Fixed income returns (standard deviations in parentheses)*

Period	Coupon (%) A	Long-term governments						Short-term governments					
		Nominal return (%)		Real return (%)		Real after-tax return (%)		Rate (%)	Real return (%)		Real after-tax return (%)	
		A	G	A	G	A	G	A	A	G	A	G
1802–1990	4.7 (1.8)	4.8 (5.4)	4.7	3.7 (8.5)	3.4	3.2 (8.4)	2.9	4.3 (2.2)	3.1 (6.2)	2.9	2.8 (6.3)	2.6
1871–1990	4.5 (2.3)	4.7 (6.5)	4.5	2.8 (8.5)	2.5	2.1 (8.3)	1.8	3.7 (2.5)	1.8 (4.7)	1.7	1.4 (4.8)	1.2
1802–1870	4.9 (0.4)	5.1 (2.7)	5.0	5.2 (8.3)	4.9	5.1 (8.2)	4.8	5.2 (1.1)	5.4 (7.6)	5.1	5.4 (7.6)	5.1
1871–1925	4.0 (0.6)	4.5 (2.9)	4.4	4.0 (6.3)	3.8	3.9 (6.3)	3.7	3.8 (0.9)	3.3 (4.8)	3.1	3.2 (4.8)	3.1
1926–1990	5.0 (2.9)	4.9 (8.4)	4.6	1.8 (9.9)	1.4	0.6 (9.4)	0.2	3.7 (3.4)	0.6 (4.3)	0.5	-0.2 (4.2)	-0.3
1946–1990	5.9 (3.1)	4.9 (9.6)	4.5	0.5 (10.5)	-0.1	-1.1 (9.5)	-1.6	4.9 (3.3)	0.4 (3.6)	0.3	-0.8 (3.3)	-0.9
1966–1981	7.2 (1.8)	2.8 (6.9)	2.5	-3.9 (7.9)	-4.2	-5.6 (7.5)	-5.9	6.9 (2.9)	-0.1 (2.0)	-0.2	-1.9 (2.0)	-1.9
1966–1990	8.2 (2.2)	7.4 (11.5)	6.8	1.6 (12.5)	0.9	-0.7 (11.3)	-1.3	7.2 (2.5)	1.3 (2.7)	1.2	-0.5 (2.5)	-0.6
1982–1990	10.0 (1.8)	15.7 (13.2)	14.9	11.3 (13.3)	10.5	7.9 (11.7)	7.3	7.9 (1.6)	3.7 (1.8)	3.7	1.8 (1.4)	1.8

* A = arithmetic mean; G = geometric mean.

252

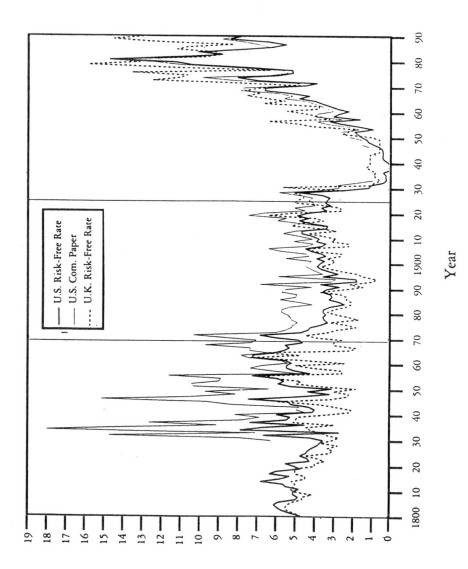

Figure 17.3 Short-term interest rates, 1800–1990

but there is insufficient information to correct the yield series for these defaults. Despite the obvious shortcomings of the data, there are few other short-term rates available for the early 19th century, and those that are available cover very short periods.

To remedy this deficiency, I constructed a **synthetic short-term government series** that removes the risk premium on commercial paper.[19] I did so by using the relation between short and long-term interest rates that prevailed in Britain during the 19th century, where the yields for long and short-term bonds were more representative of high-grade securities. The construction of the U.S. series assumes that the term structure of high-grade interest rates was the same over concurrent five-year periods in the U.S. and in the U.K. Figure 17.3 shows the short-term, risk-free series, along with other available short-term rates.

It is clear from Figure 17.1 that the total return indexes for fixed income assets fall far short of that for equity. With reinvestment of coupons, an initial investment of $1 in long-term bonds in 1802 would have yielded $5,770 in 1990; the same investment in riskfree, short-term assets would have yielded $2,680. Both these returns are less than 1% of the sum accumulated in stocks over the entire period.

Gold and Commodities

The gold series represents the value of gold measured at the market price. Until the mid-1960s, this price was controlled by the government; furthermore, U.S. citizens were not allowed to hold gold in monetary form between 1933 and 1970. Gold has nonetheless been a key asset in world monetary history and many investors still consider it an important hedge asset. One dollar of gold bullion purchased in 1802 would have been worth $15.80 by the end of 1990.

The Consumer Price Index (CPI), provided for comparison, represents the value of a basket of widely diversified goods that could be stored costlessly, with no depreciation.[20] Consumer prices increased about 11-fold from 1802 to 1990, almost all of the appreciation coming in the last subperiod. Table 17.3 summarizes the returns for gold and commodities over the various time periods.

Note that, by the end of the first subperiod, 1802–70, the accumulations in government bonds, bills and stocks were virtually identical. It is in the second and especially the third subperiods that stocks clearly dominated fixed income assets. The return on gold is clearly dominated by bonds and stocks over the entire period, but its appreciation did surpass bonds (but not stocks) over the past 65 years.

THE PRICE LEVEL AND ASSET RETURNS

The behavior of price levels is critical to any interpretation of asset price movements over time. Figure 17.4 displays various U.S. price indexes. They all tell the same story. Before World War II, the price level displayed no overall trend. Since the war, the price level has increased steadily. Prices accelerated until the 1980's, when the rate of inflation slowed. The CPI in 1990 was nearly seven times its 1945 value. Over the entire period, prices increased at an average compound annual rate of 1.3%. Inflation averaged 0.1% per year in the first subperiod and 0.6 and 3.1% in the second and third subperiods. Table 17.3 gives the statistics.

Over long periods of time, increases in the price level are strongly associated with increases in the money supply. Throughout the 19th and the early part of the 20th centuries,

Table 17.3 Economic variables (standard deviations in parentheses)*

| | Prices | | | | | | | Output | | | | S&P 500 (per share) | | | |
| | CPI (%) | | WPI (%) | | GNP deflator (%) | | Gold (%) | Real GNP (%) | | Industrial production (%) | | Real earnings (%) | | Real dividends (%) | |
Period	A	G	A	G	A	G	A	A	G	A	G	A	G	A	G
1802–1990	1.5 (6.1)	1.3	1.4 (9.0)	1.0	—	—	2.3 (14.8)	—	—	—	—	—	—	—	—
1871–1990	2.1 (5.0)	2.0	2.0 (8.1)	1.6	2.3 (5.3)	2.2	3.3 (17.7)	3.5 (5.6)	3.3	5.5 (17.7)	4.0	6.0 (25.7)	3.0	3.9 (12.8)	3.1
1802–1870	0.4 (7.5)	0.1	0.4 (10.3)	−0.1	—	—	0.5 (7.0)	—	—	—	—	—	—	—	—
1871–1925	0.7 (5.1)	0.6	0.7 (9.6)	0.2	0.9 (5.5)	0.7	−0.2 (1.2)	3.8 (4.9)	3.7	5.6 (18.2)	4.1	6.5 (31.9)	2.1	2.5 (13.4)	1.6
1926–1990	3.2 (4.7)	3.1	3.1 (6.4)	2.9	3.5 (4.7)	3.4	6.2 (23.6)	3.2 (6.1)	3.0	5.4 (17.4)	4.0	5.6 (19.1)	3.7	5.2 (12.1)	4.4
1946–1990	4.6 (3.9)	4.5	4.3 (5.3)	4.1	4.9 (4.0)	4.9	7.4 (26.5)	2.6 (4.3)	2.5	3.7 (6.1)	3.5	7.1 (14.9)	6.1	6.4 (5.9)	6.2
1966–1981	7.0 (3.3)	7.0	6.8 (4.2)	6.7	6.6 (2.1)	6.6	22.0 (39.2)	2.8 (2.3)	2.8	3.4 (5.1)	3.3	7.6 (10.8)	7.0	5.8 (4.5)	5.7
1966–1990	6.0 (3.1)	5.9	5.2 (4.1)	5.2	5.6 (2.2)	5.6	13.4 (34.4)	2.8 (2.3)	2.8	3.2 (4.9)	3.1	4.7 (12.7)	3.9	5.4 (3.7)	5.3
1982–1990	4.0 (1.2)	4.0	2.5 (2.1)	2.5	3.9 (1.0)	3.9	−2.0 (13.4)	2.8 (2.4)	2.8	2.8 (4.6)	2.7	−0.4 (14.3)	−1.4	4.6 (1.6)	4.6

*A = arithmetic mean; G = geometric mean.

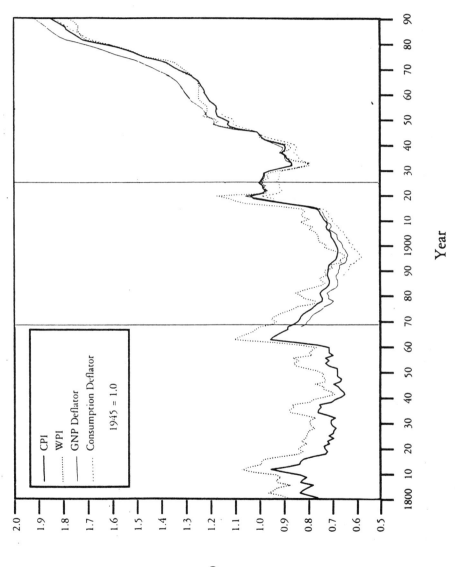

Figure 17.4 Price indexes, 1800–1990

the money stock was closely tied to the amount of gold held by the Treasury and central bank. The abandonment of the gold standard, a process that started in 1933 but gained momentum in the post-World War II period, reduced constraints on the monetary authority's issuance of money. Chronic inflation, which cannot occur under a gold standard, became the norm in the postwar period.

Figure 17.5 depicts total *real* return indexes — total (nominal) return indexes deflated by the price level. Because of inflation, real returns are much more modest than nominal returns, especially in the final subperiod. One dollar invested in equities in 1802 would have accumulated to $86,100 of constant purchasing power, or real dollars, by 1990.

Over the same period, one dollar would have accumulated to $520 in real dollars if invested in long-term governments, to $242 in real dollars if invested in short-term governments, and to only $1.42 if invested in gold. A dollar of hoarded currency, which pays no return and whose value is eroded by inflation, would have left an investor with only 9 cents of purchasing power in 1990.[21]

Taxes and Returns

Figure 17.6 displays the total return index corrected for both federal taxes and inflation. Average federal income tax rates were taken from studies by Robert Barro and Chaipat Sahasakul and are reported in Table 17.1.[22] Because no state or local taxes are considered, tax rates before 1913, when the federal income tax was instituted, are set at zero. It is assumed that dividends and interest income are taxed at the average marginal tax rate prevailing in the year they were earned and that capital gains are taxed (and losses remitted) at one-fifth the prevailing average marginal tax rate.[23] The reduced tax rate on capital gains arises primarily from the deferment of taxes on gains accrued but not realized and secondarily from the lower tax rate on realized gains.

Because a significant part of the returns on equity has been earned through capital gains, while virtually all the returns on bonds are in the form of taxable interest, the returns on equity are taxed at a lower effective rate than those on fixed income securities. In the third subperiod, 1926–90, when taxes became significant, the compound after-tax real return on stocks is reduced by 1.1 percentage points, to 5.3%; the after-tax real return on short-term bonds is reduced by 0.8 percentage points, to −0.3%, while the return on long-term government bonds falls 1.2 percentage points, to 0.2%.

These results indicate that, on an after-tax basis, investors rolling over long-term bonds in the third subperiod have barely kept up with inflation, while those rolling over short-term bonds have fallen behind inflation. In fact, investors in short-term bonds have earned *no* after-tax real return from 1900 through 1990. Over the same period, the after-tax real return index for equities increased 90-fold!

Trends in Returns

Figure 17.7 displays 30-year centered moving averages of compound real rates of return on stocks, short and long-term government bonds.[24] One of the striking aspects of these data is the relative constancy of the real returns on equity across all the subperiods. In the first subperiod, the average geometric real return on equity is 5.7%; it is 6.6% in the second subperiod and 6.4% in the third.[25] These figures imply that, although inflation increased substantially in the third subperiod, the nominal return on equity increased by an almost identical amount, so the return after inflation remained essentially unchanged. To the extent

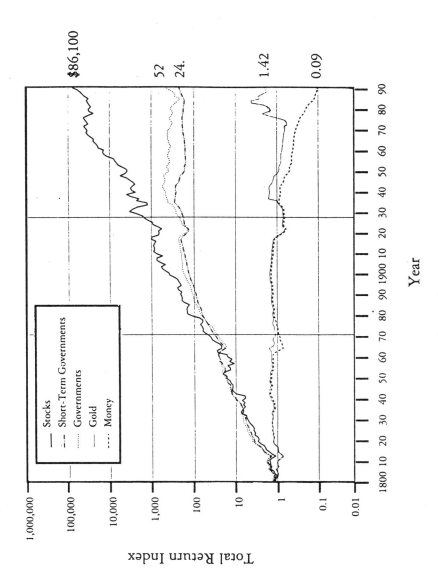

Figure 17.5 Total real return indexes, before taxes, 1802–1990

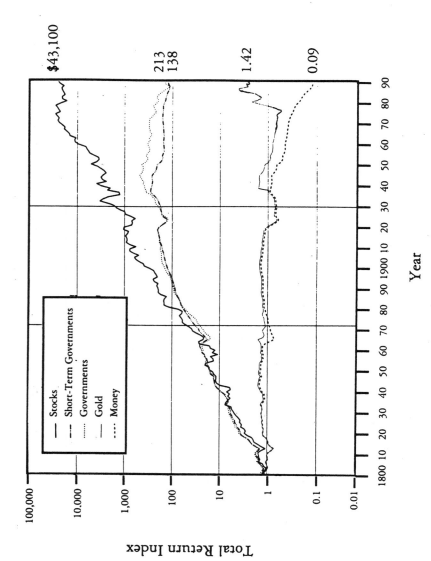

Figure 17.6 Total real returns indexes, after taxes, 1802–1990

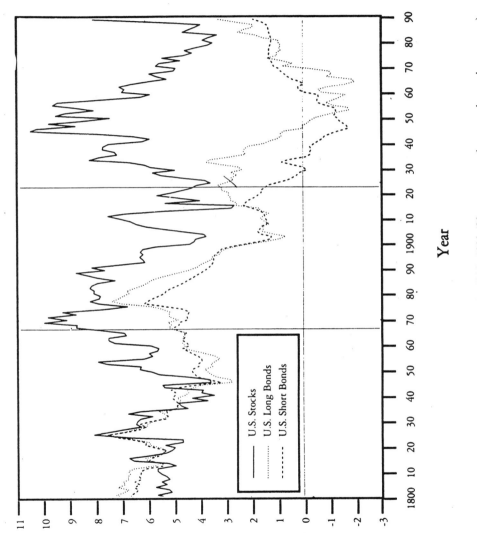

Figure 17.7 Real returns on stocks and bonds, 1802–1990 (30-year centered geometric moving average)

that stocks are claims on real assets, they might be expected to be good hedges against inflation over the long run.[26]

As noted, the average real compound rate of return on stocks over the entire period has been 6.2%. Over every 30-year period from 1802 through 1990, there have been only two when the compound real annual rate of return on stocks fell below 3.5%, and those occurred in the depths of the Depression, in 1931 and 1932. The periods of the highest real returns on stock ended in the early 1960s, when the real compound annual return exceeded 10%.

The most striking pattern in Figure 17.7 is the decline in the average real return on fixed income assets. In all 30-year periods beginning with 1888, the year that Mehra and Prescott began their analysis, the real rate of return on short-term government securities has exceeded 2% in only three periods, ending in the Depression years 1932–34. Since the late 19th century, the real return on bonds and bills over any 30-year horizon has almost never matched the average return of 4.5 to 5% reached during the first 70 years of our sample period. Since 1878, the real return on long-term bonds has never reached 4% over any 30-year period; it exceeded 3% in only six years. One has to go back to the 1831–61 period

Table 17.4 Holding-period returns on stocks, long bonds and short bonds

Holding period	Time	Stock return > long bond (%)	Stock return > short bond (%)	Long bond > short bond (%)
1 year	1802–1870	49.3	49.3	34.8
	1871–1925	56.4	60.0	65.5
	1926–1990	67.7	69.2	86.2
	1802–1990	57.7	59.3	61.4
	1871–1990	62.5	64.7	76.5
2 years	1802–1870	52.9	48.5	44.1
	1871–1925	58.2	61.8	56.4
	1926–1990	75.4	69.2	60.0
	1802–1990	62.2	59.6	53.2
	1871–1990	67.5	65.8	58.3
5 years	1802–1870	47.7	49.2	43.1
	1871–1925	67.3	67.3	60.0
	1926–1990	78.5	80.0	61.5
	1802–1990	64.3	65.4	54.6
	1871–1990	73.3	74.2	60.8
10 years	1802–1870	46.7	43.3	46.7
	1871–1925	83.6	83.6	60.0
	1926–1990	83.1	83.1	56.9
	1802–1990	71.1	70.0	54.4
	1871–1990	83.3	83.3	58.3
20 years	1802–1870	54.0	60.0	46.0
	1871–1925	94.5	100.0	52.7
	1926–1990	95.4	98.5	64.6
	1802–1990	82.9	87.6	55.3
	1871–1990	95.0	99.2	59.2
30 years	1802–1870	55.0	52.5	40.0
	1871–1925	100.0	100.0	60.0
	1926–1990	100.0	100.0	63.1
	1802–1990	88.8	88.1	56.3
	1871–1990	100.0	100.0	61.7

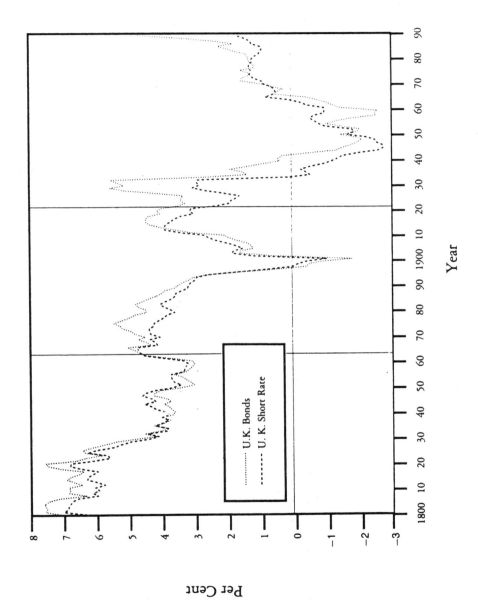

Figure 17.8 Real returns on U.K. bonds, 1802–1990 (30-year moving average)

to find any 30-year period where the return on either long or short-term bonds exceeded that on equities. The dominance of stocks over fixed income securities, so evident from Figures 17.1, 17.5 and 17.6, is borne out by examining long-term holding-period returns.

Table 17.4 compares the compound returns on stocks, long and short-term bonds. Over the entire period, stocks outperformed short-term bonds 57.7% of the time on a year-to-year basis but 88.8% of the time over 30-year horizons. Since 1871, over horizons of 20 years or longer, stocks have underperformed short-term assets only once and have outperformed long-term bonds 95% of the time. Even with holding periods as short as five years, stocks have outperformed long and short-term bonds by a four-to-one margin since 1926 and a three-to-one margin since 1872. In contrast, in 1802–71, stocks outperformed short or long-term bonds only about one-half the time over any holding period.

Trends in the U.K.

In the 19th century, as London emerged as the world's financial center, capital markets in Great Britain were far more developed than in the U.S. The British consol, depicted in Figure 17.2, is a security that pays interest only; it was first floated in 1729. The consol has long been used by economists to construct a continuous and homogeneous long-term interest rate series stretching over 250 years. British short-term interest rates are represented, with some exceptions, by the open-market rate at which high-quality commercial paper is discounted.[27] Figure 17.8 shows the 30-year average real returns on U.K. short and long-term bonds.

There is remarkable similarity in the yield trends in the U.K. and the U.S. The sharp decline in the real yields on fixed income securities in the U.S. was closely mirrored in the U.K. Statistical tests cannot reject the hypothesis that the return process was identical for both long and short-term real interest rates in the U.S. and the U.K. over the entire period.

EXPLANATIONS OF TRENDS

Although the data demonstrate that returns on equities have compensated investors for increased inflation over the postwar period, the returns on fixed income securities have not. One possible explanation is that lenders did not anticipate inflation during much of the period.

One could argue that a large part of the increase in the price level since World War II, especially since 1970, was unanticipated, hence bondholders did not have a chance to adjust their required returns. The progressive abandonment of the gold standard only slowly reduced investors' convictions about the stability of the long-run price level.

Unanticipated inflation certainly lowered the real return on long-term bonds. Buyers of such instruments in the 1960s and early 1970s could scarcely have imagined the double-digit inflation that followed. But unanticipated inflation is less important for short-term bonds. The inflationary process, although increasingly subject to long-term uncertainty, has been quite persistent and inertial in the short run. Short-term investors thus have a better opportunity to capture the inflation premium in the rate of interest as they roll over their investments. Short-term bonds should therefore provide better protection against unanticipated inflation than longer-term bonds. Of course, this protection is not perfect; unanticipated inflation may account for up to one percentage point of the decline in the real yield on short-term bonds over the sample period.[28]

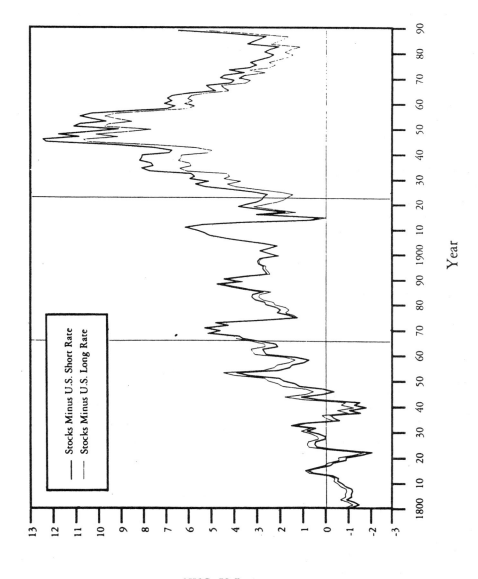

Figure 17.9 Equity risk premium, 1802–1990 (30-year centered geometric moving average)

Other Factors

Other factors influence the real rate of interest. Slower or more variable economic growth, for example, will generally lower the real rate investors demand to hold fixed income assets. Slower growth may have depressed real yields over short periods of time, including the 1970s, when real returns on short-term Treasury bills were negative. Economic growth in general, however, has been as high in the 20th as in the 19th century.

There is no evidence that the economy has become more volatile. In fact, Table 17.3 suggests that the real economy has actually been more stable since World War II, but real rates have been very low in this period. Intuition would suggest that the yield differential between risky assets such as stocks and less risky assets such as bonds would be smaller, the less risky the economy. If the real return on stocks has remained constant (and this is what the data suggest), then the real return on fixed income should have risen. The decline in the real yields on bonds suggests that changing variability of the real economy can not adequately explain the decline in real returns.

Perhaps the low real interest rates during much of this century can be explained by a combination of historical and institutional factors. The 1929–32 stock market crash and the Depression left a legacy of fear; most investors clung to government securities and insured deposits, driving their yields down. Redistribution policies undertaken by the government subsequent to the Depression may also have lowered real rates by shifting wealth to more risk-averse segments of the population. Furthermore, during World War II and the early post-war years, interest rates were kept low by the Federal Reserve. Because of its inflationary consequences, this policy was abandoned in 1951, but interest rate controls, particularly on deposits, lasted much longer.

Finally, one cannot ignore the development of the capital markets, which transformed a highly segmented market for short-term instruments in the 19th century into one of the world's most liquid markets in this century.

The Equity Premium

The decline in the real return on fixed income investments has meant that the advantage of holding equities, which have experienced a remarkably steady real return, has increased over time. The equity premium, plotted in Figure 17.9, has trended up over the last 200 years and was particularly high in the middle of this century. The premium, computed from real geometric returns, averaged 0.6% in the first subperiod, 3.5% in the second, and 5.9% in the third.

The primary source of this equity premium has been the fall in the real return on bonds, not the rise in the return on equity. Nonetheless, it is not unreasonable to believe that the low real rates on bonds may, on occasion, have fueled higher equity returns, because the costs of obtaining leverage were so low. The highest 30-year average equity return occurred in 1931–61, a period that also experienced very low real returns on bonds.

One might take an even broader view of the superior returns on equity. Certainly investors in 1802 (or even 1872) did not universally expect the United States to become the greatest economic power in the next century. This was not the case in many other countries. What if one had owned stock in Japanese or German firms before World War II? Or consider Argentina, which, at the turn of the century, was one of the great economic powers. In some sense, the returns on U.S. stocks might not be representative of the broader international context.[29]

CONCLUSIONS

The high real interest rates in the 19th century may have reflected the possibility that the U.S. would default on its bonds or abandon the gold standard. Since the inflation shocks of the 1970s, fear of outright default has been replaced by an inflationary premium in nominal interest rates. Future inflation may be caused by growing U.S. government deficits or by inflationary policies pursued by the Federal Reserve in response to political pressures or economic crises.

The last 10 years represent only about 5% of the total time examined in this study, but the period since 1980 contains the highest real long-term bond returns during any consecutive 10-year period since 1884 and the highest real short-term bond returns since the 19th century (excepting the sharp deflationary periods of the Depression). It is not unreasonable to assume that the current higher real rates will turn out to be more characteristic of future returns than the unusually low real rates of the earlier part of this century. If they do, then the advantage of holding equities over bonds will shrink from the levels reached over the past several generations. The holders of fixed income investments should enjoy enhanced real returns in the future. Equities, however, still appear to be the best route to long-term wealth accumulation.[30]

ENDNOTES

1. The average compound real return on the S&P 500 has been 6.7 % over the same period. Very small stocks (bottom quartile of capitalization) have performed better, averaging 8.2% compound real return since 1926.

2. Mehra, R. and Prescott, E. "The Equity Premium: A Puzzle," *Journal of Monetary Economics* 15 (1985), pp. 145–61. The time period covered by Mehra and Prescott was 1889–1978. The returns on stocks and bonds were very similar to the returns since 1926.

3. Some rely on non-standard preference functions; see, for example, Constantinides G.M., "Habit Formation: A Resolution of the Equity Premium Puzzle," *Journal of Political Economy* 98:3 (1990), pp. 519–43; Abel, A. "Asset Prices under Habit Formation and Catching up with the Joneses," *American Economic Review* 2:80 (1990), pp. 38–43; Benninga, S. and Protopapadakis, A. "Time Preference and the "Equity Premium Puzzle'," *Journal of Monetary Economics*, January 1990; and Weil, P. "The Equity Premium Puzzle and the Risk-free Rate Puzzle," *Journal of Monetary Economics*, November 1989. Others rely on individual stocks and segmented asset holdings; see Mankiw, N.G. "The Equity Premium and the Concentration of Aggregate Shocks," *Journal of Financial Economics* 17 (1986), pp. 211–19 and Mankiw, N.G. and Zeldes, S.P. "The Consumption of Stockholders and Non-Stockholders," *Journal of Financial Economics* 29 (1991), pp. 97–112. See Abel, A. "The Equity Premium Puzzle," Federal Reserve Bank of Philadelphia *Business Review*, September–October 1991, for a summary.

4. Schwert, William G. "Indexes of United States Stock Prices from 1802 to 1987," *Journal of Business* 63:3 (1990), pp. 399–426. Ibbotson, R. and Brinson, G. (*Investment Markets: Gaining the Performance Advantage* (New York: McGraw Hill, 1987), p. 73) report that the Foundation for the Study of Cycles, in Pittsburgh, has published data from an internal stock index entitled "Historical Record: Stock Prices 1789–Present," Data Bulletin 1975–1. However, attempts to obtain documentation for this series have not been successful.

5. Cowles, A. *Common Stock Indexes, 1871–1937* (Bloomington, IN: Principia Press, 1938).

6. In the 1970s and 1980s, Roger Ibbotson and Rex Sinquefield analyzed data on inflation, stock and bond returns since 1926 (see *Stocks, Bonds, Bills, and Inflation, 1991 Yearbook* (Chicago: Ibbotson Associates, 1991)). Several authors (see for example Wilson, J.W. and Jones, C.P. "A Comparison of Annual Common Stock Returns: 1871–1925 with 1926–85," *Journal of*

Business, April 1987, and "Stock, Bonds, Paper, and Inflation, 1870–1985," *Journal of Portfolio Management*, Fall 1987) have extended much of the data back to 1872.

7. Standard stock indexes do, however, reflect increases in the value of shares resulting from reinvestment of retained earnings and changes in the capitalization of expected earnings.

8. The data from the Foundation for the Study of Cycles (found in Ibbotson and Brinson, *Investment Markets*, *op. cit.*) show a compound return of 7.95% from 1802 through 1870 and 7.92% from 1789 through 1870.

9. The geometric, or compound, return is the nth root of the one-year returns; it is always less than the average or mean arithmetic return, except when all yearly returns are equal. The geometric return can be approximated by the arithmetic mean minus one-half the variance of the individual yearly returns.

10. Blodget, S. Jr. (*A Statistical Manual for the United States of America*, 1806 ed., p. 68) estimated that wealth in the U.S. was $2.45 billion in 1802. Total wealth today is estimated at nearly $15 trillion, of which about $4 trillion is in the stock market.

11. Homer, S. *A History of Interest Rates* (New Brunswick, NJ: Rutgers University Press, 1963).

12. The first federal government debt was the Hamilton refunding 6s of 1790, "redeemable at the pleasure of the government at 100 in an amount not exceeding 2% a year."

13. Ibbotson and Sinquefield, *Stocks, Bonds, Bills*, *op. cit.*

14. See Homer (*A History, op. cit.*, pp. 296 and 301) and Martin, J.G. (*Boston Stock Market*, 1871) for a description of these municipals. The lower yield for municipals was not due to any tax advantage, because tax considerations did not emerge until the early 20th century.

15. The Greenback period, when the government issued notes not redeemable in specie, provides a fascinating episode in monetary theory. For further discussion, see Roll, R. "Interest Rates and Price Expectations During the Civil War," *Journal of Economic History*, June 1972.

16. For a discussion of the issues involved in the bimetal standard and the potential distortion in yields see Garber, P.M. "Nominal Contracts in a Bimetallic Standard," *American Economic Review*, December 1986.

17. The magnitude of this distortion can be seen by examining the yields in 1917–20 on government bonds issued with and without circulation privileges (see Homer, *A History, op. cit.*, Table 46). The yield differential between bonds with and without circulation privileges ranged from 50 to 100 basis points.

18. Macaulay, F.R. (*The Movements of Interest Rates, Bond Yields, and Stock Prices in the United States since 1856* (New York: National Bureau of Economic Research, 1938)) reported rates for choice 60 to 90-day commercial paper after 1856, while data from 1831 through 1856 were collected from Bigelow, E.B. (*The Tariff Question* ..., (Boston, 1862)), which covers "Street rates on First class paper in Boston and New York, at the beginning, middle, and end of the month." The paper floated in Boston is said to be of three to six months in duration. See Macaulay, p. A341, for a more detailed discussion of these sources.

19. For details of the construction of U.S. short-term rate series, see Siegel, J.J. "The Real Rates of Interest from 1800–1900: A Study of the U.S. and U.K.," *Journal of Monetary Economics*, forthcoming.

20. The CPI includes services that cannot be stored. Since World War II, commodity prices have risen slower and service prices faster than the CPI. When futures markets exist, investors can buy futures, putting up margin in interest-bearing Treasury bills. This may result in returns higher than the CPI.

21. An investor would actually have done far better hoarding paper money than gold bullion. The first U.S. currency, a one dollar U.S. note issued in 1862, now catalogues for $1000 in uncirculated condition, while earlier colonial paper goes for even more. Of course, gold coins have also increased in value far more than bullion.

22. Barro, R.J. and Sahasakul, C. "Measuring the Average Marginal Tax Rate from the Individual Income Tax," *Journal of Business* 56 (1982), pp. 419–52 and "Average Marginal Tax Rates from Social Security and the Individual Income Tax," *Journal of Business* 59 (1986), pp. 555–66.

23. This adjustment is consistent with research done by Protopapadakis, A. "Some Indirect Evidence on Effective Capital Gains Tax Rates," *Journal of Business* 56 (1982), pp. 127–38.

24. The averaging period is progressively shortened to 15 years at the end points of these series.

25. If the stock data from the Foundation for the Study of Cycles (see footnote 4) are considered, the real compound annual return in equity from 1802 to 1870 is 6.8%.

26. In the short run, stocks have proved poor hedges against inflation. This is particularly true if inflation is induced by supply shocks, which affect the productivity of capital. See Fama, E.F. "Stock Returns, Real Activity, Inflation and Money," *The American Economic Review*, September 1981.

27. These series can be found in Homer (*A History*, op. cit., Table 23). He describes the paper as of "nonuniform maturity of a few months" before 1855 and thereafter "three month bills." These series are based on data compiled by the NBER from British Parliamentary papers and from various editions of *The Economist* (1858–1900). Details are contained in Siegel, "The Real Rate of Interest," op. cit.

28. This has been suggested to me by some preliminary work done by Charles Calomaris.

29. Of course, even on a worldwide basis, who might have expected the triumph of capitalism and market-oriented economies 100 or even 50 years ago? We may be living in the golden age of capitalism, the fortunes of which may decline in the next 100 years (or sooner)!

30. I thank Peter Scherer and Ashish Shah for their research assistance.

18

Risk vs. Return in Pension Fund Management

Irwin Tepper

...The optimal stock-bond mix is the single most important element of the investment policy decision. It is widely accepted that, on the average, equities will continue to yield higher long-run returns than bonds; but equities will also remain much more volatile. How can this prospect be factored into investment policy?

By means of a case study, this article analyzes a technique that allows corporate sponsors to measure the effects of various asset mixes directly and in the terms most meaningful to them — pension costs and unfunded pension liabilities. By factoring pension costs into the income statement and unfunded pension liability into the balance sheet, a company can set pension fund investment policy with the same criteria it employs to control other elements of its finances.

In focusing on investment policy, I do not consider the analysis of other important matters affecting a pension plan — that is, inflation, actuarial assumptions, or the funding policy. But the framework I discuss in this article is capable of handling many of these issues.

PLANNING FRAMEWORK

The relationship between investment policy and the future financial burden of a pension plan is influenced by many factors. Playing an important role are:

- The future population of the plan's participants (active employees, retirees, and vested terminated employees).
- The plan's benefit provisions, such as vesting and early retirement.
- The actuarial cost method, the asset valuation procedure, and the assumptions established by the plan's actuary.
- Future capital market conditions.

Reprinted from: Tepper, I. 1977: Risk vs. Return in Pension Fund Management. *Harvard Business Review*, 55, March-April, 100–107

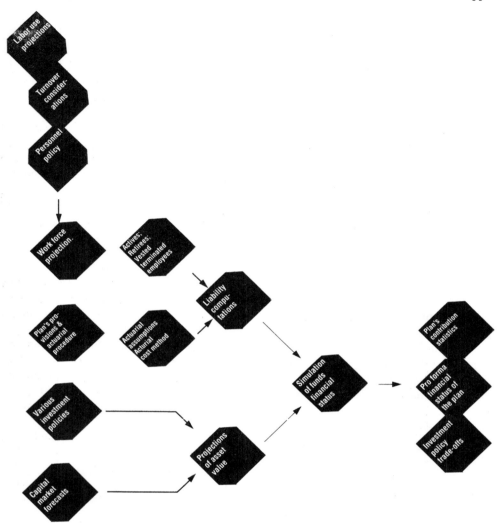

Figure 18.1 A pension fund financial planning framework

How can the sponsor bring all these factors together in order to see the net effect of investment policy in its broadest context? The most direct way is to simulate the operation of the pension fund over the spectrum of bond-stock mixes and generate a set of pro forma financial statements for the plan. Figure 18.1 is a diagram of one model used to do this. A computer-based simulation model performs all the calculations.

For each prospective investment policy, the computer projects pension costs and unfunded liability for each of the next 20 years. The steps it goes through include: (1) projecting the entries and departures of the work force and retiree pools; (2) projecting salary increases;

(3) calculating the plan's normal cost (that is, the cost of benefits created in the current year); (4) amortizing the plan's past service liability, as required by ERISA; (5) estimating the benefit payments to be made to retirees in the current year; (6) determining the earnings on the pension fund; (7) analyzing the investment experience of the plan; and (8) setting up the 15-year amortization schedules. (Some cost methods permit experience gains and losses to be built into future costs, and the computer model is modified to accommodate this factor.)

The computer model that does all this must, of course, be complex. It contains a package that analyzes the dynamics of the work force, the complete actuarial system established for the plan, and a technique for "sampling" the investment experience that the fund will encounter. Once constructed and verified, however, it is easy to use. As I shall demonstrate, the output comes in a form well suited for its intended use.

The plan's investment experience is derived from a set of forecasts of the returns that the sponsor and his money managers expect to obtain in the stock and bond markets. A realistic assessment of the manager's ability to deal with capital market uncertainties should be factored into these projections.

No one who could have anticipated the performance of the stock market in 1973 and 1974 — the worst in 40 years — would have invested in equities. Yet pension funds on the whole were saddled with substantial equity investment during that period. Since most of these funds were in the hands of money managers, it is obvious that even the professionals in the business cannot penetrate the uncertainties in the capital markets.

Of course, the 1973–1974 period is not the only one in which the stock market failed to perform according to expectations. The lesson to be learned from history is that the investment process must be accepted as a statistical phenomenon in which expected returns and risks go hand in hand. Mere point estimates of annual returns make up an incomplete and unrealistic description of the capital markets. The sponsor must specify the chances of earning each possible level of return.

The computer model simulates the investment experience of the pension fund over the 20-year period. Instead of making a point estimate of the fund's earnings, it constructs a random sample drawn from a pool of all the possible returns of the plan's investment experience. The pool is constructed so that the chances of obtaining any one occurrence depend on the odds specified by the sponsor. In the case that follows (an actual, though disguised, case), I elaborate on this procedure and other aspects of pension fund financial planning.

SUPER INVESTMENT POLICY

Prompted by the enactment of ERISA and rising pension costs, Super Co. is using a planning model to aid in a review of its pension plan's financial policies. The plan covers some 600 employees, many of whom have become eligible only recently as the result of a change in the company's benefit package. Super management anticipates no growth in the work force.

The company's profits in 1976 slipped 30% from their all-time high of two years before. The company's pension costs last year amounted to $600,000, or about 22% of pretax income. The plan has an unfunded liability of $2 million (assets equal $7 million and liabilities $9 million). In ordering the study, management wanted to know whether it could realistically expect to reduce this liability with a change in investment policy, by how much if so, and what trade-offs would be involved in pursuing a reduction.

In launching the study, Super established these actuarial policy parameters:

- It adopted an $8\frac{1}{2}\%$ interest rate assumption for the plan. This figure is somewhat higher than is usually found.

- It assumed an annual salary growth rate of 7%, a figure also somewhat higher than average, for projecting retirement benefits (the plan has a final-average pay formula for establishing benefits).

- It forecast for the foreseeable future a $5\frac{1}{2}\%$ to a 6% rate of inflation, which would be reflected not only in the payroll but also in the nominal returns the plan earned on its investments. In other words, the sponsor assumed that the relationship between inflation and the returns in each sector of the capital market would *not* continue their abnormal pattern of the last decade.

- It expected the bond market to yield a lower average return and to exhibit much less volatility than stocks.

Super's bond portfolio was to be actively managed — that is, its manager would trade when he saw incremental profit opportunities. The sponsor expected this approach to result in a modest improvement in the results that would be achieved by a buy-and-hold strategy. A different person ran the equity portfolio, which was to be diversified. He was expected to shift funds into and out of cash equivalents when he felt confident that such timing decisions would, on the average, enhance the return.

Taking into account historical relationships, forecasts of economic and financial scenarios, and the portfolio administration characteristics of each manager, Super came up with the statistical forecasts of returns on its stock and bond portfolios that can be seen in Figure 18.2. The simulation model uses these probability distributions to extract random samples of the plan's investment experience.

The exhibit shows two probability distributions, one for 100% of the stocks invested and one for 100% of the bonds purchased. This histogram indicates that, for example, there is a 13% chance of obtaining a bond return between 3% and 5%, and a 7% chance of losing between 5% and 10% of its money invested in equities.

Super was in the process of changing its asset valuation scheme, which provides the basis for determining if the plan's investment return is matching the actuarial assumption or whether a gain or a loss has actually occurred. Super had been using a formula designed to smooth fluctuations in its equity investment experience. Now the company decided to experiment with a method whereby bonds would be kept at amortized (that is, book) value and equities would be maintained at full market value. This procedure is sanctioned under ERISA.

Financial Analysis

Figure 18.3 shows how Super's investment policy affects its pension costs and unfunded liability. The data come from a simulated look at the twentieth year into the future; years 1 to 19 exhibit similar financial profiles on a somewhat smaller scale.

The percentile lines incorporate the data on the volatility, or risk, inherent in the future financial condition of the plan. For example, there is a 95% chance that the value of the quantity on the vertical axis will fall below the 95th percentile line. On the other hand,

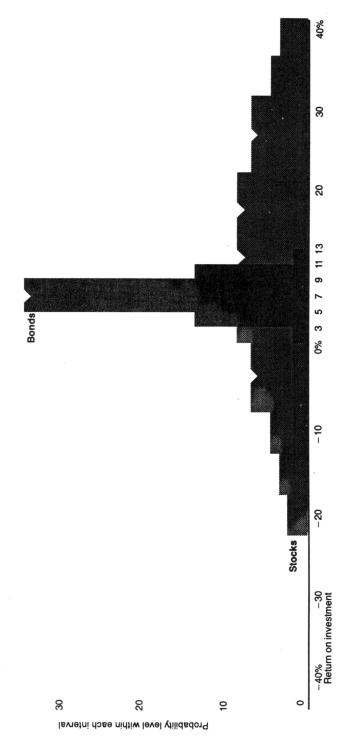

Figure 18.2 Forecasts of annual returns on stocks and bonds

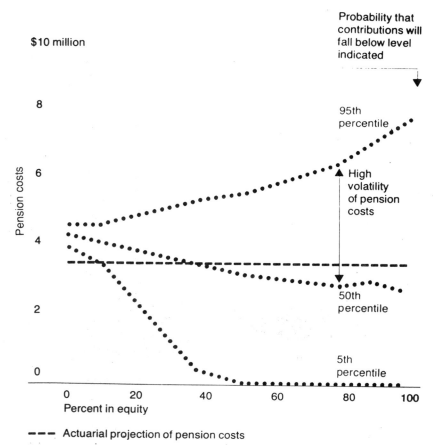

Figure 18.3 Impact of investment policy on pension costs in the twentieth year

there is a 5% chance that pension costs will exceed this value. The median (50th percentile line) is a measure of the trend in the data, since the chance of being on either side of this line is 50/50. The distances from the median to the 5th and the 95th percentiles are measures of the risk inherent in achieving results close to the statistical tendencies (that is, the median). The "bumps" in the percentiles are a product of the simulation process rather than a discontinuity in the pension finances.

The actuarial projection of costs (the dashed line) includes such estimates as the plan's normal costs and unfunded liability amortization but excludes the impact of investment experience. This projection assumes that the pension fund will earn the plan's actuarial interest rate every year. The differences between the dashed line and the dotted lines are attributable solely to the impact of investment experience (that is, all other factors in the pension system are held constant). In this manner, Super can determine whether the plan's interest rate assumption is appropriate for the investment policy selected.

Looking at the left side of Figure 18.3, Super's financial vice president observed that if the company selected an investment policy that had little equity investment, the pension contributions would be highly predictable, but the plan also would incur the highest average cost over the range of possibilities. The contributions would exceed the actuarial projection because portfolios dominated by long-term bonds are incapable of producing returns as high as the plan's $8\frac{1}{2}\%$ interest rate assumption. As a result, the plan would experience a series of actuarial losses on investments, amortizable over 15 years. Therefore, if an all-bond investment policy is chosen, the company should reduce the plan's interest rate assumption.

Increasing the proportion of stocks relative to bonds, he noticed, would reduce the average level (the 50th percentile) of pension costs. At the same time, however, the unpredictability would increase greatly, reflecting the volatility of the stock market. Eventually, the marginal benefits of rising equity investment would almost disappear as the potential risk became insupportable.

Super had figured that the actuarial projection of $3.3 million in pension costs would approximate 22% of pretax earnings in the twentieth year. That proportion was the same as the company's experience in 1976. Super was anticipating no significant growth and was assuming that its revenues and costs would grow more or less in proportion to the inflationary movement of the economy.

Using 22% as a rough bench mark, the financial staff estimated that an all-bond portfolio would lead to an average level of pension costs equal to 26% of pretax profits, whereas an all-equity portfolio would result in an 18% level. Therefore, Super could adjust the average level of pension costs, as a percentage of pretax profits, within a plus or minus 4% band around the current figure. Naturally, in pursuing a cost reduction, the company would have to accept higher risk. For example, an all-equity portfolio would expose Super to a 5% chance that pension costs would amount to 63% of pretax income 20 years hence.

The relationship between investment policy and the projected financial status of the pension plan — that is, its asset-liability balance — appears in Figure 18.4. It is evident that investment policies stressing equities tend to move the plan toward a fully funded status. This favorable funding trend accompanies the declining level of average contributions, which, of course, reflects the superior returns anticipated in the stock market.

Because the stock market is so unpredictable, however, a significant deterioration in the plan's unfunded liability may develop as soon as the manager makes any major equity investment. Equity investments in excess of 60% present troubling possibilities of unfunded vested liabilities — a critical concern for stockholders, creditors, and the Pension Benefit Guaranty Corporation. That corporation, of course, is the termination insurance fund administered by the Department of Labor, which steps in when a pension plan fails and imposes a lien on the employer of up to 30% of his assets.

Ultimate Decision

From these graphs, the financial VP could see that equity-oriented investment strategies would significantly reduce pension costs and the unfunded liability, and at the same time make pension finances unstable. The investment policy trade-offs are present throughout the spectrum of asset mixes; the appropriate one depends on the sponsor's circumstances and financial goals.

But there seemed to be little point in further consideration of the two ends of the spectrum — either at the low-risk end, with a maximum equity commitment of 10%, or at the other end, where equity investments of 70% to 80% offer little reward for taking extra risks. In the intermediate range, there is a relatively constant trade-off between expected contributions and volatility.

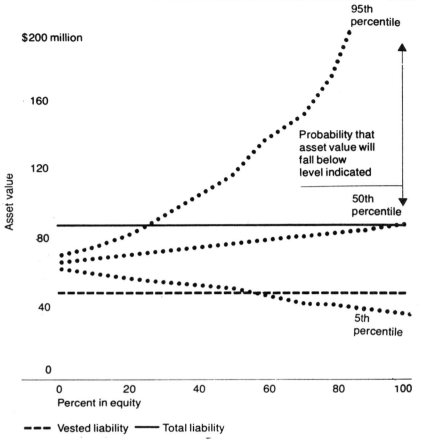

Figure 18.4 Pension plan asset value and liabilities in the twentieth year

In the five years prior to 1975, Super had experienced steady growth, and the relationships among salaries, pension contributions, and profits before taxes had been stable. In 1975 and 1976, however, the failure of revenues to rise at previous rates, while salaries and other operating expenses climbed, had disrupted these stable relationships. Therefore, the company concluded, the near-term uncertainty in the business overshadowed the risks inherent in a pension policy heavily committed to equity.

Another factor was the executives' feeling that the capital markets would be more volatile than originally assumed. They ordered a simulation rerun for a pessimistic view of the market. The results indicated that pension contributions would *rise* rather than fall as the investment in stocks increased beyond the level of 50% equities. Yet the volatility continued to rise.

On the ground that the potential rewards were justified, the financial VP and his associates decided to adopt a 50% to a 70% range in the stock-bond mix for the next few years. At the end of that period, the decision was to come under review.

INTEGRATING THE ANALYSIS

The financial planning model I have described is useful for examining a range of pension problems broader than the investment policy question. It can assist a sponsor in projecting pension costs, in testing his actuarial model against experience, and in determining the cost of proposed benefit liberalization. The analysis helps managers make explicit their assumptions about the future.

The development of a pension fund financial planning model is an interdisciplinary task requiring the participation of the plan's actuaries and money managers. Usually, these professionals have operated independently. While this stance may be acceptable at the level of policy implementation, is intolerable in policy setting. Happily, ERISA has been responsible for a new-found interest in integrating into policy making the analysis of the plan's assets and liabilities. Corporate sponsors should follow this lead in promoting a cooperative atmosphere among the pension planning participants.

It is fair to say that much of the extraordinary growth of pension liabilities, the associated corporate costs, and the attendant asset accumulation could have been predicted, and the companies that did project them knew what to expect. It is also fair to say that, given the policies their sponsors have followed, the current difficulties of many pension plans are understandable.

Despite the limitations imposed by ERISA, pension plan sponsors still enjoy broad discretion in the way they comply with the newly augmented regulations. An effort to improve pension trust management along the lines I have suggested should pay off.

―――――― 19 ――――――

The Importance of the
Asset Allocation Decision
Chris R. Hensel, D. Don Ezra and John H. Ilkiw

It is widely believed that the asset allocation policy decision of an investor is far more important than decisions such as market timing or security selection.[1] Of course, this belief reflects the practices of the *average* investor — more specifically, the average pension plan sponsor. But it is conceivable that some investors take such large bets on, say, security selection (or large departures from the composition of market indexes) that security selection has a greater impact on the achieved return of these investors than asset allocation policy. Sponsors might thus like to know how to estimate the relative impacts of different types of investment decisions on their funds' returns.

This article describes a method investors can use to analyze their returns and determine the impacts that several different risk-taking decisions have on these returns. In the course of constructing a suitable model and applying it to a very small sample of actual results, we discovered that the massive influence currently attributed to asset allocation policy depends crucially on one factor — that is, the naive alternative from which the sponsor's policy represents a departure. If the naive alternative is a reasonably diversified portfolio, then asset allocation policy may, for many sponsors, be only as important as (or not much more important than) other types of investment decisions.

PERFORMANCE ATTRIBUTION

The impact of any investment decision can be measured by comparing its outcome with the outcome of some alternative decision. This notion is frequently used to attribute pension fund investment performance to each of a number of decisions. For example, some funds compare the return on an actively managed portfolio with the return that would have been earned had funds been invested in the market portfolio instead. The difference represents the value added (or perhaps lost) by the investment judgments, which represent departures from the market portfolio.

Reprinted, with permission, from Hensel, C.R., Ezra, D.D. and Ilkiw, J.H. 1991: The Importance of the Asset Allocation Decision. *Financial Analysts Journal*, 47, July–August, 65–72. Copyright © 1991, Association for Investment Management and Research, Charlottesville, Va. All rights reserved.

While the principle is easy to understand, its application is often difficult. It is difficult to define the alternative portfolio that would be held by an investor who is devoid of investment judgment. Conventional wisdom defines the naive alternative as one that represents all available opportunities proportionately; this is usually the same as the average of what everybody else is holding.[2]

Furthermore, investment portfolios often reflect judgments of many kinds, each a departure from some naive alternative. A multilevel decision model for a pension plan sponsor (or indeed any investor) might involve three sets of asset allocations:

- the market mix, X,
- the sponsor's customized policy mix, Y, and
- the actual mix held from day to day, Z.

The corresponding trio of security weights would be:

- market weights, 1,
- the sponsor's customized "normal" weights, 2, and
- the actual weights of securities held from day to day, 3.

Allocation X could be the average weights of different asset classes held by all U.S. pension funds. Allocation Y could be the customized 60% U.S. equities/40% U.S. bonds selected as the policy for a particular sponsor's pension fund. Allocation Z on a particular day might be 55% U.S. equities, 15% U.S. bonds and 30% cash, assuming that mix were deemed by the fund's manager to be temporarily superior to the policy mix.

Weights 1 might be the weights assigned to securities in a well known index such as the S&P 500, attempting to reflect the market's opportunity set. Weights 2 might reflect specific tilts that the sponsor elects from a long-term policy perspective, such as a tilt toward long bonds rather than the intermediate length that reflects all bonds available in the U.S. Weights 3 would consist of the weights of the actual securities held in the portfolio on a particular day.

Security Weights

Asset Allocations	1: Market Security Weights	2: Sponsor's Customized "Normal" Weights	3: Actual Wts. of Securities Held from Day to Day
X: Market Mix	X 1: Basic Naive Portfolio		
Y: Sponsor's Customized Policy Mix		Y 2: Reflects Sponsor's Choices	
Z: Asset Mix Held from Day to Day			Z 3: Reflects Investment Manager's Choices

Figure 19.1 Composition of various portfolios

The basic naive portfolio consists of asset class weights X and security weights 1 (see Figure 19.1). It is conveniently labeled Portfolio X1. It earns no-judgment returns. All other portfolios reflect a choice of some kind, whether made consciously or unconsciously by representatives of the sponsor or by the investment manager (who may also be the sponsor). Portfolio Y2 is the quintessential representation of the sponsor's decisions, while Z3 represents the investment manager's decisions.

Differences between the different portfolios' returns measure the impact of various kinds of investment judgments. Thus (Y1 − X1) measures the impact of the sponsor's customized asset allocation policy as the two hypothetical portfolios differ only insofar as the sponsor's policy allocation differs from the neutral market allocation.[3]

In summary, Portfolio X1 represents the results from neutral participation in the markets. Differences between portfolio returns represent the impacts of investment decisions.

NAIVE ASSET ALLOCATIONS

We mentioned earlier the difficulty of defining the naive asset allocation. While we used the market mix to illustrate Allocation X in the model above, it is by no means obvious that this is what a naive pension plan sponsor would do.

Some candidates for Allocation X frequently found in practice include the following.

A: 100% in T-bills. This could be the minimum-risk portfolio for (1) a sponsor concerned with asset growth rather than surplus growth or (2) a sponsor concerned with surplus growth, which believes that pension liabilities are real in nature and that real interest rates tend to remain constant over time.[4]

B: 100% in bonds. This could be the minimum-risk portfolio for a sponsor concerned with surplus growth and focused on pension liabilities that are either fixed in nominal terms or inflation-sensitive up to each member's retirement but not beyond retirement.

C: The average asset allocation held by large pension funds. We assumed this to be 50% U.S. stocks, 5% international stocks, 30% U.S. fixed income, 5% real estate and 10% cash.[5] This allocation might be the naive selection of a sponsor who asks, "What is everyone else doing?"[6]

D: The asset allocation representing the "market mix." This would include all available investment opportunities. But what is "all"? Everything available to U.S. investors? Everything available anywhere in the world? Because of the difficulty in defining "all," we did not take this candidate any further.

Conceptually, we believe the appropriate hierarchy of investment policy portfolios is the one shown in Figure 19.2. We define the minimum-risk portfolio as liability-driven, in the sense that it minimizes the extent of future surplus uncertainty. For the balance of this article, we will use T-bills as the minimum-risk portfolio, without attempting to defend or convert others to this viewpoint. (Results are virtually identical if bonds are used as the minimum-risk portfolio.)

The average-risk portfolio is Naive Allocation C (i.e., "what other large pension funds are doing"), combined with market security weights. For the remainder of this article, we will refer to this allocation as the "Naive Policy Allocation." Comparing the return on this portfolio C1 with the return on T-bills reveals the reward received by the average fund for accepting risk.

Security Weights

	1: Market Security Weights	3: Actual Wts. of Securities Held from Day to Day
A: 100% in T-Bills	Minimum-Risk Portfolio	
C: Average Mix Held by Sponsors ("Naive Policy Allocation")	Average-Risk Portfolio	
Y: Sponsor's Customized Policy Mix	Policy Portfolio	Security-Allocated Portfolio
Z: Asset Mix Held from Day to Day	Timing-Allocated Portfolio	Actual Portfolio

Asset Allocations (vertical label on left)

Figure 19.2 Portfolios used in study

The sponsor's policy portfolio depends on the specific sponsor. Sponsors usually conduct periodic analyses of the characteristics of their pension assets and liabilities, as well as their own comfort levels (frequently called "risk tolerance" in the finance literature, although in practice psychological aspects of risk tend to be at least as important as financial aspects). As a result of these analyses, they adopt their own asset allocation policies, which may differ from the average-risk portfolio. Comparing the return on this portfolio Y1 to the return on the average-risk portfolio C1 reveals the impact of the sponsor's decision to depart from the implicit average risk tolerance of other sponsors.

Once this hierarchy of investment policy portfolios is established, one can proceed as follows.

- Ignore the existence of security weights 2. In effect, assume that sponsors invoke no deliberate policy tilts away from standard indexes for the relevant asset classes.
- For the impact of *market timing*, compare the returns on the timing-allocated portfolio (Z1) to the returns on the sponsor's policy portfolio (Y1), that is, market timing equals the impact (Z1 − Y1).
- For the impact of *security selection*, compare the returns on the security-allocated portfolio (Y3) with the returns on the policy portfolio (Y1). That is, security selection equals the impact (Y3 − Y1).
- The residual part of the actual return earned by each sponsor's fund is attributed to the *interaction* of market timing and security selection, as well as portfolio *activity*; all our hypothetical portfolios were rebalanced quarterly and remained unchanged throughout the quarter. Thus interaction plus activity equals the impact (Z3 − Y1 − timing − selection), which equals the impact (Z3 + Y1 − Z1 − Y3).

Table 19.1 Return variation explained

Decision level	Additional variation explained by this level	Cumulative variation explained through this level
Minimum risk	2.66%	2.66%
Naive policy allocation	94.35	97.01
Specific policy allocation	0.50	97.51
Market timing*	0.14	—
Security selection*	0.40	—
Interaction and activity*	1.95	—
Total	100.00%	100.00%

*The additional return variation explained by market timing, security selection and interaction and activity need not be sequentially cumulative. Therefore, rather than imply a specific order, they are left blank.

RETURN VOLATILITY

We examined the volatility of returns for seven Russell U.S. sponsors, using quarterly data over the 1985–88 period.[7] We regressed historical portfolio returns on five different portfolios — the naive alternatives A and C, each sponsor's policy portfolio, the timing-allocated portfolio and the security-allocated portfolio.[8] The results indicate the amount of the variability of each sponsor's returns explained by each decision level. The individual sponsors' squares (coefficients of determination) were then averaged over the seven sponsors.

For these seven sponsors over the four-year period, 97.5% of the variation in total plan returns was explained by their policy portfolios.[9] The diversified naive allocation (Alternative C: average large pension fund exposures to the asset classes) explained 97% of the variation in total plan returns. Table 19.1 gives the amount of the variation in plan returns explained by different decision levels.

Our results highlight the importance of the naive allocation. If T-bills, rather than a diversified mix, had been selected as the naive alternative, then the sponsor's choice of policy allocation would explain most of the variation in plan returns. The use of a diversified mix as the naive alternative makes the choice among different diversified mixes relatively unimportant; that choice explains only an additional 0.50% of return variation.

RETURN IMPACT OF DIFFERENT DECISIONS

We believe the most significant analysis concerns the potential impact of different types of decisions on returns themselves, rather than their variability. Table 19.2 shows the results of our return analysis.

The average quarterly return on T-bills over the period was 1.62 per cent.[10] By contrast, the Naive Policy Allocation would have resulted in an average quarterly return of 3.75%– 2.13% higher than the T-bill return. We interpret the 2.13% as the average quarterly reward over the period for the average pension fund's decision to take investment risk as a matter of policy. The reward, of course, is highly dependent on the time period under consideration. There must be periods when the reward is negative; that is the essence of risk.

The absolute size of each quarterly reward (or cost) is important. Sponsors will accept negative results if they expect that, in the long term, positive results will predominate.

Table 19.2 Quarterly return impacts of different types of decisions

Source of return	1985–1988 Average quarterly return*	1985–1988 Average quarterly contribution[†]	Potential quarterly impact as measured by average MAD
Minimum risk (T-bills)	1.62%	1.62%	—
Naive policy allocation	3.75	2.13	4.43%
Specific policy allocation			
(average of 7 sponsors)	4.24	0.49	0.79
Market timing			
(average of 7 sponsors)	—	(0.10)	0.57
Security selection			
(average of 7 sponsors)	—	(0.23)	0.85
Interaction and activity			
(average of 7 sponsors)	—	(0.05)	0.15
Quarterly total fund return			
(average of 7 sponsors)	3.86%	3.86%	5.63%

*All returns are before all fees and expenses.

[†]Returns and mean absolute deviations were computed for each sponsor and then averaged across sponsors.

The size of a decision's impact (regardless of sign) is an indication of its potential effect. It is certainly an *ex post* measure of its effect. We therefore measured the dispersions of the impacts around zero and calculated the average of the absolute values of the dispersions. This measure is the "mean absolute deviation" (MAD).[11]

For the Naive Policy Allocation, the potential impact on the fund's return, as measured by the MAD, amounted to 4.43% per quarter. The specific asset allocation policies adopted by the sponsors in the sample added, on average, 0.49% per quarter to the Naive Policy Allocation return; the policy portfolios earned an average quarterly return of 4.24%. The impact of a specific policy allocation relative to the Naive Policy Allocation was occasionally negative. The potential impact of the specific policy allocations, as measured by their average absolute size, was 0.79% per quarter.

The average quarterly return of the timing-allocated portfolios was 4.14%. That is, the average quarterly impact of market-timing decisions by sponsors was −0.10%. When the quarterly impacts were averaged in absolute terms (without regard to sign), the average was 0.57%. This is the potential quarterly impact of managers' market-timing decisions.

Security selection had an average impact of −0.23% per quarter, and a potential impact of 0.85% per quarter. Interaction and activity had an average impact of −0.05% per quarter and a potential impact of 0.15% per quarter.

FURTHER COMMENTS

Table 19.2 indicates that T-bills and the risk premium associated with the Naive Policy Allocation accounted for most of the return over the period studied. Market timing, security selection and the effect of interactions and activity all, on average, reduced returns. Specific asset allocation policy decisions added slightly to returns.

The relative magnitudes of the *potential impacts* are particularly interesting.

- The potential impact of the Naive Policy Allocation easily surpasses all other decisions.

Table 19.3 Extreme MAD results in study

Source of potential quarterly impact	Lowest quarterly MAD for any 1 sponsor	Average quarterly MAD over 7 sponsors	Highest quarterly MAD for any 1 sponsors
Specific policy allocation	0.51%	0.79%	1.53%
Market timing	0.23	0.57	0.73
Security selection	0.53	0.85	1.50
Interaction and activity	0.07	0.15	0.20

- The potential impact of interaction and activity is the smallest, when measured over one quarter.
- The potential impacts of specific policy allocation and of security selection are roughly equal in magnitude and somewhat greater than the potential impact of market timing.

The order of average magnitudes in Table 19.2 may not hold for every sponsor. Table 19.3 shows, for example, the highest and lowest potential impacts for different sponsors in the sample. One sponsor departed significantly from the Naive Policy Allocation — so much so that the mean potential impact of the specific policy allocation was 1.53% per quarter. Another sponsor departed relatively little from the Naive Policy Allocation; the mean potential impact of the difference was only 0.51% per quarter. Averaged over all seven sponsors, the mean potential quarterly impact of specific policy allocation was 0.79% per quarter, the same number shown in Table 19.2.

The potential impact of the specific policy allocation will be high for any sponsor whose attitude toward risk differs significantly from the attitude of the average sponsor. This is a decision only the sponsor can make. Similarly, the potential impacts of market timing and security selection will depend on the specific sponsor.

In our sample, the potential impacts of specific policy allocation and security selection are of roughly equal magnitude in all columns and larger than the potential impact of market timing. But there could conceivably be a sponsor with a specific policy allocation identical to the Naive Policy Allocation, which believes in holding indexed portfolios and adding value through market timing. For such a sponsor, the potential impacts of specific policy allocation and of security selection will be zero; market timing will produce the entire impact. This demonstrates the importance of each sponsor's deciding individually how much significance each type of decision should be given.

Finally, it is legitimate for the expected reward from a specific policy allocation to be negative for a sponsor that consciously decides to take less investment risk than the average sponsor. However, the expected reward from active management decisions should not be negative; if it is, the exposure to active management should be severely curtailed.

EXISTING LITERATURE

The Brinson, Hood and Beebower (BHB) study is the seminal work on performance attribution, and deservedly so.[12] Our study follows its methods to a large extent. But we made two conceptual changes.

First, in performance attribution, there is usually a base return (representing the naive portfolio) and a series of effects (representing the impacts of judgments). If the base return is itself added to one of the effects, it exaggerates the impact of the corresponding judgment. Essentially, this is equivalent to assuming that the naive portfolio always has a zero return. The naive portfolio thus implies no investment whatsoever; this is clearly unrealistic.

We were careful not to measure the impact of the sponsor's policy decision, in our numerical results, as the difference from a zero return. This reduces the explanatory power of the sponsor's policy decision as a source of return variability, relative to the results of BHB. The difference is small if the naive alternative is T-bills. The reduction is quite large if the naive alternative is a diversified portfolio.

Second, we asked ourselves what the naive alternative to a judgment on asset allocation policy would be. Experience with sponsors indicated that when they study the subject, they almost always consider the average mix held by other sponsors. Hence our decision to consider Naive Allocation C as the point of departure. The same experience underlies our concept of the policy allocation as itself representing a departure from a naive allocation, rather than from no investment whatsoever.

For most sponsors, the decision to depart from a risk-minimizing investment policy is likely to have a greater impact on total plan returns and return variability than any other single decision. Relative to a naive diversified mix, any specific asset allocation policy may have a sizable impact on total return, but nothing like the dominance frequently (and erroneously) attributed to it. Decisions regarding active management (market timing and security selection) can be as worthy of a sponsor's attention as the asset allocation decision.

ENDNOTES

1. See Sharpe, W.F. "Asset Allocation," in Maginn and Tuttle, eds., *Managing Investment Portfolios*, 2nd ed. (Boston: Warren, Gorham & Lamont, 1990), who accurately quotes the prevailing sentiment: "It is generally agreed by theoreticians and practitioners alike that the asset allocation decision is by far the most important one made by an investor." The definitive quantitative study on the subject is Brinson, G., Hood, L.R. and Beebower, G.L. "Determinants of Portfolio Performance," *Financial Analysts Journal*, July/August 1986.

2. Conventional models of economic equilibrium require that all markets clear so that there is no excess supply in any market. Thus the portfolio positions held in aggregate are the market with no ownable assets excluded. The market so defined represents a benchmark against which average performance can be measured. See, for example, Arrow, K.J. "The Role of Securities in the Optimal Allocation of Risk Bearing," *Review of Economic Studies* 31 (1963–64), pp. 91–96, or Radner, R. "Existence of Equilibrium of Plans, Prices, and Price Expectations in a Sequence of Markets," *Econometrica*, March 1972.

3. Actually, (Y2 − X2) is an equally valid measure of the impact of the sponsor's policy allocation. This illustrates the principle that there may not always be a unique "right" way to measure impacts, merely ways with different degrees of usefulness. In fact, however, Weights 2 are rarely found in practice, so (Y1 − X1) would usually be used.

4. While a discussion of the characteristics of pension liabilities and surplus is beyond the scope of this paper, an explanation is provided in Ezra, D.D. "Asset Allocation by Surplus Optimization," *Financial Analysts Journal*, January/February 1991.

5. See the 1989 *Money Market Directory for Pension Funds*, p. xvii (corporate pension funds with total assets exceeding $500 million). In different countries, of course, this allocation will be different, reflecting local preferences and opportunities.

6. A simple benchmark frequently quoted consists of 60% stocks and 40% bonds. Results using this allocation are virtually indistinguishable from the results using mix C.

7. This study is based on a small sample and a short period of time. Our purpose was to outline an approach rather than to produce definitive numerical results.

8. The asset class benchmarks were the Russell 3000 for U.S. equity; the MSCI EAFE Index for non-U.S. equity; the Shearson Lehman Hutton Aggregate Bond Index for U.S. fixed income; the Russell NCREIF Property Index (formerly FRC Property Index) for real estate; and the Salomon Brothers 3-Month Treasury Bill Index for cash. Sponsors' actual policy weights were used when available. For sponsors lacking policy portfolios or for periods prior to the adoption of a policy portfolio policy weights were inferred from the client's average actual allocations to managers for those periods. For these seven sponsors, two had policy portfolios for all quarters and two lacked any policy portfolios. The average length of time these sponsors had policy portfolios was 10 quarters. Thus, on average, the policy portfolios for the initial six quarters were inferred.

9. This result is reasonably close to the 93.6% calculated for a larger sample, and over a longer time, by Brinson, Hood and Beebower, "Determinants of Portfolio Performance," *op. cit.*

10. All quarterly return numbers can be annualized by taking the fourth power of the return relatives and subtracting one.

11. Had we used standard deviation instead, we would have measured the variation around the mean and accorded greater weight to extreme observations. We believe measuring the deviations from zero (MAD) provides a better sense of potential future outcomes and is therefore a good measure of the potential impact of different types of decisions.

12. Brinson, Hood and Beebower, "Determinants of Portfolio Performance," *op. cit.*

20

The Noise Trader
Approach to Finance

Andrei Shleifer and Lawrence H. Summers

If the efficient markets hypothesis was a publicly traded security, its price would be enormously volatile. Following Samuelson's (1965) proof that stock prices should follow a random walk if rational competitive investors require a fixed rate of return and Fama's (1965) demonstration that stock prices are indeed close to a random walk, stock in the efficient markets hypothesis rallied. Michael Jensen was able to write in 1978 that "the efficient markets hypothesis is the best established fact in all of social sciences."

Such strong statements portend reversals, the efficient markets hypothesis itself notwithstanding. Stock in the efficient markets hypothesis lost ground rapidly following the publication of Shiller's (1981) and Leroy and Porter's (1981) volatility tests, both of which found stock market volatility to be far greater than could be justified by changes in dividends. The stock snapped back following the papers of Kleidon (1986) and Marsh and Merton (1986) which challenged the statistical validity of volatility tests. A choppy period then ensued, where conflicting econometric studies induced few of the changes in opinion that are necessary to move prices. But the stock in the efficient markets hypothesis — at least as it has traditionally been formulated — crashed along with the rest of the market on October 19, 1987. Its recovery has been less dramatic than that of the rest of the market.

This paper reviews an alternative to the efficient markets approach that we and others have recently pursued. Our approach rests on two assumptions. First, some investors are not fully rational and their demand for risky assets is affected by their beliefs or sentiments that are not fully justified by fundamental news. Second, arbitrage — defined as trading by fully rational investors not subject to such sentiment — is risky and therefore limited. The two assumptions together imply that changes in investor sentiment are not fully countered by arbitrageurs and so affect security returns. We argue that this approach to financial markets is in many ways superior to the efficient markets paradigm.

Our case for the noise trader approach is threefold. First, theoretical models with limited arbitrage are both tractable and more plausible than models with perfect arbitrage. The

Reprinted from: Shleifer, A. and Summers, L.H. 1990: The Noise Trader Approach to Finance. *Journal of Economic Perspectives*, 4, Spring, 19–33.

efficient markets hypothesis obtains only as an extreme case of perfect riskless arbitrage that is unlikely to apply in practice. Second, the investor sentiment/limited arbitrage approach yields a more accurate description of financial markets than the efficient markets paradigm. The approach not only explains the available anomalies, but also readily explains broad features of financial markets such as trading volume and actual investment strategies. Third, and most importantly, this approach yields new and testable implications about asset prices, some of which have been proved to be consistent with the data. It is absolutely *not true* that introducing a degree of irrationality of *some* investors into models of financial markets "eliminates all discipline and can explain anything."

THE LIMITS OF ARBITRAGE

We think of the market as consisting of two types of investors: "arbitrageurs" — also called "smart money" and "rational speculators" — and other investors. Arbitrageurs are defined as investors who form fully rational expectations about security returns. In contrast, the opinions and trading patterns of other investors — also known as "noise traders" and "liquidity traders" — may be subject to systematic biases. In practice, the line between arbitrageurs and other investors may be blurred, but for our argument it helps to draw a sharp distinction between them, since the arbitrageurs do the work of bringing prices toward fundamentals.

Arbitrageurs play a central role in standard finance. They trade to ensure that if a security has a perfect substitute — a portfolio of other securities that yields the same returns — then the price of the security equals the price of that substitute portfolio. If the price of the security falls below that of the substitute portfolio, arbitrageurs sell the portfolio and buy the security until the prices are equalized, and vice versa if the price of a security rises above that of the substitute portfolio. When the substitute is indeed perfect, this arbitrage is riskless. As a result, arbitrageurs have perfectly elastic demand for the security at the price of its substitute portfolio. Arbitrage thus assures that relative prices of securities must be in line for there to be no riskless arbitrage opportunities. Such riskless arbitrage is very effective for derivative securities, such as futures and options, but also for individual stocks and bonds where reasonably close substitutes are usually available.

Although riskless arbitrage ensures that relative prices are in line, it does not help to pin down price levels of, say, stocks or bonds as a whole. These classes of securities do not have close substitute portfolios, and therefore if for some reason they are mispriced, there is no riskless hedge for the arbitrageur. For example, an arbitrageur who thinks that stocks are underpriced cannot buy stocks and sell the substitute portfolio, since such a portfolio does not exist. The arbitrageur can instead simply buy stocks in hopes of an above-normal return, but this arbitrage is no longer riskless. If the arbitrageur is risk-averse, his demand for underpriced stocks will be limited. With a finite number of arbitrageurs, their combined demand curve is no longer perfectly elastic.

Two types of risk limit arbitrage. The first is fundamental risk. Suppose that stocks are selling above the expected value of future dividends and an arbitrageur is selling them short. The arbitrageur then bears the risk that the realization of dividends — or of the news about dividends — is better than expected, in which case he loses on his trade. Selling "overvalued" stocks is risky because there is always a chance that the market will do very well. Fear of such a loss limits the arbitrageur's original position, and keeps his short-selling from driving prices all the way down to fundamentals.

The second source of risk that limits arbitrage comes from unpredictability of the future resale price (De Long, Shleifer, Summers and Waldmann, 1990a). Suppose again that stocks are overpriced and an arbitrageur is selling them short. As long as the arbitrageur is thinking of liquidating his position in the future, he must bear the risk that at that time stocks will be *even more* overpriced than they are today. If future mispricing is more extreme than when the arbitrage trade is put on, the arbitrageur suffers a loss on his position. Again, fear of this loss limits the size of the arbitrageur's initial position, and so keeps him from driving the price all the way down to fundamentals.

Clearly, this resale price risk depends on the arbitrageur having a finite horizon. If the arbitrageur's horizon is infinite, he simply sells the stock short and pays dividends on it in all the future periods, recognizing that the present value of those is lower than his proceeds from the short sale. But there are several reasons that it makes sense to assume that arbitrageurs have short horizons. Most importantly, arbitrageurs have to borrow cash or securities to implement their trades, and as a result must pay the lenders *per period* fees. These fees cumulate over the period that the position remains open, and can add up to large amounts for long term arbitrage. The structure of transaction costs thus induces a strong bias toward short horizons (Shleifer and Vishny, 1990). In addition, the performance of most money managers is evaluated at least once a year and usually once every few months, also limiting the horizon of arbitrage. As a result of these problems, resources dedicated to long-term arbitrage against fundamental mispricing are very scarce.

Japanese equities in the 1980s illustrate the limits of arbitrage. During this period, Japanese equities have sold at the price earning multiples of between 20 and 60 (French and Poterba, 1989), and have continued to climb. Expected growth rates of dividends and risk premia required to justify such multiples seem unrealistic. Nonetheless, an investor who believes that Japanese equities are overvalued and wants to sell them short, must confront two types of risk. First, what if Japan actually does perform so well that these prices are justified? Second, how much more out of line can prices get, and for how long, before Japanese equities return to more realistic prices? Any investor who sold Japanese stocks short in 1985, when the price earnings multiple was 30, would have lost his shirt as the multiples rose to 60 in 1986.

These arguments that risk makes arbitrage ineffective actually understate the limits of arbitrage. After all, they presume that the arbitrageur knows the fundamental value of the security. In fact, the arbitrageur might not exactly know what this value is, or be able to detect price changes that reflect deviations from fundamentals. In this case, arbitrage is even riskier than before. Summers (1986) shows that a time series of share prices which deviate from fundamentals in a highly persistent way looks a lot like a random walk. Arbitrageurs would have as hard a time as econometricians in detecting such a deviation, even if it were large. An arbitrageur is then handicapped by the difficulty of identifying the mispricing as well as by the risk of betting against it. Are economists certain that Japanese stocks are overpriced at a price earnings ratio of 50?

Substantial evidence shows that, contrary to the efficient markets hypothesis, arbitrage does not completely counter responses of prices to fluctuations in uninformed demand. Of course, identifying such fluctuations in demand is tricky, since price changes may reflect new market information which changes the equilibrium price at which arbitrageurs trade. Several recent studies do, however, avoid this objection by looking at responses of prices to changes in demand that do not plausibly reflect any new fundamental information because they have institutional or tax motives.

For example, Harris and Gurel (1986) and Shleifer (1986) examine stock price reactions to inclusions of new stocks into the Standard & Poor 500 stock index. Being added to the S&P 500 is not a plausible example of new information about the stock, since stocks are picked for their representativeness and not for performance potential. However, a stock added to the S&P 500 is subsequently acquired in large quantities by the so-called "index funds," whose holdings just represent the index. Both Harris and Gurel (1986) and Shleifer (1986) find that announcements of inclusions into the index are accompanied by share price increases of 2 to 3%. Moreover, the magnitude of these increases over time has risen, paralleling the growth of assets in index funds. Clearly, the arbitrage trade in which rational speculators sell the new stock and buy back close substitutes is not working here. And simply selling short the newly included stock on the theory that it is now overpriced must be too risky.

Further evidence on price pressure when no news is transmitted comes from Ritter's (1988) work on the January effect. The January effect is the name for the fact that small stocks have outperformed market indices by a significant percentage each January over the last 50 or so years. Ritter finds that small stocks are typically sold by individual investors in December — often to realize capital losses — and then bought back in January. These share shifts explain the January effect as long as arbitrage by institutions and market insiders is ineffective, since aggressive arbitrage should eliminate the price effects of temporary trading patterns by individual investors. Either risk or borrowing constraints keep arbitrageurs from eliminating the price consequences of year-end trading.

Less direct evidence also shows that news is not the only force driving asset prices, suggesting that arbitrage is not successful in eliminating the effects of uninformed trading on prices. For example, French and Roll (1986) look at a period when the U.S. stock market was closed on Wednesdays and find that the market is less volatile on these days than on Wednesdays when it is open. By focusing on Wednesdays, they control for the intensity of release of public information. This result may reflect incorporation of private information into prices during open hours, but it may also reflect the failure of arbitrage to accommodate intraday demand shifts. Roll (1988) demonstrates that most idiosyncratic price moves in individual stocks cannot be accounted for by public news. He finds that individual stocks exhibit significant price movements unrelated to the market on days when there are no public news about these stocks. A similar and more dramatic result is obtained for the aggregate stock market by Cutler, Poterba, and Summers (1989a), who find that the days of the largest aggregate market movements are not the days of most important fundamental news and vice versa. The common conclusion of these studies is that news alone does not move stock prices; uninformed changes in demand move them too.

INVESTOR SENTIMENT

Some shifts in investor demand for securities are completely rational. Such changes could reflect, for example, reactions to public announcements that affect future growth rate of dividends, risk, or risk aversion. Rational demand changes can also reflect adjustment to news conveyed through the trading process itself. Finally, rational demand changes can reflect tax trading or trading done for institutional reasons of the types discussed above.

But not all demand changes appear to be so rational; some seem to be a response to changes in expectations or sentiment that are not fully justified by information. Such changes can be a response to pseudo-signals that investors believe convey information about future returns but that would not convey such information in a fully rational model (Black, 1986). An example of such pseudo-signals is advice of brokers or financial gurus. We use the term "noise traders" to describe such investors, following Kyle (1985) and Black (1986). Changes in demand can also reflect investors' use of inflexible trading strategies or of "popular models" that Shiller (1990) describes. One such strategy is trend chasing. Although these changes in demand are unwarranted by fundamentals, they can be related to fundamentals, as in the case of overreaction to news.

These demand shifts will only matter if they are correlated across noise traders. If all investors trade randomly, their trades cancel out and there are no aggregate shifts in demand. Undoubtedly, some trading in the market brings together noise traders with different models who cancel each other out. However, many trading strategies based on pseudo-signals, noise, and popular models are correlated, leading to aggregate demand shifts. The reason for this is that judgment biases afflicting investors in processing information tend to be the same. Subjects in psychological experiments tend to make the same mistake; they do not make random mistakes.

Many of these persistent mistakes are relevant for financial markets. For example, experimental subjects tend to be overconfident (Alpert and Raiffa, 1982), which makes them take on more risk. Experimental subjects also tend to extrapolate past time series, which can lead them to chase trends (Andreassen and Kraus, 1988). Finally, in making inferences experimental subjects put too little weight on base rates and too much weight on new information (Tversky and Kahneman, 1982), which might lead them to overreact to news.

The experimental evidence on judgment biases is corroborated by survey and other evidence on how investors behave. For example, extrapolation is a key feature of the popular models discovered by the surveys Shiller (1990) describes. He finds that home buyers as well as investors in the crash of 1987 seem to extrapolate past price trends. Similar results have been found by Frankel and Froot (1986) in their analysis of exchange rate forecasts during the mid-1980s: over the short horizon, professional forecasters expect a price trend to continue even when they expect a long run reversion to fundamentals.

A look at how market participants behave provides perhaps the most convincing evidence that noise rather than information drives many of their decisions. Investors follow market gurus and forecasters, such as Joe Granville and "Wall Street Week." Charging bulls, Jimmy Connors and John Houseman all affect where and how people entrust their money. When Merrill Lynch changed from their charging bulls ad (filmed in Mexico) to a single bull ad ("a breed apart"), many more people chose to take their advice. Financial gurus that attract large followings never claim to have access to inside information. Rather, they insist that they are following reliable models for forecasting future returns. They "make money the old-fashioned way," which is apparently not just by reacting to changes in fundamental economic factors.

So-called "technical analysis" is another example of demand shifts without a fundamental rationalization. Technical analysis typically calls for buying more stocks when stocks have risen (broke through a barrier), and selling stocks when they fall through a floor. "Adam Smith" (1968) refers to the informal theorem of chartism that classifies phases of price movements in terms of categories — accumulation, distribution and liquidation. The suggested trading strategies then respond to the phase of the cycle the security is supposed to be in. These trading strategies are based on noise or "popular models" and not on information.

There can be little doubt that these sorts of factors influence demand for securities, but can they be big enough to make a difference? The standard economist's reason for doubting the size of these effects has been to posit that investors trading on noise might lose their money to arbitrageurs, leading to a diminution of their wealth and effect on demand (Friedman, 1953). Noise traders might also learn the error of their ways and reform into rational arbitrageurs.

However, the argument that noise traders lose money and eventually disappear is not self-evident. First, noise traders might be on average more aggressive than the arbitrageurs — either because they are overoptimistic or because they are overconfident — and so bear more risk. If risk-taking is rewarded in the market, noise traders can earn higher expected returns even despite buying high and selling low on average. The risk rewarded by the market need not even be fundamental; it can be the resale price risk arising from the unpredictability of future noise traders' opinions. With higher expected returns, noise traders as a group do not disappear from the market rapidly, if at all.

Of course, higher expected returns because of higher risk come together with a greater variance of returns. Noise traders might end up very rich with a trivial probability, and poor almost for sure. Almost for sure, then, they fail to affect demand in the long run. But in principle, either the expected return or the variance effect can dominate.

Learning and imitation may not adversely affect noise traders either. When noise traders earn high average returns, many other investors might imitate them, ignoring the fact that they took more risk and just got lucky. Such imitation brings more money to follow noise trader strategies. Noise traders themselves might become even more cocky, attributing their investment success to skill rather than luck. As noise traders who do well become more aggressive, their effect on demand increases.

The case against the importance of noise traders also ignores the fact that new investors enter the market all the time, and old investors who have lost money come back. These investors are subject to the same judgment biases as the current survivors in the market, and so add to the effect of judgment biases on demand.

These arguments suggest that the case for long run unimportance of noise traders is at best premature. In other words, shifts in the demand for stocks that do not depend on news or fundamental factors are likely to affect prices even in the long run.

EXPLAINING THE PUZZLES

When arbitrage is limited, and investor demand for securities responds to noise and to predictions of popular models, security prices move in response to these changes in demand as well as to changes in fundamentals. Arbitrageurs counter the shifts in demand prompted by changes in investor sentiment, but do not eliminate the effects of such shifts on the price completely.

In this market, prices vary more than is warranted by changes in fundamentals, since they respond to shifts in investor sentiment as well as to news (Shiller, 1981; 1984). Stock returns are predictably mean-reverting, meaning that high stock returns lead to lower expected stock returns. This prediction has in fact been documented for the United States as well as the foreign stock prices by Fama and French (1988) and Poterba and Summers (1988).

The effects of demand shifts on prices are larger when most investors follow the finance textbooks and passively hold the market portfolio. In this case, a switch in the sentiment of some investors is not countered by a change of position of all the market participants, but only of a few arbitrageurs. The smaller the risk bearing capacity of arbitrageurs, the bigger the effect of a sentiment shift on the price. A simple example highlights this point. Suppose that all investors are sure that the market is efficient and hold the market portfolio. Now suppose that one investor decides to hold additional shares of a particular security. Its price is driven to infinity.

This approach fits very neatly with the conventional nonacademic view of financial markets. On that view, the key to investment success is not just predicting future fundamentals, but also predicting the movement of other active investors. Market professionals spend considerable resources tracking price trends, volume, short interest, odd lot volume, investor sentiment indexes and numerous other gauges of demand for equities. Tracking these possible indicators of demand makes no sense if prices responded only to fundamental news and not to investor demand. They make perfect sense, in contrast, in a world where investor sentiment moves prices and so predicting changes in this sentiment pays. The prevalence of investment strategies based on indicators of demand in financial markets suggests the recognition by arbitrageurs of the role of demand.

Not only do arbitrageurs spend time and money to predict noise trader moves, they also make active attempts to take advantage of these moves. When noise traders are optimistic about particular securities, it pays arbitrageurs to create more of them. These securities might be mutual funds, new share issues, penny oil stocks, or junk bonds: anything that is overpriced at the moment. It also pays to carve up corporate cash flows in ways that make the securities with claims to these flows most attractive to investors. After all, the Modigliani-Miller theorem does not apply in a world where sentiment affects security prices and noise traders themselves do not see through the corporate veil. In such a world, securities that would otherwise be fundamentally perfect substitutes no longer are, and therefore arbitrage that undoes changes in corporate leverage is no longer riskless. Just as entrepreneurs spend resources to build casinos to take advantage of gamblers, arbitrageurs build investment banks and brokerage firms to predict and feed noise trader demand.

When they bet against noise traders, arbitrageurs begin to look like noise traders themselves. They pick stocks instead of diversifying, because that is what betting against noise traders requires. They time the market to take advantage of noise trader mood swings. If these swings are temporary, arbitrageurs who cannot predict noise trader moves simply follow contrarian strategies. It becomes hard to tell the noise traders from the arbitrageurs.

But saying that a market affected by investor sentiment looks realistic is hardly a rigorous test. To pursue this line of thought, we must derive and test implications that are not obvious and perhaps that are new. We consider first the implications of unpredictability or randomness of changes in investor sentiment. Second, we look at implications of strategies followed by investors who buy when prices rise and sell when prices fall, possibly because their expectations are simple extrapolations.

Implications of Unpredictability of Investor Sentiment

Even without taking a position on how investor sentiment moves, we can learn something from the observation that it moves in part unpredictably. Even if arbitrageurs know that noise traders are pessimistic today and hence will on average become less pessimistic in the future, they cannot be sure when this will happen. There is always a chance that noise traders become even more pessimistic first. This unpredictability contributes to resale price risk, since the resale price of an asset depends on the state of noise trader sentiment. If investor sentiment affects a broad range of assets in the same way, this risk from its unpredictability becomes systematic. Systematic risk has a price in equilibrium. Consequently, assets subject to whims of investor sentiment should yield higher average returns than similar assets not subject to such whims. Put differently, assets subject to unpredictable swings in investor sentiment must be underpriced in the market relative to their fundamental values.

De Long, Shleifer, Summers and Waldmann (1990a) describe two applications of this argument. First, stocks are probably subject to larger fluctuations of investor sentiment than bonds. In this case, equilibrium returns on stocks must be higher than warranted by their fundamentals — the latter being given by dividends and by covariation of dividends with consumption. In particular, the difference between average returns on stocks and on bonds — the risk premium — must be higher than is warranted by fundamentals. Such excess returns on stocks are in fact observed in the U.S. economy, and are known as the Mehra-Prescott (1985) puzzle. We can even reverse the argument to say that the high average risk premium is evidence of unpredictability of investor sentiment about stocks.

The second application we examined involves the pricing of closed-end mutual funds. These funds, like open-end funds, hold portfolios of other securities, but unlike open-end funds, have a fixed number of shares outstanding. As a result, an investor who wants to liquidate his holdings of a closed-end fund must sell his shares to other investors; he cannot just redeem his shares as with an open-end fund. Closed-end funds present one of the most interesting puzzles in finance, because their fundamental value — the value of the assets in their portfolios — is observed, and tends to be systematically higher than the price at which these funds trade. The pervasiveness of discounts on closed-end funds is a problem for the efficient markets hypothesis: in the one case where value is observed, it is not equal to the price.

De Long, Shleifer, Summers and Waldmann argue that investor sentiment about closed-end funds changes, and that this sentiment also affects other securities. When investors are bullish about closed-end funds, they drive up their prices relative to fundamental values, and discounts narrow or turn into premiums. When investors in contrast are bearish about closed-end funds, they drive down their prices and discounts widen. Any investor holding a closed-end fund bears two kinds of risk. The first is the risk from holding the fund's portfolio. The second is the resale price risk: at the time the investor needs to sell the fund the discount might widen. If investor sentiment about closed-end funds affects many other securities as well, bearing the resale price risk should be rewarded. That is, closed-end funds should on average sell at a discount. Put differently, the reason there are discounts *on average* is that discounts fluctuate, and investors require an extra return for bearing the risk of fluctuating discounts.

This theory explains why arbitrage does not effectively eliminate discounts on closed-end funds. An arbitrageur who buys a discounted fund and sells short its portfolio runs the risk that at the time he liquidates his position the discount widens and so his arbitrage results in a loss. An arbitrageur with an infinite horizon need not worry about this risk. But if the arbitrageur faces some probability of needing to liquidate his position in finite time, the risk from unpredictability of investor sentiment at the time he liquidates prevents him from aggressive betting that would eliminate discounts.

This theory of closed-end funds has a number of new empirical implications, investigated by Lee, Shleifer and Thaler (1989). First, it predicts that discounts on different closed-end funds fluctuate together, since they reflect changes in investor sentiment. This prediction is confirmed. Second, the theory predicts that new funds get started when investors are optimistic about funds, which is when old funds sell at a small discount or a premium. It is indeed the case that discounts on seasoned funds are much narrower in years when more new funds start. Perhaps most interestingly, the theory predicts that discounts on closed-end funds reflect the investor sentiment factor that also affects prices of other securities, which may have nothing to do with closed-end funds. Consistent with this prediction, Lee Shleifer and Thaler find that when discounts on closed-end funds narrow, small stock portfolios tend to do well. This suggests that discounts on closed-end funds reflect an individual investor sentiment that also affects returns on small stocks held largely by individuals. These findings bear on previously untested implications of the investor sentiment approach, and so dispel the notion that this approach puts no restrictions on the data.

Implications of Positive Feedback Trading

One of the strongest investor tendencies documented in both experimental and survey evidence is the tendency to extrapolate or to chase the trend. Trend chasers buy stocks after they rise and sell stocks after they fall: they follow positive feedback strategies. Other strategies that depend on extrapolative expectations are "stop loss" orders, which prescribe selling after a certain level of losses, regardless of future prospects, and portfolio insurance, which involves buying more stocks (to raise exposure to risk) when prices rise and selling stocks (to cut exposure to risk) when prices fall.

When some investors follow positive feedback strategies — buy when prices rise and sell when prices fall — it need no longer be optimal for arbitrageurs to counter shifts in the demand of these investors. Instead, it may pay arbitrageurs to jump on the bandwagon themselves. Arbitrageurs then optimally buy the stocks that positive feedback investors get interested in when their prices rise. When price increases feed the buying of other investors, arbitrageurs sell out near the top and take their profits. The effect of arbitrage is to stimulate the interest of other investors and so to contribute to the movement of prices away from fundamentals. Although eventually arbitrageurs sell out and help prices return to fundamentals, in the short run they feed the bubble rather than help it to dissolve (De Long, Shleifer, Summers and Waldmann, 1990b).

Some speculators indeed believe that jumping on the bandwagon with the noise traders is the way to beat them. George Soros, the successful investor and author of *Alchemy of Finance* (1987), describes his strategy during the conglomerate boom in the 1960s and the Real Estate Investment Trust boom in the 1970s precisely in these terms. The key to success, says Soros, was not to counter the irrational wave of enthusiasm about conglomerates, but rather to ride this wave for awhile and sell out much later. Rational buying by speculators of already overvalued conglomerate stocks brought further buying by the noise traders, and enabled the speculators to make more money selling out at the top. Soros is not alone in trading this way; John Train (1987), in his book on successful U.S. investors, calls the strategy of one of his protagonists "Pumping Up the Tulips."

Trading between rational arbitrageurs and positive feedback traders gives rise to bubble-like price patterns. Positive feedback trading reinforced by arbitrageurs' jumping on the bandwagon leads to a positive autocorrelation of returns at short horizons. Eventual return of prices to fundamentals, accelerated as well by arbitrage, entails a negative autocorrelation of returns at longer horizons. Since news results in price changes that are reinforced by positive feedback trading, stock prices overreact to news.

These predictions have been documented in a number of empirical studies. Cutler, Poterba and Summers (1989b) find evidence of a positive correlation of returns at horizons of a few weeks or months and a negative one at horizons of a few years for several stock, bond, foreign exchange, and gold markets. They report the average first order monthly serial correlation of more than 0.07 for 13 stock markets, and positive in every case. Evidence on overreaction of stock prices to changes in fundamentals is presented for individual securities by DeBondt and Thaler (1985, 1987) and Lehmann (1990), and for the aggregate stock market by Campbell and Kyle (1988). The last paper, for example, decomposes stock returns into the fundamental and noise components and finds that the two are strongly positively correlated, meaning that prices overreact to news.

The finding of a positive serial correlation at short horizons implies that a substantial number of positive feedback traders must be present in the market, and that arbitrage does not eliminate the effects of their trades on prices.

The presence of positive feedback traders in financial markets also makes it easier to interpret historical episodes, such as the sharp market increase and the crash of 1987. According to standard finance, the market crash of October 1987 reflected either a large increase in risk premiums because the economy became a lot riskier, or a large decrease in expected future growth rate of dividends. These theories have the obvious problem that they do not explain what news prompted a 22% devaluation of the American corporate sector on October 19. Another problem is that there is no evidence that risk increased tremendously — volatility indeed jumped up but came back rapidly as it usually does — or that expected dividend growth has been revised sharply down. An examination of OECD long-term forecasts shows no downward revision in forecasts of long run growth rates after the crash, even though the crash itself could have adversely affected expectations. Perhaps most strikingly, Seyhun (1989) finds that corporate insiders bought stocks in record numbers during and after the crash, and moreover bought more of the stocks that later had a greater rebound. Insiders did not share the view that growth of dividends will slow or that risk will increase and *they were right*! Fully rational theories have a clear problem with the crash.

The crash is much easier to understand in a market with significant positive feedback trading. Positive feedback trading can rationalize the dramatic price increase during 1987, as more and more investors chase the trend. Positive feedback trading, exacerbated by possible front-running by investment banks, can also explain the depth of the crash once it has started. One still needs a theory of what broke the market on October 19, but the bad news during the previous week might have initiated the process, albeit with some lag. A full theory of the crash remains to be developed: prospects for such a theory look a lot brighter, however, if it incorporates positive feedback trading.

CONCLUSION

This paper has described an alternative to the efficient markets paradigm that stresses the roles of investor sentiment and limited arbitrage in determining asset prices. We have shown that the assumption of limited arbitrage is more general and plausible as a description of markets for risky assets than the assumption of perfect arbitrage which market efficiency relies on. With limited arbitrage, movements in investor sentiment are an important determinant of prices. We have also shown that this approach yields a large number of implications about the behavior of both investors and speculative prices which are consistent with the evidence. Perhaps most importantly, we have shown that this approach yields some new testable implications about security returns. Some of these implications, such as the ones on closed-end funds, have been tested and confirmed. It is thus not the case that the investor sentiment approach deprives finance of the discipline to which it is accustomed.

Assuming that our approach has some explanatory power and therefore intellectual merit, what are its implications for welfare and for policy? There are two normative issues relevant to the evaluation of noise trading. First, should something be done to prevent noise traders from suffering from their errors? Second, do noise traders impose a cost on the rest of market participants and, if so, how can this cost be reduced? Although answers to these questions ultimately turn on open empirical problems, both theory and empirical work permit some tentative remarks.

Investors who trade on noise or on popular models are worse off than they would be if their expectations were rational (if welfare is computed with respect to the correct distribution of returns). They need not lose money on average, as the simplest logic might suggest. But even if they earn higher average returns, it is because they bear more risk than they think. And even if they get rich over time, it is only because they underestimate the risk and get lucky. If investors had perfect foresight and rationality, they would know that noise trading always hurts them.

Whether the government should do anything to save noise traders from themselves depends on the social welfare function. People are allowed to participate in state lotteries, to lose fortunes in casinos, or to bet on the racetrack even though benevolent observers know that they are being taken to the cleaners. The case for making it costly for investors to bet on the stock market to protect them from their own utility losses is in principle identical to the case for prohibiting casinos, horse races, and state lotteries.

Noise trading, however, can also affect the welfare of the rest of the community. One effect is to benefit arbitrageurs who take advantage of noise traders. These benefits accrue both to those who bet against noise traders and those who feed their demand by providing financial services. Interestingly, the combined receipts of the NYSE member firms amounted to a sixth of the total U.S. corporate income in 1987 (Summers and Summers, 1989). Of course, some of these benefits to arbitrageurs are also a social *opportunity* cost as valuable human and other resources are allocated to separating noise traders from their money.

But noise trading also has a private cost, as it makes returns on assets more risky, and so can reduce physical investment. The overall impact of noise trading on the rest of the market participants and society can be negative (De Long, Shleifer, Summers and Waldmann, 1989). Some have also argued that noise trading in foreign exchange markets distorts the flow of goods between countries and leads to inefficient choice of production. Others have argued that noise trading forces managers to focus on the short term, and to bias the choice of investments against long-term projects. The policy reaction to noise trading can be dangerous as well; for example, sharp contractions of money supply by the Federal Reserve have often been justified as responses to excessive speculation. In this case, the consequences of such policies are more costly than the speculation itself.

Awareness of these costs of noise trading raises the question of what (if anything) should be done about it. Some businessmen and economists have proposed short term capital gains taxes as a way to cripple noise trading, while others, including Summers and Summers (1989) have advocated transaction taxes to the same end. It is not our goal in this paper to evaluate these proposals. We note, however, that one benefit of the research on markets where investor sentiment matters is to allow a more systematic evaluation of these proposals.

REFERENCES

Alpert, Mark and Raiffa, Howard. "A Progress Report on the Training of Probability Assessors." In Kahneman, Daniel, Paul Slovie and Amos Tversky, eds., *Judgment Under Uncertainty: Heuristics and Biases*, Cambridge: Cambridge University Press, 1982.

Andreassen, Paul and Stephen Kraus. "Judgmental Prediction by Extrapolation," Harvard University Mimeo, 1988.

Black, Fischer. "Noise," *Journal of Finance*, July 1986, **41**, 529–543.

Campbell, John, Y. and Albert S. Kyle. "Smart Money, Noise Trading, and Stock Price Behavior," Princeton University Mimeo, 1988.

Cutler, David, M., James M. Poterba and Lawrence H. Summers. "What Moves Stock Prices?" *The Journal of Portfolio Management*, Spring 1989a, **15**, 4–12.

Cutler, David, M., James M. Poterba and Lawrence H. Summers, "Speculative Dynamics," Harvard University Mimeo, 1989b.

De Long, J., Bradford, Andrei Shleifer, Lawrence H. Summers and Robert J. Waldmann. "The Size and Incidence of the Losses From Noise Trading," *Journal of Finance*, July 1989, **44**, 681–696.

De Long, J., Bradford, Andrei Shleifer, Lawrence H. Summers and Robert, J. Waldmann. "Noise Trader Risk in Financial Markets," *Journal of Political Economy*, 1990a.

De Long, J., Bradford, Andrei Schleifer, Lawrence H. Summers and Robert J. Waldmann. "Positive Feedback Investment Strategies and Destabilizing Rational Speculation," *Journal of Finance*, 1990b.

DeBondt, Werner, F.M. and Richard H. Thaler. "Does the Stock Market Overreact?" *Journal of Finance*, July 1985, **40**, 793–805.

DeBondt, Werner, F.M. and Richard H. Thaler. "Further Evidence on Investor Overreaction and Stock Market Seasonality," *Journal of Finance*, July 1987, **42**, 557–581.

Fama, Eugene, F. "The Behavior of Stock Market Prices," *Journal of Business*, 1965, **38**, 34–105.

Fama, Eugene, F. and Kenneth R. French. "Permanent and Temporary Components of Stock Market Prices," *Journal of Political Economy*, April 1988, **96**, 246–273.

Frankel, Jeffrey, A. and Kenneth A. Froot. "The Dollar as an Irrational Speculative Bubble: The Tale of Fundamentalists and Chartists," *Marcus Wallenburg Papers on International Finance*, 1986, **1**, 27–55.

French, Kenneth, R. and James M. Poterba. "Are Japanese Share Prices Too High?" University of Chicago Mimeo, 1989.

French, Kenneth, R. and Richard Roll. "Stock Return Variances: the Arrival of Information and the Reaction of Traders," *Journal of Financial Economics*, 1986, **17**, 5–26.

Friedman, Milton. "The Case for Flexible Exchange Rates," *Essays in Positive Economics*, Chicago: University of Chicago Press, 1953.

Harris, Lawrence and Eitan Gurel. "Price and Volume Effects Associated with Changes in the S&P 500: New Evidence for the Existence of Price Pressure," *Journal of Finance*, September 1986, **41**, 851–860.

Jensen, Michael, C. "Some Anomalous Evidence Regarding Market Efficiency," *Journal of Financial Economics*, June/September 1978, **6**, 95–102.

Kleidon, Allan, W. "Anomalies in Financial Economics," *Journal of Business*, 1986, **59**, Supplement; S285–316.

Kyle, Albert, S. "Continuous Auctions and Insider Trading," *Econometrica*, November 1985, 1315–1336.

Lee, Charles, Andrei Shleifer and Richard H. Thaler. "Investor Sentiment and the Closed End Funds Puzzle," Cornell University Mimeo, 1989.

Lehmann, Bruce. "Fads, Martingales, and Market Efficiency," *Quarterly Journal of Economics*, 1990.

Leroy, Stephen, F. and Richard D. Porter. "Stock Price Volatility: Tests Based on Implied Variance Bounds," *Econometrica*, 1981, **49**, 97–113.

Marsh, Terry, A. and Robert C. Merton. "Dividend Variability and Variance Bounds Tests for the Rationality of Stock Market Prices," *American Economic Review*, June 1986, **76**, 483–498.

Mehra, Rajneesh and Edward C. Prescott. "The Equity Premium: a Puzzle," *Journal of Monetary Economics*, February 1985, **15**, 145–162.

Poterba, James, M. and Lawrence H. Summers. "Mean Reversion in Stock Prices: Evidence and Implications," *Journal of Financial Economics*, February 1988, **22**, 27–59.

Rinter, Jay. "The Buying and Selling Behavior of Individual Investors at the Turn of the Year, *Journal of Finance*, July 1988, **43**, 701–716.

Roll, Richard, R. "R-squared," *Journal of Finance*, July 1988, **43**, 541–566.

Samuelson, Paul, A. "Proof that Properly Anticipated Prices Fluctuate Randomly," *Industrial Management Review*, Spring 1965, **6**, 11–19.

Seyhun, Neijat. "Fads or Fundamentals: Some Lessons from Insiders' Response to the Crash of 1987," University of Michigan Mimco, 1989.

Shiller, Robert, J. "Do Stock Prices Move Too Much to be Justified by Subsequent Changes in Dividends?" *American Economic Review*, June 1981, **71**, 421–436.

Shiller, Robert, J. "Stock Prices and Social Dynamics," *Brooking Papers on Economic Activity*, Fall 1984, 457–498.

Shiller, Robert, J. "Speculative Prices and Popular Models," *?Journal of Economic Perspectives*, Spring 1990, 4, 55–65.

Shleifer, Andrei. "Do Demand Curves for Stocks Slope Down?" *Journal of Finance*, July 1986, **41**, 579–590.

Shleifer, Andrei and Robert W. Vishny. "Equilibrium Short Horizons of Investors and Firms," *American Economic Review Papers and Proceedings*, 1990.

"Smith, Adam". *The Money Game*, New York: Random House, 1968.

Soros, George. *The Alchemy of Finance*, New York: Simon and Schuster, 1987.

Summers, Lawrence, H. "Does the Stock Market Rationally Reflect Fundamental Values?" *Journal of Finance*, July 1986, 591–601.

Summers, Lawrence, H. and Victoria P. Summers. "When Financial Markets Work too Well: A Cautious Case for the Securities Transaction Tax," Harvard University Mimeo, 1989.

Train, John. *The Money Masters*, New York: Harper and Row, 1987.

Tversky, Amos and Daniel Kahneman. "Evidential Impact of Base Rates". In Kahneman, Daniel, Paul Slovic and Amos Tversky, eds., *Judgment Under Uncertainty: Heuristics and Biases*. Cambridge: Cambridge University Press, 1982.

21

The Stock Market Crash of October 1987

G. William Schwert

On 19 October 1987, the Standard & Poor's composite portfolio fell from 282.70 to 224.84 (20.4%) and the Dow Jones Industrial Average fell from 2246 to 1738 (23%). Table 21.1 shows that this is the largest daily percentage drop in the history of major United States stock market indices from February 1885 through October 1991. Most of the other dates on this list come from the 1929–37 period called the Great Depression, with a few dates associated with major events. For example, 14 and 21 May 1940 were days when news about the German invasion of France affected stock prices. On 14 March 1907, a financial panic affected the illiquidity of major New York banks (see Schwert 1989, 1990 and Wilson, Sylla and Jones 1988 for detailed comparisons of the 1987 Crash with prior crashes).

What caused prices to drop so drastically on 19 October and how did this crash differ from previous experiences? These questions will puzzle financial economists for many years to come. This essay will not presume to answer either of them fully, but it will review the evidence that relates to the prominent proposed explanations for the October 1987 Crash.

WHAT HAPPENED?

Figure 21.1 shows the Standard & Poor's Composite Index and the Dow Jones Industrial Average from 1 September through 30 November 1987. Two things are clear from this plot. First, both indices dropped precipitously on 19 October following declines in the prior two weeks. Second, stock prices fluctuated much more following the crash than before it. Indeed, Table 21.1 shows that the ninth largest one day percentage decline in stock prices occurred on 26 October 1987. Also, the seventh largest one day percentage *increase* in stock prices occurred on 21 October 1987 (9.1%). There is much evidence that the volatility of stock returns was unusually high during and after the crash (Schwert 1990). Despite this

Reprinted from: Schwert, G.W. 1992: Stock Market Crash of October 1987. In: Newman, P. Milgate, M. and Eatwell, J. eds. *The New Palgrave Dictionary on Money and Finance*. London: Macmillan, Vol. 3, 577–582.

Table 21.1 The 25 largest daily percentage stock market crashes, 1885–1991

Rank	Date	Percentage crash
1	19 October 1987	−20.39
2	28 October 1929	−12.34
3	29 October 1929	−10.16
4	6 November 1929	−9.92
5	18 October 1937	−9.27
6	20 July 1933	−8.88
7	21 July 1933	−8.70
8	20 December 1895	−8.52
9	26 October 1987	−8.28
10	5 October 1932	−8.20
11	12 August 1932	−8.02
12	31 May 1932	−7.84
13	26 July 1934	−7.83
14	14 March 1907	−7.59
15	14 May 1940	−7.47
16	26 July 1893	−7.39
17	24 September 1931	−7.29
18	12 September 1932	−7.18
19	9 May 1901	−7.02
20	15 June 1933	−6.97
21	16 October 1933	−6.78
22	8 January 1988	−6.76
23	3 September 1946	−6.73
24	28 May 1962	−6.68
25	21 May 1940	−6.64

Note: Based on the Dow Jones Industrial and Railroad Indices for 1885–1927, the Standard & Poor's Composite Index for 1928–62 and 1989–91, and the CRSP value-weighted index of New York Stock Exchange and American Stock Exchange stocks for 1962–89, all including dividends.

volatility, the indices were about at the same level on 30 November as they were at the close of trading on 19 October.

Because stock prices dropped so dramatically, and then fluctuated for several weeks, people became concerned about the health of financial markets in the United States and around the world. Many groups studied the events of 19 October to diagnose the cause of the sudden drop in prices. Most notable among these studies was the *Brady Commission Report* (Presidential Task Force on Market Mechanisms 1988). Despite the intense study this crash evoked, there has been no consensus on the causes and consequences of the crash.

What facts must be explained if one is to understand the 1987 Crash? First, prices of common stocks fell about 20% on most of the stock markets around the world (see Roll 1988). In some cases, such as Hong Kong, trading was halted for as long as a week, but when trading resumed, prices were at least 20% lower than their level on 16 October. Second, after falling on 19 October, there was not a general tendency for prices to rebound upwards. Thus, the crash had a permanent effect on stock prices. Finally, there was no accompanying economic or political crisis that could explain the sudden drop in stock prices throughout the world.

305

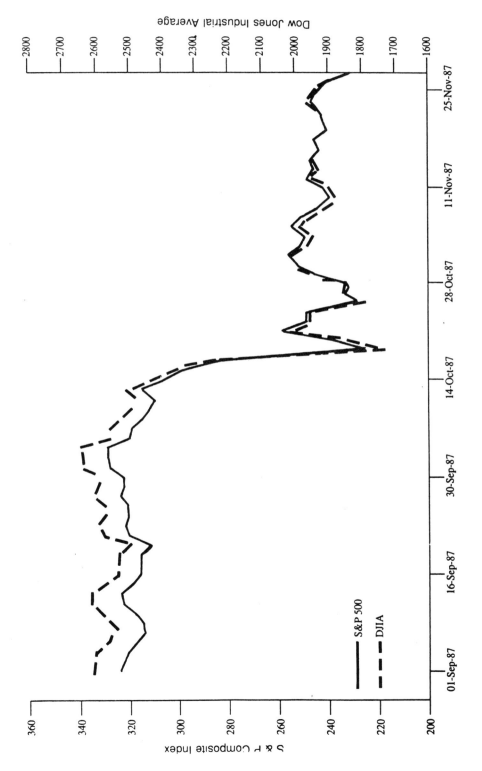

Figure 21.1 Standard & Poor's 500 and Dow Jones Industrial Average around October 1987 crash

WHAT CAUSED THE CRASH?

Many suspects have been rounded up, but there is not enough evidence to convict any of them of the crime.

Programme Trading

There was suspicion in the popular press that various strategies involving common stocks with options or futures contracts on stock indices (called 'programme trading') led to an unusual level of selling volume on 19 October. 19 October had the largest share trading volume in the history of the New York Stock Exchange (more than 600 million shares), but programme trading did not account for an unusually high proportion of the trading activity. Moreover, stock prices fell in markets around the world, irrespective of whether options or futures contracts on stock portfolios were traded on the underlying stocks (Roll 1988).

Many different trading methods are included in the term programme trading. 'Index arbitrage' involves buying (selling) futures contracts on stock indices and selling (buying) the underlying portfolio of stocks when the spread between the prices of these assets differs by more than transaction costs plus the differential yields on these investments. Such trading causes the prices of the futures and stock markets to move together.

'Portfolio insurance' is a method of reducing the risk of a stock portfolio by buying a put option on the portfolio, or by selling futures contracts on the portfolio. Among programme trading strategies, portfolio insurance is the one that might lead to sell orders triggered by a drop in prices. Thus, the drop in stock prices in the two weeks before and early on the morning of 19 October might have created some orders to sell stock or futures contracts on stock indices. There is little evidence, however, that such trades had much to do with the large volume or drop in prices on 19 October (Rubinstein 1988).

It is important to realize that programme trading can be the fastest way to execute many trades, since the computerized system used to execute trades is much faster (and cheaper) than an equivalent number of individual orders run through the specialist system on the floor of the New York Stock Exchange. Thus, even a large number of programme trades does not mean that the buy or sell decisions are made by a mechanical computer programme, which is the fear often expressed in the popular financial press.

A fact that has been studied intensively is that the futures price for the S&P 500 index fell much faster and further on 19 October than did the index, and it rebounded on the morning of 20 October (Blume, MacKinlay and Terker 1989; Furbush 1989; Harris 1989; Tosini 1988). One interpretation of this evidence is that futures prices overreacted. An alternate view, supported by the analysis of individual stock prices on the New York Stock Exchange, is that the trading mechanism on the futures exchanges responded more quickly to information on those days, while stock trading was bogged down. From this perspective, it was the inability of index arbitrage traders to execute trades in individual stocks that caused the index and the futures prices to diverge (Kleidon 1990). Thus, stock prices lagged the futures market during the hectic trading on 19–20 October due to the more cumbersome trading mechanism for trading stocks.

Illiquidity

Most people agree that the trading mechanisms in financial markets were not prepared to handle such a large flow of sell orders. Trading in many large New York Stock Exchange-listed stocks did not begin until late in the morning of 19 October because the specialists who were trying to organize trading could not find enough buyers to meet the demands of sellers at prices that were close to the levels present when trading ended on Friday 16 October. Thus, trading was halted in many common stocks.

This lack of *liquidity* may have had an important effect on the size of the drop in prices. Amihud, Mendelson and Wood (1990) argue that traders who thought they faced liquid markets in stocks learned on 19 October that they had overestimated the liquidity of the New York Stock Exchange. Since liquidity is a valuable commodity, traders reduced their valuations of the stocks that they now understood were not as liquid as they had previously thought. This may explain why the drop in prices was quick and permanent.

While the events of mid-October 1987 clearly brought bad news to stockholders about the liquidity of stock, option and futures markets, this cannot explain what caused people to decide simultaneously to start selling stocks. A trite answer is that many people decided that stock prices were too high, but it is not easy to explain what new information became available in mid-October that was not available before that time.

Trade and Budget Deficits

One economic factor that was discussed frequently in the financial press around October 1987 was the United States' trade deficit. Apparently, there was fear that continuing large deficits would cause the value of U.S. securities to fall compared with foreign securities. Figure 21.2 shows the quarterly seasonally adjusted U.S. trade deficit from 1960–90. The largest deficit occurred in the third quarter of 1987, ending in September. Information about this was announced on 14 October 1987.

While the coincidence of timing is interesting, it is hard to understand why the trade deficit would trigger a crash in the U.S. stock market. As seen in Figure 21.2, the trade deficit had been increasing steadily since late 1982 and the stock market had been rising during most of this period. Indeed, one might be tempted to conclude that stock prices fell in October 1987 in anticipation of the reversal of the trade deficit pattern that started in 1988. Foreign trade accounting requires that a merchandise deficit has to be offset by a capital flow surplus; that is, more capital was entering the U.S. than was leaving. Lowering the trade deficit is equivalent to lowering the capital surplus. Perhaps the prospect of lower rates of capital inflows contributed to a downward revaluation in U.S. stock prices.

The problem with arguments like this, however, is that it cannot explain why stock prices fell throughout the world by similar amounts. Presumably if unexpected changes in the trade deficit (or capital surplus) were bad news for one country, it would be good news for its trading partners.

There was also concern about the U.S. budget deficit, shown as seasonally adjusted annual rates in Figure 21.2. The budget deficit peaked in mid-1986 and was much smaller in September 1987 than in the previous year. As with the trade deficit, even if it is possible to tell a coherent story about why budget deficits should have a predictable effect on the value of corporate stock, it is hard to imagine what *new* information became available to investors in mid-October 1987 that would lead to an immediate 20% reduction in stock values.

Tax Legislation

Another event that may have contributed to the crash was the introduction of the Rostenkowski Tax Bill to the House Ways and Means Committee on 14 October. That bill would have eliminated the tax benefits of corporate debt used in takeovers and imposed severe

308

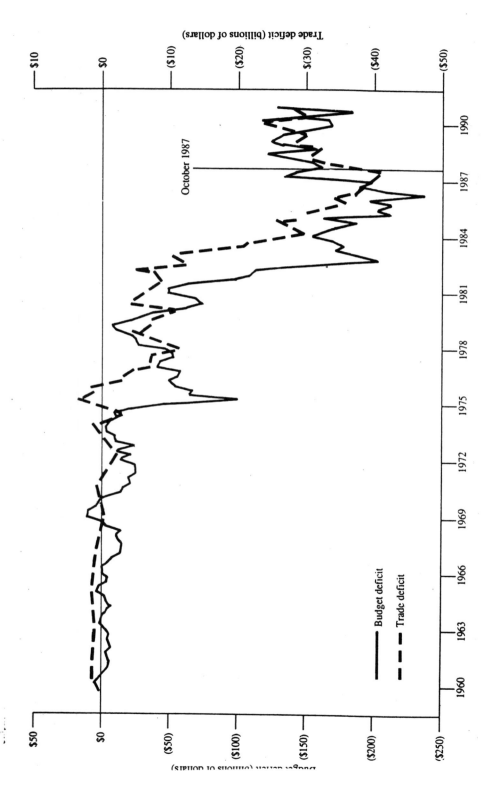

Figure 21.2 U.S. budget and trade deficits (quarterly, seasonally adjusted)

taxes on 'greenmail payments' received by large blockholders who sold stock back to the issuing corporation. The proposed legislation would have severely limited the merger and acquisition activity that had contributed to a large part of the increase in stock values during the 1980s. If incumbent managers would be sheltered from hostile takeover attempts in the future, the 'corporate control premium' would be removed from the prices of stocks that were potential targets.

Mitchell and Netter (1989) show that prices of stocks that were considered active targets fell substantially between 14 and 16 October. These were some of the first stocks to fall in value as large blocks of target stocks were sold.

Again, however, it is hard to explain how the House tax bill could have caused the crash, since it was not obvious that the legislation would be passed and implemented (in fact, it never progressed out of the Committee). Moreover, prices fell across a wide variety of stocks in the U.S. and in countries throughout the world. It is hard to imagine stock prices falling in London or Tokyo because of a tax bill aimed to limit hostile takeovers in the U.S.

Overvaluation

With hindsight, most analysts agree that stock prices were too high in September 1987. Figure 21.3 shows the Price/Earnings (P/E) and Price/Dividend (P/D) ratios for the Standard & Poor's composite portfolio from 1926–91. Both ratios had risen rapidly during 1987 as stock prices rose faster than earnings or dividends, so by October they were higher than they had been since the early 1970s. Because of the October 1987 Crash, the P/E and P/D ratios returned to their levels at the end of 1986.

Is it obvious that stock prices were too high in September 1987? As shown in Figure 21.3, these ratios were approaching historically high levels. Similar behaviour occurred before the October 1929 Crash. On the other hand, similar P/E and P/D values had been seen for most of the 1960–72 period. Thus, while there is evidence that stock prices reached high values compared with earnings or dividends in September 1987, this had not triggered crashes every time, or even most times, that it had happened in the past (see Bierman 1991 for an interesting analysis of stock market valuation before the October 1929 stock market crash).

Bates (1991) makes the interesting observation that prices of put and call options on the Standard & Poor's 500 futures contract implied fear of a crash from October 1986 to February 1987 and from June to August 1987, but not immediately before the 19 October Crash. In particular, out-of-the-money put options were overvalued compared with out-of-the-money call options during these periods. Immediately following the crash, options prices again implied an unusual fear of further crashes (which did not happen).

Volatility

Another explanation for the large drop in prices on 19 October is that risk had increased, so risk-averse investors required large expected returns to compensate them for bearing more risk. The obvious way to increase future expected returns is to reduce the current price of the asset.

As mentioned above, there is much evidence from stock and options markets that volatility of market returns increased substantially during and after the crash (e.g., Bates 1991; Franks and Schwartz 1988; Grant 1990; Schwert 1990). The rise in volatility was contemporaneous with the fall in prices, so it is hard to assign a causal role to volatility.

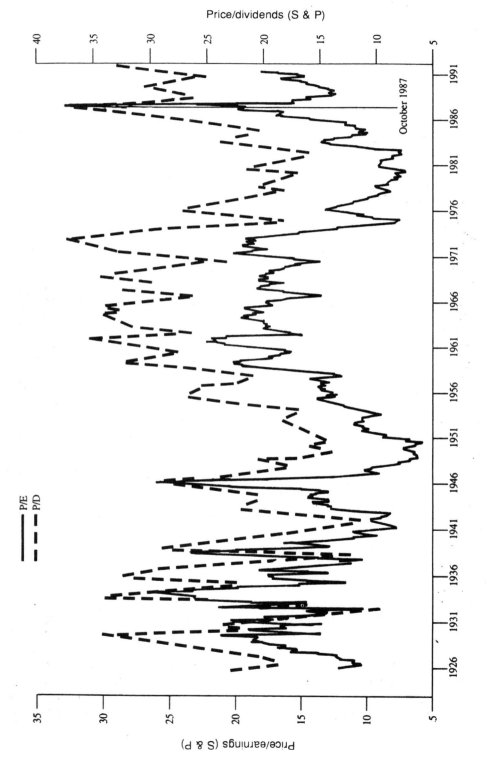

Figure 21.3 Stock market valuation measures (*P/E* and *P/D*)

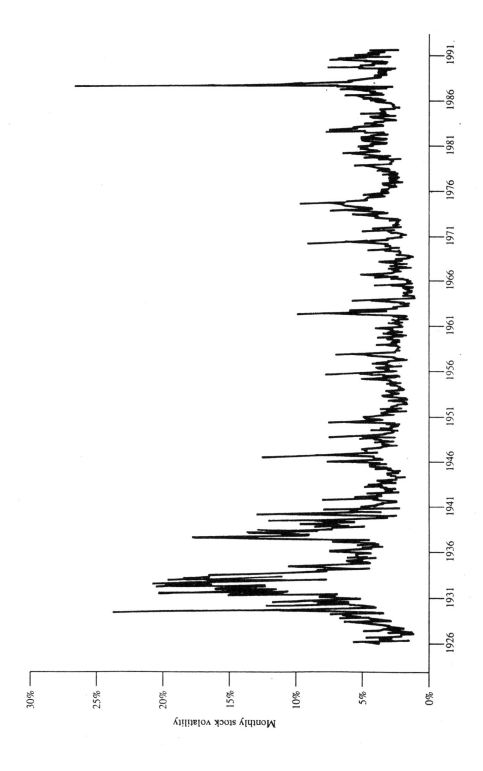

Figure 21.4 Monthly return volatility of the Standard & Poor's Composite portfolio

Moreover, as seen in Figure 21.4, stock volatility returned to pre-crash levels early in 1988, and stock prices did not immediately rebound to their pre-crash levels.

Figure 21.4 shows the standard deviation of daily stock returns within each month from January 1926 to September 1991, expressed as a monthly percent return. As with many prior crashes, such as those of 1929, 1937 and 1973–4, volatility increased during and after the fall in stock prices. What is unusual about the 1987 Crash is the size of volatility in October and November 1987, and the speed with which it returned to normal levels.

WHAT FOLLOWED THE CRASH?

Schwert (1989) shows that most previous crashes in the U.S. from 1857 to 1937 accompanied liquidity crises in the banking system. Indeed, Friedman and Schwartz (1963) and, more recently, Bierman (1991) attribute much of the cause of the 1929 stock market crash to the credit-tightening activities of the Federal Reserve Board in the U.S. (although this raises the question of why stock markets around the world also crashed at that time). In many cases, crashes preceded recessions or depressions.

None of these things happened following the October 1987 Crash. There was no recession within the next two years, there was no immediate concern about the solvency of the financial system. Indeed, markets for most other goods and services that were not directly linked to stock markets were unaffected by the crash. Barro (1990) relates real GNP and investment to past stock returns, then predicts these economic variables following the 1929 and 1987 stock market crashes. His model underpredicts the extent of the Great Depression following the 1929 Crash, but it predicts slow or negative economic growth in 1988, which was actually a year of strong real growth.

Why was the rest of the economy insulated from this stock market crash more than with previous crashes? There was much discussion in the financial press that central bankers, such as the U.S. Federal Reserve Board, responded wisely in signalling a willingness to provide credit to financial institutions that may have suffered liquidity problems due to the rapid change in stock values. In the U.S., many corporations immediately announced programmes to repurchase their own shares, showing that they felt that stock prices had fallen unnecessarily. Perhaps most important, stock prices did not fall after October 1987. In 1929, the initial crash was followed by a long sequence of further price declines as news about the economy grew continually worse. In 1987, the subsequent economic news was good, and stock prices rose to reflect that news (by mid-1991, the Dow Jones Industrial Average had passed the 3000 level, up 72% from its close of 1738 on 19 October 1987). From this perspective, the puzzle is why stock prices fell so much and so fast in mid-October, since subsequent economic news was not negative (although it was obviously worse than the market had been expecting in the first half of 1987).

CONCLUSIONS

Clearly the 19 October 1987 Crash had a large effect on securities markets. Prices fell by unprecedented amounts in a short period. Volatility of returns also reached unprecedented levels. Trading halts created by the inability of extant trading mechanisms to cope with the flood of sell orders caused many traders to revise their beliefs about the liquidity of organized securities markets.

Unlike most prior crashes, there was not a major economic downturn following October 1987. Also, there was not a liquidity crisis in the banking system or a subsequent recession such as occurred in prior crashes.

The causes of the crash remain uncertain. Among the consequences are a much increased interest by academics, regulators and participants in the market microstructure of securities markets.

REFERENCES

Amihud, Y., Mendelson, H. and Wood, R.A. 1990. Liquidity and the 1987 stock market crash. *Journal of Portfolio Management* **16(3)**: 65–9.

Barro, R.J. 1990. The stock market and investment. *Review of Financial Studies* **3**: 115–31.

Bates, D.S. 1991. The crash of '87: was it expected? The evidence from options markets. *Journal of Finance* **46**: 1009–44.

Bierman, H. 1991. *The Great Myths of 1929 and the Lessons to be Learned*. New York: Greenwood.

Blume, M.E., MacKinlay, A.C. and Terker, B. 1989. Order imbalances and stock price movements on October 19 and 20, 1987. *Journal of Finance* **44**: 827–48.

Franks, J.R. and Schwartz, E.S. 1988. The stochastic behaviour of market variance implied in the prices of index options: evidence on leverage, volume and other effects. Working paper no. 10–88, Anderson Graduate School of Management, University of California at Los Angeles.

Friedman, M. and Schwartz, A.J. 1963. *A Monetary History of the United States*, 1867–1960. Princeton: Princeton University Press.

Furbush, D. 1989. Program trading and price movement: evidence from the October 1987 market crash. *Financial Management* **18(3)**: 68–83.

Grant, J.L. 1990. Stock return volatility during the crash of 1987. *Journal of Portfolio Management* **16(2)**: 69–71.

Harris, L. 1989. The October 1987 S&P 500 stock-futures basis. *Journal of Finance* **44**: 77–100.

Kleidon, A.W. 1990. Arbitrage, nontrading, and stale prices: October 1987. Manuscript, Stanford University Graduate School of Business.

Mitchell, M.L. and Netter, J.M. 1989. Triggering the 1987 stock market crash: antitakeover provisions in the proposed House Ways and Means tax bill. *Journal of Financial Economics* **24**: 37–68.

Presidential Task Force on Market Mechanisms. 1988. *Report of the Presidential Task Force on Market Mechanisms*. Washington DC: U.S. Government Printing Office.

Roll, R. 1988. The international crash of October 1987. *Financial Analysts Journal* **44(5)**: 19–35.

Rubinstein, M. 1988. Portfolio insurance and the market crash. *Financial Analysts Journal* **44(1)**: 38–47.

Schwert, G.W. 1989. Business cycles, financial crises and stock volatility. *Carnegie-Rochester Conference Series on Public Policy* **31**: 83–125.

Schwert, G.W. 1990. Stock volatility and the crash of '87. *Review of Financial Studies* **3**: 77–102.

Tosini, P.A. 1988. Stock index futures and stock market activity in October 1987. *Financial Analysts Journal* **44(1)**: 28–37.

Wilson, J.W., Sylla, R. and Jones, C.P. 1988. Financial market volatility and panics before 1914. Working paper, Department of Economics and Business, North Carolina State University.

22
Volatility in the U.S. and Japanese Stock Markets
Robert Shiller

[...] Let me start by reviewing the evidence on the speculative nature of stock price movements. Let's go back to October 19, 1987. Between 1:15 and 4:00 that afternoon, the Dow Jones Average fell $16\frac{1}{2}\%$. As far as I know, nobody has produced a plausible economic or fundamentals-based explanation for this price movement. The only real news was the stock market crash itself; there doesn't seem to have been anything else going on.

It's true that some people have cited the tax law changes, proposed on the 14th of October, that would have discouraged takeovers. And it's a plausible enough theory that if a tax law discourages takeovers, it could significantly reduce values. In fact, there's a rather convincing paper by Mark Mitchell and Jeff Netter that produced evidence of an impact of these tax announcements on stock prices. But that impact occurred *five days before the crash*! My understanding of efficient markets theory is that the market responds *immediately* to economic news; it doesn't wait five days. Even if there are decision lags, even if people need some time to think over what this news from the House Ways and Means Committee really means, there's still no plausible reason why all investors should later reach a decision all at the same time.

The mini-crash of October 13, 1989 was different. In that case, it's very clear that the triggering event was the news of the collapse of the UAL deal — news that came just minutes before the stock market began to plunge. But, my problem with this case is that the market reaction seems disproportionate to the new information; the news just doesn't seem to be of any consequence. After all, it was news about a collapsed deal for a company whose value represents less than $\frac{1}{2}\%$ of the whole market.

But let's get back to October 1987. Merton Miller earlier argued [at the conference this paper is taken from] that, with securities of long duration like common stocks, even modest changes in expected dividend growth and discount rates could lead to significant changes in value. He was using the Gordon dividend discount model, which says that stock price (V) equals the current dividend (D) divided by the discount rate (r) minus the dividend

Reprinted by permission of Stern Stewart & Co. from: Shiller, R. 1992: Talk given at "Volatility in U.S. and Japanese Stock Markets: A Symposium", published in *The Continental Bank Journal of Applied Corporate Finance*, 5, Spring, 4–35.

growth rate (g). In equation form, $V = D/(r - g)$. In his numerical example, Professor Miller showed that just by raising r and lowering g by half a percent each, you could reduce investor's estimate of the value of the firm by 25%.

Well, there's no evidence that there was any adjustment of either "r" or "g" at the time of the stock market crash of '87. In fact, there were surveys which asked about both of those variables (although maybe not in just the right terms). In September of 1987, Richard Hoey of Drexel asked his sample of institutional investors to project their expected real bond yield; and they gave him an average number of 4%. When he asked them again two months later—that is, shortly after the crash—that expected yield had fallen to 3.7%. So there's no evidence of an increase of discount rates before and after the crash.

Moreover, Blue Chip Economic Indicators had done a survey of their 51 respondents for the first three days of October 1987, asking them to predict pre-tax profits in current dollars. In the beginning of October of 1987, these people predicted a 7.1% growth rate over the period 1988 to 1992, and 7.3% growth from 1993 to 1997. In the next survey of the same group in March of 1988, the respondents predicted a 7.0% growth rate from 1990 to 1994, and 7.5% growth from 1995 to 1999.

So there's no evidence of any change in those expectations. And it thus seems pretty clear that, during the Crash of '87, investors were responding primarily to developments in the market itself—that is, to the sharp decline in prices. It was a sort of vicious circle, with people watching prices go down deciding to sell their shares before prices dropped any further. And if that was indeed the case, then I question how we can still cling to the basic notion that markets are basically efficient.

One reaction of economists has been to dismiss the crash as an aberration. It's just one observation, one data point; and if there are such aberrations, they are rare. But I find this argument unconvincing. I think the crash is symptomatic of a larger problem, because I think that most price movements of any size are unrelated to news about fundamentals. The only reason we single out some event like the crash of '87 is that it serves as a kind of event study. For those of us skeptical about the efficiency of markets, we demand to see some plausible explanation why prices could fall by over 20% in one day.

Now, an alternative approach to explaining the crash is to argue that price movements themselves revealed important information about the market itself. For example, some studies by economists—notably, those by Bulow and Kemperer, Gennotte and Leland and Jacelyn, Kleidon and Pfleiderer—have suggested that the sudden price declines showed that there was much less liquidity in the market than investors had supposed. And viewed in this way, investors could have sharply and suddenly raised their required rates of return, thus causing prices to plummet. So, even though there was no news about fundamentals, investors learned from the abrupt decline in prices that they had overestimated the liquidity of the market—that is, the ability of investors to sell without lowering the price. And this may in turn have been the result of excessive, and mistaken, reliance by investors on various forms of "portfolio insurance," which were supposed to protect them from precipitous declines.

At any rate, I think these kinds of explanation are the way you have to go to come up with a satisfactory explanation of the crash that is consistent with market efficiency. Unfortunately, however, there's no evidence that supports that theory, or at least none that I'm aware of. There's no evidence that liquidity became abruptly lower in 1987.

The most straightforward explanation, then I think, is one that is *inconsistent* with market efficiency—namely, a speculative bubble. People were selling, in short, simply because they thought other people were going to sell.

As far as I am able to determine, I am the only person anywhere who did a questionnaire survey after the crash of '87 asking people what was on their minds on the day of the crash. Now, this may be an unreliable surveying technique, but I simply asked people what was on their mind. During the week of the '87 crash, I sent out questionnaires to 2,000 individual investors and 1,000 institutional investors, and got back a total of about 1,000 responses.

Besides asking a number of specific questions, I also asked the investors to write down their own theory of the crash. And although their interpretations were not very impressive or coherent, their response to a follow-up question was interesting. That is, when I asked them whether their own theory was "more about fundamentals, such as profits or interest rates, or more about market psychology," two-thirds of the U.S. respondents picked market psychology, and only one third chose fundamentals.

I later attempted the same experiment in Japan — with the help of Fumiko Kon-Ya of the Japan Securities Research Institute and Yoshiro Tsutsui of Osaka University. We sent out questionnaires to Japanese institutional investors asking for their views about the causes of the U.S. crash of '87. Three quarters of them thought the crash was due to market psychology, and only one quarter due to fundamentals such as profits or interest rates.

In exploring investor views of the mini-crash of October 13, 1989, I did things a bit differently. Rather than mail questionnaires, in order to get to respondents while their memories were still fresh, William Feltus and I did a survey by phone. (Unfortunately, the event came on a Friday, so we had to wait until Monday to make the calls.) And we asked investors the following question: "Which of the following statements better represents the view you held last Friday: (1) the news of the collapse of the UAL deal, because of its implications for future takeovers, is a sensible reason for the drop in stock prices; or (2) the UAL news of Friday afternoon should be viewed as a focal point, or attention-grabber, which in turn prompted investors to express their doubts about the stock market." In response, 62% picked the latter explanation, while only 38% described the UAL news as a sensible reason.

We also asked this follow-up question: "Did you hear about the UAL news before you heard about the market drop on Friday afternoon? Or did you hear about the UAL news later, as an explanation for the drop?" And 40% responded that they heard it before the drop, 60% said after. The fact that as many as 60% of these market professionals heard about the UAL deal only after the drop suggests that it's difficult to infer causality from the UAL news alone.

Now, let's turn to Japan and the stock market drop in the Nikkei.

Critics of our surveys about the U.S. crashes objected to the fact that we hadn't done any precrash surveys. So, anticipating the possibility of a crash in Tokyo, Tsutsui, Kon-Ya and I started doing surveys at six-month intervals beginning around June of 1989. We asked both Japanese and U.S. investors for their expectations over various horizons for both the Nikkei and the Dow. We asked both groups to predict both indexes. And there was a very striking difference — in fact, an incredible spread — between Japanese and U.S. investors in their predictions for the Nikkei over a one-year horizon. For example, if Japanese investors said they expected the Nikkei to go up by up 10% in the next year, U.S. investors typically said they expected it to go down by 10% — and roughly this 20% differential was present throughout the entire series of surveys leading up to the decline of the Nikkei in 1990.

Unfortunately, the drop in the Tokyo stock exchange was not a one-day event as it proved to be in the U.S. And though I don't claim to understand what happened, let me give you one result from our surveys that suggests an important role for investor speculation. We asked Japanese investors whether they thought they were in the market for the short term or the long haul. In fact, we worded the question as follows: "Although I expect a substantial drop in stock prices in Japan ultimately, I advise being relatively heavily invested in stocks for the time being, because I think that prices are likely to rise for a while." I think we can all agree that, to the extent investors endorse that statement, they are speculating.

Well, according to our first surveys conducted in mid-'89, 40% of Japanese investors said yes to that question. At the beginning of '91, after the market had fallen some 40% from its high, only 10% of Japanese investors still agreed with that same statement. So this suggests to me that there was a major speculative component underlying the large fall in the Nikkei. And I don't think it serves any purpose to try to ignore it. . . .

——— 23 ———
Were Japanese Stock Prices Too High?

Kenneth R. French and James M. Poterba

1. INTRODUCTION

Between 1984 and 1989, the Nikkei Index of Japanese stock prices rose at an average annual rate of 27.5%, and its price–earnings ratio increased from 37.9 to 70.9. These dramatic revisions in share prices and price–earnings ratios led many analysts to conclude that Japanese stocks were overpriced. For example, foreign investors were net sellers of Japanese shares in each of the last five years of the 1980s. The equally dramatic 39% decline in the Nikkei in 1990, coupled with a drop in its price–earnings ratio to 58.2, provide at least superficial support for those who viewed the high prices as a 'bubble'.

In this paper, we ask whether Japanese prices were, in fact, irrationally high in the 1980s, or whether their rapid increase and sharp decline can be explained by changing expectations about growth opportunities and changes in required rates of return. In some sense, these questions are unanswerable; any time series of prices could be justified by an appropriate set of investor expectations. Although these expectations are unobservable, we search for evidence of *changes* in such expectations, particularly coincident with share price increases or declines. We also examine the extent to which accounting conventions and tax rules can explain the high Japanese price–earnings ratios in the second half of the 1980s.

The paper is divided into five sections. Section 2 presents a stylized overview of the U.S. and Japanese equity markets. It reports the price–earnings and dividend–price ratios in both countries, and documents the relative importance of intercorporate share ownership in the two markets.

The third section explores the role of accounting and tax-rule differences in creating differences between the reported price–earnings ratios of Japanese and U.S. companies. We show that although several factors make the reported price–earnings ratios of Japanese firms systematically higher than those of their U.S. counterparts, they account for neither the increase in Japanese P/E ratios in the mid-1980s, nor the decline in 1990.

Reprinted from: French, K.R. and Poterba, J.M. 1991: Were Japanese Stock Prices Too High? *Journal of Financial Economics*, 29, 337–363.

Section 4 examines differences in required after-tax returns and expected growth rates in the two countries. We first calibrate the changes in discount factors and growth expectations that would be needed to explain the rise and decline of Japanese share values. We then consider various proxies for actual changes in required returns and growth expectations. We find that rather extreme assumptions about changes in growth or inflationary expectations would be needed to explain the post-1985 increase in Japanese share prices. The market decline in 1990, however, is easier to rationalize, since there was a coincident and significant increase in Japanese interest rates.

Finally, a brief concluding section considers the role of land-price appreciation in 'explaining' share-price gyrations.

2. OVERVIEW OF JAPANESE AND U.S. EQUITY MARKETS

The relative importance of the Japanese and U.S. equity markets shifted dramatically during the 1970s and 1980s, the result of rapid growth in Japanese share prices and depreciation of the dollar. This section provides background information on these markets.

2.1. Market size

The widely cited data from Morgan Stanley–Capital International (MSCI) *Perspectives* and others suggest that the Japanese equity market was 36% larger than the U.S. market at the end of 1989. However, these data provide a misleading measure of relative market capitalization for two reasons. First, the U.S. data include only shares listed on the New York Stock Exchange (NYSE), so they capture only about 85% of the market value of listed U.S. shares.[1] A second and more important problem is that the reported market values are not adjusted for intercorporate share ownership, which causes double-counting of corporate shares. As McDonald (1989) illustrates using a set of representative Japanese firms, such cross-ownership is much more prevalent in Japan than in the United States. Thus, the size of the Japanese equity market is significantly overstated relative to the U.S. market.

Consider the two all-equity firms in Figure 23.1. Initially, each firm has assets worth $100, there is no intercorporate ownership, and the total value of traded equity is $200. Suppose firm A now issues $50 in new shares and uses the proceeds to purchase one-half of the equity in firm B. As the second panel of Figure 23.1 illustrates, this transaction increases the market value of A to $150 ($100 in physical assets and $50 in shares of B), without affecting the market value of B. Although the value of the underlying productive assets remains unchanged at $200, the intercorporate purchase of stock raises the *apparent* value of the market to $250.

The apparent market value overstates the value of the firms' underlying assets because half of B's assets are included in the equity of both firm A and firm B. One can eliminate this double-counting and get an accurate estimate of the underlying asset value by measuring only the value of equity held outside the corporate sector. In our example, the public holds $150 of A and $50 of B, so the value of shares held outside the corporate sector is $200, the value of the underlying assets. More generally, the value of the equity held outside the corporate sector is

$$V_{\text{Outside}} = (1 - s) * V_{\text{Total}}, \tag{1}$$

where s is the fraction of the stock held by firms and V_{total} is the total value of equity, measured in the conventional way as the sum of each firm's shares outstanding times its market price.

Panel A: No Cross-Holdings			
Firm A		**Firm B**	
Assets	Liabilities	Assets	Liabilities
Physical Assets: 100	Common Equity: 100	Physical Assets: 100	Common Equity: 100
Total Assets: 100	Total Liabilities: 100	Total Assets: 100	Total Liabilities: 100

Panel B: 25% Cross-Holdings			
Firm A		**Firm B**	
Assets	Liabilities	Assets	Liabilities
Physical Assets: 100 Investments (Firm B): 50	Common Equity: 150	Physical Assets: 100	Common Equity: 100
Total Assets: 150	Total Liabilities: 150	Total Assets: 100	Total Liabilities: 100

Figure 23.1 The effect of intercorporate shareholdings on apparent market value

Table 23.1 Ownership of common stock, Japan (1989) and the United States (1987)[a]

Ownership group	Japan	U.S.
Individuals	19.9%	48.1%
Nonfinancial corporations	29.0%	14.1%
Foreigners	4.3%	6.6%
Securities companies	2.3%	0.4%
Government	0.4%	6.6%
Banks	21.3%	0.3%
Insurance companies	16.7%	23.9%
Other	6.1%	0.0%

[a]*Source*: Tokyo Stock Exchange, *1990 Fact Book*: Federal Reserve Board, *Flow of Funds* (1987) with adjustments by the authors. We use lagged U.S. data because we need tax return information. For the U.S., mutual funds are included in individual holdings. Insurance-company holdings are the sum of life, property & casualty, and pension-fund assets. The weights for the U.S. differ from the equity ownership weights in *Flow of Funds* for two reasons. First, intercorporate shareholdings are 'netted out' of the flow of funds, so nonfinancial firms appear with no equity holdings except a small stake in mutual funds. Following Tri (1971), we use IRS data on the ratio of dividends paid by U.S. corporations to domestic dividends received by U.S. corporations to estimate intercorporate holdings. Second, the flow of funds data on equity include stock in closely held corporations, worth $600 billion in 1987. We exclude this component and assume that all closely held corporations are owned directly by individuals.

Table 23.1 reports data on the aggregate ownership of traded shares in the U.S. and Japan. In the U.S., individuals hold about half of the outstanding equity, either directly or through mutual funds. Intercorporate equity holdings account for only one seventh of total equity. This fraction excludes holdings by defined-benefit pension plans, which are arguably assets of the shareholders. Including these plan holdings as corporate cross-holdings would raise the U.S. intercorporate ownership to over 20%. We do not make this correction, however, in part because of difficulties in making the analogous correction for Japanese firms. Insurance companies, with holdings for both insurance operations and pension plans, own 23.9% of the U.S. market. Slightly more than 6% of the U.S. equity is held by foreign investors and a similar fraction is held by state and local government pension funds.

Corporations of various kinds hold nearly two-thirds of the equity in Japan. These holdings include nonfinancial corporations (29%), bank (21%), and insurance companies (17%). Direct individual holdings account for only one fifth of the market value of the Tokyo Stock Exchange (TSE). Moreover, the fraction of the Japanese market held by individuals has declined through time, from nearly 60% in the early 1950s to only 20% at the end of 1989.

Table 23.2 presents a detailed example of cross-ownership, the case of Toyota Motor Company. At the end of 1988, Toyota owned more than 40% of four other firms on the TSE First Section, and at least 5% of 22 other companies. Most of these firms are Toyota suppliers. In turn, several banks owned nearly 30% of Toyota's stock. For many other firms, especially those that, unlike Toyota, are part of loosely affiliated corporate groups,

Table 23.2 Equity held by Toyota Motor Company, 1988[a]

Company name	Toyota ownership share	Net income (¥ mil)
Kanto Auto Works	49.0%	2,500
Toyota Auto Body	41.7%*	2,300
Chiyoda Fire & Marine Insurance	41.4%	6,100
Toyoda Gosei (steering wheels & hoses)	40.0%	2,400
Kyowa Leather	32.4%*	1,600
Tokai Rika (switches and seat belts)	27.8%	1,500
Toyota Automatic Loom Works	24.9%	10,100
Toyoda Machine Works	24.7%	1,600
Toyota Tsusho (trading)	23.2%*	5,400
Nippondenso (auto electronics)	22.5%*	28,000
Koyo Seiko (bearings)	22.3%	3,300
Aichi Steel	21.8%	3,150
Aisin Seiki (auto parts)	21.3%*	7,500
Chuo Spring	20.5%	1,070
Koito Manufacturing (auto lights)	19.8%	2,900
Daihatsu	15.0%	4,000
Akebono Brake	15.0%	1,250
Futaba Industrial (mufflers)	14.3%	2,350
Shiroki (auto interiors)	11.6%	1,000
Hino Motors (trucks)	11.0%	4,300
Toyoda Spinning & Weaving	8.9%*	400
Kayaba Industrial (hydraulics)	8.4%	1,200
Nippon Piston Ring	8.6%	580
Ichikoh Industries (auto lights)	7.5%	1,400
Nachi-Fujikoshi (bearings)	5.9%	1,100
Toyo Radiator	5.8%	1,100
Toyota Motors is owned by:		
Sanwa Bank	4.9%	
Tokai Bank	4.9%	
Mitsui Bank	4.9%	
Toyota Automatic Loom	4.4%	
Nippon Life	3.7%	
Long-Term Credit Bank	3.2%	
Daiwa Bank	2.5%	

[a]*Source*: Authors' tabulations from *Japan Company Handbook*, Spring 1988. Starred entries indicate substantial ownership by other firms affiliated with Toyota Motors, usually Toyota Automatic Loom.

Table 23.3 Market value of Japanese and U.S. equity markets, 1970–1990[a]

Year	Total market value (billion dollars)		Adjusted market value (billion dollars)		Percentage of total world equities	
	Japan	U.S.	Japan	U.S.	Japan	U.S.
1970	42.5	636.4	25.2	671.8	2.8	74.1
1971	67.2	741.8	39.8	784.7	3.7	72.3
1972	152.3	871.5	81.6	890.3	6.2	68.1
1973	128.6	721.0	69.2	668.2	6.6	63.7
1974	115.8	510.4	63.7	436.1	8.1	55.8
1975	135.1	683.6	75.9	660.8	6.9	60.3
1976	179.3	856.4	100.0	786.2	8.2	64.4
1977	205.1	793.9	116.1	742.1	9.3	59.5
1978	327.3	816.7	183.0	787.6	12.6	54.0
1979	274.0	960.2	153.2	923.5	9.1	55.1
1980	356.6	1240.0	200.8	1179.9	9.5	56.0
1981	402.7	1145.4	225.1	1106.7	11.2	54.9
1982	410.2	1308.3	232.2	1281.5	10.8	59.7
1983	519.2	1578.3	286.6	1506.3	11.2	59.0
1984	616.8	1593.2	327.5	1477.6	12.9	58.2
1985	909.1	1955.4	480.0	1845.7	13.7	52.7
1986	1746.2	2203.2	883.6	2187.2	18.5	45.9
1987	2978.2	2216.1	1489.1	2206.9	26.5	39.3
1988	3840.2	2480.9	1908.6	2433.9	28.7	36.4
1989	4102.1	3027.1	2038.7	2989.6	25.4	37.2
1990	3265.7	3044.4	1623.0	3006.7	20.8	38.6

[a]The 1970–1989 estimates are for the end of December. The 1990 estimate is for the end of June. The total equity values for 1970–1988 are from Tokyo Stock Exchange, *Monthly Statistical Report*, and NYSE, NASDAQ, and SEC sources described in the text. The total values for 1989 and 1990 are from Morgan Stanley–Capital International. The adjusted market values exclude intercorporate equity holdings. Our estimates of each country's weight in the world equity portfolio ignore all cross-holdings except those in Japan and the U.S.

the degree of intercorporate holding is substantially greater. [Hoshi, Kashyap and Scharfstein (1991) discuss the linkages among firms in these groups and how they affect their financial behavior.]

Table 23.3 presents both unadjusted and corrected measures of stock-market value in the U.S. and Japan. The adjustments for intercorporate holdings have a surprising effect. Although the unadjusted figures suggest that the Japanese market was larger than the U.S. market at the end of each year between 1986 and 1989, the market value of the outside equity in Japan is never more than 80% of the value of outside equity in the United States. With these adjusted estimates, Japan accounted for only 25.4% of the world equity portfolio at the end of 1989, while the U.S. accounted for 37.2%. The gap between the U.S. and Japanese market shares became even larger during the first half of 1990 as a result of dollar appreciation and the decline in Japanese share prices. At the end of June 1990, the last date for which we have complete data on the value of world equity markets, the Japanese share of the world equity portfolio was 20.8%, compared with a U.S. share of 38.6%.

2.2. Valuation, trading, and leverage trends

Table 23.4 presents price–earnings ratios and dividend–price ratios for the Nomura Research Institute 350, a broad index of nonfinancial Japanese firms, and for the S&P Industrial index

Table 23.4 Price–earnings ratios, dividend–price ratios (in %), foreign equity holdings (in %), and debt–equity ratios, Japan and the United States, 1970–1990[a]

Year	Price–earnings		Dividend–price		Foreign holdings		Debt–equity	
	Japan	U.S.	Japan	U.S.	Japan	U.S.	Japan	U.S.
1970	9.0	18.6	4.57%	3.3%	4.9%	3.7%	1.63	0.54
1971	13.5	18.7	3.57%	2.9%	5.2%	3.6%	2.13	0.50
1972	23.3	19.3	1.81%	2.5%	4.5%	4.0%	2.23	0.48
1973	13.9	12.3	2.62%	3.4%	4.0%	4.3%	1.38	0.69
1974	16.5	7.9	2.93%	5.0%	3.2%	4.5%	1.44	1.04
1975	25.2	11.8	2.20%	3.8%	3.6%	4.8%	2.13	0.78
1976	22.0	11.2	1.93%	3.7%	3.7%	4.7%	1.88	0.72
1977	19.3	9.1	2.11%	5.0%	3.0%	4.6%	1.82	0.85
1978	21.5	8.2	1.71%	5.2%	2.7%	4.7%	1.62	0.91
1979	16.6	7.5	1.78%	5.3%	3.0%	4.6%	1.78	0.83
1980	17.9	9.6	1.72%	4.4%	5.8%	4.8%	1.59	0.64
1981	24.9	8.2	1.46%	5.3%	6.4%	5.1%	1.64	0.76
1982	23.7	11.9	1.39%	4.6%	7.6%	5.3%	1.44	0.70
1983	29.4	12.6	1.15%	3.7%	8.3%	5.6%	1.03	0.64
1984	26.3	10.4	1.17%	4.1%	8.8%	5.6%	0.93	0.75
1985	29.4	15.4	1.10%	3.4%	7.4%	5.9%	0.85	0.67
1986	58.6	18.7	0.75%	3.0%	7.0%	6.7%	0.58	0.67
1987	50.4	14.1	0.72%	3.2%	5.3%	7.0%	0.52	0.73
1988	54.3	12.9	0.60%	3.0%	4.8%	7.2%	0.48	0.74
1989	53.7	14.8	0.52%	2.8%	4.3%	7.7%	0.45	0.67
1990	36.6	15.9	0.73%	3.2%	—	—	—	—

[a]*Source*: Price–earnings ratios and dividend yields for 1970–1989 are for the last trading day of each year: those for 1990 are for the last trading day of August. Foreign holdings of U.S. equity are from the Federal Reserve Board *Flow of Funds* tables. Foreign holdings of Japanese equity are from the Tokyo Stock Exchange, with 1988 value estimated from monthly net sales data in *Monthly Statistics Report*. The debt–equity ratio is defined as the book value of debt divided by the market value of equity. The debt–equity ratios for the U.S. are from the Federal Reserve Board, *Balance Sheets of the U.S. Economy*, 1988. The debt–equity ratios for Japan for 1970–1975 are from Ando and Auerbach (1988). Ratios for 1976–1989 are based on the data for 'All Industries' in *Daiwa* (1980, 1984, 1987, 1990). Debt is defined for Japanese firms as total liabilities excluding accounts payable. The Japanese data actually understate the decline in debt–equity ratios. The number of firms in the Daiwa sample increases substantially through time, and firms added to the sample in recent years had higher debt–equity ratios before they were added than did firms already in the sample.

of nonfinancial American firms. We use the NRI 350 to measure the Japanese market because other major indices have limitations for our purposes. The aggregate *P/E* ratio for the First Section of the Tokyo Stock Exchange includes financial firms, for which accounting issues are more complex than they are for nonfinancials. The MSCI indices also include financials, and they include consolidated earnings for some firms and unconsolidated earnings for others. The average *P/E* ratio reported in the *Daiwa Analysts Guide* is the ratio of the average price and average earnings based on number of shares outstanding, not value, so it is less representative of the value-weighted market than the NRI measure. The TSE, MSCI, and Daiwa *P/E* ratios were 58.3, 52.7, and 82.4 at the end of 1987. The comparable ratio for the NRI 350 was 50.4[2]

Table 23.4 documents the growth of the Japanese *P/E* ratio in 1986 and its decline in 1990. The disparity between the Japanese and U.S. *P/E*s in the second half of the 1980s is apparent. Between 1974 and 1984, the Japanese *P/E* was about twice the U.S. *P/E*. During

1986, however, the Japanese P/E ratio doubled from 29.4 to 58.6, while the U.S. ratio increased by only 21%, from 15.4 to 18.7. The Japanese P/E remained in the 50s through the end of 1989 and then fell, along with Japanese stock prices, to the mid-30s by mid-1990.

The Japanese dividend–price ratio (Table 23.4) declined throughout the 1970s and 1980s, reflecting sluggish nominal dividend payments and rising share prices. In 1970, the Japanese dividend yield, 4.57%, was higher than the U.S. yield of 3.3%. Although the U.S. yield showed no particular trend over the 1970–1989 period, the Japanese yield fell systematically, reaching 0.5% at the end of 1989.

Turnover rates, measured as the value of shares traded as a fraction of market capitalization, were similar on the TSE and the NYSE in the late 1980s. The average annual turnover rates for 1986–1989 are 70% in Tokyo and 64% in New York. (See the 1989 *TSE Fact Book* and *NYSE Fact Book*.)

Table 23.4 also documents that foreigners were net sellers of Japanese stocks during the period of most rapid price appreciation. Foreign ownership of U.S. stocks increased during both the 1970s and the 1980s, from 3.7% of the market in 1970 to 7.7% in 1989. Foreign holdings of Japanese stock also rose between the mid-1970s and the early 1980s, increasing from less than 2.7% in 1978 to 8.8% in 1984. After that, foreigners were net sellers of Japanese equities. By 1989 foreign holdings of Japanese equities (4.3%) were only 49% of their previous peak value. The persistent selling by foreigners during the second half of the 1980s is consistent with a widespread perception outside Japan that Japanese equities were overpriced.

Some have argued that high Japanese stock returns and P/E ratios during the 1980s were the result of high debt–equity ratios. This explanation is inconsistent with the data in Table 23.4 on the book value of debt divided by the market value of equity. In Japan, where most debt is short-term, the differential between market and book values for debt is small. The divergence could be larger for the United States. American debt–equity ratios show no particular trend, varying between 0.48 (1972) and 1.04 (1974). In contrast, Japanese debt–equity ratios decline during the sample period, from 1.63 in 1970 and 2.23 in 1972 to 0.45 in 1989. Although Japanese debt–equity ratios are substantially higher than their U.S. counterparts during the 1970s, they are significantly below U.S. ratios during the 1986–1989 period.

3. U.S. AND JAPANESE ACCOUNTING DIFFERENCES AND P/E RATIOS

Many analysts interpret high Japanese price–earnings ratios during the second half of the 1980s as evidence that Japanese stock prices were irrationally high. Others argue that the high P/Es are an artifact of Japanese accounting conventions. In this section we examine whether differences between Japanese and American accounting practices can explain the behavior of Japanese P/Es in the 1980s and 1990.

Two factors suggest that even if accounting considerations can explain the historical difference between U.S. and Japanese P/E ratios, they are unlikely to explain the growth of this difference in the second half of the 1980s, or its narrowing in 1990. First, changes in generally accepted accounting practices (GAAP) in Japan reduced the accounting disparities between Japanese and American firms during the period that Japanese P/Es were growing [Aron (1981, 1988)]. Second, as Figure 23.2 shows, the growth in the Japanese P/E ratio from 29.4 in 1985 to 53.7 in 1989 is dominated by rising stock prices, rather than by falling

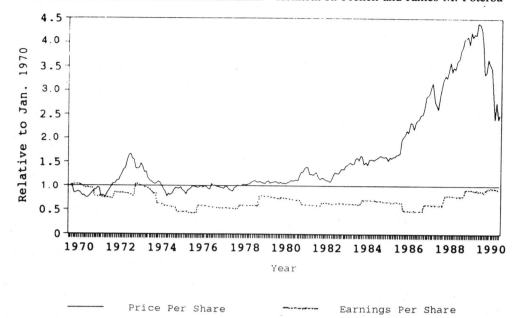

——————— Price Per Share   —·—·—·—   Earnings Per Share

Figure 23.2   Inflation adjusted price and earnings per share for NRI 350

earnings. The real price per share tracks the price–earnings ratio reasonably well. It was roughly constant from 1970 to 1980, grew gradually during the next five years, and then rose at an average annual rate of 27.1% from 1986 to 1989. In contrast, real earnings per share were roughly constant over the 1970–1990 period. A 28% decline in the earnings per share in 1986 helped double the *P/E* ratio during that year, but the ratio remained above 50 for the next three years despite annual earnings growth rates of 26%, 30%, and 18%.

Even if differences in accounting conventions cannot explain the growth of the Japanese *P/E* ratio during the second half of the 1980s, these differences may explain the smaller historical disparity between Japanese and U.S. *P/E*s. Three factors are particularly important: (i) differences in the importance of subsidiaries and the use of consolidated earnings, (ii) differences in 'reserve accounts' that permit Japanese firms to deduct significant amounts from reported earnings as advance funding for future expenses, and (iii) differences in depreciation practices. This section discusses each of these, and concludes with a brief analysis of the divergence between accounting and economic profits in Japan and the U.S.

3.1. Consolidation and intercorporate ownership

Consolidated earnings, which include the net income of subsidiaries and of firms in which the parent holds more than 20% of the outstanding equity, are the dominant measure of earnings in the United States. In contrast, unconsolidated earnings are the dominant measure in Japan. Although Japanese GAAP require firms to report consolidated earnings, unconsolidated earnings are the basis for most market analyses, and they are used in the denominator of most common Japanese *P/E* ratios, including the NRI 350 index reported here. Moreover, since intercorporate equity holdings are far more important in Japan than in the U.S., and since even consolidated earnings do not reflect the retained earnings of subsidiaries in which the parent holds less than a 20% stake, comparisons of consolidated earnings are also inappropriate. Since share prices reflect the parent companies' full claim on subsidiaries' profits, whereas unconsolidated earnings reflect only the dividends received from subsidiaries, there is a systematic upward bias in conventional Japanese P/E ratios relative to those in the U.S.

To avoid this bias, we compute price–earnings ratios based on only parent-company earnings and assets. Thus, in the spirit of our earlier adjustment for double-counting of equity holdings, we try to eliminate the effect of cross-holdings on both prices and earnings.[3]

Two adjustments are needed to correct P/E ratios for consolidation. First, we adjust prices to remove that part of value derived from intercorporate equity holdings. Since we are interested in P/E ratios for nonfinancial corporations (NFCs), the adjusted price is $P^* = (1 - \mu s')P$, where $\mu =$ (value of all traded shares)/(value of NFCs' traded shares) and s' is the share of the total market owned by NFCs. This procedure essentially redefines the market value of nonfinancial corporations as the value of outstanding equity *less* the value of shares held on corporate account.

Second, we remove intercorporate dividends from the reported earnings of parent firms. If the fraction of earnings paid out as dividends by both financial and nonfinancial corporations is d, then the relevant earnings measure is $E^* = (1 - s'\mu d)E$. The adjusted price–earnings ratio is therefore

$$P^*/E^* = [(1 - s'\mu)/(1 - s'\mu d)] * (P/E). \tag{2}$$

Note that if the dividend payout ratio of firms owned by traded nonfinancial firms is higher than the payout ratio of the traded firms, our correction will understate the actual adjustment to P/E ratios.

Table 23.5 shows the impact of the cross-holding adjustment on Japanese P/E ratios between 1975 and 1990. In August 1990, when the Japanese payout ratio (d) was 0.267 and $\mu s'$ was 0.391, the adjustment factor was 0.680. The cross-holding adjustment therefore reduces the reported P/E ratio from 36.6 to 24.9. The impact of cross-holdings on the P/E ratio grows through time. This largely reflects an increase in cross-holding during the 1980s.

3.2. Accounting for special reserves

The Japanese tax code allows firms to set aside funds each year against future contingencies including product returns, repairs, payments on guarantees, losses due to doubtful accounts, and payment of retirement benefits. Japanese workers retire when they are roughly sixty years old, and their employer typically provides a large one-time retirement payment that can equal several times the employee's annual salary. Firms can create a reserve equal to 40% of the amount workers would receive if the firm were liquidated and all workers retired. Because Japanese accounting practices require conformity between tax returns and financial statements, reductions to taxable income reduce accounting earnings as well. The net effect of contributing before-tax income to these reserves is to reduce reported earnings below what they would be in the U.S.

Aron (1988) suggests a procedure for undoing the effect of reserve contributions on reported earnings. He calculates the net contribution firms make to reserve accounts and notes that without such contributions, after-tax earnings would increase by

$$E_{\text{adj}} - E_{\text{report}} = (1 - \tau) * (\text{net reserve contribution}). \tag{3}$$

Table 23.5 Adjusted price–earnings and price-to-cash-earnings ratios, Japan and United States, 1975–1990[a]

Year	Japan Cross-holding Unadjusted P/E	Factor	Interim P/E	Reserves factor	Depreciation factor	Adjusted P/E	United States Unadjusted P/E	Adjusted P/E	Japan P/CE	U.S. P/CE
1975	25.2	0.784	19.8	0.98	0.786	15.2	11.8	11.0	6.6	6.9
1976	22.0	0.824	18.1	0.98	0.837	14.9	11.2	10.1	7.7	6.9
1977	19.3	0.797	15.4	0.98	0.866	13.1	9.1	8.1	6.2	5.6
1978	21.5	0.792	17.0	0.98	0.890	14.9	8.2	7.5	7.4	5.1
1979	16.6	0.778	12.9	0.98	0.906	11.5	7.5	6.8	6.9	4.7
1980	17.9	0.770	13.8	0.98	0.931	12.6	9.6	8.7	6.3	5.6
1981	24.9	0.764	19.0	0.98	0.910	17.0	8.2	7.6	6.9	4.6
1982	23.7	0.769	18.2	0.98	0.913	16.3	11.9	11.1	7.2	5.5
1983	29.4	0.795	23.4	0.98	0.938	21.5	12.6	11.9	9.3	6.4
1984	26.3	0.734	19.3	0.98	0.950	18.0	10.4	9.4	9.3	5.6
1985	29.4	0.694	20.4	0.98	0.928	18.6	15.4	14.2	9.0	6.9
1986	58.6	0.695	40.7	0.98	0.913	36.5	18.7	17.5	14.4	7.2
1987	50.4	0.665	33.5	0.98	0.926	30.4	14.1	12.9	14.7	6.9
1988	54.3	0.656	35.6	0.98	0.936	32.7	12.9	11.7	17.2	6.5
1989	53.7	0.663	35.6	0.98	0.936*	32.6	14.8	13.5*	18.4	7.7
1990	36.6	0.680	24.9	0.98	0.936*	22.8	15.9	14.5*	12.6	7.3

Source: Price–earnings ratios are from authors' calculations described in the text. Price-to-cash-earnings ratios (P/CE) are from Morgan Stanley–Capital International. The unadjusted P/E ratios correspond to the NRI 350 index and the S&P Industrials index. Starred values for 1989 and 1990 are estimated using 1988 data. We study the P/E ratios for the NRI 350 and S&P Industrials at the end of each calendar year for 1975–1989, and at the end of August 1990. The S&P ratio divides earnings for each calendar year by year-end prices. For the NRI 350, the Nomura Research Institute forecasts what earnings will be in the current fiscal year, which typically ends in March, and divides these forecasts by December prices. This biases the Japanese P/E ratio downward relative to the U.S. ratio when earnings are rising.

where τ is the corporate tax rate. Shoven and Tachibanaki (1987) and Aron (1988) estimate the combined marginal tax rate from national corporate income tax, enterprise tax, and local inhabitants tax at between 50% and 55%. We use a value of $\tau = 0.52$ for 1990, and lower rates earlier in the sample period. We use Aron's estimate that reserve contributions average approximately 4% of net income for large Japanese firms over the entire 1975–1990 period. The resulting adjustment factor, shown in the fourth column of Table 23.5, has a small effect on the reported price–earnings ratio.

3.3. Depreciation accounting

The last major difference between the accounting practices of U.S. and Japanese firms concerns depreciation. In the U.S., the possibility of using one set of accounting rules for tax purposes and another for financial reporting leads most firms — 75% according to Schieneman's (1986) citation of the American Institute of Certified Public Accountants — to choose accelerated depreciation for the former and straight-line depreciation for the latter. This reduces current taxable income relative to reported earnings.

Japanese firms may also choose straight-line or accelerated depreciation, but they must use the same technique for tax and financial reporting purposes. Virtually all firms choose accelerated depreciation, which minimizes current taxes, rather than straight-line depreciation, which maximizes current reported earnings. Thus, the typical Japanese firm depreciates its assets more quickly than the typical American firm; Japanese depreciation charges are higher when assets are relatively new and lower when they are old.

This difference in depreciation rules does not imply any systematic difference in P/E ratios across nations. If most firms in the rapid-depreciation nation acquired their assets in the distant past, the net effect of faster depreciation will be a *higher P/E* ratio. In practice, however, many Japanese firms were growing rapidly during the 1970s and 1980s, so they had a preponderance of young assets with depreciation deductions exceeding those of comparable U.S. firms. Therefore, the use of accelerated depreciation tends to lower reported earnings, and raise price–earnings ratios, for Japanese firms in comparison with their U.S. counterparts.

Exact comparison of the depreciation claims of U.S. and Japanese firms would require detailed information on the asset mix and investment history of firms in both nations. These data are not readily available. We can bound the effect of accelerated depreciation on Japanese price–earnings ratios, however, by making the extreme assumption that all Japanese assets were placed in service during the previous year. Since virtually all Japanese firms use double-declining-balance depreciation, straight-line depreciation would be roughly half the reported depreciation. Thus, the maximum understatement of before-tax earnings caused by accelerated depreciation is half of total depreciation claims, and the maximum understatement of after-tax earnings is $(1 - \tau)$ times this amount where τ is the corporate tax rate.

This implies that a depreciation-adjusted price–earnings ratio must be at least $E_{report}/[E_{report} + (1 - \tau) * \text{depreciation}/2]$ times the unadjusted ratio. Based on the parent-company income statement data in the 1989 *Daiwa Analysts Guide*, which covers virtually all nonfinancial firms listed on the First Section of the TSE, this lower bound for the Japanese price–earnings ratio is 24.8 at the end of 1989 and 17.3 in mid-1990.

Rather than rely on the lower bound estimates above, we estimate the depreciation-induced understatement of earnings using a simple model of continuous investment and depreciation.[4] This model assumes that firms have homogeneous assets that depreciate at a constant rate δ, and that investment in these assets grows exponentially at rate g. We also simplify the double-declining-balance technique used in Japan by assuming that accelerated depreciation charges are always 2δ times the current book value.

Each firm's investment at time t, per dollar invested at time s, is $e^{g(t-s)}$. Since accelerated depreciation reduces the book value of an $e^{g(t-s)}$ dollar investment at t ($t < s$) to $e^{g(t-s)}e^{2\delta(t-s)}$ dollars at s, the book value of a firm's assets per dollar of current investment is $\int_{-\infty}^{s} e^{g(t-s)}e^{2\delta(t-s)}dt = 1/(2\delta + g)$. Given our simplifying assumption about double-declining-balance accounting, the current accelerated (AC) depreciation expense per dollar of current investment is $AC = 2\delta/(2\delta + g)$.

To model straight-line (SL) depreciation, we define each asset's depreciable life as the time until two-thirds of the asset is eroded, $L \equiv \ln(0.67)/\delta$. This yields depreciable lives of about 15 years throughout our sample period. We also assume that, for accounting purposes, there is no salvage value. With these assumptions, the current straight-line depreciation charge per dollar of current investment is $SL = \int_{s-L}^{s} e^{g(t-s)}dt/L = (1 - e^{-gL})/gL$.

This model implies that straight-line depreciation charges would be $SL/AC = (1 - e^{-gL}) * (2\delta + g)/2\delta gL$ times accelerated depreciation charges. Thus, converting from accelerated to straight-line depreciation increases after-tax earnings by $(1 - \tau) * [1 - (1 - e^{-gL}) * (2\delta + g)/2\delta gL]$ times the accelerated depreciation actually reported by Japanese firms.

We use the ten-year change in nominal business investment, from the national income accounts, to estimate the exponential growth rate for investment, g. We estimate δ as one-half the ratio of current depreciation charges to the value of depreciable assets, since for Japanese firms using double-declining-balance methods the instantaneous depreciation rate will be approximately twice the economic rate. The accounting data for this estimate are from the *Daiwa Analysts Guide*.

As the results in the seventh column of Table 23.5 show, the conversion from accelerated to straight-line depreciation has a larger effect in the 1970s than in the 1980s. This reflects a decline in the rate of growth of nominal business investment in Japan. For example, the average annual rate of growth is 14.9% between 1965 and 1975, and 7.0% between 1975 and 1985. The earnings adjustment factor (the ratio of reported to adjusted earnings) is above 0.9 throughout the 1980s. Thus, even after we adjust for accelerated depreciation, our estimate of the Japanese *P/E* ratio is above 30.0 at the end of each year from 1986 to 1989. The adjusted ratio does fall, along with Japanese stock prices, in 1990. After converting to U.S. accounting practices, we estimate that the Japanese *P/E* ratio is 22.8 in mid-1990.

The price-to-cash-earnings (*P/CE*) ratios in Table 23.5 provide additional perspective on the impact of the different depreciation methods used by U.S. and Japanese firms. Since cash earnings are defined as the sum of reported earnings plus depreciation, they are unaffected by a company's choice of depreciation method. The U.S. *P/CE* ratio shows no particular trend during the 1975–1990 period. In contrast, the Japanese *P/CE* ratio behaves like the Japanese *P/E* ratio. It rises from 9.0 in 1985 to 18.4 in 1989, and then falls to 12.6 during the first eight months of 1990.

3.4. Adjusted U.S. P/E ratios

The adjustments for depreciation and reserves described above attempt to make reported earnings of Japanese firms comparable to those of U.S. firms. The adjustment for intercorporate holdings, however, converts Japanese earnings to a base case with no intercorporate ownership. Thus, we must also adjust the *P/E* ratio of the S&P Industrials to remove the effects of U.S. intercorporate holdings. The eighth and ninth columns of Table 23.5 present the unadjusted S&P *P/E* ratio and the adjusted series using the procedure we applied to the Japanese data. Since intercorporate holdings in the U.S. are smaller than those in Japan, the adjusted *P/E* ratio for the U.S. (14.5 in 1990) is closer to its unadjusted value (15.9).

Although accounting adjustments reduce the differences between Japanese and American *P/E* ratios, they do not eliminate them, particularly during the 1986–1989 period. For example, at the end of 1989, the adjusted *P/E* ratio is 13.5 in the U.S. and 32.6 in Japan. Moreover, like the unadjusted ratio, the adjusted Japanese ratio essentially doubles in 1986. Accounting-based hypotheses can explain much of the difference between U.S. and Japanese *P/E*s before 1986, but they cannot explain the doubling of Japanese ratios in 1986 or the high ratios during the next four years.

3.5. Accounting versus economic earnings

Our analysis has attempted to place U.S. and Japanese earnings on a comparable accounting base. It has not tried to translate accounting earnings into economic earnings. Other studies, notably Ando and Auerbach (1990) and McCauley and Zimmer (1990), pursue that issue. In principle, deviations between economic and accounting profits could cause reported price–earnings ratios in the two nations to diverge, and changes through time in this deviation could lead to divergent movements in *P/E* ratios.

Inflation is the principal source of differences between accounting and economic earnings.[5] First, because depreciation is calculated using the historical cost of physical assets, true depreciation costs are understated and profits are overstated in periods of high inflation. Second, the failure to distinguish between the real and nominal cost of debt understates earnings when inflation is high. Although the economic cost of borrowing is measured by the real interest rate, reported earnings reflect nominal interest charges. Debt–equity ratios in Japan are higher than in the U.S. during much of our sample period, so this overstatement is more important for Japanese than for U.S. earnings. Third, inflation induces spurious profits for goods held in inventory or for assets that are sold. Nominal appreciation of inventories is recorded as a profit, even though the firm receives no real gains. Similar problems arise if the firm sells appreciated assets, since accounting profits will show the nominal rather than the real capital gain.

Ando and Auerbach (1988) study the differences between accounting and economic earnings in Japan and the United States due to inflation. For the high-inflation period 1967–1983, the average reported earnings–price ratio for their sample of Japanese firms is 0.065, and that for their U.S. sample is 0.094. After correcting earnings for inflation-induced errors, they find a 'corrected' *E/P* ratio of 0.092 in Japan and 0.085 in the United States. Because of differences in leverage between U.S. and Japanese firms and differences in depreciation rates, inflation leads to overstatement of U.S. earnings but understatement of economic earnings for Japanese firms.

Inflation during the decades before 1985 causes Japanese *P/E* ratios to be higher than they would have been if accountants measured economic earnings, and has the opposite effect in the United States. Although this may further explain the historical disparity in the level of *P/E* ratios, it makes it more difficult to explain the changes since 1985. The slowing of inflation, which reduced the disparity between accounting and economic earnings, should have reduced measured Japanese *P/E* ratios and raised their U.S. counterparts. This effect is strengthened by the fact that inflation declined faster in Japan than in the U.S. after 1984. Rather than explaining recent events, the disparity between economic and accounting earnings therefore magnifies the *P/E* puzzle.

4. REQUIRED RETURNS AND EXPECTED GROWTH: JAPAN AND THE U.S.

The apparent inability of accounting factors to explain why adjusted Japanese price–earnings ratios are high in relation to historical values and in relation to U.S. P/Es during the second half of the 1980s leads us to consider two alternative explanations. First, investors may have believed that Japanese firms had extraordinary growth opportunities. Second, the required return on equity may have been lower in Japan than in the U.S., so the two markets were capitalizing earnings differently.

This section considers these explanations for the Japanese stock market boom of the mid-1980s and the collapse of 1990. It is inherently difficult to evaluate these explanations, however. First, the market's expectations about growth and required returns almost certainly vary with the forecast horizon. Most earnings- and dividend-discount models collapse the vectors of growth expectations and required returns into scalars, but this abstracts from the rich patterns of expected earnings and discount rates used by the market when setting prices. Second, the market's expectations of these variables are unobservable. Even if we were confident that our models captured the market's pricing function reasonably well, we could not be sure that we have selected appropriate inputs. The results in this section are therefore suggestive, rather than conclusive.

4.1. Growth and required returns in infinite- and finite-horizon models

Miller and Modigliani (1961), in their classic paper on share valuation, offer a convenient framework for considering the effect of expected growth and required returns on price–earnings ratios. In their model, the discount rate r is constant and firms can invest a fraction k of each period's earnings in projects that have a perpetual supernormal return of r^*. If the firms pay out their remaining earnings as dividends, earnings grow at the rate $g = kr^*$ while the supernormal investment opportunities are available.

Within this framework, one obtains the standard earnings-discount model,

$$P/E = (1 - k)/(r - kr^*) = (1 - k)/(r - g), \tag{4}$$

by making the extreme assumption that the supernormal opportunities are available forever. With the more realistic assumption that supernormal investment opportunities are available only for the next T years, Miller and Modigliani approximate the price–earnings ratio as

$$P/E = [1 + kT(r^* - r)]/r = [1 + T(g - kr)]/r. \tag{5}$$

In Table 23.6 we use these relations, along with the 1985–1986 and 1989–1990 pairs of adjusted P/E ratios, to estimate the implied growth rate g for various required returns r. Under the extreme assumption that Japanese firms will always be able to invest their retained earnings in supernormal investment opportunities (infinite T), the estimated value of $r - g$ in the first panel of Table 23.6 falls from 2.25% in 1985 to 1.37% in 1986.

This relatively small implied change in $r - g$, coupled with the large increase in Japanese asset values and P/Es over this period, illustrates the nonlinearity of equation (4). When the P/E ratio is large, the implied value of $r - g$ is small and subject to large percentage changes with relatively small absolute changes. Thus, if we are willing to assume that supernormal investment opportunities will always be available in Japan, the doubling of P/Es in 1986 can be explained by an unanticipated, once-and-for-all decline of less than one percentage point in the required return or by a similar increase in the (perpetual) growth rate.

Table 23.6 Growth rates implied by adjusted price–earnings ratios with supernormal investment opportunities of various durations[a]

Year	Required return, r								
	3.0%	3.5%	4.0%	4.5%	5.0%	5.5%	6.0%	6.5%	7.0%
Japan: 10-year horizon									
1985	−2.02	−0.70	0.63	1.96	3.29	4.62	5.95	7.28	8.61
1986	3.10	5.28	7.46	9.65	11.83	14.01	16.20	18.38	20.56
1989	2.30	4.34	6.39	8.44	10.49	12.54	14.59	16.64	18.69
1990	−0.62	0.94	2.51	4.07	5.63	7.20	8.76	10.32	11.89
Japan: 25-year horizon									
1985	0.63	1.40	2.17	2.94	3.71	4.48	5.25	6.03	6.80
1986	2.53	3.62	4.70	5.79	6.88	7.97	9.06	10.14	11.23
1989	2.43	3.50	4.57	5.64	6.71	7.78	8.86	9.93	11.00
1990	1.28	2.16	3.03	3.91	4.79	5.67	6.55	7.43	8.31
United States: 10-year horizon									
1985	−4.19	−3.23	−2.26	−1.29	−0.32	0.64	1.61	2.58	3.55
1986	−3.32	−2.20	−1.09	0.02	1.14	2.25	3.37	4.48	5.59
1989	−4.08	−3.10	−2.11	−1.12	−0.14	0.85	1.84	2.82	3.81
1990	−4.06	−3.07	−2.08	−1.09	−0.10	0.89	1.88	2.87	3.86
United States: 25-year horizon									
1985	−0.75	−0.21	0.33	0.87	1.42	1.96	2.50	3.04	3.58
1986	−0.47	0.12	0.71	1.30	1.89	2.48	3.07	3.65	4.24
1989	−0.51	0.07	0.65	1.23	1.81	2.40	2.98	3.56	4.14
1990	−0.67	−0.11	0.44	1.00	1.55	2.11	2.66	3.22	3.77

[a]*Source*: The implied growth rates are calculated using equation (5), $P/E = [1 + T(g − kr)]/r$, with T equaling 10 or 25 years.

The results for 10 and 25 years of supernormal growth opportunities illustrate that the foregoing calculations are sensitive to the assumption that new opportunities are available forever. If we use a long-term growth forecast of about 4.5% per year (which is comparable to the reported expectations of Japanese growth for 1985 discussed below) and a horizon of ten years, the estimates in the lower panel of Table 23.6 imply that the required annual return on Japanese equity was about 6% at the end of 1985. If the required return remained at 6%, the doubling of the adjusted *P/E* ratio from 1985 to 1986 implies a ten-percentage-point increase in the expected annual growth rate, to 14.5% per year for the next ten years. Alternatively, one can hold the expected growth rate fixed at 4.5%. In this case, equation (5) implies that the required return fell from about 6% in 1985 to 3.6% in 1986.

If the supernormal growth opportunities in Japan were expected to persist for 25 years, the implied changes in r and g from 1985 to 1986 are smaller, but still substantial. For example, if the expected growth rate is assumed to be 4.5% in both 1985 and 1986, the implied required return falls from 6.5% to 4.5%. This decline is more than twice the change implied by the perpetual growth model.

The calculations for the decline in Japanese share prices in 1990 suggest similarly large changes in expectations. If the required return is 5% and supernormal profits last for 25 years, the expected growth rate would have to decline by two hundred basis points to justify the downward revision in Japanese share prices. If the supernormal profits last for only ten years, the implied growth rate falls by 5%.

Assuming that supernormal profits are not available forever, the doubling of Japanese *P/E*s in 1986 and their collapse in 1990 requires a substantial shift in required returns, expected growth rates, or both. The next two subsections provide some suggestive evidence on the movements in these variables.

4.2. Evidence on changing growth expectations

Long-term forecasts by econometric forecasting firms provide some guidance on investors' growth expectations. Table 23.7 presents long-term forecasts of growth made by Data Resources, Inc., a major U.S. forecasting firm. Although these forecasts are for real GNP, not corporate earnings, they provide evidence on growth expectations during the 1980s. There is a small decline in the ten-year forecasts for the U.S. between 1984 (2.9%) and 1988 (2.3%). The ten-year growth rates forecast for Japan are surprisingly constant, varying between 4.3% in 1985 and 3.9% in 1988 and 1990. Forecasts made after the Iraqi invasion of Kuwait in August 1990 show somewhat lower Japanese growth rates, 3.3% for ten years, but this change follows the decline in Japanese share values. DRI's five-year forecasts for Japan, which span the 1985–1986 period, display somewhat greater volatility. They decline from 4.0% in 1985 to 3.3% in 1987, and then rise to 3.9% in 1988. Five-year forecasts from the Japan Center for Economic Research (4.6% in 1985, 3.0% in 1986, 3.8% in 1987, 3.2% in 1988) also suggest that growth expectations in Japan declined from 1985 to 1986.

These forecasts do not support the view that accelerating growth expectations in Japan are responsible for the 1986 rise in share values. If anything, the expected growth rate for the next decade declined. Although some might argue that equity values depend on growth forecasts over periods longer than a decade, revisions in longer-term growth prospects are not likely to explain the observed price changes. As the horizon grows, forecasts of significantly more rapid growth in one economy than in another become less reliable and less plausible. Recent empirical findings [see Barro (1989)] suggest that national growth rates exhibit mean reversion. It is also difficult to imagine the type of news investors could

Table 23.7 Expected annual growth rates and nominal and real yields on long-term government bonds, United States and Japan, 1982–1990[a]

	Expected long-term growth			Before-tax yields			
	U.S.	Japan		Nominal		'Real'	
Year	10-year	5-year	10-year	U.S.	Japan	U.S.	Japan
1982	3.2	4.6		10.3	7.8	4.0	2.4
1983	3.2		3.8	11.4	7.4	5.6	4.2
1984	2.9	3.7	4.0	11.5	6.9	6.1	4.4
1985	2.9	4.0	4.3	9.2	6.3	4.4	4.1
1986	2.6	3.6		7.3	5.5	2.6	2.9
1987	2.3	3.3		8.9	5.2	3.9	3.3
1988	2.3	3.9	3.9	9.2	4.8	4.1	3.0
1989	2.3		4.0	7.8	5.8	3.1	3.0
1990	2.3		3.9*	8.5	6.8	4.4	4.0

[a]Notes: The U.S. long-term growth forecasts are from the winter issues of Data Resources Inc.'s *Long Term Review*. For example, the 1980 forecast is from the winter 1980–81 issue. Japanese growth forecasts are from various issues of the Data Resources/Nikkei *Japanese Review*. Nominal yields are for the Nikkei Long-Term Government Bond Index and the Moody's 10-year Government Bond Index. The 'real' yields are calculated by subtracting DRI's long-term inflation forecast from the contemporaneous nominal yield.
*denotes the forecast from August 1990; the October 1990 forecast called for 3.3% annual growth.

have received that would affect growth prospects more than a decade into the future without changing near-term forecasts. Thus, we find it hard to justify the increase in *P/E* ratios as the result of increased optimism about future expected growth.

A similar argument applies to the Japanese *P/E* decline of 1990. While the Japanese economy's short-term growth prospects were reduced by fears of recession, in June and July 1990, long-term growth forecasts were only a few basis points below the projections at the end of 1989. There is consequently little evidence for concluding that declining Japanese share prices were the result of slowing growth expectations.

4.3. Required returns: Explaining the price increase

P/E ratios depend on both expected growth rates and required equity returns. Unfortunately, measuring required returns is at least as difficult as calibrating growth expectations. *Ex ante* expected returns are not observable, and neither the risk premium on equities nor the required return on riskless assets can be estimated precisely from historical data on asset returns [see Merton (1980)].

Before considering the recent changes in some proxies for required returns, it is useful to ask whether differences between required returns in the U.S. and Japanese equity markets are consistent with capital-market equilibrium. Because of the increasing integration of world financial markets, required returns in each market are linked to those in other markets. The linkage between U.S. and Japanese financial markets has grown significantly during the last decade. Before 1980, and to a lesser extent between 1980 and 1986, Japanese investors faced capital controls that limited their ability to invest in other markets. Since 1986, however, explicit barriers to capital mobility into and out of Japan have been minimal. Recent studies [see Ito (1990)] suggest that short-term riskless interest rates in Japan are now determined by world market conditions. Whether markets for long-term assets such as corporate equities are equally well integrated remains an open issue.

Required equity returns in the United States and Japan could differ for at least three reasons. First, investors may expect systematic long-term changes in real exchange rates. Frankel (1989) presents evidence of 'country effects' in real interest rates, and argues that these are the result of expected currency movements. From this perspective, lower real interest rates and required equity returns in Japan would be consistent with expectations that, after adjustment for inflation, the yen will appreciate against the dollar. There is little evidence, however, that investors expected real yen appreciation in the late 1980s.

A second possibility is that perceived risks associated with cross-border equity investments allow substantial disparities between expected returns in different markets. Despite large cross-border capital flows during the 1980s, most corporate equity is still held in the country of issue [see French and Poterba (1991)]. The cross-border equity flows may therefore be insufficient to equate expected returns. This argument is consistent with frequent claims that Japan's high savings rate has reduced required returns on Japanese assets relative to similar assets in the U.S.

Third, taxation could lead to differences in required returns for U.S. and Japanese investors. If capital markets are not perfectly integrated, differences in local tax rates can cause differences in the pre-tax returns demanded by investors in the two markets. In addition, some investors face different tax burdens on foreign and domestic securities, making these imperfect substitutes. For example, U.S. pension funds cannot reclaim the 20% withholding tax that Japan levies on dividend payments to foreign investors. Similar problems may affect some Japanese investors, since the U.S. also requires 20% withholding on dividends remitted abroad.

The foregoing considerations make it impossible to determine *a priori* whether the expected returns on long-term assets in Japanese and U.S. capital markets differ. We therefore consider the available empirical evidence on long-term real interest rates in the two nations in an effort to evaluate required returns on riskless assets; we do not attempt to measure the equity risk premium.

Nominal interest rates in both Japan and the U.S. declined significantly between 1985 and 1988. Table 23.7 reports the nominal rates on U.S. and Japanese ten-year government bonds during the 1982–1990 period. Japanese long-term rates declined by 150 basis points from 1985 to 1988, a factor that is often cited [for example by Takagi (1989)] as influential in the rise in equity prices. However, the significant increase in Japanese prices and price–earnings ratios during this period must be explained by changes in real (probably after-tax) interest rates, not nominal interest rates.

Macroeconomic forecasts of long-term Japanese inflation rates suggest that real interest rates also declined in the mid-1980s. The sixth and seventh columns of Table 23.7 report estimates of real yields calculated by subtracting Data Resources' long-term forecast of annual inflation from the contemporaneous nominal yield on government bonds. These estimates suggest that the real Japanese interest rate declined from 4.1% in 1985 to 2.9% in 1986. Similar estimates based on the five-year inflation forecast of the Japan Center for Economic Research suggest a real interest rate of 4.4% in 1985 and 3.1% in 1986, a decline of about 125 basis points during the year when *P/E* ratios doubled. Real interest rates in the U.S. declined even more. DRI's ten-year inflation forecasts imply that the real yield on U.S. government bonds fell from 4.4% in 1985 to 2.6% in 1986, a drop of 280 basis points. The real interest rates in Table 23.7 also show that, before the removal of capital controls in the mid-1980s, estimated real long-term interest rates were more than 150 basis points lower in Japan than in the U.S.

The substantial changes in these crude measures of required returns on long-term riskless assets suggest that required returns on corporate equities may also have declined, in both Japan and the U.S., during the 1985–1986 period.[6] The key questions are: 1) Is the decline in required returns in Japan large enough to explain the increase in Japanese prices and *P/E*s? and 2) If the decline in required returns in Japan does explain this behavior, can we reconcile a smaller increase in U.S. prices and *P/E*s with a substantially larger decline in the required returns on long-term riskless assets in the U.S.?

Several factors might explain why U.S. prices and price–earnings ratios increased less than their Japanese counterparts. First, since the U.S. *P/E*s began at a lower level, possibly because of higher initial discount rates, the same absolute change in required returns should have a larger effect in Japan. Second, the rise in U.S. *P/E* ratios may have been blunted by tax changes in 1986. These changes lowered marginal tax rates on interest and dividend income for top-bracket individual investors from 50% to 28%. Part of the reduction in the tax burden on dividends, however, was offset by an increase in capital-gains tax rates. For individual investors the net effect of the U.S. tax changes should have been a substitution toward debt and away from equity.

In contrast, for an important class of Japanese investors, tax changes during the mid-1980s reduced after-tax returns on debt relative to those on common stock. Before 1987, Japanese individual investors were able to avoid taxation on interest through a system of Maruyu accounts. By the mid-1980s, nearly 70% of Japan's personal savings were in these tax-exempt accounts [Japan Securities Research Institute (1988)]. The Maruyu system was largely eliminated by the 1987 Japanese tax reform. Effective April 1, 1988, households face a 20% tax on all interest income. These tax changes should have induced a substitution from debt to equity among some Japanese investors, possibly raising stock prices. These changes, however, did not affect large classes of institutional investors.

Although these factors might explain why Japanese stock prices and *P/E*s increased more than their U.S. counterparts, our rough estimate of a 125-basis-point drop in Japanese required returns seems too small to explain the doubling of *P/E*s in 1986. In the Miller–Modigliani growth model, if supernormal investment opportunities were expected to persist for 25 years and earnings were expected to grow by 4.5% per year, a 1.25% decline in the required return would have lifted the adjusted *P/E* from 18.2 in 1985 to 27.7 in 1986. This implied value is much lower than our adjusted estimate of 35.7 for 1986.

4.4. Required returns: Explaining the Japanese price decline

Movements in required returns are more successful in explaining the decline of Japanese prices and *P/E*s in 1990. Japanese real interest rates increased by approximately 100 basis points in early 1990. This change is roughly consistent with the observed change in *P/E* ratios. Consider, for example, the second panel of Table 23.7, where we examine 25 years of subnormal growth opportunities. A shift from a required return of 5% to one of 6% between 1989 and 1990 leaves the implied expected growth rate virtually unchanged, suggesting that shifts in real interest rates could be a key factor in the recent Japanese stock market decline.

Our confidence in this analysis is weakened by the behavior of the U.S. market in 1990. If our estimates of rising U.S. real interest rates and constant growth expectations are correct, the Miller–Modigliani growth model of equation (5) predicts a decline, rather than the observed increase, in U.S. share prices and price–earnings ratios during the first half of 1990.

5. CONCLUSIONS

Our analysis does not fully explain differences through time in the price–earnings ratios in the U.S. and Japanese stock markets. It does imply, however, that such differences are less puzzling than casual observation suggests. Roughly half of the discrepancy, even at the height of the Japanese market in the late 1980s, is due to differences in the accounting practices of the two countries. We estimate that if Japanese firms used U.S. accounting practices, the P/E ratio for the Tokyo Stock Exchange would have dropped from its reported value of 54.3 to 32.1 at end of 1988. Accounting differences explain much of the persistent disparity between U.S. and Japanese price–earnings ratios, but they appear unable to explain the doubling of Japanese P/E ratios in 1986, from 29.4 to 58.6, or the decline during 1990.

Because Japanese stocks have traded at higher earnings multiples than U.S. stocks throughout the last five years, a given absolute change in either discount rates or growth expectations would induce larger changes in the P/E ratios of Japanese shares than in their U.S. counterparts. We find no evidence of upward revisions in expected growth rates for the Japanese economy during this period, however. There is evidence of a substantial drop in required riskless returns between 1985 and 1986, but the decline appears to be too small to explain P/E increases as large as the actual changes. In contrast, the Japanese share-price decline of 1990 seems much easier to rationalize as the result of rising Japanese required returns.

Our analysis has focused on the relation between earnings and share prices, with no discussion of the replacement value of corporate assets or changes in this value through time. This omission is potentially important, because the rapid increase in Japanese equity values during the second half of the 1980s coincides with a similar increase in Japanese land prices. Data from the Economic Planning Agency in Japan show that the value of Japanese corporate land holdings more than doubled between 1984 and 1988. Land's share of the tangible assets in Japan also grows, from 45.8% to 56.9%. In contrast, the share for U.S. corporations remains roughly constant at just over 12%.

Some analysts argue that the increase in land prices explains much of the growth of Japanese equity values in the 1980s. This argument is not entirely satisfying because it does not explain why land prices rose. As with equities, the increase in Japanese land prices is more difficult to explain than their high level. Ito (1988) identifies several reasons why land prices in Japan should be higher than those in other nations: the tax system places very low burdens on land, especially in agricultural uses; higher population density makes the marginal product of land higher than that in many other developed nations; and the archaic system of land use precludes space-efficient development of high-rise office buildings and similar structures. None of these factors, however, seems to have changed during the 1980s.

Although Japanese land prices rose significantly in the 1980s, rents did not. For example, although the price of residential land in Tokyo was 150 times that in New York City in the late 1980s, the monthly rent on new commercial office space in Tokyo was only four times that in New York [Boone and Sachs (1989)]. Value-to-rent ratios in the Japanese land market behave like price–earnings ratios in the Japanese stock market in the 1980s.

The increases in Japanese share values and land values appear to be manifestations of a single underlying phenomenon. Arguing that high land values explain the Japanese stock market's movements is unsatisfying, since corporations hold land — either as an investment or as an input for production — because of its potential contribution to earnings. If the growth in Japanese corporate land values during the 1980s is rational, this growth must reflect an increase in land's contribution to current earnings, an increase in its expected contributions, or a reduction in the rates used to discount future contributions. These are exactly the explanations we consider for rising Japanese equity values in the late 1980s. Our incomplete explanation of the movements in Japanese share prices thus raises questions about the valuation of Japanese land as well.

ENDNOTES

1. The market value of common equity listed on the NYSE was $2,996.2 billion at the end of 1989, while that on the American Stock Exchange was $120.4 billion. Common shares of domestic corporations (excluding mutual funds) traded in the NASDAQ over-the-counter market were valued at $363.7 billion. The over-the-counter market is less important in Japan. For example, in 1986 the volume of shares traded on the First Section of the Tokyo Stock Exchange was 772 times that on the Tokyo OTC market [Japan Securities Research Institute (1988)].

2. Although some measures of aggregate Japanese P/Es were affected when the Nippon Telephone and Telegraph Company went public in 1987 with a price–earnings ratio of 285, this firm is not included in the NRI 350 index.

3. Variants of this approach are used by Ando and Auerbach (1990) and Ueda (1990). An alternative approach would involve full consolidation of the retained earnings of all subsidiaries. Our analysis neglects any capital gains that may enter earnings when a firm sells shares in other firms, an issue that McCauley and Zimmer (1990) address for financial firms.

4. Several studies, including Aron (1988), try to adjust reported earnings for different depreciation rules by assuming that the ratio of depreciation to cash earnings should be identical for U.S. and Japanese firms. Since different depreciation rates are not the only reason for differences in the amount of depreciation claimed by U.S. and Japanese firms, however, this assumption is likely to correct more than just accounting practices. It also undoes, for example, genuine differences in capital–labor ratios.

5. One other factor, of some importance in the Japanese context, is accrued but unrealized appreciation of assets that may contribute to economic but not accounting earnings.

6. The change in real after-tax interest rates in Japan is even larger, in percentage terms. With a 50% tax rate, the implied real after-tax borrowing rate in 1985 is 0.95, compared with 0.15 in 1986. Real after-tax rates are absolutely less sensitive to changes in nominal rates, but proportionally more sensitive, than the real interest rates reported in Table 23.7.

REFERENCES

Ando, Albert and Alan J. Auerbach, 1988, The cost of capital in the United States and Japan: A comparison, *Journal of the Japanese and International Economies* **2**, 134–158.

Ando, Albert and Alan J. Auerbach, 1990, The cost of capital in Japan: Recent evidence and further results, *Journal of the Japanese and International Economies* **4**, 323–350.

Aron, Paul, 1981, Are Japanese *P/E* multiples too high? (Daiwa Securities America, New York, NY).

Aron, Paul, 1988, Japanese *P/E* multiples: The shaping of a tradition (Daiwa Securities America, New York, NY).

Barro, Robert, 1989, Economic growth in a cross section of countries, Working paper no. 201 (Rochester Center for Economic Research, Rochester, NY).

Boone, Peter and Jeffrey Sachs, 1989, Is Tokyo worth four trillion dollars? An explanation for high Japanese land prices, Unpublished manuscript (Harvard University, Cambridge, MA).

Daiwa Securities Company Ltd., 1980, 1984, 1987, 1990, Analysts guide (Daiwa Securities, Tokyo).

Daiwa Securities Company Ltd., 1989, Net asset value special report: Net asset value of 450 companies and Q-ratio rankings, *Investment Monthly*, Nov., 17–69.

Frankel, Jeffrey, 1989, Quantifying international capital mobility in the 1980s, Working paper 2856 (National Bureau of Economic Research, Cambridge, MA).

French, Kenneth, R. and James M. Poterba, 1990, Japanese and U.S. cross-border common stock investments, *Journal of the Japanese and International Economies* **4**, 476–493.

French, Kenneth, R. and James M. Poterba, 1991, Investor behavior and international diversification, *American Economic Review* **81**, 222–226.

Hayashi, Fumio and Tohru Inoue, 1990, The relation between firm growth and Q with multiple capital inputs: Theory and evidence, Unpublished manuscript (University of Pennsylvania, Philadelphia, PA).

Hoshi, Takeo and Anil Kashyap, 1990, Evidence on Q and investment for Japanese firms, *Journal of Japanese and International Economies* **4**, 371–400.

Hoshi, Takeo, Anil Kashyap and David Scharfstein, 1991, Corporate structure, liquidity, and investment: Evidence from Japanese industrial groups, *Quarterly Journal of Economics* **106**, 33–60.

Ito, Takatoshi, 1988, Japan's structural adjustment: The land/housing problem and external balances, Unpublished manuscript (Hitsosubashi University, Tokyo).

Ito, Takatoshi, 1990, The Japanese economy (MIT Press, Cambridge, MA) forthcoming.

Japan Security Research Institute, 1988, Report on Japan's stock price level (JSRI, Tokyo).

McCauley, Robert and Stephen Zimmer, 1989, Explaining international differences in the cost of capital, *Federal Reserve Bank of New York Quarterly Bulletin*, Summer, 7–28.

McCauley, Robert and Stephen Zimmer, 1990, Estimating the cost of capital facing banks, Unpublished manuscript (Federal Reserve Board, New York, NY).

McDonald, Jack, 1989, The *mochiai* effect: Japanese corporate cross-holdings, *Journal of Portfolio Management*, Fall, 90–94.

Merton, Robert, 1980, On estimating the return on the market, *Journal of Financial Economics* **8**, 323–361.

Miller, Merton and Franco Modigliani, 1961, Dividend policy, growth, and the valuation of shares, *Journal of Business* **34**, 411–433.

Nagano, Atsushi, 1988, Japan, in: Joseph Pechman, ed., World tax reform: A progress report (Brookings Institution, Washington, DC) 155–161.

Norris, Floyd, 1990, Investors relish bet against Japan, *New York Times*, Jan. 15, p. D4.

Schieneman, Gary, S., 1986, Understanding Japanese financial statements: A guide for the U.S. investor (Arthur Young, New York, NY).

Shoven, John, B. and Toshiaki Tachibanaki, 1987, The taxation of income from capital in Japan, Unpublished manuscript (Stanford University, Stanford, CA).

Takagi, Keizo, 1989, The rise of land prices in Japan: The determination mechanism and the effect of taxation system, *Bank of Japan Monetary and Economic Studies* **7**, 93–139.

Tobin, James, 1969, A general equilibrium approach to monetary theory, *Journal of Money, Credit, and Banking* **1**, 15–29.

Tri, Anthony, 1971, Market value of outstanding corporate stock in the U.S. 1964–70, U.S. Securities and Exchange Commission Statistical Bulletin no. 30.

Ueda, Kazuo, 1990, Are Japanese stock prices too high?, *Journal of Japanese and International Economies* **4**, 351–370.

24

Price–Earnings Ratios as a Valuation Tool

Steven Bleiberg

Browsing through the "Business/Economics" offerings at a used book sale recently, I spotted a real classic. No, not *The Crash of '79* by Paul Erdman, although there seemed to be no shortage of that brilliant piece of prophecy. It was *The Evaluation of Common Stocks*, written by Value Line's Arnold Bernhard in 1959.

Right on page 1, Bernhard made some bold statements:

> At the time this is written, early in 1959, stock prices are high by historical standards... The Standard & Poor's industrial stock average, for example, is priced at 20 times earnings. We all recognize in retrospect that stocks were too high in 1929 when, at the very peak of the market, they also stood at 20 times earnings. By contrast, in 1949, at the beginning of this bull market, stocks were priced at only 5.4 times earnings.

On page 2, Bernhard adds that "in terms of the stock/bond yield ratio, stocks are more overvalued now than at any time of good business since their 1929 peak." Pretty scary!

There's only one problem. We now know what the stock market did in the years after Bernhard wrote those words. In the seven years from 1959 to 1965, inclusive, the S&P 500 produced an annualized return (including dividends) of 11.1%, compared to less than 5% for the bond market. During that whole stretch, the market's *P/E* never fell below 16, and spent quite a bit of time between 18 and 22, yet the market kept doing well.

It seems that making a market timing call based on *P/E* ratios can be a tricky business. We decided to see just how tricky. Specifically, how useful has the market's *P/E* ratio been as a predictor of future returns? When the market's *P/E* has moved to extreme levels, how much or how little does that tell us about what the market did next?

THE EVIDENCE

Quarterly data on the *P/E* ratio of the S&P 500 go back to 1938. (Of course, it was not always the S&P 500, but there has been a composite S&P index since that date.) Figure 24.1

Reprinted from: Bleiberg, S. 1989: How Little We Know... About *P/E*s, But Also Perhaps More Than We Think. *Journal of Portfolio Management*, 15, Summer, 26–31. This copyright material is reprinted with permission from The Journal of Portfolio Management, 488 Madison Avenue, New York, NY 10022.

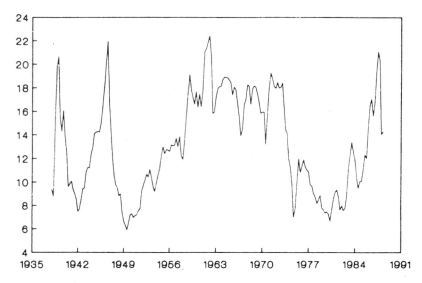

Figure 24.1   S&P 500 *P/E*

Table 24.1   Market performance by *P/E* quintile

P/E quintile	*P/E* values		S&P 500: average % change over subsequent		
	Low	High	6 months	12 months	24 months
1	17.81	22.43	−0.99	0.24	−0.68
2	14.29	17.77	5.82	6.96	8.86
3	11.23	14.28	3.34	8.09	16.57
4	9.04	11.19	4.20	8.99	25.57
5	5.90	9.01	7.99	16.21	29.79
Overall average			4.07%	8.18%	16.39%

shows the history of the index's *P/E*. It ranges from a high of 22.4 in June 1961 to a low of 5.9 in June 1949. This *P/E* is based on trailing twelve-month earnings and assumes that the earnings for a given quarter were known as of the last day of the quarter. This assumption is slightly unrealistic, but it does not produce any significant distortion in the *P/E*.

For each date, of course, we know not only the *P/E*, but also what the index did over the next six months, twelve months, twenty-four months, and so on. The first thing I did, therefore, was to sort all these *P/E* observations into quintiles, and then see what the average market performance was over various ensuing time periods for each quintile.

Table 24.1 shows the results. The first two columns in the table show the high and low *P/E* values for each quintile; the last three columns show the market's average performance over the subsequent six, twelve, and twenty-four months from each observation date. The figures show us that, *on average*, *P/E* has in fact had a relationship with how well the market did in subsequent months. Over the short term (up to one year), the relationship has been noticeable only when the *P/E* has moved to an extreme level. Over the longer term, though, the relationship has held up across all quintiles.

For example, when the *P/E* has been in the top quintile of its historic range, the average return has been −0.99% over the next six months, 0.24% over the next twelve months, and −0.68% over the next twenty-four months. At the other extreme, when the market's *P/E* has been in the lowest quintile of its historic range, the average returns have been 7.99% over the next six months, 16.21% over the next twelve months, and 29.79% over the next twenty-four months. These figures compare to overall average returns of 4.07% for six months, 8.18% for twelve months, and 16.39% for twenty-four months.

For the intermediate three quintiles, the six-and twelve-month average returns are not significantly different from the overall averages. Over twenty-four months, though, there are large differences between the average returns for the three middle quintiles. The second quintile produced an average subsequent twenty-four-month return of 8.86%, compared to 25.57% for the fourth quintile. The average return for the third quintile was very close to the overall average, as one would expect.

I stressed the phrase "on average" earlier, and that is a very important qualification. It is true that the average twenty-four-month returns produce a clear pattern in which lower *P/E*s led to better subsequent market returns. But these are just average returns. We also have to look at the distribution of the returns around those averages. When we do, we find that making specific predictions based on *P/E* is impossible, for the returns are widely scattered around the averages in Table 24.1. That is, there have been plenty of times when the market did well in the twenty-four months following a very high *P/E* value, and plenty of times when it fared poorly for twenty-four months after a low *P/E* value.

There are two ways of showing this point. First, Table 24.2 shows the frequency with which the market rose over each of the time periods measured for each *P/E* quintile. The bottom line of Table 24.2 shows that, overall, the market went up in 63% of the six-month periods, 67% of the twelve-month periods, and 76% of the twenty-four-month periods.

Now look at the top line. This tells us that, when the market has been in the highest *P/E* quintile, it has gone up 60% of the time over the next six months. This is no different, in any statistical sense, from the overall frequency of 63%. When the market has been in the lowest *P/E* quintile, it has gone up 73% of the time in the next six months. This too is not really significantly different from the overall average. It also means that the market's six-month return was negative 27% of the time even after the *P/E* was already in the lowest quintile of its historic range.

When we extend the time period to twelve months or twenty-four months, the frequencies of rising markets do diverge. Over twelve months, for example, a top quintile *P/E* reading

Table 24.2   Rising market frequency

P/E quintile	Frequency of rising market (%) over subsequent		
	6 months	12 months	24 months
Highest	60	53	54
2	60	65	70
3	58	65	73
4	65	63	85
Lowest	73	88	95
Overall	63%	67%	76%

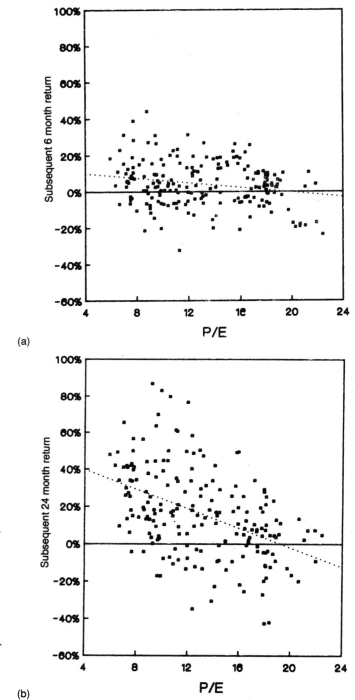

(a)

(b)

Figure 24.2 a) *P/E* versus subsequent six-month return and b) *P/E* versus subsequent twenty-four-month return

has been followed by a rising market only 53% of the time, compared to 88% of the time after a lowest quintile *P/E* reading. The three middle *P/E* quintile all have average results for the twelve-month period. Over twenty-four months, the spread between the high *P/E* quintile and the low *P/E* quintile widens farther — 54% versus 95% — and the three middle quintiles fall into an appropriate pattern as well.

Next, consider the graphs in Figure 24.2, which plot the data points in a scatter diagram, with *P/E* on the horizontal axis and subsequent return on the vertical axis. The top graph uses the subsequent six-month return; the bottom graph uses twenty-four-month returns. The dotted line in each graph shows the best fit regression line.

In general, the points fall into a pattern that slants downward from left to right, meaning that higher *P/E* is associated with lower returns over the ensuing months. But notice how widely scattered the data points are around the line. What this shows is that there were plenty of high *P/E* readings that were still followed by a rising market, and low *P/E*s that were followed by a falling market.

The point of both Table 24.2 and Figure 24.2 is that high or low *P/E* readings simply shift the probability distribution of the market's possible returns up or down. Thinking in terms of probability is the key here. Imagine the market at any given time as having a wide range of possible returns, with the "expected" return in the middle of that range. Based on the past fifty years of data, it seems that this distribution of possible returns shifts upward, as the market's *P/E* falls. This does raise the expected return, yet the range of possible returns remains just as wide as it was before, so a low *P/E* still can be followed by a falling market.

WHAT ABOUT BONDS?

Interest rates play a large role in determining the market's *P/E* ratio. And changes in interest rates figure prominently in the market's movement up or down. It makes sense to ask, therefore, how movements in the bond market affect this analysis.

For example, the market's *P/E* ratio tends to be very low when interest rates are very high. If the market in fact does go up a lot after a period of having a low *P/E*, that rally is likely to be driven at least in part by a drop in interest rates, which means that bonds will also be doing very well as stocks rise.

This complicates the asset allocation question. Earlier, we looked simply at whether *P/E* ratios have told us anything about the likelihood of the market going up or down. Now, we will see whether there is a relationship between *P/E* ratios and the subsequent performance of stocks relative to bonds.

To start, we need an index of bond market returns that goes back to 1938. The Shearson Lehman Hutton Government/Corporate index is a good index of the broad bond market, but it goes back only to 1973. For the years prior to 1973, I used a weighted average of three data series in the Ibbotson Associates data: long-term government bonds, intermediate-term government bonds, and long-term corporate bonds. Weights were determined by regressing the monthly returns for these series from 1973 to 1987 against the returns for the Shearson Lehman Hutton index over that period.

I then repeated the earlier analysis. That is, I again sorted the *P/E* observations from high to low and broke them into quintiles. But instead of looking at average absolute stock market returns over ensuing time periods, I now focused on average relative returns, calculated as the total return on the S&P 500 minus the total return on our bond market

Table 24.3 Average relative return of stocks over bonds

P/E quintile	S&P 500: average relative performance % over subsequent		
	6 months	12 months	24 months
Highest	−1.39	−0.56	−1.20
2	5.11	6.04	6.31
3	2.96	7.34	14.96
4	3.64	7.40	22.89
Lowest	7.77	16.70	32.96
Overall	3.62%	7.46%	15.57%

index. (In the earlier analysis, I actually looked at the S&P 500's price change only, not including dividends, because I was interested only in whether the index itself rose or fell.)

Table 24.3 shows the average relative returns over six, twelve, and twenty-four months for each P/E quintile. The results are quite similar to the results in Table 24.1. Over the six-month period, the top and bottom quintiles have average returns that are noticeably different from the overall average. Over all the six-month periods measured, stocks on average outperformed bonds by 3.62%. In the top P/E quintile, though, stocks underperformed bonds over the subsequent six months by an average of 1.39%. For the lowest P/E quintile, the average six-month outperformance was 7.77%. The three middle quintiles were all close to the overall average.

Over twelve months, the gap between the top and bottom deciles widens. Lowest quintile P/Es produced an average twelve-month outperformance of 16.70%, compared to −0.56% for highest quintile P/Es and 7.46% overall. Again, the middle quintiles were all close to the overall mean.

Over twenty-four months, the gap between the top and bottom quintiles widens further, and the middle quintiles begin to spread out as well. In the two years following a bottom quintile P/E, stocks outperformed bonds by an average of 32.96%, compared to an overall average of 15.57%. Meanwhile, even over two years, the average outperformance following top quintile P/Es was still negative, at −1.20%. Second quintile P/Es produced an average of 6.31% in subsequent outperformance, while fourth quintile observations led to an average outperformance of 22.89%. The average for the third quintile was very close to the overall average.

Once again, it must be stressed that these figures are averages. They do not indicate that stocks always outperformed bonds after a low quintile P/E, nor do they show that stocks always underperformed bonds after a high quintile P/E.

Repeating the earlier analysis, I looked at the distribution of the relative returns within each quintile. Table 24.4 shows the frequency with which stocks outperformed bonds over each time period within each quintile. Over all the six-month periods, stocks outperformed bonds 64% of the time. This percentage rises to 67% over twelve months, and 71% over twenty-four months.

Let's concentrate on the six-month period for a moment. In the six months following a bottom quintile P/E, stocks outperformed bonds 75% of the time; after a top quintile P/E, the frequency drops to 60%. This is really not a huge gap, nor is either figure very different from the overall frequency of 64%. These figures indicate that P/E has not been a very useful tool in making short-term asset allocation decisions between stocks and bonds.

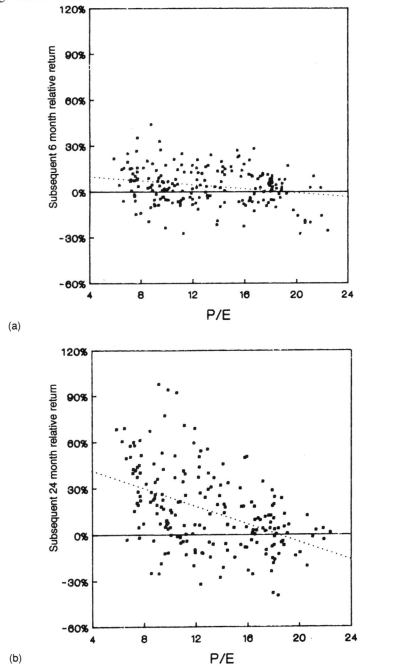

Figure 24.3 a) *P/E* versus subsequent six-month return relative to bonds and b) *P/E* versus subsequent twenty-four-month return relative to bonds

Table 24.4 Distribution of relative returns (%)

P/E quintile	Frequency with which stocks beat bonds over subsequent		
	6 months	12 months	24 months
Highest	60	53	51
2	60	65	68
3	57	63	68
4	65	68	78
Lowest	75	85	90
Overall	64%	67%	71%

Over twelve and twenty-four months, however, the gap between the figures for the top and bottom quintiles does widen. Over the twelve months after a bottom quintile *P/E*, stocks outperformed bonds 85% of the time, and over twenty-four months that figure rises to 90% of the time. This compares to frequencies of 53% and 51% for top quintile *P/E*s over twelve and twenty-four months, respectively. These are fairly large differences. Over twenty-four months, stocks are 40% more likely to outperform bonds following a bottom quintile *P/E* than following a top quintile *P/E*.

Figure 24.3 shows the scatter diagrams for the six- and twenty-four-month relative returns. These are similar to the graphs in Figure 24.2. Again, *P/E* is plotted on the horizontal axis, with the subsequent return of stocks relative to bonds now on the vertical axis. The dotted lines again represent the relationships that best fit the data, according to a regression analysis. As we saw in Figure 24.2, there is generally a downward slant to the right in the data, indicating that higher *P/E*s have been associated with poorer subsequent relative performance. But again, the points are widely scattered around the regression lines.

I HAVE SEEN THE FUTURE...

Now for the big question: Is there any way actually to use this information? This breaks down into two separate questions. First, will the future be like the past? And second, if it is, can our knowledge of the past be of any use to us? That is, knowing what we know about the historic range of *P/E* ratios and the distribution of subsequent returns, is there any way to add value to a portfolio through active asset allocation decisions that are based on the market's *P/E* multiple?

The answer to all these questions is simple: We don't know. I did perform an interesting experiment on the subject. Imagine a researcher had written this piece at the end of 1962. At that time, she would have had twenty-five years of *P/E* data from Standard & Poor's. Now suppose she decided that the data were representative of the market's long-term behavior, sorted the twenty-five years of *P/E* data into quintiles, and devised an asset allocation strategy based on those quintiles.

Asset allocation between stocks and bonds would be set each quarter. If the market *P/E* were in the middle quintile of its historic *P/E* range (based on 1938 to 1962 data), 50% of the money would go in stocks and 50% in bonds. If the market's *P/E* were in a different quintile, the equity exposure would be set differently.

Fortunately for us, she decided to try five different strategies. One strategy deals in increments of 5%. So, a second quintile *P/E* would mean 45% in stocks, and a top quintile

P/E would mean 40% in stocks. Conversely, a fourth quintile *P/E* would mean 55% in stocks, and a bottom quintile *P/E* would mean 60% in stocks. The other four strategies are basically the same, but with different increment sizes: 10%, 15%, 20%, and 25%.

Table 24.5 shows what the proportion in equities would be in each strategy for each *P/E* quintile. Note that the percent in equities could jump by more than one increment at a time. If the *P/E* goes from a second quintile value to a fourth quintile value, the proportion in equities would increase by two increments.

Twenty-five more years have passed since our intrepid asset allocator began the experiment. Remember, we are interested in two questions: Did the future turn out to be like the past, and was a knowledge of the past any use?

Tables 24.6 and 24.7 provide the answers. The first column of Table 24.6 tells us how many of the 100 *P/E* observations from 1963 to 1987 fell into each of the 1938–1962 quintiles. It turns out that 40% of the *P/E* observations from 1963 to 1987 were above the cutoff for the top quintile of the 1938 to 1962 range. The three middle quintiles from the earlier period were underrepresented in the later years, with thirteen, fifteen, and eleven observations, while the bottom quintile had almost exactly the same number of occurrences as in the earlier period. So, *P/E*s from the first twenty-five years were not a perfect guide to what the range of *P/E*s would be in the next twenty-five years, but they were not too far off.

But what about performance? Were *P/E*s from the first twenty-five years a useful guide to the market's performance in the second twenty-five years? The rest of Table 24.6 shows the stock market's average price change and its average outperformance compared to bonds for each grouping based on the 1938–1962 *P/E* quintiles. In each case, the best performance is found in the bottom quintile. That is, in the years 1963 to 1987, when the market *P/E* fell into the bottom quintile of the 1938–1962 range, the market did in fact do very well, on average, over the six-month to two-year periods.

Table 24.5 Proportion in stock for each strategy (%)

P/E Quintile	Increment size				
	5%	10%	15%	20%	25%
1	40	30	20	10	0
2	45	40	35	30	25
3	50	50	50	50	50
4	55	60	65	70	75
5	60	70	80	90	100

Table 24.6 Distribution and performance over fifty years (%)

P/E Quintile based on 1938–1962	Number of observations 1963–1987	S&P 500: average price change over subsequent			S&P 500: average relative performance over subsequent		
		6 months	12 months	24 months	6 months	12 months	24 months
Highest	40	1.70	3.19	0.97	1.55	2.73	0.41
2	13	4.90	7.36	16.28	1.99	4.87	7.52
3	15	1.17	4.85	16.64	−1.32	−2.16	5.36
4	11	1.33	8.40	24.91	−2.06	−0.41	3.08
Lowest	21	8.98	15.90	26.43	6.59	12.37	20.95
Overall	100	3.53%	7.30%	13.91%	1.84%	3.98%	7.01%

Table 24.7 Returns and standard deviations
1963– 1987 (%)

Strategy	Annualized return	Standard deviation
5% moves	8.90	10.31
10% moves	8.88	10.38
15% moves	8.84	10.60
20% moves	8.78	10.96
25% moves	8.71	11.44
Static 50/50 mix	8.91%	10.38%

The other quintiles did not hold up as well in the second twenty-five years. It is true that over the subsequent twenty-four months the forty "top quintile" *P/E* readings did produce the lowest average returns (both absolute and relative to bonds). But over the shorter time periods, the results were much more ambiguous. In the relative performance columns, for example, results show that over six and twelve months the market did better following a *P/E* reading in the top two quintiles of the 1938–1962 range than it did following a *P/E* reading in the third and fourth quintiles of that range. In fact, the *P/E*s that fell into the second highest quintile of the historic range also produced the second highest average returns in five of the six columns in Table 24.6.

This does not bode well for our asset allocator. And in fact, her efforts turn out to be rather futile. Table 24.7 shows the annualized return and standard deviation for each of the five strategies for the years 1963 to 1987, as well as the figures for a static fifty-fifty mix over the same period. Figure 24.4 shows the efficient frontier created by mixing stocks and bonds over this period. It also shows how each of the strategies did relative to that frontier.

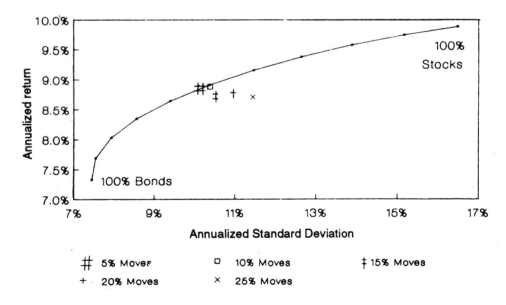

Figure 24.4 Efficient frontier, 1963–1987

Basically, only the least aggressive strategy — the one with 5% increments — was an efficient strategy. It yielded a slightly lower return than the fifty-fifty mix, but it also had slightly lower volatility, and, as Figure 24.4 shows, this strategy was right on the efficient frontier. As Table 24.7 shows, the other strategies all produced lower returns than the fifty-fifty mix while being more volatile. The more aggressively the investor tried to time the market using *P/E* as an indicator, the worse off she was. Note that the points in Figure 24.4 move farther and farther in the wrong direction as the size of the asset moves increases.

CONCLUSION

So what am I saying? Is *P/E* useless as a valuation measure? No, not that. What I'm saying is that yes, the future will be like the past, but only in broad outline. Over the long run, stocks will go up. Over most time periods longer than one year, they will outperform bonds. On average, the return on stocks (both absolute and relative) will be higher in the periods following low *P/E* values than in periods following high *P/E* values. Moreover, the likelihood that the market will do well seems to rise slightly as *P/E* falls.

But that's as far as we can go. As Arnold Bernhard found out in the early 1960s, an "overvalued" market can do well for quite a while. Historical *P/E*s are not graven in stone as valuation indicators. They do tell us something about probabilities and expected returns, but it remains far from clear how portfolio managers can use that information profitably.

25

The Equity Risk Premium and Tactical Asset Allocation

Peter Carman

I'll start by posing the two major questions about TAA. What is it, and why is everyone so interested in it? The following description has proved useful at Bernstein.

The basic assumption underlying tactical asset allocation is that it is possible to know the fair value of equities relative to other asset classes, fair value being a function of the asset classes' relative riskiness and the expected returns required to compensate investors for tolerating those risks. We define expected returns as yield to maturity for long bonds, the dividend discount model-based internal rate of return for the stock market and the current Treasury-bill rate for cash. It is assumed that, with this knowledge of fair value in hand, it is possible to shift portfolio commitments among asset classes when distortions in fair-value relationships materialize. Implemented in this manner, TAA should improve returns, reduce risk or both.

We believe that the fair expected-return premium for equities — what we call the equity risk premium — is 3.5 percentage points more than the yield to maturity on long Treasuries (Table 25.1). This means equities are fairly priced at a 3.5% spread; at that point, a portfolio targeted at 60% equities and 40% fixed income would be 60% invested in equities. If the

Table 25.1 If the proper equity risk premium is 3.5%, stocks are cheap when the spread is greater, and TAA would weight them above portfolio target

	Equity risk premium	% Invested in stocks
Stocks cheap	4.5%	90%
Fair value	3.5	60
Stocks expensive	2.5	30

TAA analytic framework for a 60/40 balanced portfolio

Reprinted from: Carman, P. 1988: *Tactical Asset Allocation: Have We Finally Found an Acceptable Name for Market Timing*? New York: Sanford C. Bernstein.

spread were to shrink by one percentage point, equities would appear expensive and, under decision rules described below, a tactical asset allocator would reduce equities to 30% of portfolio. If the spread were to widen to 4.5 percentage points, equities would appear cheap and exposure would be increased to 90%.

TAA ADDRESSES THE RIGHT ISSUES

Defined in this manner, TAA is attractive to us because it addresses the right issues. The process is price- and value-sensitive, dependent not on evaluation of near-term characteristics of the economy but on the long-term dividend-paying capability of the S&P 500. This is, in fact, the way we have always viewed relative value among asset classes.

Why is current interest in TAA so high? The answer is obvious and reasonable. Marketers of the service make the attractive claim that TAA disciplines allow practitioners to buy low and sell high. This is Nirvana. In support of the claim, we know that asset allocators were among the best-performing managers of 1987 and — since the market decline on October 19 was indiscriminate — they were virtually the only managers that protected capital during that debacle. Despite the hype and exaggeration that surrounds it because of recent performance, the process is logical, systematic and can claim attractive historical returns.

Therefore, we spent some time extending the research behind the relative returns we have always included in our quarterly equity reports, inquiring whether more active use of TAA could add return for clients. We backtested a set of decision rules that produced excellent performance in the 1980s similar to those actually achieved by TAA. The rules and results are worth reviewing.

EXCELLENT RESULTS IN THE EIGHTIES

Table 25.2 shows annualized returns from two portfolios from 1980 to 1987 — one invested 100% in the S&P 500, the other simulating use of a fairly aggressive application of tactical asset allocation, starting with a portfolio 60% invested in stocks and 40% in bonds (we felt it appropriate to compare TAA with 100% equities since, in this analysis, 100% equities was the upper limit for equity commitment in the TAA model). The TAA results are impressive: a 5.2 percentage point premium over the S&P 500 with lower volatility is nothing to sneeze at.

Now let's look at the assumptions (Table 25.3). We used only two asset classes — stocks and bonds; cash didn't make much difference. We set the fair-value spread at 3.5 percentage points. The neutral portfolio was 60% stocks and 40% bonds. Allocation shifts were made when the equity risk premium moved one percentage point.

Table 25.2 TAA beat the S&P 500 by 5.2% annualized in a 1980–87 simulation

S&P 500		(1980–87) TAA simulation (60%–40% neutral portfolio)		TAA simulation premium
Annualized return	Volatility*	Annualized return	Volatility*	
15.6%	17.5%	20.8%	14.3%	5.2%

*Standard deviation of monthly returns annualized.

Table 25.3 Our TAA simulation followed these rules

- Two asset classes: equities and long Treasury bonds
- Fair equity risk premium: 3.5%
- Portfolio 60% stocks/40% bonds with ERP at 3.5%
- Allocation shifts when ERP moved 1%
- Allocation shifts in 30% increments

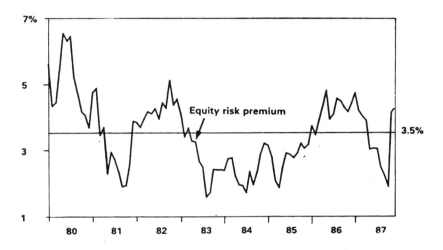

Figure 25.1 Stocks' expected return has averaged about 3.5% more than long bonds' yield to maturity

The 3.5% equity risk premium seemed reasonable based on recent history (Figure 25.1). From 1980 through 1987, the ERP has averaged about that level. The 60/40 starting allocation allowed us to benefit by shifting equity exposure both up and down at appropriate times. We shifted asset mix away from the starting point by 30 percentage points for each one percentage-point shift in the ERP away from fair value. For instance, if the ERP increased by one percentage point over fair value, to 4.5%, portfolio exposure to equities would increase from 60% to 90%.

LONGER-TERM RESULTS LESS COMPELLING

The picture for TAA is pretty compelling so far. But before we all sign up, we should review the long-term pattern of performance and the assumptions that served as basis for the decision rules. Longer-term backtest results are shown in Table 25.4. While the 1.3% premium was not so impressive as that earned in the 1980s alone, it was still pretty good, outearning the S&P 500 at lower risk.

If we divide performance into subperiods, however, TAA performance appears less compelling. Table 25.5 shows our simulated results for individual decades between the Fifties and the Eighties. Clearly, the bulk of the aggregate premium during these years was produced in the seven years of the 1980s. Aside from that, TAA performance was undistinguished relative to equities — except that, during all time periods, TAA returns were less volatile than a 100% equity portfolio.

Table 25.4 Longer term, TAA's results were less impressive than in the Eighties

S&P 500		(1951–87) TAA simulation (60%–40% Neutral portfolio)		TAA simulation premium
Annualized return	Volatility*	Annualized return	Volatility*	
11.4%	14.5%	12.7%	12.3%	1.3%

*Standard deviation of monthly returns annualized.

Table 25.5 Most of TAA's advantage in our simulation came in fairly recent years (compound annual return)

Time period	S&P 500	TAA simulation (60/40 Neutral portfolio)	TAA simulation premium
1951–59	18.2%	18.2%	0.0%
1960–69	7.8	6.2	(1.6)
1970–79	5.9	8.2	2.3
1980–87	15.6	20.8	5.2

STARTING WITH AN ALL-STOCK PORTFOLIO MADE LITTLE DIFFERENCE

Until this point we have looked at TAA starting with a 60/40 balanced portfolio. What if we started with 100% equities and shifted exposure down using the same decision rules? Results don't change much under these circumstances. On the far right of Table 25.6, note that the return premium from TAA versus all stocks for the period remained the same as that of the portfolio starting with a 60/40 mix. The positive impact of the higher average exposure to equities for the 100% starting-point portfolio offset the TAA contributions from the less-invested portfolio, which could increase equity exposure as well as decrease it.

The point is that TAA's long-term historic performance is particularly dependent on relatively recent events. Thus we had better understand whether the process's success is a temporary phenomenon, or if the key assumptions are reliable enough to depend on in the future.

Table 25.6 Starting with a fully invested portfolio rather than a 60/40 mix, TAA achieved the same moderate premium long-term

S&P 500		(1951–87) TAA simulation (beginning with 100% stocks)		TAA simulation premium
Annualized return	Volatility*	Annualized return	Volatility*	
11.4%	14.5%	12.7%	13.7%	1.3%

*Standard deviation of monthly returns annualized.

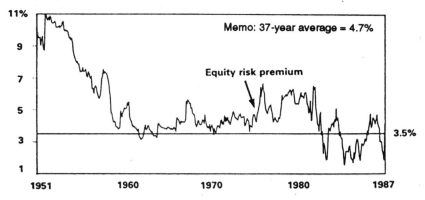

Figure 25.2 The critical factor is the proper equity risk premium — hard to estimate because it has varied so widely

IS 3.5% THE PROPER STOCK-BOND SPREAD?

The most important question is whether 3.5% is the correct fair differential between stock and bond returns. Figure 25.2 shows the expected-return premium's history during 1951–87. Note that it has ranged widely, from more than 10 percentage points in the 1950s to less than two more recently. Was it reasonable in the Fifties? I think it was. Investors and economists of the day had lived through the Depression of the 1930s and World War II; many were convinced that the Depression had ended only because of the war. It was not at all clear that the economy had any secular growth potential; it was possible that all growth was simply cyclical. Many believed the chances of a postwar depression were excellent. Under these circumstances, equities seemed an extraordinarily risky investment.

LARGE MISJUDGMENTS OF THE ERP ARE DANGEROUS

In any case, the expected-return premium has been so variable that there is potential for considerable instability. For these reasons we tested the robustness of the TAA process by using a number of expected-return premiums ranging from one to seven percentage points. Table 25.7 suggests TAA can misestimate the proper ERP by about two-plus percentage points, up or down, without producing subpar results. On the other hand, the process is sensitive to misestimations outside that range. And the potential for such large misestimation clearly existed during most of the 1950s.

The main danger is not that the ERP will turn out to be 4.5% rather than 3.5%, but that it may turn out to be 7%. And as the table indicated, returns under a seven-point ERP assumption were not very good.

Our evaluation of the 1950s' experience caused us to reassess our methodology and consider the possibility that the statistical relationship leading to the 3.5% ERP assumption would not have been obvious to investors at the time the estimates would have been made. We devised a simulation to take this into account. All assumptions were held constant except that, instead of a stable 3.5% ERP, we used a five-year rolling average to model more accurately investors' slowly changing perceptions.

Table 25.7 The ERP estimate can be off the mark by about 2% without real damage

ERP Assumption	(1951–87) TAA Simulation premium over S&P 500 (annualized return)
1%	0.2%
3	1.0
5	0.1
7	(2.8)

Table 25.8 When a rolling-average ERP was used instead of a static 3.5, TAA underperformed in the Fifties and matched all stocks over postwar history

Time period	S&P 500 annualized return	TAA simulation annualized return	TAA simulation premium
1950s	18.2%	14.7%	(3.5)%
1960s	7.8	5.9	(1.9)
1970s	5.9	7.6	1.7
1980s	15.6	19.8	4.2
1951–87	11.4	11.4	0.0

TAA simulation using rolling five-year ERP estimate

ADVANTAGE LOST UNDER VARIABLE ERP ASSUMPTION

As you can see in Table 25.8, the impact of this change was significant. Results in the 1950s were subpar. The high rolling five-year average ERP would have significantly reduced stock exposure under tactical asset allocation during that decade. Over the entire 37-year timeframe, results for TAA under these conditions were no better than those of the S&P 500.

Another problem with depending on the ERP to predict the relative performance of different asset classes is that, imbedded in virtually all TAA models is the assertion of a specific expected return for equities. That number contains important long-term forecasts including inflation and its pass-through into corporate profits, corporate profitability and real growth of gross national product. These forecasts are not easy to make.

FAULTY ECONOMIC FORECASTS CAN DESTROY ADVANTAGE

For example, under full and immediate inflation pass-through into corporate profit growth, a 1% change in inflation would affect the expected-return premium by 1%. This means that a 2% misestimate of inflation-related corporate profit growth would put an asset allocator outside the critical 2% tolerance range for mis-estimating the ERP.

Less obvious risks are difficult to quantify but, nevertheless, important. The best way to understand them is to think of TAA as the opposite of portfolio insurance, which is designed to produce acceptable results in extreme or unusual conditions. As Figure 25.3 illustrates, an insured portfolio provides downside protection and substantial upside participation: the

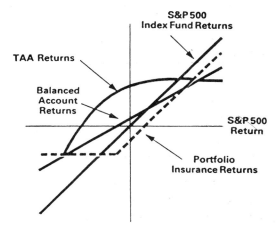

Figure 25.3 TAA does poorly in extreme markets, better at other times — the direct opposite of portfolio insurance

cost is regular, modest underperformance in the midrange, or most of the time. The return pattern of the balanced account, which represents the traditional method of dealing with portfolio risk, indicates it is something of a compromise between portfolio insurance and an all-equity portfolio. The pattern of return for TAA is very different from either of these.

TAA DOES POORLY IN EXTREMES

As the chart makes clear, TAA is likely to show poor results during dramatic extremes. It will sell out into rising markets and buy into declines, and the damage will be permanent if a sea change ever occurs in how investors view equities, or in corporate profitability and the inflation-hedge characteristic of stocks. On the other hand, TAA does very well when the market fluctuates around some trend line, which is most of the time, and which particularly characterized the 1980s.

It is paradoxical that the popularity of portfolio insurance was followed so closely by the popularity of TAA. Portfolio insurance gained prominence because of its attractive relative performance in unusual circumstances — dramatic market rises and declines. Its fall from grace was based not on change of opinion about its value in extremes, but on whether it could deliver the promised performance pattern at reasonable cost. Purchasers of TAA services may not fully understand that exposure to extremes is integral to the process.

WITH HIGH-RETURN STOCKS, TAA'S ADVANTAGE SHRINKS

Finally, we should ask if the ability to earn meaningful premiums over the S&P 500 should affect the way a manager or sponsor evaluates TAA. To answer the question, we substituted stocks chosen through Bernstein's dividend discount model for the S&P 500 as the equity position in the asset-allocation test outlined above — this time for the period 1970–87. The ERP assumption was a constant 3.5. The results appear in Table 25.9.

Table 25.9 Used with high-returning stocks like those chosen by Bernstein's dividend discount model, TAA's advantage shrinks

Results using:	TAA simulation premium (1970–87)
Bernstein Dividend Discount Model Simulated Returns	1.0%
S&P 500 Returns	3.5%

As you can see, TAA adds only a 1% premium to the simulated returns of equities chosen through Bernstein's model.[1] Thus, while some advantage remains in using TAA with high-return equities, that advantage shrinks. And the shrunken TAA premium is more likely to disappear if any of the forecast misjudgments described earlier materialize.

In sum, tactical asset allocation is a useful investment discipline with some drawbacks and areas of concern. It addresses the right questions: when stocks decline they should be more attractive and vice versa. Portfolios managed using TAA have been less volatile historically than all-stock portfolios, while providing competitive returns. On the other hand, the data on which decisions are made are not entirely reliable, and its performance advantage relative to 100% equities is uneven. There is some risk of significant relative performance penalty if there is a sea change in either corporate profitability, economic growth or investor evaluation of the risks of equity ownership. Finally, its advantage erodes if the equity investment alternative provides higher returns than the S&P 500.

ENDNOTE

1. [Discussion of this simulation has been omitted. (Note added by editor)].

26

The Markowitz Optimization Enigma: Is "Optimized" Optimal?

Richard O. Michaud

The Markowitz Mean-variance (MV) efficient frontier is the standard theoretical model of normative investment behavior.[1] Most modern finance textbooks consider mean-variance efficiency the method of choice for optimal portfolio construction and asset allocation and as a means for rationalizing the value of diversification. The Markowitz efficient frontier has also provided the basis for many important advances in positive financial economics, including the Sharpe-Lintner Capital Asset Pricing Model (CAPM) and recognition of the fundamental dichotomy between systematic and diversifiable risk.[2]

Given the success of the efficient frontier as a conceptual framework, and the availability for nearly 30 years of a procedure for computing efficient portfolios, it remains one of the outstanding puzzles of modern finance that MV optimization has yet to meet with widespread acceptance by the investment community, particularly as a practical tool for active equity investment management. Does this "Markowitz optimization enigma" reflect "a considered judgment [by the investment community] that such methods are not worthwhile," or is it "merely another case of deep-seated resistance to change."[3] The enigma is not easily dismissed by targeting the inadequate training in contemporary finance and mathematics of many practicing investment professionals. There are simplified MV-optimization procedures that are neither mathematically cumbersome nor antiintuitive.[4]

This article demonstrates that the enigma can be rationalized in many instances. The traditional MV procedure often leads to financially irrelevant or false "optimal" portfolios and asset allocations. In fact, equal weighting can be shown to be superior to MV optimization in some cases.[5] However, new techniques address some of the limitations of traditional MV optimizers, improving the practical investment value of portfolio optimization.[6]

CLASSICAL MARKOWITZ MV OPTIMIZATION

Classical MV optimization assumes that the investor prefers a portfolio of securities that offers maximum expected return for some given level of risk (as measured by the variance of return). Given estimated means, standard deviations and correlations of return for N securities, the MV-optimization procedure selects the proportions of investable wealth to devote to each security. The resulting set of prescribed portfolio weights (X_l through X_n) describe optimal solutions. (See the appendix for a mathematical formulation.)

The set of optimal portfolios for all possible levels of portfolio risk defines the MV efficient frontier. Figure 26.1 illustrates the classical MV efficient frontier in terms of the

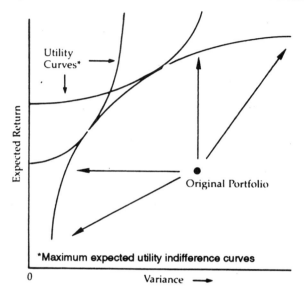

Figure 26.1   Markowitz mean-variance efficient frontier

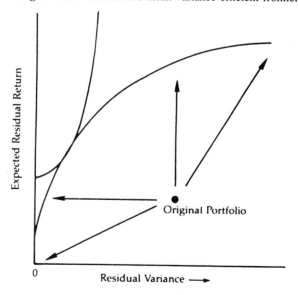

Figure 26.2   Expected residual return-risk MV efficient frontier

mean-variance of total return. Except for the names attached to the securities, the problems of equity portfolio optimization and asset allocation are equivalent in this framework. Figure 26.2 illustrates the efficient frontier in terms of the mean-variance of residual return, or "alpha"; in the case of equity portfolio optimization, alpha is usually defined as return in excess of the rate of return associated with the security's assumed systematic risk.[7] The optimal portfolio for any particular investor is the portfolio on the efficient frontier that is tangent to the "utility curve" that defines that investor's relative risk aversion.

In many cases of practical interest, the efficient frontier is defined subject to a budget constraint (sum of the proportions of invested wealth equal to one) and no short-selling (non-negative proportions of invested wealth). Other linear constraints, including trading costs, may be imposed. Computing the MV efficient frontier requires (parametric) quadratic programming.

BENEFITS OF MV OPTIMIZERS

This article focuses on the limitations of MV optimizers, but it is important to keep in mind some of the significant potential benefits of the technology. These are outlined below.

- *Satisfaction of client objectives and constraints*: Portfolio optimizers provide a convenient framework for integrating a wide variety of simple but important client constraints and objectives with portfolio structure.

- *Control of portfolio risk exposure*: Portfolio optimizers can be used to control the portfolio's exposure to various components of risk.

- *Implementation of style objectives and market outlook*: An organization's investment style, philosophy and market outlook may be reflected within the MV framework by choice of the appropriate exposure to various risk factors, the stock universe of interest and the performance benchmark.

- *Efficient use of investment information*: Optimizers are designed to use information optimally in a total portfolio context, while *ad hoc* weighting can be counterproductive with respect to available information.[8]

- *Timely portfolio changes*: Portfolio optimizers can process large amounts of information quickly, a particularly important benefit for a large institution, which needs to determine the impact of new information on all its portfolios quickly and conveniently.

SIMPLE REASONS FOR NOT USING MV OPTIMIZERS

Against these benefits of MV optimization there are arrayed some simple (though not necessarily robust) reasons for *not* using optimization. Optimizers make **conceptual demands** on portfolio managers. As products of modern finance, portfolio optimizers may seem difficult to use because investment managers are used to a more informal tradition of investment management. Optimization depends, explicitly or implicitly, on specification of an appropriate benchmark or normal portfolio, which may reflect a manager's investment style, philosophy or outlook. Consequently, information is reflected, not by the exclusion or inclusion of securities in the portfolio, but by the extent to which portfolio weights deviate from normal or benchmark weights.

Probably the single most important reason why many financial institutions don't use portfolio optimizers is **political**. This is because the effective use of an optimizer mandates significant changes in the structure of the organization and the management of the investment process. In many investment organizations the investment policy committee, which often consists of the senior officer(s) of the firm, makes the key investment decisions. An optimizer may tend to usurp many of the integrative functions of the committee.

Introduction of an optimizer will also tend to encourage the development of a more quantitative investment process, which may involve unwelcome adjustments. For one thing, it will increase significantly the level of accountability, communication and risk-sharing within the organization. This is because quantitative valuation models require that input forecasts be stated explicitly, while the valuation process itself provides return estimates that are unambiguous descriptions of value. For another, control of the optimization algorithm requires a working knowledge of basic statistical concepts and modern portfolio theory. As the ability to understand the financial meaning of the statistical characteristics of a portfolio becomes critical, quantitatively-oriented specialists inevitably assume a central role in the investment process. It is therefore not very surprising that traditional managers of large financial institutions are not eager to relinquish their positions of power and influence by allowing an optimizer and a quantitative specialist to usurp key roles in the investment process.

Organizational politics or inexperience with modern financial technology cannot fully explain the Markowitz optimization enigma. If MV optimizers added value, new investment management firms, organized and staffed to manage and leverage the technology, would eventually displace more traditional firms.

It is known anecdotally that a number of experienced investment professionals have experimented with MV optimizers only to abandon the effort when they found their MV-optimized portfolios to be unintuitive and without obvious investment value. As a practical matter, even absent the influence of organizational politics, the optimized portfolios were often found to be unmarketable either internally or externally.

SOME FUNDAMENTAL LIMITATIONS

The key operative issue in regard to MV optimizers can be stated simply, in terms of two alternative hypotheses:

(1) MV-optimized portfolios are better, even though they are difficult to understand.

(2) MV-optimized portfolios are difficult to understand because they don't make investment sense and don't have investment value.

This article argues that the unintuitive character of MV-optimized portfolios is often symptomatic of the absence of significant investment value. MV optimizers have serious financial deficiencies, which will often lead to financially meaningless "optimal" portfolios.

ERROR MAXIMIZATION

The unintuitive character of many "optimized" portfolios can be traced to the fact that MV optimizers are, in a fundamental sense, "estimation-error maximizers." Risk and return estimates are inevitably subject to estimation error. MV optimization significantly overweights (underweights) those securities that have large (small) estimated returns, negative (positive) correlations and small (large) variances. These securities are, of course, the ones most likely to have large estimation errors.

Jobson and Korkie have quantified the magnitude of the error-maximization characteristics of MV optimizers in certain cases.[9] Using a known multivariate distribution of monthly returns for 20 stocks, they found the "optimal" portfolio, defined as that portfolio on the efficient frontier with the maximum Sharpe ratio (excess return divided by the standard deviation). Then, using Monte Carlo simulations, they estimated expected returns, variances and covariances for the 20 stocks over a 60-month period and computed the "optimal" portfolio for each set of estimates. Finally, they compared the true Sharpe ratios of (1) the average of the simulated optimal portfolios; (2) the optimal portfolio derived from the known multivariate distribution; and (3) an equally weighted portfolio of the 20 stocks. The true Sharpe ratios were, respectively, 0.08, 0.34 and 0.27! Their results, illustrated in Figure 26.3, dramatically confirm the error-maximization hypothesis.

One caveat should be noted for accurate interpretation of the Jobson-Korkie results: The computed optimal portfolios did not include a short-selling constraint. Including this condition would have reduced the magnitude of the differences across the Sharpe ratios of the three portfolios. Furthermore, most financial institutions do have short-selling constraints. The Jobson-Korkie conclusions thus need to be moderated, although they are not invalidated, when applied to a realistic investment management setting.[10] These results also strongly confirm the importance of imposing financially meaningful constraints, when they are available, on the MV-optimization procedure.

A practical and general consequence of the error-maximization process is that any estimates of the statistical characteristics of optimized portfolios, if those characteristics are part of the optimization objective function, may be significantly biased. The measure of

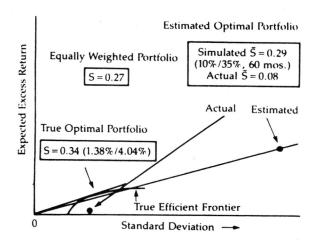

Source: Data from J.D. Jobson and B. Korkie "Putting Markowitz Theory to Work," *Journal of Portfolio Management*, Summer 1981.

Figure 26.3   The error-maximization effect

diversifiable risk produced by the optimizer, for example, is likely to be a significant under-estimate of the optimal portfolio's true level of risk.

GOOD AND BAD ESTIMATORS

An important contributor to the error-maximizing character of MV optimization when using historical data is that the usual estimation procedure — which replaces expected returns with their sample means — is (generally) not optimal.

An estimator is "admissible" if there exists no other estimator that dominates it for a given risk or loss function.[11] Stein has shown that, under standard conditions, sample means are not an admissible estimator of expected returns.[12] Intuitively, sample means are suboptimal because they ignore the inherent multivariate nature of the problem. More powerful statistical estimation techniques are required.

MISSING FACTORS AND NON-FINANCIAL STRUCTURE

MV optimization often ignores factors that are fundamentally important investment management considerations. One of the most important of these factors is liquidity, or the percentage of a company's market capitalization represented by portfolio holdings.

A portfolio of a large bank trust department or a portfolio of small-cap stocks, for example, may hold a significant percentage of a security's market capitalization. A 1% change in the portfolio may thus represent a very substantial amount of the total value of the firm. As the proportion of the total value of the company purchased (sold) by the portfolio becomes significant, the purchase (sale) price is likely to rise (fall).

Figure 26.4 illustrates the impact of liquidity on the set of efficient portfolios. Compared with the traditional (unconstrained) MV frontier, imposition of a liquidity constraint results in less return enhancement and/or less risk reduction. In an extreme case, for very large capitalization portfolios, the MV frontier may be close to the original, "unoptimized," portfolio.

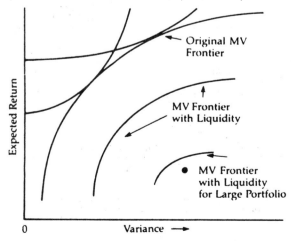

Figure 26.4   MV frontier with liquidity factor

Liquidity considerations suggest some important principles for valid portfolio optimization. (1) For a large financial institution, the "true" optimal portfolio may not differ substantially from its current portfolio. (2) Large financial institutions must necessarily use care in revising their portfolios. (3) An optimal portfolio is inherently position-dependent, even when traditional transaction costs are ignored.

MISMATCHED LEVELS OF INFORMATION

Optimizers do not differentiate between levels of uncertainty associated with the inputs. This problem is not confined to the difference in uncertainty between return and risk estimates; there are also significant differences across the levels of uncertainty associated with input estimates for various classes of stocks, such as utilities versus growth stocks.

A related problem is that, in many cases, differences in estimated means may not be statistically significant. In such cases, the primary value of MV analysis may be to reduce portfolio risk.[13]

UNSTABLE OPTIMAL SOLUTIONS

In some cases, MV optimizations are highly unstable; that is, small changes in the input assumptions can lead to large changes in the solutions. One important reason for this behavior is ill-conditioning of the covariance matrix. MV optimization requires the inversion of a covariance matrix; an ill-conditioned matrix will generally result in unstable solutions. Input assumptions that do not reflect financially meaningful estimates or the use of parameter estimates based on insufficient historical data are often associated with ill-conditioning and instability.

NON-UNIQUENESS

Optimizers, in general, produce a unique "optimal" portfolio for a given level of risk. This appearance of exactness is highly misleading, however. The uniqueness of the solution depends on the erroneous assumption that the inputs are without statistical estimation error.

As Figure 26.5 illustrates, given any point on the true MV efficient frontier, there is a neighborhood of the point (illustrated by the shaded area on and below the frontier) that includes an infinite number of statistically equivalent portfolios.[14] These "optimally equivalent" portfolios may have significantly, even radically, different portfolio structures. In effect, this means that optimal portfolio structure is fundamentally not well defined.

EXACT VS. APPROXIMATE MV OPTIMIZERS

A variety of commercially available optimization algorithms are marketed as MV optimizers.[15] Some provide "exact" (quadratic programming), others "approximate" optimal solutions. The difference determines such characteristics as (a) processing time; (b) entire frontier vs. single-point solution; (c) maximum size of the optimization universe; and (d) the ability to operate on standard personal computers.

Quadratic (parametric) programming, a generalization of linear programming, can solve for the entire MV (or alpha-diversifiable risk) efficient frontier. The primary limitations

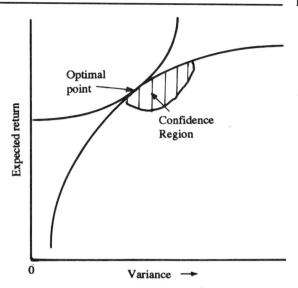

Figure 26.5 Statistically equivalent MV efficient portfolio

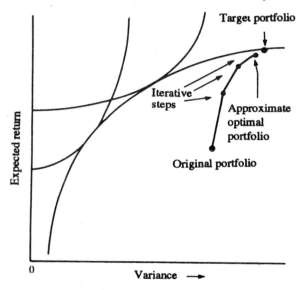

Figure 26.6 Approximate-estimate MV efficient frontier

of the procedure are a relatively small universe size and/or relatively long computational time. Although the algorithm can include transaction costs, they have often been ignored. Enhancements of the traditional algorithm, which allow for the solution of relatively large-scale optimization problems in the presence of factor models of risk, are available.[16]

Approximate MV optimizers are able to solve optimizations for "institutional-size" portfolios and generally include transaction costs and options to optimize other factors. Their important limitation is that they provide a single "optimal" portfolio that is "near" the MV efficient frontier. As Figure 26.6 shows, this procedure finds a succession of "more optimal" portfolios at each iteration, ceasing the search when a portfolio within a specified tolerance is found.

Some practitioners have claimed that MV-optimal portfolios derived from approximate optimizers don't seem particularly unintuitive. Do the characteristics of approximate and exact optimizers differ? Are approximate optimizers "better" in some fundamental, practical sense? Or are they only better at hiding the limitations of MV optimization? If both procedures solve for the same objective function under the same constraints, the results should be identical. Some reasons for any observed differences are discussed below.

INADEQUATE APPROXIMATION POWER

Approximate MV-optimal portfolios, because they *are* approximations, reflect less of the information in the input estimates, including the effects of error maximization, than exact optimizers.

This problem may be particularly acute for many PC-based optimization programs. Often used for asset allocation studies, PC optimization programs can reflect their lack of approximation power by a remarkable lack of instability in their solutions. Very different input assumptions have led to similar "optimal" allocations.[17]

DEFAULT SETTINGS OF THE PARAMETERS

Approximate optimizers solve for a single optimal portfolio near the MV efficient frontier. To single out an optimal portfolio, they must assume some value for the "target" parameter in the objective function. Risk-aversion or suitability parameters may have been set to target the more "explainable" parts of the MV frontier. At the maximum-return end of the efficient frontier, an MV-optimized portfolio has a very easily definable structure — maximize return (or alpha) and ignore risk.

Approximate MV optimizers are convenient. But the benefit of convenience should be weighed against the additional and unpredictable level of error they impose on the optimization process. Except in cases where it is computationally infeasible, parametric quadratic programming remains the algorithm of choice.

ENHANCING MV OPTIMIZATION

Procedures for enhancing MV optimization share important similarities. They are often Bayesian in character and depend on the existence of a prior, either for adjustment of the inputs or as a constraint on the optimization.

ASSET ALLOCATION WITH RESPECT TO A BENCHMARK

While it is common institutional practice to define equity portfolio optimization in terms of a benchmark such as a market index, it is infrequent in asset allocation studies. Yet in many cases MV efficiency is properly defined in terms of performance with respect to an index or a liability. (In the context of a liability benchmark, the problem is sometimes called "surplus" management.)

The MV-optimization procedure for funding a liability is called "benchmark asset allocation."[18] Liability changes represent the prior for judging the benefits of returns associated with an asset allocation in a given period. The optimization's input parameters are redefined to reflect residual returns with respect to the benchmark.

Introducing a benchmark can significantly alter the characteristics of MV-optimal asset allocations. In general, benchmark asset allocation is strongly dependent on the economic characteristics of the liabilities. It is consequently far less time-period dependent or unstable and appears to have substantially more practical investment value.

BAYES-STEIN SHRINKAGE ESTIMATORS

Bayes-Stein estimators constitute an important class of admissible estimators of expected returns when historical data are used. Observed sample means for individual assets are "shrunk" to some global mean. The global mean may represent the pooled mean, a Bayesian prior or the mean of the minimum-variance efficient-frontier portfolio. In many cases, the greater the variability in the historical data, the greater the shrinkage of sample means to the global mean.[19] Tests of Bayes-Stein estimation have shown that it can improve traditional MV optimization significantly.[20]

For a given utility function, Bayes-Stein estimation generally changes the MV-optimal portfolio, shrinking the recommended optimal mix in the direction of the minimum-variance efficient portfolio.[21] The amount of shrinkage of the input estimates generally increases as the number of asset classes increases and the number of time periods decreases. Bayes-Stein estimators represent an important emerging technology with significant potential for improving the practicality of MV optimization.

THE IC ADJUSTMENT

In many cases, financial institutions use stock valuation models, rather than historical returns, to estimate the "returns" input to an optimizer. Such "estimates" generally take the form of relative valuations, rankings or simple ordinal assignments.

The optimizer requires a ratio-scale estimate of return or alpha for each security so that the return and risk input estimates, usually derived from historical data, are on comparable scales. Ambachtsheer provides an "IC adjustment" that can be used to convert rank or ordinal valuations into inputs for optimization.[22] The appendix describes a generalization of this process.

The IC adjustment converts forecasts to a scale that represents the average return associated with the forecast. The "adjusted" returns are then on a scale comparable to the risk estimates and other constraints used in the optimization, such as transaction costs. The IC adjustment may operate as a shrinkage operator formally similar to a Bayes-Stein estimator.

While widely used, the procedure is often not well understood. Although the sole purpose of the IC adjustment is to convert forecast returns onto an economically meaningful scale, it is frequently employed as an *ad hoc* method for controlling the optimization results by adjusting the magnitude of input alphas. The IC adjustment as used in practice is thus often fallacious. In particular, as the example in the appendix shows, correct IC adjustment may not even change the size of an alpha derived from a traditional dividend discount model under common assumptions.

ALTERNATIVES TO MV OPTIMIZATION

The non-uniqueness of MV-optimal portfolios has important implications for active equity managers. Most importantly, the inherent ambiguity of optimal portfolio structure provides a rationale for choosing from among statistically equivalent optimal portfolios that portfolio most consistent with priors of financial relevance, understandability and marketability.

Understandability and financial meaning are fundamentally important practical consider-ations in defining valid portfolio construction criteria. Valid financial considerations, not the rigid application of a computer program, should dominate the portfolio construction process.

THE LINEAR PROGRAMMING ALTERNATIVE

The non-uniqueness principle allows consideration of linear programming as an alternative optimization technology. Linear programming has been successfully used by a number of organizations to optimize fixed income portfolios for a wide range of purposes. It is also an integral part of the investment process of some active equity managers.[23]

For equity optimization, linear programming provides a tool for designing portfolios with maximum (excess) return with specified financial characteristics, such as specific values or ranges of beta or yield. Simple techniques, which in many cases imitate the activities of active managers, can be used to control the overall level of diversification and extra-market risk in the portfolio. Other constraints can be imposed to take transaction costs and liquidity into account. The end result is an "optimized" portfolio with well-defined risk characteristics and readily understandable structure that avoids important errors associated with the overuse of information in statistical estimates.

Linear programming does not eliminate the problem of error maximization, although the errors may be easier to understand and correct. This is because the error-maximization process itself is linear, not quadratic; high or low concentrations in a stock or sector can easily be traced to large or small estimates of return.

"Optimal" portfolios based on linear programming may be criticized because they are not mean-variance efficient and are therefore subject to the possible misuse of valid forecast information.[24] But such theoretical criticisms have little practical relevance if the "optimal" portfolio structure cannot be unambiguously defined in the context of the statistical limita-tions of the input data. At the current state of technology, an enhanced linear programming algorithm, carefully defined and controlled, may be useful in providing a practical balance of limitations and benefits, especially for active equity management.

Ultimately, the benefits of equity optimization based on linear programming technology must be judged relative to the benefits that can be provided by carefully defined, input-adjusted, MV optimization. This is still an open issue. In many cases, however, the problems of error maximization that most limit the practical value of MV optimization seem largely attributable to estimate errors in the return, rather than the risk, dimension. This suggests that the value of linear programming technology for practical investment management may ultimately be limited.

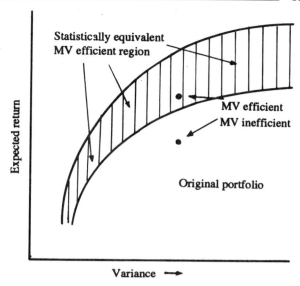

Figure 26.7   Test for MV efficiency

TESTING FOR MEAN-VARIANCE EFFICIENCY

An important alternative to MV optimization is to test for the MV efficiency of a given portfolio.[25] Figure 26.7 illustrates the procedure. The portfolio to be tested is represented by a point below the efficient frontier. The test determines whether or not the given portfolio lies within a confidence region of portfolios that are statistically equivalent to points on the MV frontier. The confidence region increases as expected return increases, reflecting the assumed lower accuracy of the estimates of expected return versus risk.[26]

Such a procedure, at least conceptually, is very attractive. Assuming that the investor or institution considers the portfolio to be tested as "optimal," the portfolio represents a revealed preference about the appropriate level of risk. The issue of which utility function to use to define a point on the efficient frontier may thus not be material.

There are two substantive problems with the approach. First, the tests have little power; the null hypothesis — MV efficiency — will often not be rejected when it is false. Second, current tests are inappropriate for many problems of practical interest; the MV efficient frontier is unconstrained, including allowance for short sales. As a practical matter, available tests have limited value as indicators of whether a given portfolio is "far" from the (unconstrained) MV efficient frontier.

SPECIALIZED APPLICATIONS OF MV OPTIMIZATION

The substantial limitations of MV optimization when applied to the general problem of optimal portfolio construction have been noted above. Some important specialized applications are discussed below.

INDEX OR TRACKING FUNDS

MV optimizers may be used to structure "index" or "tracking" funds for equity management. The objective is to structure from a prescribed set of securities a portfolio whose performance will be similar (within a specified tolerance) to that of a given index. The optimization is defined by setting the return inputs equal to zero and imposing few, if any, constraints on the solution. In this case, the MV efficient frontier reduces to a single point — the portfolio with minimum tracking error or residual variance.

Most of the problems normally associated with MV optimizers are eliminated, or greatly reduced, when MV optimization is applied to indexing. There is no error maximization resulting from errors in the return estimates. No errors are created by mismatches in the levels of uncertainty in the return versus risk estimates. Because the exact structure of the optimal solution is not the focus of the analysis, neither non-uniqueness nor unintuitiveness is an important consideration. The basic remaining source of error is the adequacy of the risk model. If the index is standard, MV optimization may provide a useful procedure for defining tracking funds. Error maximization may be exhibited primarily in terms of downward-biased estimates of the tracking error.

Nevertheless, two of the most widely used procedures for index fund management — replication and stratified sampling — do not require MV-optimization technology.[27] Replication funds index-weight the stocks in an index fund, with minimal restrictions. Stratified-sampling funds include a small number of large-capitalization securities plus a selection of securities within each industry group to match the capitalization weights of the index. The lesson of practice suggests that the strength of the error-maximization process and/or the limitations of available equity risk models may significantly limit the value of MV optimizers even when applied to structuring pure index funds.

TILTED INDEX FUNDS

Tilted index or "value-added" funds minimize tracking error with respect to the selected index while maximizing other portfolio characteristics, such as dividend yield. These additional objectives can be treated as factors in the optimization objective function. As components of a separable utility function, they operate as penalty functions trading off one portfolio attribute for another.[28] This procedure can raise problems, however, both because it is likely to introduce biased estimates of the characteristics included in the objective and because it requires assigning appropriate utility weights to the factor functions, which may be very difficult to rationalize or control.

ASSET ALLOCATION

When applied to the asset allocation problem, MV optimization aims to find an optimal mix of asset classes. The analysis may include domestic and foreign equity market indexes and various categories of corporate and government bonds. The number of assets is generally small, usually significantly less than 20.

MV-optimization estimates, even when based primarily on historical data, may be reasonably reliable in the asset-allocation context. This is because a relatively small number of estimates are required and because they are often intended to reflect the long-term structure of financial markets. The character of the "optimal" allocation may consequently be anticipated, and errors created by the input estimates more easily controlled. Benchmark asset allocation may be particularly beneficial in reducing the impact of estimation errors and focusing the optimization process on the investor's valid investment objectives.

On the negative side, asset allocation without a suitable benchmark is significantly error-prone because the focus is on the least reliable result of the optimization — the financial structure of the optimal asset mix. The most important operative issue — non-uniqueness — implies that there may be statistically equivalent MV-optimal asset allocations with very different financial structures. This effect is often observed in the time-period sensitivity of asset-allocation results. A reliable optimal asset mix recommendation requires a more than casual understanding of the characteristics of the confidence region associated with the input estimates.

CONCLUSION

Markowitz MV-optimization technology is not easy to use properly. In fact, equal weighting may significantly outperform unconstrained MV optimization in many cases. The fundamental problem is that the level of mathematical sophistication of the optimization algorithm is far greater than the level of information in the input forecasts. MV optimizers operate in such a manner that they magnify the errors associated with the input estimates. Without careful problem definition derived from sound investment judgment and sophisticated adjustment of the inputs, MV optimization may often do more harm than good.

Given the increasing potential for error maximization as the number of assets under consideration increases, the optimization process must be carefully controlled if it is to produce solutions of practical value for active equity managers. Optimization should be defined with respect to a suitable benchmark. Transaction and liquidity cost constraints and appropriate adjustment of the inputs are generally recommended. Sector and industry constraints, if available and appropriate, may be usefully included. The operative principle is that any information on the structure of the optimal prior, to the extent that it is reliable, may be included in the definition of the optimization problem.

Nevertheless, the fact that priors and constraints are generally required to derive financially meaningful optimized portfolios may indicate that MV optimization is often superfluous even counterproductive, and that simpler, more direct approaches to portfolio construction may often be advisable.

APPENDIX

Traditional Quadratic (MV) Optimization
MV optimization maximizes

$$\mu - \lambda\sigma^2$$

or

$$\alpha - \lambda\omega^2 - k(\beta - \beta_T)^2$$

subject to the following linear constraints:

$$X \geqslant 0$$

$$\sum X = 1$$

where

μ = expected portfolio return,
σ^2 = portfolio variance,
X = proportion of initial wealth invested in an individual asset,
λ = risk-aversion parameter, which varies to trace out the MV efficient frontier,
α = expected portfolio systematic risk-adjusted (residual) return,
β = estimated portfolio systematic (beta) risk,
ω^2 = estimated portfolio residual risk,
β_T = target portfolio beta, and
k = a prespecified positive constant.

The computation may include transaction cost and other linear constraints (e.g., yield or P/E portfolio values).

THE IC ADJUSTMENT

A simple use of linear least-squares regression provides a useful foundation for the IC adjustment procedure for many applications. Assume that a forecast process provides estimates of systematic risk-adjusted returns or alphas, where the cross-sectional mean is zero. Assume also that the subsequent ex post alphas for each stock are also available, with mean equal to zero. Perform a linear least-squares regression of ex post against ex ante alphas:

$$A_i = c + d\alpha_i + \varepsilon_i$$

where

A_i = ex post alpha,
c = the constant linear regression parameter,
d = the slope linear regression parameter,
α_i = ex ante alpha and
ε_i = the error term.

By assumption, $c = 0$. By definition, the regression coefficient, d, is the IC adjustment, where

$$d = \mathrm{IC}\sigma(A)/\sigma(\alpha)$$

and

IC = cross-sectional "information" correlation of ex ante and ex post alpha,
$\sigma(A)$ = cross-sectional standard deviation of ex post alpha and
$\sigma(\alpha)$ = cross-sectional standard deviation of ex ante alpha.

The product, $d\alpha_i$, is interpretable as the "excess return on average associated with forecast alpha, α_i." The IC adjustment parameter, d, provides the appropriate scale transformation of the forecast alpha with respect to ex post alpha for the given stock universe.

Note that the value of d requires three forecasts for the given stock universe — (1) the IC value; (2) the ex post level of volatility, $\sigma(A)$; and (3) the implicit forecast horizon. The values of IC and $\sigma(A)$ can be estimated from historical data or may be input as subjective estimates. For many stock valuation models, the IC is assumed to have a value of the order 0.05 to 0.20. In applications, it may be appropriate to use different values of the IC adjustment parameters, depending on the characteristics of the stock universe (e.g., growth stocks are likely to have very different IC and volatility values and forecast horizon than utility stocks).

The IC adjustment is essentially a 'two-step process — a ratio scale transformation of the forecasts, indicated by the ratio $\sigma(A)/\sigma(\alpha)$, followed by a transformation based on the level of the information in the forecasts, indicated by the IC multiplication. It is this first step that is often not well understood in traditional applications of the procedure.

For ordinal or rank data, the Ambachtsheer procedure for creating forecast alpha implies that $\sigma(A) = \sigma(\alpha)$ by construction. In this case, $d = \text{IC}$, which rationalizes common institutional practice. For the traditional dividend discount model (DDM) alpha, the simple IC procedure — multiplying alpha by the value of IC — is often not valid.[29] The problem is: Under what conditions can we assume that $\sigma(A) = \sigma(\alpha)$?

Consider the following exercise. For many traditional DDMs, $\sigma(\alpha)$ is approximately 3%.[30] Assume, as is traditional in applications associated with DDM alphas, a forecast horizon of one year and a representative capital market universe. To compute $\sigma(A)$ assume a market standard deviation of 20% and a multiplier of 1.5 for the cross-sectional standard deviation of stock alpha; i.e., $\sigma(A)$ is approximately 30%. Finally, assume an IC value of 0.1. In this case, the valid IC adjustment of DDM alpha is one; the IC adjustment is not a shrinkage operator. Valid shrinkage of DDM alphas may require a shorter forecast horizon assumption and/or lower IC value.

ENDNOTES

1. Markowitz, H. *Portfolio Selection: Efficient Diversification of Investments* (New York: John Wiley, 1959).

2. Sharpe, W. "Capital Asset Prices: A Theory of Market Equilibrium under Conditions of Risk," *Journal of Finance*, September 1964, and Lintner, J. "The Valuation of Risk Assets and the Selection of Risky Investments in Stock Portfolios and Capital Budgets," *Review of Economics and Statistics*, February 1965.

3. Gray, W. "Portfolio Construction: Equity," in Maginn, J. and Tuttle, D. eds., *Managing Investment Portfolios: A Dynamic Approach* (Boston: Warren, Gorham & Lamont, 1983), p. 415.

4. Elton, N., Gruber, M. and Padberg, M. "Optimal Portfolios from Simple Ranking Devices," *Journal of Portfolio Management*, Spring 1978.

5. Jobson, J.D. and Korkie, B. "Putting Markowitz Theory to Work," *Journal of Portfolio Management*, Summer 1981.

6. The scope of this article is limited to the assumptions implicit in the valid application of the MV efficient frontier framework. It does not address (1) time horizon and multiperiod MV efficiency, (2) the appropriate theoretical framework for defining systematic risk, or (3) optimization in the sense of strategic asset allocation with respect to the business risks of the firm or liabilities of the fund. For (1) see, for example, Markowitz, *Portfolio Selection, op. cit.*, Chapter 6; Latane, H.

"Criteria for Choice Among Risky Ventures," *Journal of Political Economy*, April 1959; Hakansson, N. "A Characterization of Optimal Multi-Period Portfolio Policies," in Elton, N. and Gruber, M. eds., *Portfolio Theory, 25 Years After* (New York: North Holland, 1979); and Michaud, R. "Risk Policy and Long-Term Investment," *Journal of Financial and Quantitative Analysis*, June 1981. For (2) see Ross, S. "The Arbitrage Theory of Capital Asset Pricing," *Journal of Economic Theory*, December 1976 and "Return, Risk and Arbitrage," in Friend, I. and Bicksler, J. eds., *Risk and Return in Finance* (Cambridge, MA: Ballinger, 1977). For (3) see Roll, R. and Ross, S. "The Arbitrage Pricing Theory Approach to Strategic Portfolio Planning," *Financial Analysts Journal*, May/June 1984.

7.   See Rudd, A. and Rosenberg, B. "Realistic Portfolio Optimization," in Elton and Gruber, eds., *Portfolio Theory, op. cit.* Equity residual return or alpha is the difference between total return and the total return associated with the level of systematic risk. Residual risk is the variance of residual return, which is parametric in the level of systematic risk.

8.   Sharpe, W. *Investments*, 3rd ed. (Englewood Cliffs, NJ: Prentice-Hall, 1985), pp. 666–670.

9.   Jobson, J.D. and Korkie, B. "Estimation for Markowitz Efficient Portfolios," *Journal of the American Statistical Association*, September 1980 and Jobson and Korkie, "Putting Markowitz Theory to Work," *op. cit.*

10. For a recent discussion, see Frost, P. and Savarino, J. "For Better Performance: Constrain Portfolio Weights," *Journal of Portfolio Management*, Fall 1988.

11. Admissibility is a minimum condition used to reduce the decision problem without loss of relevant information. See Lehmann, E. *Testing Statistical Hypotheses* (New York: John Wiley, 1959), p. 16.

12. Stein, C. "Inadmissibility of the Usual Estimator for the Mean of a Multivariate Normal Distribution," *Proceedings of the 3rd Berkeley Symposium on Probability and Statistics* (Berkeley: University of California Press, 1955). For example, vector of means, independent, normally distributed, quadratic loss functions, known covariance matrix.

13. Jorion, P. "International Portfolio Diversification with Estimation Risk," *Journal of Business*, July 1985.

14. The shaded region below the efficient frontier represents a rough illustration of a confidence region, based on some unpublished simulations provided by Jorion, P.

15. See Samuelson, P. "Computer Construction of Optimal Portfolios," in Levine, S. ed., *The Investment Manager's Handbook* (Homewood, IL: Dow Jones-Irwin, 1980) and W. Sharpe, "Microcomputer Perspectives: Asset Allocation Systems," *Financial Analysts Journal*, May/June 1985.

16. Perold, A. "Large Scale Portfolio Optimization," *Management Science*, October 1984.

17. Seidel, D. "Market Indices in the Asset Allocation Framework" (presented to the Institute for Quantitative Research in Finance, Spring 1986).

18. See Michaud, R. "Pension Policy and Benchmark Optimization," *Pension Executive Review* (Merrill Lynch, New York, July 1988) for a description of the procedure.

19. See Jorion, "International Portfolio Diversification," *op. cit.* and "Bayes-Stein Estimation for Portfolio Analysis," *Journal of Financial and Quantitative Analysis*," September 1986.

20. Jobson, "Putting Markowitz Theory to Work," *op. cit.* and Jorion, "International Portfolio Diversification" and "Bayes-Stein Estimation," *op. cit.*

21. *Ibid.*

22. Ambachtsheer, K. "Where Are the Customers' Alphas?" *Journal of Portfolio Management*, Fall 1977.

23. Farrell, J. *Guide to Portfolio Management* (New York: McGraw-Hill, 1983), pp. 168–174.

24. See footnote 8.

25. See, for example, Jobson, J.D. and Korkie, B. "Potential Performance and Tests of Portfolio Efficiency," *Journal of Financial Economics*, September 1982; Shaken, J. "Multivariate Tests of the

Zero-Beta CAPM," *Journal of Financial Economics*, September 1985 and "Testing Portfolio Efficiency when the Zero Beta Rate is Unknown," *Journal of Finance*, 1986, pp. 269–276; Roll, R. "A Note on the Geometry of Shaken's CSR T^2 Tests for Mean/Variance Efficiency," *Journal of Financial Economics*, September 1985; and Amsler, C.E. and Schmidt, P. "A Monte Carlo Investigation of the Accuracy of Multivariate CAPM Tests," *Journal of Financial Economics*, 1985, pp. 359–375.

26. I am indebted to Jorion, P. for this observation.

27. For example, Wilshire Associates' index fund management service uses index replication and stratified sampling exclusively.

28. See Rudd and Rosenberg, "Realistic Portfolio Optimization," *op. cit.*

29. Generally defined as the residual formed from the linear least-squares regression of DDM implied returns against beta.

30. See Michaud, R. and Davis, P. "Valuation Model Bias and the Scale Structure of Dividend Discount Returns," *Journal of Finance*, May 1982.

PART FIVE
Investment Asset Pot-Pourri

Part Five consists of a selection of articles that cover important topics that do not fit into other Parts.

Real estate represents a major component of world wealth. Think of all the private residences, the real estate owned by corporations and also farmland. Some years ago, Ibbotson *et al.* (1985) estimated that real estate formed about 55% of the world's physical and financial capital. Within the U.S., residential real estate accounted for about 39% of investment assets, and business real estate and farmland about 7% each. These numbers should be taken with a pinch of salt, but the importance of real estate cannot be denied. Somewhat surprisingly, the proportion of real estate in institutional investment portfolios is quite small. Amongst the largest institutional portfolios it comprises less than 5% in the U.S., about 8% in Canada and less than 10% in the U.K. These figures were higher 20 years ago. Inflation was seen as more of a problem then than it now is, and real estate was seen as an inflation hedge. An interesting international point is that real estate leases in the U.K. are different from those in most other countries because they are typically for 25 years with five year, upward only, rent reviews. This has been very attractive to institutional investors in an inflation-prone country and so it is not surprising that U.K. institutional investors have been more attracted to real estate than institutional investors in some other countries.

Recently real estate returns have been poor in all the major economies, but over the long haul returns have been attractive. These returns have been achieved with low volatility, although this is misleading. When the real estate market is weak, few transactions take place. Prices appear to be higher than they would be if a sizeable portfolio had to be liquidated. Appraisal value prices understate the volatility of prices that would be found with continuous auction trading prices. Even allowing for this, real estate offers worthwhile diversification potential. Yet institutional portfolios have low weightings in real estate relative to its market value. One reason for this might be the way most investment management firms are structured. Many handle only financial assets (cash, bonds and equities) and have no real estate expertise. Not surprisingly, many managers do not argue a case for real estate exposure, for it would mean giving up some of their funds under management and, consequently, some of their fees. Turkeys don't vote for Thanksgiving Day or Christmas. It would be interesting to know the real estate exposure of funds whose strategic asset allocation is set by consultants, who do not have the same conflict of interest as most managers.

Were real estate to be included in the strategic asset allocation decision, how might this be done and how might a real estate portfolio be put together? One approach is via efficient frontier analysis and a very clear and useful general discussion is given in Chapter 27 by

Paul Firstenberg (Prudential Realty Group), Stephen Ross (Yale University) and Randall Zisler (Goldman Sachs). In Part Four we argued that there were problems with efficient frontier analysis. This article will suggest why some investors find the analysis so seductive despite the undoubted problems. Readers should note that it has been argued that the authors do not sufficiently allow for the understated volatility of the real estate price series they use, and their suggested real estate allocation is therefore too high. (For a discussion of this, see Ennis and Burik, 1991).

Derivative instruments are increasingly important in the financial markets. The basics of both futures and options are explained in the textbooks. Here we shall look at a couple of different issues that extend the textbook treatment. The growth of futures markets has led to many calls for tighter regulation of these markets, especially in the U.S. and Japan. As we have seen (in Chapter 21) some have blamed the 1987 crash on futures: there has also been concern that the futures markets have increased volatility more generally. Some observers have been worried that the futures markets will take trade from the spot markets and that this will make the latter inefficient and more speculative. Most studies have found these fears to be unwarranted. In the U.K., the Securities and Investments Board (a regulatory body), commissioned three academics to study some of the effects of futures. Chapter 28 is a summary of their research, written by two of the academics involved, John Board of the London School of Economics and Charles Sutcliffe of the University of Southampton. Their findings are similar to the findings of other researchers for other countries. Board and Sutcliffe conclude that there is no case for regulatory intervention.

There is a lot of pressure from consultants for institutional investors to use derivative instruments. The textbooks teach us sophisticated strategies. It seems old-fashioned not to use derivatives. Few articles are written warning of the problems that arise with derivatives. In Chapter 29, Richard McEnally and Richard Rendleman, professors at the University of North Carolina, give some cautionary advice on options. Their advice is aimed at the private investor, but much of it applies to institutional investors too. I shall repeat a couple of their points and add a couple.

A major problem is that the option market appears, in general, to be priced correctly in relation to the Black–Scholes and other mathematical models. The option market is also a zero-sum game — that is to say if somebody wins, somebody else loses. Now this does not sound an intrinsically attractive game — no prizes on average and the assets properly priced. But, in addition, option costs are high — dealing costs and spreads are higher than in equity markets, at least in non-U.S. markets. In the U.K., a round trip (purchase and sale) can easily eat up 10% of the premium. In roulette, the Bank always wins, and that is with one or two zeros on a wheel with 36 other numbers. Imagine playing roulette with four zeros on the wheel — those can be the odds in the options market.

How should we assess the opportunity options offer for the transformation of risks and returns? Option writers can be covered or naked. Covered writing is a strategy that many institutional investors contemplate. It offers extra income and reduces risks. If the stock price remains unchanged the investor benefits from the premium and any dividends. If the price falls, the investor still has the premium and any dividends, so the pain is reduced. And if the price rises? Well, the investor loses the stock, i.e., foregoes capital gain, but has decided that he would want to be out of the stock at a price say 10% higher than current levels. This strategy appears to offer a return for nothing. Yet, if the market is correctly priced — but subject to costs — an investor will earn slightly less than a fair return. Further, if risk and return are related, since the strategy reduces risks it should also reduce returns.

The market's total return is achieved by a mixture of dividends and capital gains. These come from steady plodding upward moves and occasional big moves. Call writers miss the big moves. Now it is true that investors have transformed the risk-return relationship, but is it really the one they prefer? When investors sell calls because they would be happy to be out of the stock when it is, say, 10% higher, what they really mean is they would like to be out after 10% outperformance. Yet stocks typically rise strongly when the whole market rises. When the market is charging upwards, the natural instinct of many managers will be to buy back the option position rather than justify to the client why they are out of a bull market. Alas, as the market has soared, the option will be expensive to buy back. No matter, write another one at a higher price. Well the problem with this is that the client has just seen the contract note that closes a losing options position; will the client like this paper trial?

Are options an appropriate asset for the typical pension fund or charity? By their nature such funds tend to be long term with real liabilities. In terms of matching assets and liabilities, equities and index-linked securities are ideally suited to such funds. And all owners of diversified portfolios of equities can benefit from any real growth in the economy. Are options an ideal asset given their zero sum nature and short life? Some investors use options for tactical asset allocation, but this is difficult enough at the best of times. Is a tactical overlay that has to come right in a specific period asking too much?

This raises a general problem of organisational structure. The people who like playing with options tend to have different personalities and skills from those who like buying shares and visiting clients. If a fund has specialist options managers it can be very difficult to make them simply implement strategic decisions. There will be a tendency for them to start suggesting actions based more on the state of the options market than on the goals of the fund. There is a better chance of using options to efficiently implement an existing strategy if the mainstream fund manager handles the options positions. However such managers are more likely to panic when things go wrong as they are less used to the speed with which prices change in the options market. They then face the danger of either acting like a novice or becoming obsessed with watching the options positions at the expense of everything else.

Now the views expressed here are extreme, they are warning of some possible problems, and I would not deny that some empirical studies have suggested that writing covered calls is a profitable strategy and some organisations have blended option and traditional fund management successfully. Also some private investors do hit the jackpot. Still, before you put your money or neck on the line, Chapter 29 is worth reading.

For readers still interested in options, I have included an article that extends the textbook analysis of option pricing. We mentioned above the Black–Scholes option valuation formula, one of the keystones of the textbook treatment of options. The formula is widely used in the real world. The general ideas underlying the formula are reasonably straightforward although the formula itself is not for the faint-hearted. Computers, however, make light work of crunching out valuation estimates. Many students look at formulae or theorems derived in economics and finance and point out that some of the assumptions are unrealistic. The effects of this lack of realism are not always easily determined. In Chapter 30, Fischer Black, one half of Black-Scholes, points out that the famous formula depends on at least 10 unrealistic assumptions. Black argues that using more realistic assumptions hasn't produced a better formula applicable to most situations. However, if investors appear to be making one of the unrealistic assumptions, there may be a profitable strategy available that focuses on that assumption. Black, a Partner of Goldman Sachs, takes us through the unrealistic assumptions and suggests suitable strategies.

REFERENCES

Ennis, R.M. and Burik, P. 1991: Pension Fund Real Estate Investment Under a Simple Equilibrium Pricing Model. *Financial Analysts Journal*, **47**, May–June, 20–30.

Ibbotson, R.G., Siegel, L.C. and Love, K.S. 1985: World Wealth: Market Values and Returns. *Journal of Portfolio Management*, **12**, Fall, 4–23.

27

Real Estate: The Whole Story

Paul M. Firstenberg, Stephen A. Ross and Randall C. Zisler

Investors traditionally have thought of equity real estate as an inefficient market in which the key to success is in the skill with which an individual investment is selected and negotiated. The general approach seems to be to buy properties when they become available if they look like "good deals," with little regard for the equally important issue of how the acquisition fits with the other holdings in the portfolio and what effect, if any, it will have on the overall risk and return objectives of the portfolio. Only recently have some investors begun to think of the aggregate of their real estate investments as a *portfolio*, with its own overall risk and return characteristics, and to adopt explicit strategies for achieving portfolio goals.

This article takes the view that investors should examine equity real estate investments not only on their individual merits but also for their impact on the investor's overall real estate portfolio. In addition, investors need to assess how the real estate segment fits into their entire portfolio. In turn, this means:

- setting risk and return objectives for the equity real estate portfolio as a whole that are compatible with the goals for the investor's entire portfolio,

- devising a strategy for achieving these objectives, and

- evaluating the extent to which individual transactions conform to the strategy and are likely to further portfolio objectives.

These processes are, of course, familiar to anyone in the business of managing security portfolios. By contrast, there has been a nearly complete neglect of such theory and techniques in the management of real estate portfolios and in their integration into institutional portfolios. This, in turn, has deprived managers of the modern tools that they now employ when considering other financial decisions. Often, for example, the pension fund asset allocation process that results in a decision to "put 10% of the portfolio into real estate" seems governed at least as much by hunch as by any rational mechanism.

Reprinted from: Firstenberg, P.M., Ross, S.A. and Zisler, R.C. 1988: Real Estate: The Whole Story. *Journal of Portfolio Management*, 14, Spring, 22–34. This copyright material is reprinted with permission from The Journal of Portfolio Management, 488 Madison Avenue, New York, NY 10022.

Again by way of contrast, probably there is not a single major institutional portfolio in the common stock area that does not make serious use of modern portfolio techniques to continually monitor overall portfolio risk and to assess portfolio performance. These techniques are often the central mechanism for determining management strategy and selecting managers.

While some funds rely much more heavily on quantitative techniques than others do, the implementation of these procedures clearly has moved well beyond the cosmetic and lip service stage. Furthermore, a good general rule is that the larger the portfolio, the greater the reliance on such techniques. This is no doubt a consequence of the realization that even a few good stock picks will have less of an influence on the performance of a $5 billion portfolio than over-all structuring decisions will. These decisions include how much to put into different categories of assets or stocks and the overall risk level of the portfolio.

Moreover, within an asset category, the selection of sectors in which to invest is likely to have more impact on results than the choice of individual investments. These types of decisions for real estate are likely to be as critical for performance as a few good individual property "investments" and individual property asset management will be.

Our intention is to show how pension funds and other large investors can use modern portfolio techniques both to construct real estate portfolios and to allocate funds to asset categories including real estate. Our concern, however, is not with a cookbook application of some handy formulas to the real estate market.

Because the real estate market is not an auction market offering divisible shares in every property, and information flows in the market are complex, these features place a premium on investment judgment. Managers who want to own some of IBM simply buy some shares. Managers who want to participate in the returns on, say, a $300 million office building must take a significant position in the property. One alternative is to purchase a share of a large commingled real estate fund, but that does not relieve the fund's managers from the problems of constructing their portfolio.

Our aim is not to eliminate the analysis of each individual property acquisition, but rather to supplement it with a thorough consideration of its contribution to overall portfolio performance. Modern portfolio analysis provides the tool for examining the risk and return characteristics of the overall portfolio and the contribution of the individual elements. The result of its application is a method for selecting properties whose inclusion in the portfolio is of overall benefit.

Before we consider this point in more detail, we examine how real estate performance results compare with those for stocks and bonds. In this analysis, the absence of the large and continuous data record available in the securitized markets presents some special problems.

TOTAL RETURN AND REAL ESTATE DATA

In all modern investment work, the focus of interest is on the total rate of return on assets, that is, the return inclusive of both income and capital gain or loss. The logic underlying this is the basic philosophy of "cash is cash." An investment with a total return of 10%, all from capital gains, is equivalent to one with a total return of 10%, all from income, because the sale of 9% of the shares in the investment that has risen in value will realize for the holder the same cash as the all-income investment provides. This basic truth, though, does not deny the possibility that, for some holders, there may be an advantage to receiving the return in one form or another.[1]

A real estate fund might rationally have an income as well as a total return objective, yet the transaction cost of selling appreciated property to realize income is particularly severe for real estate. While we recognize that this is an important issue, space considerations do not permit us to deal with it explicitly. Fortunately, too, this is not a serious limitation to our analysis, because the income component of large real estate funds is relatively insensitive to the decision as to how to allocate the funds across different types of real estate.

To determine the total return on real estate or any other asset, we just add the income component and the capital gain or loss. The income component of an asset's return is relatively straightforward to determine, as it is just a cash flow, and good data generally are available for the computation.

The price appreciation component, however, is much more difficult to assess. If an asset is traded in a continuous auction market, like the common stock of a major company, price quotes in the market provide a good method for valuing the asset. Most real estate assets trade infrequently, however, and valuation is more problematic. For some of the commingled funds, appraisals are the only source of property valuations.

The appraisal process merits a paper of its own, but a few points are sufficient for our purposes. Appraisals usually are conducted annually and are based on one of two methods or a combination of the two. If comparable properties have recently been bought or sold, then the appraisal can use their prices as benchmarks for estimating the value of properties that have not been traded: Comparability is increasingly difficult to achieve as the number and complexity of leases increases. Alternatively, the property can be valued by the discounted cash flow (DCF) method of discounting the projected net cash flows at some discount rate determined by prevailing market conditions. Neither of these methods can be as accurate as an actual market price, but there is also no reason to think that they will be biased in the long run. Furthermore, even if appraisals are biased, the appreciation computed from appraisals will not be biased as long as the bias is constant over time.

Although appraisals are not necessarily biased, there is evidence of considerable sluggishness or inertia in appraised values. By any of the common measures of the volatility of returns, real estate returns from appraisals appear to vary far less over time than other asset return series. Standard deviation is a measure of the spread or volatility of investment returns, and we will use the standard deviation also as a measure of the riskiness of real estate returns.[2]

The data below reveal that the standard deviation of stock returns, for example, is over five times greater than that of real estate returns. The extent to which this difference is a consequence of real estate returns actually being far less volatile than stock returns or a consequence of the use of appraisal values is not really known. In the data that follow, we make a correction that raises the volatility of the real estate returns to a level that seems more reasonable to us.

The major sources of data on real estate returns come from commingled funds. We have made use of three series of aggregate real estate returns and a separate series of the returns on different subcategories of real estate. For comparison purposes, we also use returns on other assets such as stocks and bonds. The data and the sources appear in the Appendix.

Table 27.1 describes how real estate returns have compared with the returns on stocks and bonds and with inflation. As the Frank Russell (FRC) and Evaluation Associates (EAFPI) series are based on appraisals, they might move more sluggishly than a true market value series—if one were available. The two adjusted series under the FRC heading report the result of alterations in the FRC data designed to recognize this weakness. The "cap-rate

Table 27.1   Real estate series and other assets

	Annualized		
Index	Total return (%)	Standard deviation (%)	Series begins *
Real estate			
FRC	13.87	2.55	6/78
FRC (cap-rate est.)	13.04	11.28	6/78
FRC (appraisal adj.)	13.87	4.37	6/78
EAFPI	10.78	2.80	3/69
EREIT	22.26	19.71	3/74
Other assets			
S&P 500	9.71	15.35	3/69
Small stocks	14.51	23.90	3/69
Corporate bonds	8.38	11.29	3/69
Government bonds	7.91	11.50	3/69
T-bills	7.51	0.82	3/69
Inflation	6.64	1.19	3/69
Risk premium (spread over T-bills)			
EAFPI	3.27	2.43	
FRC	4.36	1.29	
S&P 500	1.48	17.54	
Small stocks	7.38	18.04	

*All series end in December 1985. For details and full titles of each series, see the Appendix.

adjusted" series estimates the change in value from a DCF model, and the "appraisal adjusted" series adjusts the standard deviation of the series upward.[3]

Even when the standard deviation of real estate returns is adjusted upward, both the return and the standard deviation make real estate an attractive asset category in comparison with stocks and bonds. Its lower risk and its comparable return partially offset the lack of liquidity inherent in real estate investments.[4]

We turn now to the issues involved in managing an equity real estate portfolio and the implications of modern portfolio analysis for real estate.

REAL ESTATE PORTFOLIOS: THE BASIC PRINCIPLES

In an imperfect real estate market, the skill with which individual assets are acquired, managed, and disposed of will be a major determinant of total return. Portfolio management is not a substitute for, nor should it divert attention from, property-specific management. Nevertheless, the composition of the portfolio as a whole will impact both the level and the variability of returns.

The twin considerations of individual property-specific management and portfolio analysis require different human skills and make use of different information. This leads naturally to a two-tiered approach to management:

- A macro analysis that employs portfolio management concepts and focuses on the composition and investment characteristics of the portfolio as a whole, identifying major strategic investment options and their long-run implications. Each property that is a candidate for acquisition or disposition should be analyzed for its impact on overall portfolio objectives.

- A micro analysis that employs traditional real estate project analysis, and focuses on the selection of the individual properties that make up the portfolio, evaluating a property's specific risk-reward potential against the investor's performance targets.

We will not have much to say here about the micro analysis; it is the traditional focus of real estate analysis. We make suggestions for it, but we do not propose changing it. Our interest is in the macro analysis.

Macro analysis derives the characteristics of risk and return for the portfolio as a whole from different combinations of individual property types and geographic locations. It establishes the trade-off between the given level of return and the volatility of return that result from different mixes of assets. Selecting the particular risk-return trade-off that best meets an investor's requirements is the most crucial policy decision one can make and is one of our major concerns.

The macro policy is implemented only through the individual selection of properties at the micro level. A thorough analysis of a property should involve an analysis of its marginal contribution to overall portfolio return, volatility, and risk exposure. The difficulty in conducting such an analysis at the individual property level is what gives rise to the separation between the micro and macro analyses. In general, the macro goals are implemented at the micro level by choosing categories of properties to examine with the micro tools, rather than by examining each individual property's marginal effect on the portfolio.

We will employ some familiar principles from modern portfolio theory as guides in portfolio construction:

- To achieve higher-than-average levels of return, an investor must construct a portfolio involving greater-than-average risk. An investor whose risk tolerance is lower than that of the average investor in the market must expect relatively lower returns. Risk may be defined as the variability or dispersion from the mean of future returns or, simply put, the chance of achieving less-than-expected returns. The variability of returns usually is measured by the standard deviation.

- It is possible and useful to measure risk and return and to develop, in an approximate manner, a portfolio strategy that balances the trade-off between these two performance criteria. Because of the difficulty and costs of transacting in the real estate market, and because of the resulting lack of precise "marked-to-market" prices for real estate, it is unrealistic to attempt to fine-tune actual investment decisions in response to risk-return estimates. Even if an investor specifies a preference for a mean return of 15% with a standard deviation of 3%, to a 14% mean return with a standard deviation of 2.5%, translating that preference into a precise strategy is probably not feasible. Broader relationships between risk and return must guide real estate investment strategy.

- The total risk on any investment can be decomposed into a systematic and an unsystematic component. Unsystematic risk will largely disappear as an influence on the return of a well-diversified portfolio. To the extent that the return on an individual property is influenced by purely local events, it is unsystematic and washes out in a large diversified portfolio.[5] A regional shopping centre, for example, might find its sales adversely affected by a plant closing. A chain of shopping centers spread across the country, however, would find total revenues unaffected by such local influences. Its revenues would depend on the overall economic conditions that affect costs and consumer demand. An investor who owned many such centers would not be subjected to the ups and downs of individual industries and markets and would be affected only by the general economic conditions that influence all retail businesses simultaneously.

- The risk from changes in economic conditions throughout the country is systematic and will influence any portfolio, no matter how large and well-diversified, because it influences each of the parts. For example, a downturn in consumer demand and a rise in wages will probably adversely affect all business, which means that even a conglomerate would suffer a decline in profits. Systematic risk can be lowered only by lowering long-run average returns. A conglomerate might attempt to lower such risks by implementing a strategic decision to sell some businesses and invest the proceeds in cash securities. The resulting revenues will have less sensitivity to the business cycle but also will have a lower average return. An investor could do the same.

In the sections that follow we will illustrate how investors can apply these principles in portfolio construction by examining how different combinations of property types and economic regions affect the risk and return characteristics of a portfolio.

Investors can reduce the unsystematic and, therefore, the overall risk level of the portfolio without sacrificing return by diversifying real estate investments among property types that have non-covariant returns and across geographic areas or leaseholds that are not subject to the same macroeconomic variables.[6] Diversification also protects the investor from over-emphasizing a particular asset class or area of the country that then falls victim to unforeseen, or more often unforeseeable, negative developments.

Spreading assets geographically has been a commonly used rough proxy for selecting areas that are economically non-covariant. A more detailed analysis, however, is required to determine whether geographically separate areas are actually subject to the same macro-economic variables. The economic base of a particular geographic area may be broad-based, with multiple and widely diversified sources of revenues, or its economy may be largely dependent on a single economic activity. The latter is obviously a riskier area in which to invest, but much of its risk is unsystematic.

As a consequence, a diversified portfolio of areas, each of which is influenced by a different industry-specific risk, can avoid such risk at no cost in returns. For instance, the economies of Houston, Denver, and New Orleans were all highly vulnerable to one variable — oil prices; San Jose, California, Austin, Texas, and Lexington, Massachusetts, are all vulnerable, to a lesser degree, to the fortunes of the hightech industries. A portfolio made up of properties in these cities is diversified geographically, but subject to significant systematic risks. By contrast, a portfolio made up of properties in Lexington, New Orleans, and, say, New York and Reno would have less overall risk.

This line of reasoning explains the power of diversification across geographic areas whose economies are independent. Within a given city, the same economic forces that influence the business demand for industrial and office space also affect the demand of workers for residential space, the demand of customers for hotel room nights, and the demand of retailers who sell to the workers. Too often, casual real estate market research leads to a claim of urban or regional diversification without an adequate analysis of the inter-industry and inter-occupational linkages affecting returns. Diversifying across different areas lowers risk to the extent to which the economies of the areas are independent of each other. Ultimately, the goal of diversifying a real estate portfolio should be to diversify across leaseholds.

Intuition also suggests that international diversification would be a powerful tool for accomplishing this goal. The question of whether a portfolio with London and New York properties is more economically diverse than a portfolio of Boston and New York is really the question of whether the underlying economy of Boston will move more or less with that of New York than will London.

REGIONAL DIVERSIFICATION

Figure 27.1 illustrates the trade-off between risk and return that is available when we break real estate investment into different regions and examine various portfolio possibilities for diversifying holdings across the regions. The four regions are the East, the Midwest, the South, and the West.[7] Figure 27.1 displays all the possible combinations of return and risk available from the different combinations of holdings across these four regions.

The expected return is graphed on the vertical scale in Figure 27.1, and the horizontal scale gives the standard deviation. The data are all historical. History is a guide to the future, but this is not to say that the next ten years will mimic the last ten. Rather, we are asking how different portfolios would have performed in the past. We contend that an intelligent look at past risk and return patterns is necessary for an understanding of the future. This, of course, is a weakness of all analysis, whether quantitative or not, but what else can we use to study the future if not the past?

By choosing different combinations of the four regions, all the points in the shaded part of Figure 27.1 are available. The labeled points describe the four pure regional portfolios.

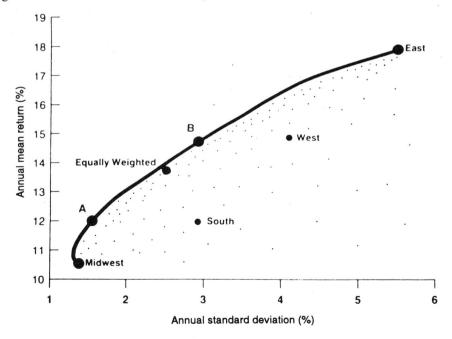

Figure 27.1 Efficient regional portfolio mixes

The East alone, for instance, shows a return of 17.9% and a standard deviation of 5.6%. The equally weighted portfolio in Figure 27.1 gives the return and the risk of a portfolio that puts one-quarter of its investment in each of the four regions.

Table 27.2 gives the background data underlying Figure 27.1. Here we have listed the return and standard deviation for each of the regions as well as the correlations in the returns across the four regions. Correlations are interpreted in the usual fashion. A positive correlation between two regions indicates that the returns tend to rise and fall together, and, as the table shows, all the regional correlations are positive. A zero correlation means that the returns tend to move independently of each other. All the correlations are low, and the correlation between the Midwest and the South is nearly zero. Combining asset categories that are only weakly correlated with each other greatly lowers overall portfolio risk. Figure 27.1 certainly reveals that this is the case for regional diversification.[8]

Using Figure 27.1, we can show that investing the entire portfolio in any single region is unnecessarily risky. For three of the regions, there is a superior alternative that involves combining the regions. The only exception is the all-East portfolio. As it had the highest return in the period used to construct Figure 27.1 (see Table 27.2), putting the entire portfolio into the East would have been the best choice, but, of course, we have no basis for assuming that the next ten years would still put the East on top.

As for the other three choices, take, for example, the South. The South had a mean return of 11.96% and a standard deviation of 2.92%. Compare these results with those of Point A, directly above the South on the curve that bounds the possible combinations of return and risk. This point has the same standard deviation of 2.92% as that of the all-South portfolio, yet its return is nearly 15%, or 300 basis points, greater than that of the all-South portfolio. Similarly, Point B, just to the left of the South, is also superior to the all-South portfolio. It has the same return of 11.96% as the all-South portfolio, but its risk level is about 1.5%, or nearly half that of the all-South portfolio. The points on the curve of Figure 27.1 are called efficient portfolios, because they give the best possible returns for their levels of risk. The points between A and B are efficient portfolios that dominate the all-South portfolio.

Table 27.3 lists the efficient regional portfolios for each level of return and shows their risk level. These portfolios are the ones that give the returns and standard deviations on the curve in Figure 27.1. Table 27.3 provides a great deal of valuable information on the optimal regional diversification of a real estate portfolio.

Table 27.2 Returns by region, 1978–1985

Region	Annualized	
	Mean return (%)	Standard deviation (%)
East	17.91	5.58
Midwest	10.49	1.44
South	11.96	2.92
West	14.83	4.11

Regional correlation matrix				
Region	East	Midwest	South	West
East	1.00	0.16	0.25	0.32
Midwest	0.16	1.00	0.04	0.14
South	0.25	0.04	1.00	0.46
West	0.32	0.14	0.46	1.00

Table 27.3 Efficient portfolio mixes by region (proportions, %)

East	Midwest	South	West	Mean (%)	Portfolio standard deviation (%)
	99		1	10.50	1.43
0%	81	18%	1	10.80	1.31
5	74	17	5	11.30	1.36
9	66	15	9	11.80	1.49
14	59	13	13	12.30	1.67
19	52	12	18	12.80	1.89
23	45	10	22	13.30	2.14
28	38	8	26	13.80	2.41
32	31	7	30	14.30	2.70
37	23	5	35	14.80	2.99
41	16	3	39	15.30	3.30
46	9	2	43	15.80	3.60
51	2	0	47	16.30	3.91
64			36	16.80	4.28
80			20	17.30	4.80
96			4	17.80	5.43

As we move from low returns to high returns — and higher risk — we see that in the range from an 11.3% return with a 1.4% standard deviation to a 15.8% return with a 3.6% standard deviation, the efficient portfolios diversify to include all the regions. In other words, as we avoid the extremes of the highest returns and risks and the lowest returns and risks, a characteristic of the efficient portfolios is that they are fully diversified. Indeed, as Figure 27.1 shows, the equally weighted portfolio that puts exactly the same investment into each region is essentially an efficient portfolio with its return of 14% and its standard deviation of 2.3%.

This is as far as this quantitative analysis can take us. At this point judgment takes over. The quantitative analysis can weed out the inferior choices, but, in the end, it cannot make the final choice for the manager. The manager is left with the central question: What combination of risk and return should be chosen and, therefore, which efficient portfolio?[9] Each investor will have particular requirements for establishing the trade-off between risk and return.

We offer here only some broad considerations. For a publicly-held fund, the basic issue is one of marketing; the combination of return and risk and, therefore, the regional diversification should be chosen according to an evaluation of the clients' demands. For a pension fund, the decision should be based on how the real estate portfolio is expected to contribute to the overall objectives of the fund. We will look at this matter more closely when we consider allocating funds across asset classes, including real estate. When regional diversification and property type diversification are combined, the resulting reduction in risk is considerable.

PROPERTY TYPE DIVERSIFICATION

Figure 27.2 illustrates the trade-off between risk and return that is available from forming portfolios of the five different property types, and Table 27.4 gives the data underlying

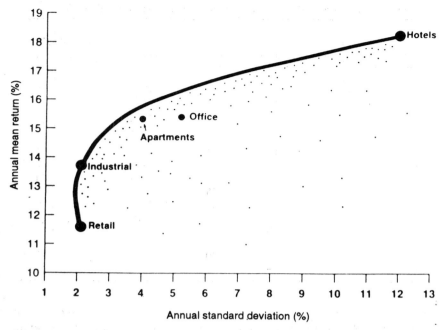

Figure 27.2   Efficient property type mixes

Table 27.4   Returns by property type, 1978–1985

	Annualized	
	Mean return (%)	Standard deviation (%)
Apartments	15.29	3.97
Hotels	18.25	12.08
Industrial	13.63	2.27
Office	15.38	4.72
Retail	11.56	2.19

Property type correlation matrix

	Apartments	Hotels	Industrial	Office	Retail
Apartments	1.00	0.56	0.41	0.21	0.13
Hotels	0.56	1.00	0.17	0.11	−0.01
Industrial	0.41	0.17	1.00	0.65	0.59
Office	0.21	0.11	0.65	1.00	0.21
Retail	0.13	−0.01	0.59	0.21	1.00

Figure 27.2. The properties are classified into five major property types: apartments, hotels, office buildings, retail properties including shopping centres, and industrial properties such as warehouses. This classification corresponds both to the available data and to an *a priori* sensible breakdown into non-covariant business-groupings. As we would expect, the efficient portfolios are diversified by property type, but here the results are different from those obtained when we consider regional diversification.

Table 27.5 Efficient portfolio mixes by property type (proportions, %)

Apartments	Hotels	Industrial	Office	Retail	Mean (%)	Portfolio standard deviation (%)
4		4		92	11.80	2.10
9		20		71	12.30	1.97
13		36		51	12.80	1.94
18		50	1	31	13.30	2.01
23		61	3	13	13.80	2.18
30		61	9		14.30	2.43
41	2	34	24		14.80	2.81
53	3	7	38		15.30	3.29
38	16		46		15.80	4.03
15	33		53		16.30	5.23
	49		51		16.80	6.67
	67		33		17.30	8.40
	84		16		17.80	10.29
	98		2		18.20	11.88

As Table 27.5 reveals, the efficient portfolios can have as few as two asset types in them. For returns above 16.3%, the efficient portfolios are dominated by hotels and office properties. For the low-risk alternatives, apartments, industrial properties, and retail dominate. At all levels of risk and return, though, some diversification is appropriate.

It is difficult to say to what extent these results predict future patterns and to what extent they are the consequence of the relatively short statistical history. There is reason to believe, though, that we should depend less on the property diversification results than on the regional analysis. For one thing, the numbers themselves are less reliable. The hotel category, for example, is based on a relatively small number of properties, and they are unduly concentrated in New York City. For another, it may well be that some of these returns reflect the economics of relatively tight leasing markets in the late 1970s and early 1980s. Furthermore, fundamental changes in the tax laws since 1986 probably will affect these property types differently.

For these reasons, we would advocate using Table 27.5 as a rough guide and tend to give greater weight to the middle region where all property types are represented. The final choice of a risk and return trade-off, as with regional diversification, rests with the manager and is governed by the same considerations as affect the regional choice.[10]

IMPLICATIONS FOR PORTFOLIO MANAGEMENT

We conclude from the foregoing analysis of the risk-return characteristics of portfolios constructed with different mixes of property types and geographic regions that:

- There is a trade-off between the riskiness (as measured by standard deviation) of a real estate portfolio and the total expected return it generates. Consistent with experience with financial assets, the degree of risk an investor is willing to assume will be the single most important factor in determining return.

- Diversifying the composition of a portfolio among geographic locations and property types can increase the investor's return for a given level of risk. Diversification among holdings with non-covariant returns will reduce risk without sacrificing return.

To construct such a portfolio, each investment category identified as offering diversification potential should be represented; the goal should be to have a substantial minimum threshold investment across property types and geographic regions (e.g., no property type or region should be below, say, 15% of the total portfolio).

- There are at least two alternative strategic approaches to diversifying a real estate portfolio. One approach calls for all investments to be made in strict accordance with diversification criteria, even though the assets allocated to different categories may exceed the minimums necessary to gain significant benefits. Under such a strict policy, an investor would not shift allocations because of perceived future changes in the payoffs from different allocations. The investor would modify the initial diversification slowly and generally only in response to some sort of significant long-term change in the marketplace. The assumption underlying this approach is that such modifications always create additional risk and that the investor lacks the forecasting ability to earn sufficient additional return to compensate for the risk.

The second approach allows for strategic deviations from the strict plan, provided that the threshold minimum allocations are met. Such an approach could reflect an investor's confidence in the ability to project changes in the risk-return differential of various geographic areas or property types. Or it could stem from pursuing a high risk-return strategy of, say, investing in development projects or in less than fully leased properties in currently out of favor markets in the hope of producing results outside of the efficient frontier of Figures 27.1 and 27.2. In such cases, the portfolio will reflect the strategic investment selections that deviate from a strict diversification policy, with the expectation that the added risk will be compensated for by additional return. One way to implement such a strategy is to divide the portfolio into a strictly diversified component (a core portfolio) and a higher risk/higher return portion (an opportunity portfolio), with the blend between the two reflecting an overall risk-return target.

In sum, an investor can target a real estate portfolio to lie at any point along the risk-return continuum; the crucial step is to articulate and explicitly adopt an investment strategy that fits this goal and that both the investor and the investment manager fully understand and agree upon. The strategies to be pursued in managing a real estate portfolio should be explicit, not unspoken.

- We need to learn a good deal more about the factors that, in fact, produce genuine diversification (i.e., non-covariant returns). Present categories of broad geographic regions or property types provide only crude guidelines for achieving efficient mixes. This lack of the proper economic classifications and the accompanying data are the most serious weaknesses of our analysis.

ASSET ALLOCATION: STOCKS, BONDS, AND REAL ESTATE

In principle, the same considerations that govern the construction of the all-real estate portfolio apply to the asset allocation decision. Table 27.1 gives the basic return and risk information, while Table 27.6 gives the correlations between real estate and other asset categories.

In constructing Table 27.6, we have treated real estate as a single category, even though different regions or property types will have different relations with other assets. Whenever we aggregate asset classes and consider their relationship with each other as classes, we

Table 27.6 Correlations among asset classes*

	FRC	EAFPI	EREIT	S&P 500	Government bonds	T-Bills	Inflation
FRC	1.00	.0.71	−0.14	−0.26	−0.38	0.30	0.38
EAFPI	0.71	1.00	−0.20	−0.28	−0.10	0.54	0.48
EREIT	−0.14	−0.20	1.00	0.78	0.36	−0.23	0.03
S&P 500	−0.26	−0.28	0.78	1.00	0.49	−0.43	−0.15
Government bonds	−0.38	−0.10	0.36	0.49	1.00	−0.09	−0.35
T-bills	0.30	0.54	−0.23	−0.43	−0.09	1.00	0.41
Inflation	0.38	0.48	0.03	−0.15	−0.35	0.41	1.00

*For details and full titles of each series, see Appendix.

always lose some of the fine detail. This is true of stocks as well as real estate. As these asset categories are managed as individual classes, however, the separation of management forces the separation of our analysis.[11]

From a portfolio perspective, the great attractive feature of real estate is its lack of correlation with other assets. Even if real estate risk is understated, the lack of correlation makes real estate a particularly attractive feature of a well-diversified portfolio.

Look first at the correlations among the three real estate indexes FRC, EAFPI, and EREIT. The two appraisal-based indexes, FRC and EAFPI, are highly correlated with each other, and both are negatively correlated with the stock market-traded REIT index, EREIT. This striking difference points up the difficulty with the real estate data. Indeed, both FRC and EAFPI are negatively correlated with the stock market as well, while EREIT with a 0.78 correlation with the S&P 500 actually looks like a stock index rather than the other two real estate indexes. (A closer look reveals that individual REITs can behave like the other real estate indexes; it all depends on the particular REIT.) Presumably, the truth lies somewhere between these two, and we can conclude that real estate returns, if not negatively correlated with those on stocks, are at least far from perfectly correlated with them.

One point with which all of the real estate indexes agree, however, is that real estate hedges against increases in inflation. All three indexes are positively correlated with changes in inflation. By contrast, the S&P 500 index has responded negatively to inflation.

Our argument for including real estate as a substantial portion of an overall investment portfolio is, thus, based on its significant diversification value in reducing risk, whatever the goal for returns.

Using the correlation data from Table 27.6 and the return data from Table 27.1, we created the efficient frontier of real estate, stocks, and bonds displayed in Figure 27.3 and tabulated in Table 27.7. We used the upward adjustment in the standard deviation of real estate in constructing Table 27.7 so as to avoid any possible underemphasis of its risk. The efficient portfolios in Table 27.7 display the same characteristics as the efficient portfolios of the real estate categories. In the middle ranges of return and risk, the portfolio is evenly diversified among the three categories, although real estate has the major share. Insofar as the risk of real estate is still understated by the 11.3% standard deviation, these numbers will overstate real estate's role in an efficient asset allocation.

To examine this matter further, we raised real estate's standard deviation to be the same as that for the S&P 500, 15.4%. The resulting efficient portfolios are given in Table 27.8. Although the increase in the risk level of real estate lowers its contribution to the efficient

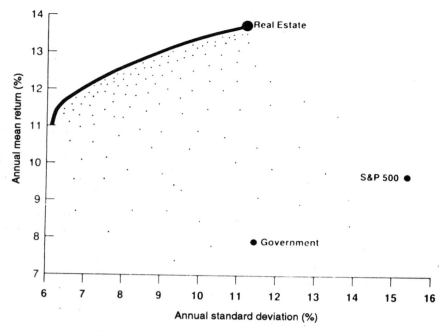

Figure 27.3 Mixes of real estate, stocks and bonds

Table 27.7 Efficient portfolio mixes of real estate, stocks, and bonds. Real estate standard deviation 'cap-adjusted' = 11.28% (proportions, %)

Real estate (FRC index)	Stocks (S&P 500)	Government bonds	Mean (%)	Portfolio standard deviation(%)
49	11	40	11.00	6.16
52	12	36	11.20	6.20
55	13	32	11.40	6.29
58	14	28	11.60	6.44
61	15	24	11.80	6.65
65	16	19	12.00	6.91
68	17	15	12.20	7.22
71	18	11	12.40	7.56
74	19	7	12.60	7.94
77	20	3	12.80	8.35
80	20		13.00	8.79
85	15		13.20	9.30
90	10		13.40	9.89
95	5		13.60	10.56
100	0		13.80	11.28

portfolios and raises the proportion of bonds, the amount of the change is surprisingly small. For example, the efficient portfolio with a 12% mean return has a 61% holding in real estate when real estate is assumed to be as risky as stocks and a 65% holding when real estate is assumed to have a risk level below that of stocks but above its measured level. Of course, this result is dependent upon the limitations of the data and our model.

Table 27.8 Efficient portfolio mixes of real estate, stocks, and bonds. Real estate standard deviation = stock standard deviation = 15.35% (proportions, %)

Real estate (FRC index)	Stocks (S&P 500)	Government bonds	Mean (%)	Portfolio standard deviation (%)
38	13	49	10.40	7.05
41	15	44	10.60	7.09
44	17	39	10.80	7.19
47	18	35	11.00	7.37
50	20	30	11.20	7.61
53	21	26	11.40	7.91
56	23	21	11.60	8.26
58	25	17	11.80	8.66
61	26	12	12.00	9.10
64	28	8	12.20	9.57
67	30	3	12.40	10.80
71	29		12.60	10.61
76	24		12.80	11.22
80	20		13.00	11.92
85	15		13.20	12.70
90	10		13.40	13.54
95	5		13.60	14.42
100	0		13.80	15.35

The important conclusion to draw from this analysis is that, even with an upward risk adjustment, real estate belongs in efficient portfolios at significantly higher levels than the 3.6% allocation for the top 200 public and private funds in 1986. Taking a pragmatic perspective, we feel that pension funds should seek initial real estate asset allocations of between 15 to 20%.

A second level of consideration in choosing among these possible asset allocations makes use of the additional data presented in Table 27.6, the correlations between asset returns and inflation and interest rates. Similar data can be collected for other major economic variables that influence asset returns, such as real productivity and investor confidence (see Chen, Roll, and Ross, 1986). We can see from Table 27.6 that real estate is positively correlated with inflation and, at least for the FRC and the EAFPI indexes, it is also positively correlated with interest rates. This is in marked contrast to stock returns, which are negatively correlated with the inflation variable and with interest rates.

This means that real estate returns have been a superior hedge against an increase in inflation or in interest rates, as compared with the experience of the stock market. As inflation or interest rates have risen, the stock market historically has tended to fall, and real estate returns have tended to rise. Of course, this will depend on the source of the increase in inflation and interest rates. The Monday, October 19, 1987, crash in the stock market produced the opposite result, where sellers of stock ran to the bond market, pushing these prices up. Rather, we are primarily concerned here with a change in stock prices accompanied by a change in inflationary expectations. This differs from a once-and-for-all shift in prices, such as a jump in commodity prices because of formation of a cartel.

A corporate pension fund that is funded ultimately by the earnings of the company would find real estate a relatively attractive asset category if its earnings tend to be negatively related to inflation. For example, suppose that a manufacturing company believes that an increase in inflation brings about a more rapid rise in its wage and material costs than in the prices of its products. A fund with a tilt toward real estate would tend to offset this profit squeeze by rising when corporate earnings fell off.

This does not mean that companies whose earnings rise and fall with inflation should shun real estate. For example, a natural resource company with relatively fixed costs would find its earnings down in a period of low inflation. But the analysis of Tables 27.7 and 27.8 is still relevant, and the pension fund of such a company should still hold a significant proportion of its assets in real estate, simply to take advantage of the return and risk diversification characteristics. The proper conclusion to draw is that such a company should hold relatively less real estate than the manufacturing company.

In the end, the allocation decision among the three categories we have studied involves a judgment that is associated with the particular needs of the fund being considered. If, in addition to the considerations of risk and return on which we have focused, there is also a concern for liquidity, this will tend to push the fund toward marketed assets such as stocks and bonds and out of real estate.[12] There is no single answer that is best for all portfolios, only a range of desirable choices. Modern portfolio analysis limits this range to the manageable alternatives presented in Tables 27.7 and 27.8.

CONCLUSION

We have shown how modern portfolio analysis can be used both to optimally diversify a real estate portfolio and to allocate overall fund assets among real estate, stocks, and bonds. Real estate is an enormous percentage of world assets, and, as our final tables show, even with an upward risk adjustment, it may belong in efficient portfolios at significantly higher levels, such as 15 to 20%, compared to the 3.6% allocation in 1986 for the top 200 public and private pension funds.

APPENDIX

Data series and sources

Source	Data description
Frank Russell Company (FRC Indexes)	A quarterly time series of equity real estate returns extending from 1978 to the present. The series is broken down by income and capital gains and also by region and property type. Currently, the data base has approximately 1000 properties owned by real estate funds with an average value of about $10 million per property.
Evaluation Associates (EAFPI)	A quarterly time series extending from 1969 to the present. It is an index constructed by an equal weighting of the returns on a number of largely all-equity real estate funds. The data base currently includes about thirty-three tax-exempt funds with a total asset value of about $25 billion.
Gs & Co. Equity REIT Returns (EREIT)	A monthly time series extending from 1974 to the present. It is an equally-weighted index constructed from thirty-three REITs holding more than 80% equity assets. In comparison with the FRC index, EREIT is more heavily concentrated in shopping centers and apartments and less in office properties.
Stock, Bond, and Inflation Data	Ibboston and Associates provide a comprehensive monthly data base that begins in 1926.

ENDNOTES

1. Regulatory and accounting conventions may lead to a preference for income over capital gains. Tax issues also influence this preference. Furthermore, some funds may be precluded from realizing income through sales, and, even if they can sell appreciated assets to generate income, the transaction costs of doing so will detract from the return. On the other side, some investors actually may prefer capital gains to income (ignoring tax effects) to avoid being faced with the need to reinvest the cash.

2. A rule of thumb is that two-thirds of the returns tend to fall within one standard deviation of the mean return and 95% of the returns fall within two standard deviations. The higher the standard deviation, the greater the range of the effective returns, and the greater the probability or likelihood of loss.

3. The first correction uses a "cap-rate" proxy in place of appraisal returns. Net operating income is a commonly used yardstick for the valuation of real estate. By treating changes in the current income stream as indications of changes in the market value of the asset, we can estimate an appreciation return. Although this approach has a number of problems, at least it allows us to base the estimate of appreciation on known data. The result is an FRC series with an annual standard deviation of 11%.
    We generated a series of appreciation returns on the change of an estimated value of the real estate index, where the value is given by the present value of a perpetual stream of income flows. The income flows are taken to be the current period income, and the discount rate can be modeled either as a spread over T-bills, or simply as a fixed rate.

    $$Cr_t = \frac{(Ve_{t-1} - Ve_t)}{(Ve_{t-1})},$$

    $$Ve_t = D_t / r_{t'},$$

where:

Cr = cap-rate return
Ve = cap-rate value
D = income per invested dollar
r = discount rate
Y = income return
I = appreciation index value

This simplifies to:

$$Cr_t = \left[\frac{I_t}{I_{t-1}} \cdot \frac{Y_t}{Y_{t-1}} \cdot \frac{r_{t-1}}{r_t} \right] - 1.$$

This method may have some validity, insofar as a similar procedure on the stock market produces estimates near the true value for volatility.

   The appraisal-adjusted series is derived from an analysis of the appraisal process and estimates a volatility of returns based on the reported data. This method is an attempt to correct returns by removing any inertia or sluggishness inherent in the appraisal process. True rates of return should be uncorrelated with each other across time. Insofar as there is excessive correlation in the FRC returns, they will not accurately reveal the true return on real estate.

   To model the appraisal process, we assumed that a property's appraised value is a mixture of the series of previous appraised values and the appraiser's estimate of the current market price the property would bring if sold. In other words, the appraiser incorporates past appraisals into the current appraisal.

   The basis of this estimation is as follows. An estimated mean return can be expressed as the true mean, M_t, and some random error term, e_t:

$$M_t = R_t + e_t,$$

where the standard deviation of e_t is the true standard deviation of returns.

The appraiser can be thought of as combining the true mean return with a lagged return to make the following estimation:

$$E[R_t] = (1 - A)M_t + AR_{t-1}.$$

More generally, the process might use a whole year's worth of past returns in combination with the true mean to produce the current estimation:

$$E[R_t] = (1 - A)M_t + a_1 R_{t-1} + a_2 R_{t-2} + a_3 R_{t-3} + a_4 R_{t-4},$$

where

$$A = a_1 + a_2 + a_3 + a_4.$$

A linear regression based on this model yields the following information:

$$R_t = b_0 + b_1 R_{t-1} + \cdots + b_4 R_{t-4} + z_t,$$

where z_t is the residual error term.

Combining these two equations, we can solve for the true mean and standard deviation from the estimates of $b_1, b_2, b_3,$ and b_4 as follows:

$$b_1 = a_1, b_2 = a_2, b_3 = a_3, \text{ and } b_4 = a_4,$$

and, therefore, the true mean:

$$M = b_0/(1 - A), b_0/(1 - A),$$

where

$$A = b_1 + b_2 + b_3 - b_4.$$

and the true standard deviation of returns is given by:

$$\sigma = \sigma(z_t/(1 - A)),$$

where $\sigma(z_t)$ is the standard deviation of the regression residual, z_t.

4. We know very little about the effect of illiquidity on investment returns beyond the intuition that liquidity is certainly no worse than illiquidity. As we do not know much more than this, we will adopt the sensible policy of not saying much more.

5. In practice, real estate managers spend most of their resources investigating local market conditions and negotiating terms of sale. Little if any attention is directed toward the role of a property in the overall portfolio. This is not as misdirected as it might seem. While diversification removes individual and unsystematic property risk, it does not help portfolio returns if misunderstanding the local markets results in overpaying for every property. Nevertheless, without understanding the marginal contribution that properties make to overall portfolio goals, the whole can be less than the sum of the parts.

6. It is important that property returns be noncovariant, that is, that they not move together, or the risk will be systematic and the advantages of diversification will be lost. For example, a $100-million stock portfolio with 100 holdings of $1 million each will not be terribly well diversified if all of the stocks are utilities.

7. Data are reported by the Frank Russell Company on a quarterly basis.

8. We have used the appraisal based returns and have not adjusted the resulting standard deviations in Table 27.2 and Figure 27.1, but the possible low volatility of appraisal returns has no effect whatsoever on our analysis. If we were to increase all of the standard deviations by, for example, a factor of two, then this would double all of the numbers on the vertical scale of Figure 27.1, but all of the points would remain in the same position relative to each other. The analysis of Figure 27.1 would change only if the appraisals distort volatility by different amounts in the different regions. However, that seems unlikely (not to mention unknowable).

9. This is probably a good place to dispel another notion that sometimes surfaces in discussions of risk and return. Often a manager will say that "Risk is important, but over the long run, the risk will wash out and all that will matter is the expected return." This is a misunderstanding of risk and its relation to return and, in fact, both the return and the risk increase over time. The exact form this takes depends on various technical features, but generally over very long periods, the greater the standard deviation of a portfolio's returns, the more likely it is that the value of the portfolio will fall below a given level.

10. It might have occurred to the reader that we should consider breaking real estate into twenty classifications according to both property type and region. For example, hotels in the West would be one of the twenty classes. This is possible, but we have chosen not to do so because of the small number of properties in some of these classes and the resulting lack of reliability of the figures.

11. A subtle technical point arises from our focus on constructing efficient real estate portfolios. Because of the different interactions between individual stock categories and real estate, we are not assured that an efficient portfolio of stocks and real estate will make use of an efficient real estate portfolio. In practice, though, the difference will be small and the data are not accurate enough to discern the difference.

12. Liquidity concerns, however, generally should not be a cause to forgo the diversification of benefits of real estate, because real estate constitutes a small percentage of most portfolios. Other assets can better serve as sources of ready liquidity.

REFERENCES

The two modern portfolio techniques used in the paper are the Capital Asset Pricing Model (CAPM) and the Arbitrage Pricing Theory (APT). Expositions of these approaches can be found in most textbooks on corporate finance. Two references are:

Brealey, Richard and Stewart Myers, *Principles of Corporate Finance*, 2nd ed. New York: McGraw-Hill Book Company 1984.

Copeland, Thomas and Fred Weston, J. *Financial Theory and Corporate Policy*, 2nd ed. Reading, Mass.: Addison-Wesley Publishing Company, 1983.

The following article outlines the APT approach to strategic planning:

Roll, Richard and Stephen A. Ross. "The Arbitrage Pricing Theory Approach to Strategic Portfolio Planning." *Financial Analysts Journal*, May/June 1984.

Other articles of interest include the following:

Chen, Nai fu, Richard Roll and Stephen Ross. "Economic Forces and the Stock Market." *Journal of Business*, July 1986.

Hoag, J. "Toward Indices of Real Estate Value and Return." *Journal of Finance*, May 1980.

Miles, M. and McCue, T. "Commercial Real Estate Returns." *Journal of the American Real Estate and Urban Economics Associations*, Fall 1984.

Zerbst, R.H. and Cambon, B.R. "Historical Returns on Real Estate Investments." *Journal of Portfolio Management*, Spring 1984.

28
Stock Market Volatility and Stock Index Futures
John Board and Charles Sutcliffe

There has been much debate about the need for financial market regulation to minimise the perceived role of derivatives markets (and in particular the market in stock index futures) in causing increased volatility in the stock market (ie the spot, or cash, market).[1]

The authors were commissioned by the Securities and Investments Board to investigate four questions:

- is the futures market more volatile than the stock market (ie the spot market)?
- has spot market volatility increased since the introduction of index futures trading?
- is the level of stock market volatility affected by the amount of trading in index futures?
- does the volume of index futures trading affect stock market volume?

While prices in spot and derivatives markets are closely linked through well known arbitrage relationships, our concern is with interactions through volatility.

To the extent that any increase in regulation weakens the economically desirable relationship between these markets, as traders no longer have unrestricted access to both markets, such regulation is costly. Therefore, at issue is whether or not the benefits of regulation (in terms of reduced volatility) outweigh the economic costs. It is worth noting that some volatility is not just inevitable but positively beneficial as, without volatility, the markets would not correctly reflect the changing values of the underlying assets. The problem is to establish whether excessive volatility is caused by futures markets.

THE DATA

The results are based on daily data on two stock market indices (FT-SE 100 and FT-A All Share Index) which are used to measure the spot price, and the prices of FT-SE 100 index futures. The FT-SE 100 and index futures data is from May 1984, and the FT-A All Share Index (FT-A) data runs from May 1977 until June 1991.

Reprinted from: Board, J. and Sutcliffe, C. 1992: Stock Market Volatility and Stock Index Futures. *Stock Exchange Quarterly with Quality of Markets Review*, Summer, 11–14.

Although the concept of volatility is simple, its precise definition is less obvious, and we, therefore, measure volatility in four ways:

- the variance of daily index levels
- the variance of daily index changes
- the variance of daily rates of return (ie the percentage change in the index)
- the daily index high-low (ie the difference between the high and low index levels during the day)

The last measure will show whether the 'normal' volatility measures are weighted against the extreme swings, which particularly concern some market participants.

All of these measures, with the exception of returns, are scale dependent; that is, they will tend to show higher volatility over time, just because the index level is higher. However, except for the high-low measure, there is a high correlation between the different measures. This suggests that, in practice, the choice of measure may be relatively unimportant.

IS THE FUTURES MARKET MORE VOLATILE THAN THE SPOT MARKET?

Theoretical models predict that the relative price volatility of the spot and futures markets should be very similar. However, empirical studies for the U.S., Australia and Hong Kong have found that the difference is much larger than suggested by the theory (index futures volatility is often double that of spot volatility), particularly when volatility is measured using high frequency data.[2]

We used the daily data discussed above to calculate monthly and quarterly volatilities for the sample period. Figure 28.1 shows the spot and futures volatilities for the FT-SE 100, and indicates, in the box at the bottom of the chart, the huge increase in the volatilities during the crash. Table 28.1 sets out some of our results for the U.K.

The numbers in the table show the percentage by which U.K. futures volatility exceeds that of the spot. Two features of these numbers are notable: first, that the futures market is considerably more volatile than the spot market, whether volatility is measured over months or quarters; second, this relationship between volatilities is of similar magnitude, however volatility is measured.[3] In keeping with most of the studies referred to above, the extra futures volatility in the U.K. is much higher than is predicted by the theory, and this suggests that there is the potential for the greater futures market volatility to transmit itself

Table 28.1   Additional futures volatilities

Volatility measure	Measured over	
	months (%)	quarters (%)
Index levels	19.5	7.2
Index changes	53.2	50.2
% change in index	45.6	41.8
Index high-low	54.1	53.3

(Futures volatility/spot volatility-1)100

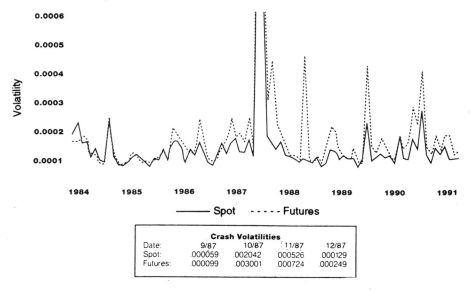

Crash Volatilities				
Date:	9/87	10/87	11/87	12/87
Spot:	.000059	.002042	.000526	.000129
Futures:	.000099	.003001	.000724	.000249

Figure 28.1 Spot and futures returns volatility

to the spot market. It was also found that the contemporaneous correlations between spot and futures volatilities are generally very high (both markets are volatile at the same time).

SOME EXPLANATIONS

Among the explanations for the extra volatility for futures are the following:

- Lower transaction costs of futures (an index transaction is in a single asset, rather than 100, and dealing is on margin), coupled with the price discovery role of futures, means that their price may respond to new information without any movement in the index. Price anomalies which are too small to justify the execution costs of trading an index basket in the spot market, may be worth trading on in the futures market.

- Stale prices. The calculation of the FT-SE 100 Index from market maker quotation mid prices may lead to an understatement of true spot price volatility if there are lags in adjusting quotations to reflect changing circumstances. In the U.S. the use of last transaction prices, rather than the price which would prevail in a current trade, has been similarly linked to the understatement of spot volatility. Since futures prices are not subject to this effect, they will have a greater volatility than the index, and will reflect true market volatility more accurately.

- As a quote driven index, the FT-SE 100 will only respond when market makers alter their views on the price. Large trades may occur outside the touch, but (unlike the, U.S. situation), these will not necessarily affect the index. This will tend to dampen index volatility so that the volatility of the FT-SE 100 may understate the real spot price volatility.

- Bid-ask bounce (successive buy and sell trades) for index futures will increase measured futures price volatility.

- The no-arbitrage (or fair) futures price used to derive the theoretical result of roughly equal price variances omits dividend risk, interest rate risk and default risk (it assumes that these factors can be predicted with certainty). In reality, these factors are uncertain, and this should make futures prices more volatile than spot prices.

- 'Noise traders' (who trade either for pleasure, or on information which they incorrectly believe is valuable) may be more active in the futures than the stock market, leading to higher futures volatility.

- Futures volatility may increase as the maturity of the contract decreases, so raising measured futures volatility.

THE EFFECT OF INDEX FUTURES ON STOCK MARKET PRICE VOLATILITY

Two basic questions were addressed:

- Does the existence of a futures market permanently affect the volatility of the underlying spot market?

- Does the level of activity in the futures market affect the volatility of the spot market?

The basic method of analysis was similar for both questions. The important feature was to separate the effects of the futures market on volatility from the effects of important, non-futures related factors which might have caused increased volatility. We made allowance for the possible effects on volatility of:

- Big Bang, to control for the institutional changes in October 1986

- general market volatility

- index levels, both to control for any tendency for volatility to rise as the index rises (as the level of the index was generally higher after 1984 than before, this might otherwise induce a spurious conclusion), and to allow for any gearing effect (when stock prices rise, leverage falls which reduces equity risk)

- the effect of lagged volatility (a number of studies of the volatility of stock market prices have found that volatility in one period is related to volatility in the next)

The analysis presented here examines the effect of futures markets over and above the effects of the above factors.[4&5]

HAS THE EXISTENCE OF FUTURES MARKETS INCREASED SPOT VOLATILITY?

Because the FT-SE 100 Index has only been computed since 1984, it is not possible to examine its volatility before the introduction of index futures in May 1984. Instead, the FT-A All Share Index (FT-A) was used to measure spot volatility from 1978 onwards. There is a high correlation between the FT-A and FT-SE 100 volatility measures, and so this switch to analyse the FT-A should not be significant.

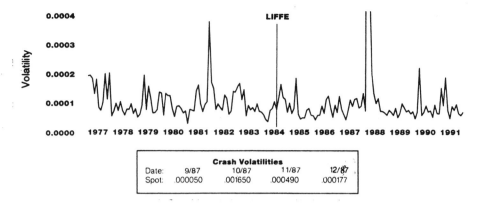

	Crash Volatilities			
Date:	9/87	10/87	11/87	12/87
Spot:	.000050	.001650	.000490	.000177

Figure 28.2   FTA returns volatility

Figure 28.2 shows the pattern of FT-A volatility over the period, and the date on which index futures trading began (denoted LIFFE).[6] Of interest is whether volatility to the right of the line which indicates the start of trading in index futures is greater than that to the left. Allowing for the Crash, it is clear that there is little difference between the periods. This suggests that spot market volatility has not been significantly affected by futures trading opportunities.

A more formal statistical test, which allows for the other effects on spot volatility discussed above, also revealed no statistically significant difference in spot volatility before and after the introduction of index futures. Therefore, our conclusion for the U.K. is consistent with that from previous studies of other markets (U.S., Hong Kong, Japan and Australia): the introduction of futures trading has not led to an increase in spot market volatility.

The results also indicate that Big Bang and the other additional variables were not associated with movements in spot volatility; indicating that spot volatility over the period was determined by variables other than those considered here.

IS SPOT VOLATILITY AFFECTED BY FUTURES VOLUME?

The hypothesis is that the larger the volume of trading in index futures, the greater the effect on spot market volatility. If there is very little trading in index futures, the presence of this market is likely to have little measurable effect on spot volatility. If the volume of the futures market is very large, it has the potential to destabilise the spot market.[7]

Figure 28.3 shows the relationship between spot volatility and index futures volume[8], and the line fitted through the non-Crash observations shows that any relationship between the two is weak with, at most, a very small positive correlation.

A statistical analysis, similar to that used in the previous section, shows that futures volume generally has a positive association with our various measures of spot volatility. Allowing futures volume to have differing effects on spot volatility in each year, reveals that the effect varies over time, but not in any systematic way. In particular, it has not increased consistently since either the introduction of index futures in 1984, or the Crash of 1987.

We interpret these results, and those of other tests, as supportive of the argument that futures volume and spot volatility are related. This might suggest that the growth of futures trading is associated, albeit weakly, with increased spot market volatility. However, it might

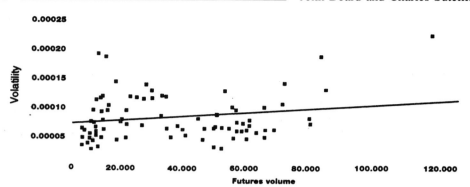

Figure 28.3 Spot volatility versus futures volume

simply be that the actual force determining both spot volatility and futures volume is the arrival of new information. This research has not established the causality if any, of this association between futures volume and spot volatility.

To investigate the relationship between futures volume and information, we repeated the above tests, substituting the previous period's level of futures trading for the contemporaneous measure, and found that this lagged variable was not related to spot volatility. Since the level of futures trading has a long term upward trend while the arrival of information does not, this result is consistent with the hypothesis that the real cause of spot volatility is information arrival, rather than any inherent destabilising effect from futures trading.

DOES FUTURES VOLUME AFFECT SPOT VOLUME VOLATILITY?

Spot volume volatility was measured as the volatility of the number of FT-SE 100 shares traded. Apart from the change in the definition of spot volatility, the model is identical to that used in the earlier sections on spot price volatility. The additional variables are also the same as those used above.

The results for spot volume volatility are broadly consistent with those for spot price volatility. Futures volume has a weak, but significant association with spot volume volatility. As with the results for price volatility, allowing the effect of futures volume to vary between years produced no consistent pattern. The use of lagged futures volume (to remove any possible information effects) led to an insignificant result. This is, again, consistent with the hypothesis that the real force driving spot volatility (prices and volume) is information arrival.

CONCLUSIONS

Our results can be summarised in the following terms:

- Futures markets are more volatile than spot markets and this finding is consistent with those of other researchers examining non-U.K. markets. This result can be partially explained by some of the factors discussed above.

- There is no evidence that the existence of futures markets has caused an increase in the volatility of the spot market.

- There is little evidence that the level of trade in index futures has increased the volatility of the spot market. The weak association which we do find may be explicable in terms of information being transmitted from futures to spot markets. If this is so, the effect may be regarded as economically beneficial.

- These results continue to hold when we change the definition of volatility, the period over which volatility is measured and when we adjust the analysis to allow for other factors which might affect spot volatility.

In terms of policy, we argue that demonstrating a link between markets is not sufficient to justify regulatory intervention. Before action is justifiable, it is necessary to show both that there are links between markets and that such linkages are economically damaging. Our findings confirm that there are links between the markets, but we do not conclude that they result in economic damage[9].

ENDNOTES

1. In part, this concern was generated by the explanations for the stock market crash of October 1987 offered in the Brady Report. The mini crash of October 1989, revived interest in the linkages between the stock market and the corresponding market in index futures.

2. However, initial results for Japan suggest that its spot market is more volatile than the futures market.

3. Exclusion of the fourth quarter of 1987 (including the 1987 Crash) leads to a large reduction in the mean price volatilities, but has little effect on the relative volatilities, and so does not affect the conclusions. We also divided the sample into pre-and post-Crash. The results were essentially unchanged, suggesting that the relationship between markets has not changed substantially over time.

4. We exclude the last quarter of 1987 from our tests. The effects of the Crash are so profound as to swamp any of the market interactions studied here. (Although they are not reported here, we carried out the same analyses without excluding the Crash, and the results were essentially unchanged.)

5. There was some suspicion that a number of these additional variables may be related to each other. Such inter-relationships can affect the validity of statistical tests applied to the variables concerned. The size and extent of the problem were investigated and no significant inter-relationships were found. Our results are, therefore, not seriously affected by this problem.

6. Because trading in the FT-SE 100 option began at approximately the same time, this variable might be regarded as a more general indicator of the existence of index derivatives markets.

7. This argument abstracts from any price discovery role that futures prices may play, which can be largely independent of futures volume.

8. Observations for the Crash period (October-December 1987) have been excluded from the chart.

9. Further details of the results reported here can be found in John Board, Charles Goodhart and Charles Sutcliffe, *Inter-Market Volatility Linkages: The London Stock Exchange and London International Financial Exchanges*. London: Securities and Investment Board, June 1992, 144 pages.

29

How to Avoid Getting Taken in Listed Stock Options

Richard W. McEnally and Richard Rendleman

In the stock market crash of 1987, investors lost hundreds of millions of dollars trading in listed stock options. How do we know? We learned as expert witnesses for individual investors who were wiped out in the crash.

One of the most distressing aspects about this experience was that many of these losses were suffered by small investors who were using options trading strategies that they never dreamed would put their wealth at risk. One of the most common laments was "I had no idea I was taking on that much risk."

The 1987 market crash was an extreme market that one hopes will not be repeated. But even in less extreme markets, unwary investors can lose badly with options, not only because of adverse market moves, but also through strategies that gradually eat away their capital.

Our objective is to alert investors to the main pitfalls in trading options — the things your broker never tells you and may not even know himself. We feel that very few people who are not trading options for a living should trade them at all. But if you are going to trade options, you need an understanding of options basics, you should know what can go wrong, and, in particular, you should be able to assess the risks you're assuming.

OPTIONS: A BRIEF REVIEW

A call option gives its owner the right, but not the obligation, to buy a stock or index of stocks at a set price (the exercise price or striking price) at any time before the option's expiration date. A put option carries the right to sell a stock or stock index at a specified price at any time before its expiration. Call options provide positive payoffs to the investor if the stock price or index value rises above the striking price. Puts provide positive payoffs when the stock or index drops below the exercise price. In these two instances, the options

Reprinted from: Richard W. McEnally and Richard J. Rendleman 1990: How to Avoid Getting Taken in Listed Stock Options. *AAII Journal*, 12, February, 8–13. Reprinted with permission of The American Association of Individual Investors, 625 N. Michigan, Chicago.

are said to be "in the money," since exercising them creates positive value. If at expiration the price of the underlying stock or index is below the exercise price of a call, or above the exercise price of a put — it is "out of the money" — then the option will be allowed to expire worthless. The buyer loses, but he loses only what was paid for the option.

In practice, it is not necessary for the owner of an option to wait until expiration and exercise in order to realize a profit or loss. "American" options can be exercised prior to expiration, but usually such premature exercise is not the best course of action. Another more common course of action is to sell the option before maturity. This normally results in a larger profit or smaller loss than exercising the option, and it is much simpler.

For every option that is bought, one must be sold. With a call option, the original option seller, known as the "call writer," agrees to sell the stock or index to the option buyer at any time before the option expires. In contrast, the writer of a put agrees to buy the stock or index from the option buyer. In both cases, the interests of the writer are the reverse of those of the buyer: The writer of a call loses when the stock or index rises above the exercise price, and the writer of a put loses when the stock or index falls below the exercise price.

Normally the option writer does not wait to get notification of exercise to close out a written position. Instead, the option is repurchased or covered through a closing transaction. The profit or loss in the transaction is simply the difference between the proceeds from writing the option and the amount that is paid to close out the position. If the option ends up out-of-the-money and is allowed to expire, the writer realizes a profit equal to the initial sales price of the option.

Puts and calls can never be bought on margin; the full purchase price must be paid to the buyer's broker. Writing options is different. For a call option, if the underlying stock is on deposit with the writer's broker, the writer is said to be "covered." The writer of a call obtains the proceeds when the initial option sale settles. On the other hand, for options on an index, where it's almost impossible for the writer to deposit the index with the broker, or where the writer simply doesn't own the underlying stock, the call writer is said to be "naked." In that case the writer must put up margin based on the value of the underlying stock or index and the price of the option.

To be covered when writing puts, a put writer would have to be short a position in stock — he would have sold shares of stock he did not own. However, few put writers are actually short the stock, and it is almost impossible to short a market index. Accordingly, writers of puts are almost always uncovered, and margin must be made to cover part of the broker's risk exposure.

Writers of both puts and calls can be required to deposit more margin when options move further into the money — as many put writers discovered to their dismay in October 1987.

OPTION PRICING THEORY AND ITS IMPLICATIONS

In 1973, two finance professors presented a theory of option pricing that has revolutionized the way professional investors approach options trading. The mathematics underlying their model (known as the Black-Scholes model after the professors who developed it) is perhaps the most complex in the entire field of finance, yet the idea behind the model is simple.

The pricing theory recognizes that if option prices are too high, investors find it attractive to write options, thereby driving their prices down. Similarly, if option prices are too low, investors buy options, and their trading activity drives prices up. The model determines the price a typical investor would consider "just right" under ideal market conditions; this is termed the "equilibrium price." At this price, the option position is in equilibrium with the stock market — under ideal market conditions, no investment strategy using options would provide investors with risk-return positions superior to those available in the stock market.

Despite the assumption of ideal market conditions, the model does an outstanding job of describing actual market prices of options. The model's assumption that options are correctly priced has a major implication for individual investors. If an investor could trade options under ideal conditions, he still couldn't consistently win in the options market if he trades at prices according to the model. However, ideal market conditions don't exist in the real world, where investors must pay commissions and taxes, and must post margin. Therefore, if investors trade at prices according to the model under everyday market conditions, they don't stand a chance of winning consistently in the options trading game.

WHAT YOU ARE BETTING ON WHEN TRADING OPTIONS

According to the pricing model, five factors determine the value of an option: the current stock price, the option's striking price, the market's perception of the volatility of the underlying stock price, the time remaining until the option expires, and the market rate of interest. As any of these factors change, the price of the option changes. Changes in the stock price and the market's perception of its volatility can create large, unexpected changes in option prices.

Most investors who buy options understand that they are betting on the future direction of the stock price. Investors who buy calls or write puts are betting that the stock price will go up. Those who write calls or buy puts are betting that the stock price will decline.

However, investors in options are also making a more subtle but highly risky bet on how the market will judge the volatility of the underlying stock or index. A sudden increase in perceived volatility can dramatically increase the prices of both puts and calls, even if the underlying stock or index price never moves. Likewise, as expectations of volatility diminish, option prices will diminish as well.

Taken together, these two bets explain why investors who had written naked put options took such a beating during the October 1987 crash. Not only did put writers lose big when stock prices fell, but they lost even more because the market raised its assessment of volatility.

WHY ANY ACTIVE OPTIONS TRADING SCHEME WILL LOSE

The options market is a "zero sum game." This means that for every winner there is a loser. It's just like betting on a football game. For every dollar bet on the winning team, an equal amount must be bet on the losing team. The world as a whole cannot get richer by placing bets on football.

The options market is also a zero sum game that is biased against the non-professional investor. Individual investors and retail brokers will most likely be on the losing end of options trading because they are competing against professional investors and floor traders whose only business is to predict stock prices and volatility. These professionals have tremendous analytical resources at their disposal. Many Wall Street firms hire in-house gurus who exclusively conduct mathematical analyses of options markets. These professional investors are likely to be taking the opposite side in many individual investors' options transactions.

Because the options market is a zero sum game, no single options strategy can make us all winners. To win consistently we must bring something special to our trading — even greater analytical capability and insight into markets than the professionals. Without such capability, any options trading strategy is doomed to failure if applied consistently over long periods of time.

BUYING OPTIONS: THE SAFEST WAY TO GO

Numerous options strategies are available to investors. The most obvious one is to buy an option. The attractions are obvious: The buyer gets high leverage and known, limited downside risk. For example, suppose IBM is selling for $120. A reasonable price for a call with three months to expiration and an exercise price of $120 would be $6. Puts are a bit cheaper than calls, so a three-month put with an exercise price of $120 might sell for $4. Since exchange-traded puts and calls are written on 100 shares of underlying stock, an investor buying options can take a position in 100 shares of IBM for $400 to $600 and profit from the upside or downside movement of an asset that otherwise would cost $12,000 — or $6,000 if bought or sold short on margin. Such leverage of 20:1 to 30:1 is far greater than the 2:1 available with a conventional margin position.

This leverage means the investor who correctly forecasts movements in a stock or market index can do spectacularly well. For example, consider what happened in October 1974 when IBM rose sharply, apparently in response to a rather far-fetched rumor that the Arabs were going to try to take over the company. On October 29, IBM common stock leaped in price from $180\frac{3}{4}$ to $191\frac{3}{4}$, a 7% increase. Action in IBM calls was even more impressive. The in-the-money January 160s jumped from $28\frac{3}{4}$ to $36\frac{1}{2}$, a gain of 27%. The out-of-the-money January 200s went up 33.3%, from $8\frac{5}{8}$ to $11\frac{1}{2}$. The at-the-money January 180s did nearly as well, up 32% from 16 to $21\frac{1}{8}$. All in all, not bad for a day's work.

Another attractive feature associated with buying options is that you know the maximum loss up front. Returning to the IBM example, the person who buys a call contract can lose only $600, but someone who goes long in the stock could potentially lose the entire $12,000 purchase price. The investor who shorts IBM could, at least in theory, have an infinite loss if IBM rises enough in price. In contrast, buying a put allows the investor to profit if IBM bombs while limiting the maximum loss to $400 if the stock price shoots upward.

Leverage and loss protection don't come free, of course. With the call priced at $6 and the put at $4, IBM stock must rise at least to $126 or fall to $116 before the option buyer walks away with a net profit.

WRITING COVERED CALLS: NO PAIN, NO GAIN

Many investors look at the prices of calls and quickly conclude that the way to increase the income of a stock portfolio without taking on additional risks is to write calls against the stock that they hold. At first blush, the math does seem convincing. An investor who owns 100 shares of IBM worth $12,000 might conclude from our example that he could write four three-month call option contracts during the course of the year at a price of $600, pocketing a handy $2,400. If the stock is called away, it is easy enough to buy more at the higher price and re-establish the call-writing program. If its price stays the same, the investor owns the stock and $2,400 to boot, representing a 20% return on a zero appreciation asset. And if the stock goes down, the $2,400 at least cushions the pain.

The problem with this strategy is that covered calls must be written in a market that is reasonably efficient. If investors write call options at efficient market prices, they will earn a fair return given the risks involved. Since writing fully-covered call options tends to reduce the risk of holding stocks, the strategy should reduce expected return, not increase it. To think otherwise denies the risk-return principle of financial markets that, on average, expected return only increases through an increase in risk.

Many call writers fail to realize the importance of large but infrequent price run-ups that account for the 12% or so average annual return investors have come to expect from owning common stocks over the long run. The call writer never gets these large returns. Call writers also forget that writing covered calls, on average, leaves them holding a portfolio of stocks that have depreciated in value. Call writing does lower the downside risk from owning stocks, but it is not as low-risk as investing in Treasury bills. On average, it should yield returns somewhere between Treasury bills and common stocks. And that's exactly what it does.

NAKED WRITING: WHAT YOU DON'T SEE CAN HURT YOU

Covered call writers at least know that the worst outcome will be either giving up profits they would have otherwise made if their stocks rise, or holding stocks they would have held anyway if their stocks fall. Investors who write naked calls and puts have no such comfort. The outcome for option writers, in fact, is that they have an absolute limit on the profit they can make, but the potential for loss is unlimited.

Many option writers do not comprehend just how much risk they are actually taking on. With naked option writing the potential losses are not at all obvious. Naked option writers can lose much more than the initial proceeds from their writing positions.

In our IBM example, for instance, the person who writes the calls exercisable at $120 receives $600 for agreeing to sell 100 shares of the stock at $120 at any time over the next three months. If IBM rises above $120, every dollar of price increase costs the call writer $100 of profit. If IBM rises to $150, the option writer will have a minimum liability of $3,000 and will lose his $600 five times over. Unlike the covered call writer, the naked call writer has no offsetting position in the stock to cushion the loss. Thus, the naked call writer has effectively the same upside risk as if he shorted the stock. Moreover, if IBM does rise above $120, additional margin will be required, and the naked call writer may have to scramble to meet the margin call.

A put writer is in the reverse position. He loses if the stock moves downward significantly; if the stock stays above the striking price, he earns only the initial put premium.

The typical brokerage statement makes the problem worse by giving the option writer an unwarranted feeling of comfort. Suppose an investor buys 100 shares of IBM for $12,000. The risk involved in this position is reasonably clear. Suppose instead that the investor deposits the $12,000 with a broker, writes five put contracts at $400 each for a total of $2,000, and invests the $12,000 plus the $2,000 received from the options in a money market fund. The total value of the account will be shown as $14,000, with a liability of $2,000 for the options written, leaving a net worth balance of $12,000 — exactly the same numbers as the investor who simply holds one hundred shares of IBM on deposit with the broker.

The $2,000 liability hardly seems intimidating, especially when compared to the $14,000 of safe assets. However, the put writer has effectively taken a long position in IBM that is much more risky than simply buying shares of stock. Suppose IBM drops to $100. The investor who bought 100 shares outright loses $2,000, or 17% of the initial investment. The put writer, on the other hand, has a liability of $10,000 based on five put options now worth $2,000 each, leaving a net worth of only $4,000. He loses 67% of the initial investment. And a margin call will surely be forthcoming.

This pattern of outcomes caused the disasters many investors experienced in the 1987 crash. These investors were writing puts on stocks and indexes in a market that was strongly bullish. The strategy seemed to work well during the first part of the year, giving investors a false sense of security and even encouraging some to increase their exposure before the bottom fell out. The pattern is characteristic of many alluring investment traps. In markets that are moving strongly in one direction or the other, either a call-writing or a put-writing program is going to look very good indeed. But naked option writing is like playing Russian roulette: Anyone who pulls the trigger several times with no bad results and concludes that the pistol isn't loaded can get a rude surprise!

STRATEGIES INVOLVING PRICING "DISPARITIES"

The last strategy we want to review involves positions that attempt to profit from perceived pricing disparities. Standard examples are time spreads, in which the investor buys options with one expiration date and writes otherwise similar options with a different expiration date, and vertical spreads, where the options differ only in the striking price. The objective is to buy options on the relatively underpriced side and write options on the relatively overpriced side, so that as the alleged mispricing corrects itself, the investor makes money.

Such strategies are the height of folly for any investor who is not in intimate contact with the options markets. Even floor traders have trouble making a profit from these positions. Individuals trading without continuous access to quotations are virtually certain to lose.

At least four problems are devastating to such strategies. One relates to correctness of prices, while the others reflect the costs of trading options.

First, the alleged imperfections rarely exist. What may seem to be imperfections are usually incomplete understandings of the considerations that enter into the valuation of options. Others reflect nonsynchronous prices. For example, two settlement (closing) prices reported in the financial press may appear inconsistent with each other, but may simply reflect trades occurring at different times between which the price of the underlying security changed. The options markets may not be perfect at pricing options correctly in a relative sense, but they come close.

Second, the trading strategy must be profitable enough to overcome trading costs. Depending on the options involved and the size of the trade, these costs can range from 1% to 10% of the option's price. In contrast, floor traders, who are the investor's primary competition, pay no commission and only a small clearing fee.

Third, the investor should be aware that there is a "bid" and an "asked" price on all options. This spread, which represents a real cost of trading, can easily run another 5%.

Fourth and finally, a very significant hidden cost is the cost of competing against floor traders, market makers and sophisticated "upstairs traders" who have immediate access to new information and can trade almost as fast. Although this cost is difficult to measure, it means the deck is very much stacked against the individual investor.

A WORD ABOUT RISK: DELTAS

A common defense of the put-writing programs that got so many investors in hot water in 1987 is that no one could reasonably have anticipated the magnitude of the October market drop. We are sympathetic to this argument, but only to a point. The essence of prudent investment is to manage a portfolio so that if a disaster does occur, the damage will be tolerable.

Portfolios containing options positions require a means of assessing exposure to adverse developments. Professional option traders routinely use a device called "delta" for monitoring their risk. Individual investors, or their brokers, can also implement the technique once they understand it.

The delta of an option is nothing more than an estimate of immediate risk measured in terms of equivalent shares of underlying stock. That is, it indicates how many shares of the underlying stock the option buyer or writer would have to be long or short in order to have the same risk as is represented by the option position.

Let's return to the example involving five put option contracts on IBM exercisable at $120 when the stock is also at $120. These options are "at-the-money." As an approximation, the delta of an at-the-money put option contract is -50 to the buyer; each option contract should provide as much immediate price action as a short position in 50 shares of stock. As long as this put is close to the money, a sudden, small change in the price of the stock will change the value of the option by about half as much, but in the opposite direction. If the stock drops $1 per share, or $100 for every 100 shares, the put should increase in value by $0.50 per share of underlying stock, or $50 per option contract. An investor could also earn $50 by shorting 50 shares of stock. Therefore, the position that results from buying these five puts has roughly the same price action as shorting 250 shares of stock.

For the investor who has written the five put contracts, the risk exposure is the opposite to that of the buyer—it is approximately the same as a long position in 250 shares of stock. The writer's immediate downside risk is the same as if he had borrowed $30,000 to buy 250 shares of IBM at a price of $120 per share ($250 \times \$120 = \$30,000$)—and that represents a lot of leverage on the initial $12,000 investment. Unfortunately, this implicit leverage will never show up on the investor's brokerage statement, and it will become even larger if the stock price begins to fall.

You can work out deltas on a hand-held calculator or personal computer programmed to perform basic options calculations. Such calculations are indispensable for anyone trading options. However, even without actually calculating deltas, several generalizations are possible:

- The delta associated with buying an at-the-money call or writing a put is approximately 50; the delta for writing such calls or buying puts is -50.

- Option positions involving buying a call or writing a put that are well in-the-money have a delta approaching 100; the delta for writing such calls or buying puts is -100.

- When option positions get well out-of-the-money, their deltas approach zero.

These observations help explain how so many investors got caught in the put-writing trap in October 1987. For the most part, they were writing puts that were well out-of-the-money at the time they were written. Such options have small deltas and, thus, the risk expressed in equivalent long positions in the underlying stock or index was also small. However, as the market dropped and these puts became increasingly in-the-money, their deltas and the associated risk became greater. Once they were well in-the-money, as many of them must have been by October 19, the deltas were close to -100 and the risk had increased by orders of magnitude. These put writers were like novice skiers who start down what seems a very slight slope, only to discover that the farther they go the steeper it gets. Unfortunately for the put writers, there was a precipice near the bottom!

One of the messages here is that you must continually monitor option positions. What starts out as a fairly innocuous position can degenerate into something far more dangerous. Options are not for the investor who cannot stay on top of positions or who cannot alter positions as their risk profile changes.

When the investor has more than one position in a stock or index — some long or short positions combined with options, say, or several options on the same underlying stock — deltas need to be aggregated over all the positions. Professional options traders and most brokerage houses trading options for their own account routinely use what is called a "risk equivalency statement." These statements work out the equivalent risk of each position and come down to a bottom line that gives the net equivalent position in the stock or index. At a minimum, these investors reassess the risks in options daily, but some do continuing re-evaluations during each trading day.

To our knowledge, no brokers provide retail customers with such statements. However, the technology is available and if enough customers insisted, these statements could be provided. While they may not be necessary for simple positions, they should be regarded as essential for complex trading strategies and naked option writing.

IF YOU MUST TRADE OPTIONS...

We hope you've gotten the message by now: Trading in options is best left to the professionals. But if you must trade options, here are a few ways to keep from getting taken.

- Never engage in any options trading program that you do not thoroughly understand. If the risks get out of hand you will never know it until it's too late.

- Use options only as a portfolio management tool to achieve a pattern of payoffs that best suits your tolerance for risk. Buy call options if you might otherwise be inclined to buy stock on margin but wish to limit your losses in the event the stock price heads south. Buy puts as an alternative to shorting stock if the risk of outright short positions bothers you. But remember, these strategies can get costly if continued for a long period of time. Alternatively, write fully-covered calls if you prefer the pattern of payoffs such a strategy provides over the outright purchase of stock. But there's no magic in this strategy either. When engaging in any of these strategies, remember that you are not likely to earn an above-average return in relation to the risks you are taking. In fact, you are likely to come out a little behind, since you must pay transaction costs to execute trades. However, if this type of investing makes you feel better from a risk-return point of view, by all means do it.

- Don't get involved in high-turnover trading strategies that attempt to take advantage of price discrepancies in the options market. Likewise, avoid strategies such as writing time spreads that purport to take advantage of the natural decline in option prices over time. No options trading strategy will always make money for everyone. In the long run, the only people who benefit from this type of trading are your broker and the professional traders who are likely to be taking the opposite side of your transactions.

- Don't allow your money to be "managed" with options by anyone who lacks a working knowledge of the Black-Scholes pricing model, deltas and other theoretical tools for managing options portfolios.

- If you trade options actively, insist that you be provided with periodic risk equivalency statements that estimate how much stock-equivalent risk is present in your options portfolio. This statement should also estimate how much this risk could change in the event of an adverse stock price movement and how much an adverse change in the market's perception of the underlying stock's or index's volatility would change the value of your portfolio.

- If your broker or any other money manager makes any guarantee whatsoever about the maximum losses that could occur in any options-writing strategy, report this individual immediately to the appropriate options exchange and the National Association of Securities Dealers.

- Never give a stock broker a power of attorney to trade stock options on your behalf.

30
How to Use the Holes in Black–Scholes
Fischer Black

The Black–Scholes formula is still around, even though it depends on at least 10 unrealistic assumptions. Making the assumptions more realistic hasn't produced a formula that works better across a wide range of circumstances.

In special cases, though, we can improve the formula. If you think investors are making an unrealistic assumption like one of those we used in deriving the formula, there is a strategy you may want to follow that focuses on that assumption.

The same unrealistic assumptions that led to the Black–Scholes formula are behind some versions of "portfolio insurance." As people have shifted to more realistic assumptions, they have changed the way they use portfolio insurance. Some people have dropped it entirely, or have switched to the opposite strategy.

People using incorrect assumptions about market conditions may even have caused the rise and sudden fall in stocks during 1987. One theory of the crash relies on incorrect beliefs, held before the crash, about the extent to which investors were using portfolio insurance, and about how changes in stock prices cause changes in expected returns.

THE FORMULA

The Black–Scholes formula looks like this:

$$w(x, t) = xN(d_1) - ce^{-r(t^* - t)}N(d_2)$$

where

$$d_1 = \frac{\ln(x/c) + (r + 1/2v^2)(t^* - t)}{v\sqrt{t^* - t}}$$

and

$$d_2 = \frac{\ln(x/c) + (r - 1/2v^2)(t^* - t)}{v\sqrt{t^* - t}}$$

Reprinted by permission of Stern Stewart & Co. from: Black, F. 1989: How to Use the Holes in Black–Scholes. *The Continental Bank Journal of Applied Corporate Finance*, 1, Winter 1989, 67–73.

In this expression, w is the value of a call option or warrant on the stock, t is today's date, x is the stock price, c is the strike price, r is the interest rate, t^* is the maturity date, v is the standard deviation of the stock's return, and N is something called the "cumulative normal density function." (You can approximate N using a simple algebraic expression.)

The value of the option increases with increases in the stock's price, the interest rate, the time remaining until the option expires, and the stock's volatility. Except for volatility, which can be estimated several ways, we can observe all of the factors the Black–Scholes formula requires for valuing options.

Note that the stock's expected return doesn't appear in the formula. If you are bullish on the stock, you may buy shares or call options, but you won't change your estimate of the option's value. A higher expected return on the stock means a higher expected return on the option, but it doesn't affect the option's value for a given stock price.

This feature of the formula is very general. I don't know of any variation of the formula where the stock's expected return affects the option's value for a given stock price.

HOW TO IMPROVE THE ASSUMPTIONS

In our original derivation of the formula, Myron Scholes and I made the following unrealistic assumptions:

- The stock's volatility is known, and doesn't change over the life of the option.
- The stock price changes smoothly: it never jumps up or down a large amount in a short time.
- The short-term interest rate never changes.
- Anyone can borrow or lend as much as he wants at a single rate.
- An investor who sells the stock or the option short will have the use of all the proceeds of the sale and receive any returns from investing these proceeds.
- There are no trading costs for either the stock or the option.
- An investor's trades do not affect the taxes he pays.
- The stock pays no dividends.
- An investor can exercise the option only at expiration.
- There are no takeovers or other events that can end the option's life early.

Since these assumptions are mostly false, we know the formula must be wrong. But we may not be able to find any other formula that gives better results in a wide range of circumstances. Here we look at each of these 10 assumptions and describe how we might change them to improve the formula. We also look at strategies that make sense if investors continue to make unrealistic assumptions.

Volatility Changes

The volatility of a stock is not constant. Changes in the volatility of a stock may have a major impact on the values of certain options, especially far-out-of-the-money options. For example, if we use a volatility estimate of 0.20 for the annual standard deviation of the stock, and if we take the interest rate to be zero, we get a value of $0.00884 for a six-month call option with a $40 strike price written on a $28 stock. Keeping everything else the same, but doubling the volatility to 0.40, we get a value of $0.465.

For this out-of-the-money option, doubling the volatility estimate multiplies the value by a factor of 53.

Since the volatility can change, we should really include the ways it can change in the formula. The option value will depend on the entire future path that we expect the volatility to take, and on the uncertainty about what the volatility will be at each point in the future. One measure of that uncertainty is the "volatility of the volatility."

A formula that takes account of changes in volatility will include both current and expected future levels of volatility. Though the expected return on the stock will not affect option values, expected changes in volatility will affect them. And the volatility of volatility will affect them too.

Another measure of the uncertainty about the future volatility is the relation between the future stock price and its volatility. A decline in the stock price implies a substantial increase in volatility, while an increase in the stock price implies a substantial decrease in volatility. The effect is so strong that it is even possible that a stock with a price of $20 and a typical daily move of $0.50 will start having a typical daily move of only $0.375 if the stock price doubles to $40.

John Cox and Stephen Ross have come up with two formulas that take account of the relation between the future stock price and its volatility.[1] To see the effects of using one of their formulas on the pattern of option values for at-the-money and out-of-the money options, let's look at the values using both Black–Scholes and Cox-Ross formulas for a six-month call option on a $40 stock, taking the interest rate as zero and the volatility as 0.20 per year. For three exercise prices, the value are as follows:

Exercise price	Black–Scholes	Cox–Ross
40.00	2.2600	2.2600
50.00	0.1550	0.0880
57.10	0.0126	0.0020

The Cox–Ross formula implies lower values for out-of-the-money call options than the Black–Scholes formula. But putting in uncertainty about the future volatility will often imply higher values for these same options. We can't tell how the option values will change when we put in both effects.

What should you do if you think a stock's volatility will change in ways that other people do not yet understand? Also suppose that you feel the market values options correctly in all other respects.

You should "buy volatility" if you think volatility will rise, and "sell volatility" if you think it will fall. To buy volatility, buy options; to sell volatility, sell options. Instead of buying stock, you can buy calls or buy stock and sell calls. Or you can take the strongest position on volatility by adding a long or short position in straddles to your existing position. To buy pure volatility, buy both puts and calls in a ratio that gives you no added exposure to the stock; to sell pure volatility, sell both puts and calls in the same ratio.

Jumps

In addition to showing changes in volatility in general and changes in volatility related to changes in stock price, a stock may have jumps. A major news development may cause a sudden large change in the stock price, often accompanied by a temporary suspension of trading in the stock.

When the big news is just as likely to be good as bad, a jump will look a lot like a temporary large increase in volatility. When the big news, if it comes, is sure to be good, or is sure to be bad, the resulting jump is not like a change in volatility. Up jumps and down jumps have different effects on option values than symmetric jumps, where there is an equal chance of an up jump or a down jump.

Robert Merton has a formula that reflects possible symmetric jumps.[2] Compared to the Black–Scholes formula, his formula gives higher values for both in-the-money and out-of-the-money options and lower values for at-the-money options. The differences are especially large for short-term options.

Short-term options also show strikingly different effects for up jumps and down jumps. An increase in the probability of an up jump will cause out-of-the-money calls to go way up in value relative to out-of-the-money puts. An increase in the probability of a down jump will do the reverse. After the crash, people were afraid of another down jump, and out-of-the-money puts were priced very high relative to their Black–Scholes values, while out-of-the-money calls were priced very low.

More than a year after the crash, this fear continues to affect option values.

What should you do if you think jumps are more likely to occur than the market thinks? If you expect a symmetric jump, buy short-term out-of-the-money options. Instead of stock, you can hold call options or more stock plus put options. Or you can sell at-the-money options. Instead of stock, you can hold more stock and sell call options. For a pure play on symmetric jumps, buy out-of-the-money calls and puts, and sell at-the-money calls and puts.

For up jumps, use similar strategies that involve buying short-term out-of-the-money calls, or selling short-term out-of-the-money puts, or both. For down jumps, do the opposite.

Interest Rate Changes

The Black–Scholes formula assumes a constant interest rate, but the yields on bonds with different maturities tell us that the market expects the rate to change. If future changes in the interest rate are known, we can just replace the short-term rate with the yield on a zero-coupon bond that matures when the option expires.

But, of course, future changes in the interest rate are uncertain. When the stock's volatility is known, Robert Merton has shown that the zero-coupon bond yield will still work, even when both short-term and long-term interest rates are shifting.[3] At a given point in time, we can find the option value by using the zero-coupon bond yield at that moment for the short-term rate. When both the volatility and the interest rate are shifting, we will need a more complex adjustment.

In general, the effects of interest rate changes on option values do not seem nearly as great as the effects of volatility changes. If you have an opinion on which way interest rates are going, you may be better off with direct positions in fixed-income securities rather than in options.

But your opinion may affect your decisions to buy or sell options. Higher interest rates mean higher call values and lower put values. If you think interest rates will rise more than the market thinks, you should be more inclined to buy calls, and more inclined to buy more stocks and sell puts, as a substitute for a straight stock position. If you think interest rates will fall more than the market thinks, these preferences should be reversed.

Borrowing Penalties

The rate at which an individual can borrow, even with securities as collateral, is higher than the rate at which he can lend. Sometimes his borrowing rate is substantially higher than his lending rate. Also, margin requirements or restrictions put on by lenders may limit the amount he can borrow.

High rates and limits on borrowing may cause a general increase in call option values, since calls provide leverage that can substitute for borrowing. The interest rates implied by option values may be higher than lending rates. If this happens and you have borrowing limits but no limits on option investments, you may still want to buy calls. But if you can borrow freely at a rate close to the lending rate, you may want to get leverage by borrowing rather than by buying calls.

When implied interest rates are high, conservative investors might buy puts or sell calls to protect a portfolio instead of selling stock. Fixed-income investors might even choose to buy stocks and puts, and sell calls, to create a synthetic fixed-income position with a yield higher than market yields.

Short-Selling Penalties

Short-selling penalties are generally even worse than borrowing penalties. On U.S. exchanges, an investor can sell a stock short only on or after an uptick. He must go to the expense of borrowing stock if he wants to sell it short. Part of his expense involves putting up cash collateral with the person who lends the stock; he generally gets no interest, or interest well below market rates, on this collateral. Also, he may have to put up margin with his broker in cash, and may not receive interest on cash balances with his broker.

For options, the penalties tend to be much less severe. An investor need not borrow an option to sell it short. There is no uptick rule for options. And an investor loses much less interest income in selling an option short than in selling a stock short.

Penalties on short selling that apply to all investors will affect option values. When even professional investors have trouble selling a stock short, we will want to include an element in the option formula to reflect the strength of these penalties. Sometimes we approximate this by assuming an extra dividend yield on the stock, in an amount up to the cost of maintaining a short position as part of a hedge.

Suppose you want to short a stock but you face penalties if you sell the stock short directly. Perhaps you're not even allowed to short the stock directly. You can short it indirectly by holding put options, or by taking a naked short position in call options. (Though most investors who can't short stock directly also can't take naked short positions.)

When you face penalties in selling short, you often face rewards for lending stock to those who want to short it. In this situation, strategies that involve holding the stock and lending it out may dominate other strategies. For example, you might create a position with a limited downside by holding a stock and a put on the stock, and by lending the stock to those who want to short it.

Trading Costs

Trading costs can make it hard for an investor to create an option-like payoff by trading in the underlying stock. They can also make it hard to create a stock-like payoff by trading in the option. Sometimes they can increase an option's value, and sometimes they can decrease it.

We can't tell how trading costs will affect an option's value, so we can think of them as creating a "band" of possible values. Within this band, it will be impractical for most investors to take advantage of mispricing by selling the option and buying the stock, or by selling the stock and buying the option.

The bigger the stock's trading costs are, the more important it is for you to choose a strategy that creates the payoffs you want with little trading. Trading costs can make options especially useful if you want to shift exposure to the stock after it goes up or down.

If you want to shift your exposure to the market as a whole, rather than to a stock, you will find options even more useful. It is often more costly to trade in a basket of stocks than in a single stock. But you can use index options to reduce your trading in the underlying stocks or futures.

Taxes

Some investors pay no taxes; some are taxed as individuals, paying taxes on dividends, interest, and capital gains; and some are taxed as corporations, also paying taxes on dividends, interest, and capital gains, but at different rates.

The very existence of taxes will affect option values. A hedged position that should give the same return as lending may have a tax that differs from the tax on interest. So if all investors faced the same tax rate, we would use a modified interest rate in the option formula.

The fact that investor tax rates differ will affect values too. Without rules to restrict tax arbitrage, investors could use large hedged positions involving options to cut their taxes sharply or to alter them indefinitely. Thus tax authorities adopt a variety of rules to restrict tax arbitrage. There may be rules to limit interest deductions or capital loss deductions, or rules to tax gains and losses before a position is closed out. For example, most U.S. index option positions are now taxed each year — partly as short-term capital gains and partly as long-term capital gains — whether or not the taxpayer has closed out his positions.

If you can use capital losses to offset gains, you may act roughly the same way whether your tax rate is high or low. If your tax rate stays the same from year to year, you may act about the same whether you are forced to realize gains and losses or are able to choose the year you realize them.

But if you pay taxes on gains and cannot deduct losses, you may want to limit the volatility of your positions and have the freedom to control the timing of gains and losses. This will affect how you use options, and may affect option values as well. I find it hard to predict, though, whether it will increase or decrease option values.

Investors who buy a put option will have a capital gain or loss at the end of the year, or when the option expires. Investors who simulate the put option by trading in the underlying stock will sell after a decline, and buy after a rise. By choosing which lots of stock to buy and which lots to sell, they will be able to generate a series of realized capital losses and unrealized gains. The tax advantages of this strategy may reduce put values for many taxable investors. By a similar argument, the tax advantages of a simulated call option may reduce call values for most taxable investors.

Dividends and Early Exercise

The original Black–Scholes formula does not take account of dividends. But dividends reduce call option values and increase put option values, at least when there are no offsetting adjustments in the terms of the options. Dividends make early exercise of a call option more likely, and early exercise of a put option less likely.

We now have several ways to change the formula to account for dividends. One way assumes that the dividend yield is constant for all possible stock price levels and at all future times. Another assumes that the issuer has money set aside to pay the dollar dividends due before the option expires. Yet another assumes that the dividend depends in a known way on the stock price at each ex-dividend date.

John Cox, Stephen Ross, and Mark Rubinstein have shown how to figure option values using a "tree" of possible future stock prices.[4] The tree gives the same values as the formula when we use the same assumptions. But the tree is more flexible, and lets us relax some of the assumptions. For example, we can put on the tree the dividend that the firm will pay for each possible future stock price at each future time. We can also test, at each node of the tree, whether an investor will exercise the option early for that stock price at that time.

Option values reflect the market's belief about the stock's future dividends and the likelihood of early exercise. When you think that dividends will be higher than the market thinks, you will want to buy puts or sell calls, other things equal. When you think that option holders will exercise too early or too late, you will want to sell options to take advantage of the opportunities the holders create.

Takeovers

The original formula assumes the underlying stock will continue trading for the life of the option. Takeovers can make this assumption false.

If firm A takes over firm B through an exchange of stock, options on firm B's stock will normally become options on firm A's stock. We will use A's volatility rather than B's in valuing the option.

If firm A takes over firm B through a cash tender offer, there are two effects. First, outstanding options on B will expire early. This will tend to reduce values for both puts and calls. Second, B's stock price will rise through the tender offer premium. This will increase call values and decrease put values.

But when the market knows of a possible tender offer from firm A, B's stock price will be higher than it might otherwise be. It will be between its normal level and its normal level increased by the tender offer. Then if A fails to make an offer, the price will fall, or will show a smaller-than-normal rise.

All these factors work together to influence option values. The chance of a takeover will make an option's value sometimes higher and sometimes lower. For a short-term out-of-the-money call option, the chance of a takeover will generally increase the option value. For a short-term out-of-the-money put option, the chance of a takeover will generally reduce the option value.

The effects of takeover probability on values can be dramatic for these short-term out-of-the-money options. If you think your opinion of the chance of a takeover is more accurate than the market's, you can express your views clearly with options like these.

The October 19 crash is the opposite of a take-over as far as option values go. Option values then, and since then, have reflected the fear of another crash. Out-of-the-money puts have been selling for high values, and out-of-the-money calls have been selling for low values. If you think another crash is unlikely, you may want to buy out-of-the-money calls, or sell out-of-the-money puts, or do both. [This refers to the situation in 1988.]

Now that we've looked at the 10 assumptions in the Black–Scholes formula, let's see what role, if any, they play in portfolio insurance strategies.

PORTFOLIO INSURANCE

In the months before the crash, people in the U.S. and elsewhere became more and more interested in portfolio insurance. As I define it, portfolio insurance is any strategy where you reduce your stock positions when prices fall, and increase them when prices rise.

Some investors use option formulas to figure how much to increase or reduce their positions as prices change. They trade in stocks or futures or short-term options to create the effect of having a long-term put against stock, or a long-term call plus T-bills.

You don't need synthetic options or option formulas for portfolio insurance. You can do the same thing with a variety of systems for changing your positions as prices change. However, the assumptions behind the Black–Scholes formula also affect portfolio insurance strategies that don't use the formula.

The higher your trading costs, the less likely you are to create synthetic options or any other adjustment strategy that involves a lot of trading. On October 19, the costs of trading in futures and stocks became much higher than they had been earlier, partly because the futures were priced against the portfolio insurers. The futures were at a discount when portfolio insurers wanted to sell. This made all portfolio insurance strategies less attractive.

Portfolio insurance using synthetic strategies wins when the market makes big jumps, but without much volatility. It loses when market volatility is high, because an investor will sell after a fall, and buy after a rise. He loses money on each cycle.

But the true cost of portfolio insurance, in my view, is a factor that doesn't even affect option values. It is the mean reversion in the market: the rate at which the expected return on the market falls as the market rises.[5]

Mean reversion is what balances supply and demand for portfolio insurance. High mean reversion will discourage portfolio insurers because it will mean they are selling when expected return is higher and buying when expected return is lower. For the same reason, high mean reversion will attract "value investors" or "tactical asset allocators," who buy after a decline and sell after a rise. Value investors use indicators like price–earnings ratios and dividend yields to decide when to buy and sell. They act as sellers of portfolio insurance.

If mean reversion were zero, I think that more investors would want to buy portfolio insurance than to sell it. People have a natural desire to try to limit their losses. But, on balance, there must be as many sellers as buyers of insurance. What makes this happen is a positive normal level of mean reversion.

THE CRASH

During 1987, investors shifted toward wanting more portfolio insurance. This increased the market's mean reversion. But mean reversion is hard to see; it takes years to detect a change in it. So investors did not understand that mean reversion was rising. Since rising mean reversion should restrain an increase in portfolio insurance demand, this misunderstanding caused a further increase in demand.

Because of mean reversion, the market rise during 1987 caused a sharper-than-usual fall in expected return. But investors didn't see this at first. They continued to buy, as their portfolio insurance strategies suggested. Eventually, though, they came to understand the effects of portfolio insurance on mean reversion, partly by observing the large orders that price changes brought into the market.

Around October 19, the full truth of what was happening hit investors. They saw that at existing levels of the market, the expected return was much lower than they had assumed. They sold at those levels. The market fell, and expected return rose, until equilibrium was restored.

MEAN REVERSION AND STOCK VOLATILITY

Now that we've explained mean reversion, how can you use your view of it in your investments?

If you have a good estimate of a stock's volatility, the stock's expected return won't affect option values. Since the expected return won't affect values, neither will mean reversion.

But mean reversion may influence your estimate of the stock's volatility. With mean reversion, day-to-day volatility will be higher than month-to-month volatility, which will be higher than year-to-year volatility. Your volatility estimates for options with several years of life should be generally lower than your volatility estimates for options with several days or several months of life.

If your view of mean reversion is higher than the market's, you can buy short-term options and sell long-term options. If you think mean reversion is lower, you can do the reverse. If you are a buyer of options, you will favor short-term options when you think mean reversion is high, and long-term options when you think it is low. If you are a seller of options, you will favor long-term options when you think mean reversion is high, and short-term options when you think it's low.

These effects will be most striking in stock index options. But they will also show up in individual stock options, through the effects of market moves on individual stocks and through the influence of "trend followers." Trend followers act like portfolio insurers, but they trade individual stocks rather than portfolios. When the stock rises, they buy; and when it falls, they sell. They act as if the past trend in a stock's price is likely to continue.

In individual stocks, as in portfolios, mean reversion should normally make implied volatilities higher for short-term options than for long-term options. (An option's implied volatility is the volatility that makes its Black–Scholes value equal to its price.) If your views differ from the market's, you may have a chance for a profitable trade.

ENDNOTES

1. See John Cox and Stephen Ross, *Journal of Financial Economics* (January/March 1976).

2. See John Cox, Robert Merton, and Stephen Ross, *Journal of Financial Economics* (January/March 1976).

3. Robert Merton, *Bell Journal of Economics and Management Science* (1977).

4. John Cox, Mark Rubinstein, and Stephen Ross, "Option Pricing: A Simplified Approach," *Journal of Financial Economics* Vol. 7 (1979), 229–263.

5. For evidence of mean reversion, see Eugene Fama and Kenneth French, "Permanent and Temporary Components of Stock Prices," *Journal of Political Economy* Vol. 96 No. 2 (April 1988), 246–273; and James Poterba and Lawrence Summers, "Mean Reversion in Stock Prices: Evidence and Implications," *Journal of Financial Economics* Vol. 22 No. 1 (October 1988), 27–60.

PART SIX
International Investment

Part Six consists of two wide-ranging international investment articles. In Chapter 31, Patrick Odier and Bruno Solnik provide an up-to-date examination of the benefits of international diversification into both bonds and equities. They conclude that international investment offers benefits in terms of risk reduction and return enhancement whatever the investor's nationality. Of course, if world markets move together more than they have in the past, the benefits of diversification will diminish. But, to date, correlations between markets have remained low. Odier and Solnik note that there is no real evidence that markets have become more volatile in recent years. However, during periods of exceptional volatility, the international markets are more likely to move together. Thus, when diversification is most needed, international diversification is least effective in its risk reduction role. They argue that there is little worthwhile that can be said about the optimal amount of currency hedging. Finally, they suggest that international indexes are far from efficient and that active international asset allocation may be profitable. Odier is Managing Partner, Lombard Odier and Cie, a private Swiss bank, and Solnik is a professor at the Hautes Etudes Commerciales — Institut Supérieur des Affaires.

Investors tend to concentrate their activities in their domestic market and to a lesser extent in the large international markets. Many investors would benefit by paying more attention to the small emerging markets. Arjun Divecha, Jaime Drach and Dan Stefek, all with the U.S. investment consulting firm BARRA Inc., provide a quantitative overview of emerging markets in Chapter 32. Amongst their many findings, they note that while individual emerging markets are very risky, the markets tend to move independently of each other. As a result, the emerging markets as a whole are much less risky than they are individually. They are not highly correlated with developed countries' markets and, if their high historical returns continue, offer superb diversification opportunities for investors in the major markets. The authors provide much useful information on whether an investor should focus on stock selection within an emerging market or should attempt to make active bets between markets. Whatever the evidence, some investors might decide that the risks of emerging markets are of a kind that they have no experience of and which demand the safety of broad diversification. Ibbotson and Brinson (1987, p. 114), discussing a different age, point out these special risks: "Eighteenth-or nineteenth-century investors who bet on the United States, Canada or Britain would have been prodigious forecasters of the world economy. In 1900, an international investor might well have bought Austro-Hungarian, Russian, and German stocks instead of U.S. and British issues. The Austro-Hungarian equities would have lost all their value by the end of World War I. The Russian equities would

have been rendered worthless by the communist government, which nationalized firms not long after the Russian Revolution of 1917. And German equity claims were wiped out by World War II."

REFERENCE

Ibbotson, R.G. and Brinson, G.P. 1987: *Investment Markets*. New York: McGraw-Hill.

31

Lessons for International Asset Allocation

Patrick Odier and Bruno Solnik

In the early '70s, U.S. pension plans held no foreign assets. A similar observation could be made for pension plans in most countries.[1] Then several studies established a strong case for international diversification, arguing that global diversification could reduce total portfolio risk while enhancing performance opportunities.[2]

A recent study by Intersec shows that total pension assets world-wide amounted to $4.6 trillion at the start of 1991, accounting for about 25% of the world market capitalization of bonds and equities combined. While global investment has risen dramatically in the past 20 years, only 7% of pension assets are invested abroad. The figure varies greatly across countries. U.S. pension funds on average have only 4% of their assets invested abroad, while U.K. pension funds invest more than 25% abroad. The percentage of foreign assets in U.S. pension plans is particularly small, given the geographic distribution of world market capitalization. As Figure 31.1 shows, non-U.S. assets represent well above 50% of the world market capitalization of bonds and equities.

The growth in international investment has been paralleled by a growth in international financial market integration. National markets have been deregulated and opened to foreign investment. Good-quality information on most markets is more easily available and transaction costs have been drastically reduced. National economies also appear to be increasingly dependent on a world business cycle. This leads one to wonder whether the advantages of international risk diversification have not been reduced.

This article investigates whether global investment is still beneficial from a risk/return viewpoint. First we restate the case for global diversification, not only for U.S. investors, but also for Japanese, British and German investors. Then we look at what has changed over the past 20 years, and how the changes affect international investment. Finally, we discuss some of the important issues for global investing in the '90s, particularly the choice of a benchmark and the currency-hedging decision.

Stock Market

June 31, 1991, Total $9.5 Trillion

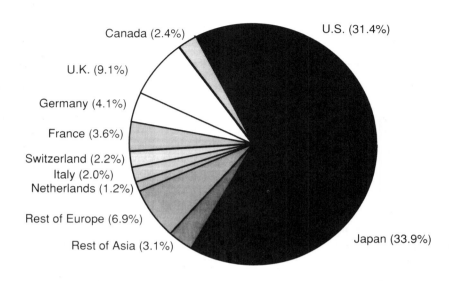

Canada (2.4%)

U.S. (31.4%)

U.K. (9.1%)

Germany (4.1%)

France (3.6%)

Switzerland (2.2%)

Italy (2.0%)

Netherlands (1.2%)

Rest of Europe (6.9%)

Rest of Asia (3.1%)

Japan (33.9%)

Bond Market

1991, Total $12 Trillion

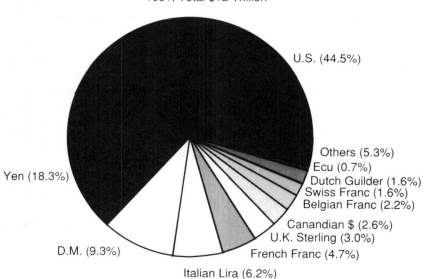

U.S. (44.5%)

Others (5.3%)

Ecu (0.7%)

Dutch Guilder (1.6%)

Swiss Franc (1.6%)

Belgian Franc (2.2%)

Yen (18.3%)

Canandian $ (2.6%)

U.K. Sterling (3.0%)

French Franc (4.7%)

D.M. (9.3%)

Italian Lira (6.2%)

INTERNATIONAL RISK DIVERSIFICATION

A major argument for investing internationally is that it increases profit opportunities while providing risk diversification. We take the viewpoint of a U.S.-dollar investor, but also present results for Japanese, British and German investors. Hence we cover the four major countries in terms of financial market size and institutional investment.

A preliminary question is the choice of numeraire for measuring return and risk. Tradition and regulation require that a U.S. pension fund measure its assets in U.S. dollars. This is not the obvious answer if the objective of the plan is to provide future pensioners with steady purchasing power at retirement some time in the future. In theory, one should optimize the real return/risk profile of a portfolio, not its nominal U.S.-dollar profile.

Foreign goods represent, directly and indirectly, a significant portion of the consumption basket, as measured by the CPI, in each country.[3] The purchasing power of U.S. pensioners is thus affected by foreign currencies, so it would seem unwise to regard an investment in nominal U.S.-dollar deposits as risk-free in terms of purchasing power. The accepted practice, nevertheless, is to optimize returns in nominal U.S.-dollar terms, and to regard as risky holdings in other currencies. We adopt this convention and demonstrate that, even with it, there remains a strong case for international diversification.

Risk Diversification

It has been repeatedly demonstrated that international diversification reduces the total volatility of a portfolio — i.e., the risk of a large loss in any given quarter or month.[4] The traditional measure of volatility is the standard deviation of return, or sigma.[5]

Table 13.1 gives the volatility of the U.S. stock market as well as that of various international stock indexes over the past 10 and 20 years. The international stock indexes are the MSCI indexes for Europe, for EAFE (Europe, Australia and the Far East) and for the world. We also report the volatility for the world index assuming that currency risk is fully hedged (unitary hedge ratio in each currency).

The volatility of the U.S. market is higher than that of a well diversified world portfolio (16.1% compared with 14.9% over the past 20 years), despite the fact that the world portfolio

Table 31.1 Total risk (% per year)

	Local-currency stocks	Europe stocks	EAFE stocks	World stocks	World hedged
U.S. dollar					
1980–1990	16.2	18.0	19.2	15.5	14.8
1970–1990	16.1	17.8	18.4	14.9	13.9
Yen					
1980–1990	20.1	17.4	15.3	15.7	14.8
1970–1990	18.4	17.4	15.6	15.4	13.9
D.M.					
1980–1990	21.7	16.9	18.4	17.3	14.8
1970–1990	18.4	16.6	17.5	16.3	13.9
U.K. pounds					
1980–1990	19.3	16.4	18.0	16.9	14.8
1970–1990	24.3	15.9	16.8	15.9	13.9

includes investments in some very volatile markets such as Hong Kong and Italy. The currency risks of foreign investments also increase the volatility of the world portfolio vis-à-vis the U.S. index; currency hedging can reduce this risk.

From the viewpoint of a Japanese investor, the benefits of international risk diversification are even greater than for a U.S. investor. Measured in yen, the volatility of the Japanese stock market has been 18.4% over the past 20 years; that of the internationally diversified portfolio represented by the world index (in yen) is only 15.4%. A currency-hedging strategy further reduces the total volatility of the world index. A similar conclusion obtains for investors of all nationalities and over all time periods covered in Table 31.1.

Although investing abroad means buying some highly volatile markets (e.g., some markets in the Far East and Italy) and bearing some additional currency risks, it appears that many of these risks get diversified away because of low correlations. The net result is an international portfolio with a lower volatility than that of a purely domestic stock portfolio.

Correlation

Figure 31.2 shows correlations of the U.S. stock market with other markets over the past 10 years. Correlation coefficients vary somewhat across countries; the coefficients are less than 0.4 for Japan and Germany and around 0.6 for the U.K. and the Netherlands.[6] The average **correlation** tends to be around 0.5; this means that only 25% (the square of 0.5) of the movements in the U.S. and any other market covered are explained by common factors. Figure 31.3a, b and c shows the correlations from the viewpoints of German, British and Japanese investors.

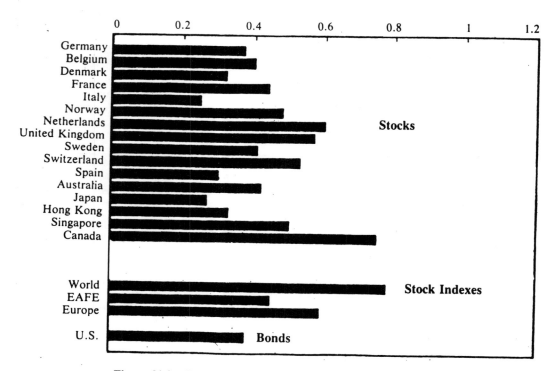

Figure 31.2 Correlations of U.S. stocks (U.S. dollars, 1980–1990)

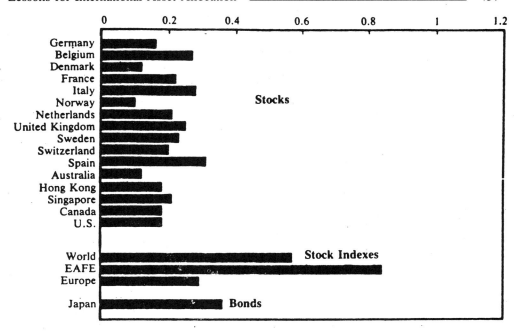

Figure 31.3a   Non-U.S. stock correlations: Japanese stocks (yen, 1980–1990)

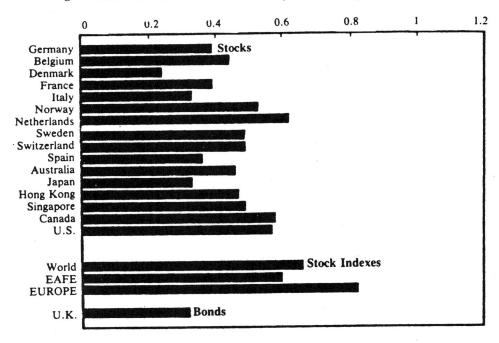

Figure 31.3b   Non-U.S. stock correlations: British stocks (pounds sterling, 1980–1990)

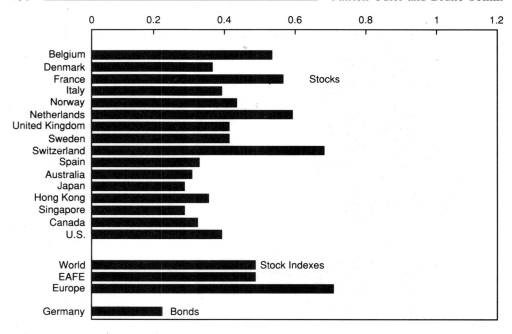

Figure 31.3c   Non-U.S. stock correlations: German stocks (deutschemarks, 1980–1990)

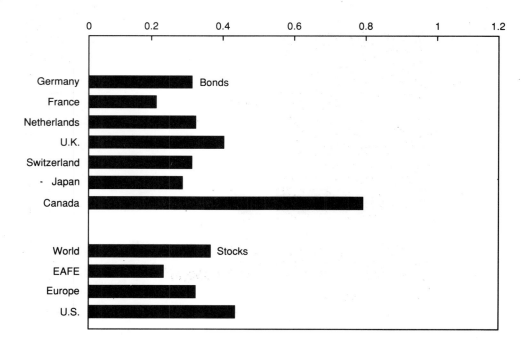

Figure 31.4   Correlations of U.S. bonds (U.S. dollars, 1980–1990)

Figures 31.4 and 31.5a, b and c show that correlations are even lower for bond markets.[7] These surprisingly low correlations reflect three factors. First, contrary to comments often made by politicians, long-term yields are not strongly correlated across countries. Second, the returns on a bond investment in a foreign country are strongly influenced by the performance of the country's currency; the currency risk is typically as large as the risk of a typical bond market measured in local-currency terms. Third, currency movements are only weakly correlated with long-term yield movements.

The general observation is that national monetary/budget policies are not fully synchronized across countries. For example, the growing U.S. budget deficit in the mid-eighties, associated with high U.S. interest rates and a rapid weakening of the dollar, was not matched in other countries. The relative independence of national monetary/budget policies, influencing both currency and interest rate movements, leads to a surprisingly low correlation between the U.S.-dollar returns of the U.S. and foreign bond markets. Foreign bonds, then, allow one to diversify the risks associated with domestic monetary/budget policies; this conclusion would be even stronger if we measured risk and return in real rather than nominal terms.

Of course, the correlations of both equity and bond markets are larger between countries with strong economic and monetary ties, such as Canada and the U.S. or Germany and the Netherlands. Altogether, however, correlations are surprisingly low and explain the good risk-diversification benefits provided by international investments.

Currency Risk

Currency risk is a component of the total risk of a foreign investment. Its impact can be estimated by comparing the standard deviation of the asset return when measured in a foreign currency with its standard deviation when measured in its domestic currency. For example, the domestic volatility of the Japanese stock market has been 20.1% per year over the past

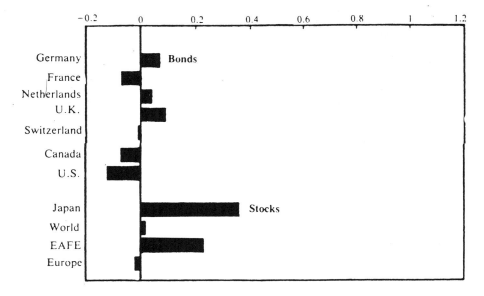

Figure 31.5a   Non-U.S. bond correlations: Japanese bonds (yen, 1980–1990)

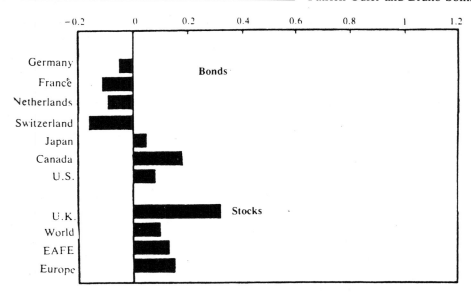

Figure 31.5b Non-U.S. bond correlations: British bonds (pounds sterling, 1980–1990)

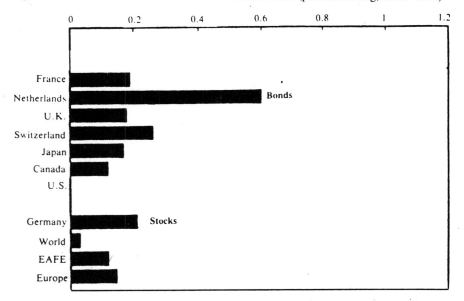

Figure 31.5c Non-U.S. bond correlations: German bonds (deutschemarks, 1980–1990)

10 years, but it increases to 25.8% when measured in U.S. dollars — an increase of over 20%. Currency risk is generally a much larger component of the total risk of a bond investment than of an equity investment. For example, the volatility of an investment in Japanese yen bonds is 6.9% in yen, but goes up to 17.0% in dollars, an increase of over 100%.

Currency risk has a stronger effect on foreign bonds than on foreign stocks because bond markets are less volatile than stock markets. One should remember that the dollar variance of a foreign investment is equal to its variance in the local currency plus the variance of the exchange rate plus twice the covariance between the investment return and the exchange rate movement. Because the covariance is usually quite small, the dollar variance is close to the sum of the two variance terms and the dollar standard deviation is much less than the sum of the two standard deviations. Of course, the contribution of currency risk varies with the currency and the countries considered and is rather small for the Canadian dollar and other currencies pegged to the U.S. dollar.

A similar qualitative conclusion holds for investors in other countries. For a German investor, currency risk adds 25% to the volatility of the U.S. stock market and 50% to the volatility of the U.S. bond market. From a German viewpoint, investments in other countries of the European Community carry less currency risk because of the European Monetary System.

While currency risk gets partly diversified away in a diversified international portfolio, the risk of an appreciation of the U.S. dollar against all or most currencies always remains for a U.S. investor. Currency risk contributes roughly 10% to 15% of the volatility of the world index, as Table 31.1 shows.

Later on, we will show that the importance of the monetary factor fluctuates over time. This means that monetary factors should be studied with great care and that they should be an important variable in the formulation of a global investment policy. It also implies that an active currency hedging policy may be valuable.

One should not forget that the objective of an optimal investment policy is not to minimize risk but to optimize risk-adjusted performance. A systematic policy of complete currency hedging would eliminate the contribution of currency risk to the total volatility of the portfolio but would also affect the return on that portfolio. Hence a systematic full hedging policy may turn out to be fairly costly in terms of performance, besides the transaction costs and the heavy administrative burden of constantly rebalancing the currency hedge. The issue of an optimal currency hedging policy is discussed later.

GLOBAL ASSET ALLOCATION

So far we have focused on the risk diversification advantage of passive international diversification. But global asset allocation can also provide better profit opportunities, hence improve a portfolio's risk/return tradeoff. Below we look at optimal asset allocations over the past 10 years.

Figure 31.6 shows optimal international stock allocations for different risk levels for the 1980–90 period.[8] Each asset or portfolio is represented by one point on the graph: The U.S. stock market has a risk of 16.2% and a total return of 13.3%. Other stock markets are more volatile, partly because of currency risk. By combining the various national stock markets we get diversified portfolios whose returns and risks can be calculated, because we know the returns and covariances of all the assets.

The well-known idea popularized by the 1990 Nobel prize winners Markowitz and Sharpe is that investors building a portfolio will try to obtain the best return while attempting to minimize the risk of loss. They will thus select asset allocations that lie in the top-left part of the figure.

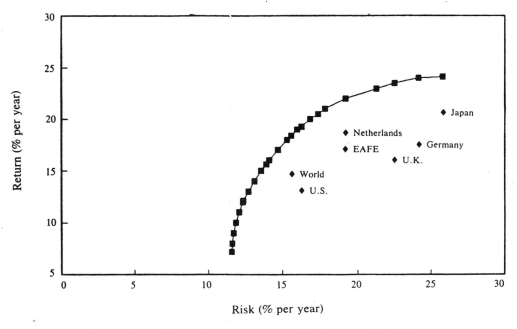

Figure 31.6 Efficient frontier for stocks (U.S. dollars, 1980–1990)

The best achievable risk/return tradeoffs — the optimal asset allocations — lie on the efficient frontier. As Figure 31.6 shows, international diversification of a pure U.S. stock portfolio would greatly enhance return without a large increase in risk. An international stock portfolio with the same risk level as the purely U.S. stock portfolio (16.2% per year) would achieve an annualized total return above 19%, compared with 13.3% for the U.S. portfolio.

The Contribution of Bonds

Can bonds help improve the risk-adjusted performance of globally diversified portfolios? The question addressed here is not whether one should prefer portfolios made up solely of bonds or solely of stocks, but whether bonds should be added to a stock portfolio in a global investment strategy. Figure 31.7 gives the efficient frontier for a global asset allocation allowing for bonds and stocks, foreign and domestic. No investment constraints other than no short-selling are applied; no currency hedging is included.

To keep the figure readable, we did not plot individual bond and stock markets, but only the U.S. bond and stock indexes as well as the world stock index. Their relative positions are consistent with theory. U.S. bonds have a lower risk and a lower return. Over the long run, riskier stock investments are compensated for by a risk premium. The U.S. equity risk premium has been around 0.5% per annum over the past 10 years. This is low compared with the risk premium observed over the past 20 years (around 2% per annum) or over longer time periods.

As noted, world stocks have had less risk and a better return than U.S. stocks.[9] The global asset allocations on the efficient frontier strongly dominate U.S. investments. The global efficient asset allocation with a return equal to that of the U.S. stock market (13.3% annualized) has a risk equal to only one-third that of the U.S. stock market. Conversely,

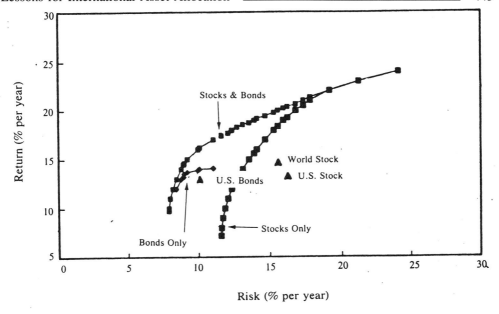

Figure 31.7 Efficient frontier for stocks and bonds (U.S. dollars, 1980–1990)

a global efficient allocation with the same risk as the U.S. stock market outperforms the U.S. stock market by 8% per annum. Similarly, any domestic U.S. stock/bond strategy is strongly dominated by a global stock/bond strategy. A domestic portfolio of U.S. stocks and bonds tends to have half the return of that on an international efficient allocation with the same risk level.

Figure 31.7 also shows the efficient international frontier for stocks only (same as in Figure 31.6), as well as the efficient international frontier for bonds only. Clearly, stocks offer a strong contribution to a bond portfolio in terms of risk/return tradeoff; the bond-only efficient frontier is dominated by the global efficient frontier. A stock-only efficient frontier is also dominated by a global strategy.

A theoretician might regard Figure 31.7 as a simple test of the efficiency of the world market portfolio. Without resorting to sophisticated econometric procedures, this figure indicates, at least visually, that the world stock index is far from efficient when the universe of all national stock markets is included.

Figure 31.8a, b and c shows the efficient frontiers for Japanese, German and British investors. All calculations are performed in the respective national currency. The conclusions derived above for an American investor also apply to the other nationalities.

International asset allocation seems to offer large potential in terms of risk-adjusted performance for investors of all major countries. This conclusion emerges from a study of the past 10 years, but a similar result would hold for a longer time period. The asset allocation strategy was kept constant over the whole period; performance could be further improved by allowing periodic revisions of the allocation over time. Also, we ruled out any form of currency hedging; systematic or selective currency hedging could have further improved the risk profile. The potential profits are large but require some forecasting skills. A major question is how much of the potential can be achieved through superior management

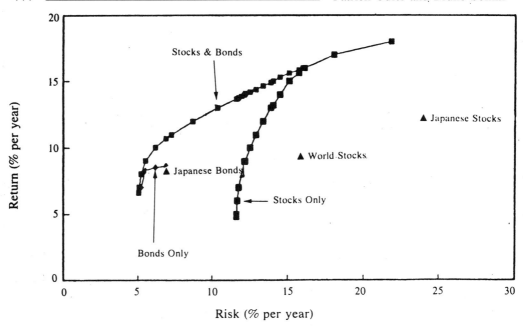

Figure 31.8a Efficient frontiers for non-U.S. investors (Japanese yen, 1980–1990)

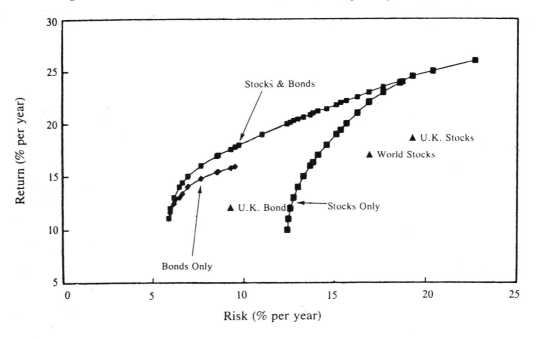

Figure 31.8b Efficient frontiers for non-U.S. investors (British pound, 1980–1990)

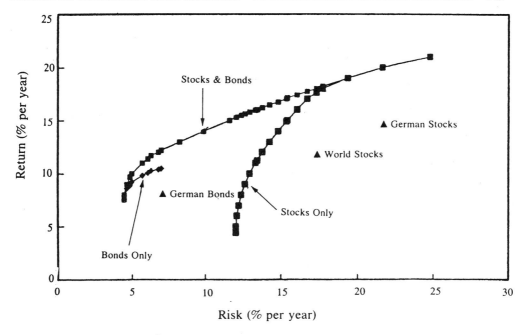

Figure 31.8c Efficient frontiers for non-U.S. investors (deutschemark, 1980–1990)

skills. Even if only 20% of the profits could be reaped, international asset allocation would seem to be very valuable in risk/return terms.

WHAT IS CHANGING?

While international diversification would have offered benefits over the past 30 years, the financial markets and their environments change rapidly.[10] Do these changes affect our conclusions?

Volatility

It is often heard that markets are becoming more volatile and unpredictable. Actually, it is hard to remember a time when money managers ever thought the markets were easy to predict (which is comforting if we believe in some degree of market efficiency). Rather than rely on short-term impressions, let's look at some statistics.

Figure 31.9 shows quarterly returns on U.S. stocks from January 1926 to December 1989. There is no clear-cut evidence of a secular increase in volatility for the stock market. While some periods of strong volatility are evident (the 1920s, 1930s and 1987), the market quickly returned to normal volatility levels.[11]

The volatility of the U.S. bond market did increase in 1979 with the new monetary policy adopted in the U.S., featuring money-supply targets rather than interest-rate targets. Figures 31.10 and 31.11 show the volatilities of the U.S. bond and stock markets over the 1970–90 period for various sub-periods of 10, five and two years. Volatility is calculated as the standard deviation of monthly returns, annualized. While the volatility of the U.S. bond market increased from the 1970s to the 1980s, this is not the case for the U.S. stock market.

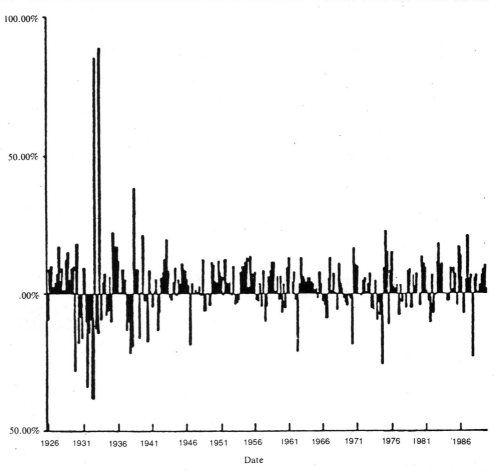

Source: Ibbotson Associates.

Figure 31.9 Volatility of U.S. stock market (quarterly U.S. dollar returns, 1926–1989)

Results for the other major world financial markets are more diverse. Figures 31.12 and 31.13 show the volatilities of these markets measured in local currencies and in U.S. dollars. Looking at the volatilities of the stock and bond markets measured in their respective currencies, it is clear that stock markets have not been stable over time. However, there is no evidence of increased volatility for all stock markets in the world. The British market was actually less volatile in the '80s than in the '70s, while the reverse holds true for Germany. The trends of bond market volatilities also varied. In local-currency terms, volatility increased in the U.S. (and to some extent in Japan), but decreased in the U.K. and was stable in Germany. These trends can be explained by national considerations — for example, the economic policy of Mrs. Thatcher in the U.K. There is no evidence of a global trend in volatility for bond markets.

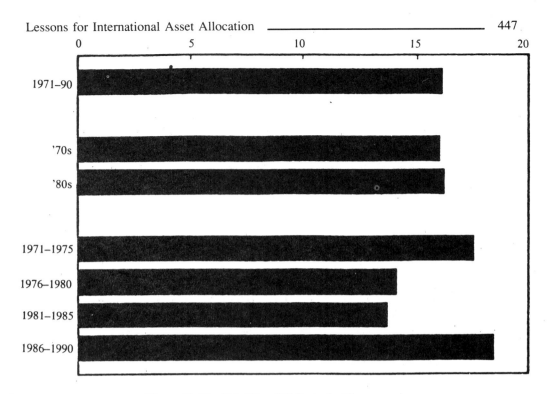

Figure 31.10   Volatility of U.S. stocks (% per year)

To summarize, bond and stock markets go through tranquil and agitated periods at different times across the world. There is little evidence of a significant trend toward more volatile markets in all countries.

Currency Risk

The contribution of currency to the performance and risk of international portfolios is significant. If we view performance in purchasing-power terms, the same conclusion holds true for a portfolio invested solely in domestic assets. For example, the depreciation of the U.S. dollar against most currencies in the late 1980s reduced the purchasing power of a U.S. portfolio invested solely in U.S. fixed-income assets.

The contribution of monetary factors to return and risk over the past 10 years can be estimated from Figures 31.12 and 31.13 showing trends in the volatilities of foreign stock and bond markets for a U.S. investor over the past 20 years. The differences between the volatilities measured in local currencies and those measured in U.S. dollars represent the contributions of currency risk. The total risk of a foreign investment can therefore be broken down into its volatility in local-currency terms and its currency-risk component. The volatility in local-currency terms equals the volatility of the investment if fully hedged against currency risk.

Several conclusions emerge from the estimates for the 1970s and 1980s. First, currency risk is a much larger relative component of the risk of foreign bonds than of foreign stocks.

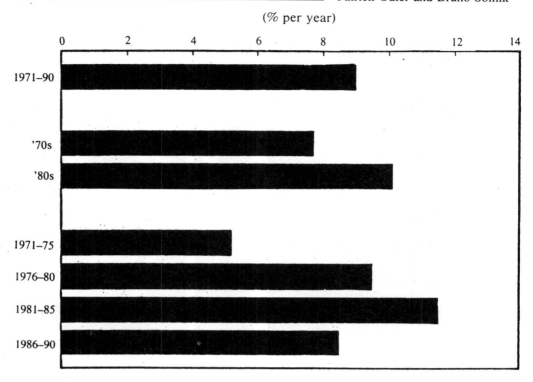

Figure 31.11 Volatility of U.S. bonds (% per year)

This is not surprising, but the magnitude of the difference is striking. Second, currency risk remains a small, although significant, component of the total risk of a foreign equity investment. Third, foreign bond markets have become quite volatile when measured in U.S. dollars. Both interest-rate risk and currency risk are monetary in nature, so any separation of the two is somewhat arbitrary; nevertheless, the currency component has been increasing over time, as can be seen in Figure 31.13.

Of course, a part of currency risk gets diversified away in an international portfolio invested in many currencies. But currency hedging has clearly become an investment decision in its own right. An important investment question is whether we should hedge and, if so, how much?

Correlation

Financial markets worldwide have certainly become increasingly integrated in terms of the physical integration of information systems, as well as the growing harmonization of trading mechanisms and transaction processing. However, the question relevant to investment management is whether financial market movements have become more synchronized. This would reduce diversification and profit potentials for international investors.

Figure 31.14 shows the correlation of the U.S. stock market with the EAFE index (representing all the major stock markets outside the U.S.) over time; all calculations are in U.S. dollars. (A correlation coefficient is a statistical average of the degree of comovement of

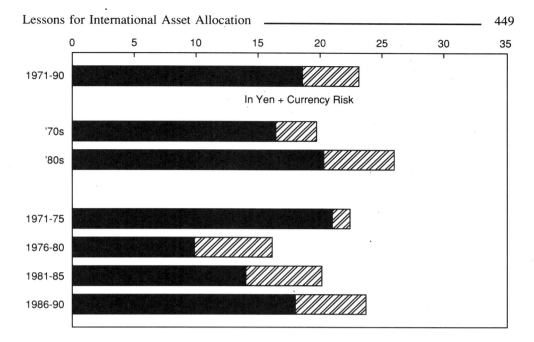

Figure 31.12a　Non-U.S. stock volatility: Japan (% per year)

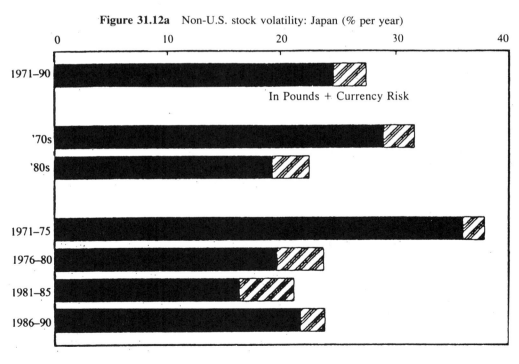

Figure 31.12b　Non-U.S. stock volatility: U.K. (% per year)

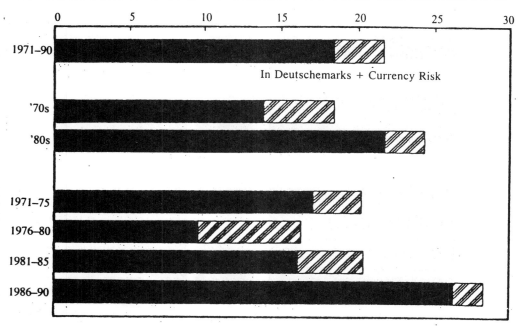

Figure 31.12c Non-U.S. stock volatility: Germany (% per year)

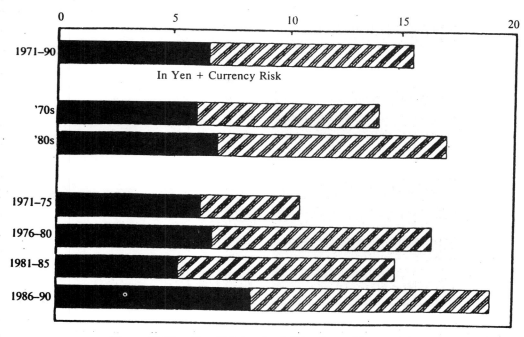

Figure 31.13a Non-U.S. bond volatility: Japan (% per year)

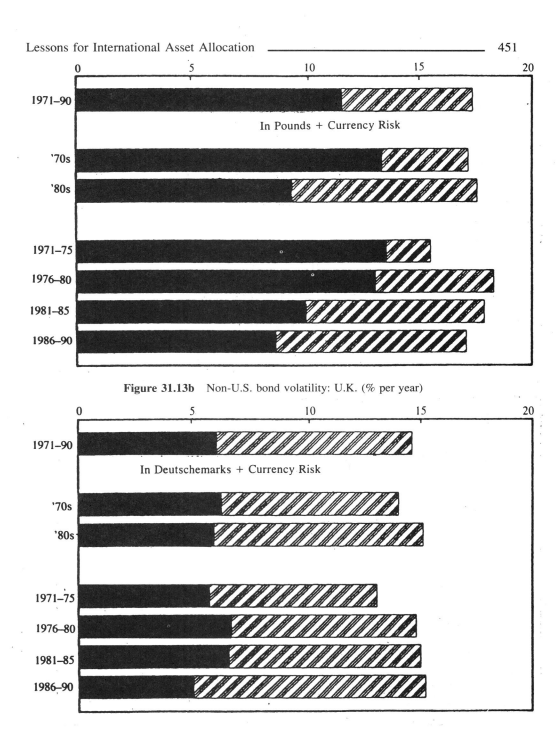

Figure 31.13b Non-U.S. bond volatility: U.K. (% per year)

Figure 31.13c Non-U.S. bond volatility: Germany (% per year)

two markets.) In some periods, the U.S. market is influenced by international factors and follows the rest of the world; at other times, it is solely influenced by specific domestic factors. The correlation coefficient gives an estimate of the average link between the U.S. market and the rest of the world.

When estimated over short periods of time, the correlation fluctuates somewhat. However, there is no obvious trend toward increased correlation. Despite the painful moments of 1987 and 1990, the correlation has stayed remarkably constant from the 1970s to the 1980s. If anything, it is less now than it was in the early '70s.

We have little evidence, here or in other studies, demonstrating a dramatic increase in correlations between stock or bond markets. Despite the media's insistence that interest rates are closely correlated across the world, the degree of correlation of bond markets (measured, for example, in U.S. dollars) is still quite low. This can be seen in Figure 31.15, which gives

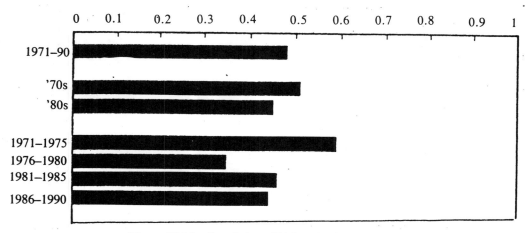

Figure 31.14   Correlation of U.S. and EAFE stocks

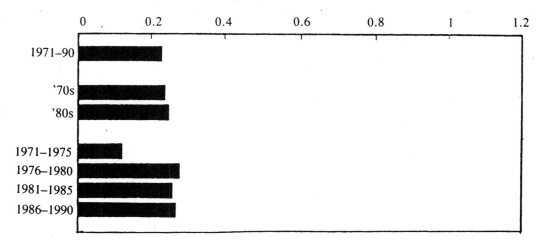

Figure 31.15   Correlation of U.S. and Japanese bonds

the correlation between the returns on the U.S. and Japanese bond markets, measured in U.S. dollars. This low correlation may be partly explained by the importance of monetary risk to bond investments, as noted above. The correlation between bond markets is much larger when measured by currency-hedged returns.

While correlations between markets have not increased, an unpleasant characteristic has appeared: Correlations seem to increase when markets are most volatile.[12] In other words, correlations are larger when market movements are large. This is bad news for a portfolio manager, because it is precisely in periods of large down movements that diversification (and low correlation) is most needed.

SOME UNRESOLVED ISSUES

Two important and related issues have been the focus of an intense debate — the choice of an international benchmark and currency-hedging policies.

The choice of a benchmark for international portfolios is controversial. Traditionally, U.S. pension plan sponsors have used separate benchmarks for separate asset classes, rather than one common benchmark including all investable assets. For example, separate benchmarks are typically used for U.S. equity and for U.S. bonds, and for non-U.S. equity and non-U.S. bonds.

Because most U.S. pension plans concentrate their foreign investments in equity, our discussion focuses on the selection of an international equity benchmark. Initially, most pension plan sponsors used as a benchmark a market-capitalization-weighted index of all non-U.S. stock markets, namely the Morgan Stanley Capital International EAFE index. Some investors now prefer to use a GDP-weighted index, which better reflects the international distribution of productive economies. Because most Japanese companies are publicly listed and trade at high price/earnings ratios compared with the rest of the world, for example, the relative stock market capitalization of Japan is higher than its relative economic production. The effect is compounded by the cross-holdings of Japanese company shares (*maoichi effect*), which artificially inflates reported market capitalization. Still other investors consider that currency risks should not be borne and use a currency-hedged EAFE benchmark.

The choice of a benchmark is important because it strongly influences the investment strategy of money managers. When a manager knows that performance is measured against a specific benchmark, deviations from the benchmark become a major source of risk. Because of the relative independence of market, and currency movements, international asset allocations that differ from that of the benchmark can lead to marked differences in performance. This shows up clearly in the huge diversity in the performances of international money managers with similar mandates, as reported by the major international performance measurement firms.

A benchmark should have at least three properties: It should be widely accepted, easy to replicate, and have a strong conceptual foundation. A benchmark that is *not* widely accepted by the profession may be useful in guiding the international asset allocation of the money manager and helping the client structure long-term strategy and set targets for the money manager. But the validity and composition of a benchmark not widely accepted or used by other sponsors and managers are subject to periodic questioning, particularly when the chosen benchmark underperforms more popular benchmarks selected by other clients.

A proper benchmark must represent an asset allocation that can be easily reproduced in the marketplace as a long-term, low-cost, passive strategy. For example, replicating the performance of an index with full currency hedging is very difficult and requires heavy costs. Currency hedges are not available in most currencies, so hedging strategies must rely on imperfect cross-hedging. Hedging also requires constant and costly monitoring to rebalance the number of currency contracts in order to reflect cross-hedge ratios, stock market price movements, changes in the portfolio composition, rollovers and so on. No investment strategy can replicate exactly the performance of this benchmark, and good tracking requires high artificial transaction costs (maybe 1% or more per year).

The benchmark must represent a passive, *efficient* alternative. It is set as the objective to match or beat because it is regarded as the best strategy *if* markets were fully efficient. The Capital Asset Pricing Model (CAPM) indicates that the market portfolio (the stock index with market-capitalization weights) is the efficient portfolio that every investor should use if the market is efficient. Empirical evidence shows that it is indeed difficult to beat the U.S. index, after risk adjustment. The important question for international investors is: What is the optimal, or efficient, portfolio under an international asset pricing theory where investors measure returns using different numeraires (currencies)?

The conclusions of international asset pricing theory are somewhat unpleasant.[13] The theory concludes that all investors should combine their national risk-free bill with a common portfolio. This common portfolio is made up of the world equity market portfolio *plus* a combination of national bills. These national bills can be viewed as foreign currency contracts, since a forward currency contract is equivalent to going short in the foreign bill and long, for the same amount, in the domestic bill. The common portfolio is thus often referred to as the world market portfolio partly hedged against currency risk.

One very serious problem with this concept is that the hedge ratios in the currencies differ depending on investors' preferences and relative wealths. Nationals of countries that are net foreign investors (like Japan) or have stronger risk-aversion, for example, would have a stronger demand than other investors to hedge foreign investment risks. Thus the neat result of the domestic CAPM, which claims that an observable market portfolio is efficient, breaks down because preferences and relative wealths, unlike market capitalizations, are not observable.

Let's be clear about what the theory says and does not say. It says that the world market portfolio (the "world index") is not in itself efficient, but only part of an efficient portfolio. Similarly, the world market portfolio fully hedged against currency risk (i.e., with unitary hedge ratios) should not be efficient by itself.[14] There does exist some universally efficient portfolio that could be used as benchmark, but its weights are neither observable nor easily estimated.

Currency Hedging

These conclusions have strong implications for the "neutral" currency-hedging policy. Basically, the efficient currency-hedging policy, consistent with market equilibrium, is not known. In the absence of an observable theory, all kinds of arbitrary *a priori* assumptions can be made. Some managers assume that currency risk carries no risk premium, hence suggest unitary hedge ratios to offset unrewarded currency risks.[15] Others claim that currency risks cancel out in the long run and that hedging policies are time-consuming and costly; they advocate a systematic no-hedging policy. Others make arbitrary assumptions about parameters of utility functions and relative wealth and derive other systematic hedging policies.[16] Many simplistic assumptions lead to many different simplistic hedging rules. Unfortunately, the theoretician can be of little help.

Another word of caution should be added. Theory tells us that the composition of the equity portfolio of each investor should be equal to the world equity portfolio and that any hedging of currency risk should take place through forward contracts, not through changes in the composition of the equity portfolio.[17] For example, if the U.S. represents 40% of world market capitalization, theory tells us that a U.S. investor should hold 40% of his equity portfolio in U.S. equity and 60% in the EAFE. Let's assume the U.S. investor decides instead to hold 90% in U.S. equity and only 10% in foreign equity; theory never says that this 10% should still be invested in the EAFE. Actually, the optimal composition of foreign holdings is likely to depend strongly on the holdings' relative importance in the total portfolio.

Similarly, the optimal currency hedging policy is likely to depend on the percentage of foreign assets in the total portfolio. Looking at risk alone, Jorion has shown that the currency contribution is hardly noticeable for portfolios with less than 10% invested in foreign-currency assets.[18] Some currency risk actually provides good diversification for domestic budget deficit/monetary policy risk.[19] This argument does not hold, however, if foreign assets represent 60% of the total portfolio. Holding 1% of a portfolio in deutschemarks or other European currencies could provide interesting risk diversification benefits for a U.S. investor. But any monetary diversification advantage would disappear if deutschemark assets represented 40% or 50% of the total portfolio. Finally, the optimal hedging policy differs between foreign equity and foreign bonds.

To summarize, we do not have, and should not expect ever to find, a widely accepted, easily replicable and conceptually sound universal international benchmark. Nor do we have a simple answer for optimal currency-hedging policy.

CONCLUSIONS

The asset allocation decision is the major contributor to the performance and risk of a portfolio. For example, Sharpe recently found that an average of roughly 90% of the monthly variation of returns on a large sample of U.S. mutual funds is explained by asset allocation, while only 10% is explained by security selection. We have shown here that international assets — both equity and bonds — should be an important component of the asset allocation of any investor. Clearly, foreign asset classes provide attractive risk diversification and profit opportunities. Even if the correlation between markets is increasing slightly, it remains quite low because of the relative independence of national economies and monetary policies. The risk and return advantages of international diversification are very large for investors in all the major countries.

It also appears that the monetary variable is an integral part of the asset allocation process. The international environment changes over time, but careful research can identify opportunities, quantify risks and identify appropriate efficient asset allocation strategies.

This article has dealt little with the international efficiency of the world financial markets. A casual look at some of the figures, however, would suggest that traditional world indexes are far from efficient. This suggests that active bets in international allocations can be taken as long as the total risk of the portfolio is carefully monitored.

ENDNOTES

1. The U.K. was the notable exception.

2. See Levy and Sarnat. "International Diversification of Investment Portfolios," *American Economic Review*, September 1970, and Solnik, "Why Not Diversify Internationally Rather Than Domestically?" *Financial Analysts Journal*, July/August 1974.

3. The percentage of foreign goods in the national CPI varies from 30% in smaller economies such as that of Switzerland to less than 10% for the U.S.

4. An extensive discussion of the benefits of international investing is found in Solnik, *International Investments*, 2nd ed. (Reading, MA: Addison Wesley, 1991).

5. Standard deviation is the familiar statistical measure of the amplitude of price swings. If we measure sigma in per cent per year, there is roughly one chance in six of a loss (or negative deviation from the mean) equal to one sigma in any given year.

6. A correlation coefficient lies between $+1$ (perfect correlation) and -1 (perfect acyclical variation). The square of the correlation, or R^2, is a good measure of the percentage of common variation of the two markets.

7. The correlation would be higher for currency-hedged bond returns.

8. The calculation of the efficient frontier is based on mean returns and covariances over the 10 years 1980–90. No short-selling or currency hedging was used. Figure 31.6 restricts the investment universe to the 15 largest stock markets: no bond investments were made but no maximum constraint on foreign investments was set.

9. A well-diversified world index tends to have a lower volatility than any of its components, as Table 31.1 shows. However, the return on a world index is simply the market-capitalization-weighted average of the national index returns; the world index is thus by definition an average return, and its volatility will be greater than that of some of its component indexes.

10. See, for example, Solnik, "Why Not Diversify Internationally," *op. cit.*

11. See also the volatility study by Schwert, "Stock Market Volatility and the Crash of '87," *Review of Financial Studies* 3 (1990).

12. See Longin and Solnik, "Conditional Correlation in International Equity Returns" (Working paper, HEC, Jouy en Josas, France, November 1991).

13. See Solnik, "An Equilibrium Model of the International Capital Market," *Journal of Economic Theory*, July/August 1974; Adler and Dumas, "International Portfolio Choice and Corporate Finance: A Synthesis," *Journal of Finance*, June 1983; Sercu, "A Generalization of the International Asset Pricing Model," *Revue Finance*, June 1980; Adler and Solnik, "The Individuality of 'Universal' Hedging," *Financial Analysts Journal*, May/June 1990; and Solnik, "Currency Hedging and Siegel's Paradox" (Working paper, HEC. Jouy en Josas, France, August 1991).

14. Similarly, the domestic CAPM tells us that IBM should be part of a larger efficient portfolio but does not say that IBM is an efficient investment on its own.

15. See, for example, Perold and Sharpe, "The Free Lunch in Currency Hedging: Implications for Investment Policies and Investment Standards," *Financial Analysts Journal*, May/June 1988.

16. See Black, "Universal Hedging: Optimizing Currency Risk and Reward in International Equity Portfolios," *Financial Analysts Journal*, July/August 1989, and Black, "Equilibrium Exchange Rate Hedging," *Journal of Finance*, July 1990.

17. This is similar in spirit to the domestic CAPM, which claims that the desired level of risk should be attained by leveraging the same equity market portfolio, not by changing the composition of the portfolio.

18. See Jorion, "International Asset Allocation." *Investment Management Review*, January 1989, and Jorion. "International Bonds: The Asset Class," in Aliber and Bruce, eds. *Quantitative Global Investing* (Homewood, IL: Dow Jones-Irwin. 1991).

19. An increase in the budget deficit can lead to inflation, higher interest rates and a drop in the value of the domestic currency.

32

Emerging Markets: A Quantitative Perspective

Arjun B. Divecha, Jaime Drach and Dan Stefek

Soaring returns and sanguine prospects for economic growth have fueled a recent surge of interest in investing in "emerging" markets. Such markets have become more accessible to the global investor. Today, there are several country funds through which investors can participate in even "closed" or restricted markets. Investment will become easier as more countries dismantle barriers to direct foreign investment.

This article presents recent research into the emerging markets from a quantitative point of view. We have developed a model for understanding the forces that drive these markets, which affords some insights for global investors.

We find that while the emerging markets are more volatile than developed markets, they tend to be relatively uncorrelated with each other and with developed markets. Thus, contrary to popular belief, modest investment in the emerging markets leads to lower, rather than higher, portfolio risk for the global investor (see also Brown [1991]). Over the past five years, a global investor who put 20% in an emerging markets index fund would have reduced overall annual portfolio risk from 18.3% to 17.5% while increasing annual return from 12.6% to 14.7%.

One unexpected result of our research is that stock returns in the emerging markets tend to be more homogeneous than in developed markets, implying that a strong market force dominates industry and stock-specific influences. In short, when the market moves, everyone goes along for the ride.

WHICH MARKETS ARE CONSIDERED EMERGING MARKETS?

Just what is considered an emerging market is frequently a matter of opinion. Narrowly defined, an emerging market:

Reprinted from: Divecha, A.B., Drach, J. and Stefek, D. 1992: Emerging Markets: A Quantitative Perspective. *Journal of Portfolio Management*, 19, Fall, 41–50. This copyright material is reprinted with permission from The Journal of Portfolio Management, 488 Madison Avenue, New York, NY 10022.

- Has securities that trade in a public market.
- Is not a developed market (as defined by countries covered within the Morgan Stanley Capital International Indices or Financial Times Indices).
- Is of interest to global institutional investors.
- Has a reliable source of data.

Table 32.1 lists the countries that we consider to be emerging markets. They fall into three regions: Asia, Latin America, and Europe/Middle East/Africa. Singapore and Hong Kong fall into most definitions of developed markets, but are included here because they are closely related to the other Asian markets. Colombia, Pakistan, Nigeria, Jordan, and Zimbabwe are not of great institutional interest at present, although Pakistan has recently opened up its economy and financial markets to foreign investors and may well be next on the list of emerging markets to attract institutional interest. Finally, Japanese over-the-counter (OTC)

Table 32.1 Emerging market characteristics

Country	Annual standard deviation(%)[a]	Market capitalization (million U.S.)[b]	Turnover ratio[c]
Argentina	108	$ 5,195	26%
Brazil	74	$ 25,112	34%
Chile	29	$ 19,563	6%
Colombia	21	$ 1,437	5%
Greece	56	$ 17,010	26%
Hong Kong	31	$ 83,600	42%
India	31	$ 27,487	57%
Indonesia	39	$ 7,998	49%
Japan OTC	20	$ 89,575	NA
Jordan	19	$ 2,166	20%
Korea	29	$ 105,051	67%
Malaysia	30	$ 58,738	22%
Mexico	56	$ 39,070	37%
Nigeria	13	$ 1,507	1%
Pakistan	10	$ 3,169	8%
Philippines	46	$ 8,940	21%
Portugal	61	$ 9,838	18%
Singapore	33	$ 55,000	59%
Taiwan	63	$ 124,038	710%
Thailand	31	$ 34,996	96%
Turkey	84	$ 18,819	31%
Venezuela	44	$ 9,332	27%
Zimbabwe	20	$ 2,399	2%
Developed Markets			
Japan	22	$ 2,917,679	54%
U.K.	19	$ 867,599	32%
U.S.	17	$ 3,072,303	58%

[a]Predicted annual standard deviation in %, based on BARRA's Emerging Markets Equity Model.
[b]As of June 30, 1991.
[c]This is defined as the ratio of annual trading volume (in U.S.$) divided by beginning of year market capitalization (in U.S.$), for 1990. *Source*: International Finance Corporation.

stocks are included in the list because they tend to behave (and are perceived) differently from listed Japanese stocks.

RETURNS AND RISKS OF EMERGING MARKETS

The casual reader of the financial press knows there have been stories of incredible returns (high and low) in the emerging markets. The Venezuelan stock market was up about 450% in U.S. dollar terms during 1990. On the other hand, the Taiwanese Stock Exchange Index started out 1990 at about the 5,000 level, went up to 12,600 during the first quarter and collapsed to near 2,500 during the third quarter. What makes this even more interesting is that the Taiwanese market is only the fourth or fifth most risky emerging market! During the first half of 1991, Latin American countries dominated all others; in U.S. dollar terms, they were up over 100%.

Overall, the emerging markets have done better than the developed markets over the past five years. During this period, the annualized total return to the International Finance Corporation's (IFC) Emerging Markets Composite Index was 19.7%, as compared to 12.6% for the Financial Times World Index.[1]

Table 32.1 shows predicted risks according to BARRA's risk model of each of the emerging markets as well as for a few developed markets. Clearly, these markets are extremely risky when compared with developed markets. Apart from the obvious risks (political instability, insider trading, etc.), there are a number of possible reasons why these markets are extremely volatile.

First, they tend to be fairly concentrated; that is, the larger stocks have a high proportion of the over-all market capitalization. As a result, there are fewer opportunities for diversification, and returns to these large stocks dominate the overall market return. Second, unlike the developed markets, which tend to have forces that affect diverse sectors of the economy differently, the emerging markets tend to have a strong market-related force that affects all stocks within a market. This tends to accentuate volatility.

There are some apparent anomalies in these results. Pakistan, Jordan, Colombia, Nigeria, and Zimbabwe appear to have had relatively low risk over the last five years. We believe that these low figures reflect the lack of liquidity in these markets, so observed volatilities (and correlations with other markets) must be viewed with caution. When we look at the turnover ratio (value traded/market capitalization) for each market, we find that these five markets rank in the bottom six (shown in Table 32.1). The real volatility is likely to be much higher, if and when these markets become more liquid.

When we look at the emerging markets as a group (the BARRA Emerging World Universe of about 4,000 stocks), we find that it has much lower volatility than most of the individual markets. This is because of low correlations between these markets. The diversification that these low correlations offer the global investor is one of the biggest benefits of investing in the emerging markets. The volatility (over the past five years) of the BARRA Emerging World Universe was about 28.0%, as compared to about 18.8% for the S&P 500 or 22.8% for the Morgan Stanley Europe, Australia, and the Far East (EAFE) index.

A MODEL TO UNDERSTAND RISK AND RETURN

To analyze risk and return in these markets, we developed a multi-factor model similar to one previously constructed for the developed markets (see Grinold, Rudd, and Stefek

[1989]). At the core of the model is a hierarchical decomposition of portfolio return into various components. This is illustrated in Figure 32.1.

We focus on excess return, return beyond the risk-free rate. This return is initially broken down into currency return and excess return earned in local markets. Local excess return is decomposed further into country factor return, industry return, and return accruing to salient attributes of the companies in the portfolio, e.g. the price/earnings ratio. These latter sources of return are called risk indexes.

The return to a global portfolio depends on the numeraire or home country of the investor. More precisely, the excess return to an investment abroad is the product of the return of the investment in its local market, $1 + r_l$, and the exchange return $1 + r_x$. With a little manipulation, this can be expressed as the sum of three components:

$$\text{Excess Numeriare Return} = (r_x + r_{fl} - r_f) - (r_l - r_{fl}) + r_x \times r_l, \text{ or,} \qquad (1)$$

$$\text{Currency Return} - \text{Local Excess Return} + \text{Cross-Product}$$

where r_f is the risk-free rate of return in the country of the investor, and r_{fl} is the risk-free rate in the market where the investment is being made. The first term in Equation (1) is the currency return, reflecting both the exchange return and the differential in interest rates between countries. The second term is the local excess return of the investment in its own market.

The final term, $r_x \times r_l$ (also known as the cross-product) poses a problem for development of a linear model. For most countries, this cross-product term is typically small and can be disregarded for the purposes of forecasting risk. For example, ignoring the cross-product reduces the annual risk of the Korean market by 51 basis points (from 29.62% to 29.11%), and of the Taiwanese market by 103 basis points. In such cases, one can safely ignore the cross-product because it is small relative to overall market risk.

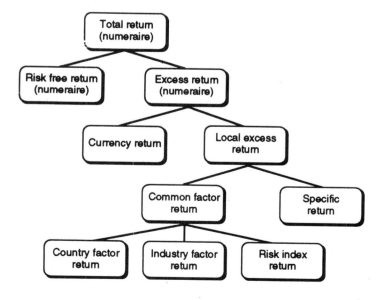

Figure 32.1 Emerging markets model

This is not true for Argentina or Brazil, where there are huge swings in exchange rates. Over the past five years, ignoring the cross-product would have changed the annual risk of the Argentinean market by 17% and the Brazilian market by 4%.

To circumvent this difficulty, we do not try to decompose the Brazilian and Argentinean asset returns into local and currency components but rather model these assets from the U.S. perspective. In other words, we translate the prices of Brazilian and Argentinean assets into U.S. dollars and model the U.S. dollar-denominated returns of these assets. Happily, this approach is consistent with investors' tendency to think of these assets in U.S. dollars.

Next, local excess return is broken down into three components: country factor return, industry return, and risk index return. The amount of an asset's return arising from each component depends on its exposure to that source. The exposure of an asset to the country factor is its beta with respect to that market. Moreover, assets are exposed only to their own local markets. In contrast, industry and risk indexes are global factors in the model, i.e., it is assumed that these factors apply equally across countries.

Industry exposure is defined using the Financial Times World industry classification. Each asset is assigned to exactly one of the thirty-six industry categories.

The risk indexes include size, success, yield, variability in markets, earnings-to-price ratio, book-to-price ratio, and liquidity. Exposures to these risk indexes are normalized within each country. Thus, these exposures measure how an asset compares to the rest of its local market.

A formal statement of our model for monthly local excess return is for asset n:

$$r_l(n) - r_{fl}(n) = \sum_k \beta(n, k)h(k) + \sum_j y(n, j)g(j) + \sum_i x(n, i)f(i) + u(n). \qquad (2)$$

Local Excess = Country Factor + Industry Factor

+ Risk Index Factor + Specific Return

$k = 1$, number of countries

$j = 1$, number of industries

$i = 1$, number of risk indexes

where $\beta(n, k)$, $y(n, j)$, and $x(n, i)$ are the exposures of asset n to the kth country factor, the jth industry, and the ith risk index, respectively. Variables $h(k)$, $g(j)$, and $f(i)$ are returns to these factors. In estimating the factor returns, the exposures are determined from the beginning of month data. The part of the return that is not explained by these factors is called the specific return, $u(n)$; it is unique to the company.

The model was estimated for assets from the twenty-three markets listed in Table 32.1 over the period February 1986 to July 1991. Data are drawn from numerous sources including the International Finance Corporation and proprietary sources in thirteen countries.

The results of the modeling process reveal some interesting differences between emerging and developed markets. The overall proportion of variance explained by the emerging markets model (adjusted R^2) is 50%, as compared with 38% for a similar model that covers the developed markets (countries covered by the Financial Times Indices). At first glance it may seem surprising that a quantitative model would explain a greater proportion of return in the emerging markets than the developed markets. In order to understand this further, we looked at two submodels.

The first submodel was built using only industry factors; i.e., we looked at what proportion of return is explained by the industry that a company is in, ignoring the country factors and risk indexes. Thus, a definition of this model is:

$$r_l(n) - r_{fl}(n) = \sum_j y(n, j)g(j) + u(n). \qquad (3)$$

Local Excess Return = Industry Factor + Specific Return

We find the adjusted R^2 for this model for the emerging markets to be 16%, compared with 22% for the developed markets. This is a measure of how "global" or integrated industries are across countries. It stands to reason that the developed markets have industries that are better integrated than the emerging ones, but the fact that the difference is small implies that there are cross-country industry commonalities in the emerging markets as well.

The second submodel was built using only country factors. Thus, we looked at what proportion of return is explained by country factors alone, ignoring the industry factor and risk indexes. The definition of this model is:

$$r_l(n) - r_{fl}(n) = \sum_k \beta(n, k)h(k) + u(n). \qquad (4)$$

Local Excess Return = Country Factor + Specific Return

The adjusted R^2 for this model for the emerging markets is 46% compared with 30% for the developed markets. Clearly, this country factor is the major force driving emerging markets. As one would expect, industries play a larger part in explaining return in the developed markets, while country differences play a larger role in the emerging markets.

HOMOGENEITY WITHIN MARKETS

The fact that country factors explain such a large proportion of variance (in absolute terms and when compared with the developed markets) in the emerging markets bears a closer look. That is, stock returns tend to be more homogeneous (within a market) in the emerging markets than in developed markets. In other words, when the market moves, there is a strong tendency for all stocks in the market to move with it.

This difference in the proportion of return explained by the market factor (46% in emerging markets versus 30% in developed countries) is not a function of capitalization weighting (which leads to larger companies dominating the regression). Even when we equally weight each stock in the regression we find the same effect persists. The comparable R^2 when equally weighting all stocks in the emerging markets is 42% (compared with 29% in the developed markets).

At first appearance, it may seem odd that the proportion of variance explained by the market factor is so large in these markets. In order to understand this, we look at various effects that may cause this to happen.

First, it may result from a concentration effect, a few large companies so dominating the market that they are, in effect, the market. Second, it may well be that these markets are actually more homogeneous (i.e., all the stocks tend to move together). Finally, there tends to be a positive correlation between the magnitude of returns within a market and the R^2, i.e., to some extent, the high R^2 is a natural by-product of high volatility.

We first look at the concentration effect; that is, whether these markets tend to be dominated by a few large stocks. Table 32.2 shows the proportion of market capitalization that the top ten stocks represent in each market.

Most emerging markets are more concentrated than the developed markets. Hong Kong and Singapore, perhaps the two most developed of the emerging markets, are highly concentrated by this measure. On the other hand, Malaysia, Brazil, India, and Korea are not significantly more concentrated than the U.K. Of course, simply looking at the biggest ten stocks in a market is not a particularly insightful way to judge concentration because it ignores all the other companies.

Table 32.2 shows two other more meaningful measures of concentration: asset concentration and sector concentration. Concentration is defined as (similar to Roll [1990]):

$$\text{Concentration} = [(N/N - 1) \times \sum (h_n - 1/N)^2]^{0.5} \tag{5}$$

Table 32.2 Emerging market statistics

Country	Proportion of capitalization in top 10 companies(%)*	Asset concentration factor	Sector concentration factor	Average correlation between stocks
Argentina	65.60	0.26	0.43	0.92
Brazil	26.60	0.17	0.38	0.70
Chile	50.90	0.18	0.26	0.59
Colombia	75.10	0.18	0.39	0.34
Greece	50.40	0.18	0.44	0.72
Hong Kong	45.20	0.17	0.44	0.69
India	29.40	0.13	0.48	0.55
Indonesia	53.40	0.17	0.43	0.71
Japan OTC	28.40	0.15	0.32	0.34
Jordan	66.20	0.55	0.62	0.21
Korea	28.90	0.16	0.28	0.56
Malaysia	25.10	0.12	0.28	0.57
Mexico	38.40	0.21	0.42	0.70
Nigeria	52.50	0.17	0.66	0.23
Pakistan	24.40	0.14	0.33	0.17
Philippines	65.20	0.33	0.57	0.70
Portugal	44.20	0.17	0.40	0.80
Singapore	54.50	0.18	0.46	0.75
Taiwan	41.30	0.13	0.37	0.77
Thailand	32.70	0.11	0.42	0.47
Turkey	53.10	0.23	0.36	0.81
Venezuela	64.20	0.26	0.49	0.60
Zimbabwe	41.20	0.25	0.43	0.25
Developed markets				
Japan	16.70	0.08	0.29	0.46
U.K.	25.50	0.11	0.30	0.56
U.S.	11.90	0.08	0.32	0.49

*Source: International Finance Corporation

where:

$N =$ Total number of stocks (or industries), and

$h_n =$ Weight in asset (or industry) n.

Asset concentration looks at how different a market is from being equally weighted. If each stock in the market had exactly the same market capitalization, this measure would be zero. If the entire market capitalization were concentrated in one company, the measure would be one.

In an extremely diversified market like the U.S., the score is 0.08. Looking at this measure for the emerging markets, we can clearly see that they are more concentrated, but that the larger ones (Taiwan, Korea, Thailand, Malaysia, etc.) tend to have numbers that are not much larger than the developed markets. The average for these four markets is 0.13. Thus, while asset concentration plays an important role in understanding why these markets appear homogeneous, there must be other factors at work as well.

Another measure of concentration is sector concentration. If most of the stocks in a market are concentrated in one industry, it would make sense that they would tend to move together. Table 32.2 shows a measure of sector concentration, defined in a similar fashion as asset concentration. A score of zero implies that companies are equally distributed across all industries, while a score of one implies that all the companies are in one industry.

The indication is that the emerging markets are more concentrated than the developed markets, but not much more so (although there is a popular perception that many emerging market countries are highly concentrated in certain sectors). In fact we see that Korea, Chile, and Malaysia have less sector concentration than the U.S., U.K., and Japan. The countries that are most highly concentrated in a few sectors are the smaller ones like Jordan and Nigeria. It seems clear from these results that the emerging markets are quite diversified across industries; the perception that their returns are driven by the fortunes of a single sector (like natural resources) is erroneous.

What then explains the fact that stocks in these markets tend to move together? We looked at the possibility that these markets are indeed more homogeneous, after adjusting for the concentration effect. One way to do this is to look at the average correlation of total monthly stock returns within a market, over a period of time. Table 32.2 shows the average (i.e., unweighted) correlation between all stocks within each market (over the past five years).

This is clearly higher for most of the emerging markets than the developed markets. With the exception of the Japanese OTC market, all the other large emerging markets have high average correlations. Taiwan has an average correlation of 0.77, Turkey 0.81, and Brazil 0.70. By comparison, the U.S. has an average correlation of 0.49 and Japan 0.46. Because these correlations are unweighted, market capitalization does not play a role in determining this number.

This implies that a single market force tends to have a large impact on the movement of stock prices in these markets. Even though we saw that these markets are fairly well-diversified across industries, these industry differentials are overwhelmed by the dominant market force.

Another reason for the high R^2 numbers in the emerging markets is the fact that there is likely to be a positive relationship between R^2 and market volatility. For example, if the market moves up 50% in a month, the likelihood is that almost all stocks in that market will also move up. Thus, one would expect to see higher R^2 for the more volatile markets.

We find that this is indeed true; if one excludes the most risky markets (Argentina, Brazil, Turkey, and Taiwan), and the low liquidity ones (Pakistan, Jordan, Colombia, Nigeria, and Zimbabwe) the average R^2 for the emerging markets is similar to that for the developed markets.

Overall, from a global investor's viewpoint, this homogeneity phenomenon implies that being in the right market at the right time is more important than the ability to pick good stocks within that market. Clearly, if you are going to be in Brazil in a month when the market moves up 50%, the high within-market correlations (0.70 for Brazil) are likely to ensure that any diversified portfolio will experience high positive returns. From a global investor's point of view, the impact of this conclusion is accentuated by the low across-market correlations.

HETEROGENEITY ACROSS MARKETS

This phenomenon of homogeneity does not apply across markets. In fact, we see that the emerging markets are much less correlated with each other than are the developed markets. Table 32.3 shows the correlations of emerging markets with each other. While we see that some markets tend to move together (Malaysia, Hong Kong, and Singapore), most markets tend to have very low correlations with each other. In fact, the average correlation between the emerging markets was 0.07 over the past five years, implying that they are essentially uncorrelated.

We propose two explanations as to why they have been uncorrelated with each other. First, many of the emerging markets have (or had) few economic and trade links with each other. Consequently, their economies tend to be unrelated to each other.

Second, many have (or had) severe restrictions on outsiders participating in their markets. Therefore, they are somewhat insulated from worldwide (or even regional) patterns in stock market returns. For example, in October 1987, while the world's markets were crashing, the Indian stock market was up modestly.

Now the current trend is for most of the emerging economies to develop greater trade links with the developed world and each other. Most of the countries that are closed to foreign participation in their stock markets are also in the process of liberalizing rules for foreigners to participate in their markets. With these increasing links between markets, we should expect to see correlations between the emerging markets increase in the future.

When we contrast these low correlations with the correlations between developed markets (Table 32.4), we see that they have much higher correlations with each other. A quick glance at Tables 32.3 and 32.4 confirms that the developed markets are much more correlated with each other than the emerging markets are. The average correlation between the developed markets was 0.49 (over the same five-year period). While all the correlations between the developed markets were positive, 89 of the 276 correlations between the emerging markets were negative (over this five-year period).

From a global investor's point of view, a more interesting question is not so much how the emerging markets relate to each other, but how they relate to the developed markets, individually and as a group. Overall, the correlation between the IFC Emerging Markets Composite Index and the Financial Times World Index was 0.35 over the past five years.

Table 32.5 shows the cross-correlations between emerging markets and developed markets. As far as individual countries are concerned, correlations between the U.S. market and emerging markets range from −0.14 for India to 0.70 for Malaysia. As one would

Table 32.3 Correlations between emerging markets (February 1986–March 1991)

	ARG	BRA	CHI	COL	GRE	HKE	IDN	IND	JOR	JPE	KOR	MAL	MEX	NIG	PAK	PHI	POR	SIN	TAI	THA	TUR	VEN
Brazil	0.02																					
Chile	0.02	0.21																				
Colombia	-0.12	-0.09	0.30																			
Greece	0.12	0.03	0.13	0.38																		
Hong Kong	-0.14	0.20	0.42	0.19	0.21																	
Indonesia	-0.29	-0.28	0.15	0.14	0.19	0.23																
India	0.20	0.03	-0.16	-0.07	-0.01	-0.08	0.03															
Jordan	-0.18	-0.15	0.07	0.15	0.15	0.20	-0.01	0.51														
Japan OTC	-0.13	0.03	-0.07	0.19	0.20	0.60	0.07	-0.02	0.25													
Korea	-0.24	-0.08	-0.05	-0.04	-0.20	0.12	0.07	0.17	-0.08	0.37												
Malaysia	-0.01	0.14	0.23	0.01	0.05	0.64	0.47	-0.07	0.09	0.63	0.18											
Mexico	0.13	-0.04	0.25	0.08	0.08	0.36	0.18	0.04	0.00	0.61	0.27	0.40										
Nigeria	0.10	0.00	0.11	0.05	0.14	-0.10	0.21	0.18	0.04	0.36	0.04	-0.18	0.07									
Pakistan	-0.03	-0.06	0.03	0.11	-0.12	0.08	-0.10	-0.03	-0.02	0.18	0.14	-0.17	-0.07	-0.11								
Philippines	-0.12	0.13	0.25	0.08	0.10	0.34	0.47	0.09	0.25	0.36	0.20	0.33	0.14	0.10	-0.11							
Portugal	0.02	0.03	0.13	0.27	0.41	0.35	0.16	-0.02	0.07	0.47	0.07	0.30	0.41	-0.21	-0.01	-0.05						
Singapore	0.00	0.14	0.25	0.00	0.07	0.68	0.44	0.25	0.15	0.68	0.21	0.90	0.43	-0.22	-0.01	0.37	0.31					
Taiwan	0.02	0.04	0.28	0.11	0.02	0.29	0.35	0.15	0.17	0.24	0.01	0.25	0.37	-0.22	-0.03	0.04	0.45	0.35				
Thailand	0.13	0.14	0.33	0.11	0.28	0.56	0.37	0.14	0.14	0.69	0.01	0.50	0.44	-0.03	0.00	0.33	0.37	0.58	0.40			
Turkey	0.25	0.13	0.02	0.02	0.24	0.13	0.29	-0.09	-0.09	0.32	0.01	0.31	0.24	0.04	0.04	0.11	0.32	0.31	0.13	0.24		
Venezuela	-0.05	-0.26	-0.13	-0.10	-0.07	-0.07	-0.15	-0.14	-0.14	-0.45	-0.11	-0.14	-0.19	-0.03	-0.01	-0.22	-0.08	-0.13	-0.28	-0.32	-0.15	
Zimbabwe	-0.26	-0.06	0.00	0.24	-0.04	-0.08	-0.15	-0.04	0.06	-0.20	-0.07	-0.17	-0.19	-0.05	0.21	0.00	0.08	-0.30	-0.13	-0.17	0.01	0.06

Source: BARRA.

Table 32.4 Correlations between developed markets (February 1986–March 1991)

	AUS	AUT	BEL	CAN	DEN	FIN	FRA	GER	IRE	ITA	JPN	NET	NOR	NZE	SAF	SPA	SWE	SWI	UKI	U.S.A.
Austria	0.18																			
Belgium	0.33	0.31																		
Canada	0.64	0.19	0.57																	
Denmark	0.17	0.33	0.52	0.34																
Finland	0.50	0.48	0.39	0.51	0.34															
France	0.29	0.40	0.76	0.47	0.61	0.36														
Germany	0.30	0.64	0.74	0.39	0.54	0.41	0.76													
Ireland	0.42	0.43	0.52	0.47	0.51	0.51	0.50	0.46												
Italy	0.22	0.46	0.64	0.42	0.52	0.33	0.69	0.64	0.41											
Japan	0.12	0.15	0.53	0.27	0.45	0.34	0.51	0.34	0.47	0.48										
Netherlands	0.43	0.39	0.73	0.71	0.49	0.46	0.66	0.75	0.59	0.57	0.45									
Norway	0.49	0.43	0.55	0.61	0.37	0.61	0.46	0.54	0.49	0.38	0.30	0.66								
New Zealand	0.76	0.26	0.28	0.47	0.05	0.40	0.20	0.31	0.41	0.25	0.11	0.39	0.52							
South Africa	0.51	0.33	0.37	0.51	0.31	0.59	0.34	0.41	0.32	0.35	0.28	0.44	0.50	0.41						
Spain	0.44	0.40	0.58	0.47	0.45	0.51	0.54	0.47	0.54	0.46	0.60	0.56	0.45	0.42	0.31					
Sweden	0.48	0.38	0.55	0.41	0.29	0.57	0.47	0.51	0.56	0.50	0.51	0.52	0.53	0.52	0.35	0.55				
Switzerland	0.43	0.44	0.67	0.59	0.53	0.44	0.67	0.78	0.53	0.65	0.45	0.77	0.54	0.48	0.43	0.62	0.59			
United Kingdom	0.56	0.38	0.56	0.67	0.45	0.61	0.51	0.54	0.66	0.50	0.47	0.73	0.66	0.43	0.45	0.57	0.61	0.67		
U.S.A.	0.49	0.14	0.55	0.82	0.30	0.42	0.48	0.39	0.47	0.34	0.25	0.69	0.55	0.39	0.24	0.49	0.46	0.61	0.67	

Source: BARRA.

Table 32.5 Correlations Between Developed and Emerging Markets (February 1986–March 1991)

	ARG	BRA	CHI	COL	GRE	HKG	IDN	IND	JOR	JPE	KOR	MAL	MEX	NIG	PAK	PHI	POR	SIN	TAI	THA	TUR	VEN	ZIM
Australia	0.06	0.13	0.08	−0.01	0.13	0.61	0.12	0.14	0.20	0.31	0.08	0.50	0.33	−0.17	0.02	0.13	0.24	0.54	0.29	0.48	0.14	−0.08	−0.30
Austria	−0.10	0.12	0.15	0.20	0.24	0.31	0.70	0.12	0.12	0.57	0.12	0.36	0.05	0.11	0.15	0.24	0.14	0.31	0.23	0.26	0.27	−0.28	−0.02
Belgium	0.00	0.02	0.20	0.06	0.23	0.47	0.23	−0.06	0.10	0.60	0.18	0.44	0.43	0.06	−0.07	0.32	0.21	0.55	0.21	0.55	0.16	−0.07	−0.23
Canada	0.04	−0.01	0.30	0.05	0.15	0.59	0.22	−0.02	0.12	0.19	0.31	0.62	0.38	0.08	−0.12	0.28	0.18	0.63	0.18	0.48	0.04	−0.03	−0.25
Denmark	0.10	0.03	−0.05	0.07	0.11	0.16	0.30	0.23	0.17	0.59	0.10	0.29	0.04	0.19	0.02	0.19	0.11	0.30	0.06	0.25	0.20	−0.17	0.04
Finland	−0.18	0.20	0.22	0.10	0.14	0.46	0.54	0.02	0.22	0.59	0.33	0.48	0.32	−0.02	0.01	0.22	0.27	0.46	0.35	0.37	0.12	−0.29	−0.14
France	0.04	−0.05	0.17	−0.02	0.30	0.39	0.15	0.07	0.10	0.69	0.07	0.38	0.25	0.05	−0.06	0.21	0.17	0.41	0.20	0.40	0.02	−0.14	−0.20
Germany	−0.04	0.02	0.19	0.10	0.21	0.35	0.40	−0.05	0.11	0.63	0.06	0.36	0.23	0.15	0.03	0.25	0.13	0.41	0.17	0.46	0.12	−0.25	−0.16
Ireland	−0.12	0.15	0.31	0.12	0.22	0.63	0.36	−0.06	0.34	0.72	0.42	0.55	0.37	0.08	0.09	0.38	0.35	0.57	0.27	0.49	0.22	−0.26	−0.02
Italy	−0.02	0.02	−0.04	0.02	0.33	0.30	0.41	0.01	0.16	0.69	0.06	0.41	0.09	0.06	−0.07	0.22	0.24	0.47	0.07	0.42	0.04	−0.23	−0.16
Japan	−0.12	0.01	−0.02	−0.01	0.09	0.27	−0.16	−0.16	0.11	0.68	0.37	0.30	0.24	0.04	0.01	0.23	0.33	0.39	0.25	0.32	0.07	−0.21	0.03
Netherlands	−0.06	0.04	0.19	0.07	0.23	0.54	0.20	−0.07	0.09	0.58	0.33	0.56	0.34	0.22	−0.03	0.36	0.22	0.59	0.07	0.48	0.12	−0.15	−0.21
Norway	−0.12	0.11	0.22	−0.03	0.17	0.52	0.47	0.00	0.05	0.40	0.20	0.62	0.39	−0.03	−0.04	0.13	0.38	0.60	0.27	0.45	0.24	−0.13	−0.08
New Zealand	0.13	0.22	0.10	−0.01	0.20	0.56	0.07	0.01	0.01	0.30	0.13	0.40	0.27	−0.17	−0.02	0.18	0.36	0.50	0.25	0.56	0.16	−0.17	−0.32
South Africa	−0.01	−0.04	−0.03	−0.10	0.12	0.22	0.38	0.04	0.17	0.37	0.25	0.26	0.21	−0.05	−0.08	0.11	0.22	0.32	0.25	0.29	0.27	−0.10	−0.14
Spain	0.07	0.15	0.22	0.24	0.35	0.59	−0.08	0.00	0.08	0.70	0.19	0.43	0.36	0.25	0.11	0.32	0.36	0.51	0.24	0.44	0.32	−0.17	−0.11
Sweden	0.02	0.34	0.11	0.04	0.26	0.52	0.11	−0.04	0.18	0.74	0.26	0.57	0.42	−0.23	0.06	0.24	0.30	0.64	0.21	0.58	0.14	−0.22	−0.12
Switzerland	0.05	0.05	0.21	0.18	0.30	0.48	0.16	−0.16	0.19	0.61	0.10	0.48	0.31	0.22	−0.16	0.27	0.22	0.55	0.09	0.54	0.12	−0.25	−0.18
United Kingdom	−0.15	0.07	0.11	0.18	0.19	0.62	0.09	−0.05	0.24	0.57	0.27	0.67	0.24	0.05	−0.03	0.19	0.33	0.63	0.21	0.40	0.08	−0.04	−0.01
U.S.A.	0.09	0.09	0.33	0.09	0.15	0.59	0.14	−0.14	0.08	0.25	0.22	0.70	0.48	0.11	−0.28	0.24	0.20	0.70	0.23	0.45	0.05	−0.06	−0.32
All Emerging Mkts	−0.01	0.23	0.38	0.10	0.11	0.65	0.42	−0.03	0.16	0.60	0.19	0.59	0.53	−0.17	−0.01	0.24	0.43	0.68	0.82	0.60	0.27	−0.33	−0.24
FT-World	−0.06	0.08	0.15	0.06	0.18	0.57	−0.01	−0.15	0.16	0.68	0.36	0.63	0.41	0.08	−0.11	0.29	0.36	0.69	0.31	0.51	0.11	−0.20	−0.15

Source: BARRA.

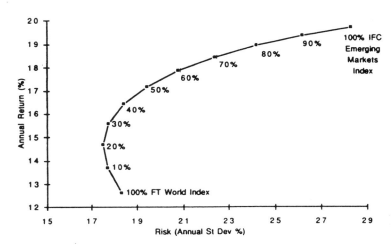

Figure 32.2 Impact on portfolio risk for a global investor

expect, Japan is most highly correlated with countries with which it has strong economic links, such as Singapore, Korea, Thailand, Hong Kong, and Taiwan. A closed market (and economy) such as India had negative correlations with ten out of the twenty developed markets. In fact, its average correlation with the developed markets was −0.01, with the highest being 0.23 with the Danish market!

Clearly, the fact that the emerging markets (individually, and as a group) have low correlations with the developed markets implies that there is an opportunity for diversification. We can illustrate this with an example. Figure 32.2 shows the risk and return (over the past five years ending March 1991) of a global portfolio as varying proportions of the IFC Emerging Markets Index are stirred into the Financial Times World Index.

Until reaching about 20% in the Emerging Markets Index, the risk of the overall portfolio decreases, because of the low correlations between the two. After that, portfolio risk starts increasing as the higher overall volatility of the Emerging Markets Index kicks in. Thus, even if one does not expect the emerging markets to outperform the developed markets, an investment of up to 20% would have reduced (rather than increased) risk for a global investor.

During this five-year period, the emerging markets outperformed the developed markets, so a 20% investment in emerging markets would not only have reduced annual risk by 0.81%, but would have increased the annual return by 2.1% as well.

IMPLICATIONS FOR PORTFOLIO MANAGERS

Even though emerging markets are risky individually, low correlations between them and with developed markets lead to risk reduction for modest investments. As these markets develop greater links (financial and trade) with the developed markets, they will undoubtedly become more highly correlated. Thus, there is a "diversification free lunch" currently available — one should indulge while the opportunity exists. One does not need to have high return forecasts for these markets to enjoy the fruits of diversification.

The flip side of the low correlations across markets and homogeneity within markets is that country selection becomes more important for the active manager. There is greater volatility and greater return associated with country selection than in the developed markets. Managers interested in entering the emerging markets arena should give great consideration to their country allocation process, perhaps more so than they do in the developed markets. This does not imply that stock selection by active managers is any less important or easier, simply that country selection has a bigger impact on overall portfolio returns.

To the extent that one decides to focus on country selection rather than stock picking, the homogeneity within markets comes to one's aid. A consequence of the homogeneity within markets is that one can construct baskets of stocks that will mimic the performance of the overall market index with relatively low tracking error. This is particularly important in the emerging markets, because the smaller stocks tend to be extremely illiquid. Thus, one can form baskets of relatively liquid stocks that will track the overall index fairly well.

Figure 32.3 shows the number of stocks required to track the SET index in Thailand, the TAIEX Index in Taiwan, and the S&P 500. If one wants to construct a basket of stocks whose performance will track the relevant index to within 1% per year (with a two-thirds probability), one would need about 75 stocks in Taiwan, 90 in Thailand, and 135 in the U.S.[2] When one accounts for the fact that the Thai and Taiwanese indexes have fewer stocks than the S&P 500, all three require about the same proportion of stocks to track the index with similar tracking error.

Finally, given that many of the emerging markets are projected to have higher real economic growth than the developed markets, one would expect that stock market return (over the medium to long term) would reflect this. Coupled with the diversification benefit, one can make a strong case for global investors to add investments in the emerging markets to their portfolios.

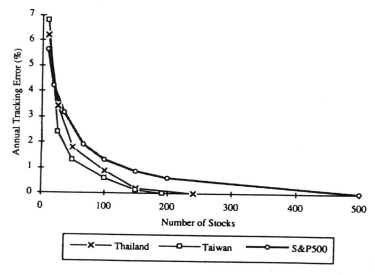

Figure 32.3 Comparison of tracking error in different markets: number of stocks required to track the index

ENDNOTES

1. Sources: "Emerging Stock Markets Factbook 1991," published by the International Finance Corporation; BARRA.
2. According to BARRA's Emerging Markets Equity Model.

REFERENCES

Brown, Rob. "Risk and Return in the Emerging Markets." *Investing*, Spring 1991.

Grinold, Richard, Andrew Rudd and Dan Stefek. "Global Factors: Fact or Fiction?" *Journal of Portfolio Management*, Fall 1989, pp. 79–88.

Roll, Richard. "Industrial Structure and the Comparative Behavior of International Stock Market Indices." Working paper, June 1990.

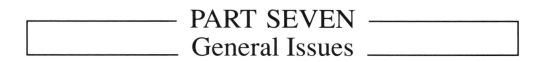

PART SEVEN
General Issues

Part Seven consists of two general and unrelated issues. The first deals with chaos theory and the second with short-termism.

The whole world seems to have either read *Jurassic Park* or seen the movie, so everybody must have heard of chaos theory, although not everybody will have understood it. Chaos theory is of potential interest to investors and a few words on it here may be worthwhile.

The word chaos, as used by mathematicians, doesn't imply chaos in the usual sense. What chaos theory tells us is that there are equations which generate observations that look random and will fool most statistical tests yet, underneath the seemingly random data, there is a pattern. Now this could be interesting for investment research. A lot is made of random walks, or a lack of a pattern in financial data, but could there really be an underlying pattern after all, could we be using the wrong statistical tests? Some work has been done along these lines by various researchers but it is a bit early to give a firm view as to whether this research is an advance or a dead end.

A second interesting aspect of chaos theory is that it is possible to produce equations that generate patterns which suddenly change into completely different patterns. Nothing in the underlying process has changed, but the observable data appears different. Economic forecasters have had a poor record in recent years — could it be that the economy is described by a chaotic process? Are economic forecasters simply extrapolating from one observed pattern, without really finding the true underlying process? When the economy switches to the second pattern, the forecasts fail. There is no evidence that this is so, but again it is an interesting issue.

Chaos theory involves a lot of mathematics and, as a result, most of us never get to first base with the notions of chaos theory. Many popular expositions are quite misleading. In Chapter 33, William Baumol, a competent mathematician as well as an excellent economist, and a professor at both Princeton and New York Universities, gives an introductory exposition that appears to be maths-free (he actually sneaks an equation into a footnote and graph). This exposition is general and not tied to investment *per se*, although it does discuss economic forecasting. Readers with good maths skills and a liking for diagrams, might wish to go on to Baumol and Benhabib (1989). The article printed here has been slightly abridged: ellipses mark the omissions.

The second article in Part Seven deals with a broad social issue. The financial markets raise many social issues that are worth discussing but space constraints allow just one to be raised here. Paul Marsh, a professor at the London Business School, tackles the issue of whether the financial markets are too short-term in their orientation. For some years it has been argued that the U.S. and U.K. markets focus only on the short-term and this forces industrialists to adopt a short-term horizon too. As a result, U.S. and U.K. industry under-invests in research and development, fixed capital investment and all the other good, but long-term things, necessary for a prosperous future. Marsh concludes that short-termism is more a problem of perception than reality, but he thinks that this is still a matter for concern lest the perception becomes reality. Marsh's article provides a good starting point for discussions of many aspects of the social consequences of the investment industry, and pondering such issues is a good way to end an investment book, especially for readers in, or those planning to enter, the investment industry.

REFERENCE

Baumol, W.J. and Benhabib, J. 1989: Chaos: Significance, Mechanism, and Economic Application. *Journal of Economic Perspectives*, **3**, Winter, 77–106.

33

The Chaos Phenomenon: A Nightmare for Forecasters

William J. Baumol

The role of the forecaster is difficult enough in a world where economic developments can be affected profoundly by unanticipated innovations or preference changes, where circumstances the day after tomorrow can be turned on their head by tomorrow's developments in the Middle East, and where even the economic relationships that underlie the economic phenomena themselves are imperfectly understood. But recent mathematical discoveries, which have already substantially affected ways of thinking in ecology, physics and meteorology, suggest that the obstacles to success in forecasting may in some circumstances be far greater than had previously been suspected. Moreover, no one is yet in a position to guess how common those troublesome circumstances may be. All one has to go on so far is the logic of the analysis which suggests that the circumstances giving rise to the problem — the so-called chaos phenomenon — can arise 'very easily.'

This paper will describe what is meant by the mathematical concept of chaos and will indicate how it can arise in economic behaviour. It will undertake to suggest the logical explanation of chaotic manifestations and then will show how the presence of the chaos phenomenon undermines all of the systematic techniques upon which economic forecasters have come to rely.

CHAOS VS. RANDOMNESS

The term 'chaos' suggests a course of events denuded of all systematic structure, one which defies analysis because no rules apply. It would appear to refer to randomness taken to its ultimate stage.

However, as used by mathematicians, the term refers to something very different. It deals with a sheep in wolf's clothing; with a set of relationships that is completely deterministic in the sense that one who knew *every decimal place* of the underlying relationships could, at least in principle, predict the future with absolute precision. Moreover, the logical structure

Reprinted from: Baumol, W.J. 1988: The Chaos Phenomenon: A Nightmare for Forecasters. *LSE Quarterly*, 1, March, 99–114.

of chaotic behaviour is so simple that an introductory analysis can be taught in a matter of an hour or two to students who are rather unsophisticated mathematically. In addition, considered conceptually, its patterns exhibit a degree of uniformity and beautiful simplicity that may well be considered unusual.

What then can be said to be chaotic about so apparently straightforward a set of relationships? The new discovery of the mathematicians is that despite the orderliness and simplicity of the relationships involved,[1] they can generate a pattern of behaviour over time that has all four of the following properties (which, for the sake of concreteness, can be envisioned to involve something like the use of a hypothetical supply curve and a hypothetical demand curve to calculate a time series of monthly price statistics):[2]

1. Even though the statistics that describe the behaviour at issue are not subject to an iota of randomness they will have all the appearance of being disturbed by powerful and, sometimes, rather abrupt random influences. A chaotic time path so effectively mimics random behaviour that it can pass any of the standard statisticians' tests of true randomness;[3]

2. The behaviour of such a chaotic time series is oscillatory (*quasi* cyclical) but no pattern ever repeats itself, no matter how long a period elapses;

3. The time series is subject to sharp and substantial breaks in qualitative pattern which are completely unportended by what went before. For example, I have generated such a time path from the equation in Note 1 in which twenty-five periods of cycles of substantially constant amplitude are succeeded all at once by virtual disappearance of the cycles for ten periods, whereupon this is suddenly followed by the reappearance of a new set of cycles very different from the first (see Figure 33.1, below);

4. The qualitative behaviour of a chaotic time series is subject to complete upheaval in response to the most microscopic change in the values of the underlying parameters, say, a miniscule change in savings rate or a microscopic shift in the demand for a product, if those are the matters at issue. The example described in the preceding paragraph is generated when we start off from an initial value of the statistical series equal to 0.99, and a value of the parameter k in the equation of Note 1 equal to 3.94. The shape of the graph of the data, however, changes unrecognisably when the initial number in the time series is either reduced to 0.989 or raised to 0.999 or when k is reduced to 3.935 or raised to 3.945!

This extreme sensitivity of the behaviour of the observed statistics in response to miniscule changes in the generating data has received an evocative description from meteorologists who concern themselves with chaotic phenomena. They have referred to it as 'the butterfly's wing manifestation' meaning thereby that if the weather in London is chaotically determined, a capricious flap of its wings by a butterfly in Tasmania can generate a powerful storm over Gatwick Airport.

By now the reader will have the general idea. In an economy in which chaotic relationships were to play a significant role many things would appear to become drastically unstable and unreliable. Non-random behaviour would become sufficiently disorderly to pass for random developments. New trends would appear, apparently from nowhere, and would disappear just as unexpectedly. Above all, small disturbances in the established state of affairs, introduced perhaps by non-economic developments, can cause a major upheaval in the economy's behaviour patterns. Obviously, none of this is apt to make the forecaster's task any easier.

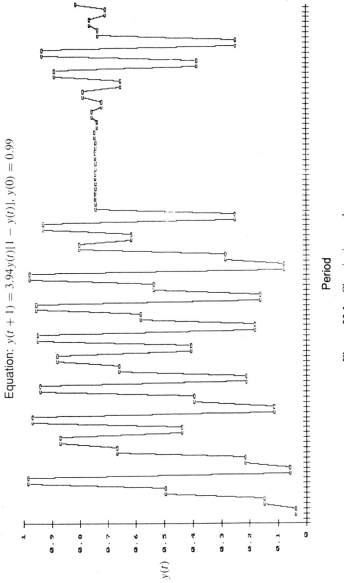

Equation: $y(t + 1) = 3.94y(t)|1 - y(t)|$, $y(0) = 0.99$

Figure 33.1 Chaotic time path

But before we return to the forecaster's activities in any detail it will be necessary to offer some hints of the nature of the mechanism that produces chaotic behaviour and some indication of its possible role in the workings of the economy.

WHAT CAUSES CHAOS?

In order to avoid any explicit mathematics, the workings of the engine of chaotic behaviour will have to be suggested by analogy. As already noted, chaos analysis has been used by ecologists and a vastly oversimplified ecological analogy may stimulate the reader's imagination. Consider a colony of microscopic animals that live on plant food. The organism's fertilising waste products stimulate the growth of its plant nutrients and that, in turn, enables the animal colony to multiply. However, once the colony grows beyond some critical size it begins to deplete the plants on which it feeds and that results in undernourishment and decline in the animal population.

It is easy to see that this process involves cyclical behaviour. One can envision the cycle as a four stage process: (i) a small initial animal colony permits moderate plant growth; (ii) the expanded food supply stimulates growth in the animal population which, up to a point, also encourages plant multiplication; (iii) beyond the critical point in animal colony size food scarcity sets in; and (iv) the animal population falls back, perhaps exactly to its initial level.

This time path can, then, in theory repeat itself exactly; with the animal population rising then falling then rising once more and so on *ad infinitum*. If it does so, it traces out as simple a cyclical time path as one can imagine, with the animal population oscillating from its lowest level, L, to its highest, H, in the sequence $L, H, L, H, L. \ldots$

However, to introduce the first step toward chaos imagine that at the end of stage (iv) the animal population, instead of having fallen back to its initial level, L, is just a bit larger, L^*, than it was earlier in stage (i). This, in turn, stimulates slightly faster plant growth than occurred before in (ii), and expands the animal colony somewhat more quickly, leading to a rather earlier and sharper depletion of the plant supply at animal population $H^* < H$. Suppose, finally, that this time as a result, the size of the animal colony falls all the way back to its initial level, L with the entire process starting all over again. We now have a time path involving a more complicated cycle — one of sharper amplitude in the expansion of animal population followed by a more moderate cycle, then another larger amplitude cycle followed by a more moderate one and so on, *ad infinitum*. The time path described in this paragraph, $L, H, L^*, H^*, L, H, L^*, H^*, L, \ldots$ is obviously more complicated than the one laid out in the previous paragraph. But there is much more to be learned from the metamorphosis than the mere increase in complexity. Indeed, the first step has just been taken toward a fully chaotic regime. What has occurred in the transition involves several remarkable features which are essential to understanding of the chaos phenomenon:

1. In basic appearance, while the first time path is extremely similar to the second, the latter seems 'messier', that is, it seems somewhat less orderly.

2. In fact, despite the appearance of disorder the second trajectory is extremely orderly and systematic — only a bit more complex than the first. Instead of repeating itself *precisely every two* periods, as it did before, it now repeats itself in an approximate way every two periods, and repeats itself precisely only once every four periods.

3. Now, in addition to the relatively big moves that are all very similar to that from L to H and back, the time path has two repetitive 'ups' and 'downs', one in its

cycle peaks—the sequence H, H^*, H, H^*, H, ... and a second such 'wobble' in its troughs—the sequence L, L^*, L, L^*, L, ... These wobbles repeat themselves every four moves.

4.   Mathematicians describe what has happened as follows: The second time path of the animal population continues to involve cycles which approximate a two period repetitive path; however, the two period path is complicated by the addition of a pair of four period repetitive wobbles to the basic cyclical movement.

This may all at first glance appear to have little connection with the forecasting issue that is our concern here. However, the relationship will soon become clear. The ecological example just needs to be carried a little bit further.

It can well be imagined that if one modifies the relationship between plant growth and animal population size still further, the time path of population size will be changed again. It is surely plausible that some curvatures will lead to trajectories even more complicated than L, H, L^*, H^*, L, ... the population size may undergo far more convoluted sequences, perhaps never returning to exactly its original magnitude altogether.

Mathematicians have, as a matter of fact, confirmed that conjecture, and a good deal more. Specifically, they have shown that as the curvature of the graph relating plant growth to animal colony size becomes increasingly sharp, that is, as it approximates the shape of a hill of increasing steepness, the trajectory will always grow increasingly complex in the manner just shown. Starting from two period path replications as in L, H, L, H, ... it will always ultimately be replaced by a two period cycle with four period wobbles as in L, H, L^*, H^*, L, ...; then each of the wobbles will develop (4 period) wobbles of its own, and so on *ad infinitum*.

When a stage has been reached at which the time path of the population size has a super-structure of so many wobbles superimposed upon other wobbles which, in turn, have been added to its predecessor wobbles, etc., a graph tracing out the time path of the population size will obviously look a mess—it will have the appearance of chaos, and that is precisely how chaotic time series are generated.

There are two features which are essential to this generation mechanism: first it must involve an oscillatory process; second, the mechanism that generates it, like our curved graph, must involve non linearities. It is these that cause the oscillations to miss perfect replication. The result is then unavoidable. Mathematical analysis assures us that a suitable .degree of non-linearity, or curvature, will inevitably involve the superimposition of cycles upon cycles in such numbers and diversity as to yield all the attributes of chaos that have already been enunciated.

ECONOMIC EXAMPLE

But what has all of this to do with economic behaviour? Dynamic models in economics have long exhibited a propensity to produce cyclical behaviour. The cobweb model of the 1930's shows that fluctuations are apt to be engendered by lags between price changes and ensuing output responses. A high price of pork leads to expansion of the number of pigs raised by farmers; the pigs' simultaneous arrival on the market depresses prices, which in turn reduces hog supplies several seasons later and so on. By the 1940s Professor Samuelson's brilliant multiplier-accelerator model also demonstrated the cyclical behaviour that can emerge from macroeconomic relationships. In that model, during an upswing national income may continue to rise but rising savings can slow down its rate of advance. That, in turn, may lead to a decline in the absolute level of construction of plant and equipment which, when it becomes sufficiently severe, is capable, ultimately, of reversing the course of national income into a downward direction, and so on.

The literature of economics is full of such cycle generating models and many of them are accompanied by a mathematical analysis that shows they really can work as the verbal description suggests. However, for the sake of analytic tractability the relationships were generally assumed, usually with explicit apology, to be linear. At least in the algebraic formulations, pig demand and supply curves were taken to be straight lines and the marginal propensity to save was assumed constant. Phenomena such as diminishing returns were implicitly banished from the models. We know that reality is often quite different. Linearity assumptions in economics (as is sometimes also true in physics) are justified only as a necessary oversimplification, not as a representation of the facts.

However, as we have seen, it is non-linearity alone that is capable of introducing chaotic behaviour. Put the other way, the assumption of linearity introduced to make cyclical models tractable analytically effectively blinded us to the possibility that chaotic behaviour patterns would emerge. The very fact that non-linearities are likely to arise in almost any real economic relationships means that we are not entitled to rule out the possibility of chaotic regimes in any of the abundant harvest of mathematical cycle models.

It is hardly surprising, then, that in the past few years the economic literature has already produced a crop of models capable of displaying chaotic properties. For example, models showing the possibility of chaotic behaviour have been constructed for lagged relationships between production and demand, IS-LM macro analyses, union growth processes including the involvement of optimising agents, investment by the firm with financial constraints, and overlapping generations issues. In addition, various empirical studies now under way are seeking evidence that can distinguish deterministic chaotic behaviour from random behaviour in time series of stock prices, GNP, industrial production and employment, both aggregated and disaggregated.

Besides merely listing available chaos models and referring to the search for empirical evidence of the presence of chaotic manifestations in the economy, I can provide a brief intuitive description of an elementary chaos model drawn from economics. This is a formalisation of the advertising budgeting decision in the business firm, a model designed for expository simplicity rather than realism.

Consider a business firm in which a fixed proportion of last year's total profits is set aside for this year's advertising. Assume also that within the pertinent range additional advertising outlays always increase sales volume, but with diminishing marginal returns. Moreover, while marginal advertising revenue is positive throughout, after some point additional advertising outlays yield negative marginal profit returns, i.e. an additional pound spent on advertising brings in less than an additional pound in revenues. If the firm's objective is maximisation of revenues rather than profits *per se*, such an incremental expenditure may even be rational.

It is now easy to see how cycles can arise in such a model. Year one's high profits produce a high level of advertising expenditure in year two. That, in turn, reduces year two profits and so cuts down the advertising budget in year three, raising profits in year three and advertising in year four. The oscillatory pattern and its explanation should be clear and a formal model readily confirms that it can 'easily' occur.

More to the point, a given oscillation may well be only an imperfect replica of its immediate predecessor. Profits are high in both years one and three but one may be slightly or even considerably higher than the other. Like the second stage in our ecological analogy, one oscillation may undergo a near miss in its replication of the one that came before it. Once this is recognised it should be clear that all the qualitative observations derived from the animal colony time path are applicable to the advertising model and why, at least with some configurations of the pertinent relationships, the time paths of the firm's profits and advertising outlays will satisfy the requirements of a chaotic regime. Mathematics readily confirms all this. When marginal returns to advertising diminish at a sufficient rate (the required magnitude, is, incidentally, easy for a mathematician to calculate), chaotic behaviour will automatically be generated by the advertising model.

The conclusion from all this is that the presence of chaotic behaviour has so far *not* been established anywhere in economics. On the other hand, it has been shown that there is hardly a corner of the discipline in which it is not a plausible possibility. At this point one can only surmise how widespread it is in fact.

IMPLICATIONS FOR FORECASTING

The attributes of chaotic behaviour indicate clearly that it must complicate the task of the economic forecaster. However, we can learn much more by careful examination of the sources of the difficulties.

First, it will be helpful to review in very general terms the basic techniques that forecasters have adopted in their work. Aside from a number of approaches that have the hallmarks of witchcraft, all of the many methods that have been employed can be classified into two broad categories; extrapolation techniques and econometric model estimation. The logic of the former is obvious. The prognosticator focuses upon past behaviour of one or a number of variables or of some attributes of those variables such as their average, their ratios or their rates of change, and assumes that whatever behaviour those focal attributes have manifested in the past can be relied upon to continue itself in the future. For example, they may assume that the share of GNP that goes into savings may change at approximately the same annual rate that it did on the average over the past X years. In short, the extrapolator's procedure is founded on a continuity premise that claims the future will share certain preidentifiable characteristics with the past.

The econometric model builders work in a different way, though their procedure must obviously also rely on knowledge derived from the past. They seek to go behind the phenomena observed in the statistics and hope to be able to reconstruct from those data the underlying economic relationships that account for the behaviour of the statistics. The time path of national income may be used to derive functions explaining the demand for plant and equipment and the size of the market for consumers' goods. Or the past prices and sales of a commodity may be used to derive demand and supply curves for that time. This step is referred to as 'estimation of the underlying model.'

Once the estimation work is completed, econometric forecasters assume that they have derived a valid representation of the mechanism that generates the statistical data. The next step rests on the reasoning that if the mechanism correctly generates the observed statistics of the past (e.g., if the numbers the model grinds out as its estimates of past GNP approximate closely the actual GNP data) then the estimates the same model grinds out for the future can serve as acceptable forecasts. The econometric forecasting procedure, thus, moves from observed data to the construction of a model used, in turn, to produce numerical values which, it is hoped, will approximate the statistics of the future.

It transpires that chaos has very different implications for the two types of forecasting approach. It handicaps the extrapolator in a straightforward manner, but the problems it poses for the econometric model builder are rather more subtle.

The sharp discontinuities that chaos injects into the time path of an economic variable constitutes its fundamental threat to the work of the extrapolator. If twenty-five years of fairly steady cyclical behaviour can be followed by the virtual disappearance of all cycles for a ten year period and the equally sudden re-emergence of cycles of a different description from their predecessors at the end of the ten year hiatus (see Figure 33.1 for an actual chaotic time path of this sort), the continuity of behaviour on which the extrapolator relies breaks down completely. In a chaotic world, extrapolation of any trend line is, in short, never justified.

Moreover, it cannot be overemphasised that in a chaotic regime abrupt and unheralded breaks in pattern of behaviour such as have just been described require absolutely no change in the underlying relationships — no change in consumer preferences, no techno-logical breakthroughs, no new mineral discoveries. Precisely the same equations and the same parameter values that governed the data before the change in behaviour pattern also govern it thereafter. This means that the extrapolators cannot hope to find signals such as a sudden change in savings behaviour that warn them of the need to modify their trend lines.

The implications of chaos for the econometric model building approach are quite different. Contrary to what may be expected, chaos need constitute no insuperable barrier to the step of estimation of the model from the observed data. No matter how bizarre the patterns exhibited by chaotic statistics, one may be able to use them to find reasonably good repre-sentations of the underlying models. For example, chaotic time series of savings, interest rates and GNP may suffice to provide an estimate of the propensity to save equation which is surprisingly accurate. This has been confirmed by simulation experiments in which an imaginary savings function has been employed to generate chaotic statistical behaviour and those statistics have then been used successfully to rederive with an extremely high degree of accuracy the original savings function from which the data were obtained. Though the fact that chaos does not preclude such analysis may seem curious, its explanation is straight-forward. By definition, a chaotic relationship is perfectly deterministic — it is beset by none of the manifestations of randomness that are the bane of econometric model estimation. Thus it is, at least in principle, easier to estimate a model from very chaotic statistics than it is from non-chaotic data subject to even moderate random influences.

If one can hope for a rather accurate estimate of the pertinent econometric model despite the presence of chaos, how can chaos constitute a serious impediment for the econometric approach to forecasting? The answer lies in another of the attributes of chaotic regimes — the extreme sensitivity of their behaviour patterns to miniscule modification of the underlying relationships. In one experiment, two statistical time series, A and B, were calculated, differing only in that A was rounded after the seventh (!) decimal place. When the two series were generated by an equation whose parameter values were chosen to lie just outside the range that causes chaotic behaviour, after more than 6,000 calculations (i.e., 6,000 'months' of simulated data) the figures generated by procedure A remained virtually identical with those derived from procedure B. The calculation was then repeated, but this time the parameter values of the generating equation were chosen to lie within the chaotic range. In this case the A and B series of statistics lost all resemblance to one another before thirty 'months' of calculations had been made. That is, in the presence of chaos even errors in the eighth decimal place in the estimate of the generating equation can change a set of forecasts unrecognisably. The moral is clear. In econometrics, accuracy even to the first decimal place is often an unattainable ideal and calculations to the third decimal place may constitute mere 'statistical noise'. Consequently, though it may be possible even in chaotic regimes to use the observed data to estimate the underlying model with what for other purposes constitutes more than tolerable accuracy, because of the butterfly's wing manifestation this offers little or no hope that such a model can be used to provide forecasts of any degree of reliability.

WHAT CHAOS THEORY MAY BE ABLE TO EXPLAIN

It is, of course, difficult to predict on what economic phenomena so new a technique as chaos theory may be able to offer illumination. The subject areas in which chaos models are available in the literature have already been described. Aside from these, the statistical records provide us with a variety of time series in which the pattern of behaviour displays what appear to be sudden and sharp qualitative breaks, which are not presaged by the preceding time path. No doubt many such cases are to be attributed to exogenous developments, but attempts to provide such evidence have not always proved easy. . . .

CONCLUDING COMMENT

So far, chaos theory has been most fruitful in the warnings that it provides. Let the consumer and the supplier of forecasts, alike, beware. While we do not know any one place where chaotic behaviour has actually intruded upon economic activity, its threatened presence seems to lurk everywhere and, for all we know, it may widely pervade the body economic. Where this is so, neither extrapolation nor calculations derived from economic models would appear to merit much confidence, even as portents of the broad qualitative properties of prospective developments. Chaotic regimes do not make for an easy life for the forecaster.

ENDNOTES

1. Chaos can be generated even by a regime that is so simple that it is governed by what is referred to technically as a first order difference equation. The most commonly cited illustration of a chaotic equation is $y_{t+1} = ky_t - ky_t^2$, where k is a constant.

2. As in the economists' 'corn-hog' or 'cobweb cycle' model.

3. It can even be argued that some of the published tables of random numbers are really chaotic, and so are not actually random, in the sense that they can be replicated precisely by anyone following exactly the same calculation procedure.

4. See (John Kendrick) U.S. Bureau of Census, *Long Term Economic Growth 1860–1970*, Washington DC, June 1973.

34

Short-Termism

Paul Marsh

Short-termism has now been a 'hot issue' for several years, and the debate has been joined by industrialists, the financial community, academics, politicians and policy-makers. Broadly, the main propositions of the short-termism position are as follows. Financial markets, together with the major players in them — investment analysts, fund managers and institutional investors — are too short-term orientated. As a result, the stock market places too much weight on current profits and dividends. This in turn causes companies to be managed according to the same short-term horizons as their investors. For if firms fail the stock market's myopic test, their share prices will drop, making them vulnerable to takeovers. Companies are thus inhibited from undertaking long-term investment in fixed capital, R&D, and training. Myopia on the part of Wall Street and the City of London has therefore been detrimental to economic growth and industrial competitiveness in the U.S.A. and U.K., relative to Germany and Japan, which have so-called 'bank-based' financial systems.

These views, or close variants on them, are frequently put forward by many industrialists (e.g., see Business Week/Harris Poll 1987, 3i 1990, Laing 1990); by politicians and governments (for selected quotations, see Marsh 1990); by popular writers on management (e.g., see Hayes and Abernathy 1980, Drucker 1986, Jacobs 1991); and also by a number of economists and other academics (e.g., Ellsworth 1985, Dertouzos *et al.* 1989, and Wass 1990). Many other economists, while not supporting the allegations of stock market myopia, have nevertheless been concerned with the issue of short-termism and possible underinvestment within firms (e.g., Stein 1989, Myers 1989 and Hirshleifer and Chordia 1991).

The purpose of this essay is to help structure the debate on short-termism, and to establish whether the propositions above are substantiated by the evidence. We begin in Section I by examining whether stock markets undervalue the long term. We conclude that there is no convincing evidence that they do. Section II then argues that if short-termism is a problem, the direct perpetrators must anyway be managers, and not financiers or shareholders. But managers may nevertheless be acting under duress from the financial system. Section III examines this possibility and concludes that the major source of duress arises from contested takeovers. Section IV therefore looks at takeovers and short-termism, and finds again that many of the popular views are simply not supported by the evidence.

Reprinted from: Marsh, P. 1992: Short-Termism. In: Newman, P. Milgate, M. and Eatwell, J. eds. *The New Palgrave Dictionary on Money and Finance*. London: Macmillan, Vol. 2, 446–453.

If many of the accusations put forward against the financial markets are myth rather than reality, then why has long-term investment been lower in the U.K. and U.S. than in Japan and Germany? Section V reviews the many factors which may have contributed to this, and argues that these dominate concerns about the financial markets. Section VI then looks briefly at some possible remedies.

I. IS THE STOCK MARKET SHORT-TERMIST?

If stock markets are short-termist, this implies that share prices place too much weight on short-term profits and dividends. But despite the widespread belief that this is the case (see above), the main evidence put forward to support this view relates to the short-termist way in which investment analysts and fund managers *appear* to behave (e.g., see Ellsworth 1985, Innovation Advisory Board 1990).

What is at issue, however, is not how analysts and fund managers talk, or appear to behave, or even how they actually behave. Instead, the question is one of how *share prices* behave, and whether they fairly reflect both short-and long-term prospects, or whether they tend to overvalue the short-term and undervalue the long. No reliable evidence has yet been put forward to support the claim of short-termism in share prices.

To be fair, conclusive, direct evidence would be hard to obtain. First we would need to define giving 'too much weight to the short-term'. In theory, a company's share price should reflect the present value of its stream of future cash flows (e.g., see Miller and Modigliani 1961). This implies that near-term cash flows should necessarily be given more weight since future cash flows must be brought back to present values by taking account of the cost of capital. Short-termism thus needs to be redefined as 'giving more weight to the near term than is justified by the cost of capital'.

Unfortunately, it is impossible to utilize the discounted cash flow approach to determine whether a particular company's share price is undervaluing the long term. The reasons for this relate to the essentially subjective nature of the future forecasts which would have to be used (see Marsh 1990). Instead, however, we can appeal to the very large body of evidence on share price behaviour and market efficiency.

Economists define an efficient market as one in which prices reflect all information. If stock markets are efficient, we should not be able to find any trading rules based on publicly available information which work; nor should there be any category of information which is not already fully discounted in share prices, or group of individuals with access to such information. Market efficiency has been subjected to very extensive testing, and any balanced assessment of the resultant evidence has to conclude that the theory is remarkably well supported by the facts. (For reviews, see Fama 1970 and 1991, Brealey 1983, Foster 1986, Richards 1979 and Keane 1985.)

If markets are efficient, then clearly they should reflect all information — including that relating to a company's long-as well as its short-term prospects. The claim that share prices are short-termist is thus itself an allegation that the stock market is inefficient. We cannot simply dismiss this, since although market efficiency is well supported by the evidence, there is also an anomalies literature (see Jensen 1978, Dimson 1988 and Fama 1991), including a more controversial literature on 'fads', speculative bubbles, excessive volatility and the alleged predictability of long-run returns (see Shiller 1981 and 1984, Shleifer and Summers 1990 and Fama 1991). Instead, therefore, the specific allegations of short-termism need to be put to the test by translating them into trading strategies, to see whether there is any evidence to support them.

The Market is not Myopic

For example, if the stock market places too much weight on current dividends, then presumably low-yielding stocks are undervalued, relative to their expected future cash flows. Long-term investors in such a short-sighted world could therefore make money by buying low yielders and holding them long term, when true value must be realized if the short-termist proposition is valid. Similarly, if the market undervalues future prospects, investors could again make money by buying growth stocks (i.e. shares with high price–earnings (PE) ratios, but where the PEs should presumably be even higher), and holding them long term. Or if the market marks down the prices of companies which invest for the longer term, investors would simply need to identify companies which were about to announce major capital investments or R&D expenditure, and then sell them short, or at least avoid them (until after the announcement, when presumably they might be good long-term buys).

These issues are all testable propositions, which have been subjected to scientific enquiry. But the results do not support the proposition that the market is short-termist. For example, the evidence on dividends is that historically the U.S. and U.K. markets have had a preference for capital gains, with high-yielding shares being more lowly valued (see, for example, Blume 1980, Litzenberger and Ramaswamy 1982 and Levis 1989). This apparent anomaly, however, is more likely to be attributable to historical taxation considerations than to the stock market being overly long-termist. Similarly, with PE ratios, the only controversy arising out of careful empirical research in Britain and America is a concern that the shares of companies with good growth prospects may have been *overvalued* rather than *vice versa* (see, for example, Reinganum 1981, Basu 1983 and Levis 1989).

Finally, a growing number of studies have documented how share prices react to announcements of decisions on capital expenditure, R&D and investment in new products (see McConnell and Muscarella 1985, Woolridge 1988, Jarrell, Lehn and Marr 1985, Chaney *et al.* 1989, and Chan, Martin and Kensinger 1990). These studies indicate that, far from causing alarm and dismay, such announcements are regarded as good news, and result, on average, in share price increases. Announcements of decreases in planned capital expenditure or R&D are, on the other hand, associated with share-price falls. The researchers in question have also partitioned their samples to seek to explain differential reactions to various types of announcement by different groups of companies. The evidence from such partitioning is consistent with the notion that the market responds rapidly to information about new long-term projects, based on a rational assessment of the likely profitability of the project in question.

The evidence cited above has a direct and obvious bearing on the short-termism debate. However, there is also much indirect evidence — related, for example, to the way the market reacts to earnings announcements, dividend announcements, changes in accounting practices, fund raising operations, and mergers and acquisitions (see Fama 1970 and 1991, Brealey 1983, Foster 1986, Richards 1979 and Keane 1985). This extensive 'event-study' literature (see Fama 1991) supports the general hypothesis that the stock market is broadly efficient, and that it is concerned with, and on average correctly discounts, the long-term as well as the short-term implications of relevant news items and key events.

II. THE PERPETRATORS OF SHORT-TERMISM

The actual evidence is thus that to blame the stock market's pricing mechanism for the ills of American and British industry is to pick the wrong target. This is not to imply that Wall

Street and the City of London are necessarily blameless, nor that financial institutions should receive a clean bill of health in the debate on short-termism. All that we have exonerated so far is the measuring rod—namely the stock market's pricing behaviour.

Before looking more closely at the possible role of the financial institutions in fostering short-termist behaviour, it is important to establish what short-termism actually involves, and who carries out such acts. Ultimately, short-termism is the failure to undertake profitable, long-term investments. By profitable, we mean investments which are expected to make shareholders wealthier, that is, investments with positive net present values. In an efficient stock market, with well-informed investors, these are precisely the kinds of investment which should lead to an increase in the company's share price when the market first learns about them.

Short-termist Behaviour

One reason why managers may shun long-term investments is that they can depress short-term accounting profits. The latter are defined as revenues less expenses, where expenses can in turn be broken down into operating costs and investments. Operating costs include all the immediate expenditures incurred in producing and delivering existing products and services. Investments, on the other hand, are all the expenses which are incurred today in the hope of generating longer-term benefits, that is greater or at least sustained profits in the future. Examples include investments in capital expenditure (where the expense item is an increase in the depreciation charge); and expenditures on research and development, training, preventive maintenance, product improvements, distribution and strategic marketing, including advertising, promotion, the building of brands and price cutting to obtain market share.

A manager wishing to maximize short-term accounting profits can do so by increasing revenues, decreasing operating costs or cutting investments. The short-termist manager will thus aim to milk and exploit the company's current products and services, while at the same time forgoing potentially profitable investments. This will maximize immediate profits, but only at the expense of the future, that is, it will not maximize shareholder value.

Are Managers Myopic and Why?

By definition, therefore, if short-termism is a problem, it must be because managers in firms are underinvesting in this way. This raises two fundamental questions. First, do managers behave in this myopic way? And second, if so, why?

Curiously, despite the extensive debate on short-termism, there is very little systematic evidence which demonstrates that British and American managers are short-termist (Hirshleifer and Chordia 1991). It is often inferred that they are, simply because British and American firms have invested less than their Japanese and German counterparts (e.g., see CBI 1987, Wass 1990). However, different firms in different countries face different opportunity sets. Thus British and American managers may not have underinvested. Instead, they may have accepted every project with a positive net present value, but simply found too few of these 'on offer' (see also Section V below). The strongest direct evidence that short-termism is a problem is in fact anecdotal, and comes from business executives describing their own perceptions and behaviour (e.g., see Dertouzos *et al.* 1989, Innovation Advisory Board 1990).

But while managers often admit to short-termist behaviour, they argue that there are extenuating circumstances and that they are acting under duress from the financial community to meet Wall Street or the City's short-termist requirements (e.g., see Ellsworth 1985, Dertouzos *et al.* 1989). On this view, the real culprits for short-termism are investment analysts, fund managers and institutional investors.

III. ANALYSTS, FUND MANAGERS AND THE INSTITUTIONS

If share prices are long-termist, but managers believe that the financial markets and community are short-termist, this constitutes a dangerous misunderstanding, which could itself cause short-termist behaviour. But why should such misunderstandings arise? And what forms of 'duress' or pressure do investment analysts, fund managers and institutional investors exert on companies?

The Behaviour of Analysts

Investment analysts often appear to be excessively preoccupied with short-term earnings and dividends (see Business Week/Harris Poll 1987 and 3i 1990). But while this can convey an impression of short-termism, attention to the current year's results need not imply that analysts are taking too short-term a view. First, dividend and earnings announcements are a very important source of company news. And second, they can convey (and are generally accompanied by) significant information about the future. Companies, for example, frequently attempt to manage and 'smooth' their future dividend and earnings growth paths (see, for example, Lintner 1956, Watts 1973, Edwards and Mayer 1984 and Marsh and Merton 1986). This means that earnings and dividend announcements provide important signals, not simply about the current trading position, but also about the longer term, and management's own (inside) knowledge and judgements about the future. Analysts and fund managers would therefore be negligent to ignore them.

Furthermore, the evidence from price–earnings ratios confirms that investors are not simply focusing on current earnings per share. Research studies indicate that PE ratios vary widely across stocks, and depend — as theory indicates they should — on prospective long-term earnings growth, the retentions needed to finance this growth, the rate of return needed to compensate for the risks involved, and the precise accounting methods used (see Whitbeck and Kisor 1963, Beaver and Morse 1978, Beaver and Dukes 1973 and Foster 1986).

There is therefore much evidence to indicate that analysts take a very broad view when valuing shares, and use far more data than just the current results. Nevertheless, analysts as a group may well be guilty of 'conduct likely to mislead'. The quality of analysts is often uneven, and while poor analysts may have little influence on share prices, companies are exposed to the poor analysts as well as the good. By their behaviour, and by the questions they ask — and fail to ask — analysts can undoubtedly sometimes convey an unhelpful impression of short-termism to industrialists (e.g., see CBI 1987, Innovation Advisory Board 1990).

Fund Managers and Quarterly Performance Measurement

Fund managers are also often viewed as short-termist, and this is widely attributed to the pressures they themselves face from short-term quarterly performance measurement (e.g., see Ellsworth 1985, Wass 1990, Innovation Advisory Board 1990, etc.). However, this concern that performance measurement prevents fund managers taking a long-term view is misplaced. It is a misconception which almost certainly arises from inappropriate comparisons with managers in industry. The latter, if faced with pressures to maximize *accounting profits*, might be tempted to sell the firm's long-term future short by cutting back on investments in R&D, training, fixed assets, etc. (see Section II above).

Fund managers, however, are evaluated quite differently. Faced with the demand for better short-term performance, the fund manager, unlike his or her industrial counterpart, cannot sell the future short. The only way he or she can outperform is to identify undervalued shares and buy them, and/or overvalued shares, and sell them. This is no easy matter, given the competition they face (as borne out by the many studies which indicate that consistent outperformance is very rare; see, for example, Jensen 1968, and Bogle and Twardowski 1980). Indeed, the only way they can succeed is through careful analysis of a company's short- and longer-term prospects — something widely held to be a good thing.

Indeed, to maximize their own short-run performance, fund managers need to be concerned with companies' long-term prospects. Any insights the manager has about even the company's very long-term future get incorporated into the share price almost immediately, partly because of competition between investors, and partly because dealing activity itself alerts others that there may be information around, causing prices to adjust accordingly. By spotting mispriced shares, fund managers thus help to keep the market efficient. Their short-term actions often reflect long-term views, and their own short-term performance will reflect changes in the capitalized value of the longer-term prospects of the shares they hold.

Institutional Investors: Speculators or Owners?

Institutional shareholders are often criticized for behaving more like speculators than owners (e.g., see Ellsworth 1985, Charkham 1990, Wass 1990). In particular, they are accused of excessive turnover ('churnover'). This, in turn, is felt to have an adverse effect on relationships between shareholders and companies, on accountability and on shareholder loyalty.

Again, misunderstandings abound. First, any suggestion that turnover is bad *per se* is misguided. Much turnover is not speculative, but is for liquidity or rebalancing reasons, or else is part-involuntary (e.g. reinvestment of dividends). It is a fundamental function of stock markets to provide the 'liquidity' to facilitate such dealings, and this type of turnover is a healthy sign of a well-functioning capital market. Indeed, it would be far harder to establish an efficient primary market, where companies can raise money for new investment, without the existence of a liquid secondary market.

Turning to so-called 'speculative' turnover, it might be more instructive (and less emotive) to relabel this as information-motivated turnover. Such turnover occurs whenever investors believe they have identified mispriced shares. However, as noted above, such dealing activity alerts others, including market makers, to any element of mispricing, and prices will therefore adjust quickly. Such turnover by informed investors is essential to keep the market efficient and to keep prices in line with underlying values. Indeed, even economists who claim that stock markets are inefficient argue that the reason for this is that there is *too little* trading activity by informed investors and 'arbitrageurs' (e.g., see Morck, Shleifer and Vishny 1990). In itself, therefore, turnover is not detrimental to market efficiency, but is instead a very important part of the mechanism for keeping markets efficient.

There is a deeper concern, however, relating to the impact of turnover on relationships between companies and their institutional shareholders. If one accepts the view that shareholders have responsibilities towards, and at least some role to play in the affairs of, the companies in which they invest, then this argument would have some force—at least if turnover levels were excessive. There is no evidence, however, that they are. U.S. and U.K. turnover rates are currently lower than those in Germany and Japan, and in the U.K., for example, the major shareholding institutions currently have an average holding period in excess of seven years.

Takeover Activity: Direct Duress

Unfortunately, perceptions, even if they are wrong, can still influence behaviour. Thus while the conduct of analysts, fund managers and institutional shareholders may be perfectly reasonable, it may nevertheless convey a general short-termist impression to corporate managers which may be setting the wrong tone and climate. Unless the financial community devotes more resources to setting the record straight via more effective two-way communications and relationships, then there is a danger that managers in companies may feel under pressure to act in a short-term manner, simply because they—incorrectly—assume that this is what, for example, Wall Street and the City of London want.

But while the financial institutions may give companies the impression that they are short-termist, the behaviour we have outlined above hardly amounts to coercing companies into short-termism, or to the kind of direct duress referred to in the previous section. The one very important exception here is the threat of an unwanted takeover bid. This is the one source of direct duress which is brought to bear on companies. It therefore lies at the very heart of the popular concerns about short-termism.

IV. TAKEOVERS AND SHORT-TERMISM

It is frequently argued that the fear of an unwanted takeover bid can coerce managers into short-termism (e.g., see Stein 1988, Dertouzos *et al.* 1989 and Laing 1990). The usual contention here is that bids encourage managers to maximize short-term profits and dividends in the hope that this will boost their share price and keep the predator from the door. This causes them to cut back on long-term investment.

There is a fundamental problem with this view, however, namely that companies are unlikely to bolster their share prices by cutting back on potentially profitable long-term investments—in fact quite the opposite, as we noted in Section I above. As a defence against unwanted bids, such a strategy seems fundamentally flawed. Indeed, there is no evidence that companies which are investing heavily for the future are more likely to get taken over, and, if anything, the reverse is true (see Jarrell, Lehn and Marr 1985). Furthermore, the large body of empirical research on takeovers (see, for example, Jensen and Ruback 1983, Dodd 1983, Marsh 1986 and 1990, Jensen 1986 and Franks and Harris 1989), suggests that it is the worse performing companies which tend to get taken over by their better-performing counterparts. Nor is there any persuasive evidence that acquisitions herald general cutbacks in investment spending or R&D in the post-merger period (see Healy, Palepu and Ruback 1990). Indeed curiously, there is some evidence that after adopting *anti*-takeover amendments ('shark repellents') firms reduce their R&D spending (Meulbroek *et al.* 1990).

Furthermore, writers who contend that barriers to take-over may be needed to discourage myopic behaviour by managers (e.g., Stein 1988) also need to take into account the now considerable body of empirical evidence (see the studies in the previous paragraph) which suggests that shareholders have gained from mergers, and that takeovers have led to efficiency gains. Indeed, all studies indicate that takeovers have resulted in large gains to the acquirees' shareholders. Acquirers, for their part, appear on average to have broken even or reaped modest gains, even after taking account of the premia they have paid. On average, therefore, the combined entity has enjoyed a higher market capitalization than the sum of its two components when run separately. Acquisitions have thus historically allowed companies to reap economic and efficiency gains, and on this dimension, acquisitions appear to have been a virtue rather than a vice.

The above findings need some qualification. First, they relate to average behaviour. Thus although, on average, mergers have increased shareholders' wealth, many have failed. And while takeover victims have tended to be poorer performers, well-managed, long-termist companies also sometimes get taken over against their managements' (but not their shareholders') will. Second, the available evidence relates mostly to shareholders' interests. Possibly, shareholders' gains have been counterbalanced by welfare reductions for consumers and other stakeholders. The evidence we have on this, however, suggests that it has not been the case (see Healy, Palepu and Ruback 1990).

Third, the published evidence does not take account of the hidden costs and benefits of takeover activity. For example, there are substantial costs — in terms of fees, management time and employee motivation — associated with failed bids. Furthermore, costs may arise from short-termist behaviour on the part of managements who find themselves under the threat of a bid — however counterproductive to their intended cause these actions may be. Furthermore, the possibility of a future takeover may undermine contractual relationships between investors and employees and managers, making the latter reluctant to invest in firm-specific assets and longer-term investments, if they may later be denied the benefits of such investment because of a change in ownership (see Franks and Mayer 1990). Balanced against these costs are the substantial benefits which can flow from the threat of takeovers and the value of 'keeping managements on their toes'. Indeed, in the U.K. and the U.S.A., contested takeovers are one of the most effective disciplinary devices available — both as a deterrent and as a measure of last resort.

This raises the obvious question of whether there might be better, cheaper ways of ensuring effective corporate control than leaning so heavily on acquisitions. Indeed, two of the most successful industrialized nations, Japan and Germany, have done very well without the disciplinary mechanism of contested bids. If improvements in relationships between companies and their shareholders, together with more effective corporate governance, could yield shareholders the same gains they have achieved from takeover activity without the associated costs, including short-termism, this would clearly be worth striving for.

V. THE REAL REASONS FOR UNDERINVESTMENT

If many of the short-termist accusations put forward against the financial markets are myth rather than reality, then why have capital formation and R&D expenditure been relatively lower in the U.K. and U.S. than in Japan and Germany? One explanation could be that managers believe the mythology and act accordingly. But there are many other possible contributory factors. We examine just three of these below, namely managerial short-termism, cross-country differences in the cost of capital, and supply-side factors.

Managerial Short-termism

'Managerial short-termism' can be defined as a tendency by corporate managers to favour the short term independently of any spur from the financial markets.

There are many aspects of managerial practice and systems in the U.K. and U.S. which can mitigate against a long-term orientation. First and perhaps foremost, there are remuneration and reward systems. Most executive incentive systems link remuneration to accounting profit, typically assessed over short horizons, no greater than a year, rather than to long-term measures of value. This is not true of remuneration schemes in Japan. Furthermore, several studies show that more long-term-orientated incentive schemes serve to extend managers' planning horizons, and increase corporate investment (see, for example, Larcker 1983).

A closely related issue is managers' time horizons within jobs. The relatively high rates of executive mobility in the U.S. and U.K. contrast starkly with the Japanese system of so-called 'lifetime employment'. This, in turn, may make managers more concerned with short-term results, and less ready to make long-term investments.

Finally, the managerial systems used to appraise new investments could be causing short-termism in many U.S. and U.K. companies. Many companies still seem to overemphasize payback, a notoriously short-termist measure. But even where greater reliance is placed on discounted cash flow approaches, many companies appear to use excessively high discount rates, or to misapply the technique through failing to value strategic options properly or to assess terminal values correctly (see Marsh 1990 for a more detailed discussion).

Cross-country Differences in the Cost of Capital

Several studies have purported to show that the cost of capital is higher in the U.K. and U.S.A. than in Germany and Japan. But these have been flawed. Some have incorrectly focused on nominal rather than real interest rates. But even the more sophisticated studies (e.g. McCauley and Zimmer 1989) have used inappropriate measures of the cost of equity, such as the earnings yield. This results in the erroneous conclusion that equity is cheap in countries with good growth prospects and hence high PE ratios, such as Japan.

A proper assessment requires an international comparison, first of real interest rates, and second of equity risk premia. In fact, average real interest rates have been broadly similar in the U.S.A., Japan and the U.K. throughout the 1970s and 1980s. Equity risk premia have differed between countries, and have, in fact, been highest in Japan. The rankings, though, accord with the differences in investment risk between countries, suggesting that the equity risk premium per unit of risk has been roughly the same worldwide (see Baldwin 1987). Differences in the cost of capital have therefore been much exaggerated. Japanese and German firms may enjoy some advantage, arising from their large domestic savings flows and their greater use of debt, but the benefit here seems likely to be quite modest (for a fuller discussion, see Baldwin 1987 and Marsh 1990).

Even if the true cost of capital were identical everywhere, however, it is still possible that managers in, say, Japan, may *act* as though they have a lower cost of capital. There is some evidence of this (Hodder 1986), just as there are indications that U.S. firms may use discount rates that are too high (Myers 1984). Arguably, therefore, this could be another area where incorrect perceptions have generated their own reality — of lower U.S. and U.K. investment levels.

Supply-side Factors

There may be many other explanations for international differences in investment levels. In the postwar period, for example, Germany and Japan's higher investment reflects their greater scope for reconstruction and catching-up. Meanwhile, the principal war victors remained burdened with heavy defence spending, which may have pre-empted scarce resources. Macroeconomic policies also undoubtedly played their part, particularly in the U.K., with its 'stop-go' policies, exchange rate instability and higher inflation.

Most important of all, however, are supply-side factors, particularly those relating to the education, skills, working practices, attitudes and productivity of the work force; to engineering, product design, manufacturing and marketing skills; and to the quality, training and attitudes of management. Indeed, conventional wisdom needs to be turned on its head here. The popular belief is that the U.S.A. and U.K.'s lower economic growth rates have *resulted* from too little investment. In reality, however, both the lower growth rate and the lower investment levels are the consequence of supply-side weaknesses — at least by comparison with the strength of the German and Japanese competition. These competitive weaknesses not only depress the profitability of existing activities, but also reduce the attractiveness of new investment (for a more detailed discussion, see Caves and Krause 1980, and Crafts 1988).

VI. REMEDIES

The problems of short-termism induced by the U.S. and U.K. financial systems thus relate more to perceptions than to reality. They cannot however be dismissed, lest perceptions become reality. If industrialists believe that the financial community is short-termist, they may act accordingly, cutting back on long-term investment.

Yet many of the 'remedies' put forward for short-termism — such as share turnover taxes, penal rates of tax on short-term capital gains, or 'throwing sand in the takeover machine' — are predicated on the false premise that the financial markets are to blame. If implemented, such measures would yield perverse results, by lowering market liquidity, increasing the cost of capital and reducing economic efficiency.

Measures aimed at closing the perceptional gap, however, seem worthy of serious pursuit. These include improving relationships between companies and their institutional share-holders; better communications and greater disclosure; selective (and collective) direct interventions by share-holders; a greater emphasis on shareholder responsibilities, especially during contested bids; and better board structures and corporate governance — which, if successful, might anyway make contested takeovers less necessary, and hence less prevalent.

It is important, however, to keep these measures in perspective, and be realistic about what they might achieve. In particular, it would be a great pity if industry became sidetracked from the central issues it faces — international competitiveness, market orientation, innovation, quality and excellence — by further talk about short-termism from the financial markets. Indeed, there is a real congruence of interests here. The very activities required to enhance business competitiveness, and to improve the prospects for, and levels of, future investment, are the self-same actions required to enhance share prices, create shareholder value, deter corporate raiders and improve investor relations. Quite simply, the way ahead for both the financial community and industry is to get on with managing as if tomorrow mattered.

BIBLIOGRAPHY

Baldwin, C.Y. 1987. Competing for capital in a global environment. *Midland Corporate Finance Journal* **5**: 43–64.

Basu, S. 1983. The relationship between earnings' yields, market value and the returns for NYSE stocks: further evidence. *Journal of Financial Economics* **12**: 129–56.

Beaver, W.H. and Dukes, R.E. 1973. Tax allocation and depreciation methods: some empirical results. *Accounting Review* **11**: 549–59.

Beaver, W.H. and Morse, D. 1978. What determines price–earnings ratios? *Financial Analysts Journal* **34(4)**: 65–76.

Blume, M.E. 1980. Stock returns and dividend yields: some more evidence. *Review of Economics and Statistics* **62**: 567–77.

Bogle, J.C. and Twardowski, J.M. 1980. Institutional investment performance compared: banks, investment counsellors, insurance companies and mutual funds. *Financial Analysts Journal* **36(1)**: 33–41.

Brealey, R.A. 1983. *An Introduction to Risk and Return from Common Stocks.* 2nd edn, Cambridge, Mass.: MIT Press.

Business Week/Harris Poll. 1987. Survey of corporate attitudes. *Business Week* 23 October: 28.

Caves, R.E. and Krause, L.B. (eds) 1980. *Britain's Economic Performance.* Washington, DC: The Brookings Institution.

CBI. 1987. *Investing for Britain's Future: Report of the City/Industry Task Force.* London: Confederation of British Industry.

Chan, S.H., Martin, J.D. and Kensinger, J.W. 1990. Corporate research and development expenditures and share value. *Journal of Financial Economics* **26**: 255–76.

Chaney, P.K., Devinney, T.M. and Winer, R.S. 1989. The impact of new product introductions on the market value of firms. Report 89–105. Marketing Science Institute, Cambridge, Mass.

Charkham, J.P. 1990. Are shares just commodities? In *Creative Tension?*, National Association of Pension Funds, London: NAPF.

Crafts, N.F.R. 1988. British economic growth before and after 1979: a review of the evidence. In *The British Economy Since 1945*, ed. N.F.R. Crafts, B. Duckham and N. Woodward, Oxford: Oxford University Press.

Dertouzos, M.L., Lester, R.K. and Solow, R.M. 1989. *Made in America.* Cambridge, Mass.: The MIT Commission on Industrial Productivity.

Dimson, E. ed. 1988. *Stock Market Anomalies.* Cambridge: Cambridge University Press.

Dodd, P. 1983. The market for corporate control: a review of the evidence. *Midland Corporate Finance Journal* **1**: 6–20.

Drucker, P. 1986. A crisis of capitalism. *Wall Street Journal* 30 September: 31.

Edwards, J. and Mayer, C. 1984. An investigation into the dividend and new equity issue practices of firms: evidence from survey information. Institute of Fiscal Studies working paper 80, London.

Ellsworth, R.R. 1985. Capital markets and competitive decline. *Harvard Business Review* **63**: 171–83.

Fama, E.F. 1970. Efficient capital markets: a review of theory and empirical work. *Journal of Finance* **25**: 383–417.

Fama, E.F. 1990. Efficient capital markets: II. *Journal of Finance* **46**: 1575–1617.

Foster, G. 1986. *Financial Statement Analysis.* 2nd edn, Englewood Cliffs: Prentice-Hall International.

Franks, J.R. and Harris, R. 1989. Shareholder wealth effects of corporate takeovers: the U.K. experience 1955–85. *Journal of Financial Economics* **23**: 225–49.

Franks, J.R. and Mayer, C. 1990. Takeovers: capital markets and corporate control: a study of France, Germany and the U.K. *Economic Policy* **10**: 189–231.

Hayes, R.H. and Abernathy, W.J. 1980. Managing our way to economic decline. *Harvard Business Review* **58**: 67–77.

Healy, P.M., Palepu, K.G. and Ruback, R.S. 1990. Does corporate performance improve after mergers? Working paper 3149–90. MIT Sloan School of Management.

Hirshleifer, D. and Chordia, T. 1991. Resolution preference and project choice. Working paper. Anderson Graduate School of Management, UCLA, August.

Hodder, J.E. 1986. Evaluation of manufacturing investments: a comparison of U.S. and Japanese practices. *Financial Management* **15(1)**, Spring: 17–24.

Innovation Advisory Board. 1990. *Innovation: City Attitudes and Practices.* London: Department of Trade and Industry.

Jacobs, M. 1991. *Short-Term America: The Causes and Cures of Our Business Myopia.* Boston: Harvard Business School Press.

Jarrell, G.A., Lehn, K. and Marr, W. 1985. Institutional ownership, tender offers, and long-term investments. Washington, DC: Office of the Chief Economist, Securities and Exchange Commission.

Jensen, M.C. 1968. The performance of mutual funds in the period 1945–64. *Journal of Finance* **23**: 389–416.

Jensen, M.C. 1978. Some anomalous evidence regarding market efficiency. *Journal of Financial Economics* **6**: 95–101. (The June 1978 issue of the *Journal of Financial Economics* was given over to a Symposium of Some Anomalous Evidence on Capital Market Efficiency.)

Jensen, M.C. 1986. The takeover controversy: analysis and evidence. *Midland Corporate Finance Journal* **4**: 6–32.

Jensen, M.C. and Ruback, R.S. 1983. The market for corporate control: the scientific evidence. *Journal of Financial Economics* **11**: 5–50.

Keane, S. 1985. *Stock Exchange Efficiency: Theory, Evidence and Implications*. Oxford: Philip Allan.

Laing, H. 1990. The Balance of Responsibilities. In *Creative Tension?*, National Association of Pension Funds, London: NAPF.

Larcker, D. 1983. The association between performance plan adoption and corporate capital investment. *Journal of Accounting and Economics* **5**: 3–30.

Levis, M. 1989. Stock market anomalies: a re-assessment based on the U.K. evidence. *Journal of Banking and Finance* **13**: 675–96.

Lintner, J. 1956. Distribution of incomes of corporations among dividends, retained earnings, and taxes. *American Economic Review* **46**: 97–113.

Litzenberger, R.H. and Ramaswamy, K. 1982. The effects of dividends on common stock prices: tax effects or information effects. *Journal of Finance* **37**: 429–43.

Marsh, P.R. 1986. Are profits the prize of the prey or the predator. *Financial Times Mergers and Acquisitions*, May: 4–7.

Marsh, P.R. 1990. *Short-Termism on Trial*. London: Institutional Fund Managers Association.

Marsh, T.A. and Merton, R.C. 1986. Dividend variability and variance bounds tests for the rationality of stock market prices. *American Economic Review* **76**: 483–98.

McCauley, R.N. and Zimmer, S.A. 1989. Explaining international differences in the cost of capital. *FRBNY Quarterly Review*, Summer: 7–28.

McConnell, J.J. and Muscarella, C.J. 1985. Corporate capital expenditure decisions and the market value of the firm. *Journal of Financial Economics* **14**: 399–422.

Meulbroek, L.K., Mitchell, M.L., Mulherin, J.H., Netter, J.M. and Poulsen, A.B. 1990. Shark repellents and managerial myopia: an empirical test. *Journal of Political Economy* **95**: 1108–17.

Miller, M.H. and Modigliani, F. 1961. Dividend policy, growth and the valuation of shares. *Journal of Business* **34**: 411–33.

Morck, R., Shleifer, A. and Vishny, R.W. 1990. The stock market and investment: is the market a sideshow? *Brookings Papers on Economic Activity* **2**: 157–215.

Myers, S.C. 1984. Finance theory and financial strategy. *Interfaces* **14**: 126–37.

Myers, S.C. 1989. Signaling and accounting information. Working paper IFA-120-89, London Business School.

Reinganum, M. 1981. Misspecification of capital asset pricing: empirical anomalies based on earnings' yields and market values. *Journal of Financial Economics* **9**: 19–46.

Richards, P.H. 1979. *U.K. and European Share Price Behaviour: The Evidence*. London: Kogan Page.

Shiller, R.J. 1981. Do stock prices move too much to be justified by subsequent changes in dividends? *American Economic Review* **71**: 421–36.

Shiller, R.J. 1984. Stock prices and social dynamics. *Brookings Papers on Economic Activity* **2**: 457–98.

Shleifer, A. and Summers, L.H. 1990. The noise trader approach to finance. *Journal of Economic Perspectives* **4**: 19–33.

Stein, J.C. 1988. Takeover threats and managerial myopia. *Journal of Political Economy* **96**: 61–80.

Stein, J.C. 1989. Efficient capital markets, inefficient firms: a model of myopic corporate behavior. *Quarterly Journal of Economics* **104**: 655–70.

3i. 1990. Corporate attitudes to stock market valuations: 3i shareholder value survey. *plc U.K.* 1 (entire issue), London: 3i.

Wass, D. 1990. Innovation and industrial strength. *Policy Studies* **11**: 10–17.

Watts, R. 1973. The information content of dividends. *Journal of Business* **46**: 191–211.

Whitbeck, V.S. and Kisor, M. 1963. A new tool in investment decision-making. *Financial Analysts Journal* **19(3)**: 55–62.

Woolridge, J.R. 1988. Competitive decline: is a myopic stock market to blame? *Journal of Applied Corporate Finance* **1**: 26–36.

Index

Index compiled by Michael Heary